SAGE was founded in 1965 by Sara Miller McCune to support the dissemination of usable knowledge by publishing innovative and high-quality research and teaching content. Today, we publish over 900 journals, including those of more than 400 learned societies, more than 800 new books per year, and a growing range of library products including archives, data, case studies, reports, and video. SAGE remains majority-owned by our founder, and after Sara's lifetime will become owned by a charitrust that secures our continued independence.

Los Angeles | London | New Delhi | Singapore | Washington DC | Melbourne

International Relations

International Relations

Theories and Approaches

Amartya Mukhopadhyay
Former Professor, Department of Political Science,
University of Calcutta, West Bengal, India

SAGE | TEXTS

Los Angeles | London | New Delhi
Singapore | Washington DC | Melbourne

First published in 2021 by

SAGE | TEXTS

SAGE Publications India Pvt Ltd
B1/I-1 Mohan Cooperative Industrial Area
Mathura Road, New Delhi 110 044, India
www.sagepub.in

SAGE Publications Inc
2455 Teller Road
Thousand Oaks, California 91320, USA

SAGE Publications Ltd
1 Oliver's Yard, 55 City Road
London EC1Y 1SP, United Kingdom

SAGE Publications Asia-Pacific Pte Ltd
18 Cross Street #10-10/11/12
China Square Central
Singapore 048423

Published by Vivek Mehra for SAGE Publications India Pvt. Ltd. Typeset in 9.5/11.5 pt Bookman Old Style by Zaza Eunice, Hosur, Tamil Nadu, India.

Library of Congress Control Number: 2021942276

ISBN: 978-93-91370-99-2 (PB)

SAGE Team: Amit Kumar, Indrani Dutta, Shruti Gupta, Sonam Rana, Aishna Bhatt, Madhurima Thapa and Kanika Mathur

To

Late Captain Sridhar Prasad Mukherjee (1936–1973), eldest brother, sailor, visionary and my maker. From him wafted my way the heady scent of foreign lands.

Ruby Mukhopadhyay, my beloved wife, ever beautiful and ever young.

CONTENTS

DETAILED CONTENTS

LIST OF ILLUSTRATIONS

Figures

Tables

Boxes

LIST OF ABBREVIATIONS

AAI	Arms and Influence
AH	After Hegemony: Cooperation and Conflict in World Political Economy
AP	Anarchy problématique
APEC	Asia-Pacific Economic Cooperation
ASCs	Amalgamated security communities
ASEAN	Association of Southeast Asian Nations
BCTIP	British Committee on the Theory of International Politics
BOP	Balance of power
BOPS	Balance of power system
BOTS	Battle of the sexes
BPM	Bureaucratic politics model
BTTF	Back to the Future: Instability in Europe after the Cold War
CAC	Choice and Consequence: Perspectives of an Errant Economics
CACM	Central American Common Market
CESO	Centro de Estudios Socio-Económicos
CFE	The Choice for Europe
COEr	Council of Europe
CPC	Communist Party of China
CRINTHEO	Critical international theory
CRITHEO	Critical international theorist
CSCE	Conference on Security and Cooperation
CT	Critical theory
CW-E	Capitalist world-economy
DDIR	Data Development for International Research
DMA	Decision-making approach
DNTS	Détente system
DOV	Diplomacy of Violence
EC	European Community
ECLA	Economic Commission for Latin America
ECOWAS	Economic Community of West African States
ECSC	European Coal and Steel Community
EJ	Environmental justice
ENA	Essential national actor
EPT	Environmental political theory
ERT	Ecology and Revolutionary Thought
ES	English School
EU	European Union

EUE	Ecologically unequal exchange
FDI	Foreign direct investment
FPDM	Foreign policy decision-making
G7	Group of Seven
G8	Group of Eight
GATT	General Agreement on Tariffs and Trade
GDP	Gross domestic product
GEDS	Global Events Data System
GEFP	Global ecological footprint
GEP	Global environmental politics
GG	Green growth
GIRT	Greening of international relations theory
GNP	Gross national product
GPE	Global political economy
GPM	Governmental politics model
GPPs	Green political parties
GPT	Green political thought
GREECOSM	Green cosmopolitan theory
GRIPE	Green international political economy
GST	General systems theory
GTA	Green theory of agency
GTV	Green theory of value
HINS	Hierarchical international system
HOTPWA	History of the Peloponnesian Wars
HST	Hegemonic stability theory
IBRD	International Bank for Reconstruction and Development
ICBMs	Intercontinental ballistic missiles
IGO	Intergovernmental organization
ILO	International Labour Organization
ILPES	Instituto Latinamericano de Planificatión Económica
IMF	International Monetary Fund
INDS	Incomplete nuclear diffusion system
IP	International politics
IPE	International political economy
IR	International relations
IRT	International relations theory
ISA	International society approach
ISI	Import substituting industrialization
LBPS	Loose bipolar system
LI	Liberal intergovernmentalism
LOH	Level of hostility
LSE	London School of Economics
LTG	Limits to growth
MAD	Mutually assured destruction
MERCOSUR	Comisión Sectorial para el Mercado Común del Sur
MID	Militarized Interstate Dispute
MNCs	Multinational corporations
MSW	Man, the State and War

MWS	Modern world-system
NAFTA	North American Free Trade Agreement
NATO	North Atlantic Treaty Organization
NGO	Non-governmental organization
NIEO	New international economic order
NRA	New regionalism approach
NSAs	Non-state actors
OAS	Organization of African States
OC	Operational code
OCAM	Organization Commune Africaine et Malgache
OECD	Organisation for Economic Co-operation and Development
OPEC	Organization of the Petroleum Exporting Countries
OPM	Organizational process model
OSCE	Organization for Security and Co-operation in Europe
OSE	Our Synthetic Environment
PAIR	Power and Interdependence Revisited
PAIWPIT	Power and Interdependence: World Politics in Transition
PAN	Politics among Nations
PD	Prisoner's dilemma
PE	Political economy
POK	Politics of knowledge
POS	Philosophy of science
PPE	Positive political economy
PSC	Pluralistic security community
RAM	Rational actor model
RBA	Region-building approach
SAARC	South Asian Association for Regional Cooperation
SADC	Southern African Development Community
SALT	Strategic Arms Limitation Talks
SD	Sustainable development
SEA	Single European Act
SOC	Strategy of Conflict
SOCAOE	Strategies of Commitment and Other Essays
SON	State of nature
SOPs	Standard operating procedures
TBPS	Tight bipolar system
TGS	The Green State
TIP	Theory of International Politics
TLC	Toward a Liberatory Technology
TNCs	Transnational corporations
TPNZSG	Two-person non-zero-sum game
TPZSG	Two-person zero-sum game
TRAWP	Transnational Relations and World Politics
TSR	Transnational social relations
TTOGPP	The Tragedy of Great Power Politics
UN	United Nations
UNCED	United Nations Conference on Environment and Development
UNCTAD	United Nations Conference on Trade and Development

UNGA	United Nations General Assembly
UNSC	United Nations Security Council
USBS	Unstable bloc system
UVIS	Universal system
UVTS	Unit veto system
VLBS	Very loose bipolar system
WSA	World-systems analysis
WSP	World-systems perspective
WST	World systems theory
WTO	World Trade Organization

PREFACE

Advanced, ambitious and fat, this textbook on international relations (IR) theory is way more comprehensive than most recent and not-too-recent attempts in not missing neither most of the old and new 'isms' invading IR nor the 'theories' or approaches developed in or imported to it. It is organized around three paradigms, self-images and world views of the discipline: realism, pluralism and globalism, first crystallized during the inter-paradigm debate of the 1970s and the early 1980s, and has loose elective affinity with it. But finally, the book breaks out of the shackles and limitations of this debate. The introductory chapter discusses the nomenclature, origins and three paradigms supposedly constitutive of IR, and the resultant identity—defining 'great debates' or 'waves', normally counted as three, but four by my counting. Section IA, concerned with the realist/power-theoretic approaches, contains six chapters, reflecting the continuing overwhelming dominance of the realist paradigm and approach in the IR theory field. Section IB, dealing with systems theories and approaches, also falling under the realist paradigm, contains three chapters. So together with game theory in Chapter 11, the realist paradigm alone accounts for 10 units. The pluralist paradigm has four units, including two sub-chapters in Chapter 13. The globalist paradigm has seven chapters. The section on postpositivism contains four chapters, beyond the inter-paradigm debate, belonging to the fourth great (postpositivist) debate between rationalists and reflectivists, from Chapters 23 to 26. Among them, critical theory (Chapter 24) is on the left; postmodernism (Chapter 26) is on the left but can also be on the right; and the English school (Chapter 23) and constructivism (Chapter 25) are in the middle of the theory road.

This textbook has some additional merits over others in the market apart from its comprehensiveness. The first is that it addresses the excessive American centricity and Eurocentrism of the discipline of IR, without overdoing it in any foolish hope of bringing IR theory 'back home'. American centricity is addressed through substantial references in the text to Martin Wight and Hedley Bull among English school theorists, and to other continental scholars, apart from a whole chapter (Chapter 23) dedicated to the English school, rather than treating it as a minor and parochial variant of realism, and through remembrance that besides English E. H. Carr and French Raymond Aron, realism had other proponents on the other side of the Atlantic too. As regards addressing West centrism/Eurocentrism, the space and importance accorded in the book to Kautilya from India and Master Han Fei Tzu from China, given short shrift in conventional books because of the Western bias of the discipline, will be convincing. Further, in my next book on discussion of concepts, issues and concrete patterns of IR, I will accommodate references to ancient, premodern, modern and current international practices in non-Western settings wherever possible and relevant.

Due to the sheer size of the book, Chapters 3, 9, 11, 13B, 19 and 25 have been put on the companion website for this edition to maintain its financial affordability. But buyers/readers should and would have free access to them. The book is an integrated, self-sufficient unit, written in a way that advanced undergraduate, inquisitive postgraduate students, research scholars and teachers need not have to search for additional books and references. Since the textbook is of semi-research type, consulting as far as possible all iconic books and articles of the areas covered by the chapters, readers of different levels will benefit from it in different ways. The book covers the syllabi for IR in all undergraduate, postgraduate and MPhil courses in Indian and foreign universities, without addressing that of any one specific university.

ACKNOWLEDGEMENTS

As regards initial inspiration behind the writing of this book, I would first remember Professor Rakhahari Chatterji of Calcutta University, my teacher and research supervisor, and direct student of Hans Morgenthau. He introduced me and other students to the intricacies of realism in IR in the classroom. Professor Radharaman Chakrabarti and Late Professor Deb Kumar Banerjee kindled my interest in diplomatic history and in the events, practices, concepts, issues and patterns in international politics, which will figure in the second volume of this work. Students in my IR classes at the University of Kalyani for 26 years and at the University of Calcutta for the final 12 years also deserve acknowledgement for raising searching, agreeable and disagreeable questions that compelled me to rethink my understanding of the discipline.

I thank and acknowledge the National Library, Kolkata, and the Central Library and Campus Library of the University of Calcutta for the innumerable books that I could browse and read to get a better grasp of all the theories and approaches. I thank books.google.co.in for the books in public domain that I consulted, and JSTOR.org for the books and journal articles that I have used and cited.

I thank and acknowledge Mr Amit Kumar of SAGE for persuading, sticking to and believing in me for a long time. Without his indulgence, this book could never have been written. Indrani Dutta, also of SAGE in Kolkata, has been a reassuring spirit. Finally, I thank my dear wife, children and grandson for suffering the privation of commiseration and company that the writing of the book caused them. Whatever limitations and shortcomings the book has are, however, mine alone.

ABOUT THE AUTHOR

Amartya Mukhopadhyay is a retired professor of political science and one-term chair at the University of Calcutta. He was formerly professor of political science, departmental chair for seven terms and dean, Faculty of Arts and Commerce, at the University of Kalyani. He has published in diverse areas, including social and political thought (in book *Politics, Society and Colonialism: An Alternative Understanding of Tagore's Responses*, 2010); postcolonial theory (in book *India in Russian Orientalism: Travel Narratives and Beyond*, 2013); public policy analysis (in book *Politics of Implementation: Mass Transportation Policy for Calcutta 1947–1989*, 2002, and 'Politics of Power Crisis in West Bengal: Linkages between Technical and Political Aspects of Policy Making', in *Politics in West Bengal: Institutions, Processes and Problems*, ed. Rakhahari Chatterji, 1985); Indian politics (as in 'Bearing Unusual Fruit: What Ails the Civil Society in (West) Bengal', in *Rethinking India's Democracy*, eds Malyasree Mukherjee and Nivedita Saha, 2017, and 'Civil Social Initiatives in Bengal', in *West Bengal under the Left, 1977–2011*, eds Rakhahari Chatterji and Partha Pratim Basu, 2018); IR theory and practice (in 'Constriction of Choices and the Kashmir Solution', in *Conflict Resolution in the Post-Cold War Era*, ed. Arun Kumar Banerji, 2000, and 'Theories of Foreign Policy Decision Making: Indian Context', in *Socialist Perspective* XII, nos. 1 and 2, June 1984); and Bengali and English literature. He is a regular contributor to various webzines on cultural aspects of Bengali and Indian life. At present, he is engaged in and is much advanced in his translation of iconic Bengali folk tales and has taken to writing a novel. Father of two well-established children, Mukhopadhyay spends his time in reading, writing, performing daily chores and taking care of his wife. Mukhopadhyay is a loner and has modern Bengali poetry as his lifetime obsession.

CHAPTER

1

Introduction

CHAPTER OUTLINE

- Name and Origins
  - *International Relations or Interstate Relations*
  - *IR or International Politics*
  - *World Politics, Global Politics or IRs*
  - *Origins: Analytical Tradition and Historical Tradition*
- Three Images or Paradigms of IR
- 'Great Debates' or 'Waves' of the Discipline
  - *The First Great Debate: Context, Contenders, Contentions, Critiques*
  - *The Second Great Debate: Context, Issues, Contenders, Outcome*
  - *The Third Great Debate/Inter-paradigm Debate: Context, Contenders and Contentions*
  - *The Fourth Great Debate in IR*

This introductory chapter will discuss the nomenclature of the discipline and its origins and attendant disputes. After touching upon the alternative images, paradigms or world views of the discipline, it will embark on an exploration of the four contours-defining debates in the discipline to give students a fair idea of the nature and scope of the discipline, even before they turn to individual chapters.

NAME AND ORIGINS

International Relations or Interstate Relations

The issue of the appropriateness of nomenclature arises from the fact that during much of its existence, the discipline of international relations (henceforth IR) simply signified interstate relations. Because of this, some think the term IR is a misnomer.[1] It is no use invoking Barker's definition of the state as 'the juridically organized nation'[2] against this charge because it is inevitably premised on the concept of the nation state, which was beset by what Benedict Anderson calls the 'impending crisis of the hyphen that for two hundred years yoked nation and state'[3] caused by the failure of the promise of states, as also by the expanding spectacle of stateless nations. The number of nation states is very limited in the world. Connor, for examples, counts only 12 out of the existing 132 states in the 1970s as nation states and calls the League of Nations and the United Nations (UN) as misnomers and malapropisms, to bluntly claim that '(t)he discipline called International Relations should be designated Interstate Relations.'[4] And when we remember that member states in the UN, at odds on nearly every conceivable issue, agree only in resisting any change in their frontiers,[5] we fully understand the problem of the appellation of IR. In many North Indian languages, 'international' means 'āntarjātik', and 'jāti' can mean caste, community, ethnicity or even nation but never state. Rabindranath Tagore, one of India's iconic poets, littérateurs and linguists, unequivocally said that the word 'nation' has no Bengali equivalent.[6] Still, the discipline goes by the name of IR. The reigning unhappiness with the resultant confusions about the dimensions of the discipline will be reflected not only in my mode of analysis but also in the range of topics chosen for discussion.

IR or International Politics

The most appropriate name cannot be international politics (henceforth IP), for it is a narrower field than IR and forms part of it. In contradistinction to IP or foreign policy, IR 'may refer to *all* forms of interaction between members of separate societies, whether government sponsored or not', including 'the analysis of foreign policies or political processes between states'. With its interest in 'all facets of relations between distinct societies, IR would include, as well, studies of international trade unions, the International Red Cross, tourism, international trade, transportation, communication and the development of international values and ethics', all neglected by the student of IP, '*except where they impinge upon official governmental objectives or where they are employed by governments as inducements to achieve military or political objectives* [italics by author].'[7] The next Olympics, wherever held, might be a truly international event but still would not be the stuff of IP, unless they throw up some events or issues with potential political implications. Another problem with nomenclature IP is that when IR is taught as a sub-discipline in political science, international political relations may get some primacy over international social or cultural or economic relations. But this would not be the case when IR is taught as a sub-specialization in the disciplines of law, philosophy or economics or separate discipline itself.

World Politics, Global Politics or IRs

This is the third issue in nomenclature. Spiro pointed out in 1966 that the substitution of international for the world has taken a far longer time than Morgenthau's substitution of politics for relations in the title of his iconic 1948 book. It 'began much more recently and has gained a much narrower acceptance'. The pace of these changes in terminology is not just academically driven but 'reflect changes in reality which the words seek to describe' and even more 'changes in our perception of that reality'. Since, 'there was no world politics' till 'roughly the end of the Second World War', and relations among a limited number of sovereign national states did affect many parts of the world but not the whole of it, two of the greatest military conflicts in the history of mankind somewhat wrongly got the epithet of 'world war'. The first was fought by and large in Europe. The second had its most important theatres in the Pacific area, in Asia and Africa, but was mostly centred on the aims and aspirations of European states, despite the US's (however, late) entry; Canada and many Latin American states' role as signatories of anti-German alliances, and Japan's transformation from a minor belligerent in the first war into a major partner of the Axis alliance in the second. Neither of these two international conflicts posed a direct threat to a very large 'proportion of the surface of the globe'. The main reason why some scholars started taking a global perspective upon what was till recently seen as IR is that only recently, a 'global community of mankind ... is coming into existence in the consciousness of human beings', whether positively because of the 'rapidly and radically improving technology, especially of transport and communications' or negatively due to 'the expanding scope of destructive weapons' in a world riven by the Cold War.[8]

Why the same set of positive and negative factors would substitute the word 'world' with a host of other adjectives, including 'global' in three decades and a little more? Suggesting the term 'postinternational politics', Rosenau identified the following five parametric transformations' that caused its emergence.

- 'The shift from an industrial to a post-industrial order' brought about the 'microelectronic revolution' that has vastly shortened social, economic and political distances; made the movement of ideas, pictures, currencies and information immensely faster, and has, as a result, increased the interdependence of people and events.
- New issues, such as environmental degradation, terrorism, drug trafficking, currency crises and AIDS, emerging as direct products of the new technologies or the world's enhanced interdependence, making them so much different from traditional issues because of their transnational nature.
- The weakening capability of nation states and governments to arrange adequate solutions of the principal issues on their agenda, first, because the new issues are not confined to their jurisdictions and, second, because even traditional issues have developed strong international dimensions.
- Systematic devitalizing of 'whole systems' and acquisition of corresponding effectiveness and salience, thereby nurturing 'tendencies towards decentralization', which run athwart the otherwise dominant centralizing tendencies.

- Resulting from all the foregoing processes, emergent 'skills and orientations of the world's adults who comprise the groups, states and other collectivities', in the course of coping with the 'new issues of interdependence' and adapting 'to the new technologies of the post-industrial order', proving them not only enhanced skills, orientations and responsibilities but also new sensibilities.[9]

Preferring to call the new IP 'global', McGrew claims that it is an academic response to the recognition that 'the scale of political life' has been changed 'fundamentally' so much so that politics in the sense of a set of activities devoted to the establishment of order and justice is no longer 'confined within territorial boundaries'. From that perspective, it questions the validity and usefulness of 'the distinction between the domestic and the foreign, inside and outside the territorial state and the national and the international'. Since, these days, decisions and actions taken in a particular region touch the well-being of communities in several distant parts of the globe, 'domestic politics is internationalized, and world politics becomes domesticated.' Even power in the global system is no longer held in monopoly by nation states but is, even if unevenly, diffused among a motley group of private and public actors and networks, ranging from international and/or intergovernmental agencies, multinational corporations (MNCs) or transnational corporations (TNCs), non-governmental organizations (NGOs). Likewise, authority is shared not only by 'supra-state bodies', like regional organizations (European Union [EU], Association of Southeast Asian Nations [ASEAN], South Asian Association for Regional Cooperation [SAARC]) but moves down to regional assemblies, sub-state bodies and even private agencies. Although nation states still possess the trappings of sovereignty as a juridical principle, increasingly, sovereignty is also distributed among local, national, regional and global bodies. McGrew confidently asserts that in 'an age of globalization, national politics no longer function as bounded or closed systems'. Rather global politics ensures that 'all politics—understood as the pursuit of order and justice—are played out in a global context'.[10]

Despite keeping IR in this book's title, I will, in the course of my discussions of theories, approaches, issues and patterns, make the discipline take on the dimensions of other names. Let us now move on to the origins of the discipline.

Origins: Analytical Tradition and Historical Tradition

The question of when the discipline emerged has got interestingly entangled with the name of the discipline. Knutsen clarifies two meanings of IR, both of which buttress our point about the problem of the name of the discipline. According to him, the first meaning of this 'vague' term relates to 'interactions among states and between states and state-based actors across state boundaries' and its coinage dating back to Jeremy Bentham's 1789 book, *An Introduction to the Principles of Morals and Legislation.* The second meaning of the term refers to an autonomous field of academic enquiry, distinct from other social sciences, and takes the first as 'its object of scholarly scrutiny'. When Knutsen says that IR, in this second sense, 'effectively originated in 1919' with the founding of the Woodrow Wilson Chair of IP at the University College of Wales, Aberystwyth, by philanthropist merchant David Davies; he is admittedly taking IR in this second sense.[11]

So by far, the most dominant view of the origins of the discipline regards IR as a product of the First World War. Surely, organized academic activity is seen more in this period, as exemplified by the lecture tour on IR in the USA by British political scientist Lord Bryce.[12] Still, is it possible to say that before the war, any study of IR was absent, considering that this orphan discipline lovingly calls Thucydides father? Knutsen rightly traces any confusion about the origins of international relations theory (henceforth, IRT) to an 'unclear idea of what tradition means' and makes a distinction between a 'historic tradition' and an 'analytic tradition' of IR to bring greater clarity. The former signifies 'a self-constituted pattern of conventional practice', while the latter is defined as 'an inherited pattern of thought or a sustained intellectual connection through time along which scholars stipulate certain concepts, themes and texts as functionally similar'. A 'historic tradition' of IR looks back to antiquity 'to Xenophon, Thucydides, Herodotus, Plutarch and other ancient authors, who discussed causes of war and described practices of balance and counterbalance'. But since 'one cannot safely infer from political practices the existence of political theories', an 'analytic tradition' of the study of IR does not date back to more than a few centuries. Although many authors, including Thucydides, point out the existence of a balance of power (henceforth, BOP in the rest of the book) practices and even theory and, moreover, draw lessons from contemporary history for the posterity, 'neither Thucydides nor any other classical author can alone demonstrate the existence of a 3,000-year-long tradition in IR; their accounts do not add up to a sustained intellectual connection across ages'. Their arguments lost colour in the Western scholarly tradition, 'once Greece fell to Macedon and Rome. And when Rome collapsed, they slipped out of view altogether'.

While Knutsen traces the beginning of the 'analytic tradition' of IR from the collapse of Rome,[13] some other scholars trace the 'historic tradition' of IR far beyond Westphalia or even beyond the collapse of the Roman Empire. For example, deploring the fact that, until recently, 'mainstream IR theorists have shown virtually no interest in examining IR from a world-historical perspective', Buzan and Little use the framework of their international systems to identify 'three significant turning points in the world history of international systems'. The first occurred more than 40,000 years back when hunter-gatherer bands first embarked on a form of exchange that 'resulted in long-distance movement of goods and ideas, over hundreds and sometimes thousands of miles', resulting in indirect linking and contact between numerous hunter-gatherer bands and providing the first signs of 'pre-international systems' that were accountable for global colonization that eventually spread to almost every part of the habitable world, 'last vestiges of which can still be dimly discerned today'. The second turning point occurred 5,500 years back with the emergence and interaction of 'state-like units', mutual interactions between them providing the backbone of the 'first fully fledged international systems'. The major components of them became increasingly diversified to embrace agrarian empires, nomadic empires, chiefdoms, city-states and city leagues. The characteristic diversity of the ancient and classical historical era left scope for a juxtaposition of 'pre-international systems' and 'international systems'. The former were far from extinction even at the end of the second transformational stage and not only prevailed in large sections of the globe but also continued to penetrate 'increasingly inaccessible and previously uninhabited regions'. Yet 'international systems' continued to expand, come into contact with each other and coalesce, even if mainly in the economic and cultural sectors without establishing political or military contact and notwithstanding pieces of evidence of systems coalescence, allowed a large number of discrete international systems to maintain their existence throughout the period. But at the onset of the third turning point that started only 500 years ago, a new kind of political actor, the modern sovereign state, emerged, and after leading to the elimination of units in 'pre-international systems' and diversity of actors in both eras, it covered the entire globe by the end of the 20th century. The 'international systems' that had emerged and developed in the five millennia after the second turning point now 'coalesced remarkably swiftly' to engender a single international system dominating all the lands and seas of the Earth. While this process was completed more than 150 years ago, culminating in 'the fully global international system, which, in turn, gave birth to the self-conscious study of IR', the world-historical transformation was far from complete. Amid debates about whether the Westphalian state was yielding place to a post-modern state and about whether military-political relations are ceding primacy to socio-political ones, the 'historic tradition' of IR remains open. To Buzan and Little, this historico-theoretical foray establishes that 'the development of theory in IR has been held back by its confinement to the theoretical strait-jacket'.[14]

Long before Buzan and Little, K. J. Holsti compared such diverse historical international systems as those of the Chou dynasty (1122–221 BC), the Greek city-states (800–322 BC), the interstate system of Europe (1648–1814 AD) and the contemporary global system, which, though not historicized, dated from the Vienna Congress (1815) and evolved all through the next 175 years.[15]

This argument about the pre-Westphalian roots of IR is valid and allows us not to exclaim like Alice, 'a grin without a cat! It's the most curious thing I ever saw in my life.'[16] Since the cats (of pre-international and international systems) existed for so long, it is impossible that a disciplinary IR grin never lit up their faces. Making this distinction between two traditions does not necessarily breed 'confusion between an analytical and a historical tradition' that Schmidt warns about. Nor does it lead to the historically 'mistaken belief that the contemporary configuration of the discipline can be explained by a continuous tradition that reaches back to classical Athens and extends forward to the present'.[17] It only guards against the opposite error of brags about theoretical novelty that Morgenthau so wisely warned for international theory.[18]

THREE IMAGES OR PARADIGMS OF IR

In any discipline where several approaches, conceptual frameworks and theories contend, some are more affine than others, making a grouping of those normatively or epistemologically kindred approaches and theories advisable, whether as filing systems, 'paradigms' (in dilution of its Kuhnian meaning),[19] 'alternative images' after Viotti and Kauppi[20] or 'diverse world views' underpinning contemporary IRT in the manner of Martin Griffiths.[21] Viotti and Kauppi think that of these 'alternative images', the first set focuses on 'the key *actors*, or *units*', (generating 'unit assumptions') and the second set involves '*assumptions* made about them' (engendering 'agenda assumptions'). Viotti and Kauppi elaborate three images or paradigms of IR: realism, pluralism and globalism.

Realism has three key unit assumptions and one agenda assumption. The first unit assumption is: 'states are the principal or most important actors', starting from the times of Greek city-states down to the modern times of nation states. Even those realists who make allowance for the concept of the *system* take it to be an international system of states and discount the impact of non-state actors (NSAs) on states' primacy. Intergovernmental actors, including the UN, are not thought to have achieved sufficient clout as independent international actors to be able to question this primacy, not to talk of other NSAs such as MNCs, terrorist groups and other transnational and international organizations. The second unit assumption takes the state as a unitary and monolithic actor covered by a 'metaphorical hard shell', which confronts the world outside as an integrated unit. Since political disputes and discords within the state are resolved authoritatively, at any specific moment, the state speaks in only one voice and has only one position on any given issue, differences in responses of ministries, departments or personalities being quickly ironed out. In the third unit assumption, consonantly with this state-centric view of IP, the state is seen as 'essentially a rational actor', pursuing a rational foreign policy that includes a 'statement of objectives'; a list of 'all feasible alternatives'; the possibility of attaining these objectives through these alternatives, and the benefits and costs entailed by each alternative, assuming that the official decision-makers evaluate each alternative and choose the one that optimizes all the utilities, even though this is assumption counterfactual assumption. In circumstances of uncertainties, incomplete information, constraints of time and limits to data processing powers, such a rational course is seldom possible, even without taking into account the factor of human biases and predilections. Realists know that 'satisficing' behaviour and suboptimal solutions accordingly become inevitable. But they would not let go this presumption of, even if 'bounded', rationality. The upshot of all these considerations is the inescapable conclusion that there is a hierarchy in international issues where national security predominates; military and political issues dominate the agenda of IP; power is the key concept, and in the graded IP agenda, 'high politics', understood as a concern with security or strategic issues, takes precedence over 'low politics' or mundane internal welfare issues.

The pluralist image/paradigm questions all these assumptions of realism. First, it views NSAs as no less important entities in IR. International organizations, pluralists believe, have already become independent actors, and their decision-makers, bureaucrats and other associated bodies already wield considerable influence in the agenda setting of IR—no more feckless and inert forums which sovereign states use to pursue their ends. Similarly, MNCs have also gathered enough clout in an interdependent world economy, being able not only to bypass the directive of the state but also sometimes bend the state to their wishes. Second, rather than being a unitary actor, the state is an abstraction that hides the stuff of politics within it and is a conglomeration of individual bureaucrats, interest groups, leaders and other personalities and organizations that seek to formulate or influence foreign policy through 'competition, coalition building, conflict and compromise'. To understand the politics, it is necessary to 'disaggregate the state—break it into its component parts' instead of treating it as an integrated whole with a single will and immune to outside forces. Pluralists think that states and governments have a porous outer shell, which non-governmental actors can pierce, to take actions that have grave policy implications for the state. Pluralists, thus, not only consider interactions between NSAs and governments within states but take into reckoning the transnational dimensions of the state to grasp these interactions across national borders. Any unitary view of the state will miss the very essence of this complex politics. Third, pluralists question the realist view of the state as a rational actor. In the pluralist image of the disaggregated state, in which foreign policy decisions emerge from 'clashes, bargaining and compromise'—as also coalitions and counter-coalitions between and among so many different actors, and achieving 'a minimum winning coalition' becomes the only condition and criterion of policy—any premise of state rationality would be highly questionable. 'Satisficing' and suboptimal decisions would not be a conceptual irritant but an inevitable reality. All these would have implications for the agenda of IP, which will not be hierarchical but extensive. Military security issues will not predominate, and 'low politics' will be as important as 'high politics'.

While the realist and the pluralist image/paradigm address their assumptions and propositions to each other, the globalist paradigm, comparatively a recent one, puts up independently its unit-and-agenda assumptions. First, focusing neither on the state nor on NSAs, globalists take, as the analytical starting point, the entire 'global context within which states and other entities interact'. The 'big picture' is important because understanding the external behaviour of states needs going beyond factors internal to a state and attempting to grasp how the structure of the system compels or induces actors to behave in certain directions. Second, even while conceding the importance of states as actors, international organizations and transnational actors and coalitions, globalists emphasize how these and other factors constitute 'mechanisms of domination' which enable some states, classes or elites to reap greater benefit from the international system at the cost of others' sufferings. This leads them to explore the development and maintenance of dependency relations between the Northern industrialized states, on the one hand, and the poor, underdeveloped and industrially backward states in Asia, Africa and Latin America on the other. They are in the 'periphery' of the international system, and their underdevelopment is premised to be the precondition as well as the outcome of the development of the northern 'core'. Third, the globalists' agenda assumption is that IR is best viewed from a historical perspective. Since globalists of both Marxist and non-Marxist orientations share the belief that the present international system is predominantly capitalist, they undertake an examination of the rise of capitalism in Western Europe and its development and transformation down to its culmination in the world capitalist system. Finally, goaded by the first three points, globalists uphold the 'critical importance of economic factors' as keys to the understanding of the dynamics of the international system. While realists place political–military issues above economic ones and pluralists treat them at par, globalists differ from both of them to posit economics as fundamental to the creation, evolution and working of the contemporary world system. They equally spurn the realist reification of the state with its hard shell and the pluralist fragmentation of it as contrary to the structuralist image of the world system, since any bargaining between multiple actors, whether inside or across state borders, is predetermined if it has a North–South dimension. This is because all state interactions are guided and controlled by class forces that aim to maintain an exploitative and dependent relation between developed states in the North and underdeveloped states in the peripheral South.

However, these images or paradigms are ideal types and pure types, which in their zeal to highlight what 'a number of seemingly diverse theoretical approaches have in common' ignore the differences in the thinking of many theorists of any one image. Besides, though they give the impression that the three images are mutually exclusive, many notable writers in IR share many of the assumptions of each image.

Finally, many IR specialists cannot be conveniently fixed in any one image/paradigm. Still, inasmuch as the vast majority of writers within the field 'tends to be associated with one of the three perspectives', even these 'notable exceptions' do not in their view detract from the merit and value of this division and differentiation of images/paradigms. They also make a few additional points about the images. These are as follows:

- They are more concerned with what is studied in IR than with how to study these, rendering any dispute between quantitative or non-quantitative approaches in IR, as the behaviouralist–traditionalist controversy, secondary.
- Recent attempts at predicting global futures through complex modelling can be anchored in any one or other of the images.
- Known methods in the field of decision-making or public choice theory and other economic models applied to political decision-making, such as public or collective goods theory, game theory, econometrics and other approaches, emerging in the burgeoning field of international political economy (IPE) transcend these world images.
- Finally, the three images are not *theories* but general perspectives on IR, which can be home to different theories.[22] Griffiths says that they, however, 'shape the questions we ask and provide some of the key interpretive concepts that are employed to build theories', apart from representing 'a distinctive set of ideas and arguments about IR'. But from the way Griffiths' co-authors talk about such world views in his edited volume (such as Realism, Liberal Internationalism, Marxism, Critical Theory (CT), Constructivism, the English School (ES), Poststructuralism, Feminism and Theories of State Formation), the distinction between world views and theories gets blurred.[23] Anyway, in my book, many of Griffiths' world views are classed as theories or approaches, locatable under any one of the three images or paradigms.

'GREAT DEBATES' OR 'WAVES' OF THE DISCIPLINE

It is fitting that from an exploration of the alternative images of the discipline of IR, I will proceed to a brief discussion of its 'great debates', which are deeply interwoven with the self-images of the discipline at different times of its evolution, although not all scholars are agreed on the constitutive role of the 'great debates' for the disciplinary self-imagining of IR, some even branding hem as parts of a 'stylized version of the history of international relations theory (IRT)' that 'haunt countless undergraduate and graduate course descriptions'.[24] Still, we state them briefly because inside 'the orthodox historiography of IR, it has been through the organizing device of the *image* of a series of 'great debates' that the story of the field's development has been framed.' And the belief that the history of the discipline is encapsulated in three successive debates is so ingrained that it hardly leaves any other alternative in telling the history of the discipline'. The 'great debates' provide one of the 'most dominant self-images of the field' and earn the status of 'defining debates'.[25]

The First Great Debate: Context, Contenders, Contentions, Critiques

The best way of understanding each of the debates would be to situate it in its context. The First Great Debate is believed to have taken place between the interwar 'idealists' and the post-war 'realists'. Amid a worldwide pacifist sentiment engendered by the horrors of the First World War, enthused by Woodrow Wilson's Fourteen Points programme and the establishment of the League of Nations and its undergirding concept of collective security, some thinkers, somewhat inappropriately called 'idealists' and 'liberal utopians', started thinking that the real interest and enthusiasm of the people were for lasting peace. So if democratic states and governments were given a fair chance, they would seek to realize these hopes and aspirations of the people on the international plane. Believing that undemocratic, tyrannical and militaristic states equipped with the most lethal weapons were the worst enemies of peace (exemplified by Germany, Austria-Hungary and Russia before 1914 and manifest in military interventions of Italy in Abyssinia—now Ethiopia—and of Japan in China and Manchuria in the 1930s), 'idealists' and 'liberal utopians' took democratic governments in the domestic sphere and an international organization (like the League in the external sphere) as the surest guarantees against the scourge of war. They also placed great faith in the mechanisms of the pacific settlement of international disputes in the League Covenant.

But with increasing warlike activities of democratically formed governments in Germany, Italy and Japan in the 1930s, poverty of this idealist–utopian thought became supposedly apparent. This induced a number of scholars on both sides of the Atlantic to question the assumptions and premises of the 'idealists' and League of Nations' goal of the outlawry of war and search for more practical methods for the attainment of a workable peace. Among them were an American theologian and ethicist named Reinhold Niebuhr and three academicians, E. H. Carr, Nicholas J. Spykman and Hans J. Morgenthau. Aware that anxiety 'is the inevitable concomitant of the paradox of freedom and finiteness in which man is involved,'[26] which leads to a will to power, reflected in the international plane in the mutual and unceasing conflicts of nations and convinced that 'the most significant moral characteristic of a nation is its hypocrisy', Niebuhr doubted if 'conscientious pacifism on the part of 2 per cent of a national population could actually prevent future wars'. Let alone the contemporary radical pacifism, Niebuhr grudged any truck with moderate pacifism. For him, no world state but only a policy of BOP could ensure lasting peace.'[27] So he pilloried 'the perfectionists', that is, liberal utopians for wrongly 'making no distinction between an individual act of self-abnegation and a political policy of submission to injustice, whereby lives and interests other than our own are defrauded or destroyed.'[28] Distinguishing between individual and state morality, Morgenthau, discussed shortly below, said similarly that 'the individual may say for himself: "Fiat justicia, pereat mundus (Let justice prevail, even if the world perish)," but the state has no right to say so in the name of those who are in its care.'[29]

On the other side of the Atlantic, Carr, a noted neo-Marxist historian, bemoaned 'the almost total neglect of power' in 'nearly all thinking, both academic and popular, about IP in English-speaking countries from 1919 to 1939', by British (and American) 'utopians', wedded to a normative agenda which took scant notice of the world around them while focusing on ways to bring in a Manichean change in the ways states related to each other.[30] The reason why liberal theory dominated IR discourse despite failing to deliver was that the discipline was supposedly still 'in its infancy', and the first generation of IR theorists, who stood in the same relation to modern 'realists' as alchemists to the sophisticated chemists, were 'utopians'. Carr criticized their vision of a natural 'harmony of interests', coining the term from the Smithian concept of the 'invisible hand'. World history, being conflictual in this concept, while contentious before, was even more anachronistic in the 1930s, given the saturation of colonial markets. The attendant competition for them increased manifold the possibility of war. But unfortunately, 'harmony of interests', concealing under its liberal veneer, 'nothing but the ideology of a dominant group', seeking political and cultural domination in the guise of universal good, merely helped in obscuring the power relations between classes and states. Fitting it into the terms of the idealist–realist debate, it was a refutation of Sir Norman Angell's contention in 1912 that a large-scale war between the great powers was not rational in view of the interdependence or world markets and industry.[31]

Spkyman's realist book[32] never mentions the debate, probably, because his critique of idealist internationalism, set in the background of his prescription for US proper geopolitical strategy, is more nuanced. He did not think that the League of Nations, which President Wilson made a part of his peace settlement plan and which, in his thinking, should have replaced 'the discredited BOP system as an instrument for the prevention of war', was actually workable. He contended that had the USA even joined the League and other great power members did not have 'failed to attune their policies to the spirit of the Covenant', the League could not have arisen from its ideological morass. 'The idealists were wrong in thinking that its procedures represented a radical departure from the policy of power politics. The League changed the legal obligations of states, but it did not basically alter the organization of force in the international community', with control of the armed by sovereign independent states, possessing a veto power on collective decisions its major features. The system of collective security was a misnomer.[33]

Morgenthau, the last of the four early stalwarts of neo-classical realism, built his arguments around the key concepts of national interest and the international BOP, a 'particular general social principle to which all societies composed of a number of autonomous units owe the autonomy of their component parts' so that 'policies aiming at its preservation are not only inevitable but are an essential stabilizing factor in a society of sovereign nations'.[34] A realist and rational theory of IP grounded in the concept of 'interest defined in terms of power', guards against two 'popular fallacies: the concern with motives and the concern with ideological preferences'.[35] Although Morgenthau did not specifically mention it, both the fallacies were presumably associated with liberal utopianism.

Critics of the First Great Debate have questioned its authenticity from various angles. Some argue that both idealism and realism were, in fact, parts of traditional theory, the same 'paradigm' in Kuhnian terms. Systematized over centuries in the works of Thucydides, Hobbes and Rousseau, this was carried over into post-World War IR and held sway till the onset of the Second World War. So it was far less 'significant and fundamental' than the later debate between behaviouralists and traditionalists.[36] Smith thinks the first debate or even the next one (between traditionalists and behaviouralists) was less a debate than 'a series of statements of faith with political and sociological factors determining which voice was heard.'[37] Another scholar calls it a 'sterile standoff' which was inadequate to 'meet the normative challenges confronting the world after the Second World War'.[38]

Further, a new group of disciplinary historians doubts if this debate had at all taken place, first, because 'the scholarship of the interwar period cannot, in any meaningful way, be characterized as an idealist or utopian', despite Carr's clever coinage 'for discrediting a whole range of things he happened to disagree with' with a 'realist category of abuse'. Second, they refuse to accept that in the late 1930s or the early 1940s 'any meaningful intellectual exchange' took place between 'interlocutors holding opposing "idealist" and "realist" points of view'. Wilson even did not hesitate to term the debate a 'myth'.[39] The revisionists deny any serious differences between these two schools for three reasons. First, the concepts of anarchy and state sovereignty bothered the so-called idealists as much as realists. The interwar scholars had no doubt that their subject matter was inextricably linked with causes of war and peace and could not avoid the reality of sovereign states functioning in a situation of anarchy. Second, ever since the 1920s, critics of the juristic theory, including pluralists, pointed to the interdependence of the world. Their heritage and legacy were lost because the 'idealist tag' was unjustly attached to their findings. Third, the 'idealist tag' stood in the way of observing how, while studying international organization and security, the interwar scholars were keenly aware of the limitations of the new international organization in altering fundamentally by itself the logic of IP.[40]

Moreover, the 'idealist' paradigm was home to a mind-boggling array of beliefs, convictions and characteristics and subsumed a wide variety of other doctrines, including 'universalism, cosmopolitanism, humanism, liberalism, socialism, pacifism, anarchism, internationalism, "idealist nationalism" and chiliasm'. By throwing away such a richly stowed pack as idealism, realism rendered itself 'an exceptionally bleak and deterministic doctrine', which denied the possibility of progress and the application of reason except in a narrowly interpreted managerial sense, imparted to all purposeful progressive change pejorative connotations of 'unworldliness, impracticality and untruth' and reserved positive overtones of 'worldliness, practicality and truth' only for realist premises of 'fatalism, international stasis, human impotence'.[41]

Some writers, however, not only contend that a debate had actually taken place but also insist that the Great Debate framework does perform some 'useful disciplinary functions', which necessitates retaining the story of the First Great Debate despite its imprecision and ambiguities.[42] Osiander pointed out that since the signal difference between idealism and realism lies in their 'respective theories of history', for a proper understanding of idealist IR thinking, 'it is essential to realize the extent to which it relies on the notion, not so much of progress (as is usually asserted) as of an inescapable, directional historical process', which was entirely misconstrued by Carr.[43]

Even after these qualifications, the exchange between idealists and realists led to a change in emphasis in IR after the Second World War, as can be seen from Box 1.1.

The Second Great Debate: Context, Issues, Contenders, Outcome

While in the First Great Debate, a whole corpus of international thought was attacked by 'realists' under the rubric of 'idealism', in the sacred cause of a rational/scientific theory, in the Second Great Debate of the 1950s and 1960s, popularly known as the

BOX 1.1
The First Great Debate in IR

Utopian Liberalism	*Realist Response*
1920s *Focus*	1930s–1950s *Focus*
• International Law	• Power politics
• International organization/collective security	• Security/BOP
• Interdependence	• Aggression
• Cooperation	• Conflict
• Peace	• War

Source: Adapted from Jackson and Sørensen, *Introduction to International Relations*, 44.

traditionalism–behaviouralism debate, realism itself came under attack in the name of 'traditionalism'.[44] In Smith's words, this debate 'took the 'rhetorical' arguments about science and gave them methodological substance.'[45] Despite their arguments—even if sometimes hesitant—for an autonomous discipline or a specific science of IR, methodologically, the 'realists' were in the same boat with the 'idealists', owing to their close connections to history, philosophy and law and training, like their 'idealist' brethren, in history and the methods of the diplomatic historian and the art of judgement of the functioning diplomat. Accordingly, they could not escape their concern with moral questions. The resultant tension between rationalist aspirations and normative considerations is clear in Morgenthau's iconic text, to be 'read' in the next chapter.

The context of the debate is provided by the post-Second World War's rapid and huge expansion of the academic discipline of IR, particularly in the USA, financially and logistically sponsored by government agencies and private foundations for research that will serve US national interest and the resultant arrival of a new crop of IR scholars from not only political science, economics and other social sciences but also, sometimes, mathematics and other natural sciences. Their ideas about how IR should be studied drew sustenance from the current behavioural revolution raging in other social and natural sciences, buttressed by a philosophy of science (hereafter POS) called positivism. What they wanted for IR was not so much a new theory as a novel methodology which will make the pursuit of international studies 'scientific' in the Positivist sense. The version of positivism, which behaviouralists in IR were promoting among others and which believed in the unity of the sciences, posits that scientific knowledge emerges only with collection of sufficient observable data. When analysed after being subjected to the standard processes used for measurement, classification, generalization and finally validation of hypotheses, it helps identification of patterns facilitating formulation of laws, the same kind of objective and verifiable laws that seek to explain the physical world are achievable in the world of IR as well by separating facts from values. This stress on observable facts and measurable data, precise calculation and collection of data in order to discover or discern recurring behavioural patterns that would yield 'laws' of IR led positivists-cum-behaviouralists to lay down specific steps in theory construction and criteria of 'good' theories, all of them standard in the positivist POS. We are presenting the steps of scientific theory construction pursued/prescribed in Box 1.2.

The steps of theory construction as detailed above would suggest that for the positivists-cum-behaviouralist the criteria of 'good' theories, as detailed in Box 1.3.

It is from this perspective on the theory that the exponents of the new scientific model challenged realists' and other traditionalists' view of science, charging that many of the central concepts of 'classical' realism lacked specificity and amenability to measurement and that if power and national interest were to be tested on the anvil of the new science, they had to be invested with higher levels of clarity and specificity

BOX 1.2
Steps in Scientific Theory Construction

Formation of hypothesis

Validation through testing, involving:

- Design of a verifying experiment
- Collection of empirical data in other ways
- Careful observation, recording and analysis of results of data-gathering effort
- Discarding, modifying, reformulating or confirming hypothesis
- Publication of findings and inviting others to duplicate this knowledge-discovering adventure and to confirm or deny

Source: Adapted from James Dougherty and Robert L. Pfalzgraff Jr.'s exposition in *Contending Theories of International Relations: A Comprehensive Survey*, Fifth Edition (New York: Longman, 2001), 46.

BOX 1.3
What Good Theories Should Be

- Accurate
- Falsifiable
- Capable of evincing great explanatory power
- Progressive as opposed to degenerating in terms of their research programme(s)
- Consistent with what is known in other areas
- Appropriately parsimonious and elegant

Source: John A. Vasquez, 'The Post-Positivist Debate: Reconstructing Scientific Enquiry and International Relations Theory after Enlightenment's Fall,' in Ken Booth and Steve Smith, *International Relations Theory Today* (University Park, PA: Pennsylvania State University Press, 1996), 230.

and that anything that failed the test of measurement and testing was to be exorcized from the new disciplinary dispensation.

The traditionalists defied these criticisms because many of them felt that the core concepts of the discipline left little scope for the kind of data collection and measurement procedures that the behaviouralists favoured. A debate naturally ensued, as a duel between ES theorist Hedley Bull from the traditionalists and Morton Kaplan from the 'scientists', but was later joined in by even earlier realist defenders of science in IR like Morgenthau and later scienticist realists such as David Vital, Oran Young, J. David Singer, Robert A. Jervis and Marion J. Levy Jr.[46]

The root cause of the debate was of course the widely divergent views on methodology. The traditional approach, holistic in nature because of its acceptance of the complexity of the human world and of IR as part of it, was basically interpretive in approach. It sought to *understand* this world by getting *inside* it. It called for *understanding* the minds of the statesmen by values, orientations, situations, ethics and moral dilemmas. The behaviouralist approach, on the other hand, discounted morality or ethics in the study of IR because values cannot be studied scientifically, that is, objectively. The scholar is expected to stand *outside* the world and *explain* it from there. It was a reflection of the wider debate in the social sciences between positivist and anti-positivist approaches and, to that extent, irresolvable. The basic differences between the two approaches are provided in Box 1.4.

As regards scores, while the first debate was claimed to have been won by realists, however, contentiously, the second debate is seen as having ended in a tame draw and, compared to the wealth of literature about the first debate, far less 'carefully and systematically investigated' and consequently far less 'well understood'. Thus, despite

BOX 1.4
The Second Great Debate in IR

Traditionalist Vision of IR	*Behaviouralist Vision of IR*
Nature of the Discipline • Part of the social sciences	**Nature of the Discipline** • Specialized, technical and specific field of knowledge
Function of Theory • Interpretation from inside • Intuitive understanding • Providing holistic knowledge	**Function of Theory** • Explanation from outside • Explanation, prediction and control • Providing specific and atomistic knowledge
Focus • Norms and values • Application of informed judgement • Qualitative analysis • Historical knowledge	**Focus** • Hypothesis and facts • Design of experiment/systematic collection of data • Quantification and measurement • Scientific and empirical knowledge

Source: Adapted from Jackson and Sørensen, *Introduction to IR* (1999), 48.

the academic consensus that it was a debate about the scientific reorientation of the field, four completely divergent accounts of the status of the controversy vie for attention. First, George Liska branded the very decade during which the debate occurred as the 'heroic decade', in which a narrow, specialized construction of the field was staked out against a broader social scientific orientation to it, and Arendt Lijphart described the second debate as more substantive and fundamental than the earlier debate for generating a new behavioural paradigm. Second, John Vasquez in *The Power of Power Politics* (1983) and Stefano Guzzini, Martin Hollis and Steve Smith and K. J. Holsti saw it as a 'pseudo debate' that eschewed substantive aspects of the subject matter and focused on narrow methodological questions within the close confines of the realist paradigm.[47] Third, Finnegan asserted that before burning itself out, the Second Great Debate had ushered in a compromise in the discipline, interpretable as 'different ends of a continuum of scholarship than different games' where 'each type of effort' fertilized the other while checking on the excesses 'endemic in each approach',[48] and Black doubted 'how much impact it had on theoretical formulations', for two reasons: (a) 'competing methodological preferences were compatible both with the dominant emphasis on national conflict and with a continuing minority interest in co-operation and the growth of supranational actors' and (b) both traditionalists and scientists were visible on opposing sides of such momentous and divisive issues as the American intervention in Vietnam.[49] Fourth, Wæver said that even though no side apparently won the debate, 'substantial 'paradigms' as to assumptions (ontology) of IR remained with realism, while the 'scientific' challenge had left a decisive mark within realism itself, and the second debate was to be won through delayed effect in the 1980s' through Waltz's *Theory of International Politics (TIP)*. Wæver would not call this debate minor. It not only helped to 'professionalize' the discipline but was also a 'major move in the construction of a self-referential, inner-directed debate defining a separate scientific "sub-system"'. Whereas the first debate was merely the 'academic reflection of a more general exchange about foreign policy', the second primarily addressed and attracted the 'members of the profession'.[50]

I subscribe to Finnegan's position, as it helps refute the claim that the debate had only a 'delayed effect' and only through Waltzian positivism. While the thought patterns of realism were clearly visible in the systems models of Morton Kaplan in the late 1950s and the capability analyses of M. D. Wallace (*War and Rank among Nations*) and of W. H. Ferris (*The Power Capabilities of Nation-states*), both published in 1973, the debate was coincident with the emergence of new scientific approaches. Examples are Richard Snyder, H. W. Bruck and Burton Sapin's early decision-making theory; Karl Deutsch's communications approach; Thomas C. Schelling's early game theory, and J. David Singer and Melvin Small's huge data collection to unravel the correlates of war.

The Third Great Debate/Inter-paradigm Debate: Context, Contenders and Contentions

Compared to its predecessors, the third debate had a much fuzzier identity, so much so that in it, two debates of vastly different concerns got melded. There is wider agreement among scholars that an inter-paradigmatic debate that was waged in the late 1970s and the early 1980s among three dominant schools of the time, namely realism, liberalism (embracing pluralism, interdependence and world society) and Marxism (covering radicalism, structuralism and globalism) is to be given the status of the Third Great Debate.[51] Yet some reserve this ordinal for the more fundamental post-positivist debate that happened much later.[52] Fuzziness of the debate also stems from the failure of participating scholars to agree on the nomenclatures and contents of the paradigms. While most prefer the epithet realism, Holsti wants to replace it with 'classical tradition' and counts two other paradigms as neo-Marxism and global society. Viotti and Kauppi compare 'images' of as realism, pluralism and globalism. McKinlay and Little call them realist, socialist and liberal to make them more amenable to political science. From the perspective of IPE, Gilpin meshes realism and mercantilism into nationalism and adds liberalism and Marxism as two other perspectives.[53] The debate turned triangular between the mid-1970s and the mid-1980s with transnationalism and interdependence posing serious theoretical challenges to realism, and dependency theory and Marxism also staking their claim as legitimate alternatives to the realist orthodoxy. Once the challenge of transnationalism struck firmer roots in the discipline, the later years of the decade were marked by a feeling that a new debate had started. It took paradigmatic overtones towards the end of the 1970s and invaded the contents of academic journals and books in the early 1980s. It began to be called the 'inter-paradigm debate' in the UK and the 'realism versus and globalism' debate, the 'debate over interdependence' and 'paradigms in IR' in the USA, till Maghroori and Ramberg put the final seal of the 'third debate' on it in 1982.[54]

The most familiar explanation of the debate's origins traces it to the bad times that realism fell in the 1970s, owing to developments not only in the international political and economic sphere but also in matters of peace and security that seemed to belie many of the basic assumptions of realism about IP. This mismatch between theory and reality brought into sharper focus alternative conceptualizations of IP and society, such as Robert Keohane and Joseph Nye's theory of 'complex interdependence'; Immanuel Wallerstein's 'world-systems theory' (WST), and dependency theory of A. G. Frank, Fernando Cardoso and others. They criticized not only realism's methodology, world image, state centrism, power monism and consequent efforts at clear demarcation between 'high politics' and 'low politics' but also its blindness to processes operative at domestic and transnational levels and beyond the political–military sphere.

Beyond criticisms, the detractors of realism also offered alternative conceptions of the international system based on regional integration, transnationalism and interdependence and a pluralist system composed of a plethora of sub-state and trans-state actors. Both the state and the system were robbed of their former conceptualizations since power was no more tied to states but was wrested by multiple political arenas all connected to one big game or 'picture'. So instead of focusing on actions of major states, it was considered more productive to identify specific issue areas, their distinctive distributions of and even forms of power and then to construct discrete theories of how issue linkages came about as also of how issues were politicized and depoliticized for agenda setting.

But it became evident shortly that in the debate between realists and pluralists/ liberals, no clear winner would emerge. While the realist image had great appeal for actual decision-makers still operating in a state-centric world, the new image was still far from finding solid ground beyond being a good site for viewing the complications, limitations and shortcomings of realist theory. Besides, the two paradigms viewed different realities, and when proceeding to 'test' their theories 'tested them against different material'. Each arranged the world in terms of different concepts and different types of empirical knowledge. There was no way to *prove* one against the other. Against what Keohane and Nye wanted, the disciplinary self-perception that emerged was that the field was witnessing the emergence of 'competing theories', each having its own 'confirmatory stories, its own data and its own preferred issues'.

To complicate matters further, Marxism gained salience as a third paradigm, back from its strange and protracted exile, ironical because Lenin's *Imperialism, the Highest Stage of Capitalism* (1917) had been written full three years before the first university department of IR was created, occasioning bloodier debates than the ones in the disciplinary confines of IR, and neo-Marxist Carr had such exalted stature in the discipline. But in the 1970s, Marxism's potential as an alternative image of IR was seen in a new light, only partly because of Lenin's modification of the Marxian class primacy into the new formulation that the backward nations are carriers of progressive consciousness. Additionally, Lenin's focus on backward nations appealed to dependency theorists and world-system theorists. Now Marxism became important to provide a structuralist view of world politics that relied more on the 'big picture'.

Stated in simplest terms, the basic point of departure for each of the paradigms was its focus: states for realists, individuals and groups for pluralists/liberals and classes or world capitalism for Marxists/globalists/structuralists/radicals. So while realists concentrated on the conflictual relations among states, pluralists/liberals focused on the non-strategic (meaning economic and social) relations within and across societies in which these relations are embedded, and radicals/Marxists/globalists saw the conflicts that realists focused on as located not among states but within and across them. Metaphorically speaking, the 'billiard-ball' model of the realists and the 'cobweb' model of the pluralists was confronted by the 'octopus' model of the Marxists.

But in Wæver's view, the third debate was not triangular as claimed since despite claims of paradigmatic triangularity, most of the debate took place on the side of realism and liberalism. It was still different from its predecessors through (a) location of the area of differences 'ontologically', as divergent conceptions of the nature, units and content of IR, (b) portrayal of three 'schools' as contenders and (c) 'self-conception as "incommensurable paradigms".' The term 'inter-paradigm' was, however, not a harmless pedagogic device. Rather, it had other serious problems. Apart from 'its tendency to produce straw men, not least of the realists', the debate is self-referential and 'self-steering' and is yet unmindful of the dangers of 'counting wrongly' theories and theorists in paradigms where do not always naturally fit or belong.[55] Schmidt charged that the third debate even denied its own nomenclature by calling itself third without giving 'due attention to the field's earlier disciplinary history' and thereby missing 'a favourable intellectual opportunity to explore the historical roots of the discipline'.[56]

Smith makes an interesting point that the inter-paradigm debate shifted attention away from the narrow methodological issues in the second debate of the 1960s mainly because of 'a general shared commitment to the principles of science', stemming from the acceptance by all the contenders in it of a broadly conceived positivist view of science, which had mellowed the maniacal concern of the early behaviouralists with data collection, hypotheses testing, measurement and quantification.[57] This methodological and normative truce owes much to the impact of Thomas Kuhn and his view of scientific revolutions, positing paradigmatic succession through 'adversary proceedings' in the 'revolutionary phase' to an era of 'normal science' when a single paradigm holds sway, around which research converges. But the unresolved problem was how to compare the three paradigms and decide which paradigm, incomparable because incommensurable, the discipline was to cast anchor in, except as a matter of choice. And after Lakatos and Musgrave gave wider currency to Kuhn's theory in the social sciences in the 1970s,[58] scholars increasingly accepted that relations among competing general theories could not be assessed in terms of any encompassing neutral knowledge or tertium quid. By constructing its own basic units, concepts, founding questions, data, criteria of judgement and versions of the paradigmatic experiment, each paradigm becomes self-referential and incommensurable.[59] This is why Wæver quips that the third debate was 'seen as a debate not to be won, but a pluralism to live with'.[60]

But such a solution based on 'pluralism, relativism and incommensurability' would reduce the various paradigms to 'idealist world views or "texts"' with 'a contested correspondence with reality'. The only available alternatives would be 'relativism, hegemonic synthesis or simple reversion to realism'. Keenes's suggestion was to give the debate a 'renewed direction' by not considering the paradigms merely 'as "theory" (in the Waltzian sense), as "text" (in the deconstructionist sense) or as world views (in the Kuhnian sense)' but by taking them as 'logical and internally consistent, yet partial accounts of history', each representing 'distinctive forms of political action and political space'. Keenes wanted this historical reading of paradigms for imparting the insight that the 'making of the Westphalian world which began 300 years ago is today barely complete, and in the meantime, industrialization and capitalism have added distinctive features to the mix: conservatism, liberalism, socialism, independence, interdependence and dependency'. Realism is incapable of fully grasping it. What is needed is a new 'paradigmatic discourse' wound around a view of global politics which concedes 'ontological prominence and legitimacy to interests and praxis which are cosmopolitan and not simply national', upheld by ecologists, pacifists, feminists and so on. It requires unravelling of the complex and uneven layering of the cosmopolitan and Westphalian industrial capitalist interests and concerns. Paradigmatic pluralism is acceptable only when allowing it.[61]

The Fourth Great Debate in IR

The methodological truce and reprieve of the inter-paradigm debate was, however, short-lived and reappeared bull blown during the fourth debate which arose shortly thereafter, termed the third debate by Lapid,[62] but kept apart and distinct as fourth debate by Wæver because (a) 'it is much more philosophical', (b) has 'a different pattern' with 'new lines of controversy' and (c) 'does not organize itself through the idea of incommensurability'.[63]

The opposing disciplinary positions in the fourth debate have been differently conceived by different commentators and presented through different binaries of easily discoverable commonalities. Smith's binaries around the role of science are explaining versus understanding; positivism versus post-positivism, and rationalism versus reflectivism. Wæver focuses on the extended meanings of epistemology and ontology, as also on the impact of 'continental' philosophers, particularly post-structuralists and Habermas. Lapid also searches for the sources of the debate in the ontological, epistemological and axiological ferment following the 'demise of the empiricist-positivist promise for a cumulative behavioural science'. I take up Smith first.

Explaining versus Understanding

To Max Weber, *'erklären'* means explaining from the outside in a positivist vein, following scientific methods aimed at discovering general causes expressible in universal laws, and *'verstehen'* means understanding from the inside, in the interpretive/hermeneutic sense, pursuing social meanings, language and beliefs that provide the bases of the 'action' by the subjects. While not wholly discounting the role of social meanings, language and beliefs in social 'action', explanatory theorists fail to see how these can be accommodated in a scientific framework of analysis that depends on empirical justification. Contrarily, interpretivists are unwilling to sacrifice beliefs, ideas or meanings for a pre-commitment to an analytic procedure that calls itself science. So while explanatory theorists seek to focus only on those ontological aspects of the social world that are observable, measurable and verifiable, the interpretivists reject such reduction. Driven by a positivistic belief in the unity of sciences, explanatory theorists give priority to quantitative methods or seek to quantify even qualitative data. But zealous of a separate space for the human sciences, the supporters of understanding prefer interpretive methods and concentrate on the qualitative, the discursive and the historical.

Positivism versus Post-positivism

The explanatory alternative is controlled by a positivist–empiricist view of science. As a distinct epistemological position, empiricism posits that all genuine knowledge derives from 'facts' experienced through senses, and there is no a priori source of knowledge, scientific knowledge being certain only with empirical validation. Positivists also prioritize observation, empirical data and measurement. Its other assumptions are as follows:

- Science must generate a set of logically rigorous guidelines regarding appropriate methodological techniques and standards for systematic observation and root knowledge claims in them so that a valid distinction between genuine knowledge and 'belief' is possible.
- Masses of collected data produced through repeated instances of systematic observations will reveal regularities that reflect the operation of general laws or forms of relationships between patterns among observable events. All attempts to smuggle in non-observable processes, mechanisms and events as explanations are unwelcome since causal relations are discoverable only through detections of regular patterns of observable behaviour.
- Because of this stress on observability, true to the precept of *esse est percipi* (to be is to be perceived) and downgrading of 'realities' not susceptible of observation, all thinking about 'deep ontological systems' that try to tackle non-observable entities like 'discourses' or 'social structures' is discouraged.
- Knowledge cannot rest with being truthful but must also be useful, and hence, meta-theory in IR is not legitimate.

Of course, to cope with doubts about its applicability in the social sciences, positivism has been changing itself in subtle ways since the 1960s, culminating into a 'soft' post-behaviourist positivism that allows both quantitative and qualitative dimensions of inquiry and recognizes the role of observation and measurement but wants to rescue social science from speculative and unsystematic inquiry and prove that the 'scientific logic of inference' can apply also in qualitative studies. King, Keohane and Verba aspire to 'encourage qualitative researchers to take scientific inference seriously' and 'incorporate' them in a 'unified logic of inference', which will integrate two styles of research in 'one logic of inference'.[64]

Still, this positivist monomania of an even reformed 'science' of human behaviour has been critiqued by a diverse range of post-positivist positions, which transcend the hermeneutic/interpretive mode of inquiry, to draw from a much wider spectrum of intellectual traditions, their only common point being a near total rejection of positivism as a valid way of studying social processes. They are as follows:

- A non-positivist version of science, which equally spurns the positivistic view and its hermeneutic alternative (demanded by some of the post-positivists and post-positivist feminist theorists).
- A claim that social science should be able to accept the importance of meanings, beliefs and language without being anchored in a hermeneutic perspective (demanded by postmodernists and post-structuralists).
- Belief that meanings and beliefs are the most important data in the study of social processes, and the task of social science is unearthing of deep meanings submerged under surface reality (insisted on by interpretivists).
- Position that naïve reliance on meanings should be replaced by a 'hermeneutics of suspicion' that extends to all positivistic knowledge claims (represented by post-structuralists).

This makes it clear that a whole range of new social theories and philosophies were taking shape in the social sciences, whose only unifying point was opposition to positivism, but their significant differences in other matters would make unsound any attempt at putting them in a strait-jacket of interpretive philosophy and methodology, the positivist/postpositivist debate too would have fuzzy boundaries.

Rationalism and Reflectivism

The rationalist–reflectivist divide subsumes the previous two binaries along with its own additional points and implications. It is itself a fallout of what Wæver familiarized in the discipline as the 'neo-neo synthesis' or the synthesis between later developments in realism and liberalism. While explaining this synthesis, it is instructive to remember that in the triangular inter-paradigm debate the Marxist/structuralist side never got the same importance as 'interdependence' thinking. But realism fought 'interdependence' by offering more 'scientific' versions of itself, as in Tucker's *The Inequality of Nations* (1977), Waltz's *Theory of International Politics* (1979) and Gilpin's *War and Change in World Politics* (1981). The newness of Waltz's 'neo-realism' lay less in its substantive tenets than in its concept of science, that is, a restatement in the form of theory understood as a system of concrete and testable propositions. The liberal theory witnessed a similar transformation. Shunning a general interpretation of IR, it focused on asking a few precise questions, mainly concerning the impact of 'variations of institutionalization of world politics' on the 'behaviour of governments'.

To test its premise that 'patterns of cooperation and discord can be understood only in the context of the institutions that help define the meaning and importance of state action', it used the anarchy assumption of neo-realism differently. Through arguing that even in a world marked by restrictive realist portrayal of egoistic, rational states and institutions are possible, liberal theory became 'neo-liberal institutionalism'. Thus, both approaches became 'leaner and meaner'.

Rationalism was first imported in the field of IR by Robert Keohane from positivistic rational choice theory (RCT), which would not deny the general complexity of the social world but would still gloss over much of it to facilitate predictions premised upon an understanding of individuals—and by extension, of states—as utility optimizers, ignoring every other dimension of their social being. This reductionism has resorted not because it affords the best representation of what an individual is, but because it might facilitate a slew of well-grounded predictions concerning human behaviour rooted in observed outcomes. While differing from previous forms of positivism in its greater reliance on the deduction, rational-choice-theoretic analysis has the same penchant for observation, measurement and discovery of general laws. Despite being in sync with the greater positivist tradition in IR, RCT is distinctive and has almost monopolized the term rationalism in its new meaning in post-1980 IRT.

To distinguish rationalism from a host of newly emerging adversarial theories, such as CT, constructivism, post-structuralism and feminism, Keohane christened them as reflectivism in common. They were dubbed 'reflectivist' because they spurned the classical positivist/explanatory path in IRT and research and highlighted reflexivity and the partisan nature of all political and social explanation. While not denying their potential to enrich the discipline, Keohane suggested that they first come up with a research programme, which will move beyond criticism of the mainstream and undertake substantive researches establishing the validity of their various claims. However, many reflectivists viewed Keohane's concession as another carefully laid trap through which they were being tempted to adopt the positivistic model of science.[65]

To Lapid, the fourth debate is as methodological as the second debate, though on a higher plane.[66] For Wæver, while the second debate was wedded to the ascendance of positivism in Western social science, the fourth debate owed, 'historically and intellectually, to the confluence of diverse anti-positivistic philosophical and sociological trends'. Pondering over the 'frenzy of words such as "epistemology" and "ontology"' buzzing during the fourth debate (although with altered meanings), Wæver reminds us that the 'quintessential second debate exchange between Kaplan (1966) and Bull (1966) was not only about techniques (social science quantification and modelling versus classical reflection) but largely about epistemology: what kind of knowledge can be gained about IR, by what means and with what degree of certainty.' The main difference of the fourth debate was that in it, the terms epistemology and ontology got more enriched in meaning and signification. This is because the new crops of writers were unwilling to fall into the traps laid by traditional mainstream scholarship and chose to concentrate on how meaning is constituted. Epistemology now meant 'how do we know that we know what we know'. Even ontology transcended its literal meaning of questioning 'what is', which in the context of the third debate referred to the 'stuff of IP', to become a deeper Nietzschean or Heideggerian way of questioning the core categories of mainstream international discourse, including the state.

The changed meanings of epistemology and ontology owed much to the post-structuralist writings of Jacques Derrida, Jean Baudrillard, Julia Kristeva, Gilles

Deleuze and Paul Virilio and more systematic use of Habermasian debate. The feature that sets apart the new IR debates from earlier ones is their reliance on philosophies that interrogate 'the general philosophical outlook', characterizing most of the social sciences. Everything is questioned, including its assumptions about language, identity, 'the subjectivity of subjects, the objectivity of object, the subject/object distinction', the whole idea epistemology as a set of rules prescribing 'how to produce secure knowledge' and also ontology understood as 'problematic assumptions about extra-textual pre-givens'.[67] For Wæver, the fourth debate moved beyond the 'neo-neo synthesis' or the synthesis between later developments in realism and liberalism, which he terms as 4A, towards an 'absolute/relative gains debate, which he terms as 4B. The graphic comparison between the third debate and the fourth debate that he provides[68] is very instructive to get at their basic differences (see Box 1.5).

Since the late 1980s, another attempt at a synthesis from constructivism, in which its leading spokesperson Alexander Wendt has tried to reach up to Keohane and liberal institutionalism, as also to Ned Lebow, cognitivism's leading light, generated another debate. Wendt told liberal institutionalists that in order to convince realists that cooperation is possible, they did not have to adopt a framework that made state identities and interests irrelevant. A model in which identities and interests evolve through interaction would better shore up the possibilities of cooperation. To the cognitivists, particularly those engaged in foreign policy analysis, Wendt's message was that their approach, despite its lack of philosophical sophistication, is in essence constructivist. Despite these overtures, social constructivism continues to have its strong differences with the mainstream, which congeals the general debate between rational choice theorists and social constructivists, Wæver detects in it a potential challenger to mainstream rational institutionalism. In his view, it can provide competing explanations of not only institutions but concepts like security in ways unfamiliar

BOX 1.5
The Third and Fourth Debates Compared

	Debate 3 (Interparadigm Debate)	*Debate 4A (Reflectivist versus Rationalist)*	*Debate 4B (Absolute versus Relative Gains)*
Relationships among debaters	Incommensurability	War	Differences within a research programme
Theme of disagreement	World view	Philosophy	Empirical question to be settled or finding a coefficient
Combatants	The three paradigms	Neo-neo synthesis against postmodernists	Neo-realists versus neo-liberal institutionalists

Source: Adapted from Wæver, 'Figures of International Thought', 23–24.

to the mainstream. To Keohane's 1988 exhortation to reflectivists to design alternative research programmes, Wendt's replied that he can offer better explanations than Keohane even without it. Of course, these claims did not mollify critical theorists or post-structuralists, like Richard Ashley or James Der Derian, who argued that it was a misrepresentation of their aims and designs in its disrespect of difference and was to that extent another instance of mainstream repression and naiveté. From the reflectivist perspective, mainstream constructivism may have softened up the rationalist mainstream and may have made it malleable for new questions. But for this, it excluded the more radical issues and aspirations of the post-structuralists as well as the critical work done by them and early non-mainstream constructivists.

Wæver thinks that this makes a new debate between constructivists and deconstructionists likely in the future. But he is still willing to take the constructivist response seriously because of its untapped potential to accommodate a vast range of theories, including their concepts, structures, mechanisms or units, in its fold. This can be done just by showing that these are socially constructed, right in substance though amiss in the ontology. He finds the same merit of eclectic inclusiveness in ES also. But we will talk about both later, as 'after the fourth debate' middle roaders in **Chapters 23** and **25**.

Counting the benefits and disadvantages of the construction of the fourth debate, Wæver says that on the positive side 'it offers better strategic guidance and is a relatively up-to-date mapping of the terrain over which major battles have been fought'. However, the negative side of the debate is that it first replicates Keohane's false aggregation of 'reflectivists'; it is false because it steamrolls over sharply divisive differences among them. Second, in its desperate attempt to create 'a linear debate along one axis', it relegates to the background major theoretical challenges such as the IPE, feminism and historical sociology, which not only cross sharp swords within the contours of IR but also press them so hard that they threaten to burst at the seams. Third, as a corollary to the two desiderata, it is reductionist.[69] The second point is very important because Sandra Whitworth's pointer to the absence of attention to gender in all the strands of the inter-paradigm debate—for her, realism, pluralism and CT[70]—applies even for the fourth debate.

Not everyone, however, ends one's comments on the debate on such a sad note. For example, instead of defining the debate as 'linear' or reductionist like Wæver, Lapid expresses 'a vague uneasiness over the fact that no reduction seems to be obtaining in the diversity of conceptualizations and higher-order theories'. Adopting Anthony Giddens' response of cautious celebration and systematic reconstruction of the post-positivist heterodoxy, Lapid finds two significant commonalities among the seeming cacophony of positions. These are (a) end of the sway of the positivist epistemological consensus left unscathed by the "history versus science" controversy' and (b) 'a shared appreciation' that the field is caught up in a process of restructuring directly occasioned by debates taking place in contemporary social and political theory. On the basis of these commonalities, Lapid identifies the themes that are vital in setting the 'the tone, agenda, and mood' of the fourth debate. These are (a) dominating concern with meta-scientific units or 'paradigmatism', (b) quest for 'underlying premises and assumptions' or 'perspectivism' and (c) shift towards 'methodological pluralism' or 'relativism'.[71]

With these discussions of nomenclature, origins and images of the discipline and four debates on it, we move to the next section, dealing with the realist paradigm in its six chapters.

REVIEW QUESTIONS

1. What are the merits and disadvantages of calling the discipline IR, interstate relations, IP, world politics and global politics?
2. Comment on the origins of IR, including its analytic and historic tradition.
3. Discuss the three images or paradigms of IR.
4. Critically examine the debate on the authenticity of the First Great Debate in IR.
5. Describe the context, issues, contenders and outcome of the Second Great Debate.
6. 'Compared to its predecessors, the third debate had much more fuzzy identity'. Discuss.
7. What are the differences between 4A and 4B in the Fourth Great Debate?
8. Identify the opposing positions in the Fourth Great Debate.

NOTES AND REFERENCES

1. Walker Connor, 'Nation-Building or Nation-Destroying,' *World Politics* 24, no. 3 (1972): 320; Walker Connor, 'Terminological Chaos ("A Nation is a Nation, Is a State, Is an Ethnic Group, Is a …"),' in Connor, *Ethnonationalism: The Quest for Understanding* (Princeton, NJ: Princeton University Press, 1994), 8, 39, 96.
2. Ernest Barker, *Principles of Social and Political Theory* (Oxford: Oxford University Press, 1951), 56.
3. Benedict Anderson, 'Introduction,' in *Mapping the Nation*, ed. Gopal Balakrishnan (London; New York, NY: Verso, 2012), 8–9.
4. Connor, 'Nation-Building or Nation-Destroying,' 97.
5. See Burton and Värynen, 'The End of International Relations?' in *Contemporary International Relations: A Guide to Theory*, ed. A. J. R. Groom and Margot Light (London and New York, NY: Pinter Publishers, 1994/1999), 69.
6. Rabindranath Tagore, 'Nation Kī (What Is a Nation?),' *Ātmaśakti*, in *Rabīndra Rachanābalī* (Collected Works of Tagore, Vol. 2, Kolkata: Visvabhāratī, 1986–1991), 619; low-priced edition on the occasion of Tagore's 125th birth anniversary.
7. K. J. Holsti, *International Politics: A Framework for Analysis* (New Delhi: Prentice-Hall of India, [1972] 1995), 18–19.
8. Herbert J. Spiro, *World Politics: The Global System* (Homewood, IL: The Dorsey Press, 1966), 1–3.
9. James N. Rosenau, 'Previewing Post-international Politics,' in *Global Politics in a Changing World: A Reader*, ed. Richard W. Mansbach and Edward Joseph Rhodes (Boston, MA: Houghton Mifflin, 2009), 13–18.
10. Antony McGrew, 'Globalization and Global Politics,' in *Globalization and Global Politics: An Introduction to International Relations*, ed. John Baylis, Steve Smith, Patricia Owens (Oxford: Oxford University Press, 2013), 29.
11. Torbjørn Knutsen, 'The Development of International Relations,' Encyclopedia of Life Support Systems, Available at: www.eolss.net/Sample-Chapters/C14/E1-35-01.pdf (accessed on 19 March 2021).
12. Viscount James Bryce, *International Relations: Eight Lectures Delivered in the United States in August 1921* (New York, NY: Macmillan, 1922).
13. Torbjørn Knutsen, *A History of International Relations Theory* (Manchester: Manchester University Press, 2007), 10–11.

14. Barry Buzan and Richard Little, *International Systems in World History: Remaking the Study of International Relations* (Oxford: Oxford University Press, 2000), 1–7.
15. K. J. Holsti, *International Politics: A Framework for Analysis* (New Delhi: Prentice Hall of India, 1995), 23.
16. Lewis Carroll, 'Pig and Pepper,' in Carroll, *Alice's Adventures in Wonderland* (London: Macmillan, 1865), Chapter VI.
17. Brian C. Schmidt, 'The Historiography of Academic International Relations,' *Review of International Studies* 20, no. 4 (1994): 349–367, Available at: http://www.jstor.org/stable/20097385 (accessed 19 March 2021).
18. Hans J. Morgenthau, *Politics among Nations: The Struggle for Power and Peace* (Calcutta: Scientific Book Agency, [1948] 1966), 4.
19. For explications of Thomas Kuhn's influential concept of paradigm in *The Structure of Scientific Revolutions* (1962) and its 21 different definitions, the most basic of them being a 'disciplinary matrix'. See, George Ritzer, 'Paradigm,' in *Encyclopedia of Social Theory*, Vol. 2, ed. George Ritzer (Thousand Oaks, CA: SAGE Publications, 2005), 543; Ian Hacking, 'Introductory Essay,' in *The Structure of Scientific Revolutions: 50th Anniversary Edition*, ed. Thomas S. Kuhn (London, Chicago: Chicago University Press, 2012), vii–xxxviii. For its popularization and legitimization in IR during the 'inter-paradigm debate', see Brian C. Schmidt, 'On the History and Historiography of International Relations,' in *Handbook of International Relations*, Walter Carslnaes, Thomas Risse, and Beth A. Simmons (Thousand Oaks, CA: SAGE Publications, 2002), 8–10.
20. Paul R. Viotti and Mark V. Kauppi, *International Relations Theory: Realism, Pluralism, Globalism*, Maxwell Macmillan International Editions (New York, NY: Macmillan, 1990), 5.
21. Martin Griffiths, ed., *International Relations Theory for the Twenty-first Century* (London: Routledge, 2007), 1.
22. Viotti and Kauppi, *International Relations Theory*, 5–15.
23. Griffiths, *International Relations Theory*, 1–2, passim.
24. Miles Kahler, 'Inventing International Relations: International Relations Theory after 1945,' in *New Thinking in International Relations*, ed. Michael W. Doyle and G. John Ikenberry (Boulder, CO: Westview Press, 1997), 21.
25. Schmidt, 'History and Historiography,' 10.
26. Robin W. Lovin, 'Introduction,' in *The Nature and Destiny of Man: A Christian Interpretation, Volume 1: Human Nature*, ed Reinhold Niebuhr (Westminster: John Knox Press, [1941] 2004), 182.
27. Cornel West, 'Foreword,' in *Moral Man and Immoral Society: A Study in Ethics and Politics* (1932), ed. Reinhold Niebuhr (Louisville, KY: John Knox Press, 2013), 93–94, 231–232.
28. Reinhold Niebuhr, 'The Christian Faith and World Crisis,' in *Love and Justice: Selections from the Shorter Writings of Reinhold Niebuhr* (1957), ed. D. B. Robertson (Louisville, KY: John Knox Press, 1992), 280.
29. Morgenthau, *Politics among Nations*, 10.
30. Carr, *The Twenty Years' Crisis*, 2nd edition (New York, NY: Palgrave, 2001), p.cv, cited by John Mearsheimer, 'E. H. Carr vs. Idealism: The Battle Rages On,' *International Relations* 19, no. 2 (2005): 139–152, doi: 10.1177/0047117805052810.
31. See Seán Molloy, *The Hidden Hand of Realism: A Genealogy of Power Politics* (New York, NY: Palgrave Macmillan, 2006), 37–38; Stefano Guzzini, *Realism in International Relations and International Political Economy: The Continuing Story of a Death Foretold* (London: Routledge, 1997), 20; Jeanne Morefield, *Covenants without Sword: Idealist Liberalism and the Spirit of Empire* (Princeton, NJ: Princeton University Press, 2005), 7.
32. Francis P. Sempa, 'Introduction,' *America's Strategy in World Politics: The United States and the Balance of Power*, ed. Nicholas J. Spykman (New Brunswick, NJ: Transaction Publishers, [1942] 2007).
33. Ibid.,' 108–109.

34. Morgenthau, *Politics among Nations*, 168.
35. Ibid., 6.
36. Arend Lijphart, 'International Relations Theory: Great Debates and Lesser Debates,' *International Social Science Journal* 26, no. 1 (1974): 1–20, especially 20.
37. Steve Smith, 'The Self-Image of a Discipline: A Genealogy of International Relations Theory,' in *International Relations Theory Today*, eds. Ken Booth and Steve Smith (Cambridge: Polity Press, 1995), 17.
38. Patrick Hayden, ed., *The Ashgate Research Companion to Ethics and International Relations* (Farnham: Ashgate, 2009), 1.
39. For revisionist scholars who stake these two claims, see Brian C. Schmidt, *International Relations and the First Great Debate* (Abingdon: Routledge, 2012), 1; Peter Wilson, 'The Myth of the "First Great Debate",' in *The Eighty years' Crisis: International Relations, 1919–1999*, eds. Ken Booth, Michael Cox, and Tim Dunne (Cambridge: Cambridge University Press, 1998), 1, 16.
40. Schmidt, 'History and Historiography,' 13.
41. J. H. Herz, 'Idealist Internationalism and the Security Dilemma,' *World Politics* 2, no. 2 (1950): 157–180; cited in Wilson, 'The Myth,' 8–10.
42. For relevant citations, see Schmidt, *International Relations and First Great Debate*, 1–2.
43. See Andreas Osiander, 'Rereading Early Twentieth Century IR Theory: Idealism Revisited,' *International Studies Quarterly* 42, no. 3 (1998): 409–432; cited in Schmidt, *International Relations and First Great Debate*, 133–136.
44. The following account of the Second Great Debate draws upon: Robert Jackson and Georg Sørensen, *Introduction to International Relations* (Oxford: Oxford University Press, 1999), 45–48; Steve Smith, 'Introduction: Diversity and Disciplinarity in International Relations Theory,' in *International Relations Theories: Discipline and Diversity*, eds. Tim Dunne, Milja Kurki and Steve Smith (Oxford: Oxford University Press, 2007), 17–18; Ole Wæver, 'Figures of International Thought,' in *The Future of International Relations: Masters in the Making?* ed. Iver B. Neumann and Ole Wæver (London: Routledge, 1997), 8–12; Walter Carslnaes, Thomas Risse, and Beth A. Simmon, *Handbook of International Relations* (Thousand Oaks, CA: SAGE Publications, 2013), 11–12.
45. Smith, 'Introduction,' 17.
46. Klaus Eugen Knorr and James Nathan Rosenau, *Contending Approaches to International Politics* (Princeton, NJ: Princeton University Press, 1969).
47. Schmidt, 'History and Historiography,' 11, 13–14.
48. R. B. Finnegan, 'International Relations: The Disputed Search for Method,' *Review of Politics* 34, no. 1 (1972): 40–66.
49. Naomi Black, review of *Globalism versus Realism: International Relations' Third Debate*, by Ray Maghroori and Bennett Ramberg, ed., *International Journal* 38, no. 4 (1983): 722–724, Available at: http://www.jstor.org/stable/40202213 (accessed on 21 March 2021).
50. Wæver, 'Figures of International Thought,' 12.
51. Schmidt holds this view. See Schmidt, 'History and Historiography,' 11.
52. See, for example, the title of the paper by Yosef Lapid, 'The Third Debate: On the Prospects of International Theory in the Post-Positivist Era,' *International Studies Quarterly* 33, no. 3 (1989): 235–254.
53. See K. J. Holsti, *The Dividing Discipline: Hegemony and Diversity in International Theory* (Boston, MA: Allen & Unwin, 1985); Viotti and Kauppi, *International Relations Theory*; R. D. McKinlay and R. Little, *Global Problems and World Order* (Madison, WI: University of Wisconsin Press, 1986); Robert Gilpin, *The Political Economy of International Relations* (Princeton, NJ: Princeton, 1987)—all cited in Ernie Keenes, 'Paradigms of International Relations: Bringing Politics Back In,' *International Journal* 44, no. 1 (Winter, 1988/1989): 41–67, especially 46.
54. Ray Maghroori and Bennett Ramberg, *Globalism versus Realism: International Relations' Third Debate* (Boulder, CO: Westview Press, 1982).

55. Wæver, 'Figures of International Thought,' 12–14, 15.
56. Schmidt, 'Historiography of Academic,' passim.
57. Smith, 'Diversity and Disciplinarity,' 18.
58. *I. Lakatos and A. Musgrave, Criticism and the Growth of Knowledge* (Cambridge: Cambridge University Press, 1970) is being referred to.
59. Wæver, 'Figures of International Thought,' 13–14.
60. Ole Wæver, 'The Rise and Fall of the Inter-Paradigm Debate,' in *International Theory: Positivism and Beyond*, eds. Steve Smith, Ken Booth, and Marysia Zalewski (Cambridge: Cambridge University Press, 1996), 155.
61. Keenes, 'Paradigms of International Relations,' passim.
62. Lapid, 'The Third Debate,' 235–254.
63. Wæver, 'Figures of International Thought,' 15.
64. G. King, R. Keohane and S. Verba, *Designing Social Inquiry: Scientific Inference in Qualitative Research* (Princeton, NJ: Princeton University Press, 1994), ix, 3.
65. The discussion of the first two strands of the fourth debate has, thus, far closely followed Smith, 'Diversity and Disciplinarity,' 21–22.
66. Lapid, 'The Third Debate,' pp. 236–237.
67. Wæver, 'Figures of International Thought,' 16–17.
68. Ibid., 23–24.
69. Ibid., 24–26.
70. Sandra Whitworth, 'Gender in the Inter-paradigm Debate,' *Millennium* 18, no. 2 (1989): 265, doi: https://doi.org/10.1177/03058298890180020201, 265–272.
71. Lapid, 'The Third Debate,' 238–244.

SECTION I

THEORIES OF THE REALIST PARADIGM

IA. Realist Theory and Its Variants

IB. Systems Theory and Its Variants

Chapter 8
General Systems Theory and Morton Kaplan's Application in IR

Chapter 9
Systems Theory: From Modelski to Singer
[Available on the Companion Website]

Chapter 10
Critique and Evaluation of Formulations of Systems Theory

IC. Game Theory

Chapter 11
Game Theory or the Theory of Interdependent Decisions
[Available on the Companion Website]

IA. REALIST THEORY AND ITS VARIANTS

CHAPTER

2

Early Classical Realism

CHAPTER OUTLINE

MEANING OF 'REALISM'

Chapter 2 best starts with what the term 'realism' *really* signifies in this eponymous paradigm-cum-approach in IR. For, it has diverse and sometimes even antagonistic meanings in the areas of art, literature, epistemology, jurisprudence, metaphysics, moral philosophy and politics. Etymologically, realism involves a particularly dispassionate way of looking at the world; a readiness to 'focus on the most salient dimensions of a given situation' irrespective of its conformity with our preferences or desires; a boldness to take on 'reality' by the horns and a distrust for easy answers and uninformed optimism. Derivatively, in IR, realism has become the trade name for a wide array of approaches that 'focus on the sources, modalities, and effects of power'. Its arguments meet at the intersection of two discrete though related literatures of (a) the post-1919 'analytic tradition' of IR and (b) the 'historic tradition, giving, in both, primacy to politics over morality. When popularly equated with *realpolitik*, which frankly fetishizes the state and military power, realism is an offshoot of the *machtpolitik* of the 19th-century German state theories; and the philosophy of power manifest in Bismarckian statecraft; a position that is blatantly antithetical to ethical reflection. But though *realpolitik* had its proponents both in politics and academia,[1] it will be seen in the course of our discussion that neither can realism be reduced to *realpolitik* nor can all of its variants be considered essentially amoral. The gamut of the term's mixed meanings comes out in the following quote.

> Realism was first used in political discourse to denote the doctrine that universals exist outside the mind. In political theory, however, the term has come to be reserved for the theorists of raison d'ètat or Realpolitik. It denotes a school which holds that there are real forces operating in the world beyond our immediate perceptions of them, that these forces are revealed by the historical process and that the able practitioner takes account of these forces and incorporates them into his political conceptions and his political acts.[2]

EARLY CLASSICAL REALISM

Early classical realism dates back to ancient Greece, India, China, and medieval and early modern Europe and is represented by Thucydides (c. 460–390 BC), Kautilya (c. 321–296 BC), Chinese realists (legalists) including Master Han Fei Tzu (c. 280 BC), Machiavelli (1469–1527) and Hobbes (1588–1679).

Thucydides

Thucydides has lasting importance. Crane wonders that even after living through the shattering experience of the Second World War, the Vietnam War and the struggle with fascism, we can relate to Thucydides' masterful analysis of the Peloponnesian War. Some even compare the confrontation or stand-off between the USA and the Soviet Union during the Cuban Missile Crisis with that between Athens and Sparta. Morgenthau looked upon Thucydides as the first member of the neoclassical realist school, and Gilpin doubted if 24 centuries really added many new insights after into how states relate to each other and why wars waged.[3]

The perceived relevance is astonishing, considering that what we call IR would hardly apply to his times, since his *History of the Peloponnesian Wars* (hereafter HOTPWA) basically dealt with competitions and conflicts between Greek city states of the cultural linguistic entity called Hellas and contiguous non-Greek empires of Macedonia and Persia, termed 'intermunicipal relations' by some.[4] Thucydides accepted the inequalities in capabilities between small city states of Greece and adjacent landmasses, and a few 'great' powers such as Athens, Sparta and the Persian Empire as 'natural', to be adapted to by states if they wanted to survive and prosper. Pointing to the debris of ruined states and empires in ancient Greek history as empirical evidence of failure to do so, he harped on the limited choices and restricted manoeuvring space available to statespeople in the conduct of their foreign policies, as well as to the ethics of prudence, caution, foresight, justice and self-restraint.[5]

Ned Lebow points out that, like Morgenthau later, and unlike naïve realists, Thucydides was not constrained by the 'generic distinction' between anarchical international and well-ordered domestic realms. Describing the internal political developments in Athens with the same intensity as external developments in the various 'theatres of war', he provides a near scalar depiction of city states which range from the highly ordered and consensual on one end to those ravaged by anarchy and civil war on the other. Their differences have less to do with the coercive capacity of the city states than with their communal cohesion or 'homonoia', which facilitated, in Periclean Athens and Greece before the Peloponnesian War, the reign of 'nomos'—laws, rules or conventions, and chastened both individuals and city states.

In the same Morgenthauian nuanced manner, Thucydides discounts military capability and alliances as the panacea for all interstate problems that endanger peace. If Athens' alliance with Corcyra—or present-day Corfu—embroiled the Corinthian fleet in a bloody war and precipitated a confrontation with Sparta, her subsequent preemptive action against Megara and Potidaea made the war imminent by straining the already fragile unity of the Hellenic League. Sparta's alliance with Corinth made a war with Athens difficult to avoid, despite her disinclination. Thucydides does not provide a single instance of an alliance preventing or deterring war, though the whole logic of BOP stands on this deterrent impact. Rather, his telling of the Mytilenean Debate[6] and the Melian Dialogue[7] provides insights about why this impact might not happen, because of the tendencies of the powers to cherish and attempt unrealistic goals, indulge in wishful thinking, underestimate the enemy, ignore risks and exaggerate probabilities of success.

For Thucydides, another factor that led to the defeat of deterrence before the Peloponnesian War was the erosion of the community and the conventions which made it possible after Athenians fell into self-aggrandizing tendencies or *pleonexia*. In the Sicilian Debate in 415 BC, Nicias' wise warning to Athenians about the size, population and military strength of Sicily, particularly of the large and prosperous city of Syracuse, and the folly of setting off for a distant island, with undefeated enemies close to home remaining unguarded against, went unheeded because Alcibiades succeeded in playing on the avarice of the Athenians, and appealing as a trump card to the glorious history of the Greeks since the Persian Wars. Even Nicias' further attempt at dissuasion by pointing out the need for a much larger fleet, arms, materiel and provisions failed to dissuade the Athenians. Impervious to the voice of reason, the Athenian Assembly was convinced by Alcibiades to vote to launch a massive naval campaign against the large island of Sicily and committed their second mistake after striking an allegiance with Corcyra.

Again, like Morgenthau, and unlike many lesser realists, Thucydides did not consider the tension between interest and justice irreconcilable but rather thought them complementary and constitutive on a higher plane. Although Pericles had described Athens in his oration as the annual public funeral for the war-dead as *dēmokratia* (democracy), the outcome of the reforms between 462 BC and 461 BC was a mixed form of government (*zunkrasis*), where Pericles' rule was behind the façade. The democratic ideology softened class antagonisms and made the democratic and political privileges of the elite tolerable to the *dēmos*; however, he was cold to it. But the more the post-Periclean demagogues laid bare the gap between rhetoric and practice through their behaviour, the more acute did class conflict become. Politics also became more contentious, leading finally to a violent subversion of democracy by the regime of the thirty tyrants in 404 BC and a just as violent restoration one year later. Thucydides deduced from this that justice, or at least a perception of it, was a basic prerequisite for community.

True to his insight into a linkage between the inside and the outside, Thucydides showed how Athenian imperialism underwent a parallel transformation. The empire was solid as long as power was exerted according to the social norms informing Greek speech and behaviour. But after post-Periclean Athens chose power over principles, the loss of Athens' *hēgemonia* caused estrangement of its allies and resultant loss of its power base. In Cleon's words in the Mytilenean Debate, the *archē* or empire had degenerated into *turannis* or despotism, whose only assets were military power and the fear it generated. As seen in the Melian Dialogue, the Athenian commissioners' division of the people into the rulers (*archē*) and the ruled (*hupōkooi*) facilitated unbridled imperialism. Thucydides argued from these parallels between domestic and IP that coercion is an inadequate and self-destructive basis of influence. Drawing 'an analogy between individual pursuit of wealth and Athenian pursuit of power' (manifest in her efforts to build the largest navy in Greece), Thucydides cautioned that Athens built up its hegemony (*hēgemonia*) by showing generosity (*charis*) to its allies through conferring and not receiving favours. He taught that to create a synthetic order that combined the best in the old and the new, one needed to remember that the best in the old was its stress on excellence of virtue (*arête*), which educated the elite to restrain their hunger for wealth and power.[8]

Crane detects four types of realism in Thucydides' *HOTPWA*: 'procedural', 'scientific', 'ideological' and 'paradigmatic'. It is 'procedural' because of its stress on 'observational accuracy' and 'scientific' not only because of his conviction that 'there really are objective facts out there' but also because he wanted to transcend them to discover general laws in them. Although keenly conscious of inadequacies and errors of observation, Thucydides still insisted that if historians and statesmen could transcend the pressures of the moment and concentrate on 'the facts themselves' (*auta ta erga*), then a true account of events would surely be available. Thucydides' realism is supposedly ideological in the sense that he uses his 'claim to positive knowledge as a stick to beat' his critics and detractors. And finally, it is 'paradigmatic' for 'seeing some phenomena more clearly' and attempting to achieve 'a better view of the whole, but at the expense of simultaneously minimizing or ignoring other factors' more emphasized by his predecessors.[9]

Kautilya

Although known and appreciated less outside India, true to the Western bias of the discipline of IR, Kautilya was in no sense a lesser realist than Thucydides. Max Weber linked his realism to the 'Hindu way of life', which prescribed 'a separate ethical code, a Dharma' for different 'callings', later solidified into a 'strict hierarchy of rank', all of which helped brew a culturally rooted but richer realism.

> This specialization of ethical codes made it possible for Indian ethics to treat this royal art in a wholly consistent way, by following only the inherent laws of politics and even radically strengthening them. Truly radical 'Machiavellianism'...is classically expressed in the *Arthashâstra* of Kautilya (written long before the birth of Christ, ostensibly in the time of Chandragupta): compared to it, Machiavelli's *Prince* is harmless.[10]

Indian historians go one over Weber to claim that the 'Indian treatise worked infinitely better in practice for its time and place' than its Greek counterpart (Koshambi); Kautilya was far above Machiavelli in 'intellectual acumen and comprehensiveness of outlook' (Roy); Kautilya was 'a practical statesman', giving empire-building advice to Chandragupta Maurya, 'whereas the Florentine diplomat's experience was only of a few years in a subordinate department of the state' (Indra).[11] Bandyopadhyay rues the fact that modern realists neglect or miss him, though 'Kautilya was a more sophisticated political thinker than Machiavelli'.[12] Behera traces this sidelining of Kautilya in the theoretical literature of IR to the 'impoverishment of traditional IR's political thought', the 'Gramscian hegemony' of Western IRT over traditional IR and its 'disciplinary gate-keeping practices', because of which the progenitor of *realpolitik* was neglected in the discipline, and 'the universal applicability of his ideas is not acknowledged—almost universally'.[13]

When comparing Kautilya with Thucydides, the centre of Thucydides' realist analysis was a war. For Kautilya, it was an empire. Of course, commentators differ on what Kautilya was talking about in his book, whether it was the extant Mauryan Empire or the principles and policies according to which a polity ought to rule. Indian historians, such as K. A. Nilakanta Sastri, Romila Thapar, Purushottam Lal Bhargava, V. R. Ramachandra Dikshitar and Radha Kumud Mukherjee take the second view, but not too definitively, switching between citing *Arthaśāştra* as an authoritative source on the basis and general policy of the Mauryan Empire and speculating how, as the principal adviser of Chandragupta, he must have put into practice many of the ideas and insights of his books. Indra argues that unlike Plato's *Republic*, *Arthaśāştra* was not merely theoretical, being written for the use of Chandragupta, the emperor.[14] Mookerjee cites British and Indian authorities to claim that 'whatever might be the time of its composition in its present form, it is a picture of the early conditions applicable to Mauryan India', and that it is the only sourcebook on the Mauryan polity's land system, fiscal system, laws and social system, literature and religion, a picture that could be embellished only after *Āin-i-Akbari* in Akbar's time.[15] Shah's comment that the book contains 'a structure of thought, pertaining to the management of the affairs of the state, with reference, but not confined to the *Arthasastra*' seems more apt.[16]

There are many reasons why Kautilya looks so familiar to a modern political realist in IR. First, he wrote a book 'analyzing how the political world does work' than 'stating how it ought to work' and, like Machiavelli, 'discloses to a king what calculating and sometimes brutal measures he must carry out to preserve the state and the common good'.[17] Second, Kautilya is strikingly far ahead of his times in the settlement of disputes or resolution of conflicts, a very important theme of modern realism, with his stipulation of four factors as important in conflict resolution: dharma ('code of conduct' or 'ethical code' for Weber), *vyabahāra* (the actual transaction in a particular case), *caritra* (the history of similar cases, tradition) and *rājāsana* (the order of the king) and their different bases, namely truth for dharma, witnesses for *vyabahāra*, history for *caritra* and the king's decision for *rājāsana*. Kautilya's originality lies not in enumerating these factors but in showing how they operate in the implementation of dharma, and in demonstrating their interrelationships. Evidently, though dharma provides the proper rule, law or code in the settlement of a dispute, it cannot encompass or exhaust all possible situations. So, even to enforce a law, not only should *rājāsana* know all transactional facts (*vyabahāra*) beforehand but also the history of similar cases if uniformity in implementation in situations where facts are same is to be preserved.

Kautilya uses a phrase in respect of the relation of these factors—*paścimo pūrvabādhakah*, which literally translates as 'the latter factor supersedes or is superior to the former', which brings out his clear realist position. Shah thinks this phrase admits of only one exception to the pre-eminence of dharma in the whole book, namely where there is a conflict between rational or just decision, or *dharmanyaya* and dharma, the latter should prevail.[18] If one asks if these rules of conflict resolution are as applicable to IP as to domestic politics, my answer would be that Kautilya's politics is always outward-looking. For, of the seven constituent elements (saptāṃga) of the state (swamī, amātya, janapada, durga, koṣa, daṇda, mitra iti prakrityah), the seventh, 'mitra' or allies, is not only transnational but also located outside the boundary of the state.[19]

Third, in *Arthaśāṣtra*, Kautilya 'offers a work of genius in matters of foreign policy and warfare, including key principles of international relations from a realist perspective and a discussion of when an army must use cruel violence', and when it would find being humane more beneficial. Boesche finds the amorality of views on IR to be not less, but rather more vigorous than Machiavelli's, for example, in Kautilya's forthright advice to a king to violate treaties when they are useless or are thorns for his expansionist plans. Because,

> In reality, international relations for Kautilya are lawless struggles among those who are strong and those who are weak. Whatever 'laws' exist are temporary treaties among those roughly equal, among those who find peace temporarily beneficial. Diplomatic missions do not serve the cause of peace, but rather they help with the timing of the conquest.

The king is enjoined to attack a neighbouring kingdom if his country is stronger than it; if a neighbour suffers a calamity; and if a treaty is no longer useful. Coupled with this is Kautilya's brutal Machiavellian honesty in discussions of warfare; instructions to a king to employ all means, good and evil, to win a war, including propaganda, disinformation, use of religion to boost the morale of the king's own troops or weaken those of the enemy troops, planting of plausible lies to confuse and frighten troops of bellicose kings and widespread use of spies and saboteurs, particularly beautiful women, to plant discord among opposing generals, ministers or aspirants to enemy thrones. Also germane is Kautilya's astute classification of wars into open, hidden and silent. Alongside traditional open war of armies positioned against each other is hidden war, akin to modern guerrilla warfare, employing harassment of enemy troops by surprise attacks, ambush and other ruses. In duplicitous silent warfare, the king overtly praises a rival king as a friend and ally while simultaneously plotting calamities and assassinations against him and instigating quarrels among his high-ranking officials through spies and provocateurs.[20]

Boesche harps on the following similarities between Kautilya with Machiavelli:

- Kautilya is 'an immoral thinker' (though Boesche once admits that 'maybe it is more complicated than that').
- Kautilya's efforts at tying up the warring pieces of India and bringing peace through uniting them in an empire are venturesome and sordid undertakings, where moral sermons about goodness and virtue did not fit.

- Kautilya's warning that admonitions about being virtuous might be appropriate at times of stability, but not in crisis situations, in which the king or leader's reliance on traditional norms of morality may invite disaster and ruin for himself and his people.
- Kautilya's explicit statement that the ugly facts of the political world are not our creation.
- Kautilya's affirmation that the survival of the state is of primary importance, because the spiritual, material and sensual goods of life are preserved only by the state, and his specification of the rules of survival in this world.
- Kautilya's counsel to the king to judge political and military not by intentions but by results bearing echoes of Machiavelli born some 18 centuries later and Morgenthau 22 centuries later.[21]

I can add that while Kautilya was searching for the implementer of law (given by him) in his emperor-king or *vijīgīṣu*, Machiavelli was searching for him in his prince. While for Kautilya the goal was unity of India's warring kingdoms into an empire, the goal, for Machiavelli, was the unification of Italy's city states to reclaim Italy's pride before its West European neighbours. And for Morgenthau, the goal was to guide US foreign policy after its emergence as a leading power. But we should still mull over if the adjective 'amoral' would apply for Kautilya, though it could easily stick to Machiavelli, considering Kautilya's preoccupation with dharma and his insistence that its pre-eminence can be waived only in cases of conflict between rational, just decision or *dharmanyaya*. In fact, *Arthaśāstra* is replete with words that problematize the claim that the acquisition of royal power was the only goal of Kautilya's foreign policy, which required renouncing treaties right and left; and that he discounted the moral foundation of other goals. A verse in *Arthaśāṣtra*, *sāma vyayamau yogakṣemayoryonih*, has been translated by Natarajan as the 'welfare of a state', and interpreted in the context of foreign policy as 'ensuring the security of a state within its existing boundaries and acquiring new territory to enlarge it' by 'adopting a policy of non-intervention or overt action'. Kautilya makes yoga dependent on *sama*, mentioned only in another verse (7.17.1), where it comes along with *saṃdhi* (peace treaty) and samadhi (treaty with hostage). If someone still persists with the misperception that Kautilya advised breaking treaties with playful abandon, then one can just see the objective of the three words given in the next verse (7.17.1,2), stated as 'means for creating confidence between kings'. Natarajan translates *sama* as non-intervention and interprets it as 'not a policy of doing nothing but the deliberate choice of a policy of keeping away from foreign entanglements, in order to enjoy the fruits of past acquisitions by consolidating them'.[22] Besides, even in the matter of the king's waging war, Kautilya's counsel is that 'it is better to attack an unrighteous king than a righteous king' (verse 7.13. 11–12); and one mark of just behaviour is that a king shall not take land belonging to his ally, even if it is offered to him by someone else.[23]

In words that could impress a Morgenthau, Spykman or Schelling, Kautilya affirms that 'The welfare of a state depends on an active foreign policy.'[24] An active and pragmatic foreign policy comprises these six methods: (a) saṃdhi, or 'agreement with pledges'—a policy of peace (pursuable by a king with powers inferior to his opponent); (b) 'vigraha', or the policy of hostility (best suited to a king with superior powers); (c) 'asana', or the policy of staying quiet or 'indifferent' (opportune for one thinking he can neither hurt one nor be hurt by one); (d) yāna or the policy of marching, or 'making preparations' for an expedition (befitting king capable of setting off against his enemy); (e) śanśraya, seeking shelter or protection of another king in a fort—an alliance-based policy (appropriate for a king lacking sufficient power to defend himself) and (f) dvaidibhāva, or the dual policy of simultaneous peace with one king and hostility with another (appropriate for a king needing external help to achieve an objective).[25] But more than mere knowledge of these six methods, a good foreign policy decision-maker should understand 'the interdependence of the six methods of foreign policy' (verse 7.18.44).[26] Apart from these six methods, the four methods of achieving one's objective, with their components, suggested by Kautilya, are also highly relevant to foreign policymaking even today, namely *sāma*, praise or persuasion; *dāna*, gifts or monetary allurements; *daṇḍa* or punishment and *bheda* planting discord among others, and, as resultant of them, by diplomacy.[27]

Apart from these insights, Kautilya's greatest and finest contribution to IR is his *maṇdala* theory of foreign policy or interstate relations, meant to advise the king about how to set about building an empire, and judged by Bandyopadhyay as 'the first theoretical work on an ancient system of kings, kingdoms and empires...that can be considered as analogous to a model of international relations'.[28] Kautilya places his conqueror or potential emperor (*vijigīṣu*) in the centre of a well-mapped circle of 12 kings, where the position of each other king determines his potential response to him as well as the vijigīṣu's possible policy to him. The first principle of this theory is that kings of any two kingdoms sharing a common border are natural enemies of each other. Similarly, a king whose realm has shared borders with that of the enemy is an enemy of the enemy and automatically a friend of the king. From this central assumption that a state regards its immediate neighbours as its enemies but views the state on the others side of a neighbouring state as an ally, Kautilya counts 12 kings in his international system (verses 65.2.17–22 and 6.2. 24–27). Counting the conquest-aspirant once, in front are (a) the conqueror in the centre (*vijigīṣu*); (b) the enemy (*ari*) (c) the friend (*mitra*) or enemy of the enemy; (d) the enemy's friend (*arimitra*); (e) the friend's friend (*mitrāmitra*) and (f) the enemy's friend's friend (*arimitrāmitra*). Making up the rear are the *vijigīṣu* again, not counted; (g) the enemy (*pārśanigraha*); (h) the friend (*ākranda*); (i) the enemy's friend (*pārśanigrahasāra*) and (j) the friend's friend (*ākrandasāra*). In addition, there is (k) a middle king (*madhyamā*), intermediary and mediator; and a (l) neutral king (*udāsīna*). Location-wise, *madhyamā* rules a territory very close to both *vijigīṣu* and *ari*, and capability-wise is able to help both, whether united or disunited, and resisting either individually. The *udāsīna* king, however, is situated beyond the realms of any one of the 10 kings. He is mighty enough not only to help the *vijigīṣu* but also the *ari* and the *madhyamā*, or to take any one of them individually. The basic international system is shown in Figure 2.1.

Together, the key kings conqueror, friend and friend's friend in the front form a circle of states in any frontal attack. But the enemy, the mediator and the neutral kings are also possible conquerors, with their own circles of three key kings. The actual direction of attack is immaterial. Only then the *vijigīṣu* will have to enlist the support of the *ākranda* and *ākrandasāra* to counter the combination of *pārśanigraha* and *pārśanigrahasāra*, neutralize the ambitions of *madhyamā* and maintain the neutrality of *udāsīna*. In order to secure his interests, *vijigīṣu* will have to institute both in the front and the rear a circle of kings composed of outstanding allies (verse 7.18.42). In any venture, the six methods of foreign policy and the four techniques of achieving an objective must be considered.[29] What Kautilya says about *maṇdala*

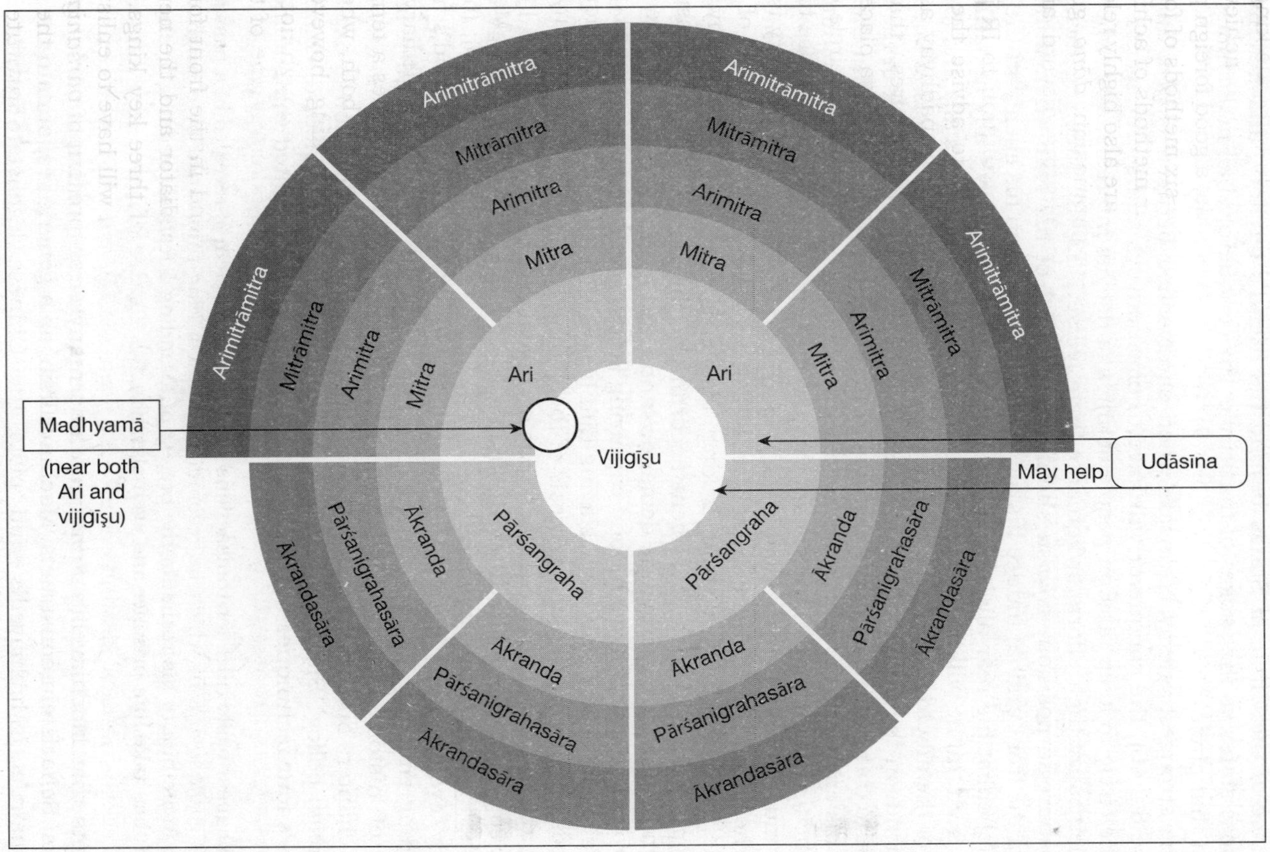

FIGURE 2.1 Kautilya's International System

Source: Author's graphical representation, reconstructed from Kautilya's text.

theory could impress modern geopoliticians: 'The Conqueror shall think of the circle of states as a wheel—himself at the hub and his allies, drawn to him by the spokes though separated by intervening territory, as its rim (verse 6.2.39)'[30]; or 'Throwing the circumference of the Circle of States beyond his friend's territory, and making the kings of those states as the spokes of that circle, the conqueror shall make himself as the nave of that circle'.[31]

Since the strongest enemy is unsafe when sandwiched between *vijigīṣu* and his allies (verse 6.2.40), the conqueror will have to plant envoys and secret agents in all states of the circle to keep tabs on people acting against his interests, and, wherever possible, neutralize their efforts or liquidate them (verse 7.13.43). Tailoring strategies to his geostrategic position, *vijigīṣu* should be mindful of his rear when initiating attack from the front and (a) induce his ally-in-the-rear to keep his enemy-in-the-rear busy and (b) enlist his rear-ally's friend to take on his rear enemy's ally in battle. To secure his front, (a) he will have to use his ally to take on the enemy's ally and (b) use the friend of the ally to take on the enemy's ally's friend. The objective is to keep the enemy's friends in the front and the rear occupied. When initiating attack in the rear, he will have to transfer the same strategy backwards, inducing his own ally in the rear to embroil his enemy in the rear in battle to secure his own rear, and then joining his ally by launching an attack on the enemy in the rear. But in a situation where *vijigīṣu* is himself under attack, he will enlist his ally to first attack the rear of the enemy and to induce the friend of his ally to launch an attack on the enemy.

When he faces attack by a stronger king, *vijigīṣu* is to distinguish among three types of aggressors and mete treatment accordingly: the righteous one wants only capitulation by him; the greedy one demands lands and goods as compensation and the monstrous one would move beyond capturing lands, goods, wives and sons of the conqueror's lands to stop only after slaying him (verse 12.1.10–16). Along with these tactics of positional war, the long exegesis of the six methods of foreign policy, briefly mentioned above, for stronger, equally strong and weaker kings[32] testifies to the high theoretical sophistication of Kautilya's maṇdala theory, which Bandyopadhyay calls 'model of the inter-state metasystem'.[33]

Tragically, even modern Western scholars of IR do not give Kautilya his due, save condescending endnote. Offbeat systems theorist Kai Holsti misses Kautilya in his discussion of 'historic international systems', except making two brief mentions of him in his chapters on 'foreign policy actions' and 'law and world opinion in explanations of foreign policy'. Silence in the first chapter is followed by a neutral comment on Kautilya's four techniques in the second, and a very short-sighted wry comment.

> Lack of the most basic rules for transactions in the Hindu system is revealed in a passage of Kautilya's *Arthasastra*, in which he recommends that a king threatened by a neighboring sovereign invite him to his realm on the pretext of attending a festival, wedding or elephant hunt and then take him prisoner and even slay him.[34]

Holsti forgets that Machiavelli's *Prince* contains many such prescriptions for confidence tricks. Scharfstein constructs 'Machiavellism' as a generic realist category and further constructs 'Machiavellis' and plots the Chinese legalists, Kautilya and Machiavelli himself in it in a somewhat topsy-turvy chronology.[35] Waltz grants only a dry footnote that 'Since Thucydides in Greece and Kautilya in India, the use of force and the possibility of controlling it have been the preoccupations of international-political studies'.[36] Indian scholar Sil tries to do some justice by comparing Kautilya with Plato, Aristotle and Machiavelli.[37] Chandrasekaran differentiates between Kautilya and Machiavelli on the twin grounds of empiricism and linguistic felicity, and gives greater credits to Machiavelli on both counts, but seems to indicate in a muddled fashion the greater breadth of Kautilya's work, so much so that 'Machiavelli's work can be considered as one of the possible subsets of Kautilya's statecraft'.[38]

Anyway, a recent revival of interest in Indian IR reinstates Kautilya in his deserved status. Behera seeks to use Kautilya in her re-imagining of Indian IR as part of a 'new IR'.[39] Gautam seeks to rehabilitate Kautilya beyond the confines of realist theory by pointing to the 'eigenvalue'—in Weberian terms—of the Kautilya *Arthashastra* and claiming that Machiavelli was 'narrower in focus' than Kautilya for 'leaving out the question of the economy'.[40] Let us turn to another breed of Scharfstein's 'Machiavellis', Chinese legalists, who however predate Machiavelli.

The Chinese Legalists and Han Fei Tzu

Chinese legalists (480–221 BC), an integral part of classical realism, have produced a huge corpus. Sadly, from these, I can pick up only Han Fei as the most famous, and that too sketchily, for reasons of space constraints in a textbook, that too because the oversight of this tradition in books on realism pains me for two reasons. First, the period between 551 BC and 233 BC, famous for the flowering of the legalist school, and known as the 'Period of the Hundred Contending Schools...in Chinese history', is coeval or contemporaneous with the Hellenic Age in Europe.[41] Second, even almost 1,800 years before Machiavelli, Chinese legalists' 'body of writings' are more 'contemporary in tone and more Machiavellian' than the eponymous thinker himself. Besides, two centuries before the advent of the Christian era, the 'level of the refinement and subtlety of statecraft' that the Chinese legalists achieved excelled 'in many respects that of [the] most eminent later day Western writers'. May be the imprint the legalists left on China's historical development was shrouded by Western and popular perceptions of China's cultural moorings as exclusively Confucian. But despite classical Confucianism's potent influence on Chinese culture and the end of China's imperial dynastic era in 1911, the imprint of the legalists on China's state practices lingered far beyond that period, far longer than the imprint of Machiavelli on Western political discourses. Indicators of this lingering influence are as follows: (a) the admission of many of the institutions and political practices of present-day China of their intellectual roots to Chinese legalism; (b) initiation of a nationwide campaign with Mao Zedong's support to popularize the teachings of the legalists instead of the Confucians in late 1973 by the Communist Party of China (CPC), which ended only with the official termination of the Cultural Revolution in 1976; (c) the proof provided by the campaign that both Mao and the CPC leadership regarded themselves as 'true successors of the legalist heritage'[42] and (d) the lingering appeal of Han Fei's writings for the Japanese Sinologues of the Tokugawa period,[43] testifying to his general impact in the Far East.

Among the extant works of eminent pre-Qin legalists are Master Guan Zhong (*Guanzi*); Master Shen [Dao] (Shen Zi); Shen Buhai (Shen Buhai or 'Fragments of Shen Pu-hai'); Gongun Yang or Wei Yang (*Shangjun shu* or *Book of Lord Shang*); Master Han

Fei Tzu (*Han Fei Zi* or *Works of Master Han Fei*); three short essays of Li Si (*Shi Ji* or *Records of History*) and a few others. The rest are lost. While the main tenets of their thought developed between 380 BC and 230 BC and the 'Warring States Period' (475–221 BC), unlike other pre-Qin schools of thought and much like modern realism, they 'had no commonly recognized founder' from whom teachings descended to disciples. Rather, it was a group, christened by the members' 'shared doctrinal theses', whose remarkable consistency and commonalities, particularly in the themes and doctrines of more than six eminent legalists[44] make it easier for me to choose one, Master Han Fei, because he had a great impact on the consolidation of the Qin (aka Ch'in) dynasty and the unification of China under it, and was taken as their intellectual guide.

Born in c. 280 BC in the royal family in the state of Han in central China, received with honours in the Qin court by the youthful First Emperor Qin Shi Huang (Ch'in Shih-huang), who had ascended the throne in 246 BC, finally fallen a victim to his fellow student's intrigue, and executed on the basis of false charges in 233 BC, Han Fei Tzu did not witness the full spread of the Qin empire during 221–207 BC. After his regular letters to two successive kings of Han, highlighting the sorry state of his native state, went unheeded, he wrote a book that Qin Shi chanced upon and greatly admired, as did the second emperor. Like Machiavelli's *The Prince*, with which it has been often compared—or even like Kautilya's *Arthaśāştra* that Boesche compared it with[45]—*Han Fei Zi* was a handbook for the prince and his ministers, guiding in the political vacuum created after the loss of control of Zhou rulers and the rise of powerful feudal leaders.

Han Fei did not create *fajiya* or more authentically 'fa-chia', the legalist or the realist school but, much like Kautilya and his final compendium of *Arthaśāştras*, merely perfected it.[46] Gleaning the best portions of *Guanzi*, *Shangjun shu*, *Shen Zi*, *Shen Buhai* and thoughts of their writers, and meshing them in a comprehensive whole, Han Fei created a new treatise. It lived on,[47] much like the terracotta figures of it hidden in subterranean chambers, even after the Qin dynasty went out of existence in 207 BC, subverted by internal insurrections.[48]

Classical legalism like realism too treats human nature as an important variable. 'Han Fei', says Bárcenas, 'discusses the issue of the natural tendencies of humans... on more occasions than the three most prominent members of the so-called Legalist school combined—Guanzi, Shen Buhai and Shang Yang', and the influence of his master-cum-intellectual rival Xunzi on this has been subject of much speculation.[49] But his writings demonstrate a particularly low assessment of human nature, against the Confucians and the Mo-ists, who cited history to argue that human nature was not always that bad. *Han Fei Zi* systematically sourced history to get its 'catalogue of human follies and idiocies', draw anecdotes from historical times or legends of late Chou times, establish the validity of legalist principles or decry other schools of thought; all later emulated by Morgenthau. He even predates Carr's critique of the vision of a natural 'harmony of interests',[50] arguing that more peace and order in ancient times was not attributable to the moral influence and direction of the sages, but to the availability of more goods with 'fewer men to scramble for them'. He regarded all efforts to educate and ennoble the common people as futile. Rather, to succeed, the ruler must dispense with 'all impulses toward mercy and affection and be guided only by enlightened self-interest'. He even anticipates Morgenthau's statesman and his omniscient national interest and, like Thucydides, Machiavelli and Morgenthau, makes it applicable both in external politics and domestic politics, where he differentiates inept bureaucracies from adept ones, which can make national interest the sure lens of national weal.

> Find men who have a clear understanding of what is beneficial to the nation and a feeling for the system of laws and regulations, and place them in charge of lesser officials,... Find men who have...the judgement to weigh issues properly, and put them in charge of foreign affairs; then the ruler can never be deceived in his relations with other powers of the world.[51]

Like Machiavelli, neither Han Fei nor other Chinese legalists had any truck with morality, and Han Fei would have approved of Machiavelli's maxim of mere appearance of virtuousness, but still they were different. Womack branded Machiavelli as an 'entrepreneurial realist', idolizing Cesare Borgia for his struggle with fortune, and Han Fei as a 'bureaucratic realist', content with observing from his 'place of darkness' 'the weaknesses of others', with even more cynicism than Machiavelli, if possible.[52] The block quote below from Han Fei Tzu would make it self-evident.

> A ruler's troubles come from trusting others, if he trusts others, he will be controlled by them...ministers spy on their lord's heart without even a moment's respite, while the ruler dwells above them, indolent and haughty. This is why, in our time, lords are bullied and rulers are assassinated. If a ruler puts great trust in his son, treacherous ministers will... take advantage of the son, and fulfill their private interests. Thus [minister] Li Dui mentored the King of Zhao [i.e., Huiwen, r. 299–266 BC] and starved the Ruler's Father [i.e., King Wuling, 325–299, who had abdicated in favour of his son]. If a ruler puts too much trust in his wife, treacherous ministers will...take advantage of the wife, and fulfill their private interests. Thus Jester Shi mentored Lady Li [d. 651 BC], killed [Crown Prince] Shenseng [d. 656 BC] and installed [her son] Xiqi [665–651 BC] If someone as close as his wife cannot be trusted, then none among the rest can be trusted either.[53]

Enriched with profuse historical examples from ancient pre-Qin Chinese history, this paean of distrust lends credence to a modern Chinese scholar's branding of Han Fei as an 'offensive realist', together with Shan Yang (390–339 BC) and Kautilya, centuries before Machiavelli.[54]

Because human nature is basically evil, Han Fei placed great faith in law; combined the three elements of law (*fa*), method (*shu*) and position/power (*shi*) into 'a structured approach to ruling a stable state'; and sought to place authority within law, not in good men or their rule in a Confucian manner or in nature in a Daoist manner. According to Bárcenas, Han Fei thought it 'crucial that the laws put an end to the pervasive aristocratic privileges during his time and, for that matter, that the law became equally applicable to all members of society'. In Han Fei's words:

> The law (fa 法) does not favor people of high status like the plumb line does not bend to accommodate a crooked place in the wood...when faults are to be punished, the highest minister cannot escape; when good capabilities are to be rewarded, the lowest person must not be neglected.[55]

But even while thinking about a law-governed ideal state

> Han Fei was conscious of the possible dire consequences (not to mention the difficulty of overcoming social inertia) of attempting to make deep changes in any society. In effect,

> among many reforms, limiting hereditary privileges and most of all attempting to provide guidelines and limitations on the power of a king was, to say the least, a dangerous enterprise

so much so that in Chapter XIII of *Han Fei Zi*, he even predicted his own death for his views, by remembering the tragic destiny of Wu Chi and Shang Yang.[56]

It is said that 'Han Fei's multi-faceted commitment to safeguarding the ruler's authority stands out as his most outstanding contribution to Chinese political theory'. But it merits recalling that Han Fei was the first-ever Chinese thinker to differentiate public (*gong*) from private (*si*) realm. And as Pines says, 'Han Fei ends with the same bottom line as most thinkers of the Warring States period: the ruler should be omnipotent as an institution but nullified as an individual.'[57] A secular state morality can be easily inferred from all this, which would make Han Fei comparable with Machiavelli, who will be discussed next.

Niccolò Machiavelli

Machiavelli, quintessential realist, is known mostly for his *The Prince*, which—just as Kautilya's *Athaśāştra* was a compendium of various previous *Athaśāştras*—is also the most famous and perfect utterance of a dominant tradition of books for princes and courtiers, generally called the 'mirror-for-princes' literature.[58] The Florentine diplomat has earned many epithets for his realism, such as 'fundamental realism' (Michael Doyle), 'empirical realism' (David Boucher), one of the 'six realist paradigms' (Jack Donnelly), realpolitik even before the term was coined (Howard Williams) and a relentless espousal of raison d'état (Friedrich Meinecke). Some have sought to rescue him from the realist label. While Benedetto Croce pitied him as a humanist victim of the struggle between the exponents of 'what is' and 'what ought to be', and Skinner views him as the defender of classical republicanism and of a different notion of freedom, others (Boucher, Donnelly) pleaded that his realism was more complex and less amoral than is made out to be.[59] Post-structuralists have found his realist reading a caricature.[60] But these rescue acts are as unnecessary because, like Thucydides and even Kautilya before him, Machiavelli too seldom sacrificed norms of justice, decency, communal bonds, order and so on at the altar of power and interest to entertain a banal realism.

Machiavelli's *The Prince* was written for private circulation much before its wider publication well after his death in 1532, before his more elaborate book *Discourses on the First Ten Books of Livy* (1531), *The Art of War* (1521), *Florentine Histories*, dedicated to the Medici Pope Clement VII (1525), a report to Clement on the fortifications of Florence and plays including *Mandragola* (1524).

Some of Machiavelli's realist credentials, traceable from his views on 'the nature of man, the definition of values, the state, glory and virtue, and conflict' in *The Prince*, *Discourses* and *The Art of War*, are as follows:

- The contention, different from Plato and Aristotle, that the 'the security and well-being of the community rather than the higher moral ends' are the supreme values in politics.
- Affirmation that the social and political outcomes of political acts are more important than the moral intentions of decision-makers, reminiscent of

Morgenthau's warning against 'the concern with motives and the concern with ideological preferences' of statesman.[61]

- View on conflict, constituted by the three beliefs that (a) conflict is not only universal but also a permanent condition in society, rooted in human nature; (b) the medieval faith in harmony, faith and reason as solvents of conflict in society is chimerical and (c) endemic conflict between social and political groups at the domestic and international levels is less explicable in economic and class terms than in terms of the fundamental struggle for power and domination.
- Defence of the state as the most effective means of chastening man's essentially selfish nature towards socially desirable ends, and as the provider of security, enabling one to say that the state 'has no higher end or spiritual purpose than its preservation'; and to regard policies of raison d'état 'as the prudent calculated acts of statesmen' to secure secular aims.
- Machiavelli's writing about politics in the language of war, requiring as much readiness, flexibility, capacity to surprise and employ deception as war does; besides the abilities of diplomacy, foresight, secretiveness and initiative to hatch conspiracies and counter-conspiracies that most political situations involve.[62]
- Machiavelli's symbols of the lion and the fox as signifiers of opposed qualities of power and deception, both of which are required for the successful conduct of foreign policy.

The main task of the ruler is to defend national freedom and the interests of the state to ensure its survival. The ruler has to be as strong and heroic as a lion to ward off layers of traps seeking to take advantages of its weaknesses, that is, other states. But he must also bc cunning and sharp-eyed like a fox to discern any trap that has been laid. The world being at the same time a dangerous and an opportune place, to survive here, it is as much important to be aware of the dangers as of the opportunities, and the conduct of foreign policy is essentially a Machiavellian act of measuring one's power and interests against those of rivals or competitors. Historical examples of statesmen who possessed these qualities are Cesare Borgia, Maximilian and Pope Julius II, with different abilities. If the ruler is to practise Machiavellian methods of statecraft, he (a) must be aware of the events occurring; (b) must not wait for things to happen but pre-empt them through a shrewd analysis of the motives and actions of others and (c) react before they act. So if the ruler or statesman wants to avoid disaster or ruin of his subjects, he cannot afford to act according to the norms of Christianity.[63]

For many, Machiavelli's supposed amorality is a mark of realism, in the twin senses of 'a particularly dispassionate way of looking at the world' and an empirically derived 'deep anthropological pessimism', beyond his numerous cynic utterances. The best proof of this are the reasons behind his famous resolve to posit, in a passage in Chapter XV of *The Prince*, 'what will be useful' and 'what really happens', against 'theories or speculations'.

> For, many have imagined republics and principalities that have never been seen or known to exist. However, how men live is so different from how they should live that a ruler who does not do what is generally done but persists in doing what ought to be done will undermine his power rather than maintain it.

The reasons for acting immorally stem from this reality: 'If a ruler who wants always to act honourably is surrounded by many unscrupulous men his downfall is inevitable. Therefore, a ruler who wishes to maintain power must be prepared to act immorally when this becomes necessary.'[64] Moreover, for Machiavelli, the purpose of praising the Romans against his degenerate times was to be rooted in facts and derive educative lessons for the young from them for the benefit of Italian unification, 'so that the minds of young men...may turn from the one [evils] and prepare to imitate the other [virtù] whenever fortune provides them with occasion for so doing'.[65]

In the backdrop of these utterances, Shakespeare's phrase 'murderous Machiavel'[66] or Voltaire and Frederick II's denigration of him in *Anti-Machiavel*[67] are startling. For, Machiavelli was till death a Christian; and his assault on the Church was more 'anticlerical' than 'antireligious', aimed at the Popes' profligacy and the obstacles they put before the unification of Italy. The relationship between glory and *virtù* is said to contain 'the essence of Machiavelli's normative thinking'. Virtù signifies the qualities of the soldier in battle, including virility, self-control, responsibility and purpose, in the contexts of struggle with *Fortuna* (the Renaissance Goddess) who symbolizes 'chance, capriciousness and change' and of solid republicanism. For, in the *Discourses*, Machiavelli says that virtù can prosper only in a republican society where liberty is alive and is protected by a citizens' army.[68] In tune with humanists' confidence that *virtù vince fortuna* (meaning *virtù* is capable of overcoming the powers of *fortuna*), Machiavelli says in the *Discourses* that 'only where men have but little *virtù*', we find *fortuna* making a great show of her powers. For, *fortuna* has no powers over great men, since 'they stay firm even when faced with her greatest malevolence'.[69] Moreover, Machiavelli followed Polybius in contending that conflict and power can be used for socially useful purposes if there were mechanisms for it, as in the Roman republic, where the discord between the patricians and the plebeians was resolved in the Senate.[70]

But still, for far more scholars, Machiavelli is a realist in the normal sense of the term in IRT. Steven Forde says that Machiavelli presents 'the realist argument in its purest form, arguing that the nature of international politics absolves states of any moral duties whatsoever'. Openly supporting unbridled imperialism and the indiscriminate subjugation of weaker nations by stronger ones, he 'develops a new, amoral basis for the community', in line with his perception of the requirements of contemporary IP and his rejection of the status of widely recognized moral principles. His political treatises are nothing but guidebooks on how to survive in a 'completely chaotic and immoral world'. For example, in *The Prince*, Machiavelli endorses the imperialistic efforts of the ancient Romans as worthy of emulation by prudent princes and states (*The Prince*, III, XII–XIII) and justifies Roman expansionism as a pre-emptive effort to counter a possible future threat from the King of Syria because of the nature of the international environment. Such defence of pre-emptive advances even in the absence of actual provocations confuses all possible distinctions between just and unjust wars and between aggression and defence. Machiavelli shows how Rome profited by not making this distinction, going so far as to say that they brought the (Western) world under their control just from considerations of self-defence, which was a rational reaction to a hostile environment.

For Forde, this argumentation reveals that 'Machiavelli's analysis of international politics overrides moral duties by extending the plea of self-defense to all states.' Machiavelli 'casts himself in the role of a doctor...diagnosing the danger [in IP] and prescribing the cure—preemptive attack', in the manner of Romans, and 'argues that the moral rules simply do not correspond to the "order of things". Indeed the natural order punishes those who attempt to play not by its rules but by moral rules instead'.[71]

Beitz assesses Machiavelli's position on morality in the context of what he calls 'international scepticism', expressed in American realists' claims that (a) 'moral judgments have no place in discussions of international affairs or foreign policy'; and (b) 'there are moral restrictions on individual action, but no such restrictions on the actions of states.' Since 'one cannot consistently maintain' this distinction, his advice is that any position that 'purports to be an international morality' and yet 'extends beyond the lowest common denominator of the various social moralities will be insecure in foundation'. And still this lowest-common-denominator-based position would leave most of the international conflicts unsettled, because at bottom these conflicts are about 'which principles to apply to given situations, or which goods should be sacrificed when several goods conflict'. And the principles which would be required to resolve these conflicts being 'fundamentally insecure', the sceptic would be justified in arguing that no normative international theory worth its name is sustainable.[72] Beitz does not accept that the concept of national interest can serve as a surrogate for international morality, however much Morgenthau may contend 'that a ruler, and especially a new ruler, cannot always act in ways that are considered good because, in order to maintain his power, he is often forced to act treacherously, ruthlessly or inhumanly, and disregard the precepts of religion'.[73] So how would he react to Machiavelli's statement that the prince should not 'deviate from right conduct if possible, but be capable of entering the path of wrongdoing when this becomes necessary'.[74]

Beitz argues that Machiavelli is neither implying that princes are free to behave as they please nor that their official actions are free from searching scrutiny. The principal issue here is what criteria should be applied to justify or question a prince's official actions, not private virtues such as liberality, kindness and charity, which are not only not virtues but veritable vices in the public sphere simply because observing them will harm the well-being of the state, and the rule 'preserve the state' ranks highest in the prince's order of moralities and overwhelms all others.

Beitz wonders if this stance of Machiavelli amounts to international scepticism. Should the contention that the prince has some leeway while striving to promote national interest be true, 'then Machiavelli's views and its contemporary variants' do not qualify as forms of international scepticism. The latter do not contend that moral judgements are inappropriate in international relations, but only that 'moral evaluations of a state must be cast in terms of the state's actions and its own interests'. The difference between international scepticism and Machiavelli's concession for state actions strongly resembles, or at least parallels, 'the distinction between moral skepticism and ethical egoism. One pair of views denies the possibility of morality altogether, while the other pair advances a substantive moral principle.' After conceding Machiavelli, the possibility of a republican or even international morality, Beitz goes one step further to ask if 'international morality' is at all a viable concept. 'Why should we say that right conduct for officials of a state consists in action that promotes the state's interests'? If it is not self-evident that the quest for self-interest by individuals does not naturally or automatically lead to morally right action, then 'it is no more obvious in the parallel case for officials of states.'[75]

Ernesto Landi makes the case of Machiavelli's amorality stand on a difference between his key books. Machiavelli's bad reputation supposedly comes from assessing him only on the basis of *The Prince*, though a close reading of his ideas in *Discourses* and the *History of Florence* would present Machiavelli as both a realist and a visionary, whose only quarrel with Christianity was that it did not facilitate *virtù*. While his exposure to the Italian Dominican reformer Savonarola and his views on the role of violence in politics made Machiavelli nonchalant about, and even hostile to, Christianity and its avowedly human institutions, in real fact, his most original insight was into the existence of two moralities, political/public and private. Landi links Machiavelli to Galileo—for making observation the fulcrum of his theory of politics—and to Marx—for showing how to read and take control of the future by using the laws of history.[76]

But can we agree with Landi that there are two Machiavellis—of *The Prince* and the *Discourses*? I think not. For, even in the *Discourses*, we find a chapter titled 'That One Comes from Base to Great Fortune More through Fraud than through Force' not tied to *staatsraison* alone.[77] This Machiavellian permission for fraud and concealment, and any use of it, has made his name synonymous with hypocrisy in foreign policy-making in a democracy and has also placed him in an unfavourable comparison with Thucydides. In the context of American realists' grouse during the last four generations against the resistance of democratic politics to their preferred policy choices since the time of Morgenthau, Forde writes that Thucydides would not view this resistance as 'simply naïve', but as indicative of one perennial problem of realism, that communities fight unmixed realism 'partly out of a need to protect their moral consensus'. So, while engaging with national hypocrisy to a degree, a Thucydidesian statesman will temper his realism not merely because of considerations of expediency even relating to long-term survival of the community, 'but out of an independent moral concern'. Machiavelli, however, would look askance at any such 'tempering or realism' as an uncalled-for hazard in questions of security, and would have no compunction about statesmen covering their realism under complete hypocrisy and deceit. The targets of such hypocrisy would be not only aliens but also fellow citizens, both in republics and autocratic regimes. And he says this not only in *The Prince* (Chapter 18) but also in the *Discourses* (1.13–14, 47, 48).[78] He would feel that Kautilya and Han Fei are more understandable.

Thomas Hobbes

Hobbes' exposure to realism was academic, at Oxford University while studying Aristotle, while studying mechanical science at Paris and as competent translator of Thucydides into English. His two books which concern us are (a) *Leviathan; Or The Matter, Forme and Power of a Commonwealth, Ecclesiasticall and Civil* (1651), and (b) *De Cive* ([1642]1647), *Philosophical Rudiments Concerning Government and Society* in its first English translation (1651).

Hobbes' realism (he never termed it so) was occasioned not by the international political developments but by the turbulent domestic politics of pre- and-post Civil War England[79] and by the concept of the 'state of nature' (SON) which he developed to describe it and other such situations. But realists have swooped upon this concept, whether to adopt it as their 'mantra' or to question its applicability to IP. The acceptability of the concept is mind-boggling, since from 'Hobbes to Raymond Aron, there is an unbroken chain or writers referring explicitly to the state of nature when describing international relations'. Different thinkers from Spinoza, Locke, Rousseau in *Emile*, Bodin, Hume, Fénelon, the Marquis de Mirabeau, Henri Bergson and Aron have referred to the concept in their different senses and contexts, both domestic and international, whether as a depiction of reality or a proffering of solutions.[80] Hobbes' explication of SON has become the defining feature of realist thought, and his 'notion of the international state of nature as a state of war is shared by virtually everyone calling himself a realist'. For Morgenthau, it provides the 'stock in trade' of the discipline of IR.[81]

The pre-civil condition, called SON in Hobbes' formulation, implies a sorry plight for everyone that was as adverse as disorderly. Conflict was as inevitable as it was endemic, since men driven by natural passions collided with others some natural bodies in 'free motion'. Conflict existed because of certain ingrained attributes of human beings, such as (a) capability of rationality; (b) fear of violent death at others' hands; (c) equal vulnerability in the sense of the weakest possessing enough strength to kill the strongest; (d) constant desire to increase power and prestige; and (e) natural independence and freedom. All of these assumptions created a situation where rational individuals interested in self-preservation, equally able to inflict harm on others and equally vulnerable to similar capability of others, and equally eager to extend domination on others, were living in a pre-social condition, without keepers or interpreters of rules that restrict such freedoms; and without any central authority that would supervise the allocation of scarce resources. This not only made 'the life of man [please don't mind] solitary, poor, nasty, brutish and short' but also created a situation of war of all against all.[82]

Hobbes provided the escape route from this jungle of SON into a civilized commonwealth through his famous 19 'laws of nature', the first three of which are enough to show how these wild rational persons become amenable to the creation of a commonwealth. The first law stipulates that 'every man ought to endeavour Peace, as farre (far) as he has hope of obtaining it; and when he cannot obtain it, that he may seek, and use, all advantages of Warre (war)'. The second law states that

> a man may be willing, when others are so too, as farre-forth (far forth), as for Peace and defence of himselfe (himself) he shall think it necessary, to lay down this right to all things; and be contented with so much liberty against other men, as he would allow other men against himself

followed by its corollaries. The third law states that 'men performe (perform) their Covenants made: without which Covenants are in vain, and but Empty words...' In *Leviathan*, the primary meaning of injustice is non-performance of covenants, though many other meanings exist. Along with the laws of gratitude (fourth), and mutual accommodation (fifth), the remaining 14 specify how to prevent war in the commonwealth and escape SON.[83]

Does SON refer to any historical reality? If so or not, what is its relevance to IRT? Some scholars think that SON is an ahistorical and imaginary point reachable after mentally dissolving the bonds of civilized society and then extrapolating forward from there. Bronowski and Mazlish show how Hobbes arrived at this conceptual device through his axiomatic method, method of 'causal definition', and his 'scientific materialism', backed by Euclid's geometry, read accidentally backwards from the final 47th theorem of Pythagoras, and 'back to the elementary axioms'. So he 'was not trying to depict a historical development but a logical one'.[84] Some others too regard this pre-civil condition as a 'thought experiment that strips away social artifice to reveal a fixed, constant core of human nature',[85] or as not any historical circumstance lodged in the distant past, but 'an ever-present abyss which we skirt daily, and thankfully but unwisely forget'.[86] But Hobbes visualizes SON differently in two different books. In *De Cive*, it is offered to readers as a 'thought experiment'. But in *Leviathan*, SON is stated to be observable in actuality in three types of historical circumstances: in primitive societies, at the height of civil war and in IR.[87] I support Hayden and produce one quote of Hobbes' view of SON in *Leviathan*.

> It may peradventure be thought, there was never such a time, nor condition of warre (war) as this; and I believe it was never generally so, over all the world: but there are many places, where they live so now. For the savage people in many places of America...live at this day in that brutish manner.... Howsoever, it may be perceived what manner of life there would be, where there were no common Power to feare (fear); by the manner of life, which men that have formerly lived under a peacefull (peaceful) government, use to degenerate into a civil Warre.

SON assumes a different, more permanent shape in IR.

> But though there had never been any time, wherein particular men were in a condition of warrre one against another; yet in all times, Kings, and Persons of Soveraigne (sovereign) authority, because of their Independency, are in continuall (continual) jealousies, and in the state and posture of Gladiators; having their weapons pointing, and their eyes fixed on one another; that is their Forts, Garrisons, and Guns upon the Frontiers of their Kingdoms; and coninuall Spyes upon their neighbours; which is a posture of War.

Of course, Hobbes is quick to point out the differences between the SON that prevails in international relations, however anarchic, and that which prevails in other situations. This is 'because they [states] uphold thereby the Industry of their Subjects; there does not follow from it that misery, which accompanies the Liberty of particular men'.[88] It was unlikely that a man of Hobbes' acumen would not see the difference. But could he really understand the import of what is called the 'security dilemma'[89] in IR too? I think he could! Jackson and Sørensen say that the statist solution to the problem of order in the SON—through personal and domestic security through the state—replicates another SON in the international sphere. There is no escape from it comparable to that from the pre-civil condition due to many reasons: (a) the greater reluctance of sovereign states to relinquish their independence to facilitate any global security guarantee; (b) the less alarming and hazardous aspect of the international SON, compared to the primary SON, as states can more easily guarantee security for their subjects on their own and (c) the lesser vulnerability of states compared to men in the primary SON, even as the international SON remains a condition of actual or potential war. But Hobbes would add that states can also conclude treaties with one another to create a legal basis for their relations.[90]

Williams says that from this perspective, Hobbes' realism is very different from what he is thought to represent in IR. 'Far from yielding an international order directly analogous to his SON, Hobbes seeks to construct a practice of sovereignty that supports a politics of limits—and to construct an international order on the basis of the reconstruction of sovereignty'.[91] Oakeshott points out the oddity of the Hobbesian situation of self-interested men and women cooperating politically because of their fear of getting hurt or killed by neighbours, and in effect being 'civilized by fear of death'.[92] This constructive function of fear was familiar to Hobbes, fond of saying that 'my mother gave birth to twins: myself and fear', since his mother delivered him prematurely on hearing the fearful news that Spanish Armada was invading England.[93] So given this 'fear' and the 'passions that encline men to peace'[94] that Hobbes talks of, can we not imagine a world where nuclear fear has prompted sovereign states to cooperate?

Can we in these circumstances place Hobbes squarely in realist IR? There are as many scholars who say 'aye', as others who say 'nay', and both sides include big names. Wight, doyen of ES, implants Hobbes firmly in IRT, and even terms the realist school as 'the Hobbesian or realist tradition', since Hobbes' view of SON as 'a state of war of all against all' depicts IR as 'an arena of struggle', where 'pure conflict between states...resemble a game that is wholly distributive or zero-sum'. Some other scholars have recognized the international implications of Hobbesian SON and re-explored its umbilical relationship with the realist approach in IR. They have also applied game theory and gaming models to the Hobbesian SON to show how the 'natural conditions' of mankind inevitably lead to it. But there are detractors of this view. Some among them think that Hobbes was never preoccupied with IR. His references to them are an 'offshoot, a subordinate part of his explanation of domestic politics', which make it truly problematic that these 'few and brief references' have been given such canonical importance in a wanton attempt to fit Hobbes into IRT.[95] Malcolm thinks that this portrayal of Hobbes' IR 'appears to be based, for the most part, on a handful of passages in one or two of his works'.[96] As Forsyth says, for students of political theory, the 'external relations of Leviathan are...on the fringes of Hobbes' theory', even though students of IR 'invoke Hobbes' name frequently as a kind of shorthand' for realism in IR.[97]

On the 'aye' side, even after conceding that Hobbes was a theorist of the sovereign state more as 'sovereign over its subjects, rather than a sovereign among sovereigns', Armitage regards any view that 'the balance of Hobbes' writings supports the greater focus on "the internal dimension of the state"' as an incomplete reading of Hobbes. For, if one makes a thorough historical survey of Hobbes' conceptions of the relations among states spread over his entire academic career, one will find a far more 'expansive and nuanced set of reflections on the state in its international capacity'. Still, the 'standard account of Hobbes as an international theorist arose in conditions of not of his own making'. In circumstances of positivists battling naturalists over the reconcilability of law of nations with law of nature, pluralist theorists of the state criticizing juristic/monistic theorists of legal personality, and political scientists upholding their discipline against international law and IR, 'Hobbes could be invoked on both sides of each dispute'.[98] He is rightly invoked. Thompson says that 'Hobbes' contention that the relations among states and Kings are in "a condition of mere nature" presages the clash between realists and idealists'.[99] Gauthier says that equal nuclear vulnerability would make the analogy between IR and the Hobbesian SON more plausible.[100] We understand Hobbes' relevance to realism even in circumstances of limitation of nuclear arms, amid our Hobbesian 'fear' that they might fall in the hands of rogue states and terrorist groups. And here Hobbes' sonorous words about the distinction between war and peace, as psychological states, in the context of fear caused by the absence of common sovereign power, would continue to remain relevant not only for realism but for IP in general, its anarchic nature qualifying as a state of war.

> Hereby it is manifest, that during the time men live without a common Power to keep them all in awe, they are in that condition which is called Warre; ...as the nature of Foule (foul) weather, lyeth (lies) not in a showre (shower) or two of rain, but an inclination thereto of many dayes (days) together: so the nature of War consisteth not in actual fighting, but in the known disposition thereto, during all the time there is no assurance to the contrary. All other time is PEACE.[101]

CONCLUSION

In her psychological account of the theoretical variants of realism, Annette Freyberg-Inan differentiates Thucydides' 'Athenian justifications of power politics, and the "first indications of the realist psychology", from Machiavelli's "Classical Ideological Realism", and Hobbes' "Classical Paradigmatic Realism"'.[102] We have seen the epithets 'fundamental', 'empirical' and 'entrepreneurial' being applied before Machiavelli's realism, and 'bureaucratic' before Han Fei's realism. Then what unifies the motley group of classical realists? The first factor is that all of them view the human condition as one of endemic insecurity and conflict that has to be addressed through a strong state or empire. The second is that all of them proffer keys to it from a body of political knowledge that they have created or perfected. The third is that none of them believe that there is a permanent escape from this condition since it is a reflection of basic human nature. The fourth which is a corollary of the above three is the pessimism of all the proponents. In the next chapter,[103] we will focus on the development, decay and regeneration of geopolitics, which is an important application of the realist perspective to spatial reality and imaginings.

REVIEW QUESTIONS

1. Compare Thucydides and Morgenthau as realists and explain Thucydides' lasting importance and relevance.
2. What are the reasons that Kautilya looks so familiar to a modern political realist in IR?
3. Assess the position of Han Fei among early classical realists and show from Han Fei Tzu why he remains relevant to modern mainstream IRT.
4. Would you agree to the statement that 'there are two Machiavellis—of *The Prince* and the *Discourses*'? State with reasons.
5. How does Hobbes point out the differences of the SON that prevails in IR, however anarchic, from that found in other situations?

NOTES

1. For these various meanings, see Duncan Bell, 'Introduction: Under an Empty Sky—Realism and Political Theory', in *Political Thought and International Relations: Variations on a Realist Theme,* ed. Duncan Bell (Oxford: Oxford University Press, 2008), 1–2.
2. Cornelia Navari, 'Hobbes, and the "Hobbesian Tradition" in International Thought', *Millennium* 2, no. 3 (1982): 207.
3. Gregory Crane, *Thucydides and Ancient Simplicity: The Limits of Political Realism* (Berkeley, CA: University of California Press, 1998), 1–2. Available at books.google.com/ *books?isbn=0520207890* (accessed on 29 July 2014).
4. See William Eliot Butler, ed., *On the History of International Law and Organization: Collected Papers of Sir Paul Vinogradoff* (Clark, NJ: Lawbook Exchange, 2009), 75.
5. Jackson and Sørensen, *Introduction*, 70–72.
6. The Mytilenean Debate was occasioned by the misadventure of the city state of Mytilene against Athens in 428 BC, even after enjoying privileged status in the Athenian empire, by its ill-judged request to Sparta for help, Sparta's non-response and Mytilene's fall before Athenian siege. The debate in the Athenian Assembly in 427 BC concerned reprisals proposals by Athens and their softening after a debate between hawkish Cleon and moderate Diodotus. Thucydides reconstructed this debate in Book Three of *HOTPWA*. For a good description and interpretation of the Mytilenean and the Sicilian debates, see Josiah Ober, *Political Dissent in Democratic Athens: Intellectual Critics of Popular Rule* (Princeton, NJ: Princeton University Press, 1999), 94–107.
7. The Melian Dialogue is a fictionalized speech put into *HOTPWA* by Thucydides, occurring during 416–415 BC in the 16th year of a 27-year ruinous war between the Athenians and the helpless people of a small island state called Melos. Faced with two options from the Athenians, surrender of their city and payment of tribute or total destruction, the Melians pleaded for their right to remain neutral and appealed to the Athenians' sense of justice towards a small, peaceful, defenceless city, eventually spurned by the Athenians on the ground that questions of justice did not arise between unequal powers. For a translated version of Melian Dialogue, see Viotti and Kauppi, *International Relations Theory*, 78–84.
8. For this section, see Richard Ned Lebow, 'Classical Realism', in *International Relations Theories: Discipline and Diversity*, eds. Dunne, Kurki and Smith (Oxford; New York, NY: Oxford University Press, 2007), 53–64; 'Alcibiades and Sicilian Debate' in http://historum.com/ancient-history/62552-alcibiades-sicilian-debate.html (accessed on 28 July 2014) and Thomas R. Martin, 'The Peloponnesian War and Athenian Life, The Course of the Peloponnesian War', in *An Overview of Classical Greek History from Mycenae to Alexander*, ed. Thomas R. Martin (New Haven, CT: Yale University Press, 2000); this portion available at www.perseus.tufts.edu/hopper/text?doc=Perseus%3Atext%3A1999.04 (accessed on 28 July 2014).
9. Crane, *Thucydides and Ancient Simplicity*, 38–60.
10. Max Weber, 'Politics as Vocation', in *Weber: Selections in Translation*, ed. W. G. Runciman, tr. Eric Matthews (Cambridge: Cambridge University Press, 1985), 220.
11. D. D. Koshambi, *An Introduction to the Study of Indian History* (Bombay: Popular Prakashan, [1956]1994); Somendra Lal Roy, *Diplomacy in Ancient India: From the Early Vedic Period to the End of the Sixth Century A.D.* (Calcutta: Charu Publishing Co., 1978) and Indra, *Ideologies of War and Peace in Ancient India* (Hoshiarpur: Vishveshvaranand Institute Publications, 1957); all cited in Roger Boesche, *The First Great Political Realist: Kautilya and His Arthashastra* (Lanham, MD: Lexington Books, 2002), 17.
12. Jayantanuja Bandyopadhyay, *General Theory of International Relations* (New Delhi: Allied Publishers Limited, 1993), 137.

13. Navnita Chadha Behera, 'Re-imagining IR in India', in *International Relations of the Asia-Pacific* 7 (2007): 341–348, here 341 and 352. Courtesy Google scholar, doi:10.1093/irap/lcm014.
14. Boesche, *The First Great Political Realist*, 15–16.
15. Radha Kumud Mookerjee, *Chandragupta Maurya and His Times* (Delhi: Motilal Banarsidas, 1966), 4–5.
16. K. J. Shah, 'Of Artha and the Arthasastra', in *Comparative Political Philosophy: Studies under the Upas Tree*, eds. Anthony J. Parel and Ronald C Ketih (New Delhi, California, London: SAGE Publications, 1992), 141.
17. Boesche, *The First Great Political Realist*, 18–19.
18. Shah, 'Of Artha and the Arthasastra', 148–151.
19. For a translation of the verse 6.1.1 see Kautilya, *The Arthashastra*, edited, rearranged and introduced by L. N. Rangarajan (New Delhi: Penguin Books, 1992), 119, 547.
20. Boesche, *The First Great Political Realist*, 8, 109–110.
21. Ibid., 110–111.
22. Kautilya, *Arthashastra*, Rangarajan, 546, 548–549.
23. Ibid., 548.
24. Ibid., 541.
25. For a more detailed version of these six methods, see Kautilya, *Arthashastra*, Rangarajan, 548–549, 563–579; Bandyopadhyay, *General Theory of International Relations*, 140–141; S. D. Chamola, *Kautilya Arthshastra and the Science of Management: Relevance for the Contemporary Times* (Gurgaon: Hope India Publications, 2007), 31–32.
26. Kautilya, *Arthashastra*, Rangarajan, 541.
27. Ibid., 113–115; Chamola, *Kautilya Arthshastra*, 32.
28. Bandyopadhyay, *General Theory of International Relations*, 137.
29. Kautilya, *Arthashastra*, Rangarajan, 555–561; students may also see R. Shamasastry, *Kauṭilya's Arthaśastra* (Mysore: Wesleyan Mission Press, 1929), 289–292.
30. Kautilya, *Arthashastra*, Rangarajan, 561.
31. Shamasastry, *Arthaśāstra*, 269.
32. Kautilya, *Arthashastra*, Rangarajan, 563–579, especially 566–567.
33. Bandyopadhyay, *General Theory of International Relations*, 136.
34. See Holsti, *International Politics*, Chapters 2, 5 and 13, pp. 23–51 for silence and pp. 126 and 291 for neutral mention and the biased one, based on George Modelski, 'Kautilya: Foreign Policy and International System in the Ancient Hindu World', *American Political Science Review* 58 (1964): 559–560, especially 553, 556.
35. Ben-Ami Scharfstein, *Amoral Politics: The Persistent Truth of Machiavellism* (Albany, NY: State University of New York Press, 1995).
36. Kenneth Waltz, *Theory of International Politics* (Long Grove, IL: Waveland Press, 2010), 186, fn. 33.
37. Narasingha Prosad Sil, *Kautilya's Arthaśāstra: A Comparative Study* (Calcutta, New Delhi: Academic Publishers, 1985), *passim.*
38. Pravin Chandrasekaran, 'Kautilya, Politics, Ethics and Statecraft', Munich Personal RePEc Archive, MPRA Paper No. 9962, posted 12 August 2008. Available at http://mpra.ub.uni-muenchen.de/9962/ (accessed on 12 May 2015), 15.
39. See note 13 above.
40. P. K. Gautam, *One Hundred Years of Kautilya's Arthasastra*, IDSA Monograph Series, No. 20 (New Delhi: Institute for Defence Studies and Analysis, 2013).
41. Zhengyuan Fu, *China's Legalists: The Earliest Totalitarians and Their Art of Ruling* (Armonk, NY: Sharpe, 1996), 3.
42. Ibid., 7–8.
43. R. H. van Gulik, 'Review' of *The Complete Works of Han Fei-Tzu*, translated from the Chinese with introduction, notes, glossary and index by W. K. Liao, Probsthain's Oriental

Series, vol. xxv (London, 1939), *Monumenta Nipponica* 3, no. 2 (1940): 674–676. Available at http://www.jstor.org/stable/2382614 (accessed on 15 May 2015).

44. Fu, *China's Legalists*, 9, 11; Han Fei, *Han Fei Zi: Basic Writings*, trans. Burton Watson (New York, NY: Columbia University Press, 2003). Available at books.google.com/books?isbn=0231521324 (accessed on 22 March 2021), 4.
45. Roger Boesche, 'Han Feizi's Legalism versus Kautilya's *Arthashastra*', *Asian Philosophy* 15, no. 2 (2005): 157–172.
46. Shamasastry, *Arthaśāstra*, 1.
47. Fei, *Han Fei Zi*, ix–x, 1–5; *Basic Writings of Mo Tzu, Hsun Tzu, and Han Fei Tzu*, tr. Burton Watson, UNESCO Collection of Representative Works, Chinese Series (New York, NY: Columbia University Press, [1963]1964). Available at books.google.com/books?isbn=0231521103 (accessed on 12 August 2014), 1–4.
48. Yu Yonqui, 'A Two-Thousand-Year-Old-Underground Empire'; Lucas Nickel, 'The Terracotta Army', in *The First Emperor: China's Terracotta Army*, ed. Jane Portal (London: British Museum, 2007), 152–179; Hung Shi-Ti, 'The Age in which Ch'in Shih-huang Was Born', in *The First Emperor of China*, ed. Li Yu-Ning (first published 1978; London; New York, NY: Routledge, 2018), 3–16.
49. Alejandro Bárcenas, 'Xunzi and Han Fei on Human Nature', *International Philosophical Quarterly* 52:2, no. 206 (2012): 135–148, here 140–141.doi:10.5840/ipq201252214.
50. See note 31 of 'Introduction'.
51. Fei, *Han Fei Zi*, 10–13, Section 6, 'On Having Standards', 21–22; *Basic Writings of Mo Tzu*, 10–11.
52. Brantly Womack, *China among Unequals: Asymmetric Foreign Relationships in Asia* (Hackensack, NJ: World Scientific, 2010*), 171.*
53. For the whole bigger quote, see Qiyou Chen, *Han Feizi, with New Collations and Commentary* (Shanghai: Guji, 2000), 5.17, 321–322, cited in Paul R. Goldin, 'Introduction', in *Dao Companion to the Philosophy of Han Fei, ed. Paul R. Goldin* (New York, NY: Springer Verlag, 2013), 2–3.
54. Shiping Tang, *A Theory of Security Strategies for Our Time: Defensive Realism* (New York, NY: Palgrave Macmillan, 2010), 173–174.
55. Fei, *Han Fei Zi*, Chapter VI, cited in Alejandro Bárcenas, 'Han Fei's Rule of Law and Its Limits', in *The Bloomsbury Research Handbook of Early Chinese Ethics and Political Philosophy*, ed. Alexus McLeod (New York, NY; London: Bloomsbury, 2019), 155–183, here 158.
56. *Ibid., 173.*
57. Yuri Pines, 'Submerged by Absolute Power: The Ruler's Predicament in the Han Feizi', in *Dao Companion to the Philosophy of Han Fei*, ed. Paul R. Goldin, 73–74, 85.
58. Quentin Skinner, *The Foundations of Modern Political Thought: Volume One, The Renaissance* (Cambridge: Cambridge University Press, [1978]1988), 118–128.
59. For citations of these authors, see Gabriella Slomp, 'The Origins of Realism Revisited', in *The Ashgate Research Companion to Ethics and International Relations*, ed. Patrick Hayden (Farnham and Burlington: Ashgate, 2009), 16–18.
60. Notes 63–65 of Chapter 26.
61. See Morgenthau, *Politics among Nations*, 6–7.
62. Kenneth W. Thompson, *Fathers of International Thought: The Legacy of Political Theory* (Baton Rouge, LA: Louisiana State University Press, 1994), 62–67.
63. Jackson and Sørensen, *Introduction*, 72–74.
64. Quentin Skinner and Russell Price, ed., *Machiavelli, the Prince* (Cambridge: Cambridge University Press, 1988), Chapter XV, 54.
65. Machiavelli, 'The Preface to Book Two', in *The Discourses of Niccolò Machiavelli*, translated from the Italian with and introduction and notes by Leslie J. Walker, with a new

introduction and appendices by Cecil H. Clough (London; Boston, MA: Routledge and Kegan Paul, 1975), Paragraph 7, pp. 355–356.

66. William Shakespeare, *King Henry the Sixth*, in *The Complete Works of William Shakespeare* (New Delhi: Oxford & IBH Publishing Co. Pvt Ltd, 2005), Part III, Act III, Scene II, Line 193.
67. Voltaire (François Marie Arouet) and Frederick II of Prussia, trans. P. Sonnino, *The Refutation of Machiavelli's Prince: or Anti-Machiavel* (Athens, OH: Ohio University Press, 1981).
68. Thompson, *Fathers of International Thought*, 64–65.
69. Skinner, *The Foundations of Modern Political Thought*, 187.
70. Thompson, *Fathers of International Thought*, 66.
71. Steven Forde, 'Classical Realism', in *Traditions of International Ethics*, eds. Terry Nardin and David R. Mapel (Cambridge: Cambridge University Press, 1999), 64–66.
72. Charles Beitz, *Political Theory and International Relations* (Princeton, NJ: Princeton University Press, 1999), 15–17.
73. Morgenthau, *Politics among Nations*, 10.
74. Skinner and Price, *Machiavelli*, 62.
75. Beitz, *Political Theory and International Relations*, 20–23.
76. Ernesto Landi, 'Machiavelli', in *Niccolò Machiavelli: An Annotated Bibliography of Modern Criticism and Scholarship*, ed. Silvia Ruffo-Fiore (New York, NY: Greenwood Press, 1990), 208.
77. Niccolò Machiavelli, *Discourses on Livy*, trans. Harvey C. Mansfield and Nathan Tarcov (Chicago, IL: University of Chicago Press, 1996), Second Book, 13, p. 155.
78. Steven Forde, 'Varieties of Realism: Thucydides and Machiavelli', *The Journal of Ethics* 54, no. 2 (1992): 372–393, especially 388.
79. Thompson, *Fathers of International Thought*, 76–77; Slomp, 'The Origins of Realism Revisited', 18–19.
80. Marcel Merle, *The Sociology of International Relations* (Bloomsbury, NY: Bloomsbury Academic, 1977), 40–47.
81. *Michael J. Smith, Realist Thought from Weber to Kissinger* (Baton Rouge, LA: Louisiana State University Press, 1986), 13; Hans Morgenthau, *Scientific Man versus Power Politics* (Chicago, IL: University of Chicago Press, 1946), 113, both cited in Michael C. Williams, *The Realist Tradition and the Limits of International Relations* (Cambridge: Cambridge University Press, 2005), 19.
82. See Thompson, *Fathers of International Thought*, 77–78; Slomp, 'The Origins of Realism Revisited', 19.
83. Thomas Hobbes, *Leviathan* (Harmondsworth: Penguin Books, 1968), 189–214. See for their summary, Bruce K. Alexander and Curtis P. Shelton, 'Materialism: Thomas Hobbes and the Human Machine', in *A History of Psychology in Western Civilization*, eds. Bruce K. Alexander and Curtis P. Shelton (Cambridge: Cambridge University Press, 2014), 238–239; *Thompson, Fathers of International Thought*, 78.
84. Jacob Bronowski and Bruce Mazlish, *Western Intellectual Tradition: From Leonardo to Hegel* (London: Hutchinson of London, 1960), 195–196, 198, 204.
85. Jack Donnelly, *Realism and International Relations* (Cambridge: Cambridge University Press, 2000), 15.
86. K. R. Minogue, 'Hobbes and the Philosophy of Absolutism', in *Political Ideas*, ed. David Thomson (Harmondsworth: Penguin Books, 1977), 59.
87. Slomp, 'The Origins of Realism Revisited', 20.
88. Hobbes, *Leviathan*, 187–188.
89. John Herz, 'Idealist Internationalism and the Security Dilemma', *World Politics* 2, no. 2 (1950): 157–180.
90. Jackson and Sørensen, *Introduction*, 74–76.
91. Williams, *The Realist Tradition and the Limits of International Relations*, 21.

92. M. Oakeshott, *Hobbes and the Civil* Association (Oxford: Basil Blackwell, 1975), 36, cited in Jackson and Sørensen, *Introduction*, 74.
93. Bernard Gert, *Hobbes: Prince of Peace* (Cambridge: Polity, 2010), 1.
94. Donnelly, *Realism*, 14–15.
95. For citations of M. Wight, *Power Politics* (London: Royal Institute of International Affairs, 1946), and other detractors, see Slomp, 'The Origins of Realism Revisited', 20–21.
96. Noel Malcolm, *Aspects of Hobbes* (Oxford: Clarendon Press, [2002]2004), 435.
97. Murray Forsyth, 'Thomas Hobbes and the External Relations of States', *British Journal of International Studies* 5, no. 3 (1979): 196–209, especially 196.
98. David Armitage, *Foundations of Modern International Thought* (Cambridge: Cambridge University Press, 2013), 59–60, 72.
99. Thompson, *Fathers of International Thought, 78.*
100. D. Gauthier, *The Logic of Leviathan* (Oxford: Clarendon Press, 1969). Slomp, 'The Origins of Realism Revisited', 21.
101. Hobbes, *Leviathan*, 185–186.
102. Annette Freyberg-Inan, *What Moves Man: The Realist Theory of International Relations and Its Judgment of Human Nature* (Albany, NY: State University of New York Press, 2004), 9.

CHAPTER

3

Geopolitics*

CHAPTER OUTLINE

* This chapter is available on the companion website.

CHAPTER

4

Neoclassical Realism

CHAPTER OUTLINE

- Introduction
- Methodology
- General Assumptions
- Propositions
- Niebuhr's Christian Realism
- Carr's Neo-Marxist Realism
- Morgenthau's Realist Search for Peace
- The 'Six Principles'
- Morgenthau beyond Six Principles
- Conclusion

INTRODUCTION

This chapter will deal with neoclassical realism, alternatively called realism, power politics or power approach, by different IR scholars, which got branded as classical realism after Kenneth Waltz launched neorealism in the late 1970s. But this book uses classical realism, with the prefix 'early' only for classical precursors of realism in political theory in **Chapter 1**, and neoclassical realism for theories dominating the interwar years and continuing through the post-Second World War era up to and beyond the turn of the 20th century. This chapter will eschew the detailed contextual origins of realism, being already covered in **Chapter 1**, save saying that, for Carr, apart from these historical factors, the rise of realism over idealism was also a result of IR's growing maturity, in which 'the element of wish or purpose' gave over to 'the inclination to analyse facts': 'Like other infant sciences, the science of intentional politics has been markedly and frankly utopian...in the initial stage in which wishing prevails over thinking...'[1]

Anyway, realism appeared as a body of shared beliefs of scholars from both sides of the Atlantic, in iconic books of Carr, Schwarzenberger and Wight in Britain, and of Schuman, Niebuhr and Morgenthau in the USA. Despite a decline in the 1950s, it survived in the writings of Aron, Organski, Rosecrance, Spanier, Thompson, Schelling, Waltz and very lately John Mearsheimer.[2] The way the resultant assemblage of modern classics dominated the IRT field led Wohlforth to say that

> It is only a slight exaggeration to say that the academic study of international relations is a debate about realism. Realism provides a foil against which many other schools of thought define themselves and their contributions. Take realism out of the picture and the identities of these other schools as well as the significance of their arguments become much less clear.[3]

But what are the methods, assumptions and propositions that knit these major and lesser-or-partial realists together beyond the terms of the First Great Debate? I state and test them below through views of a few realists.

METHODOLOGY

Methodologically, the first point is the multiple roles of history in realist analyses, not only as a source of inspiration for hypotheses but also as a touchstone for their accuracy, making it the living laboratory for realists, where 'generalizations about international politics can be tested'.[4] Speegle draws attention to 'the remarkable, though often unnoticed fact' that amid multiple differences, Carr, Sir Herbert Butterfield, Wight, Morgenthau, Friedrich Meinecke, George Kennan, Kenneth Thompson, Aron (among others), 'shared a deep sense of the many ways in which international politics is bound up with historical concepts, categories and methods'.[5] However, not all realists used history in the cautious and self-conscious way that Morgenthau did, and were guilty of the selective fallacy, in which historical instances that supported their hypotheses were only chosen, not discordant ones.[6] The preoccupation with history shows realists as successors to Thucydides, dealt with in **Chapter 2**.

The second most important aspect about realist methodology is the place of political philosophy, even though mostly confined to Enlightenment thinkers who portrayed the darker sides of human nature, such as Machiavelli and Hobbes, also introduced in **Chapter 2**. Whelan includes Hume as an intellectual source since a sizeable portion of Hume's thought and philosophy 'is historical, an orientation that kept him securely in touch with the world of actual political events', and evidences 'numerous specifically Machiavellian elements'.[7] But the extent of his influence is questionable. Carr quotes Hume once while showing how the 'Soldan of Egypt' or the Emperor of Rome treated 'harmless subjects' like 'brute beasts', and 'the mamelukes or praetorian bands' they led 'like men by their opinions'.[8] Leaving Hume out in his main book, Morgenthau merely mentions Hume's seminal works in two areas in his bibliography,[9] problematizing Levy's claim that Morgenthau's description of BOP as an 'iron law of politics' is inspired by Hume.[10] Surely, Wolfers regards Hume's arguments for BOP as 'empirical rather than normative theory', 'based on generalizations concerning the way states as a rule have behaved in the past and are likely to behave in the future, the emphasis being on factors that induce them to push beyond the point of equilibrium'.[11] But Wolfers is generally more catholic than other realists in his quest of classical thinkers for guidance and picks out 'non-normative aspects of earlier thinking on the subject', even if they are 'less obvious'. Hume includes unlikely figures such as Alexander Hamilton and Francis Bacon, together with 'a More, Hume or Bentham', as thinkers for whom the 'problem of self-preservation in the light of extreme danger, of expansion into new territories or contraction, of intervention in the affairs of another, of alliances, peacemaking, and the conduct of wars' were no less 'matters of concern and controversy' than today.[12] But, normally, realists stick with Machiavelli and Hobbes, at most with India's Kautilya or China's legalists, whose pessimistic political philosophies form the 'traditional paradigm' in IR, or at least in the dominant realist view of it.[13]

Other methodological points are secondary and unevenly distributed, only the first three being noticeable in Morgenthau. For the remaining two, the names of their makers are given in brackets. These are as follows: (a) prediction is not possible in IR theorizing beyond a surmise about the most possible tendencies; (b) social scientists cannot achieve absolute truth since they cannot be objective even in choosing their research problems; (c) autonomy of IR from other social sciences is necessary and justifiable; (d) though political realism does not normally search for methodological inputs in social and natural sciences, materials from psychology and sociology can help in describing human nature and the resultant forms of political organization (Schuman) and (e) the sociological concept of cross-cutting loyalties can be used to explain how multipolar systems derive stability, since two states at loggerheads with each other over one issue may have shared concerns about another (Karl Deutsch and J. David Singer).

Besides, in the Second Great Debate, realists had at least one, though weaker, leg in the latter camp through lesser-and-partial exponents. Morton Kaplan's systems theory has power as an important component, but he took delight in model building. Again, J. David Singer, many of whose ideas are fully compatible with the power politics framework, resorted to quantification, as evidenced in his monumental volume on the 'correlates of power'.[14] Finally, M. D. Wallace (*War and Rank among Nations*, 1973) and W. H. Ferris (*The Power Capabilities of Nation States*, 1973) made complex statistical exercises in their capability studies, which generated concrete indicators of power.

GENERAL ASSUMPTIONS

As for assumptions, first the state is personified as a purposive actor, as 'at least a necessary fiction or hypothesis' (Carr). As shown in **Chapter 1**, pluralists rejected it to demand a disaggregation of the state and opening of the black box. **Chapter 12** will show how Richard Snyder and Graham Allison demolished the 'Rational Actor Model' of decision-making. Second, following from the rational purposiveness of states, each of them has a 'national interest' or interests, amid minor differences about its/their meaning: for Schuman survival; but more power than security for Morgenthau, delimited only by the interest it serves. Some like C. V. Crabb, Jr, find it difficult to distinguish between power and security.[15] But national interest exists, is quite easy to find and makes theoretical models based on 'rational action' both possible and plausible. Third, unlike domestic politics, IP is primarily the sphere of interaction between these purposive sovereign authorities. Fourth, anarchy is the defining characteristic of this sphere, understood as the competitive quest for national interest, whether as security or power, in a situation lacking any superior, controlling authority. Fifth, this anarchic condition creates some compulsions in the relations between states, resulting in the operation of the complex system of BOP, understanding which is tantamount to understanding IP. Sixth, a bleak view of human nature is stressed by Machiavelli and Hobbes, and embellished by later exponents, such as Schwarzenberger's view of *Homo sapiens*, which mirrors Sigmund Freud's view of human nature, constituted by 'love, fear, and lust for power'; and by Aron's finding in strength not only the instrumental value of ability of imposing one's will more easily over others but also an intrinsic satisfaction that needs no other justification. Seventh, as a corollary to all of these, political realism says that conflict is natural and inevitable in IR.[16]

As recast by Wohlforth, realism's assumptions comprise the following:

- *Groupism:* Group solidarity in domestic politics contrasts with group conflict in IP, mainly between nation states, with nationalism being the most important residence of in-group cohesion. The same in-group cohesion that makes survival above subsistence level possible produces the potential for conflicts among different groups.
- *Egoism:* Particularly when acting politically is innate to human beings, being only temporarily chastened or submerged by international political structures, institutions and values.
- *Anarchy:* Caused by the absence of world government imposes clear limits on the capacities of international actors in achieving their purposes without increasing group egoism.
- *Power politics:* Results from the mix of groupism and egoism in a condition of anarchy.[17]

PROPOSITIONS

The above assumptions privilege the following propositions of realism:

- In the absence of any central authority to settle differences and allocate scarce resources, every state has to fend for itself, making IR a self-help system.
- State behaviour is induced by the system, irrespective of the states' cultures or ideologies. Martin Wight, whom we will discuss in **Chapter 23**, said that power politics is nothing but relations between independent powers. So Schwarzenberger and Schuman see states ever ready for the worst possible situations and constantly matching other state's capabilities, ignoring their expressed intentions. In this perpetual conflict scenario, cooperation is

possible only when it serves the national interest of the cooperating state and not any common goal, as shown in Rousseau's cautionary tale of the stag hunt.

- Power is not only a means to an end, but it is also a goal in itself. Modelski, Schuman, Schwarzenberger and Butterfield find the only test of a successful foreign policy in its capacity to increase a state's power resources, making identification of the sources of power the major task of statesmen. However, Carr and Niebuhr add moral foundations of other goals to this power monism.
- Spiegel, Wallace and Midlarsky, among others, equate power with military capabilities, though peripheral or modified. Realists such as Brown, Knorr and Kindleberger stress economic and other types of power. The conviction about the priority of military strength as 'naked power' has been aptly described with disapproval by Russell and explicated with approval by Osgood and Tucker. A modified version of this realization is seen in Waltz's statement: 'Strong states cannot do everything with their military forces... but they are able to do things that militarily weak states cannot'.[18]
- The conceptual priority of military strength foregrounds the question of its distribution and leads to BOP, which is the basic structural guarantee of minimum order in a system of multiple states. BOP retained its importance in all realist writings, though its meaning remained imprecise, sometimes referring to equal (Speier and Kahler), or unequal distribution of powers among five states, or sometimes to just multipolarity. Some BOP theorists present clear superiority of one power over others as the surest guarantee of peace (writings of Organski, Gelber, Jones, Dutt and so on), while others regard such superiority as the begetter of expansionism and provoker of counterproductive opposition. Some theorists on the Left wing, though not solely, claimed that such expansionist tendencies are tempered by democracy.[19]
- The behaviour and operation of these states, and the resultant international political system, rule out any major change in the future and preclude any hope of a functionalist reorganization of the international system.
- Any hypothetical overthrow or reform of the state system is thought futile, just replacing interstate wars by intergroup wars or 'international war'.[20] The full weight of this assumption is understandable from Wohlforth's reminder that 'realism makes no assumption about the nature of the polity' being applicable 'to any setting where groups interact'.[21]

These major assumptions and propositions of realism are recast by a Carr scholar as 'loosely' implying 'excessive respect for power, structural constraints, and the state, together with a pessimistic attitude towards projects for radical political reform'.[22] But is a 'signature argument' from these broad statements and their summaries, understood as a running 'intellectual thread that provides coherence to the realist tradition' possible? Wohlforth thinks that the answer is no.[23] Rosenberg warns that anyone

> seeking to reconstruct realism as a school might reasonably expect, on turning to its classic texts, to find these state-centric tenets argued for and grounded in a broader concept of political science—or at least stated in propositional form. Yet this is often not the case.[24]

His point will be proven from our reading of Niebuhr, Carr and Niebuhr.

NIEBUHR'S CHRISTIAN REALISM

As has been shown in **Chapter 1,** Niebuhr's realism is grounded in a modified Biblical view of human nature, distinguishing the divergent ethics of private/individual morality and political policy, and finally finding the recipe for peace in 'an uneasy BOP' in a state-centric IP.[25] Being a collective resultant of the individual human being's hunger for power, national power was subject to even fewer moral restraints than that of an individual acting alone.[26] Understandably, Niebuhr's concrete realistic propositions derive their distinctiveness from his 'Christian realism', informed by its context of the Great Depression in the early 1930s, which made Americans reluctant to think about great power politics. The tenacity, endurance and European spread of the Depression left even moderate social democrats and new radicals in wonderment if capitalism was not seriously flawed, needing a comprehensive overhaul of the system. The economic turmoil, and Japanese, Italian and German totalitarian policies and adventures made Americans think if history itself was not 'engulfed in evil'. Amid real advances in science, technology and industrial capacity, social degeneration mocked the meliorist 19th and early 20th centuries, and Niebuhr angrily jarred the optimism about human nature cherished by both the liberals and the Marxists in *Moral Man and Immoral Society.*[27]

Niebuhr was the spokesman of a school of thought called 'religious realism' or 'realistic theology, connected with the Yale Divinity School and advocating for watch over the powers and interests influencing current events. These young theologians and ethicists derided the Social Gospel Movement and its hollow belief in the capacity of moral exhortation to induce people to work for justice. Probing both contemporary middle-class morality and the revolutionary ethics of the impoverished and the powerless, *Moral Man and Immoral Society* found a 'contest' between 'hypocrisy and brutality and between sentimentality and cynicism' that left a candid acknowledgement of the encompassing rule of self-interest insufficient for realism. Recognizing that moral commands to love one's own neighbour would never get the better of self-interest was also inadequate. For, the capacity of moral ideas and commitments to create pressures on the course of events, and their reality in this sense, was undeniable.[28] For Niebuhr, realism was nothing but 'the disposition to take all factors in a social and political situation, which offer resistance to the established norm, into account, particularly the factors of self-interest and power'. 'Christian realism' was nothing but the Biblical sensitivity that saw human nature through the lenses of the fall from innocence and dissociation from God.[29]

From this perspective of a Christian sensitization to types of economic and political power operative in history, Niebuhr identified the inadequacies of American attitudes to foreign policy: primarily, imperviousness to power as a dominant motive in IR, stemming from Americans' prolonged isolation from the power theatres of Europe; and their delusion that the founding fathers' dream of America as the embryonic virtuous polity was still valid when she was being dragged into a struggle for world power. He considered the frantic efforts of the American idealists to hide this reality under 'schemes of an ideal world order' as insensitive to present dangers and pressing duties. Strongly believing that defeat of Nazi Germany was the first prerequisite of European peace, Niebuhr said at the end of the War that world security requires 'much more abridgement of national sovereignty than either the great or the small nations are willing to grant'. But that, without world government there would be no reprieve from frequent wars, did not mean that it was easily achievable. Rather, the world was likely to continue to live in such insecure convictions. The theological concept of original sin, meshed with a realist assessment of the contemporary international situation, convinced Niebuhr of the impossibility of freeing IR from conflict. So, in spite of their limitations, the Dumbarton Oaks and Yalta proposals for an international organization were preferable to the mirage of an ideal world government, which found no support in the 'traditions, and habits, the collective instincts and impulses of the nations'. The two main fallacies of the concept of world government were that (a) 'governments cannot be created by fiat (though sometimes they can be imposed by tyranny)' and that (b) 'governments have only limited efficacy in integrating a community,' itself being a product of community and only secondarily its generator.[30]

While considering conflict as a defining feature of intergroup and IR, Niebuhr did not deduce amorality of statesmen from it. Rather, realism must engage with morality since nations have to turn power into 'an instrument of justice and a servant of interests broader than their own'. An overemphasis on 'national interests' was mistaken because egotism, whether at the individual or the international level, was never the antidote to a blundering idealism. Since each state defines justice from its own angle, and not from its rival's, the maxim that statesmen must form policies on the basis of their 'national interests' cannot be operationalized. BOP is the only mechanism through which a semblance of justice can be achieved in all forms of human relations.

Niebuhr believed that frequent moral ambiguities confronting political leaders can be better addressed in a constitutional democracy than in a communist oligarchy. But America's status of a constitutional democracy did not mean that she was free of the power motivation that was driving other nations of the world. After having started imperialist adventures, America must look more closely at her strong self-image of a nation with an international mission, discard her illusions of any special national innocence and rectitude, and not invest her search of power with 'more virtue...than the facts warrant'.[31]

Niebuhr neither rued the loss of America's innocence nor basked in the glory of America's transformation into a superpower. As Diggins says insightfully, regarding the dismissal of *The Irony of American History* as a timely 'apology for American power during the first years of the Cold War':

> Niebuhr...did not ask the nation to reject a destiny that had been thrust upon it by world events. America in the 1950s was a morally self-righteous nation that believed its survival rested on its possession of the atomic bomb and its willingness to use.... But Niebuhr believed America's world leadership was based on its extraordinary economic prosperity and technological progress, not its eagerness for power politics, and he feared American innocence more than American experience. He urged the nation to surrender its illusions of 'winning' the Cold War.... The danger was that a militarily strong America might confuse its 'mastery of nature with the *mastery of history*' [italics ours].[32]

In a world where the post-Cold War triumphalism of the USA is manifested in Francis Fukuyama's words 'End of History', Niebuhr's caution against this confusion is remarkable. It tempered the realism of his intellectual disciples, such as George F. Kennan and Morgenthau.

CARR'S NEO-MARXIST REALISM

If Niebuhr deviated significantly from realism's 'signature argument', Carr deviated further. He does not figure in Dougherty and Pfalzgraff's consideration of the 20th-century realists, being ambiguously mentioned separately, as a critic of utopianism.[33] Jones makes Carr personally responsible for this, for having made continuous efforts 'to situate himself precisely halfway between utopianism and realism', though more scholars and historians agreed about his realist credentials than those who did not. Jones explains why the ambiguity still persisted. First, in his decade-long writings on foreign policy, nationalism and IR, after quitting the British Foreign Office, Carr invariably prioritized power against assumptions of harmony of interests. Still, amid the association of realism after 1945 'with the political right in Britain and North America, and a hawkish resolve to resist Soviet aggression', his Leftist credentials created embarrassment. Second, Carr remained elusive to 'easy textbook classification' of realism, partly because *Twenty Years' Crisis*, his most famous book, 'is probably the least realist of his works'; and judging the book by its two chapters (Chapters 3 and 6), 'too rich and flamboyant, too clever by half, too revealing, and too ambitious' to serve as a politically effective treatise in spite of its publication during the War. As Jones further says, 'Carr saturated his best works in kerosene. Opponents had only to toss a match to start the conflagration'.[34]

Another more fundamental reason why Carr is de-emphasized as a founder of modern realism, despite getting far more endorsing citations than opposing ones, is the extreme variety and complexity of his thinking, due to which he has followers in different, even opposed camps. As Kubálková explicates:

> Carr has been seen as the forefather of the realism and the 'post' movement, as well as a 'proto' constructivist.... This means that were he alive, Carr could do a circus act at IR conferences by sitting alone at a roundtable discussing three positions at the same time.

Fittingly, together with Bull and Lapid, who embodied the Second and the Third Great Debates, Carr has been identified by Robert Cox as 'an intellectual progenitor' of a 'critical approach' to IR; and, complicating matters further, earned kudos from the most prominent Trotskyists of the day. Kubálková frets about what to make of this.[35]

Truly, in the post-First World War days of disenchantment, Carr not only pitted realism against utopianism but also chided naïve realism, saying that IR 'took its rise from a great and disastrous war'; and that the cause of the modern international crisis was 'the collapse of the whole structure of utopianism based on the harmony of interests'. His diagnosis that the reigning international morality of the interwar years was a camouflage for the interests of the victorious, English-speaking, status quo seeking 'haves' of IP against those of the 'have-nots' was apparently realist. But shortly after this, Carr censures the utopians and the realists in the same breath. While the idealists, in their imperviousness to the lessons of history, wrongly inflated the freedom of choice of statesmen and roped in universal moral principles to sanitize their concept of national interest, the realists unnecessarily magnified fixed causality to lapse into a regrettable determinism, resorted to destructive cynicism and failed to 'provide any guide for purposive and meaningful action'. Downgrading the importance of purpose as a framework of observation, they forgot that a platonic vision was a precondition of an Aristotelian analysis, and that political theories could combine elements of ethics and politics, utopianism and realism, and power and moral values.[36]

So what are the (realist) virtues and defects of Carr's books that commentators identify? Robert Kaufman lists five virtues. First, Carr bases his theorizing of IP on a dialectical tension between utopia and reality, which demonstrates their inseparability as well as antithesis. This unfolds dichotomies in his analysis of free will versus determinism, theory versus practice, and 'the sense of right and the strong arm of authority', which are resolvable by '[m]ature thought' that 'combines purpose with analysis' and utopia with reality as 'the two facets of political science'. Second, while decrying the utopians' implicit faith in the moral force of public opinion, the harmony of states' interests and misplaced trust in the ability of the League of Nations and its underlying principle of collective security to establish durable world peace, Carr named only English idealists for pillorying, but allowed its implication to encompass Wilson and American idealists. All were chastised for failure to recognize that 'power is an essential element of politics' that 'has hitherto vitiated all attempts to establish international forms of government and confused nearly all attempts to discuss the subject'. Third, Carr underscored the crucial significance of economic power and economic conflict, and the inseparability of politics and economics, through his classic analysis of the origins, manifestations and impacts of British economic power in the 19th century, which laid the foundations of contemporary realist analyses of IPE. This inspired later realists of the 1970s, such as S. Brown, Klaus Knorr and Charles Kindleberger. Fourth, Carr rightly rebuked realists for their bad habit of mistaking particular for universal good, and personal for international morality, ignoring Machiavelli's insight that morality is a creation of power, and fulminations on international morality have always come from dominant nations, right from the Roman to the Soviet Empire. Fifth, Carr showed that the solution to the problem of dynamism and change has to be sought through the 'process of give and take...within the existing order'. For, those who profit most by it can reasonably continue to do so for a longer time frame only by 'making sufficient concessions' to those who profit least by it.[37]

But, says Kaufman, notwithstanding Carr's attacks upon the fallacies of utopianism, certain grievous errors make his policy prescriptions unacceptable. First, his inordinate moral relativism could imply that might makes right, even after his correctly branded unalloyed realism as 'nothing but a naked struggle for power which makes any kind of international society impossible'. For, his recipes of a 'neo-Marxist sociology of knowledge' and his resort to a 'dual morality governing the actions of states and individuals' mislead his quest of principles that could temper this struggle in desirable ways. What bring Carr dangerously close to a neorealist view of IR are as follows: his use of the 'weapon of relativity of thought' to 'demolish the utopian concept of a fixed and absolute standard' as a judge of policy and action; his debunking of international morality as a smokescreen of power and his undue valourization of 'moral intuitions of the ordinary man' as the source of his conception of relative morality. Because, for Carr, as well as neorealism, the difference between individual and state morality is caused by the constraints of the international system; and for both the structure of domestic politics and the regime's ideological leanings are irrelevant. Kaufman thinks this moral relativism made Carr impervious to the seriousness of the Nazi and Soviet threats to international peace; induced him to hail the Munich Agreement reached by Germany, Britain, France and Italy on 30 September 1938 to allow Germany to annex Sudetenland in Western Czechoslovakia, as 'the nearest approach to the settlement of a major international issue by the procedure of peaceful change'; and persuaded him to mistake Germany as just another revisionist state seeking to redress the inequities of the Treaty of Versailles, which will rest content after acquiring Sudetenland.

Kaufman criticizes Carr also for his mistaken equation of the USA and the Soviet Union as 'morally equivalent superpowers', and praise of the achievements of the Soviet Union as a collectivist state in *The Soviet Impact*. Miller pleaded not to overemphasize Carr's wrong guess on Hitler in measuring the value of his work.[38] But Kaufman regards Carr's 'advocacy of appeasement and his moral disarmament of the Versailles settlement' not as aberrant but reflecting 'the logical culmination of his extreme moral relativism, his excessive structuralism, and his exaltation of power as the ultimate standard of international morality'. He finds the 'content of Carr's idealism as problematic as the content of his realism', whose merit lies in 'diagnosing than providing a cure for the disease of naive utopian prescriptions that slight the struggle for power and the recalcitrance of human imperfectability'.[39]

Was then Carr a confused realist? Perhaps not, since recent scholarship has found new virtues in the book. Reading it after the end of the Second World War, the onset of which supposedly marred the book's short-time end, Miller found in it 'a revelation that had nothing to do with Hitler or Chamberlain', but inhered in

> the book's abrupt dismissal of politicians' cant about foreign policy, in its demonstration of the plurality of national interests, in its description of the forms that power might take and uses to which they might be put, and in its almost brutal neglect of how power might triumph in spite of the efforts of moralistic men and women.

Miller says that what binds Carr's extremely varied works together is 'an interest in power, so obvious that many of Carr's critics accused him of mistaking power with destiny, and of making power the test of political success'. Carr placed Hitler and Stalin on a par because they had been in the helms of the affairs of their countries, effecting radical changes by employing all the different aspects of power. His detractors overlooked this. Carr's demarcation of 'status quo' powers and 'have-not states' or 'anti-status quo states' has not stood the test of time. A similar fate has befallen his prediction about the decline in the status of nation states (at least minor ones); his diagnosis in *Twenty Years' Crisis* of 'a trend toward the concentration of political or economic power in the hands of six or seven highly organized units', surrounded by 'lesser satellites' and his belittling of the notions of 'international opinion' and 'international society'.[40] But all of these were perhaps examples of Carr's complaint against 'rhetoric' in international affairs.[41]

So *Twenty Years' Crisis* is not Carr's 'period piece'. Amusingly, Carr is now praised for its 'serious defects'. For each berating from the realist mainstream, Carr gets a positive post-positivist response. Against Kaufman's branding of his realism is 'amoral and unrealistic', Beer and Harriman call him an 'ambivalent realist'. Jim George, post-structuralist, regards him as a 'dialectician'.[42] Howe finds in his book *What Is History*, and its flawed philosophy, early dawning of CT.

> His account of global politics bears many similarities to that propounded by today's critical theorists. …Carr takes exception to the stagnation and conservatism embedded in the traditional realist approach. A review of Carr's work…reveals a thinker in possession of a coherent and provocative philosophy and a commentator on international affairs sensitive to the inertial forces tending to perpetuate an atomistic international system….[43]

Miller says, 'Carr's realism—tempered, wherever possible, by the prudent utopianism that he saw as a necessary corrective—is needed as we confront the ostensibly different world of today, which is so often similar to the one about which he wrote'.[44] Linklater deplores the fact that by

> showing that new forms of political organization were already immanent in existing societies, Carr avoided the naivety of utopianism and the sterility of realism. But somehow his reputation for realism has obscured these aspects of his thought, and his writings have too frequently been used to legitimize a discipline with limited normative assumptions.[45]

Kubálková provides an 'overlooked clue' to the seeming inconsistencies of Carr's realism that Carr was not only 'a dialectician' but was writing from the perspective of a 'non-Marxist Marxism, 'Westernized' by himself; and that his texts, especially, *Twenty Years' Crisis*, need 'deciphering' in that light. Carr was 'neither realist nor idealist'. But, as realists claim about their wisdom that 'it is all in Thucydides', we can claim about the paradigmatic Third Debate that 'it is all in E. H. Carr'. He not only 'anticipates an application of the dialectical approach to IR', but 'champions intellectual pluralism' in it, and is the forerunner of the IPE approach.[46]

Now that Carr is shown to be the most deviant realist, what about Morgenthau, the last and most famous of the holy realist trinity, if I may bypass Spykman, who has already been covered in **Chapter 3**?

MORGENTHAU'S REALIST SEARCH FOR PEACE

Few modern realists match Morgenthau's popularity and stature. *Politics among Nations* (henceforth *PAN*)is also rated very highly by eminent modern realists such as Robert Gilpin, John Mearsheimer[47] and Richard Ned Lebow (he calls Morgenthau the 'intellectual father of postwar realism'.[48] William finds impossible to overlook 'the importance of Morgenthau in the evolution of the field, and his role in placing Realism in the centre of that evolution'.[49] Morgenthau was rated as the 'single greatest contributor to the field' in a survey of the IR faculty in the USA in 1972, and he was still ranked 18th in a global survey of most influential thinkers in 2009 (29 years after his expiry).[50] *PAN* is a source of common quotes for power politics in IR, which[51] 'like all politics, is a struggle for power' (p. 28); 'aspiration for power being the distinguishing element of international politics as of all politics'; it is 'of necessity power politics' (p. 31); the 'struggle for power is universal in time and space and is an undeniable fact of experience'[52] and the 'main signpost…through the landscape of international politics is the concept of interest defied as power' (p. 5).

But this reputation has come with a cost. A post-structuralist's comment, 'texts have effects without being read,'[53] applies with full force to *PAN*. Because of this, Morgenthau 'has been reduced by both his supporters and his critics primarily to an implacable opponent of liberalism and an advocate of power politics'.[54] Jervis is sad that though Morgenthau is a 'rare, if partial exception' in a 'trendy discipline' like IR, where ideas and their progenitors die young, scholars cite from *PAN* without reading it carefully, 'even if their main objective is to attack it'.[55] Consequently, 'there have been relatively few systematic or sympathetic attempts to unpack the theory' unfolded in *PAN*, except rummaging the text for convenient quotations.[56] This is scant justice for a man whose magnum opus *PAN* has 'made the field'.[57]

Reading *PAN* is challenging because, though started in the 1930s long before Morgenthau became prominent, it has evolved right from the first edition (1948) to the seventh (2006). The 'Six Principles of Political Realism', the quintessential and succinct statement of Morgenthau's realist philosophy, entered the text in the 1954 edition. Morgenthau's ambitious claims of theory building appeared in the second edition; and preoccupations with the fear of the thermonuclear revolution changed many contents of the text in even later editions. So Guilhot identifies 'as many Morgenthaus as there are editions of *PAN*'. The book is 'a geological sedimentation of successive intellectual layers, each reflecting a particular historical context and a specific stage' in the reflections of an émigré scholar on the aberrations of a decaying European civilization 'from the shores of a hegemonic power…lacking the tragic sense of history that alone sustained political wisdom',[58] much like Hans Castorp of Thomas Mann's *Magic Mountain* (1924), reflecting on pre-war Europe from a Swiss sanatorium.

But the multiplicity of texts cannot be the only source of imperfect or partial reading, since Morgenthau had complained even in the Preface of the second edition for having been 'blamed for ideas he has not only never expressed, but which he has explicitly and repeatedly refuted and which are repugnant to him', quoting a passage from Montesquieu where he requests his readers to 'not judge by a few hours' reading the labour of 20 years. In the Preface to the third edition, he not only reiterated his grouse against this misfortune of misinterpretation but also identified the broad areas where he was being misunderstood, such as beliefs 'in the prominence of the international system based upon the prominence of the nation state', and success as 'the standard of political action', despite refutations of these misunderstandings way back in 1955.[59] So I suggest that we read for ourselves this dauntingly fat book, starting with the famous six principles.

THE 'SIX PRINCIPLES'

Among these six principles, the first, directly, and the second, less directly, explain why Morgenthau's theory is rightly or wrongly called 'human nature and biological Realism'.[60] The first, 'politics, like society in general, is governed by objective laws that have their roots in human nature', ordains any efforts to improve society to unavoidably understand these laws, which are 'impervious to our preferences' and challengeable 'only at the risk of failure'. Being supposedly objective, these laws promise the possibility of developing a rational theory that reflects, however partially, their operation. That the history of the theory of BOP dates back to thousands of years does not make it 'outmoded and obsolete' if it meets the dual criteria of the validity of a good theory, of reason and experience, ascertaining facts properly and giving them meaning through reason. But since there is an element of guess in the functioning of reason, while ascertaining the character of a foreign policy through 'an examination of the political acts performed' for it, 'we can surmise what their objectives might have been' only from the 'foreseeable consequences of these acts', the element of guess is to be kept within limits. So when trying to 'give meaning to the factual raw material of foreign policy', the analyst needs to go with 'a rational outline, a map', charting out the 'possible meanings of foreign policy' as an interpretive tool (though Morgenthau does not explicitly say it). For, it puts the realist analyst 'in the position of a statesman', who, while meeting a certain foreign policy problem under spatiotemporal circumstances, must ask himself what might be the 'rational alternatives' before that statesman doing this 'in a rational manner'. The constitutive function of a theory, which imparts 'meaning to the facts of international politics, is "the testing of this rational hypothesis against the actual facts and their consequences"'.

The second, perhaps most cited principle, upholds 'the concept of interest defined as power', guiding us through the labyrinth of IP by not only linking reason to the facts but also turning politics into an autonomous domain of 'action and understanding' distinct from other such domains. This assumption is yet another interpretive tool that enables us 'to retrace and anticipate, as it were, the steps a statesman—past, present, or future—has taken or will take'; to kind of eavesdrop on his activities and get under his skin. For, by using thinking through this concept, the analyst would think just as he does, and understand his thoughts and actions 'perhaps better than he...does himself'.

These last words remind us of neo-Kantian hermeneutical contention that the reader 'has to understand the author better than he understood himself'.[61] To be foolproof, the concept of 'interest defined as power' should guard against 'two popular fallacies: the concern with motives and the concern with ideological preferences'. The first is avoidable not only because motives are the 'most illusive of psychological data' but also because they can provide 'only one among many clues' to the possible trajectory of any foreign policy, but no one sure clue. Besides, good intentions of a statesman are seldom a guarantee of 'a morally praiseworthy or politically successful foreign policy'. Morgenthau here gives contrasting examples of Robespierre and Chamberlain, on the one hand, and Churchill on the other hand. For the former two, good motives led to disastrous (foreign) policies; in the latter case, far 'inferior motives' resulted in foreign policies of a 'superior...moral and political quality'. Deducing the foreign policies of a statesman from his philosophical and political sympathies is also fallacious because these ideological leanings are often facades for personal agendas of these statesmen. Realism dislikes both because without belittling political ideals and moral principles, it enjoins 'a sharp distinction between the desirable and the possible'. Foreign policies do not always pursue such a 'rational, objective and unemotional' course because of various 'contingent elements of personality, prejudice, and subjective preference', particularly in situations of democratic control. But a rational theory of foreign policy has to 'abstract from' these irrational intrusions in order to present a rational portrait of foreign policy which would be different from an all-encompassing photograph.

The third principle counsels against giving the concept of 'interest defined as power' a fixed, permanent meaning, even though from Thucydides' times up to Weber's, interest has been regarded as the prime mover of actions. For, the kind of interest shaping political action has always been determined by 'the political and cultural context within which foreign policy is formulated'. The same temporal and contextual relativism applies to the concept of power and the manner of its use. So political realism does not view 'the contemporary conditions, under which foreign policy operates, with their extreme instability and the ever present threat of large scale violence' as immutable. Noticing that BOP has functioned even under relative stable conditions of 'peaceful conflict' in domestic pluralistic societies, as in the USA, Morgenthau posits that that if the factors that begot these taming conditions could be replicated in the international plane, they could reproduce similar chastening effects even there. This is more so because even though interest remains the perennial touchstone for testing the nature and direction of political action, 'the contemporary connection between interest and the national state' is not permanent. Being a 'product of history', the nation state is 'bound to disappear in the course of history'. So realism does not contradict the contention that 'the present division of the political world into nation states will be replaced by larger units of a quite different nature', more attuned to the technical possibilities and moral needs of the modern world. It only states that such great transformation can be reached only 'through the workmanlike manipulation of the perennial forces that have shaped the past as they will (shape) the future', and not through 'confronting a reality' grounded in its own laws with an intractable 'abstract ideal'.

The fourth principle accepts the ineluctable moral significance of political action but cautions against overlooking the inescapable tension between moral imperatives and the requirements of successful political action. It eschews the mistaken attempts to apply universal moral principles unalloyed by adjustment to the 'concrete circumstances of time and place', to the actions of states; and without remembering during its application the crucial distinctions between the private individual and the state, the actor and the agent. As a moral subject, the individual can sacrifice everything for the sake of moral principles, but not states, which have to consider prudence, or the rational calculation of the political consequences of apparently moral action, as the touchstone of political morality. Assessment of action through its compliance with the moral law is permissible under abstract ethics. But political ethics can only assess actions by their political consequences.

The fifth principle cautions against a nation's mistake of equating its 'moral aspirations' with universal moral laws, and against all temptations, recognizing that the blithe, morally unjustifiable and politically deleterious 'equation between a particular nationalism and the counsels of Providence' is a common vice, curable through the concept of 'interest defined as power'. This 'moral excess and political folly' can be avoided if the analyst looks at nations, including his own, as pursuing similar interests and judges other nations as 'we judge our own'.

The sixth or final principle builds on all the five above to carve out a separate niche for political realism and IR while allowing the economist, the lawyer and the moralist to maintain the autonomy of their domains. Even after recognizing the existence and relevance of other modes of thought different from the political one, the realist seeks to subordinate politics to the political mode of reasoning, fending off other irrelevant modes. Morgenthau cites three historical examples to substantiate the difference of this mode of reasoning from the 'legalistic–moralistic approach', that is, liberal utopianism. The first is the decision of Britain and France to leap to the defence of Finland when the Soviet Union attacked it in 1939, first by expelling the Soviet Union from the League of Nations, and then by joining Finland in its war against her, a rash move that was curbed only by Sweden's opposition to the passage of their troops through Swedish territory. The second was the dilemma for Western governments regarding the recognition of Communist China. The third was the British decision to go to war with Germany in 1914, when she violated the neutrality of Belgium in 1914 only because she was the guarantor of Belgium's neutrality. In each case, the political realist would have advised that a positive or negative decision could only come from whether and how the offending actions and the counteractions would have affected the concerned state's interests and the existing distribution of powers between or among them. And lastly, Morgenthau says that even though political realism had 'a pluralistic conception of human nature', it gave political man priority over economic, moral or religious man.[62]

MORGENTHAU BEYOND SIX PRINCIPLES

Gallarotti offers a good synoptic reading of *PAN*,[63] which I will use to supplement my own reading. He argues that even though Carr or his *Twenty Years' Crisis* finds scanty mentions in Morgenthau's book,[64] still 'in structure, logic and spirit', *PAN* is a 'true progeny' of Carr's book. Just like Carr, Morgenthau also has a positivist urge for discovering 'objective laws' and, after a methodological prelude aimed at enriching the ontological worth of *PAN* (Chapters 1–2), comes up with a 'hard power rhetoric' adored by realists. After identifying three sources of political power, such as expected benefits, fear of punishment and respect or love for men and institutions (Chapter 3), Morgenthau shows three corresponding ways of nations' exercise of it, namely policies of status quo, imperialism and prestige (Chapters 4–6). But even though he starts with an exegesis (Chapter 8) and analysis of the tangible aspects of national power, such as geography, natural resources, industrial capacity, military preparedness and population (Chapter 9), he appends soft elements to his elastic concept of power. Not only are the 'content and the manner of use' of (interest defined as) power 'determined by the political and cultural environment (p. 9), but political power 'must be distinguished from force in the sense of the actual exercise of military violence' (p. 28). For Morgenthau, from 'the militaristic error follows the equation of national power with material force' and the resultant 'paradox that a maximum of material power does not necessarily mean a maximum of over-all national power'. He warns states against attempting total disempowerment of other powers to avoid being 'confronted with the maximum effort of all its competitors to equal or surpass its power'. History shows the futility of such efforts against a combined challenge, and states like Great Britain were spared such fate only for using their superior power with self-restraint, which endeared themselves to powerful allies (pp. 162–163).

The importance Morgenthau gives to softer elements of national power is proven by the inclusion of national character and national morale as its components (pp. 126–139). National character has roots in 'national culture', or the 'anthropological concept of the "cultural pattern", i.e., "certain qualities of intellect and character" that "occur more frequently and are more highly valued in one nation than in another"' (p. 126). But national morale is more political, being 'the degree of determination with which a nation supports the foreign policies of its government in peace or war' (p. 133), which in turn 'influences the determination with which the government pursues its foreign polices' (p. 135–136). A 'truly representative government' has a better chance of getting such popular support than an autocratic government. For, the closer the people identify with the actions and objectives of their governments, the more likely they are to fight for them. So, finally, 'the power of a nation, in view of its national morale, resides in the quality of the government' (p. 138). The final and 'the most important' intangible element of national power is the quality of diplomacy, which processes all the aforesaid elements or 'raw material' into 'an integrated whole'. It is the 'brains' of national power, just as national morale is its 'soul' (p. 139). Diplomacy, which aims at the 'promotion of the national interest by peaceful means' (p. 539), uses 'persuasion, compromise, and threat of force'; puts 'the right emphasis at any particular moment on each of these three moments at its disposal' and promotes national interest without getting the state embroiled in war (p. 541).

The aim of a political policy being to 'keep', 'increase', or 'demonstrate' power, 'three typical international policies' correspond to 'these typical patterns of politics'. States that want to preserve their existing power adopt foreign policies of 'the status quo'. States aspiring after more power than they have go for a 'policy of imperialism'. States seeking to show off their actual power, either to preserve it or add to it, adopt a policy of prestige (p. 39). Empowerment on the basis of status quo legitimizes the search for political power, being executed through legally and morally justified institutions. But the word *imperialism* no more remains 'a term of opprobrium'. Discarding the Marxist, liberal and the '"devil" theory of imperialism', Morgenthau argues that the 'true nature of imperialism as a policy devised to overthrow the status quo' is understandable only in terms of the three 'subjective and objective conditions necessary for an active foreign policy', or so to speak the 'inducements': (a) an anticipated 'victorious war'; (b) a lost war threatening to establish a permanent status of subordination for the victim and (c) the 'existence of weak states or politically empty spaces'. The goals of imperialism can be a global empire, a continental empire or a local preponderance. Its three methods are military, economic and cultural. Just as 'international policies' are different, so must then be policy responses to it: appeasement for a policy of status quo seeking minor adjustments in the distribution of powers; and containment or a 'fear of hostile alliances' for a policy of imperialism (pp. 39–71). The policy of prestige can have two inducements: 'prestige for its own sake or, much more frequently, prestige in support of a policy of the status quo or of imperialism'. A policy of prestige can be pursued either through a strategy of 'diplomatic ceremonial' or that of a 'display of military force'. But its effectiveness will depend on just not hard military power but also on the 'reputation for power tempered by self-restraint' (pp. 81, 72–85).

For Morgenthau, ideologies are not just smokescreens that muffle the relentless search for power. Although 'frequently its basic manifestations do not appear as what they actually are', it would be wrong to treat all of them as 'the accidental outgrowth of the hypocrisy of certain individuals' at the helm of policymaking. Rather, Morgenthau reminds us that 'the very nature of politics' compels the domestic or international actor 'to use ideologies in order to disguise the immediate goal of his action'. Besides ideologies of the status quo and imperialism, typical ideologies of foreign policy, there are ambiguous ideologies from which the ideology of anti-imperialism draws its sustenance. The UN was originally established by the founding members to help preserve the status quo emanating from their victory in Second World War, but it was immediately thereafter used by other states to justify their different, contradictory interpretations of this status quo and to have their own distinctive claims on this organization adequately camouflaged (pp. 87–95).

Conceptual discussion of BOP is presented in Chapters 11–14, though it is strewn throughout *PAN*. Some critics label them as 'ahistorical, ambiguous and incoherent'; displaying 'open contradictions, ambiguity and vagueness', 'uninteresting tautology, vague and unhelpful generalities' and 'patent absurdity'[65]; a little undeservedly, since Morgenthau does not give BOP an incorrigible hard power definition, as 'a necessary outgrowth' of power politics. Rather, international BOP is no more than a 'particular manifestation of a general social principle' characterizing 'all pluralist societies', 'an essential stabilizing factor in a society of several nations', whose instability is caused not by the shortcomings of the principle, but by the 'particular conditions under which the principle must operate' (p. 167). This is why Morgenthau harps on the importance of domestic and international social elements that held together the pre-1914 older BOP system, after a discussion of BOP through two main patterns of direct opposition and competition (pp. 173–177); different methods of divide and rule, compensations, alliances and holder of the balance (pp. 178–197); its structure (comprising dominant and dependent systems in it) and structural changes in it (pp. 198–203) and its evaluation in terms of its uncertainty, unreality and inadequacy (pp. 204–216). Little says that this is inconsistent, revealing within *PAN* 'two interconnected dynamics' associated with BOP. The first, presented in mechanistic terms, makes BOP precarious and dangerous. The second dynamic, visualized as social in orientation, helps soften the effects of the first dynamic to generate a much more stable and self-consciously managed BOP.[66]

But Morgenthau was *not* describing two parallel BOP dynamics in *PAN*. His Thucydides-like evocation of moral consensus and community as restraining influences on BOP pervades *PAN* from the beginning, as when he deplores the replacement of the past, Europe-centred multi-state system by 'a worldwide, bipolar system', in which '*the moral unity of the political world*, which distinguished Western civilization during most of its history' has degenerated into two incompatible systems of thought and action, vying 'for the allegiances of men' (pp. 22–23; italics ours)'. Not for nothing Morgenthau cites classical authors on European history, showing that the confidence in the stability of the modern European state system, which their writings exuded, emanated not from the BOP 'but from a number of elements, intellectual and moral in nature' (pp. 216–220), creating a 'moral consensus' whose loss was the source of the later 'inflexibility of the new balance of power'. In Europe, this 'intellectual and moral consensus...restrained the struggle for power for almost three centuries' and provided BOP 'the vital energy that made it a living principle of international politics' (p. 346).

Gallarotti suggests that to see through the apparent 'contradictory arguments as inconsistencies' of Morgenthau, we should put his 'caveats' into a 'perspective' that would reveal his steadfast commitment to an Aristotelian–cosmopolitan mean. He interrogated the competence of softer elements in IP (Chapters 15–18),[67] such as international morality (pp. 245–259), world public opinion (pp. 260–271), international law (pp. 275–311) and the nature of state sovereignty and 'the functions it performs for the modern state system' (pp. 313–331), mostly to explore the present state of the 'heritage' of the old BOP that undergirded the modern state system till the onset of the First World War, and the nature of the consensus that unites nations in the post-Second World War era (p. 335). What he found saddened him because (a) 'the moral limitations upon the struggle for power on the international scene' had appreciably weakened; (b) the international morality that checked individual nations' power aspirations had degenerated into the 'morality of individual nations', which disregarded higher moral obligations; (c) world public opinion had become mere 'ideological shadow' of the 'common valuations' shared by at least the 'international aristocracy' in olden times and (d) 'supranational forces, such as universal religions, humanitarianism, cosmopolitanism, and all other personalities, institutions and organizations that bind individuals together across national boundaries', had faded before the forces that valued only national boundaries and not 'the rest of humanity'.

Morgenthau blamed the misdoing of the 'new moral force of nationalistic universalism' for all these maladies of the present international order, loath, much like Hobsbawm,[68] to equate it with the older 19th-century nationalisms because of its essentialist ardour. This made it arrogate for one nation state 'the right to impose its valuations and standards of action upon all the other nations', like [as he unjustifiably singles out] Soviet communism, launching a "struggle for the minds of men" through new forms of propaganda' (pp. 335–345), and injecting new inflexibilities into the new BOP. These inflexibilities were manifested in the new bipolarity; the rise of a two-bloc system without a balancer; the mirage of a 'third force'; the 'continuation of the Cold War' and so on (pp. 346–364). In the context of the 'mechanization' of warfare, weapons, transportation and communication, and the 'overall mechanization of culture', of which these were but partial 'manifestations' (pp. 373–386), a perturbed Morgenthau searched for the means of winning peace in this troubled world in a total of 10 chapters in the last three parts of *PAN*. At the end of his search, Morgenthau makes explicit why, like Carr, he dissociated himself from liberal utopianism, and why the book's final 32nd chapter was devoted to diplomacy, in a prosaic fashion, not choosing 'the radical simplicity of a formula that with one sweep seems to dispose of the problem of war once and for all', as exemplified by 'such solutions as free trade, arbitration, disarmament, collective security, universal socialism, international government and world state'. Just as 'the integration of domestic society and its peace' result from the workaday and quotidian processes of 'accommodation and change', the ultimate goal of international life in an integrated supranational society 'must await its realization from the techniques of persuasion, negotiation, and pressure, which are the traditional instruments of diplomacy' (p. 568).

CONCLUSION

This chapter has described the methods, general assumptions and propositions of (neoclassical) realism in the writings of both its major and lesser-and-partial exponents to spell out a common realist position a 'signature statement' of realism after Wohlforth and Jones, questioning if the major exponents of realist theory and analysis, such as Niebuhr, Carr and Morgenthau, are to be captured by these. It sees that Rosenberg is right that it is not possible. And this is precisely why these authors are still relevant today. Critique and evaluation of their thought is provided in **Chapter 7** containing all internal/in-house and external criticisms of realism.

REVIEW QUESTIONS

1. State how the methodology of neoclassical realism has evolved.
2. Analyse the assumptions and propositions of realism and the 'signature arguments' of realism that have been teased out from these.
3. Discuss Niebuhr's 'Christian realism' in the light of its concordance and deviation from the 'signature argument' of realism.
4. How relevant is Niebuhr's realism at present?
5. Do you think that Carr's 'serious defects' in *Twenty Years' Crisis* and his equidistance from the 'naivety of utopianism and the sterility of realism' have made him a precursor of recent critical turns in IRT? State with reasons.
6. Assess Carr's contribution to IRT in the light of contemporary evaluations of his deviation from textbook realism.
7. Morgenthau is 'the intellectual father of post-war realism'? Argue in support or refutation.
8. Point out the commonalities and differences among Niebuhr's, Carr's and Morgenthau's statements of realism.

NOTES

1. E. H. Carr, *The Twenty Years' Crisis 1919–1939: An Introduction to the Study of International Relations* (London: Macmillan, 1956), 5–6.
2. Their most representative works are Carr, *The Twenty Years' Crisis*; George Schwarzenberger, *Power Politics* (Cambridge: Cambridge University Press, 1941); Martin Wight, *Power Politics* (New York, NY: Continuum, 1946); Robert Schuman, *International Politics* (New York, NY: McGraw-Hill, 1933); Niebuhr, *Moral Man and Immoral Society*; Morgenthau, *Politics among Nations*; Raymond Aron, *Peace and War: A Theory of International Relations* (Piscataway, NJ: Transaction Publishers, 1966); A. F. K. Organski, *World Politics* (New York, NY: Alfred A. Knopf, 1958); Richard Rosecrance, *International Relations: Peace or War* (New York, NY: McGraw-Hill, 1973); John Spanier, *Games Nations Play* (Thousand Oaks, CA: Sage Publications, 1972); Kenneth W. Thompson, *Political Realism and the Crisis of World Politics: An American Approach to Foreign Policy* (Princeton, NJ: Princeton University Press, 1960); Thomas Schelling, *The Strategy of Conflict* (Cambridge, MA: Harvard University Press, 1960); T. C. Schelling, 'The Diplomacy of Violence', in *Theories of Peace and Security*, ed. John Garnett (London: Palgrave Macmillan, 1970), 64–84; Waltz, *Theory of International Politics*; John J. Mearsheimer, 'Back to Future: Instability in Europe after the Cold War', *International Security* 15, no. 1 (1990): 5–56; John J. Mearsheimer, 'A Realist Reply', *International Security* 20, no. 1 (1995): 82–93.
3. William C. Wohlforth, 'Realism', *The Oxford Handbook of International Relations*, eds. Christian Reus-Smit and Duncan Snidal (Oxford: Oxford University Press, [2008]2010), 131.
4. Rosecrance, *International Relations*, 25, quoted in Trevor Taylor, 'Power Politics', in *Approaches and Theory in International Relations*, ed. Trevor Taylor (London; New York, NY: Longman, [1978]1984), 125.
5. Roger D. Speegle, *Political Realism in International Theory* (Cambridge; New York, NY: Cambridge University Press, 1996), 162.
6. Taylor, 'Power Politics', 125.

7. Frederick Whelan, *Hume and Machiavelli: Political Realism and Liberal Thought* (Lanham; Oxford: Lexington Books, 2004), 2.
8. Carr, *The Twenty Years' Crisis,* 132.
9. Morgenthau, *Politics among Nations,* 601–602.
10. Jack S. Levy, 'What Do Great Powers Balance against and When?' in *Balance of Power: Theory and Practice in the 21st Century,* eds. T. V. Paul, James J. Wirtz and Michel Fortmann (Stanford, CA: Stanford University Press, 2004), 29.
11. Arnold Wolfers, *Discord and Collaboration: Essays on International Politics* (Baltimore, MD; London: The John Hopkins Press, [1962]1968), 235.
12. Ibid., 235, 247, 249.
13. Arendt Lijphart, 'The Structure of the Theoretical Revolution in International Relations', *International Studies Quarterly* 18, no. 1 (1974), 49, cited in Taylor, 'Power Politics', 126.
14. J. David Singer, *Measuring the Correlates of War* (Ann Arbor, MI: University of Michigan Press, 1990); Taylor, 'Power Politics', 125–127.
15. C. V. Crabb, Jr, *Nations in a Multipolar World* (Manhattan, NY: Harper and Row, 1968).
16. Taylor, 'Power Politics', 127–129.
17. Wohlforth, 'Realism', 132–134.
18. S. L. Spiegel, *Dominance and Diversity: The International Hierarchy* (Boston, MA: Little, Brown and Company, 1972); M. I. Midlarsky, *Power, Uncertainty and the Onset of International Violence* (Ann Arbor, MI: University of Michigan Press, 1974); S. Brown, *New Forces in World Politics* (Washington, DC: Brookings Institution, 1974); Klaus Knorr, *Power and Money* (London: Palgrave Macmillan, 1973); Charles Kindleberger, *Power and Money* (Berlin: Springer, 1970); Bertrand Russell, *Power* (London: Allen and Unwin, 1938); R. Osgood and R. Tucker, *Force, Order and Justice* (Baltimore, MD: Johns Hopkins Press, 1967); K. N. Waltz, 'International Structure, National Force, and the Balance of World Power', *Journal of International Affairs* 21, no. 2 (1967): 219—all cited in Taylor, 'Power Politics', 131–132.
19. Hans Speier and Alfred Kahler, eds., *War in Our Time* (New York, NY: W. W. Norton, 1938); L. Gelber, *Reprieve from War: A Manual for Realists* (New York, NY: Macmillan, 1950); F. E. Jones, *The Battle for Peace* (London: V. Gollancz, 1938); R. P. Dutt, *World Politics* (Vancouver: Read Books, 1936)—all cited in Taylor, 'Power Politics', 132–133.
20. Taylor, 'Power Politics', 134–135.
21. Wohlforth, 'Realism', 133.
22. Charles Jones, *E. H. Carr and International Relations: A Duty to Lie* (Cambridge: Cambridge University Press, 1998), xi.
23. Wohlforth, 'Realism', 134–135.
24. Justin Rosenberg, *The Empire of Civil Society: A Critique of the Realist Theory of International Relations* (London: Verso, 1994), 10.
25. See 'Introduction', Notes 26–28.
26. Dougherty and Pfalzgraff Jr, *Contending Theories of International Relations,* 92–94.
27. Introduction by Langdon B. Gilkey, in Niebuhr, *Moral Man and Immoral Society,* xvi–xvii.
28. Robin W. Lovin, 'Introduction', in *The Nature and Destiny of Man: A Christian Interpretation, Volume 1: Human Nature,* ed. Reinhold Niebuhr (Louisville, KY: Westminster John Knox Press, 1996), xii.
29. Reinhold Niebuhr, *Christian Realism and Political Problems* (New York, NY: Charles Scribner's Sons, 1953), 119–123.
30. Reinhold Niebuhr, 'The Spiritual Problem of the Coming Decades', *Christianity and Society* 10, Summer (1945): 7; 'Is This "Peace in Our Time"?' *The Nation* 160, April (1945): 383; *Christian Realism and Political Problems,* 17—all cited in Ronald H. Stone, *Professor Reinhold Niebuhr: A Mentor to the Twentieth Century* (Louisville, KY: John Knox Press, 1992), 157–158.
31. Niebuhr's words in these contexts are cited by Dougherty and Pfalzgraff Jr, from *The Irony of American History* (New York, NY: Scribner's, 1952), 2, 35, 40, 148; 'The Illusion of World

Government', *Bulletin of Atomic Scientists* V, October (1943): 290; *Christian Realism and Political Problems*, 36. For the citations and analysis, see Dougherty and Pfalzgraff Jr, *Contending Theories of International Relations*, 93–94.

32. John P. Diggins, *Why Niebuhr Now?* (Chicago, IL: University of Chicago Press, 2011), 95–96.
33. Dougherty and Pfalzgraff Jr, *Contending Theories of International Relations*, 4–7.
34. Jones, *E. H. Carr and International Relations*, 144–145.
35. Vendulka Kubálková, 'The Twenty Years' Catharsis: E. H. Carr and IR', in *International Relations in a Constructed World*, eds. Vendulka Kubálková, Nicholas Onuf and Paul Kowert, first published by M. E. Sharp in 1998 (London; New York, NY: Routledge, 2015), 25–26.
36. Carr, *The Twenty Years' Crisis* (London: Macmillan and Company Ltd., 1956), 8, 62 and generally 60–62, 92, 5–6, 20–21, 93–94.
37. For Kaufman's quotes from Carr's *The Twenty Years' Crisis* (1942), *Nationalism and After* (1945), *The Soviet Impact on the Western World* (1947) and explication of virtues, see Robert G. Kaufman, 'E. H. Carr, Winston Churchill, Reinhold Niebuhr and Us: The Case for Principled, Prudential, Democratic Realism', in *Roots of Realism*, ed. Benjamin Frankel (London; New York, NY: Routledge, 2013), 318–325.
38. J. D. B. Miller, 'Review: E. H. Carr: The Realist's Realist', *The National Interest* 25, Fall (1991): 65–71. Available at http://www.jstor.org/stable/42894766 (accessed on 14 June 2015).
39. Kaufman, 'E. H. Carr', 323–325.
40. Miller, 'Review', 68–69.
41. Charles Jones, 'E. H. Carr: Ambivalent Realist', in *Post-Realism: The Rhetorical Turn in International Relations*, eds. Francis A. Beer and Robert Harriman (East Lansing: Michigan State University, 1996), 95–119.
42. Kubálková, 'The Twenty Years' Catharsis', 27.
43. Paul Howe, 'The Utopian Realism of E. H. Carr', *Review of International Studies* 20, no. 3 (1994): 277–297.
44. Miller, 'Review', 71.
45. Andrew Linklater, 'The Transformation of Political Community: E. H. Carr, Critical Theory and International Relations', *Review of International Studies* 23, no. 3 (1997): 321–338, here 338.
46. Kubálková, 'The Twenty Years' Catharsis', 27–33.
47. Giulio M. Gallarotti, *Cosmopolitan Power in International Relations: A Synthesis of Realism, Neoliberalism and Constructivism* (New York, NY: Cambridge University Press, 2010), 128.
48. Richard Ned Lebow, *The Tragic Vision of Politics: Ethics, Interests and Orders* (Cambridge: Cambridge University Press, 2003), 216.
49. Williams, *The Realist Tradition and the Limits of International Relations*, 82.
50. Arash Heydarian Pashakhanlou, *Realism and Fear in International Relations: Morgenthau, Waltz and Mearsheimer Reconsidered* (Cham: Palgrave Macmillan, 2017), 8.
51. In-text page numbers for Morgenthau are *Politics among Nations* (Calcutta: Scientific Book Agency, 1966), 28.
52. This quotation is in the book's first edition of *Politics among Nations* (New York, NY: Knopf, 1948), 17.
53. Nicholas Royle, *After Derrida* (Manchester: Manchester University Press, 1995), 2–7.
54. Williams, *The Realist Tradition and the Limits of International Relations*, 82.
55. Robert Jervis, 'Hans Morgenthau, Realism, and the Scientific Study of International Politics', *Social Research* 61, no. 4; Sixtieth Anniversary 1934–1994: The Legacy of Our Past (Winter 1994): 853–876, here 853.
56. Richard Little, *The Balance of Power in International Relations: Metaphors, Myths and Models* (New York, NY: Cambridge University Press, 2007), 92.

57. Jervis, 'Hans Morgenthau', 853.
58. Nicolas Guilhot, 'Politics between and beyond Nations: Hans J. Morgenthau's Politics among Nations', in *Classics of International Relations: Essays in Criticism and Appreciation*, eds. Henrik Bliddal, Casper Sylvest and Peter Wilson (Abingdon; New York, NY: Routledge, 2013), 70.
59. Morgenthau, *Politics among Nations.*
60. Donnelly, *Realism*, 44, 47.
61. Wilhelm Dilthey, 'The Understanding of Other Persons and Their Life Expressions', in *Hermeneutics Reader: Texts of the German Tradition from the Enlightenment to the Present*, ed. Kurt Mueller Vollmer (New York, NY: Bloomsbury Publishing, 2006), 162.
62. Morgenthau, *Politics among Nations*, 4–15.
63. Gallarotti, *Cosmopolitan Power in International Relations*, 144–153.
64. See Morgenthau, *Politics among Nations*, 237, 597, 600, 603, 604, 605.
65. For critics and critiques, see Little, *Balance of Power*, 91, 94–95.
66. Ibid., 97.
67. Gallarotti, *Cosmopolitan Power in International Relations*, 154.
68. E. J. Hobsbawm, *Nations and Nationalism since 1780: Programme, Myth, Reality*, Canto Edition (Cambridge: Cambridge University Press, 1995), 163–192.

CHAPTER

5

Neorealism: Kenneth Waltz, His Images and Level of Analysis

CHAPTER OUTLINE

INTRODUCTION: ORIGINS AND NATURE

I start this chapter by stating the material factors behind the emergence of neorealism. Even before the onset of the 1970s, the practical influence of realism as a theory had started waning. The post-war realism was no more helping an America facing a weakening of control over IP, manifested in differences between the USA and European nation states over questions of security and trade, the shocking debacle of the USA in the Vietnam War and the overheating of the American economy because of this war or the 'first oil shock' of 1973. Moreover, ever since the end of Bretton

Woods in 1973, persistent misalignments in exchange rates and periodic bursts of serious over-valuations of the Dollar were hurting American industries, prompting demands for, even if sector-specific, protectionism. Some historians, energy policy analysts, politicians and political observers sought evidence of America's declining hegemony in the Organization of the Petroleum Exporting Countries (OPEC) oil embargo and showed it 'as a profound national crisis, one that revealed that the nation had lapsed from a state of independence into one of dependency (in this case, dependency on Middle Eastern oil)'. While the American public was divided and uncertain about the causes of the embargo, opinion polls suggested that for them 'it constituted solid evidence of national decline in the immediate wake of the Vietnam war.'[1] Also, in the 1970s

> economic interdependence among countries seemed to have as much importance as balance of military power, whether through the ability of relatively weak states to cripple the world economy with the OPEC oil embargo, or through the integration of western Europe into the European Economic Community.[2]

In the resultant impression of decline of American hegemony,[3] the impact of the Arab–Israeli War of 1973 also added to the conviction that military power could no more be the most important factor in IR. A theoretical edifice that had depended for its origins and succour on American power and hegemony in world politics suddenly found itself sort of suspended in thin air. It was at this time that Keohane and Nye raised the demand for a 'world politics paradigm' in 1971.[4] A decade later, Mansbach and Vasquez also called for 'a new paradigm for global politics' in 1981.[5] While a buoyant pluralism and transnationalism started recognizing new developments to challenge the old state centricity of realism, American imperialism responded to the new liberalism through neorealism. It was in this way that a 'non-state structuralism' (in Keohane and Nye's terms), 'structural realism', or neorealism came to dominate the post-1970s theoretical field in IR and found its best expression in Kenneth Waltz's iconic book *Theory of International Politics* (henceforth *TIP*).

Neorealism is the most self-conscious attempt to present a general theory of IP that revolved round the concept of the international system. It is not that the concept was altogether unknown in IR. Already in the writings of Morton Kaplan, Richard Rosecrance, Kai Holsti and others, the systems concept had been applied in IR in different conceptualizations. Even the writings of the ES rest on a different view of international system.[6] But Waltz set the systems concept in a full realist framework that differed from neoclassical realism mainly in methodology and view of science, though Waltz never admitted it. Claiming to have produced the first authentic 'systemic' theory in the world, where all previous theories were 'reductionist', Waltz seemed to claim the status of a pioneer in IR theorizing. But to understand Waltz's full-blown neorealism, spelt out in *TIP* properly, we must first look at his earlier book, *Man, the State and War* (henceforth *MSW*; 1959), dealing primarily with the causes of war, where he was showing the first signs of breaking out of the bounds of realist theory, and then compare it with *TIP*.[7] Mouritzen says, the

> 'object of explanation' in *MSW* is clear and precise, the phenomenon of war or its absence. By contrast, the object of explanation in... *TIP* is more vague, international politics in general.... Waltz consistently uses the double formulation 'behavior and outcome' about his object of explanation here.

This should logically imply that his theory is concerned both with foreign policy, that is, behaviour of units, and IP as their 'outcomes for the international system as a whole'. But Waltz self-consciously eschews any preoccupation with foreign policy.[8]

MAN, THE STATE AND WAR, AND LEVELS OF ANALYSIS

Answers to the question 'Where are the major causes of war to the found?' are 'bewildering in their variety and in their contradictory qualities'. But Waltz thinks this variety could be made manageable by arranging them under 'three headings: within man, within the structure of the separate states, within the state system'. The resultant 'images of international relations',[9] generate theories about the causes of war at the individual, state and systemic levels.[10] Waltz brushes away explanations at the first two levels as inadequate, the individual level explanations because, 'While human nature no doubt plays a role in bringing about war, it cannot explain both war and peace except by the simple statement that man's nature is such that sometimes he fights and sometimes he does not'.[11] For Waltz, the 'causal importance of human nature' is exaggerated by first image/level theorists. Both pessimistic and optimistic views of human nature fail to explain war. The former cannot say why wars do not happen all of the time, and the latter cannot explain why they occur some of the time. Besides, we see both good and bad men making war. Because human nature is too complicated to offer direct or sole explanations for the causes of war, theories based on human nature have to invoke social or political institutions that limit the likelihood of wars, that is, second-level images. But these are also similarly handicapped because, just like individuals, there are both good and bad states. Explanations based on internal organizations of states and societies are inadequate because, first, if bad states are warmongers, we should know what will transform them into good states.[12] Second, second-level image theorists do not agree on what constitutes a good state, whether it is good internal governmental arrangement or something else. Are good states monarchical, democratic or socialist?[13] Third, even if they could agree on this, there is no guarantee that even a world full of good states will be peaceful. For, just as good men do, good states too sometimes wage wars. Theories of the first two levels can explain specific wars at best. They cannot provide answers to the question of why wars in general occur. Thus, the state-level answers also refer us to the third or international level. This is because 'the international political environment has much to do with the ways in which states behave'.[14] To facilitate an understanding of the international system, Waltz refers to Rousseau's famous cautionary tale of the stag hunt. Elaborated in Rousseau's *Discourse on the Origin of Inequality* (1755), the tale is about a group of hunters' attempt to trap a stag in the SON. Five hunters position themselves in a forest in a day-long attempt to trap it. The success of the venture depends on none of the hunters evading his responsibilities. But lacking 'foresight' and uncertain of the outcome of the hunt, each of the hunters will leave his position to catch a fleeing hare, allowing the stag to escape. Waltz extends this logic to the international system and shows that in a condition of anarchy, with no overarching authority to discipline any defector state(s), cooperation is possible only to the extent that a state does not deviate like a stag hunter to pursue its short-term interests to the detriment of the common venture.[15] Jervis describes the dilemmas of uncertain cooperation in an anarchic situation well and makes Waltz's meaning clearer.

> If they cooperate to trap the stag, they will all eat well. But if one person defects to chase a rabbit—which he likes less than stag—none of the others will get anything. Thus, all actors have the same preference order, there is a solution that gives each his first choice: (1) cooperate and trap the stag (the analogue between international cooperation and disarmament); (2) chase a rabbit while others remain at their posts (maintain a high level of arms while others are disarmed); (3) all chase rabbits (arms competition and high risks of war); and (4) stay at the position while another chases a rabbit (being disarmed while others are being armed).[16]

So the third image mirrors a situation where 'many sovereign states' exist, 'with no system of law enforceable among them, with each state judging its grievances and ambitions according to the dictates of its own reason or desire…'. Here, 'conflict, sometimes leading to war' is inevitable. The relation between anarchy and the occurrence of war is clear and direct.

> In anarchy there is no automatic harmony…. A state will use force to attain its goals, if after assessing the prospects for success, it values those goals more than it values the pleasures of peace. Because each state is the final judge of its own cause, any state may at any time use force to implement its policies.

In a scenario where there is no higher authority to resort to, states would have to fend for themselves. Having no other agency to rely on for succour and constantly aware that other states may deviate from any cooperative venture at any time, states live in a situation where any dispute may erupt into violence.[17] The systemic roots of war are all too clear.

> Wars occur because there is nothing to prevent it. Among states, as among men, there is no automatic adjustment of interests. In the absence of a supreme authority, there is then constant possibility that conflicts will be settled by force.[18]

Although the third level has to be brought in to compensate for the deficiencies of the first two levels or images, Waltz advises exploring the relationship among the three levels/images rather than laying an exclusive emphasis on the third level. The third level has better explanatory potential because its anarchy assumption makes clear why neither individuals nor particular types of states can be held responsible for all types of war despite having waged wars sometimes. Better explanation is facilitated by the differentiation made possible by the anarchy assumption between the 'efficient' and the 'permissive' causes of war. Efficient causes apply to wars waged over particular interests, both territorial and others. But permissive causes are those that make wars generally likely and are, in the case of IR, typified by anarchy. However, like Emile Durkheim's differentiation between 'egoistic' and 'anomic' suicide, the difference between them is also thin, because very often when one state wages a preventive or pre-emptive war against another, fearing its power potential after a few years, the 'efficient cause of such a war is derived from the cause that we have labelled permissive'. In short, the Hobbesian fear, caused by insecurity, itself a result of anarchy, can be as much a prolific source of wars as any specific reasons. Since in the absence of any central authority states have to fend for themselves, the fear of attack in the near or distant future by another state, gathering power, will predispose them to preemptive attack.[19] So the international system itself becomes a subject of focus. While unable to explain by itself why wars occur, it can show why their particular causes remain unrestrained at this level.

WALTZ'S OEUVRE AND *TIP*

Waltz's oeuvre after *MSW* included *Foreign Policy and Democratic Politics* (1967), which compared foreign policymaking in the UK and the USA; 'Theory of International Relations', in *Sage Handbook of Political Science* (1975), which contained the essence of Waltz's 'theory'; Waltz's response to critiques of him by critics in Keohane's edited book *Neo-Realism Its Critics* (1986), the sole example of a one-volume debate between positivism and its critics in IR and quite a few articles addressing the post-1989 world from his theoretical standpoint. However, *TIP* is the book by which Waltz stands or falls, and here there is no more mention of the three levels/images, as if the issue has been decisively settled in *MSW*. Let me present the book.

Written 20 years after *MSW*, *TIP* is a complex book of four identifiable parts. The first part sets about discussing the function and role of theory in the social sciences. The second criticizes existing theories of IR, especially those with systemic pretensions that are, according to Waltz, actually 'reductionist'. He promises to provide a truly 'systemic' theory minus their problems, including those arising from wrong levels of analysis. The third delineates the theory, while the final seeks to test the theory with historical examples as the laboratory.[20] Within these parts, Chapter 1 deals with his understanding of theory. Chapters 2–4 summarize the efforts to develop a theory of IP before his book, their failures and the causes of them. Finally, Chapters 5–9 delineate his own theory and its pay-offs for understanding the intricacies of IP and the validation of his claim that it is the only authentic theory of IP.

AGAINST INDUCTION: OF LAWS, MODELS, THEORIES AND WALTZ'S PHILOSOPHY OF SCIENCE

Exploration of the nature of theory in IR is an important theme in *TIP* because Waltz wants a non-inductive, 'new style of theory' for IP. I have shown in **Chapter 1** how for many IR scholars 'the disciplinary transition from realism to neorealism' was 'a delayed and displaced victory for the "scientific" side of the second debate'.[21] Molloy says that *TIP* is 'one of the last great entries' in this methodological debate 'between the scientific and classical wings of international theory', turning realism into 'a rationalist, structural theory of international politics' in a clear 'inversion of the epistemological position taken by two of its most important founders', namely Carr and Morgenthau. So Waltz conscientiously makes his 'epistemological groundwork' preparatory to explicating this theory in the second part of *TIP*: unlike his realist predecessors, a self-conscious positivist view of science. He downplays the problems of applying the methodology of physical sciences to social sciences; soft-pedals Morgenthau's distinction between the human and the social sciences in *Scientific Man versus Power Politics* (1946) and finally subsumes 'the social under the scientific method associated with disciplines such as physics', taking microeconomics as 'the poster boy of such attempts'; all this to tide over the basic problem with IRT, namely its imperviousness to POS. Endeavouring to make IR thinking amenable to its principles, Waltz first constructs 'a theoretical taxonomy of the necessary mental apparatus for the construction of theory—ideas, laws, theory, and science'.[22]

This taxonomy starts with a distinction between laws and theories, which is often missed by students of IR, who 'use the term "theory" freely, for any work that departs from mere description and seldom adopt philosophy-of-science standards'. Laws 'establish relations between variables' but vary in their rigour which depends on the frequency of repetition of the relation and its expectations about 'specified probability'. But let alone social sciences, even in the natural sciences, 'even probabilistic laws contain a strong imputation of necessity'. The social sciences abound in examples of 'law-like statement(s)', the suffix '-like' conveying a 'lesser sense of necessity', though even a 'probabilistic' law would not pass for a law unless the discovered relation is so regular that prediction of its future occurrence in roughly equal probability is high.

For theories, a less demanding meaning makes them 'collections or sets of law pertaining to a particular behavior or phenomenon'. It is visible in attempts to find the link between a specified income and support for a political party by supplementing it with probabilistic associations between voters' education, religion, political commitments prevalent in the family and so on, providing 'higher correlations' between aspects of a voter's social profile (independent variables) and his choice of party (dependent variable). Here also, theory is more complex than laws, but only in a quantitative sense, allowing no qualitative difference. Most of the theoretically minded social scientists, 'collecting carefully verified, interconnected hypotheses', take theory in this diluted sense, unconcerned that 'a coefficient of correlation, even a high one', does not indicate a causal connection in still not having 'accounted for that connection in the sense of having explained it'. Besides, the inductive methodology underlying and inducing such careful collection of data and hypothesis ignores the truth that what passes for reality is itself an elaborate process of historical construction and reconstruction, foregrounded by 'our selection and organization of materials that are available in infinite quantity'. So more than 'being mere collections of laws, theories are statements that explain them', thus 'qualitatively different from laws'. For, while 'identifying invariant or probable associations', theories alone 'show why these associations obtain'.

This type of theory has additional epistemological aspects: (a) all its 'descriptive terms' are directly placed under 'observational and laboratory procedures', accepted as laws only after clearing associated tests; (b) these are supplemented by certain theoretical conceptions, minimizing the reliance on induction. Waltz compared Aristotle's physics with Galileo's, and then with Newton's, to show that theoretical notions are invented, not discovered, and are explainable by taking increasingly bolder 'steps away from the real world' and 'our sense experience'. He added that a theoretical notion, either as a concept or an assumption, does not explain or predict anything simply because assumptions are never 'assertions of facts'. The truth or falsity of theoretical notions is immaterial, being legitimized or validated only in the 'success of theories that employ them' and (c) laws are judged by their truth contents, but theories by their 'explanatory power'. Newton's theory of universal gravitation is superior to Aristotle's law-like statement about the possibility of displacement of a particular body in a fixed time 'through a distance proportional to the force available' in the following areas: its ability to bring under one explanatory system all the previously discordant empirical generalizations regarding these phenomena; the number and range of new hypotheses it engenders or suggests and new experimental laws that its hypotheses gave rise to. So while laws are observed facts, theories are nothing but 'speculative processes' that seek to explain them. And though experimental results are permanent, theories, however mightily buttressed by experiments, are rarely so.

Waltz chooses theory in its second meaning, though it is prevalent in the natural sciences and some social sciences, particularly economics, rather than in its 'usage in traditional political theory', involving 'philosophical interpretation' more than 'theoretical explanation'. But theory in such a natural scientific sense is possible only when it distances itself from the world, with 'reality' being 'congruent neither with a theory nor with a model that may represent it'. Political scientists mistakenly believe that 'the best model is one that reflects reality most accurately'. So Waltz teaches them the difference between a model and a theory. A model either 'represents a theory' or 'pictures reality by simplifying it' either 'through omission or through reduction of scale'. Unlike theories, models cannot deviate too far from reality without getting useless. But the explanatory power of a model also increases the more it moves away from reality. For a theory, a fuller realistic description lessens its explanatory power, and 'an elegant theory' of maximum explanatory power would be at the greatest remove from reality, as in physics. This departure from reality is not intrinsically good, but otherwise one can just describe and never explain, let alone control. Accordingly, a good model of any theory should improve: be 'as far removed from reality as the theory it represents'; employ 'symbolic ways of depicting a theory rather than the reality it encapsulates' and present the theory 'with its theoretical notions necessarily omitted, whether through organismic, mechanistic, mathematical or other expressions'.

This harangue on models was targeted at political scientists who envision only models of the 'airplane sort'; object to the state-centric model of IP for its deviation from reality and aspire after models that 'mirror reality' even more truly, not realizing that success of their endeavours would make models and the real world nearly indistinguishable. After invoking Kant and Einstein in support of his position, Waltz emphatically asserts that there is no straightforward road to theory through induction. 'To claim that it is possible to arrive at a theory inductively is to claim that we can understand phenomena before the means for their explanation are contrived.'

Waltz needs to explain how theories are arrived at after dismissing induction, which works at the level of hypotheses and laws and not of theories (more so because hypotheses are derived not only from induction but also from theories and, if 'confirmed quite conclusively', also become laws); showing that a direct leap from law to theory is not possible (laws being discovered but theories being constructed) and claiming that the leap from law to theory, from the fashioning of hypotheses to the development of explanations is not possible (through collating information as evidence, however comprehensive, or through continuing to discover further associations). It can only be done by raising questions about how things are caused and hang together. After this rationalist reduction, a theory becomes

> ...a picture, *mentally formed*, of a bounded realm or domain of activity...a depiction of the organization of a domain and the connection among its parts. The infinite materials of any realm can be organized in endlessly different ways. A theory indicates that some factors are more important than others and specifies relations among them. In reality, everything is related to everything else.... Theory isolates one realm from all others in order to deal with it intellectually. To isolate a realm is a precondition to developing a theory that will explain what goes on within it. If the precondition cannot be met...then the construction of theory...is impossible. The question...is not whether the isolation of a realm is realistic, but whether it

> is useful...judged by the explanatory and predictive powers of the theory that may be fashioned.

After establishing that theories are only indirectly connected with reality, they 'do construct *a* reality', but not '*the* reality' due to 'an infinity of data and an equal infinity of the possible explanations of them'; 'facts do not determine theories' as 'more than one theory can match any set of facts' and, besides, no theory does 'explain facts conclusively' so that 'a good theory' can always be 'replaced by a better one'. Waltz asserts that theories are made 'creatively' since even an endless regress of trials and errors will not lead to theory construction until 'at some point a brilliant intuition flashes and a creative idea emerges'. These intuitions and ideas help in the organization of the subject matter by conveying a 'sense of the unobservable relations of things'; disclosing 'connections and causes by which sense is made of the things observed'; making 'significance of the observed...manifest'; arranging phenomena 'so that they are seen as mutually dependent'; connecting 'otherwise disparate facts' and revealing the way 'changes in some of the phenomena necessarily entail changes in others'.

This nature of theory gives rise to its identifiable elements of simplification, theoretical assumptions and an adroit combination of deduction and induction. Simplification is needed for ascending from causal speculations grounded in factual studies to theoretical speculations, and it is reached through four primary routes of 'isolation', 'abstraction', 'aggregation' and 'idealization'. Its goal is to identify 'a central tendency' amid a welter of propensities, a driving principle amid many other principles that are active and to locate essential factors among many other non-essential ones.

Theoretical assumptions are elemental because theories are constituted by descriptive and theoretical statements, the latter being non-factual elements included not from whim but from the need to facilitate explanation. Finally, both deduction and induction are involved in theory construction, which is not reducible to performing only 'logically permissible operations on observed data'. Deduction, by itself, explains nothing. It proceeds from 'initial premises' and lacks novelty in its provided answers since what is deduced was already present in the major theoretical and minor empirical premises. Induction does provide answers more deftly, but they are weak in the uncertainty and inability of multiple observations to generate a universal statement. The strength of theory lies in its capacity to use both induction and deduction adroitly in service of a 'creative idea' that has emerged.

The complications of the task of verifying theories stem from the puzzling relation between theory and observation or between theory and fact, since theoretical notions 'have no meanings outside of the theory in which they appear' and are defined by that theory. While the terms 'space, energy, momentum, and time' have carried different meanings in physical theories, terms such as 'power, force, pole, relation, actor, stability, structure, and system' have been invested with widely divergent meanings in the field of IP too. For, in weak and contradictory theories, such as those in IR, the meanings of terms become even more divergent. Here, even very crucial points such as 'the closeness of national interdependence, the stability of particularly configurations of power, the usefulness of force' have been employed by users in so many senses and to encapsulate so many different realities as to render them useless for discussion and debate. Any progress in clarification of their meanings is hamstrung by these theorists' unawareness of the problems of meaning and eagerness to operationalize the term as a technical solution to a semantic problem. Moreover, apart from theoretical notions, circumscribed in meaning by their theoretical contexts, even descriptive and factual terms acquire new meanings as theories change, particularly because theories go beyond defining terms to even suggest the operations required for it; indicate the extant connections; show how they are 'made' or 'hang together' and delimit the structure and contours of the 'realm of enquiry'. Theory is needed because, without it, correlation efforts would start from the illusion that 'international realm variables are directly connected, without any structural constraints operating on them' and that the phenomena under investigation are operative at a single level.

Methodologically, while constructing a theory, the theoretician has to ascertain whether his/her object of investigation allows for the (a) employment of the classical method of analytical physics, exploring interactions of two variables while controlling for others; (b) the employment of statistics, as applicable when the number of variables is numerous or (c) neither approach, demanding instead a systemic one. If the investigator is faced with 'organized complexity', as in IP, and his/her answer to the last question is predictably affirmative, he/she will have to test his/her theory through the seven steps specified by Waltz.

- State the theory being tested.
- Infer hypotheses from it.
- Subject the hypotheses to experimental or observational tests.
- In taking steps two and three, use the definitions of terms found in the theory being tested.
- Eliminate or control the perturbing variables not included in the theory under test.
- Devise a number of distinct and demanding tests.
- If a test is not passed, ask whether the theory flunks completely, needs repair or restatement or requires a narrowing of the scope of its explanatory claims.[23]

For Waltz's conception of theory, its scientific pretensions are its Achilles' heel for critics. When an IR author presents his 'thinking...so clearly stated and neatly packed' theoretically, and so unceasingly eulogizes POS standards, a comparison with Karl Popper becomes inevitable, as with any work that grounds itself in POS. All debates about POS engaged in by positivists/empiricists, Marxists and neo-Marxists, relativists (comprising idealist philosophers of language, Kuhnian philosophers of science and instrumentalists of various hues) have pilloried Popper. But Waltz's self-representation is not strictly Popperian. Although IR theorists such as Keohane, Cox and Ashley have branded his approach as 'positivist', Jones has described it as 'an 'inconsistent blend of various traditions'. Waltz himself talks of undifferentiated POS standards, or sometimes of microeconomic theory,[24] as his two starting blocks, specifically mentioning 'a theoretical breakthrough in a related field: economics' for its role in 'clarifying some problems in the framing and applying of international–political theory'. He brands Aron and Morgenthau, with their 'old' realism, as 'physiocrats in international politics'. Physiocrats, with their single-factor analyses, knew not how to relate 'the parts of an economy to one another and to the economy as a whole', being unable to invent 'the concept of an economy as distinct from the society and the polity in which it was embedded'. But the Waltzian 'new realism, in contrast to the old', 'begins by proposing a solution to the problems of distinguishing factors internal to the international–political systems from those that are external', aware that the task of all theory is to isolate 'one realm from the others to deal with it intellectually'. So, according to Waltz, only through 'depicting an international–political system as a whole, with structural and unit levels at once distinct and connected, neorealism established the autonomy of international politics and thus makes a theory about it possible'. This is why some also call it 'structural realism'. Waltz asserts that the 'idea that international politics can be thought of as a system with a precisely defined structure is neorealism's fundamental departure from traditional realism'.[25]

AGAINST REDUCTION: OF REDUCTIONIST AND SYSTEMIC THEORIES

Equipped with mixed positivism, Waltz looks at the state of theory in IR and finds that one of the 'depressing features of international–political studies' is the insignificant pay-off in 'explanatory power' of preceding decades' research. There, 'nothing seems to accumulate, not even criticism'. While diagnosing the causes of this theoretical malaise in Chapter 2 of *TIP*, Waltz finds the reductionism of the extant works as the troubling virus. So, instead of locating, as before (in *MSW*), the causes of war or the conditions of peace in terms of the three levels of causation, he makes 'a still simpler division' in *TIP* between theories 'that concentrate on causes at the individual or national level' (now termed 'reductionist') and 'theories that conceive of causes operating at the international level' (termed 'systemic' as before). In a reductionist view, 'the whole is understood by knowing the attributes and interactions of the parts', as exemplified by efforts to 'understand the behavior of a group through the psychological study of its members'; 'understand international politics by studying the behavior of national bureaucrats and bureaucracies' and, as the most classic instance, the once atomistic attempts at understanding 'organisms by disassembling them and applying physical and chemical knowledge in the examination of their parts', true to the maxim that the whole is knowable through the study of its parts.

Waltz believes that in IP, the enticement to such reductionism has come from its successes and prestige in physics and chemistry, and the pitfalls of explanation of international–political events through psychological factors or social–psychological phenomena, or national political and economic characteristics. But still he considers the resultant 'reductionist urge' unfortunate, as here it could have been caused less 'from failures of work done at the international–political level' than from its 'successes of other possibly pertinent disciplines'. He analyses the best, as most impressive, of such reductionist approaches, 'the Hobson–Lenin theory of imperialism', to show why they would not do. Since the assumptions of this theory are economic rather than political, its validity as an example of imperialism and war would depend on (a) its tenability as economic theory; (b) the availability of 'the conditions envisioned in the theory' in most of the imperialist countries and (c) the presence of imperialist tendencies in most of the countries where these conditions obtained. But, after pointing out several anomalies of the theory, which we do not have time to go into, Waltz argues that since imperialism is 'at least as old as recorded history', and its assigned cause, namely advanced capitalism, 'is much younger than the effect than it produces', both Hobson and Lenin should have pointed out 'what caused imperialism in bygone periods, and why those old causes of imperialism no longer operate, why these have been replaced as causes by capitalism'.[26]

For Waltz, the main problem of economic theories of imperialism, neocolonialism and war is that while they 'assign specific causes of war', it is on record that every kind of state with 'every imaginable variation of economic and social institution and political ideology' has engaged in wars. 'Internationally, different states have produced similar as well as different outcomes, and similar states have produced different as well as similar outcomes. The same causes sometimes lead to different effects, and the same effects sometimes follow from different causes'. But still, while admitting the legitimacy of the resultant suspicion that reductionist explanations of IP are inadequate and 'analytic approaches' and must be replaced by 'systemic ones', Waltz concedes that the 'failures of some reductionist approaches' would not prove that no reductionism would 'succeed'. Even if their 'defects' throw light on general problems witnessed in 'concentrating on explanations of international politics at national or lower levels', they guarantee that all such reductionist theories will similarly fail.[27] Noting how reductionist, and even avowedly systemic, theories have found similarity and repetition in international outcomes in spite of the 'wide variety in the attributes and interactions of the agents that supposedly cause them' baffling,[28] Waltz argues that other, systemic, forces must have been operative in producing them.

Among all forms of reductionism, economic reductionism is of special distaste to Waltz, perhaps because he wants to theorize an autonomous international political sphere away from economy. So he begins Chapter 3 on reductionist approaches and theories with a scathing attack on Marx's reduction of the politics of nations to their economics and Immanuel Wallerstein's efforts to explain both national and international politics by the effects of 'the capitalist world-economy'.[29] So Waltz directs our attention to what systemic theories mean and how they are constructed. To do that, he again starts with a distinction between 'analytic', that is, atomistic and reductionist, and 'systemic' approaches. While the former valourized in classical physics 'as *the* method of science' mandates 'reducing the entity to its discrete parts and examining their properties and connections', the latter enjoins 'conceiving of political systems in ways compatible with usage in systems theory and cybernetics'. There, a system is defined as a 'set of interacting units', which at one level 'consists of a structure', which is the 'systems-level component that makes it possible to think of the units as forming a set as distinct from a mere collection', while at 'another level the system consists of interacting units'.[30] This structure, however, would not be amenable to visual experience and is decipherable only though an abstract model of it. For Waltz, a 'political structure is akin to a field of forces in physics: interactions within a field have properties different from those they would have if they occurred outside of it, and as the field affects the objects, so the objects affect the field'.[31] So while defining the structure, one 'must leave aside, or abstract from, the characteristics of the units, their behaviour, and their interactions...so that we can distinguish between variables at the level of the units and variables at the level of the system.'[32]

In this model, the political structure of the international system is composed of three elements: (a) the system's ordering principle; (b) the functional differentiation, or specificities or characteristics of the units and (c) the distribution of capabilities or resources among the units. The first element is fully structural. In national political systems, the ordering principle is hierarchical, with superordinate–subordinate relations. But here, anarchy or the absence of such authority, 'orderer' or world government is operative, making survival the prime will of the government. The second structural feature is the character of the units that Hobden finds 'slightly more problematic'.[33] Functional differentiation would obtain if something akin to social division of labour exists in the international system. But here states are 'functionally undifferentiated' and perform the same tasks. The logic of anarchy dictates that all states are forced to focus on their central preference, which is the maintenance of sovereignty. Since the 'international imperative is: "take care of yourself"',[34] anarchy makes the international system a 'self-help system'. A state 'decides for itself how it will deal or cope with internal or external problems'.[35] The third structural feature of the international system, or the distribution of capabilities among nation states, refers to power relations among discrete states. It may be mistaken as a concession to the national or sub-systemic level, but Waltz says that it is not, since his concern is not with the capabilities of individual states but with their distribution across the system. Even if 'capabilities are attributes of units, the distribution of capabilities across units is not'. It is rather a 'system-wide concept' and a structural feature.[36]

The distribution of capabilities, a very powerful determinant of the form or character of the system at a specific point of time, is also different from the first and second structural features of the system in two important ways or respects: (a) the first two elements are relatively more stable than the third and (b) any changes in them would entail a total change *to* and *of* the system, while for the third, they would lead to changes *in* the system. For, Waltz, however, the only systemic change that can be considered significant is from an anarchical order to a hierarchical one, facilitated by the rise of a world government. Waltz gets the concept of anarchy, in the special sense in which it is employed, that is, 'the order of international politics...understood in the absence of an "orderer"', through an 'extended analogy to microeconomics and the theory of the market'. The condition of the coexistence of states is likened to the condition of the coexistence of firms to show how structure emerges from this coexistence and why 'intentionality is not an issue' behind the emergence of international anarchy.[37] In Waltz's words, 'The market arises out of the activities of separate units—persons and firms—whose aims and efforts are not directed toward creating an order but rather toward fulfilling their own internally defined interests by whatever means they can muster.'[38]

Compared to such change *of* the system, change *in* the system is worked by the distribution of power. Since Waltz cares only for the great powers, such distribution may take three directions: the international system may take a unipolar turn (with domination by a powerful hegemon); it can turn bipolar, with two great powers ruling the roost as during the entire Cold War period or it can turn multipolar, with more than two powers.[39] In Chapters 7–9, Waltz discusses the relative merits of the bipolar and multipolar systems and seems to find the former more stable. He points to 'the effects on the European states of the shift from a multipolar to a bipolar system. So long as European states were the world's great powers, unity among them could only be dreamt of'. But post-shift, 'politics among European states changed in quality after World War II.'[40] Pre-empting the question of how then could European multipolarity have lasted three centuries, he said that such stability had been possible only 'because as some states fell from the top rank others rose to it through the relative increase of their capabilities. The system endured even as the identity of the members changed'.[41] But problems of multipolar systems are as follows: the existence of too many powers in such systems 'to permit any one of them to draw clear and fixed lines between allies and adversaries'[42]; and states frequently 'pool their resources to serve their interests', though in bipolar systems 'alliance leaders make their strategies mainly according to their own calculations of interests'.[43] Their strategies can be more synoptic and rational because their 'extraordinary positions in the system' embolden them to undertake tasks that other states have neither the incentive nor the ability to attempt.[44] As we will see later, this reliance on bipolarity as a more stable system became one of neorealism's weakest theoretical spots.

FROM SYSTEMIC STRUCTURE TO THEORETICALLY RESULTANT BIPOLAR INTERNATIONAL POLITICS

What new light does this perspective on the structure of the international system throw on IP and its polarity? How does theoretical structure conceptually affect the behaviour of individual actors so that states are seen compelled to act under conditions of anarchy? For both questions, Waltz enlightens us that the 'first concern of states is not to maximize power but to maintain their positions in the system'.[45] Unlike traditional realists, who maintain that states want only to maximize their relative power, Waltz avers that, in vital situations, 'the ultimate concern of states is not for power but for security. This revision is an important one'.[46] Moreover, structure controls the outcome of behaviour irrespective of the intentions and motives of the actors,[47] even though structure is a resultant of their own actions.

International–Political System and Markets

To show how structure is a resultant of unit actions, Waltz draws on the analogy of markets and the international–political system, showing the autonomy of the market after its birth from the activities of buyers and sellers, that is, the co-action of units, from which emerges a structure that affects and constrains all of them. Once formed, a market becomes a force in itself, and a force that the constitutive units acting singly or in small numbers cannot control.[48] Immediately thereafter, he focuses on the similarities (and also differences) between international–political systems and economic markets, both constituted by 'co-actions of self-regarding units'.

> International–political systems, like economic markets, are individualistic in origin, spontaneously generated, and unintended. In both systems structures are formed by the coaction of their units. Whether those units live, prosper, or die depends on their own efforts.... To say that the two realms are structurally similar is not to proclaim their identity. Economically, the self-help principle applies within governmentally contrived limits. Market economies are hedged about in ways that channel energies constructively.... International politics is more like a system where anything goes. International politics is structurally similar to a market insofar as the principle of self-help is allowed to operate in the latter.[49]

Waltz, however, does not accord full causative power to structures. Structures are surely causes, but not in the sense of A causing X and B causing Y.[50] Structures merely 'shape and shove'.[51] The looseness of causal structural determinism is manifested in the way actors respond to structural pressure. The ingrained propensity of the international system to equilibrium notwithstanding, behaviour of states is not 'determined by structure', more than being shaped and shoved. States are 'free to do any fool thing they care to' in a self-help system, but they are restrained by the thought they will be 'rewarded for behavior that is responsive to structural pressures and punished for behavior that is not.'[52] The probabilistic BOP-seeking tendency of states is also probabilistic since, in a self-help system, states which 'do not help themselves...will fail to prosper, will lay themselves open to dangers'. It is the dread of such unexpected outcomes which 'stimulates states to behave in ways that tend toward the creation of balances of power'. So 'the theory' presented here 'requires no assumptions of rationality or constancy of will on the part of all of the actors'. It just shows that if by following this tendency 'some do relatively well, others will emulate them or fall by the wayside'. But the system 'will continue to work if some states do, while others do not, choose to lose their political identities, say, through amalgamation'. Waltz also reminds us that his theory has no need to 'assume that all of the competing states are striving relentlessly to increase their power'. However, the 'possibility that force may be used by some states to weaken or destroy others' would 'make it difficult for them to break out of the competitive system'.[53]

Waltz stresses that the point of departure of such a systemic explanation of 'BOP theory' from earlier reductionist theories is that while they attribute the 'maintenance of a balance' to the motives of separate states, this

> theory explains to claim a result...which may not accord with the intentions of any of the units whose actions combine to produce that result. To contrive or maintain a balance may be the aim or one or more states, but then again it may not be.

But in his systemic theory, 'balances of power tend to form whether some or all states consciously aim to establish or maintain a balance, or whether some or all states aim for universal domination'.[54]

Polarity

Another area where Waltz's structural perspective differs from 'old' realism and its BOP theory is the way it relates the concepts of anarchy and polarity to this balance formation. It is anarchy which primarily induces BOP politics, prevailing 'the only two conditions are met: that the order be anarchic and that it is populated by units wishing to survive'.[55] But polarity, which Waltz takes up early in *TIP*, since 'well-known theories...refer to numbers of great powers or polarities', is also important. Waltz only wants to discourage widely variant definitions of polarity 'in terms of countries or blocs' and counting of poles 'sometimes according to the physical capabilities of nations or of alliances, sometimes by looking at the pattern or national interrelations, and sometimes by awarding or denying top status to those who get or fail to get their ways'. Against such 'confused, vague and fluctuating definitions' of this important variable,[56] Waltz defines pole status in terms of 'combined capabilities'. In a self-help system, states 'have to use their combined capabilities in order to serve their interests'. But pole status of the system will depend less on the will or compulsions of individual states in the system than on how they 'score on *all* of the following items:

size of population and territory, resource endowment, economic capability, military strength, political stability and competence'.[57] Since in terms of these criteria the 'barriers to entering the superpower club have never been higher and more numerous' than in 1979, the club 'will long remain the world's most exclusive one', the system will stay bipolar.[58]

CONCLUSION

This chapter has shown the origins of neorealism situationally in the perceived decline of American hegemony post-1970, and theoretically in the related decline of neoclassical realism and the resultant demand for a 'world politics paradigm'. We know that it was provided by Waltz first in *MSW*, as the third 'image' or 'level' of IP, and then in *TIP* as a 'systemic' theory of it. I have shown that the moorings of Waltz's theory lie in a mixed positivist view of science that is less Popperian than influenced by the microeconomic theory of markets. I have shown that Waltzian theory is not fully determinist structurally but shows how the anarchy assumption and the BOP politics resulting from it predispose the international system towards bipolarity as the present and most stable outcome. Its concept of structure is best given in Waltz's own words:

> Neorealism develops the concept of a system's structure which at once bounds the domain that students of international politics deal with and enables them to see how the structure of the system, and variations in it, affect the interacting units and the outcomes they produce. International structure emerges from the interaction of states and then constrains them from taking certain actions while propelling them toward others.[59]

Since criticism and evaluation of neorealism will be provided in **Chapter 7**, I am concluding this chapter with this observation that neorealism finally turned out to be a pessimistic 'theory of great power politics, specifically great power politics in the European mainland'.[60] In the next chapter, I will take up two other important variants of modern realism, strategic realism of Thomas Schelling and offensive realism of John Mearsheimer, and their affinity to Waltz's thought.

REVIEW QUESTIONS

1. Discuss Waltz's view of three 'images' of IR in connection with the decline of neoclassical realism in the 1970s and the demand for a 'world politics paradigm'.
2. Point out the similarities and differences between Waltz's statements of structural realism in *MSW* and in *TIP*.
3. Give a brief review of Waltz's view of science.
4. How are Waltz's invectives against 'induction' in natural and social sciences and 'reduction' in IR theory related?
5. Summarize Waltz's 'systemic' view of IP as given in *TIP*.
6. Show in what sense Waltz's neorealism is not fully structural.

NOTES AND REFERENCES

1. Natasha Zaretsky, 'In the Name of Austerity: Middle-Class Consumption and OPEC Oil Embargo of 1973–1974', in *The World the Sixties Made: Politics and Culture in Recent America*, eds. Van Gosse and Richard R. Moser (Philadelphia, PA: Temple University Press, 2003), 138.
2. Matthew A. Shadle, *The Origins of War: A Catholic Perspective* (Washington, DC: Georgetown University Press, 2011), 58.
3. Zaretsky, 'In the Name of Austerity', 138; T. V. Paul, *International Relations Theory and Regional Transformation* (Cambridge; New York, NY: Cambridge University Press, 2012), 127; Stephen Gill, *American Hegemony and the Trilateral Commission* (Cambridge; New York, NY: Cambridge University Press, 1991), 17–19; Martin Griffiths, *Fifty Key Thinkers in International Relations* (London; New York, NY: Routledge, 1999), 14–16.
4. Joseph S. Nye and Robert O. Keohane, 'Transnational Relations and World Politics: An Introduction', *International Organization* 25 (1971): 329–349.doi: 10.1017/S0020818300026187.
5. Richard Wallace Mansbach and John A. Vasquez, *In Search of Theory: A New Paradigm for Global Politics* (New York, NY: Columbia University Press, 1981).
6. M. A. Kaplan, *System and Process in International Politics* (New York, NY: Wiley, 1957); R. N. Rosecrance, *Action and Reaction in World Politics: International Systems in Perspective* (Boston, MA: Little Brown, 1963); K. J. Holsti, *International Politics: A Framework for Analysis* (Englewood Cliffs, NJ: Prentice Hall, 1988); H. Bull, *The Anarchical Society: A Study of Order in World Politics* (London: Macmillan, 1977).
7. Kenneth Waltz, *Man, the State, and War: A Theoretical Analysis* (New York, NY: Columbia University Press, [1959]2001); Kenneth N. Waltz, *Theory of International Politics* (New York, NY: McGraw-Hill, 1979; reissued by Long Grove, IL: Waveland Press, 2010).
8. Hans Mouritzen, 'Kenneth Waltz: A Critical Rationalist between International Politics and Foreign Policy', in *Neumann and Wæver, The Future of International Relations*, 72–73.
9. Waltz, *Man, the State, and War,* 12.
10. Ibid., Chapters 2-5.
11. Ibid., 29.
12. Ibid., 114.
13. Ibid., 120.
14. Ibid., 122–123.
15. Ibid., 167–168.
16. Robert Jervis, 'Cooperation under the Security Dilemma', *World Politics* 30, no. 2 (1978): 167–214, here 167–168.
17. Waltz, *Man, the State, and War,* 160.
18. Ibid., 188.
19. Ibid., 232–234.
20. Stephen Hobden, *International Relations and Historical Sociology: Breaking Down Boundaries* (London; New York, NY: Routledge, 1998), 50.
21. See notes 50 and 65 of 'Introduction'.
22. Seán Molloy, *The Hidden History of Realism* (Berlin: Springer, 2006), 116.
23. Waltz, *Theory of International Politics,* 1–14.
24. Charles Jones, 'Rethinking the Methodology of Realism', in *The Logic of Anarchy,* eds. Barry Buzan, Charles Jones and Richard Little (New York, NY: Columbia University Press, 1993), 169–231, here 185, cited in Mouritzen, *'Kenneth* Waltz', 72.
25. Kenneth Waltz, 'Realist Thought and Neorealist Theory', in *Controversies in International Relations Theory: Realism and the Neoliberal Challenge*, ed. Charles W. Kegley Jr (New York, NY: St. Martin's Press, 1995), 67–74.
26. Waltz, *Theory of International Politics,* 18–25.

27. Ibid., 37.
28. Ibid., 67.
29. Ibid., 38.
30. Ibid., 39–40.
31. Ibid., 73.
32. Ibid., 79.
33. Hobden, *International Relations and Historical Sociology*, 54.
34. Ibid., 107.
35. Ibid., 96.
36. Ibid., 98.
37. The quote is from Molloy, *The Hidden History of Realism*, 120.
38. Waltz, *Theory of International Politics*, 90.
39. Ibid., 98.
40. Ibid., 70–71.
41. Ibid., 162.
42. Ibid., 168.
43. Ibid., 170.
44. Ibid., 199.
45. Ibid., 126.
46. Kenneth Waltz, 'The Origins of War in Neorealist Theory', *Journal of Interdisciplinary History* 18, no. 4 (1988): 616; reprinted in Robert I. Rotberg and Theodore K. Rabb, *The Origin and Prevention of Major Wars* (Cambridge; New York, NY: Cambridge University Press, 1988), 40.
47. Waltz, *Theory of International Politics*, 74.
48. Ibid., 90.
49. Ibid., 91.
50. Ibid., 74.
51. Kenneth N. Waltz, 'Reflections on Theory of International Politics: A Response to My Critics', in *Neorealism and Its Critics*, ed. Robert Keohane (New York, NY: Columbia University Press, 1986), 322–345, here 343.
52. Kenneth Waltz, 'Evaluating Theories', *American Political Science Review* 91, no. 4 (1997): 915, cited in Siegfried Schieder and Manuela Spindler, *Theories of International Relations* (Abingdon; Oxon; New York, NY: Routledge, 2014), 43.
53. Waltz, *Theory of International Politics*, 118–119.
54. Ibid., 119.
55. Ibid., 121.
56. Ibid., 15.
57. Ibid., 131.
58. Ibid., 183.
59. Kenneth N. Waltz, *Realism and International Politics* (New York, NY: Routledge, 2008; a comprehensive collection of Kenneth Waltz's major articles), 73–74.
60. Miroslav Nincic and Joseph Lepgold, *Being Useful: Policy Relevance and International Relations Theory* (Ann Arbor, MI: University of Michigan Press, 2000), 270.

CHAPTER

6

Strategic Realism and Offensive Realism

CHAPTER OUTLINE

SCHELLING: STRATEGIC REALISM

Introduction

Strategic realism is associated with the name Thomas Crombie Schelling (1921–2016). From material context, it is a product of the Cold War, compelling Ned Lebow to offer justifications to his readers why he discusses Schelling, 'when there is no longer a Berlin Wall, Cold War or Soviet Union'. From the perspective of disciplinary evolution, it appeared at a time when the behaviouralist revolution, with its quest for a positivist social science of IR, was transforming realist approaches.

Schelling abjured normative analysis as Waltz did. Instead, he focused on the instrumental aspects of foreign policy diplomacy. So '[i]f Hans Morgenthau expounded the fundamental tenets of realism and described its principal strategies, Thomas Schelling theorized its tactics'.[1]

Oeuvre

Schelling has authored many books, some of them quite recently.[2] *SOC* was replete with concepts and ideas prized by contemporary IR literature, like 'commitment strategies, tacit bargaining, strategic interaction, randomized behaviour, agenda setting, threats, promises, secrecy and revelation', and 'non-zero-sum games'. Although Schelling's greatest impact is in the area of international security, his influence spilled over into IPE through his book *International Economics* (1958). *CAC* (1984) threw light on game theory, strategic analysis, the strategy of inflicting costs and nuclear terrorism, among others.[3] 'DOV' expatiated on the extremely important concept of 'coercive diplomacy'. *SOCAOE* talks on subjects as diverse as global warming, cigarette smoking, rationality, prices and warfare. A realist, he got a peace medal, Award for Behavioral Research Relevant to the Prevention of Nuclear War in 1993, and the Nobel Prize in Economics for creative application of game theory in 2005. *SOC* is praised by Myerson as 'a masterpiece...one of the most important and influential books in [the] history of social science', since 'in just the first three chapters, Schelling introduced enough ideas to revolutionize social theory'.[4] I start reading it for my readers.

The first chapter, 'The Retarded Science of International Strategy', offers 'a new theory of interdependent decisions to provide a framework for analysing problems of conflict and deterrence'. Schelling distinguishes theories 'that treat conflict as a pathological state and seek its causes and treatment' from theories 'that take conflict for granted and study the behaviour associated with it'. He further subdivides the second type between those 'that examine the participants in all their complexity' with an eye to 'both "rational" and "irrational" behaviour, conscious and unconscious, and to motivations as well as calculations' and 'those that focus on the more rational, conscious and artful behaviour'. Choosing the latter kind in the second type of theories, treating 'conflict as a kind of contest, in which the participants are trying to "win"', he reserves the name of 'the *strategy* of conflict' for it. For he seeks to study 'conscious, intelligent, sophisticated conflict behaviour' to find 'rules of "correct" behaviour in a contest-winning sense'. Avowedly, Schelling takes the word from game theory.[5]

Chapter 2 of *SOC* 'An Essay on Bargaining', introduces the 'tactical approach to bargaining' both 'explicit' and 'tacit', 'in which adversaries watch and interpret each other's behaviour, each aware that his/her actions are being interpreted and anticipated, each acting with a view to the expectations he/she creates'. Leaving theoretically unproductive bargaining that seeks 'mutually profitable adjustments', Schelling concentrates on 'the "distributional" aspect of bargaining', highlighted in situations in which a better bargain for one entails a loss for the other; situations in which each party is driven by his/her expectations of what the other will concede, expectations which are inevitably 'compounded' until a deal is struck when one party 'makes a final, sufficient concession', in his/her perception that the other will not accept anything less. So a 'range of alternative outcomes' emerges 'in which any point is better for both sides than no agreement at all' (the 'saddle point' or 'equilibrium point', to be discussed in **Chapter 11**). Any party which considers any of these points is engaging in 'pure bargaining' and would be ready to 'recede' if the needs of the agreement make this important. Since all parties know the limits of this range, 'any outcome is a point from which at least one party would have been ready to retreat, which the other party knows. So even the saddle point affords 'no resting place'.[6]

This chapter draws attention to a particular type of tactic that is most 'appropriate to the logic of indeterminate situations', which has timeless importance for all international bargainers and negotiators. A few peculiarities of these tactics provide extremely important insights for realism since:

- These tactics presuppose 'some voluntary but irreversible sacrifice of freedom of choice', demanded by 'the paradox that power to constrain an adversary may depend on the power to bind oneself...to capitulate'.
- The concepts of 'bargaining power', 'bargaining strength' or 'bargaining skill' never suggest that advantages in bargaining go to 'the powerful, the strong or the skilful', except when taken tautologically as meaning that 'negotiations are won by those who win'. But if greater intelligence, debating skills, material resources, physical might, military capability or 'ability to withstand losses' are deemed to always provide more advantages in bargaining, then they do a 'disservice'. For rather than being universal assets in bargaining situations, they can be liabilities.
- The accomplished negotiator can seldom share the irrationality and pre-commitment of a 'truly obstinate man' due to the uneasy implications of irrationality and pre-commitment for decision-making discussed in **Chapter 11,** along with gaming models such as chicken and prisoner's dilemma (PD). For Schelling, in the field of international bargaining, even 'the threat of mutual destruction' is useless for deterring 'an adversary who is too foolish to appreciate it' or 'too weak to enforce his/her will on those he/she represents'.
- Bargaining power is not always helped by the capacity to fool and bluff. For bluffing has types where the bluffer may get away by distorting or misrepresenting facts like when lying about his/her resources or condition and types where bluffing alone does not suffice and is purely tactical. Situations where each bargainer 'knows everything about the other and each knows what the other knows' allow no scope of fooling anyone. When the buyer sticks to a price fully knowing that he/she may have to pay more, and the seller capitulates, we cannot decide if he/she was 'fooled' or 'convinced of the truth', not knowing if the buyer really knew 'what he/she would do next if the tactic failed'. Despite all bragging by the buyer after the bargain is struck, the resultant situation 'is not adequately conveyed by the notions of bluffing and fooling'.
- The situation's dynamics is rather revealed by Schelling's suggestion that the success of the buyer will depend on the extent to which he/she makes his/her 'reservation price' seemingly 'true' or credible, and also on commitments, in a situation where not knowing the other's reservation price, each party makes frantic efforts to gauge the other's mind and mystify his/her

> own as in normal bargaining. The ensuing 'process of creating and discovering commitments' irrevocably alter the "true" reservation prices'. The difference in commitments explains the difference in one's 'asserting' and the other's matching of the reservation price. *Extending this insight to international politics*, Schelling argues that in negotiations with other governments on subjects like desirable uses of 'foreign assistance' or 'tariff reduction', the government had better prefer Congressional surveillance to decisions by the executive branch. For where the executive branch enjoys such freedom, 'it may be unable to make any position stick'. But where executive leeway is 'constrained by law', making it fairly obvious that Congress would not be called to session to alter that law within the time period of the negotiations, the firm position of the executive branch will be credible to its negotiating partners. This is why in complex bargaining situations, national negotiators frequently take to 'issuing public statements', designed to manufacture a public opinion that precludes further concessions.

With these examples and insights, Schelling establishes that firmness in bargaining depends not on commitments incurred but on 'communicating it persuasively to the other party'.[7]

Chapter 3 speaks about 'tacit bargaining—bargaining in which communication is incomplete or impossible' in vastly different situations, including 'limited war, jurisdictional manoeuvres and jockeying in a traffic jam'. The goal is to develop a 'modus vivendi' for bargaining in situations where 'one or both the parties either cannot or will not negotiate explicitly or when neither would trust the other in respect of any agreement explicitly reached', be they of common interest or 'situations where their interests are divergent'. Analysing *nine such situations of tacit bargaining under common interests*, Schelling ventures that people may concert their intentions or expectations with others 'if each knows that the other is trying to do the same'. So most of these situations instantiate 'coordinating behaviour', where the key or the solution is provided by 'imagination more than logic', by 'analogy, precedent, accidental arrangement, symmetry, aesthetic or geometric configuration, casuistic reasoning, and who the parties are or what they know about each other'. *For situations of divergent interests*, Schelling gives eight further examples of tacit bargaining to show that everywhere 'the outcome is determined by something fairly arbitrary' and unfair, either from the participants' or the observers' points of view. Still the clinching factor in all these cases pertained to 'coordination for a common gain', even amidst 'rivalry among alternative lines of common action' and within the available choices a single or a few showed the potential of a 'coordinator'.[8]

The concept of coordination developed to explain tacit bargaining applies to situations of 'explicit bargaining' also. Although in the presence of verbal communication or exchange and external clues or links that impacted outcomes, the need of 'intuitive rapport' decreases, still factors of coordination remain influential, as is evident in monetary bargains of high values where the final agreement is frequently precipitated by an agreement to 'split the difference', and the difference is non-trivial. Even more illustrative is the remarkable frequency with which protracted negotiations over 'complicated quantitative formulas or *ad hoc* shares in some costs or benefits' suddenly concur on such mundane solutions as 'equal shares', commensurate with common magnitudes, say of gross national product (GNP), population and so on, inexplicably dominated by reference to precedents (whether in the settlement of a strike or of 'international debt', return to *status quo ante* or 'natural boundaries' and so on). In other bargaining situations, precedents even sometimes 'seem to reduce the scope of bargaining skill' in the 'configuration of the problem itself' and the location of the 'focal point' in it. Through these examples Schelling establishes the point that even explicit bargaining needs some coordination of participants' expectations for an ultimate agreement, within 'some range of possible outcomes within which each party would rather make a concession than fail to reach agreement at all'. Such being the case, no analysis of explicit bargaining can do without the communication inherent in bargaining situations that pertain to 'the signals' that the participants decipher in the intangibles of the case.

The logical corollaries of these considerations are that: (a) instead of being 'thoroughly separate concepts', both tacit and explicit bargaining demonstrate ascension from minimal, incomplete, faulty or limited communication to full communication, all of which betoken some 'dependence on the need to coordinate expectations', because of the participants' dependence on and awareness of their shared 'inability to keep their eyes off certain outcomes'; and (b) even though the focal points of bargaining in a situation where speech is allowed would differ from where it is not, 'what may be the *main* principle in tacit bargaining apparently may be *one* of the important principles in explicit bargaining'.[9] The insight from 'this line of analysis' is that 'it is possible to find limits to war—real war, jurisdictional war or whatever—without overt negotiation'. For example, war was 'limited in Korea and gas was not used in the Second World War'.[10] I can add that nuclear weapons have not been used in any theatre of war after 1945, including in the Indo-Pak frontier.

There is a large body of literature, comprising Schelling's own writings in *SOC*,[11] and other writings,[12] and of other scholars[13] on how Schelling has reoriented game theory in his study of interdependent decisions and conflict, which I exclude here to avoid repetition with **Chapter 11**.

Predictably for a tactical theoretician of realism, Schelling devotes attention to foreign policy decision-making, particularly questions of diplomacy, bargaining, force, threat, coercion, warfare, 'hurting' and so on. *AAI* (1966) has a total of seven chapters: 'The Diplomacy of Violence' (Chapter 1), 'The Art of Commitment' (Chapter 2), 'The Manipulation of Risk' (Chapter 3), 'The Idiom of Military Action' (Chapter 4), 'The Diplomacy of Ultimate Survival' (Chapter 5), 'The Diplomacy of Mutual Alarm' (Chapter 6) and 'The Dialogue of Competitive Armament' (Chapter 7) as themes and chapter names.[14] Because of space constraints and thrust of the present discussion, we focus on diplomacy of violence which brings out his thought on diplomacy as the cornerstone of foreign policy.

For Schelling, the distinction between diplomacy and force lies not in the replacement of bullets by words but in 'the relations between adversaries', transformed by 'the interplay of motives and the role of communication, understandings, compromise and restraint'. Being essentially bargaining, diplomacy aims at outcomes that are not being 'ideal for either party', is still preferred to some other alternatives. For, here each party partly limits what the other seeks. That is done more through 'compromise, exchange and collaboration' than through arrogating things by disregarding the other's wishes. The bargaining may be impolite, combine threats with offers, uphold a status quo, disregard rights or privileges of the other, be among friends or antagonists, and rooted in mistrust rather than trust, the only condition being, 'there must be some common interest, if only in the mutual avoidance of damage, and an awareness of the need to make the other prefer an outcome acceptable to oneself'.[15]

For Schelling, 'common interest' as basis of diplomacy is the fountainhead of some rules of the game that the states obey in common, thereby making diplomacy and the foreign policy it supports a 'rational instrumental activity'. This facilitates employment of 'a form of logical analysis' in the shape of game theory,[16] where concepts of force, hurt, coercion, threat, warfare and so on operate at different levels of depth. Force is to diplomacy what scarcity, and its opposite plenty, is to economics. Just as plenty all around would leave no scope for economics, so 'enough military force all around'—where a country can have and keep all 'by sheer strength, skill and ingenuity', and that too 'forcibly, accommodating only to the opposing strength, skill, ingenuity'—would leave no space for bargaining. Echoing the political theoretic distinction between power and authority, Schelling distinguishes brute force from coercion, because force is successful only when *used*, 'whereas the power to hurt' best succeeds when *kept in reserve*. The threat of increasing damage and 'latent violence' elicits compliance better than actual damage. So to acquire the 'capacity to hurt' and inflict damage, the intender needs to know what it is that the adversary/opponent prizes and fears the most and needs to signal to him/her what kind of behaviour on his/her part might attract violence and what other kind would keep it 'withheld'. Likewise, the targeted country has to know what is wanted of it and what is not. In his psychology of coercion, Schelling argues that even coercion by threat or damage requires that the interests of the countries inflicting and receiving it are not drastically opposed. Where one country's pain is the source of the other's rapture, and its satisfaction is the 'greatest woe', coercive diplomacy has little scope. After proposing that the difference between brute force and coercion may lie 'as often in the intent as in the instrument', Schelling illustrates their difference with two historical examples, the first provided by the Texas–Comanche or Texas–Indian Wars between 1820 and 1875, and the second by the strategy of Genghis Khan. In the first, hunting down Comanches and exterminating them exemplified brute force, but raiding their villages 'to make them behave was coercive diplomacy, based on the power to hurt'. In the second, Genghis Khan discarded his earlier strategy of killing everyone from the vanquished enemy, which was brute force, later in favour of 'forcing captives—women, children, aged fathers, favourite sons—to march ahead of his army as the first potential victims of resistance', an example of coercive diplomacy.

With these insights into bargaining and coercive diplomacy, Schelling looks at modern warfare as the site of coercive violence, exemplifying the 'distinction between the power to hurt and the power to seize or hold forcibly'. Presently, especially after the advent of nuclear weapons, rather than the amount of military strength, the 'power to hurt' has been the most important criterion of military capabilities. It has turned war into less 'a contest of strength' than 'one of endurance, nerve, obstinacy and pain'; less 'a contest of military strength' than a 'bargaining process—dirty, extortionate and often quite reluctant bargaining on one side or both'. The difference is more fundamental than one between 'the *use* and *threat* of force'. The actions entailed by accomplishing something forcibly and by 'fulfilling a threat' can be considerably dissimilar, since occasionally 'the most effective direct action causes enough pain or cost on the enemy, sometimes not'. So Schelling considers unproductive the contemporary US threat of near complete annihilation of the society and population of the Soviet Union if it initiated a surprise attack on the US, because 'the threat is to do it all afterward anyway'. Tracking down and liquidating the enemy's entire military force to inflict a crushing defeat on enemy armies may have been 'the avowed purpose and the central aim of American strategy in both the World Wars', but it saw military action as an *alternative* to bargaining, not a *process* of bargaining'.

According to Schelling, the reason states adopted 'counterforce' strategy (of targeting enemies' forces, sparing their cities) was not that the countries had become 'civilized' and 'averse to hurting people' or that they chose pure military wars. Had it been so, they would not have resorted to 'blockade' or 'strategic bombing of homelands'. The simple reason why hurting people was not the primary aim of wars may have been that 'the technology and geography of war, at least for a war between anything like equal powers during the century ending in the Second World War, kept coercive violence from being decisive before military victory was achieved'.

What is the difference in language of coercion after the invention of nuclear bombs? It lies not in the number of people they can exterminate 'but in the speed with which it can be done in the centralization of decision, in the divorce of war from political processes,...in computerized programs that threaten to take the war out of human bonds once it begins' and in their capacity 'to compress the fury of global wars into a few hours'. Another epoch-making difference of wars fought with nuclear weapons would be that for the first time in history victors alone would not be able to do what they want with the enemy. For doing 'monstrous violence to the enemy without first achieving victory' would be conceivable for both. But one problem with nuclear weapons is that though capable of hurting the enemy 'decisively enough to make the military engagement academic', it is probably 'all they can do' in a major war. This vital point is missed because nuclear war 'is often discussed as though it will be a contest in national destruction'. But if, with nuclear weapons, annihilation of places and their populations becomes the central object of war, then it will mean that 'the sequence of war has been reversed'. For, in place of liquidation of the enemy's forces as a prerequisite of 'imposing one's will on the enemy nation', the only course available would be destroying the nation preparatory to destroying the enemy forces. The victor does not even have the choice of 'sparing the conquered nation'. So the change introduced by nuclear weapons in warfare lies not just in the achievable amount of destruction but also in the 'role of destruction and in the decision process'. Besides changing the speed, control and sequence of events, nuclear weapons can also alter 'the relation of the victor to the vanquished, and the relation of homeland to the fighting front'. It makes deterrence contingent on the 'threat of pain and extinction, not just on the threat of military defeat'.

To bring out the significance of hurting as a means of coercion, Schelling takes us from the 'battlefield of warfare to the diplomacy of violence' and shows the changing status of hurting in war in the special context of non-combatants in wars who, in spite of the founding of the Red Cross in 1863, have remained prime subjects of war since the Second World War till now. Unless we attribute it to 'a depravity peculiar to the 20th century', we have to look at the changes in the nature of war in Europe for 300 years. In the first stage, stretching from the Westphalia treaty to the Napoleonic era, when wars were affairs of monarchies, fought with mercenary armies for closely defined territorial, monetary and dynastic aims, hurting people was not a desirable strategy, since hurting people and destroying property only decreased the value of potential gains or spoils. Besides, warring monarchs often shared more non-material things with each other than with their subjects and, therefore, hated discrediting the social institutions of their opponents and circumventing them to take the war directly to their people, because of its potential disruptive implications. The position changed in the Napoleonic wars because in a situation of national mobilization and people's concern with and for the outcome of the war, the relationship of the people to the war changed from that of passive fearful onlookers to active participants in direct and even indirect ways. So non-combatants lost their right to immunity. The post-Second World War third stage has changed this relationship of the people to war even more, resulting in a new equation between 'civilian violence and warfare'. If because of great improvements in nuclear and conventional weapons, enough pain and damage can be caused to the enemy during the war itself, then there is no need to 'wait for the surrender negotiations that follow a military decision'. In this situation, it is less 'victory' than 'the influence that resides in latent force', 'the bargaining power that comes from the capacity to hurt', that a democratic nation wants from its armed forces. Schelling warns that the third stage can be experienced in two vastly different manifestations. In the first, 'sheer pain and damage are primary instruments of coercive warfare and may actually be applied to intimidate or deter', while in the second, 'pain and destruction in war are expected to serve little or no purpose but prior threats of sheer violence, even of automatic and uncontrolled violence....'[17]

Evaluation

This is a clear-headed, even if amoral, explication of strategic realism. It is strategic but not offensive in its version of 'limited war', where application of military force should rest on countries' tacit understanding or each other's war aims; its warning that the 'danger to all-out war is almost certainly increased by the occurrence of a limited war'[18]; its difficulty 'to imagine that the tacit agreement that nuclear weapons would be as powerfully present on the occasion of the next limited war after they have already been used in one'.[19] Schelling praised the 'attitude, or convention or tradition that took root and grew over the past six decades', since the time of John Foster Dulles, which continued to obey the 'taboo' he attached to nuclear weapons, even after it became possible after the end of the Eisenhower administration to make 'little' nuclear weapons, 'as an asset to be treasured', and what policies would 'preserve this inhibition' a fit subject for research.[20]

Zeckhauser pointed out that 'Schelling's lessons about tacit communication are more important than the simple scenarios...he uses to capture their essence', since the USA and the USSR 'regularly engage in such communication, for example, in determining the meaning of "glasnost"'. His lasting message is that 'in any interactive situation it is vitally important to look at matters from the side of the other party', from what Zeckhauser calls the 'other-people's-shoes approach'. To underscore the importance of Schelling in realism as theory, we are tempted to quote another utterance of Zeckhauser the full import of which you will understand when we come to game theory: 'Even a genius such as Clausewitz did not clearly perceive the non-zero-sum nature of war, the fundamental property around which Schelling builds his models of cooperation and conflict—the yin and yang of most interactive situations'.[21]

We now turn from Strategic to offensive realism (John Mearsheimer).

MEARSHEIMER: OFFENSIVE REALISM OR NEOREALIST STABILITY

Theoretical/Practical Context: Benefits of Cold War Bipolarity

John J. Mearsheimer's offensive realism arose from his reaction, along with scholars like Schelling and John Gaddis, to popular beliefs about the Cold War and its deleterious consequences for international politics. For his thoughts in this regard, we will read his article 'BTTF I'; iconic book *TTOGPP*; his other writings, particularly his correspondences relating to 'BTTF I' with Stanley Hoffmann and Robert Keohane, in 'BTTF II'; and correspondences with Bruce M. Russett and Thomas Risse-Kappen in 'BTTF III'.[22]

We have already shown in **Chapter 5** how Waltz viewed the bipolar concentration of power during the Cold War as a better insurer of international stability. Schelling, master strategist, took the Cold War as 'a game that had to be played right the first time'; advised America's foremost foreign policy and military strategists present at Camp David during the height of the Berlin Crisis in September 1961 from his academic lair at Harvard as 'one of the Cold War intellectuals at Rand, the Air Force's research arm; and used game theory to dissect the possibility of an event no one had experienced: thermonuclear war'.[23] He could not be a denouncer of the Cold War bipolarity. But Gaddis explicitly recognized it as a harbinger of peace and stability in war-torn Europe since it: (a) 'realistically' depicted the facts relating to the residence of power at the end of the Second World War; (b) simplified the resultant structure of international politics, obviating the need of 'sophisticated leadership to maintain' it; and (c) in consequence of this simplicity of structure, rendered alliances in the bipolar system proved more durable than any in the 19th century or in the 20 years between 1919 and 1939, thereby making NATO more long-lasting than pre-World War alliances.[24] And the Cold War, supposedly 'the most dangerous, bitter and protracted rivalry between great powers in modern history, did in time become the most protracted period of freedom from great power war in modern history'. Howsoever one might disapprove of 'the means by which this happened', and 'the way it happened', the stark fact remained that 'the Cold War did evolve into a long peace'.[25]

Dystopia about a Post-Cold War World

Mearsheimer joined this tradition of the Cold War apologists to point to the absence of great power war between 1945 and 1990 and prognosticate a far less stable situation if the Cold War came to an end, and the two superpowers, especially the USA, withdrew from Western and Central Europe. Trashing the expressions of optimism surrounding the imminent end of the Cold War, he disagreed that the 'profound changes now underway in Europe' would usher in 'a new age of peace' with the lifting of 'the threat of war that has hung over Europe for more than four decades'; harmony would reign among the states and peoples of Europe; and military bases of 'Central Europe, which long groaned under the massive forces of the two military blocs', would convert into industrial parks, playgrounds and condominiums'; enabling theorists of security to shift their gazes from 'military doctrine and balance assessments' to 'finding ways to prevent global warming and preserve the ozone layer' and European leaders to contemplate how to spend peace dividends'.[26]

Against this rosy picture of a peaceful post-Cold War world, Mearsheimer conjures up a situation where Soviet Union has withdrawn 'all of its forces from Eastern Europe, leaving the states in that region fully independent'; this has generated vocal academic and popular demands in the USA, Britain and Germany for withdrawal of all their military forces in Germany, since they 'have lost their principal raison d'être', as a result of which NATO and the Warsaw Pact would have to 'dissolve', and even if alive on paper, cease to function as an alliance; and 'the bipolar structure that has characterized Europe since the end of the Second World War is replaced by a multipolar structure'. Mearsheimer contends that 'the prospects for major crises and war in Europe are likely to increase markedly if the Cold War ends and this scenario unfolds. The next decades in a Europe without the superpowers would probably not be as violent as the first 45 years of this century but would probably be substantially more prone to violence than the past 45 years'.

Mearsheimer's reason behind this dystopian prediction is that the Cold War preserved peace and its disappearance would exacerbate chances of war. From his central argument that 'the distribution and character of military power are the root causes of war and peace', he posits that the unwarlike situation in Europe since 1945 was an offshoot of three interrelated factors: 'the bipolar distribution of military power on the continent; the rough military equality between the two states comprising the two poles in Europe, the United States and the Soviet Union; and the fact that each superpower was armed with a large nuclear arsenal'. Domestic peace preservers, like the decline of that hyper-nationalism since 1945 which also facilitated the two World Wars, are of secondary importance to 'factors of military power' which were of primary causal importance in 'shaping past events' and will remain so in the future. The exit of the superpower would return Europe to a new multipolarity, where besides the old giants of Germany, France, Britain and the Soviet Union (a major power, even after clipping of its superpower status), Italy might emerge as a new major player. The resultant multipolar system of 'five major powers and a number of lesser powers' would be heir to all the problems of such systems, including proneness to power iniquities and instability. Moreover, since the exit of the superpowers would be accompanied by the removal of 'the large nuclear arsenals they now maintain in Central Europe', thereby depriving Europe of 'the pacifying effect that these weapons exercised on her politics', this could set in motion four alternative scenarios: (a) Europe would become denuclearized, thereby 'eliminating a central pillar of order in the Cold War era'; (b) the European states might not widen their stockpiles enough to make up for the nuclear denudation caused by the exit of the superpowers' weapons; (c) nuclear proliferation would continue, but in a more or less mismanaged manner, where appropriate steps have not been taken to control the numerous built-in dangers of the proliferation process; and (d) nuclear proliferation will continue in Europe but under the surveillance of the existing nuclear powers who would institute all safeguards that would 'deter preventive strikes on emerging nuclear powers...set boundaries on the proliferation process by extending security umbrellas over the neighbours of emerging nuclear powers... help emerging nuclear powers build secure deterrent forces, and...discourage them from deploying counterforce systems that threaten their neighbours' deterrents'. This was the least dangerous of the storylines and the best provider of hope for maintenance of the long peace in Europe, though slightly more dangerous than the 1945–1990 period. But Mearsheimer considered hopes of such efficient management as remote.

While unfolding this pessimistic array of possible post-Cold War futures, Mearsheimer rubbishes the three standard countervailing arguments against them: (a) that 'the peace will be preserved by the effects of the liberal international economic order that has evolved since the Second World War'; (b) that since the already extensive spread of democracy in Europe, including 'the ongoing democratization of Eastern Europe' has secured the bases of peace, wars would definitely be less likely; (c) that the historical learning of the Europeans from past experiences of the century teaches them that wars, whether fought with conventional or nuclear weapons are destined to be so costly that they should be avoided at all costs. But Mearsheimer thinks that just as the theoretical underpinnings of these arguments are amiss, their predictions are also 'flawed'. Being so, the appropriate policy responses of the USA to the new situation should be threefold: (a) to 'encourage a process of limited nuclear proliferation in Europe' and allow only Germany to acquire nuclear weapons, since 'Europe will be more stable if Germany acquires a secure nuclear deterrent', but to permit no one else; (b) not to 'withdraw fully from Europe, even if the Soviet Union pulls its forces out of Eastern Europe'; and (c) to 'take steps to forestall the re-emergence of hyper-nationalism in Europe'.[27]

Superiority of Bipolarity: Deductions and Empirical Evidence

If these policy prescriptions were premised in the proposition that the long peace was a result of the Cold War bipolarity backed by nuclear weapons, to become precarious after the Cold War, the theoretical task was to identify what theories best explain the period of violence before the Cold War and the 45-year peace after it, and what other theories, even when deficient in explaining these two periods, would still be more adept at prognosticating what might happen to a Europe unprotected by Soviet and American military presence.[28] True to his realist upbringing, Mearsheimer brings in the anarchy assumption in IR and the compulsions it imposes on state behaviour to support the three interrelated factors that imported peace in Europe and the theories that undergird them and to posit that the resultant 'competitive world is peaceful' only when 'it is obvious that the costs and risks of going to war are high' compared to the benefits. The 'two aspects of military power' that inform this 'incentive structure' are 'the nature of the military power available to them' and their 'distribution', which again 'is a function of the number of poles in the system and their relative power', since these directly determine 'the costs, risks, and benefits of going to war'. The potential belligerents will take into reckoning factors like whether 'the military weaponry available guarantees that warfare will be very destructive' or whether 'available weaponry favours the defence over the offence' and 'tends to equalize the relative power of states'. If the answers to these queries are affirmative, they will be deterred and discouraged. Additionally, if available 'military weaponry makes it easier to estimate the relative power of state', wars born of unjustified optimism or gross miscalculation will be unlikely. All these make bipolarity a better distribution of power for three reasons: (a) 'the number of conflict dyads is fewer, leaving fewer possibilities for war'; (b) deterrence is more easily achieved, since 'imbalances of power are fewer and more easily averted'; and (c) 'prospects for deterrence are greater because miscalculations of relative power and of opponents' resolve are fewer and less likely'. That is why the bipolar system dominated by two powers is a better candidate. For here minor and lesser powers not only 'find it difficult to remain unattached to one of the major powers' but 'have little opportunity to play the major powers off against each other'. In contradistinction to it, in a multipolar system dominated by three or more, minor powers have much broader leeway regarding alliance partners and can afford to be 'free-floaters'. Contrasted with a single-dyad bipolar system, in a multipolar system of numerous dyads, major power dyads are not only more numerous but the potential conflict situations outnumber them, since conflicts can occur between both major and minor powers of major dyads, and dyads of minor players. Although wars would be less encompassing and devastating, even local wars can escalate into major and systemic ones. Besides, deterrence is also more difficult, since 'power imbalances are commonplace, and these are generative of conflict in two directions: when two states 'gang up to attack a third state' and when through its 'superior strength' a major power simply bullies a weaker one in 'a one-on-one encounter, pushing it into a corner. BOP dynamic can sometimes counter such imbalances, but not always, whether because of problems of geographical non-contiguity or insurmountable coordination. War can break out 'when a state underestimates the willingness of an opposing state to stand firm on issues of difference', such miscalculations being endemic under multipolarity, not only because 'the shape of the international order tends to remain fluid, due to the tendency of coalitions to shift', but also because they lead to constant changes in 'the international "rules of the road"—norms of state behaviour and agreed divisions of territorial rights and other privileges'. Wars are also probable when states miscalculate the relative power of an opposing coalition, from underestimating the number of states who will oppose them or exaggerating the number of allies. On all these counts, bipolar system is according to Mearsheimer superior to a multipolar system.

Mearsheimer admits the absence of empirical studies adducing irrefutable evidence regarding effects of bipolarity and multipolarity on chances of war. For different forms of multipolarity were witnessed in Europe between 1648 and 1945, but instances of bipolarity before the period 1945–1990 are scarce, sketchy and incomplete, save instances of Athens and Sparta, and Rome and Carthage. So he uses certain deductions for pointing out their relative merits to compensate for lack of empirical demonstration. Since the polarity of an international system and the degree of power equality in it are causally related, 'bipolar systems tend more toward equality, because...states are then compelled to balance by internal methods, and internal balancing is more efficient than external balancing'.[29] The differing stabilizing potentials of internal balancing (meaning balancing by reliance on other members of the respective bloc) and external balancing (signifying balancing by roping in powers outside the bloc)—their difference dramatized by George Canning's famous boast in 1826 in the British Parliament, to have 'called the New World into existence, to redress the balance of the Old'[30]—makes bipolarity superior to multipolarity, despite not being tension free. In a bipolar system, the number-two state might resort to 'mobilizing its own resources to reduce the gap' from the leader, lacking potential major alliance partners. Contrarily, in a multipolar system, the second strongest state can seek security through alliances with others, instead of building up its own strength. While attractive, being 'cheap and fast', the demerit of external balancing is that it 'leaves intact the power gap between the two leading states, and thus leaves in place the dangers that such a power gap creates', while bipolarity brings 'greater tendency for its poles to be equal'.

So the virtues of power equality are better preserved under bipolarity, as are those of nuclear deterrence since deterrence works best when 'the costs or risks or war' are not only excessively high but 'conquest is most difficult'. On both counts, nuclear weapons are better guarantors of peace. Since as 'weapons of mass destruction', particularly under scenarios of mutually assured destruction (MAD), they make conquest more unthinkable, 'international conflicts revert from tests of capability and will to purer tests of will, won by the side willing to run greater risks and pay greater costs'. Besides, MAD-like situations support peace not only by 'moving power relations among states towards equality' but also by 'clarifying the relative power of states and coalitions'. Furthermore, nuclear bipolarity reduces the virulence of 'hyper-nationalism', a very important cause of war. Although of second-order importance, being 'domestic', 'its causes lie in the international system'; and nuclear bipolarity is not congenial for it, as 'hyper-nationalism is least likely when states can rely on small professional armies or on complex high-technology military organizations that do not require vast manpower'.[31]

After these deductive system-wide comparisons, all favouring nuclear bipolarity, Mearsheimer embarks upon the empirical evidence of their contribution to the long peace, beyond the high positive correlation between 'bipolarity, equality of military power and nuclear weapons, on the one hand, and the long peace, on the other'. While this high correlation testifies to the validity of 'the bipolarity theory, the equality theory and the nuclear theory of the long peace', empirical evidence is needed to eliminate other factors, or what prefer to call, 'free variables', that might have influenced this outcome. Aware that 'correlation alone does not prove causation', he points to the dangers of multipolarity and their effects on European peace before the onset of the Cold War. The picture was messy even before the First World War: intensified interactions among the five major powers of Britain, France, Russia, Austria-Hungary and Germany, and the two minor powers of Serbia and Belgium; as also minimally the 'six significant adversarial relationships' they generated, between Germany versus Britain, France, Russia, and Belgium on the one hand, and Austria-Hungary versus Serbia and Russia on the other. Likewise, before the Second World War interactions among the five great powers of Britain, France, the Soviet Union, Germany and Italy and seven lesser powers of Belgium, Poland, Czechoslovakia, Austria, Hungary, Romania and Finland generated at least 13 important conflicts. These pitted Germany against Britain, France, the Soviet Union, Czechoslovakia, Poland and Austria; Italy against Britain and France; the USSR against Finland and Poland; Czechoslovakia against Poland and Hungary; and Romania against Hungary. This welter of conflicts and the interconnections among the state interests at stake in each of them culminated into the Great War. The confusions born of this multiplicity of conflicts helped Germany to combine with others against some minor powers, with Poland and Hungary against Czechoslovakia and with the USSR against Poland. But whether because of geographic factors or 'buck passing', England before 1914 and the USSR, France and Britain, and even the USA, till the end before 1939 failed to balance efficiently against aggression and come to the aid of the victims. The messy scenario and its attendant miscalculations complicated the process of deterrence, partly owing to the superiority of German strength over her immediate neighbours. All these typified 'the risks that arise in a world of pure conventional deterrence in which weapons of mass destruction are absent'. Even German 'hyper-nationalism' and its resultant aggressiveness, though not unprecedented in European history, were a good example where domestic and international factors met. 'The policy of murder arose chiefly from domestic sources; the wars arose mainly from aspects of the distribution and character of power in Europe'.[32]

Against this shabby history of multipolarity for Europe's peace, Mearsheimer measures the report card of the Cold War bipolarity. All the three factors that were contributory for this bipolar shift assured peace in diverse ways: 'the near-complete destruction of German power, the growth of Soviet power and the permanent American commitment to the European Continent'. While Allied occupation divided and debilitated the German Reich, the Soviet Union extended westward, but unlike her predecessors without disturbing West Europe's peace by attempts to spread her hegemony. Mearsheimer traces this self-restraint of the USSR partly to bipolarity, nuclear weapons and the resolve of the USSR and the USA to eschew hyper-nationalism. Bipolarity helped reduce the axis of friction to the East–West conflict and facilitated: a neat division of spheres of influence, save the 'few unprotected weak states' in the East which the USSR was left to bully to submission; a tacit consensus 'on the division of rights in Austria, Berlin and elsewhere in Europe; a proscription on secret unilateral redeployment of large nuclear forces to areas contiguous to the opponent; mutual toleration of reconnaissance satellites; agreement on rules of peacetime engagement between naval forces; and so forth'. This emergence of norms of the game explains the rarity of superpower frictions between 1963 and 1990. Since bipolarity allowed the same two superpowers to be there for an extended period and know each one better, both knew how to understand and respect each other's interests and avoid conflicts with them. It left less scope for 'miscalculation of both resolve and capability' of the opposing coalitions in the context of the 'horrendous results' that an unwinnable nuclear war would produce, due to which none of the superpowers ever resorted to 'brandishing' nuclear weapons in any crisis. Additionally, nuclear weapons established a rough 'equality and clarity on the power relations between the superpowers' which effaced the 'sharp power inequalities and miscalculations of relative power' of the non-nuclear past. Finally, during the Cold War period, 'the locus of European politics shifted to the USA and the Soviet Union—two states that, each for its own reasons, had not exhibited nationalism of the virulent type found earlier in Europe'.[33]

Inadequate Theories of the Long Peace

To establish the sufficiency of his three theories of 'bipolarity, equality and nuclear weapons' in explaining the 45-year-long period of stable peace, Mearsheimer now takes on the three rival theories claiming to explain them too, namely 'economic liberalism', 'peace-loving democracies' and 'obsolescence of war'. Economic liberalism, which reposes faith in a liberal economic order as the bulwark of peace, is inapplicable because all through these 45 years economic exchange either between the Soviet Union and the West has been negligible, or that between Eastern and Western Europe has been only slightly better. Similarly, the peace-loving democracies position, which says democracies are averse to war against other democracies (though not against authoritarian states), is untenable since the Soviet Union and her allies never became liberal democracies. The third theory, the obsolescence of war position, that even the contemporary modes of conventional war had become so murderously destructive by the 20th century that it had been rationally absurd and morally reprehensible to wage it 'as a sensible means to achieve national goals', looks more persuasive than the other two, but is still problematic for many reasons. First, were it true, then the states and their elites or decision-makers would never have fought the Second World War after the First. Second, apart from failing to distinguish between unwinnable nuclear wars and winnable conventional wars, proponents of this theory do not realize that unlike the First World War, on the Western front, conventional wars need not always be prolonged and gory tests of attrition, endurance and nerve, but can sometimes be quickly won. And since conventional weapons, however advanced, are never as destructive and annihilative as nuclear weapons, conventional deterrence also is not as easy to implement as nuclear deterrence.[34]

The Best Theoretical Arrangements

Theorizing the future of peace in Europe after this comparison of pre-Cold War chaos and Cold War stability, against myopic optimists, Mearsheimer mulls over the best arrangements that would prevent the post-Cold War balkanization of Europe after the exit of the Soviets and Americans with their nuclear installations, and the dissolution of the Cold War order. He is sure that in the consequent multipolarity, Europe would experience the same uncertainties, miscalculations of capabilities and intentions, deterrence failures and nagging armed conflicts. Since 'distribution and deployment patterns of nuclear weapons in the new Europe are the least certain, and probably the most important, element of the new order', he visualizes the consequences of 'the four principal nuclear worlds that might develop: a denuclearized Europe, continuation of the current patterns of nuclear ownership, and nuclear proliferation either well or ill-managed'. He prefers most 'the limited, managed proliferation of nuclear weapons', as 'more dangerous than the current order, but considerably safer than 1900–1945'. The 'worst order' would be 'a non-nuclear Europe in which power inequities emerge between the principal poles of power...perhaps almost as dangerous as the world before 1945. Continuation of the current pattern, or mismanaged proliferation, would be worse than the world of today, but safer than the pre-1945 world'.

Mearsheimer places the problems of peace under these imaginary scenarios and critiques the three alternative theories—the obsolescence of war position, the peace-loving democracies position and the economic liberalism position—that foretell a peaceful situation in denuclearized post-Cold War. I have already given a glimpse of their weaknesses.[35] But his conclusions after these critiques startlingly show how realism can spin a web around itself and be shackled by it. Convinced that the collapse of the Cold War order would only increase the chances of war and major crises in Europe, he offers a 'straightforward, if paradoxical,' lesson from his theoretical engagement with the bipolar, nuclear-powered long peace of Europe:

> The West has an interest in maintaining peace in Europe. It therefore has an interest in maintaining the Cold War order, and hence has an interest in the continuation of the Cold War confrontation; developments that threaten to end it are dangerous...a complete end to the Cold War would create more problems than it would solve.[36]

Apparently paradoxically, but actually explicably, this interest of the West would also have to maintain the role of the Soviet Union as a prime balancer, even if it requires maintenance of East–West tension in prophylactic doses. For being the 'only superpower that can seriously threaten to overrun Europe', she supplies 'the glue that holds NATO together'. The moment the Soviet Union and the USA decide to exit from Europe, the bipolar order would cave in, returning Europe to her troubled pre-war days. To Mearsheimer, in a dramatic departure from the history of the late 1940s, 'the West paradoxically has an interest in the continued existence of a powerful Soviet Union with substantial military forces in Eastern Europe'. Muscle flexing by the Soviet Union is necessary because: (a) otherwise, the very idea of stationing large forces just to entice the Soviet Union into order-sustaining competition will appear crazy and ridiculous to Americans; (b) the 'idea of propping up a declining rival' goes against the basic instincts of states under anarchy assumptions and (c) even such a Manichean reversal of practice would not stop the Soviet Union, already leaving Eastern Europe and drastically pruning its military forces and presence because of its tottering economy, just because her arch-rival wants her to be there.

With a Soviet Union hell bent on exiting from Europe, what are Mearsheimer's policy recommendations for peace for a multipolar Europe? These are three: (a) the USA should approbate a limited and carefully managed nuclear proliferation in Europe, extending to Germany but ideally travelling no further; (b) Britain, the USA and the Continental states should 'balance actively and efficiently against any emerging aggressor to offset the ganging up and bullying problems' that characterized pre-war European politics and are sure to raise their heads in new multipolar Europe. In operational terms, this would mean that both insular England and extra-continental USA should station armies and military forces on the Continent, ready to deter potential aggressors and disturbers of the balance at the first instance. For gaining popular consent for such a strategy, they must 'sensitize "their publics" to the importance of this 'Continental commitment', however difficult the task might be; (c) the USA and Britain should make a coordinated effort to fend off hyper-nationalism, especially in Eastern Europe since, with 'deep roots' all over Europe, this potent factor was a prolific sub-systemic source of many past international conflicts'.[37]

Manifestations of Mearsheimer's Hard Core

This hard-core realist position stems from Mearsheimer's five basic realist assumptions about the international system, and state behaviour in it, best described in Chapter 2 of *TTOGPP*[38] and in an article,[39] wound around his central argument that great powers always seek opportunities to acquire power over their competitors. The first of these assumptions, that 'the international system is anarchic' echoes Waltz. The second views great powers as inherently possessing 'some offensive military capability, which gives them the wherewithal to hurt and possibly destroy each other', and accordingly being more dangerous than other states. The third thinks states are aggressive, being unsure whether 'another state will not use its offensive military capability to attack the first state' and never being certain about one another's intentions. This is no matter of 'hostile intentions', for even in a system of 'reliably benign' states, gauging their intentions with absolute certainty will be difficult, especially because in the presence of multiple intentions no state can be sure which one of them would motivate the potential aggressors. This uncertainty is related to the fourth assumption that 'survival is the primary goal of great powers' and to the fifth that 'great powers are rational actors'. At the end of these assumptions, Mearsheimer says in the next section about 'state behaviour' that it is driven by fear and by the absence of no one to turn to when attacked. To highlight the situation, he points to the problem of the absence of a 911 number in international politics.[40]

These assumptions and attendant state behaviours tell us nothing new except replacing the word 'powers' with 'great powers'. So where is 'structural realism' different? It is possibly in the answer to the question 'what causes great power war', that even though 'isolating a particular cause of all wars is not a fruitful enterprise, structural realists maintain that the likelihood of war is affected by the architecture of the international system'. Mearsheimer considers in turn theories offered by realists based on the 'polarity of the system', distribution of powers among the units in 'a balanced and imbalanced manner', 'dynamic of the balance of power' or 'balance shifts' in it and the 'offence–defence debate' as looked at by 'defensive realists'.[41] Since all these have been discussed in detail in 'BTTF I', I choose not to repeat them.

But what are the other aspects of his realist credentials? One is his amoral view on international politics. He seemed to justify the false claim of President Bush Jr to have declared war on Iraq because of President Saddam Hussein's alleged confirmation of the latter's possession of weapons of mass destruction, which was but subsequently nailed,[42] arguing that while lying is a 'reprehensible behaviour in ordinary life, it is accepted conduct in international politics because there are sometimes good strategic reasons for leaders to lie to other countries, and even to their own people'.[43] In a 'self-help world', where the 911 number is absent, states 'have to do whatever is necessary to provide their own security. If that means lying and cheating, so be it'. That is why, 'a leader who is discovered to have lied even to his/her public about a particular policy' gets away with 'it if it works' and does not have to pay much of a political price'. Through churning of the history of state interactions and the lies told by different leaders, Mearsheimer seeks to 'consider the benefits and costs of the various kinds of lies that statesmen and diplomats tell each other', differentiates between 'strategic lies and selfish lies'[44] and suggests that inter-state lying has systemic causes. It is 'the lack of trust between states', which 'explains in good part why there is lying between states'.[45]

It was as a staunch hardcore realist that Mearsheimer wrote about the military thought of Basil Henry Liddell Hart, English military historian and theorist (1895–1970),[46] as expressed in: (a) his post-First World War 'infantry tactics' and (b) his 'indirect approach...articulated between 1925 and 1931', mistakenly confused with Hitler's *blitzkrieg*, although formulated as 'an alternative to that armoured strategy' and his pleas about 'the superiority of defence in an armoured war'. Mearsheimer reassessed Hart's ideas, including his theorization about 'conventional war' in the age of nuclear parity and his excogitations on the policy debates of the 1930s concerning the 'grand strategy' and Britain's desirable position on the 'Continental commitment', as especially helpful to scholars debating the pros and cons of America's withdrawal of ground and tactical air forces from Europe and keeping only her navy stationed to ward off Soviet aggression.[47] It was natural because the new relevance of effective deterrence achievable by conventional forces during the mid-1980s was largely due to his 1983 book *Conventional Deterrence*. I mention all this to show Mearsheimer's over-reliance on the military dimension of power.

Mearsheimer has no doubts that his neorealist stability theory built around 'security competition and war among the great powers' will continue to hold its pre-eminence, in spite of disparagement by academicians and even American presidents (like Bill Clinton in 1992 and 1997). Since we still inhabit 'a nasty and brutish world' of great powers' competition, the only discordant voices against realism will come from inside the academia. Since the end of the Cold War, notwithstanding 'the basic structure of the international system remains largely unchanged', even from 1990 to the present, there is little reason to expect that state behaviour will differ much 'from what it was in the past centuries'. This was evidenced by two US wars since 1990, against Iraq in 1991 and in Kosovo in 1999. Outside the US, potential theatres of war that would prevent realism from being 'outmoded' are: South Asia with its Indo-Pak rivalry; the Persian Gulf, where Iraq (before America's successful 2003 invasion) and Iran 'were' nuclear power aspirants; and Africa where interstate conflicts have been on the ascendant after 1990. We already know what he has to say on Europe after the Cold War's end. So academia remains the only place where intense dislike or realism reigns.[48]

Predictably, this raucous realism leaves no room for liberal institutionalism in its scheme of things. For Mearsheimer, major IR theories that employ institutions as a core concept are 'liberal institutionalism', 'collective security' and 'critical theory'. He thinks institutions have a very negligible impact on the behaviour of states and for that reason 'holds little promise for promoting peace in the post-Cold War world'.[49] Policymakers are advised not to take them seriously, because they 'do not accurately describe the world' and 'policies based on them are bound to fail'. As a structuralist, he accepts that the 'international system strongly shapes the behaviour of states, limiting the amount of damage that false faith in institutional theories can cause'. However, despite the constraints imposed by the international system, states, especially great powers, 'will have considerable leeway'.[50]

CONCLUSION

From these two very brief renderings of Schelling's strategic realism and Mearsheimer's neorealist stability theory, both Cold War centred and smitten by belief in its contribution to the long peace, backed by the superpower's strategic use of nuclear weapons for deterrence, my readers will find that while Schelling's realism is grounded in a new theory of interdependent decisions based on tacit consent, Mearsheimer's realism is more great powers and weapons oriented. But just as Schelling propounded nuclear deterrence is a proponent of limited war, Mearsheimer also devoted attention to conventional deterrence. Both again were preoccupied with America's role in world politics during and after the Cold War. Now, we turn to **Chapter 7**, reserved for all 'internal' and 'external' critiques, where schools of realism will talk to each other and other schools of IR will talk with realism.

REVIEW QUESTIONS

1. Discuss Schelling's tactical approach to bargaining with special reference to tacit bargaining and the concept of coordination developed in the context of tacit bargaining.

2. Show how Schelling makes the concept of coordination applicable in both tacit and explicit bargaining.
3. Show how Schelling's insights into bargaining and coercive diplomacy help him theorize modern warfare as the site of coercive violence.
4. The *strategy of conflict* offers 'a new theory of interdependent decisions to provide a framework for analysing problems of conflict and deterrence'. Discuss.
5. 'Mearsheimer continued in this tradition established by Cold War apologists such as Waltz, Schelling and Gaddis.' Comment.
6. How does Mearsheimer establish that the Cold War preserved peace and its disappearance would exacerbate chances of war?
7. How does Mearsheimer establish the superiority of bipolarity over multipolarity through deductions and empirical evidence?
8. How, according to Mearsheimer, 'economic liberalism', 'peace-loving democracies' and 'obsolescence of war' are no match for his three theories of 'bipolarity, equality and nuclear weapons' in both explaining the long peace and the post-Cold War likelihood of chaos?
9. Comment on the amorality of Mearsheimer's theory in the light of his assumptions, justification of lies in international politics, study of Liddell Hart's strategies and focus on conventional deterrence.

NOTES AND REFERENCES

1. Richard Ned Lebow, 'Thomas Schelling and Strategic Bargaining', in *Coercion, Cooperation and* Ethics *International Relations*, ed. Lebow (New York, NY: Routledge, 2007), 255.
2. Thomas C. Schelling, *The Strategy of Conflict*, with a new Preface by the author (Cambridge, MA: Harvard University Press, 1960/1980), hereafter *SOC*; Thomas C. Schelling, *Choice and Consequence*: *Perspectives of an Errant Economics* (Cambridge, MA: Harvard University Press, 1993), hereafter *CAC*; Thomas C. Schelling, 'Diplomacy of Violence', in *The Art of War in World History: From Antiquity to the Nuclear Age*, ed. Gérard Chaliand (Berkeley, CA: University of California Press, 1994), 1013–1022, hereafter DOV; and Thomas C. Schelling, *Strategies of Commitment and Other Essays*, (Cambridge, MA: Harvard University Press, 2006), henceforth *SOCAOE.*
3. David A. Baldwin, 'Thomas Schelling', in *Routledge Encyclopedia of International Political Economy*, ed. R. J. Barry Jones, vol. 3 (London: Routledge, 2011), 1364–1365.
4. Roger B. Myerson, 'Learning from Schelling's Strategy of Conflict', *Journal of Economic Literature* 47, no. 4 (December 2009): 1109–1125, here 1109.
5. Schelling, *The Strategy of Conflict*, 3.
6. Ibid., 22–23.
7. Ibid., 23–28.
8. Ibid., 53–65.
9. Ibid., 67–74.
10. Ibid., 75.
11. Ibid., Section II, Chapters 4–6, 81–172.
12. Thomas C. Schelling, 'The Strategy of Conflict: Prospectus for a Reorientation of Game Theory', *Journal of Conflict Resolution* 2, no. 3 (September 1958): 203–264.
13. Myerson, 'Learning from Schelling', 1109–1125.
14. Thomas C. Schelling, *Arms and Influence* (New Haven, CT: Yale University Press, 1966), hereafter *AAI.*

15. Schelling, 'Diplomacy of Violence', 1013.
16. Jackson and Sørensen, *Introduction*, 81.
17. Schelling, 'Diplomacy of Violence', 1013–1022.
18. Schelling, *The Strategy of Conflict*, 190.
19. Ibid., Appendix A, 265.
20. Thomas C. Schelling, 'The Legacy of Hiroshima', in *Strategies of Commitment and Other Essays*, (Cambridge, MA: Harvard University Press, 2006), 313–326.
21. Richard Zeckhauser, 'Distinguished Fellow: Reflections on Thomas Schelling', *Journal of Economic Perspectives* 3, no. 2 (Spring 1989): 155, 158.
22. John J. Mearsheimer, 'Back to the Future: Instability in Europe after the Cold War', *International Security* 15, no. 1 (Summer 1990): 5–56, hereafter BTTF I; Stanley Hoffmann, Robert O. Keohane, and John J. Mearsheimer, 'Back to the Future, Part II: International Relations Theory and Post-Cold War Europe', *International Security* 15, no. 2 (Fall, 1990): 191–199, hereafter BTTF II; Bruce M. Russett, Thomas Risse-Kappen, and John J. Mearsheimer, 'Back to the Future, Part III: Realism and the Realities of European Security', *International Security* 15, no. 3 (Winter, 1990–1991): 216–222, hereafter BTTF III; John J. Mearsheimer, *The Tragedy of Great Power Politics* (New York, NY: Norton, 2001); hereafter *TTOGPP*; John J. Mearsheimer, *Conventional Deterrence* (Ithaca, NY: Cornell University Press, 1983); and others as incidentally cited.
23. Tim Harford, *The Logic of Life* (London: Little Brown, 2008), excerpted in Robert V. Dodge, *Schelling's Game Theory: How to Make Decisions* (Oxford: Oxford University Press, 2012), 38–39.
24. John Lewis Gaddis, *The Long Peace: Inquiries into the History of the Cold War* (New York, NY: Oxford University Press, 1987), available at http://jstor.org/stable/253891 (accessed on 23 May 2016).
25. John Lewis Gaddis, 'The Cold War, the Long Peace and the Future', in *The End of the Cold War: Its Meaning and Implications*, ed. Michael J. Hogan (Cambridge: Cambridge University Press, 1992/1994), 21.
26. Mearsheimer, 'Back to the Future', Part I, 5.
27. Ibid., 6–8.
28. Ibid., 9.
29. Ibid., 12–19.
30. See *Hansard*, XVI (NS), 390–398, excerpted in Dr Marjorie Bloy, 'A Web of English History: The Peel Web', available at www.historyhome.co.uk/polspeech/portugal.htm (accessed on 31 May 2016).
31. Mearsheimer, 'Back to the Future', Part I, 19–21.
32. Ibid., 21–26.
33. Ibid., 26–29.
34. Ibid., 29–31.
35. Ibid., 31–51.
36. Ibid., 52.
37. Ibid., 52–56.
38. All references to and citations from this chapter are from www.ucs.mun.ca/~russellw/Teaching_files/Mearsheimer%20-%20Realism.pdf (accessed on 3 June 2016).
39. John J. Mearsheimer, 'Structural Realism', in *International Relations*, eds. Tim Dunne, Milja Kurki, and Steve Smith (Oxford: Oxford University Press), 71–88; and John J. Mearsheimer, 'The False Promise of International Institutions', *International Security* 19, no. 3 (Winter 1994–1995): 5–59, here 9–10.
40. Mearsheimer, *The Tragedy of Great Power Politics*, 54–56.
41. Mearsheimer, 'Structural Realism', 78–82.
42. John J. Mearsheimer, *Why Leaders Lie: The Truth about Lying in International Politics* (Oxford: Oxford University Press, 2011), 5, 51–55.

43. Ibid., 6.
44. Ibid., 6–14.
45. Ibid., 100.
46. Mearsheimer, *Liddell Hart and the Weight of History* (Ithaca, NY: Cornell University Press, 1988/2011).
47. Ibid., 5–10.
48. Mearsheimer, 'Realism, the Real World and the Academy', in *Realism, Institutionalism and International Studies*, eds Michael Brecher and Frank P. Harvey (Ann Arbor, MI: University of Michigan Press, 2002), 23–33.
49. Mearsheimer, 'The False Promise of International Institutions', 7.
50. Ibid., 49.

CHAPTER

7

Internal and External Critiques of Realism

CHAPTER OUTLINE

INTRODUCTION

This last chapter of Section IA contains 'internal' and 'external' critiques of realism[1] in general terms (where Morgenthau and Carr are targets of barbs), as well as in the context of individual schools 2–6 (of which 3 is available on the companion website). Donnelly privileges 'internal' critique over 'external' critique, even if its acceptance of realism's terms of reference limits criticisms to 'critique of its coherence and consistency', because internal critiques can avoid 'fruitless controversy over first principles and basic assumptions' and 'achieve a special power and leverage'. But external critiques attack realist assumptions directly.[2] I will take up internal critiques of realism first. Although more concerned with the internal schisms of realism, these too reveal inadequacies of realism, more so when they are critiqued by outsiders even after attacking inadequacies of their theoretical kinsmen, thereby revealing weaknesses of the paradigm. The best start would be with Waltz's critique of neoclassical realism and Morgenthau.

INTERNAL CRITIQUES

Waltz's Uneven Critique Neoclassical Realists

In *MSW*, the fulcrum of Waltz's critique of neoclassical realism and Morgenthau is the mistaken choice of 'images' or 'levels of analysis' rooted within man and within the structure of the separate states (the first- and the second-order images) rather than those located 'within the state system' or the systemic and international level. The section on *MSW* in **Chapter 5** has already stated his arguments on this point.[3] *TIP* criticizes them for choosing 'reductionist' theories in place of 'systemic' ones.[4] To put Morgenthau's 'reductionism' in perspective, Waltz picks up a half-jocular quote from Blaise Pascal in an article titled 'International Relations: Quantitative and Qualitative Approaches' about whether the history of the world would have been different had Cleopatra's nose been a bit shorter, and asking readers 'How do you systematize that?'[5] It was a research question, once put by Lacan too, with explanations of its entry into the world's discourse,[6] and Morgenthau justifiable for raising it, there having been some quantitative approaches to the explanation of 'rare events' in IP, with lamentation that 'the data collection strategies used in IP are grossly insufficient'.[7] But Waltz derives from this rhetorical question an example of his and other realists' sub-systemic focus, and their poor understanding of the meaning of 'theory' in IR. With great ire, he told Morgenthau and Aron, who 'gave us six well-known reasons why you can't have a theory of international politics', that a 'theory is not about accidentals and peculiarities. You don't put that into theory'.[8]

Niebuhr, largely spared, 'hovers over Waltz's text but...is permitted to alight, nowhere', possibly because 'Waltz did not want to get on the treacherous ground of theology or anything that smacked of "metaphysics"'.[9] The lone mention is in Waltz's review of Niebuhr's *The Structure of Nations and Empires*, where Waltz advised 'a more careful and thorough examination of economic and social, military and political conditions than here is given' to unravel the meaning of states and empires over time,[10] thereby unwittingly invoking attention to sub-systemic focus. Dunne is astonished that Waltz does not mention or target Carr as a serious exponent of reductionist realism, though he is the only British scholar to be ranked alongside Niebuhr, Morgenthau, George Kennan and Schelling.[11] Save mention in in the bibliography of *TIP*, Carr himself or *Twenty Years' Crisis* is largely ignored. In an interview with Halliday and Rosenberg, Carr was brought out twice. But Waltz did not commit himself much.[12]

This downgrading of Carr is doubly surprising because his position on the role of morality in IR was diametrically opposite to that of Waltz, and so a likely target of direct critique. When Carr 'emphasizes the intimate dialogue of power and morality', and the fatally mistaken separation of them, because 'morality—if only the morality of safety and prudence in an uncertain and dangerous world' is 'an integral and explicit element' of his realism, Carr's realism becomes most distant from the 'amoral...positivist social science realism' of Waltz.[13] Besides, Carr predates Waltz's concerns for the systemic causes of war and the importance of great powers in it. Beyond listing the human desire for power and the desire for scarce goods as the two most important sources of conflict, Morgenthau said little about the causes of war. And Waltz could not have missed Carr's hypotheses in Chapter 13 of *Twenty Years' Crisis* that the risk of war increases when stronger states enjoy lesser privileges than their capabilities should provide in the system, and that war is more likely in multipolar rather than bipolar systems.[14]

Aron finds mention, as an exponent of reductionist, sub-systemic realism, mentor of Stanley Hoffman[15] and source of 'explanations of the type of inside–outside variety'.[16] His fault is that, even after discovering 'the distinctive quality of international politics in "the absence of a tribunal or police force, the right to resort to force, the plurality of autonomous centers of decision, the alternation and continual interplay between peace and war"', he could neither differentiate between 'the descriptive, explanatory and predictive potentialities of the two levels of analysis: the national and the international', like J. David Singer, nor 'mention the contextual difference between organized politics within states and the formally unorganized politics among them'.[17] But Waltz does not take up for frontal attack Aron's attention to the role of moral and social causes on IR, particularly his contention that the type of a political regime has a near-determining impact on its foreign policy; and Aron's point that Soviet foreign policy was ideology-driven, although his theory is most distant at these points from Waltz's preoccupation with the anarchy problematique, Waltz being convinced that the diplomatic–strategic behaviour of states is induced only by inflexible laws caused by the absence of an international moderator or referee and the immoderation of states. But, after seeing the differences of the foreign policy behaviour of 'post-Communist Russia' from what would have been of a 'still-extant Soviet Union, we know that ideology matters; and that in trying to extend a "partial truth" too far and "a conceptual logic beyond its proper measure"', Waltz's belittling of the compulsions of domestic politics[18] resulted from his insensitivity to the subtler realizations of European realists.

Schelling's Critique of Morgenthau

Thomas Schelling did not take on Morgenthau for any direct critique. But he 'improved on' Morgenthau's description of power, which even though fine-spun and subtle, covering hard and soft bases of it, '*conflated* power and *influence*, and sometimes used these terms interchangeably', surprisingly for a theorist of such calibre. Schelling broadened the horizons of our understanding of power. He focused on the importance of signalling and commitments; included willingness to use power and credibility about it as elements no less important than capability; mentioned show of respect to commitments as an important aid to credibility; considered reputation as a subtle but important element of power and showed that reputation could be harmed by the failure to honour even secondary and 'peripheral' commitments. However, evidence from the Cold War showed that Schelling's revision of Morgenthau contained in 'this proposition was not only wrong but also bordered on the paranoid, as did the greatly exaggerated concern for credibility within the national security community'. Further, Schelling retained Morgenthau's stress on material bases of capability, but overlooked his forewarning about the limitations of translating power into influence, which sometimes made Schelling's analysis of America's response to events in Indochina far less incisive.[19]

However, both Morgenthau and Schelling have shared beliefs that render these differences non-fundamental. As de Wit and Meyer rightly point out, though 'in most respects differences between Morgenthau Schelling could not be more pointed', a proper assessment of the extent to which each relies on Model 1 (i.e., the Rational Actor Model of Foreign Policy, which we will discuss in **Chapter 12**), 'reveals basic similarities among Morgenthau's method of "rational enactment", and Schelling's method of "vicarious problem solving", family resemblances among Morgenthau's "rational statesman" and Schelling's "game theorist"'.[20]

Offensive Realist/Mearsheimerian Critique of Neoclassical Realism and Morgenthau

Mearsheimer is not much critical of either Morgenthau or Waltz. Rather, while claiming that conflict is 'common among states because the international system creates powerful incentives for aggression', he cites with approval both *PAN* and *TIP* as the 'two classic works on this subject'.[21] But in his iconic *The Tragedy of Great Power Politics*, Mearsheimer regards Morgenthau and *PAN* as an example of 'human nature realism', avowedly defective compared to later-day realist theories.[22] To Toft, while Mearsheimer's preoccupation with the 'power structure of IP' accords perfectly with that of Waltz, the dreary atmosphere of his portrayal of IP contrasts sharply with 'the more benign realism' of Waltz, which traces 'the outbreak of international wars and security competition' not to 'overt calculated aggression as argued by Mearsheimer' (in Part II of *The Tragedy of Great Power Politics*), but to 'miscalculation and overreaction in a "world populated by states with inherently defensive motives trapped in a security dilemma"'. The bleak picture of the international system drawn by Mearsheimer echoes more the sentiments of 'human nature realists' as of Morgenthau, Niebuhr and Henry Kissinger. But apart from this shared pessimism, while the later search for the causes of war and security competition in the international sphere in the human nature of will to power and domination, Mearsheimer locates them in true Waltzian fashion at the systemic or structural level of IP, the dynamics of which locks inherently security-seeking states in aggressive competition.[23]

Defensive Realist Critique of Neoclassical and Structural Realism

Since, due to space constraints, defensive realism was not treated as a separate brand of realism in this section of my book, a brief glimpse into its theoretical contentions would be fitting before turning to defensive realists' critique of mainstream realism and Morgenthau. Among their many differences, a key assumption that sets off defensive realists such as Charles Glaser, Robert Jervis and Jeffrey Taliaferro from proponents of other forms of realism including offensive realism is that *states are not inherently aggressive*. This key, nodal assumption is followed by other auxiliary assumptions. Four of Taliaferro's are as follows: (a) security dilemma is an intransigent aspect of anarchy; (b) 'structural modifiers', meaning factors such as offence–defence balance and geography affect the gravity of security dilemma between states; (c) material factors are mediated by leaders' calculations and perceptions before shaping states' foreign policies and (d) domestic politics set precise limits to the capacity of a state's response to the external environment.[24] Besides, defensive realism differs in its doubts about the pervasiveness and inescapability of mistrust in IP.[25]

Despite being 'the logical extension' of Waltz's structural realism, defensive realism's later dramatic divergences from its predictions owe to three modifications wrought in it, the first and second consisting in 'correcting deductive errors', but the third in 'introducing structural variables' that facilitate different takes on the 'constraints and opportunities facing states'. The first disputes the commonest proposition of the anarchy assumption that the international structure itself engenders 'a tendency for security-seeking states to compete' because of the resolve to avoid the risk of cooperation and neutralize vulnerability. Defensive realism argues that competition being no less risky than cooperation because of the uncertainty of its outcome and the possible damage that a loss in it can entail for a state's security, the very internal logic of structural realism would require states to weigh the relative merits of cooperation and collaboration, rather than allowing any one strategy to dominate their behaviour.

The second modification renovates structural realism by not only stressing the role of the security dilemma, barely mentioned by Waltz, but also by showing that, apart from power, offence–defence variables inform the choices of states about security. Jervis explains how the 'offence–defence balance' (referring to 'the relative ease of attack', or the 'cost ratio of offence and defence') and the offence–defence differentiability (referring to 'whether weapons and policies that protect the state also provide the capability for attack') determine whether the security dilemma obtaining in a situation is 'severe or mild'.[26]

The third revision interrogates the widely accepted theoretical belief that realism urges states to think the worst about their enemies' objectives and intentions, and to concentrate on the enhancement of their military capabilities on the following grounds: (a) as a third image and systemic theory, structural realism dissuades states from looking into the domestic policies and politics of their opponents, thereby lacking crucial information needed for judging their schemes and purposes and (b) in the absence of any certainty of others' intentions, states cannot hope that they would make use of opportunities made available by their military advantages. Glaser however contends that reliance on such worst-case policies may be counterproductive since 'under a range of conditions states have preferable alternatives'.[27] Elsewhere, terming his approach as 'contingent realism', Glaser claims that since it makes 'conditional predictions about cooperation and competition, any structuralist–realist case against cooperation must demonstrate that the conditions necessary for cooperation have not occurred....'[28]

These modifications themselves provide clues to the possible lines of critique of structural realism/neorealism by defensive realists. However, their disaffection for certain aspects of Waltzian theory notwithstanding, they agree with neorealists to abjure Morgenthau's 'human nature realism' and adopt as their 'starting point Waltz's theory of the anarchical structure of international politics'. But still, like early realists, they produce 'explicit theories of the domestic politics of foreign policy' and go one over them 'in seeing democratic public opinion as an enforcer of realist prudence in foreign policy against self-interested or ideological elites'.[29]

While considering Waltz's structural realism, his view of systemic theory and international structure, Jervis questions Waltz's assumption that 'states seek to maximize not power but security' since 'the idea of seeking to maximize power unilaterally makes no sense' to a systems theorist. But while keeping the dependent and the independent variables on the systemic level, Waltz's theory tends to sustain more than one kind of analysis, like other theorists, which 'spans two boxes', the bulk of their attention going towards phenomena in which both independent and dependent variables are systemic, but simultaneously analysing 'the system's impact on foreign policies'.[30] Claiming that 'variables at the system level rarely determine the nature of international politics, let alone the foreign policy of individual states', and enlisting Stanley Hoffman,[31] to his aid, Jervis contends that even though 'international outcomes', rather than foreign policies of states, are Waltz's objects of explanation, it is never clear just 'how much and what variation of state behaviour is compatible with his ideas'. Waltz's systemic logic would have been impossible if 'crucial states', such as America, did not appreciate or comprehend their 'place in the structure'. Waltz could reply that the USA's departure from its isolationist course to assume global responsibilities against its political traditions itself proves the 'power of systemic imperatives'. But for Jervis, 'an alternative reductionist explanation' might more problematize Waltz's answer if it asks whether bipolarity would have produced anything like the Cold War had the Soviet Union been a democracy, and Britain and France been totalitarian regimes. For, regime factor incompatibility explains a large part of Soviet Union's unproductive gambits and America's zealous counter-moves. Even more surprising is Waltz's denial of any causal influence to the characteristics of the units over 'dominant international outcomes as long as the structure remains the same', because of his own admission that 'structural change begins in a system's unit', even though in the context of 'its power more than its ideology'.

Jervis has reservations about Waltz's argument that the international system chastens unit behaviour through mutually reinforcing socialization and natural selection, and his supporting examples: Soviet leaders' reversion to foreign policies indistinguishable from their tsarist predecessors; Russian Bolsheviks' adoption of their tsarist ancestors' 'frock coats'; their alliance patterns including the Rapallo Treaty (1922) and the Nazi–Soviet pact (1939) that allowed the partition of Poland just before the Second World War and the similarities of American and Russian actions during the Cold War. These supposedly indicated the limitations of reductionist accounts. But Jervis doubted if 'internationally driven states' are so easily 'tamed'. The role of the Comintern, with its communist world view and the domestic system as an important determinant, is difficult to discount in explaining the extremely bitter relations between the USSR and the Western world, including the USA. France's socialization happened only after protracted wars that had changed the shape of her domestic and IP. Hitler proved impossible to socialize, as did post-Khomeini Iran. Jervis questions Waltz's claim that recalcitrant or intractable states 'fall by the wayside'. For, at the time he wrote 'few modern nations had died'. Even if the later dissolution of the Soviet Union, and more so of Yugoslavia and Czechoslovakia, could be dubbed as a result of their 'failure to meet international competition, in general it is hard to see much natural selection working this way'. Vicissitudes of domestic politics and internal dynamics had more to do with Britain's decline before and during the Cold War or the growth of German and American economies in the late 19th and early 20th centuries. So Jervis can only partly accept that the international system compels states.

Jervis finds problems in Waltz's concept of structure too, which he views as rather 'austere', for demarcating the 'systemic from the unit attributes' so 'rigorously' that it leaves too little space for other factors, even those with 'considerable explanatory power'. Besides, Waltz supposedly makes an overly simplified distinction between hierarchical and anarchical structures. Despite the fact that the international system has no sovereign, it would be as mistaken to magnify 'the role of superordinate authority in domestic society' as to believe that hierarchy is the only possibility of a non-anarchical organization of the system. This is because, to a considerable extent, states can also take initiatives in forming 'anarchical society' with attendant 'shared values, principles, norms and practices'. So, rather than treating the states and the international system as distinct levels of analysis and taking the existence of states as a given, theories should better accept that they are accorded this existence 'by the standing and legitimacy given them by other actors and the system they constitute'. Jervis thinks that to get rid of this 'dualism' of agency and social structure that permeates 'individualist and collectivist ontologies', we need "structurationist ontologies" advised by liberal institutionalists and constructivists, Alexander Wendt and Raymond Duvall, which provide a frame of reference that takes into account the "codetermined irreducibility" of these two fundamental units of analysis'.

Jervis has reservations against Waltz' conception of structure also for ignoring the 'second dimension of structure', because the international system is anarchical, and states being ever ready to wage wars with one another, so no diversification among them is possible, which essentially compels states to be alike in almost all vital respects.[32] I leave this point here to be taken up during the external critiques of Waltzian structuralism.

Taliaferro calls Waltzian structural realism as BOP theory instead of neorealism. For, in his view, the term *neorealism* 'also applies to several systemic realist theories that often make predictions that diverge sharply from Waltz's theory'.[33] He objects to Waltz's diagnosis that even great powers either adopt adaptive strategies or 'fall by the wayside', since Waltz does not focus on the internal dynamics of the state units, that is, 'does not explain why and how states choose between different types of "internal" balancing strategies'.[34] Elman argues that, while Waltz would not have anything to do with sub-systemic, reductionist things, 'several neorealists and their critics have attempted to make foreign-policy predictions' and 'despite his protestations, even Waltz appears to do so', for example, by arguing that the 'foreign policies of nations are affected in important ways by the placement of countries in the international–political system, or more simply by their relative power'. Examples of such placements affecting external behaviour of states and 'systemic factors' inducing 'specific foreign policies' from Greek times to Cold War years exist in *TIP*, where 'Waltz also uses his version of neorealist theory to predict German and Japanese foreign policies in the post-Cold War world'.[35]

Why amid the general silence of offensive realists about Waltz, defensive realists critiqued him, even if mildly? The answer lies in the second post-war crisis for realism, sparked off by the theoretical arrival of neorealism in IRT, which was no less bitter than the 'anti-realist storm' that had raged and assaulted Morgenthau in the 1960s and 1970s. Originating *before* the collapse of the Berlin Wall and gathering momentum *after* the Cold War petered out, the failure of Waltz and his neorealism to foresee this demise of the Cold War made the heat of the debate felt even within the closed confines of structural realism. Scholars realized that pitted against 'real-world conditions', Waltz's core assumptions did allow divergent predictions. Neorealism just overlooked this because of its highly abstract nature, which allowed it to gloss over significant variations in IR, including effects of geography and technology.

Defensive and offensive realists read the effects of these factors differently. After Jervis' 1986 study and others, Taliaferro argued that, in certain very familiar circumstances, the conflict-generating powers of even anarchy are enfeebled. Van Evera argued from the signature realist assumption of groupism that the more group identity would become solidary, as seen happening in the modern era of nationalism, the more difficult would it be to defeat and subjugate sub-systemic groups, thereby rendering states more secure and the systemic logic less. Others add factors ranging from technology to nationalism as rendering harder the conquest of states (especially those possessing the capacity for nuclear strike-back). Similarly, even after conceding Waltz's point about the difficulties of security in an anarchical world, Glaser shows that, under the conditions referred to above, states can find ways to defend their autonomy without scaring others, and/or convey their peaceful intentions, all of which promise an international system which has more ingrained potentials for peace than realists were earlier prepared to accept.

By contrast, offensive realists focused on the war-engendering structural properties of anarchy, in which states, shorn of all authority to sanction or wrest agreements, can never be sure that the current peacetime condition will prevail even in the foreseeable future. Even if factors of geography, technology and group identity render conquest a remote possibility today, there is no certainty that tomorrow a devilish state would not find a way of neutralizing these obstacles. So, rarely complacent about their security, states watch the augmentation of power of their neighbours and competitors nervously, disturbed by the prospects of expansion and strengthening of their powers and contraction, and weakening of others to seek survival. All of this ensures that the competitive nature of life under anarchy is perpetuated.[36]

INTERNAL CRITIQUES AND THE DIVIDED HOUSE OF REALISM

The foregoing internal critiques show that realism is 'a house divided'.[37] While classifying the discords in it, van Evera enumerates five 'pairs' of them, where

- The first two pairs of the debate, that is, (a) 'hawkish realists'/'dovish realists' and (b) 'pessimistic realists'/'optimistic realists' are subsumed in the debate between 'offensive realists' and 'defensive realists'.
- The third pair, occurring between 'third-image' and 'second-image realists'; between those stressing the role of the structure and the international system in determining state behaviour and those emphasizing the importance of domestic institutions, politics and culture, including misperception and bias; corresponds to but transcends the debate between structural realists and non-structural reductionist realists.

- The fourth pair covers structural (or third-image) realists and 'human nature realists', the first emphasizing structural causes and systemic determinants but the second focusing on man's sinful and rapacious disposition.
- The fifth pits 'amoral realists' against 'moralist realists', the former seeing no scope of reconciling moral principles or ethical issues with the making of foreign policy, but the latter seeing no innate contradictions between efforts to maximize national interest and the observance of moral standards.[38]

Following Wolfers, some scholars reduce these five pairs to just two divergent types of explanations: (a) 'human nature realism', underlining humans' supposedly 'insatiable lust for power or *animus dominandi*; (b) 'vicious circle theory', underscoring 'a general human craving for security', heightened by the 'insecurity of an anarchical system of multiple sovereignty', which, by 'a tragic irony', compels actors to seek maximum power even against their real desires. It is kinder to statesmen and people than the '*animus dominandi* theory' since it replaces the 'mad Caesar' epithet which Harold Lasswell reserves for his '*homo politicus* of the pure power model' with the 'hysterical Caesar', who is led astray by the fruitless search for 'the will-o'-the-wisp' or mirage of 'absolute security'.[39] Of course, some realists (like Morgenthau) would straddle across this overly broad typology, and some (like Carr) would not be captured by either this reduction or Evera's five pairs. Still, this is a good summary of the internal critiques and has been refined by Spirtas as the two schools of 'tragedy' and 'evil'.[40] But Wolfers' or Spirtas' reductions of types of realist theory would not capture the intricacies of intra-realism debates, because of the immense variety of realist schools, as captured in their fine-tuned enumeration by Glenn Snyder and collated by Tang. With my minor modifications aimed at capturing the temporal progression of realism, these are classical realism (Carr, Niebuhr, Morgenthau, Spykman), neorealism (Waltz), modified realism (S. D. Krasner), defensive realism (Jack Snyder), contingent realism (Glaser), cultural realism (Alastair Iain Johnston), modern realism (Benjamin Frankel), post-classical realism (Stephen G. Brooks), soft realism (Deborah Welch Larson), motivational realism/Bayesian realism (A. H. Kydd), human nature realism (Mearsheimer), neoclassical realism (Gideon Rose), offensive realism (Mearsheimer), general realism/specific realism (Richard Rosecrance), Bayesian realism[41] and so on.[42] Hansen et al. mention additional types of 'the post-Cold War era', such as 'state-centric realism' (F. Zakaria), 'fine-grained structural realism' (van Evera), 'Machiavellian fundamentalism', 'Hobbesian structuralism' and 'Rousseauian constitutionalism' (Michael W. Doyle), 'romantic realism' (G. Liska), 'subordinate realism' (Mohammed Ayoob), 'peripheral realism' (Carlos Escudé), and 'contingent and universal realism' (Anders Wivel).[43]

This excursus into different typologies of realism in the context of internal critiques of realism is theoretically productive because the sub-schools identified within realism 'help the student figure out the intellectual connections between scholars' and their progression. This is important because 'realist theories which do the real work of explanation are far more diverse than any one theoretical sub-school within realism'. Accordingly, Wohlforth identifies BOP theory, balance-of-threat theory (Stephen M. Walt), security dilemma theory (of Herz, Jervis, Glaser and Barry Posen), offence–defence theory, which is a spin-off of Jervis's development of the security dilemma theory, further enriched by Glaser, Evera and others, hegemonic stability theory (HST) (Robert Gilpin) and power transition theory (Ronald L. Tammen et al.).[44]

This somewhat tedious long list of brands of realism indirectly betokens the endless conversations going on within realism, which are no less noteworthy than the debates between realism and non-realist schools of IR, which are discussed below.

EXTERNAL CRITIQUES

Stanley Hoffmann's Paradigm-free Charge against Morgenthau

Stanley Hoffman, a famous proponent of 'analytic eclecticism' and of thinking 'beyond paradigms' in IRT,[45] makes a thorough critique of Morgenthau's realism,[46] which supposedly fails 'as a general theory', for seeing the world as a 'static field', where 'power relations reproduce themselves in timeless monotony'. Here, Morgenthau's 'main signpost' of national interest provides no 'reliable "map", first because the Realist concept of power is "debatable"'. Second, Morgenthau's demand for the autonomy of the domain of politics makes sense in two alternative situations: (a) when the domain is focused on 'a specialized and limited number of variables' or (b) when 'it is connected with *all* the variables with which the various specialized spheres deal'; the first representing *residual*, and the second *architectonic* status positions. However, Morgenthau veers between them. First, he wants theory to organize a hierarchical integration of the various disciplines for a richer study of IR, and he gives politics the architectonic status of a 'common integrating core'. Second, claiming a residual position for realist politics, he urges realists to 'think in terms of interest defined as power', just as economists, lawyers and moralists think in terms of their relevant concepts. The equation of politics and power is, however, permissible only when power is viewed as 'a complex and diffuse balance' between all the organizing ideas that construct the different social sciences, precluding either taking 'a limited and specific set' of variables or equating politics with the human 'lust for power'. Given the existing 'drive for participation and community' in world politics, 'the image of the political man', of monomaniacal preoccupation with the control of actions of others, is a shaky basis for theory. For, the evil of power, both international (or domestic), 'is rooted not in the sinfulness of man but in a context, a constellation, a situation in which even good men are forced to act selfishly or immorally'.[47]

Hoffmann has at least six reasons why the realist 'map' is distorted, limited and inadequate. First, it gives power—a merely instrumental concept—excessive explanatory importance, though power is but a means to a huge number of unspecified ends, and the desirable quality and quantity of it depends on the 'purposes' to which it is put, necessitating a theory of ends. Yet realism relegates to the background 'all factors that influence or define purposes', all domestic factors, including 'the nature of the regime, the structure of power, beliefs and values' that shape the goals of the nation and the motivations of the statesmen, in short, what later theorists would term 'innenpolitik'.[48] Anticipating the constructivists, Hoffmann grieves that in its scheme of things, internationally shared beliefs and purposes are left out to provide us a mechanical if not 'oversimplified' view of reality where the only function of the statesman is to adapt national power to an unchanging array of contextual imperatives. Even if Morgenthau's goal of a 'rational' theory of politics was achieved, which would be a portrait bringing out 'the human essence of the person portrayed' than a photograph, we would still have to take cognizance of 'all the twists and vagaries of a person's existence' and not pretend that these can be 'easily deducible' from the former. So it would not be wise to 'put so much methodological weight' upon the concept of power even if its role was as central as claimed without differentiating diverse meanings of power, such as 'power as a condition of policy, and power as a criterion of policy; power as a potential and power in use; power as a sum of resources and power as a set of processes'.

Second, apart from using a 'timeless concept of power', Morgenthau's and other realists' theories also seek to perpetuate BOP as a historical pattern by offering the 'highly embellished ideal-type of 18th- and 19th-century IR' as a 'norm both for empirical analysis and for evaluation'. This 'optical illusion' that takes 'a particular historical system' as the norm for a scientific system discourages all discussions of ends and removes it from the processes and pressures of domestic politics.

Third, the concept of national interest constitutive of Morgenthau's map is skewed, being applicable only for stable periods and circumstances in which the actors of the international system pursue 'limited ends, with limited means'; domestic kibitzers and players do not scuttle their moves and their survival is seldom in jeopardy, so that 'more stable and far less vital interests' can be easily graded. But in circumstances where great technological breakthroughs have irretrievably disturbed the constancy of these factors, state survival is continually threatened, and the most dissimilar and atypical courses of action can be touted as legitimate strategies for survival, and where far less exacting or constraining factors vie for the status of vital interests, all understandings of national interest become purely subjective.

Fourth, the position that 'national interest carries its own morality' also holds true only in a stable and consensual era where accommodation of national objectives is possible, and 'conflicts of interest are not struggles between competing international moralities'. The empirical and normative 'philosophical pluralism' underlying realist theory presupposes a system of 'stability and moderation' resulting from a 'basic agreement on values', unavailable in periods of 'nationalistic universalism', in which 'secular religions and incompatible ideologies' dominate.

Fifth, for Hoffmann, the map's penchant for stressing the 'rationality' of foreign policy and exclusion of all 'irrational elements' makes sense only under 'cabinet diplomacy', that is, deliberations under common rules of the game, where rationality consists in simply adapting means to widely recognized and stable ends. This is not opportune in turbulent or revolutionary times, when political struggles settle the determination of ends, rendering any exclusive reliance on such instrumental rationality inadequate. Besides, panegyrics on instrumental rationality for selection of ends may throw up formulas like advocacy of limited nuclear war as the most effective way of putting into use the military resources of the West. That a theory of world polices has to be rational does not mean that the reality it depicts has to be 'generally rational too'.

Sixth, Morgenthau's map omits from its purview all activities not engaged in by states or governments, or not related to unequivocal efforts to gain control over other nations, pardonable only in those times when a large spectrum of activities that only tangentially touches the jurisdiction of states is left in the hands of private citizens, or when these activities are conducted 'unobtrusively within the common framework in which "power politics" operates'. But even in the analysis of such calm and stationary times, the total omission of these activities is inopportune, because their temporary removal from the disciplinary agenda of IR is precisely its 'underpinning and one of the defining features'.

For Hoffmann, these inadequacies have two effects. First, it is overly static, and while setting to find the 'timeless features' of the international–political domain it glosses over processes of change. In its zeal to secure the autonomy of IR, it keeps out of its view the forces ushering in change, which even while cutting across states, affect their behaviour. The premises of the permanence of power not only shift from a diagnosis to a goal but also allow a confusion between the truth of power conflicts and the impermanent forms and institutions they have been instantiated in. The vocal reminder that 'power is here to stay' can never mean that 'the present system of nation states would continue' (though readers please remember that Morgenthau never said it either).

Second, any theory that foregrounds necessity than choice in policymaking, 'adjustment to the environment or to the existing element of national power than value objectives and the orientation of the "givens" to such purposes', and preservation of the present units than winds of change, has 'disturbing normative implications', the least of which is being a pseudonym for sophisticated 'success philosophy'. The paradox of realist theory is a combination of 'a Hobbesian image of naked power politics' with a foredoomed effort to show that states would nevertheless be assured of an existence that is more than 'nasty, brutish and short' because of discordant trust in 'voluntary restraints, moderation and the underlying assumptions of possible harmony among national interests'.[49]

Feminist Critique of Morgenthau's Six Principles and J. Ann Tickner

Leaving the feminist and gender-based critique of mainstream IRT for detailed treatment in **Chapter 20,** here Tickner's demolition and reformulation of Morgenthau's six principles is being presented as a small but concave lens on external critiques of realist malestream.[50] Tickner looks at Morgenthau's six principles, summarized in **Chapter 4,** mainly to answer the question why 'international politics is perceived as a man's world'. She chooses these principles despite their 'lack of scientific rigour' and ambiguities of language, because of their constitutive role in the framing of the discipline since 1945, and their role in providing at least a 'partial description' of the international system, despite being grounded in 'assumptions about human nature that are partial and that privilege masculinity'. She starts from the position that masculinity and femininity are temporally and spatially varying 'constructed categories', rather than 'biological determinants', and questions the conceptual binaries prevalent in the West such as 'objectivity vs subjectivity, reason vs emotion, mind vs body, culture vs nature, self vs other or autonomy vs relatedness, knowing vs being, and public vs private'. Knowing that psychological tests made on people across diverse socio-economic groups in the USA indicated that they were employed to bring out differences between males and females by both feminists and non-feminists; and that of these, traits associated with masculinity were accorded higher value both my men and women, she first attacks the hidden masculine overtone of the concept of objectivity, upon which Morgenthau's goal of a rational and non-emotional theory of IP rests.

For Tickner, the positivist expectation that the universe studied is explicable through concepts 'shaped not by language but only by the demands of logic and experiment...beyond the relativity of language' is a ruse to legitimize and enforce 'a coercive, hierarchical and conformist' form of scientific enquiry. Besides denying the possibility of 'finding a universal and objective foundation of knowledge since all knowledge is socially constructed', feminists claim that since it is language through which knowledge is disseminated, 'the use of language' and its pretension to objectivity should also be put under scrutiny. She cites Keller's contention that objectivity as perceived in Western culture is dominantly 'a set of cultural values that simultaneously (and conjointly) elevates what is defined as scientific and...masculine',[51] for revealing how it ensures the divorce between subject and object that is the hallmark of positivist science, and springs from a felt need for control, being thereby a tool for power and domination.

Morgenthau's quest for an objective, rational theory seeking to 'impose order on a chaotic and conflictual world' avowedly springs from this need for control. Fully knowing that 'real men, like real states, are both moral and bestial', he invokes the abstraction of the 'political man, a beast completely lacking in moral restraints', because states seldom abide by 'universal moral laws that govern the universe' and perish if they do. To resolve this dilemma, Morgenthau demarcates from the domain of domestic politics a Hobbesian international domain, where the amoral behaviour of the political man is appropriate and 'prudent'. But wedded to the slogan 'the personal is political', most feminist theorists spurn the plea for an autonomous political sphere that will have its own admissible forms of conduct. They denigrate the separation between public and private as a stratagem that both defends the contour lines of the political and captures its 'content and style'. Morgenthau's political man offers, at best, a partial view of human nature, since it does not say what place women occupied in the Hobbesian SON, though surely engaged in activities of propagation and child rearing in place of destructive warfare if life was to continue in past generations. But Morgenthau's stress, and of his ilk, on the conflictive aspects of IP, deliberately soft-pedals these cooperative and germinal elements of IR; and his conceptualization of an amoral sphere of IP politics as a resolution of the tension that exists between universal 'moral laws' and 'requirements of successful political action' is nothing but a ruse and allowance for states' pursuit of their own national interests while using morality as a cloak for it.

Even Morgenthau's hierarchical ordering of morality is shown to have had affinity with American psychologists such as Lawrence Kohlberg, whose experiments on the moral development of American boys have been critiqued by Carol Gilligan because its stages exude masculine standards. On Kohlberg's scale, women rarely get beyond the third and contextual of the six stages, being conditioned into a mentality that is 'contextual and narrative' instead of being 'formal and abstract'.[52] But the ingrained tendency in IR of viewing morality either as 'abstract, universal and unattainable' values, or as merely 'instrumental' considerations (as by Morgenthau), belittles women's ability to accommodate cultural differences and engage in community building in spite of them. So, convinced that Morgenthau's efforts to design an objective, universal theory wholly on the basis of masculine assumptions of human nature and morality and virile nation states cannot be a sound basis for IRT, particularly in the nuclear age, where 'increasing power by increasing security could be suicidal', Tickner offers a 'feminist perspective on IP' and an inkling of a feminist epistemology of IR that would prepare the ground for a feminist reformulation of Morgenthau's six principles and the edifice political realism erected on it.

Morgenthau's concept of power, as control of man over man, which has signally influenced the definition of power in IR, is also critiqued for privileging masculinity. Tickner pits alternative conceptions of power in the writings of Nancy Hartsock, Hannah Arendt and so on embodied in 'stress energy, capacity and potential'; 'the human ability to act in concert' or the capacity 'to take action with others who have similar concerns'. These come very near David McClelland's description of 'female power', since being 'shared rather than assertive', having lesser control of instruments of coercion, women are more prone to resort to 'power as persuasion'. Tickner shows how this feminist view of power 'as a relationship of mutual enablement' or as 'female strategy of coalition building', finds parallels in IR, mostly in institutional attempts at regional integration or the creation of regional infrastructure rooted in 'mutual cooperation and collective self-reliance', as manifest in the activities of the European Economic Community, the Southern African Development Coordination Conference or in the underpinning vision Karl Deutsch's concept of the 'pluralistic security community'.[53]

Similarly, Tickner wrenches the concept of security away from its monomaniacal moorings in military strength, which to her (somewhat unjustifiably) accords with Morgenthau's conceptualization of national interest, for being not only partial but anachronistic in today's world of 'technologically advanced' and 'highly interdependent states' possessing weapons of mass destruction. This security discourse becomes doubly deficient when one shifts it from East–West to North–South perspectives, where the insecurities faced by a large part of the world population concern more 'satisfaction of basic material needs' than 'military threats'. Security as gratification of basic needs applies more to women, who, despite being 'providers of basic needs', as recognized in current development literature, are traditionally victims of a lack of them. Tickner also mentions another challenge to national security, largely ignored in contemporary mainstream theories. Drawing from Carolyn Merchant's berating of the 'mechanistic view of nature' (in *The Death of Nature*, 1980), which ignored the 'age-old association' between women and nature depicted throughout 'culture, language and history,'[54] she contends that reflection on 'military, economic and environmental security in interdependent terms' towards 'mutually beneficial rather than zero sum outcomes' is exemplified by Sara Ruddick's concept of 'maternal thinking'. It wants to nurture a domestic environment through preservation of tranquillity and avoidance of conflict as much as possible, striving for it non-violently and re-establishing community at the end. Its fondness for 'contextual judgements' in place of 'absolute standards' has close affinity to Gilligan's description of 'female morality'. Accordingly, the crux of the feminist perspective on IR is how to make such 'maternal thinking', shared by men as well women operative in the public sphere, an essential prerequisite of survival in this nuclear age that has put into question the whole notion of winners and losers.[55]

Tickner teases out some unifying themes of various feminist literatures to construct a feminist epistemology of IR. First, against Morgenthau's injunction 'to stand back from the world' to construct a rational map of universal applicability, she underscores themes such as 'connection and contingency', and what Keller calls 'dynamic objectivity' (essentially type of knowledge that concedes 'independent integrity' for the world outside, coupled with our connection with it). Second, it urges for the adoption of what Sandra Harding called 'an African world view', 'where the individual is seen as part of the social order, acting within that order rather than upon it', athwart the 'Western liberal notion of rational economic man, an individualist and a welfare maximizer', a close affine of the 'rational political man', the basis of realism's theoretical edifice. Tickner offers the feminist view of the individual that combines Merchant's holistic perspective and 'ecological thinking', stressing the interconnections of all things, cultural, social and natural, Keller's dynamic objectivity and Harding's African world view. It makes possible 'an appreciation of the "other" as a subject whose views are as legitimate as our own'. This feminist individual is the fulcrum of a reformulation of Morgenthau's six principles as stated below.

1. Since 'objectivity, as it is culturally defined' has deep masculine overtones, and the alleged 'objective' laws of human nature are rooted in a 'partial, masculine view' of it, a 'connected view of objectivity' has to accommodate as much 'elements of social reproduction' as those of 'political domination' through dynamic objectivity.
2. Since national interest is 'multidimensional and contextually contingent', it is wrong to define it exclusively 'in terms of power', especially because in present times national interests require 'cooperative rather than zero sum solutions' for problems and issues impinging on nuclear risks, economic welfare and environmental decay.
3. It would be mistaken to invest power with a timeless and universally applicable meaning, since power, viewed only through the lenses of domination and control not only 'privileges masculinity' but misses the 'possibility of collective empowerment...often associated with femininity'.
4. The realist injunction that moral command be separated from political action is misleading since there is no political action devoid of moral sanction. The realist programme of consolidating order through power and control also accords pre-eminence to 'the moral command of order over those of justice and the satisfaction of basic needs' so essential for social reproduction.
5. Even though it would be wrong to confuse 'the moral aspirations of particular nations' with 'moral laws that govern the universe', it is perfectly legitimate to search for 'common moral elements in human aspirations', since they are important bases for 'deescalating international conflict' and constructing 'international community'.
6. The 'autonomy of the political' acclaimed by realists is inadmissible because it too is hopelessly tied up with masculinity as defined in Western culture and with discipline-defined attempts to offer us a world view that is not premised in a 'pluralistic view of human nature' consonant with feminist perspective and epistemology. Firming up boundaries around a closely circumscribed political realm interprets political in a way that debars the 'concerns and contributions of women'.[56]

The Ecological/Environmentalist Critique of Realism

The environmentalist and ecological critique targets realism's failure to address, and the growing irrelevance or inadequacy of answers it provides to, the problems of security, liberty, peace and happiness in the backdrop of the environmental crisis that has already arrived. In the realist world view, where everyone is an unencumbered and atomized individual, and other individuals and nature are potential opportunities or obstacles to his/her chances of material acquisitions and prosperity, and power is the key to fulfilment of material ambitions, there is every chance that it will be monopolized by elites, depriving others, resulting in the degradation of politics to a game of 'value extraction...an ontology of competition'. For

> the politics of realism,...with the extractive individualized self arraigned against the nature and other human beings as the 'other' and identified with elite group, class or nation's global control and homogenization as the sole objective can never be the realm of the expanded or universal self.

Consequently, the ecological approach to IR looks for alternative ontologies, epistemologies and ethical/political norms that put under strain conventional mainstream approaches that rely on the benefits of 'force, materialism, elitism, homogenization' and extravagant consumption and consumerism. It decries the reigning positivist epistemology in IR, which seeks 'objectification and control' against the normative goals that stem from ecology. It believes that since the egotistic individual, with his profligate lifestyle and dependence on fossil fuel-dependent industrial development, is at the root of the ecological crisis, which challenges the sovereign state system's claims to provide security for its citizens and the legitimacy derived from them, realist theory needs some urgent self-introspection. This would involve a reconsideration of its views on reality and human nature, its mechanistic weltanschauung and its dreary conception of security, peace and freedom. It should take a 'leap of faith' towards what Aldo Leopold calls a 'land ethic', which believes that no mode of thinking is right and proper unless it seeks to 'preserve the integrity, stability and beauty of the biotic community'.[57]

Realist theory, as it is presently constituted, cannot avowedly take this 'leap of faith' because of five vices in its thought structure: (a) 'ontology of conflict and aggression'; (b) 'hierarchical orientation'; (c) 'emphasis on homogeneity'; (d) 'materialistic ideology' and (e) 'reductionist ideology (in the component literature)'. The first vice starts from assumptions about human nature and their projection onto larger units of states to view states as both 'death-fearing and power-seeking' rational actors in 'perpetual motion' that will anytime collide with such others. The consequent stress on 'threats from outside' reduces the state's ability to foresee threats from inside or 'from transnational processes, such as environmental decay or longer-term processes such as global warming'. The second concerns the structure of the international system, viewed as a conflictual and anarchical world, which requires that national 'units' are hierarchically placed. The resultant elitist perspective on human affairs enjoins acceptance of power and authority, and suppression of important aspects of freedom for the sake of immunity to external assaults on political independence. Third, even though realism's legitimization of hierarchy allows for 'difference in social stature and power relations' of and between states, the third vice in realist thought that impels it to favour homogenization is its view of history as a site of sameness, marked by 'a series of recurrences' or 'cycles of power assertion and displacement' that either culminate in or stem from war. Homogeneity stems from the supposedly unchanged substances and processes of global politics and their underpinning human disposition and behaviour, amid the succession of drastically different types of international systems from the Greek city state system to Westphalian system and beyond. The materialist world view imparted by these three vices of realism, consisting in the pre-eminence of survival, and the deliverance from uncertainty through meeting physical force by greater force require 'harnessing of matter' and 'transformation of nature as a means to that end', necessitating the adoption of an unabashed 'utilitarian ecological perspective'. Finally, not only in its contemporary formulations and utterances but also embryonically in classical writings, realism has adopted 'a positivist, reductionist epistemology', which would be regarded by radical ecologists as part more of the problem than of the solution.[58] The full weight of the ecological critique will be clear when I take green politics as a separate theme in **Chapter 21**.

THE POSTPOSITIVIST CRITIQUE OF REALISM/NEOREALISM

Postpositivist critiques, whether coming from CT, postmodernism/post-structuralism or constructivism, are aimed mostly against neorealism, though neoclassical realism is not wholly exempt. Such critiques 'range from (John) Ruggie's perceptive identification of neorealism's inability to explain the nature of international systemic origins and transformation, to the epistemological critiques of Richard K. Ashley'.[59] Ruggie shows how the choice by American comparative and IP scholars of 'social totalities as the appropriate unit of analysis' is a revival from oblivion of the holistic 'social milieu' conceptualized by Durkheim as 'the system formed by [individuals'] association' 'by the fact of their combination'. Locating Waltz's 'argument within its self-consciously Durkheimian problematic' and treating it as a 'mirror image' of Immanuel Wallerstein's world system approach (to be discussed in **Chapter 18**), Ruggie seeks 'to assess, modify and extend it on its own terms' in the interest of 'a more synthetic neorealist formulation'. For, Waltz's failure to portray a unit-independent international structure partly resides in his 'errors or omission and commission', and partly arises from the very nature of the 'enterprise' he has taken up. Accordingly, Ruggie sets to consider the emendations that are necessary in Waltz's theory.

Regarding Waltz's claim about the high constancy of the 'texture of IP', proven by recurrence and repetition of its patterns,[60] Ruggie's objection is that it ignores 'the most important contextual change in this millennium: the shift from the medieval to the modern international system'. Even if the medieval system was also anarchical, any attempt to capture its difference from the modern international system only through the 'differences in the distribution of capabilities among the constituent units' is 'historically inaccurate'. Waltz does not notice this because 'a dimension of change' is absent in his scheme, and this is because he excludes 'the second analytical component of political structure, differentiation of units when discussing international systems'. A crude understanding of the sociological term 'differentiation' as something implying *differences* rather than *separateness* makes him overlook the fact that the 'modern system is distinguished from the medieval not by "sameness" or "differences" of units, *but by the principles on the basis of which the constituent units are separated from each other*' (italics author's). While anarchy indicates that the political system has metameric segmentation, differentiation instructs us about the *basis* on which the segmentation operates. The gain from this clarification is awareness that, far from disappearing, 'the second conception of structure' not only 'stays in' but also functions as a prolific source of 'structural variation'. For Ruggie, where the medieval and the modern international system differed most was in their systems of property rights and authority. The main characteristic of the modern international system is consolidation of 'absolute' and 'exclusive' private property away from 'fiefs' and lord–vassal relations in the medieval state and juxtaposed with it 'institutionalization of public authority' as sovereignty. From the Roman era to modern times, in both domestic and international systems, private property rights and sovereignty perform comparable functions in three crucial areas: (a) 'they differentiate among units in terms of possession of self and exclusion of others'; (b) since any mode of differentiation involves a 'corresponding form of sociality', they also 'establish systems of social relations among their respective units', like that of 'possessive individualists' under the modern international system and (c) the most influential and impactful theorists of the two domains 'developed an autonomous legitimation of the political order based on the minimalist social needs of its component units'. Ruggie argues from this that if the significance of the concept of differentiation is properly grasped, the second structural level of Waltz's model not only persists to 'depict the kind of institutional transformation illustrated by the shift from the medieval to the modern international system' but also 'serves as a dimension of possible future transformation, from the modern to the postmodern international system'. That 'not only a dimension of change is missing from Waltz's model' but also 'a determinant of change' is traceable to Waltz's misreading of Durkheim's structuralism and consequent overlooking of Durkheim's stress on the 'growth in the volume of dynamic density of societies' as a critical factor that 'modifies the fundamental conditions of social existence'. To redress this oversight, which leads to the limitations of Waltz's model, Ruggie offers his concept of an alternative structure as a cure.[61] But I am skipping it for reasons of space.

Startlingly, Ashley finds the main fault of neorealist structuralism in its tendency of reductionism. For him, neorealism betrays both the 'realist revolution against idealism and the scientific revolution against traditionalism', the first because of its tendency to reduce 'political practice to an economic logic' and the second (and its 'critical faculties') due to 'swallowing methodological rules that render science a purely technical enterprise'. Of course, it seems to have 'cut through the subjectivist veils and dark metaphysics of classical realist thought…the normatively laden metaphysics of fallen man…including concepts of power and national interest, securely in the scientifically defensible terrain of objective necessity'. But if neorealism wants to exult in its structuralist accomplishments, it should answer for its structuralist limitations, as 'a self-enclosed, self-affirming joining of statist, utilitarian, positivist, and structuralist commitments', which within neorealism are tied together 'in machine-like, self-enclosing unity', in which resides the neorealist counterpart of Althusser's 'orrery of errors'. Let alone interrogate 'common sense appearances', neorealism 'hypostatizes them', and, let alone try to extend the contours of international political discourse, debars from consideration all viewpoints that would bring out to light the shortcomings of the 'given order of things'.

Preparatory to his attack on structuralism, Ashley critiques the statist, utilitarian and positivist aspects of neorealism. The 'state-as-actor assumption' of neorealism does not have to be gleaned from individual utterances of neorealists on the state and foreign policy, being 'a metaphysical commitment prior to science and exempted from scientific criticism'. Its brag about 'hard falsifying tests' as the precondition of theoretical advance notwithstanding, the immunity enjoyed by this assumption is manifest in the absence of any 'historically testable hypothesis that the state-as-actor construct might be not a first-order given of international political life, but part of a historical justificatory framework by which dominant coalitions legitimize secure consent for their precarious conditions of rule'. Two argumentative consequences of this 'state centricity' are (a) the inability to recognize and even 'comprehend those global, collectivist concepts that are irreducible to logical combinations of state-bounded relations' and (b) sanction not only for the 'priority of structure over practice' but also for the unshakeable 'predominance of the whole over the parts', leading to the expectation that neorealists would confer upon the structure of the international system 'an identity independent of the parts or units'. But any such hopes are unfounded, since to neorealists, 'the state is ontologically prior to the international system'.

For Ashley, neorealism is in a broader, non-Benthamite, sense 'utilitarian'. For, to the neorealist, 'states are rational individual actors whose interests and calculations give form and moment to the international system'. Neorealism's commitment to American positivism also fights shy of many of the positive facets of philosophical positivism, and 'its rich currents of meaning in recent European, Latin American sociology, philosophy, and anthropology', to equate positivism with 'the essential objectivity of technical rationality'. Neorealism's promise of a 'structuralist turn' is also finally disappointing, because neorealists 'slide all too easily between two concepts of the whole, and conflate them'. Instead of understanding structure as 'a deep, internal relation prior to and constitutive of social actors', Waltz sees it as an external joining of states-as-actors, invested with precise boundaries, common sense, ends and self-perceptions. Pitted against 'the idealized point of view of the lone, isolated state-as-actor', the imperfectly understood 'independence of the structured whole' admits no possibility of change. For, the units can neither 'alone alter the whole' nor enlist the aid of similar others. So neorealism offers 'the worst of two worlds', 'atomism's superficiality' with 'structuralism's closure'.

Ashley argues that neorealism's totalitarian or totalizing impulses stem only partly from 'its celebration of power before order'. They are also evident in its 'silence' on those aspects of history that are distasteful to or problematic for it. This silence covers four dimensions of history that Ashley calls its '"four p's": process, practice, power and politics'. Neorealist structuralism 'denies *history as process*', because of two of its characteristics: (a) the rigid 'fixity of its theoretical categories', such that 'each is a category of stasis even when it is set in motion among other moving parts' and (b) all mobility is constrained because it occurs within a 'closed field whose limits are defined by the pregiven structure'. Second, in common with all other 'modes of historicism', neorealism denies the historical 'significance of *practice*', or the juncture at which 'men and women enter with greater or lesser degrees of consciousness into the making of their world', taking them as mere Althusserian 'subjects', inserted and performing their roles. Third, in spite of its preoccupation with 'power politics', neorealism has a poor understanding of the 'social basis and social limits of power', which is mechanically reduced to a litany of 'capabilities or means under the control of an unreflective actor whose status as actor is given from the start'. Finally, its raucous defence of political autonomy and denigration of 'economism' of other perspectives notwithstanding, neorealist historicism 'reduces' politics to only those considerations that are susceptible to analysis wholly 'within a framework of economic action' and undertaken 'under structural constraints'. All possibilities of interrogating this economic framework for its unstated 'political content' are foreclosed, and politics is denuded of any 'practical basis' that might facilitate reflective 'resistance to strictly economic demands'. Ashley thinks that, despite Waltz's denigration of them as 'unscientific', Morgenthau and Wight's neoclassical realism provides 'greater insights' into 'the traditional practice of world politics'. But, since like neorealism, neoclassical realism too is a 'closed system of thought', Ashley offers, like Ruggie, an alternative, which he calls 'a dialectical competence model' and spells out its epistemological advantages.[62]

Some commentators, however, say that Ashley's employment of Althusser's conception of structure to criticize Waltz's is ill applied. Waltz's concept of structure is akin to 'the sociological structural tradition' enriched by Durkheim, Robert Merton and Talcott Parsons, whereas Ashley subscribes to a model 'associated with Durkheim, Althusser, Lévi Strauss and Saussure', better known as structuralism, and hence is not fit for comparison with the sociological tradition.[63]

CONCLUSION

This chapter has dealt with both internal critiques (neorealists, strategic realists, defensive realists and offensive realists against realists, neorealists and one another) and external critiques (Hoffmann, Tickner and feminist, ecologists, Ruggie, Ashley and other postpositivists). We have seen for ourselves how the internal critiques of realism are no less important than the external criticisms. But criticism of the realist paradigm and particularly of its 'anarchy assumption' is far from complete because the arguments in **Chapters 20, 21, 22, 24, 25** and **26** will impinge on the 'anarchy assumption' in important ways.

REVIEW QUESTIONS

1. Summarize Waltz's critique of Morgenthau and Carr/neoclassical realism, and comment on the significance of Cleopatra's nose in the critique.
2. State in brief the strategic realist criticism of neoclassical realism and Morgenthau.
3. Describe the offensive realist/Mearsheimerian critique of neoclassical realism and Morgenthau.
4. Give the essence of the offensive realist/Mearsheimerian critique of neoclassical realism and Morgenthau.
5. Why would you consider realism as a 'house divided'?
6. Give an outline of Stanley Hoffmann's critique of Morgenthau and show how it presaged later postpositivist critiques of Morgenthau.
7. Write an essay on Tickner's feminist critique of Morgenthau and his six principles.
8. Give a brief note on the ecological/environmentalist critique of realism.
9. Analyse the postpositivist critique of realism after Ruggie and Ashley.

NOTES AND REFERENCES

1. While

   > an 'internal critique' accepts the theory's objectives as given and identifies problems within the theoretical formulation arising from various logical or explanatory inadequacies; the 'external critique', in contrast appraises the theory's objectives itself and identifies problems with respect to either the adequacy or scope of those objectives.

   Ashley J. Tellis, 'Reconstructing Political Realism: The Long March to Scientific Theory', in *Roots of Realism*, ed. Benjamin Frankel (London; Portland, OR: Frank Cass, 1996), 61.
2. Jack Donnelly, *Realism and International Relations* (Cambridge: Cambridge University Press, 2000), 2.
3. Apart from Section 2 in Chapter 5, see Waltz, *Man*, 114, 120, 122–123, 167–168.
4. See Section 5 of Chapter 5.
5. For Pascal's exact quote, see Blaise Pascal, *The Thoughts, Letters and Opuscules of Blaise Pascal*, trans. O. W. Wight, with Notes from All the Commentators (New York, NY: Derby and Jackson, [1859]1861), 225. Available at https://books.google.com/books?id=eiJHAAAAIAAJ (accessed on 7 June 2016). For Morgenthau's reference, see Henrikki Heikka, 'Beyond Neorealism and Constructivism: Desire, Identity and Russian Foreign Policy', in *Understandings of Russian Foreign Policy*, ed. Ted Hopf (University Park, PA: Pennsylvania State University Press, 1999), 58.
6. Jacques Lacan, *Écrits* (New York, NY: W. W. Norton & Company, 2007), cited in Ibid.
7. Gary King and Langche Zeng, 'Explaining Rare Events in International Relations', *International Organization* 55, no. 3 (2001): 693–715.
8. Anna Cornelia Beyer, *Kenneth Waltz's Life and Thought. An Interview* (2015). Available at https://books.google.com/books?isbn=1312889705 (accessed on 8 June 2016), 30.
9. Jean Bethke Elshtain, 'Niebuhr's "Nature of Man" and Christian Realism', in *Reinhold Niebuhr and Contemporary Politics: God and Power*, eds. Richard Harries and Stephen Platten (Oxford: Oxford University Press, 2010), 44.
10. Campbell Craig, *Glimmer of a New Leviathan: Total War in the Realism of Niebuhr, Morgenthau and Waltz* (New York, NY; Chichester: Columbia University Press, 2003), 120.
11. Tim Dunne, 'A British School of International Relations', in *The British Study of Politics in the Twentieth Century*, eds. Jack Hayward, Brian Barry and Archie Brown (Oxford: Oxford University Press, 2003), 395.
12. Fred Halliday and Justin Rosenberg, 'Interview with Kenneth Waltz', *Review of International Studies* 24, no. 3 (1998): 371–386, here 385.
13. Robert Jackson, 'Is there a Classical International Theory?', in *International Theory: Positivism and Beyond*, eds. Steve Smith, Ken Booth and Marysia Zalewski (Cambridge: Cambridge University Press, 1999), 211–212.
14. Stephen van Evera, 'Introduction', in *Causes of War: Power and the Roots of Conflict* (Ithaca, NY: Cornel University Press, 1999), excerpted in Colin Elman, Michael Jensen, eds., *The Realism Reader* (London; New York, NY: Routledge, 2014), note 10, p. 155.
15. Waltz, *Theory of International Politics*, 43–49.
16. Ibid., 47.
17. Ibid., 61.
18. Brian C. Anderson, *Raymond Aron: The Recovery of the Political* (Lanham, MD: Rowman & Littlefield, 1997), 128.
19. Simon Reich and Richard Ned Lebow, *Good-Bye Hegemony: Power and Influence in the International System* (Princeton, NJ; Oxford: Princeton University Press, 2014), 28–30.
20. Bob de Wit and Ron Meyer, *Strategy: Process, Content, Context* (Hampshire: Cengage Learning, 2010), 143.

21. Mearsheimer, 'Back to the Future', 12.
22. Mearsheimer, *The Tragedy of Great Power Politics*, 18.
23. Peter Toft, 'John J. Mearsheimer: An Offensive Realist between Geopolitics and Power', *Journal of International Relations and Development* 8 (2005): 381–408, especially 388–390. Available at https://doi.org/10.1057/palgrave.jird.1800065 (accessed on 13 March 2020).
24. Shiping Tang, *A Theory of Security Strategy for Our Time: Defensive Realism* (New York, NY: Palgrave Macmillan, 2010), 3, 11–15.
25. Andrew H. Kydd, *Trust and Mistrust in International Relations* (Princeton, NJ; Oxford: Princeton University Press, 2005), 16.
26. Robert Jervis, 'Cooperation under the Security Dilemma', *World Politics* 30, no. 2 (1978): 167–214, here 178, 187–207; Charles L. Glaser and Chaim Kaufman, 'What Is Offense–Defense Balance and How Can We Measure It', *International Security* 22, no. 4 (1998): 44–82, here 46; Marco Nilsson, 'Offense–Defense Balance, War Duration, and the Security Dilemma', *The Journal of Conflict Resolution* 56, no. 3 (2012): 467–489.
27. Charles L. Glaser, 'The Necessary and Natural Evolution of Structural Realism', in Elman and Jensen, *The Realism Reader*, 246–247.
28. Charles L. Glaser, 'Realists as Optimists: Cooperation as Self-Help', *International Security* 19, no. 3 (1994–1995): 50–90, here 54.
29. Jack Snyder, 'Tensions within Realism', in *The Invention of International Relations Theory: Realism, The Rockefeller Foundation and the 1954 Conference on Theory*, ed. Nicolas Guilhot (New York, NY: Columbia University Press, 2011), 68.
30. Robert Jervis, *System Effects: Complexity in Social and Political Life* (Princeton, NJ: Princeton University Press, 1997), 75–76, 92.
31. Stanley Hoffman, *Gulliver's Troubles, or the Setting of American Foreign Policy* (New York, NY: McGraw Hill, 1968).
32. Jervis, *System Effects*, 103–109.
33. Jeffrey W. Taliaferro, 'Security Seeking under Anarchy: Defensive Realism Reconsidered', *International Security* 25, no. 3 (2000–2001): 128–161.
34. Jeffrey W. Taliaferro, 'Neoclassical Realism and Resource Extraction: State Building for Future War', in *Neoclassical Realism, The State, and Foreign Policy*, eds. Steven E. Lobell, Norrin M. Ripsman and Jeffrey W. Taliaferro (Cambridge: Cambridge University Press, 2009), 196.
35. Colin Elman, 'Horses for Courses: Why Not Neorealist Theories of Foreign Policy', *Security Studies* 6, no. 1 (1996): 7–53, here 10.
36. Jervis, 'Cooperation under the Security Dilemma'; S. van Evera, *Causes of War: Structures of Power and Roots of International Conflict* (Ithaca, NY: Cornel University Press, 1999); Glaser, 'Realists as Optimists'. For all the citations and comments, see William C. Wohlforth, 'Realism and Security Studies', in *The Routledge Handbook of Security Studies*, eds. Myriam Dunn Cavelty, Victor Mauer and Thierry Balzacq (Abingdon; Oxon; New York, NY: Routledge, 2010), 14.
37. Michael Spirtas, 'A House Divided: Tragedy and Evil in Realist Theory', in *Realism: A Restatement and Renewal*, ed. Benjamin Frankel (London; Portland, OR: Franks Cass, 1996), 385–424.
38. Stephen van Evera, 'Elements of the Realist Paradigm: What Are They?' (typescript, 27 January 1992), 4, cited in Frankel, *Realism*, xix.
39. Wolfers, *Discord and Collaboration*, 83–84.
40. Spirtas, 'A House Divided', *passim.*
41. Kydd, *Trust and Mistrust in International Relations.*
42. For these, see Tang, *A Theory of Security Strategies for Our Time*, 9.
43. For these additional brands, see Birthe Hansen, Peter Toft and Anders Wivel, *Security Strategies and American World Order: Lost Power* (London; New York, NY: Routledge, 2009), 9, 155.

44. See for these types of realist theory and citations, Wohlforth, 'Realism and Security Studies', 15–17.
45. Rudra Sil and Peter J. Katzenstein, 'Preface', in *Beyond Paradigms: Analytical Eclecticism in the Study of World Politics* (New York, NY: Palgrave Macmillan, 2011), xiv–xv.
46. Stanley Hoffman, *Contemporary Theory of International Relations* (New Delhi: Prentice-Hall of India (Private) Ltd, [1960]1964).
47. Hoffman, *Contemporary Theory of International Relations*, 30–38.
48. Hans J. Morgenthau, *Dilemmas of Politics* (Chicago, IL: University of Chicago Press, 1958), 98–100, cited in Hoffman, *Contemporary Theory of International Relations*, 30.
49. Hoffman, *Contemporary Theory of International Relations*, 30–38.
50. J. Ann Tickner, 'Hans Morgenthau's Principles of Political Realism: A Feminist Reformulation', in *Gender and International Relations*, eds. Rebecca Grant and Kathleen Newland (Bloomington, IN; Indianapolis, IN: Indiana University Press, 1991), 27–39.
51. Evelyn Fox Keller, *Reflections on Gender and Science* (New Haven, CT: Yale University Press, 1985), 89, cited in Ibid., 30.
52. For Kohlberg's enumeration of levels of moral development and Gilligan's critique of them, see Robert Kegan, *The Evolving Self: Problem and Process in Human Development* (Cambridge, MA: Harvard University Press, 1982), Chapter 2; Carol Gilligan, *In a Different Voice: Psychological Theory and Women's Development* (Cambridge, MA: Harvard University Press, 1982), Chapter 1; both cited in Ibid., 31–32.
53. I will have more to say on this in **Chapter 13A**.
54. Carolyn Merchant, *The Death of Nature: Women, Ecology and the Scientific Revolution* (New York, NY: Harper and Row, 1982), xv, cited in Tickner, 'Hans Morgenthau's Principles of Political Realism', 34.
55. Sara Ruddick, 'Maternal Thinking' and 'Preservative Love and Military Destruction: Some Reflections on Mothering and Peace', in Joyce Treblicot, *Mothering: Essays in Feminist Theory* (Totowa, NJ: Rowman and Allenhead, 1984).
56. Ibid., 35–37.
57. Narottam Gaan, *Relevance of Environment: A Critique on International Relations Theories* (Delhi: Kalpaz Publications, 2005), 202–205.
58. Eric Laferrière and Peter J. Stoett, *International Relations Theory and Ecological Thought: Towards a Synthesis* (London; New York, NY: Routledge, 1999), 75–105, especially, 83–86.
59. Molloy, *The Hidden History of Realism*, 121.
60. Waltz, *Theory of International Politics*, 66.
61. John Ruggie, 'Continuity and Transformation in World Polity: Toward a Neorealist Synthesis', in *Neorealism and Its Critics*, ed. Robert O. Keohane (New York, NY: Columbia University Press, 1986), 131–157.
62. Richard K. Ashley, 'The Poverty of Neorealism', in Ibid., 255–300.
63. Colin Wight, *Agents, Structures and International Relations: Politics as Ontology* (Cambridge: Cambridge University Press, 2006), 123–124.

IB. SYSTEMS THEORY AND ITS VARIANTS

CHAPTER

8

General Systems Theory and Morton Kaplan's Application in IR

CHAPTER OUTLINE

INTRODUCTION: ORIGINS AND GENERAL SYSTEMS THEORY

Systems theory predates Kenneth Waltz's neorealism as an application of the scientific method in IR but is still belated in its arrival. Some scholars trace this late entry to the relatively delayed impact of the behavioural persuasion in theoretical IR amidst the dominance of realism here.[1] However, this is only partly true. For, the discipline of IR remained immune and impervious to the impact of behaviouralism more because its emphasis on individual and small group behaviour did not suit a domain of social enquiry centred on nation states and sometimes larger entities. Of course, to circumvent the problem, some researchers started studying the relation between 'individual stereotypes' and attitude-formation towards other countries, or insights into in social and political psychology regarding the impact of individual leaders on international political processes and their outcomes. But researches of this type seemed quite distant from the chosen areas of most IR experts. A transition was needed.

Developments in the 20th-century POS that made this transition possible were led by a group of scholars at the behavioural science centre in Stanford in 1954–1955, who founded the Society for General Systems Research, later made an integral part of the American Academy for the Advancement of Science. In its yearbooks, Bertalanffy, Boulding and others wrote a few articles to state the main propositions of general systems theory (GST) and their possible applications in the natural and social sciences.[2]

If in these essays Bertalanffy noticed 'a general tendency towards integration of the various sciences, natural and social', apparently 'centred in a general theory of systems', promising achievement of the goal of the unity of science through 'developing unifying principles running "vertically" through the universe of the individual sciences',[3] Boulding detected the increasingly felt need 'for a body of systematic theoretical constructs which will discuss the general relationships of the empirical world'. After examining the various instances of interdisciplinary ferment among and cross-fertilizations of disciplines, Boulding detected two feasible alternatives for the organization of GST: (a) surveying 'the entire empirical universe...to pick out certain general phenomena which are found in many different disciplines', and constructing 'general theoretical models relevant to these phenomena'; and (b) arranging 'the empirical fields in a hierarchy of complexity of organization of their basic "individual" or unit of behaviour', and trying to 'develop a level of abstraction appropriate to each'. Thus conceptualized, GST would provide 'the skeleton of science' on which 'can be hung the flesh of particular disciplines and particular subject matters in an orderly and coherent corpus of knowledge'.[4]

From a historical perspective, it is astonishing that the concept of systems should seem so novel in political theory, rich with such major forms of holism as: Plato's suggestion about the big tabloid of the state; Rousseau's description of 'general will' as something different from the sum total or collective of individual wills; Adam Smith's 'concept of the self-regulating market and of non-purposive social formations in general', where in the interplay of their actions each individual is 'led by an *invisible hand* to promote an end which was no part of his/her intention'[5]; Kant's view of nature 'as a great artist...whose mechanical process makes her purposiveness visibly manifest, permitting harmony to emerge among men through their discord, even against their wills'[6]; Hegel's view of the 'clear, dialectical connection' between the 'unfolding of the Spirit in the world' and the actualization of the modern state[7]; and Marx's ideas of totality, retaining the influences of Hegelian holism.[8] And in IR too holism was manifested in BOP theories, premised in holistic characteristics of IP rather than in attributes of individual members dominated. So what is the source of this amnesiac feeling of novelty of the systems concept, if not caused by disinterest in behaviouralism?

The last suggestion seems plausible if we look at the epistemological see-saw in the history of science between atomistic and holistic modes of reflection. The dominance of atomism with its attendant mechanistic implications, established ever since the 17th-century physics adopted it in the form of 'corpuscularianism' under the leadership of Galileo, Descartes and finally Newton as part of a new cosmology initiated by Copernicus' heliocentric view, needed the new atomist physics to buttress it and was supported in the social sciences by Hobbes and Locke.[9]

Word Help

Corpuscularianism, blended with alchemy by early scientists such as Robert Boyle and Isaac Newton in the 17th century, is akin to the theory of atomism, except that while atoms were supposed to be indivisible, corpuscles could in principle be divided.

Early systems thinkers disliked the dominant atomistic mode of thinking because its mechanistic assumptions about the relationship between the variables unmediated by any intervention from any environment could at best tolerate closed systems, whose problems with closed system models were first noted by biologists. They denied that the changing behaviour of a living organism faced with threat was comparable to that of a gas increasing in volume when temperature is raised under constant pressure. This called for a new model that would give closer attention to their environment and their dynamic, often versatile, interactions with it. The main problem here was the supposition of 'conscious purposes' in their doings because of the uncomfortable implications of some 'telos' or 'entelechy' serving as a substitute for these organisms' cerebral or at least thinking abilities. It was resolved or circumvented once the concept of 'feedback' was developed in the field of cybernetics, manifested by sophisticated machines, and even cruder and simpler communications machines showed that it could create illusions of purposeful behaviour simply with a sensor.

The masterly statement of the role of feedback 'both in engineering design and biology' by Norbert Wiener[10] and others opened the way for treating both closed and open systems from an integrated conceptual framework. Physicists were already grappling with the problem of 'how living matter, while not eluding the "laws of physics" as established up to date, is likely to involve "other laws of physics" hitherto unknown'.[11] As Bertalanffy argued, there is need for 'an extension and generalization of the principles of physics and physical chemistry, complementing the usual theory of reactions and equilibria in closed systems, and dealing with open systems, their steady states, and the principles governing them'.[12] These new developments paved the way for the entry of GST in the social sciences and in IR with appropriate concepts.

SYSTEMS THEORETIC CONCEPTS

Before applying the systems concept to IR, it is important to clarify the meaning of the word 'systems' in close compliance with its meaning in GST and other disciplines, so as not to confuse it with systems analysis which is basically a management technique and involves breaking down tasks to treat problems in a phased and systematic manner, though sometimes illustrious thinkers like David Easton and some commentators on him use this epithet for their systemic frameworks.[13] To remove confusion, systems analysis is sometimes termed as 'systems integration', but it is no widely accepted.[14]

Oran Young proposed a good schema of systems approaches, distinct from systems analysis, using three broad groups of GST concepts, dealing with (a) the definition of systems in their entirety; (b) the processes of systems regulation and maintenance; and (c) innate propensities of growth and decay in systems.[15]

About the first group, bidding adieu to widely different numerous meanings of the word systems in physical, organismic, physiological, biological, electrical, electronic and social contexts,[16] and the minimal definition of system as 'simply a set of interrelated elements', for its woeful incompleteness in capturing complex social entities such as nation states and international politics and their environments, I choose a three-stage definition by John Lovell's with clarifications by Morgan:

- 'A set of component parts which together can perform some purposeful activity' (Morgan stresses 'purposeful', because although technically many systems lack purpose, only rarely will a study of a foreign policy system be unconcerned with its goals).
- 'Functional interrelationship of the parts' (important where 'the components work together', because if 'some are absent or do not work properly, the system will fail to work to capacity, or may even break down').
- 'An ongoing interrelationship between this set of component parts and the environment' ('system monitors the environment, responds to it, may even be able to influence it').[17]

The environmental component helps us differentiate closed inanimate systems from open living systems and centralized systems from decentralized ones. While all biological systems are open/centralized, social systems, including the international system, are open/decentralized. The concept of isomorphism allows us to compare different types of systems, identify their functional correspondences and apply GST for their understanding. Both analogies ('explanations done by relating something not yet understood to something understood') and isomorphism (present when 'common characteristics, structures, formulas and forms of organization are in accordance with different systems', i.e., 'when formally identical laws governing the functioning of materially different phenomena exist') are important for comparing between systems. Isomorphism facilitates 'indirect study of systems in terms of other systems (simulation) and the use of content-independent methods within different scientific areas'.[18]

Among the second category of GST concepts are: system equilibrium (both stable and unstable). Homeostasis or stable equilibrium says that a 'system survives only so long as all essential variables are maintained within their physiological limits'; and control functions create 'the state of dynamic equilibrium in a healthy organism', plus 'the ability of the body to maintain a narrow range of internal conditions in spite of environmental changes'. Integration, another concept, refers to the principles of organization and institutions holding the system together. Viability is 'a function of the proper balance between the autonomy of the sub-systems and their integration within the whole system', or of the balance between stability and adaptation.[19] Pattern maintenance and adaptation, two other important concepts of this group, refer to the 'preservation of identity' within systems.[20]

Among the third group of concepts, entropy and its negative are most important. Entropy as a 'fundamental law of physics' is 'just the natural tendency of things to approach the chaotic state', unless countered. When expressing in terms of this theory, the 'statistical concept of order and disorder', or 'the marvellous faculty of a living organism, by which it delays the decay into thermodynamic equilibrium (death)', one shows that it 'feeds upon negative entropy, attracting, as it were, a stream of negative entropy upon itself to compensate for the entropy increase it produces by living and thus to maintain itself on a stationary and fairly low entropy level'. Since 'entropy, taken with the negative sign, is itself a measure of order', Schrödinger preferred 'sucking out orderliness from the environment' to the 'awkward expression' of 'negative entropy'.[21]

APPLICATION OF GST TO SOCIAL SCIENCES EXAMINED

GST was applied in sociology by Talcott Parsons. His functionalist social analysis substituted the concept of society by 'the 'social system' and drew upon both the advances in GST in his time and his reading of Pareto in the 1930s. A social system is a 'system of interdependent structures and processes such that it tends to maintain a relative stability and distinctiveness of pattern and behaviour as an entity by contrast with its social or other environment'. Here, the 'functional significance' of roles and institutions could be explored either in the light of their 'function' for the system's internal *integration* or in the light of their impact on the system's *adaptation* to its environment. Functional structures and processes can perform either *instrumental* or *consummatory* tasks. While the former is about the means or resources required by a system, the latter is about the ends and goals to which it is directed. From the cross-cutting of these four italicized dimensions follows four functional processes of 'adaptation', 'goal attainment', 'integration' and 'latency'.[22]

Of course, Parsons' theory of social system does miss out many implications of GST as enunciated by Bertalanffy. Although both view systems as open, detect the presence of order in social groups and provide integrative viewpoints, they have important differences. While Bertalanffy sees order as 'negentropy' (highlighting negative entropy), Parsons sees it as mere equilibrium. He lacks Bertalanffy's rigour in resorting to verbal analysis sans mathematics and violates the second law of thermodynamics in making the suggestion that change will return either to the previous equilibrium or usher in a new one. Where Bertalanffy details a concrete system, Parsons visualizes an abstract one. Finally, in place of Parsons' part/whole analysis, Bertalanffy stresses on interactions among all parts of the system.[23]

David Easton's application of GST to political science may not have been directly rooted in the tradition of 'systematic politics', spearheaded by Karl Mannheim (in *Systematic Sociology: An Introduction to the Study of Society*, 1936) or Charles E. Merriam (in *Systematic Politics*, 1945). But while defining politics as 'authoritative allocation of values'[24] he was surely influenced by Harold Lasswell's conceptualization of 'Politics' as '*Who Gets, What, When and How*' (1936). While desisting from attempting a description of Easton's systems theory, encapsulated in three of his major books,[25] I stress that while developing a unified theory of politics applicable to all political systems and helpful in identify the conditions of their survival, Easton says that the explanation of political reality requires the linking of all the sciences. This is because 'the social sciences are analytic. Social problems are totalistic',[26] not amenable to discipline-defined packaging.

Easton saw the political system as a living open system, 'a boundary-maintaining set of interactions embedded in and surrounded by social systems to the influence of which it is constantly exposed'. It adjusts to changes in its environment through a dynamic equilibrium that preserves those characteristics which help us recognize that it is essentially the same system. Essentially, 'a set of interactions abstracted from the totality of social behaviour', through which values are authoritatively allocated in a society, the political system is a massive conversion process. It turns the 'demands' made upon it with the backing of 'supports' into 'inputs' which enter it and after being processed, result in 'outputs' in the form of legislations, executive acts or decrees. The latter again circulate in the environment and generate new demands backed by new supports, which enter the throughput via a feedback loop. In order to survive, the political system must pre-empt any demand stress either in the shape of information feedback from its output(s) or from the potential input overload emanating from the environment. The responses of the system may range from concrete outputs to 'symbolic outputs' or 'symbolic gratification'. It has to also cope up with support stresses resulting from failures of members, structural failures or output failures. These stresses can never be allowed to reach 'critical range' since at that juncture, 'authoritative allocation of values' goes haywire to an extent where the society, lacking a 'system of behaviour' which enables it 'to fulfil one of its vital functions', collapses. Easton did, however, admit that systems very rarely break down and political life, in whatever form, goes on.[27]

Systems theory was applied in comparative politics by Almond and Powell in a broad Eastonian framework.[28] Political systems were arranged in terms of their 'capabilities, conversion functions, and system maintenance and adaptation functions' and their interrelations. While capabilities are of different types, comprising 'extractive', 'regulative', 'distributive', 'symbolic', 'responsive', and 'domestic and international' dimensions, conversion processes relate to the structures they possess for the performance of the same input and output functions as well as their culture. For Almond, structure means 'the observable activities which make up the system', while political culture means 'the pattern of individual attitudes and orientations towards politics among members of a political system'. The major input functions are 'interest articulation', 'interest aggregation', 'political communication' and 'political socialization', while the major output functions are 'rule making' 'rule application' and 'rule adjudication'. The interrelation between the structures and cultures of political systems in the performance of these functions help us in comparing types of political systems such as 'primitive and traditional', and 'modern democratic and authoritarian'.[29]

THE SYSTEMS PERSPECTIVE: DO THE REALITIES OF IR FIT INTO IT?

Systems theorists would answer the question in the affirmative from theoretical reasons. First, since GST reduces the entire reality of the world to a dozen bio-physical and chemical principles, all areas of knowledge can be explained from this gestalt-oriented perspective. Only, to explain the behaviour of a particular 'unit', one should pitch its explanation holistically at a higher level by locating the 'unit' in a broader systemic framework. This is a point which has long been recognized by structural anthropologists, as for example in Lévi-Strauss's concept of a system including 'both the concept of system and that of structure'[30] and in his concept of 'order of order' or the 'interrelationship between the levels to which structural analysis can be applied'.[31]

Second, in the case of IR, the systems theorist would empirically argue that without resort to it, international politics will be nothing but a total of discrete actions of or bi- or multipolar interactions between states. For only the systems perspective can unearth the underpinning principles which give rise or scope to the particular configurations of relationships and identify a set of structures which give some meaning to the complexity and confusion coming from the welter of myriad interactions. Accordingly, systems theorists take the international system as the appropriate level of analysis, with the state providing the lower sub-systemic level, though some theorists circumvent state centricity to advocate a world society based approach where the individual will be the unit of analysis in place of states.[32]

Third, the four Parsonian functions of social systems—pattern maintenance, adaptation, goal attainment and integration—are minimally performed in international politics.[33]

- Pattern maintenance in the shape of interactions among nation states upholding their autonomy, avoiding both the possibility of world government or empire, and nuclear holocaust in its absence; adaptation, in the shape of the international political system's unfolding adjustment with the post-Westphalian and an emerging Eastphalian environment.[34]
- Goal attainment in the process and sense of survival of the system, amidst intermittent hiccups.
- Integration evidenced in the remedial attempts of the parts of the system to strike common ground even after drifting too far apart from or acting too much against each other, as in the case of the USA and the USSR throughout the history of the Cold War.

So the final verdict of Lieber is that 'while IR, in terms of an international system, are not characterized by a high degree of coherence or centralized authority, nor always by clear boundaries', they nonetheless more than satisfy the minimal definitional characteristics of an international political system.[35]

Since acknowledging the existence of a system does not automatically generate willingness to use a systems approach', as evident in the quarrels of the behaviouralists and structuralists in the field of linguistics,[36] even with such a broad-based approach as GST, interactions in any mechanical, biological or social systems, or in international politics can be studied from this framework, only if there is willingness. Morton Kaplan, dealt with in the following section, showed willingness in ample measure.

APPLICATION OF GST TO IR: MORTON KAPLAN

General Framework

The 'Preface' of *SAPIIP*[37] promises 'an attempt to analyse international politics systematically and theoretically'. Its first part describes 'alternative models of the possible international systems' together with the 'environmental circumstances' or 'conditions' under which they will either 'persist' or 'be transformed' into another alternative system. Some 'consequences' of his theory are hypothesized to be more verifiable empirically, such as comparison of national interactions under the more fluid alliance structures of the 'balance of power system' (hereafter BOPS), with its interest-centric, short-term and diverse groupings and of the less fluid alliance systems of the 'loose bipolar system (LBPS)', hinged on long-range interests and ideology, making some alliances or alignments probable than others. The second part of *SAPIIP* states 'a number of regulatory and integrative propositions', while the third explores 'propositions concerning the relationship between values, value change, information and social structure'. The fourth and final chapter focuses on 'game theoretic concepts' to tackle problems arising from 'the fitting of various models to the social structure of the international system'.

Since a theory of international politics 'normally cannot be expected to predict individual actions because the interaction problem is too complex, and because there are too many parameters', Kaplan allows expectation only of prediction of 'characteristic or model behaviour within a particular kind of international system'.[38] His writings since 1957[39] offer only 'macromodels' of international politics which evince patterns of recurrent and replicable characteristic behaviour, stemming from the consistency of their elements and their capability to fulfil national and international needs. These patterns have close connections with the types of actors operating in international politics, and also with military, economic, technological, demographic and other factors.[40] Later, he clarified that these 'macromodels' are not 'models of foreign policy process', although recent studies of Italian city–state system and Chinese Warlord system indicate that they can also be applied to relationships between regional and intranational systems, and regional and international systems.[41] However, to hope that the loose bipolar model would unravel the varieties of behaviour within the African sub-system despite being designed as 'an overarching system of international politics' would be as foolish as applying 'a model of monopolistic competition to explain the economics of the garment trade on the east coast of the USA'. Such confusion of different aims, structural levels of analysis, levels of complexity, levels of abstraction, levels of concreteness or descriptivity, and of 'the differences between the theoretical and the descriptive' would stall all moves for advancement of the discipline.[42]

His goal being discovery of regularities which would enable 'the organization of the materials of international politics within a simple framework of reasonable explanatory or predictive power', Kaplan searched for analytical tools that would 'abstract systematically the materials of international behaviour from their biographical and historical setting' and 'organize them into a coherent body of timeless propositions', applicable for all types of international actors and covering all issues of equilibrium and dynamic change. He hypothesized that: (a) a system will retain its equilibrium until a parameter value undergoes change and the system gets disturbed; (b) if a system with a 'locally stable equilibrium' is affected by a disturbance possessing critical strength, it will either reach a new state of equilibrium or cease being a recognizable system; (c) should the 'parameter value', that is, the disturbance which has brought about the change in the equilibrium, revert to its previous value and not be accompanied by any other 'critical change', and should the system still not revert to its original state of equilibrium, the change will be designated as 'system change' to mark it off from 'equilibrium change'. It means that even though ultrastable, the system is irreversibly transformed.

Kaplan thinks identification of the state of the system is possible only when 'values are assigned' to the five types of variables, 'the essential rules of the system, the transformation rules, the actor classificatory variables, the capability variables and the information variables'. The essential rules are those propositions which state general relationships between the actors of a system or which assign definite systemic role functions to actors, thereby containing 'the most important descriptive properties of the systems'. Transformation rules are those which match 'given sets of essential rules to given parameter values or step level functions'. They are important as indicators of the 'the behaviour necessary to maintain equilibrium in the system' and, with some knowledge of the existing state of the system and the value of its parameters, as prognosticators of the future trajectory of the system. When environmental circumstances are potent enough to produce changes in essential rules of systems, transformation rules detail the changes in that behaviour. The actor classificatory variables detail the 'structural characteristics' of the actors, important as the behaviour of units such as nation states, alliances and international organizations will differ according to their structural characteristics. The capability variables concern the ability of actors to initiate particular types of actions in certain 'specified settings' and comprise territory, population, industrial strength, different types of skills, military strength, amenities of transport and communication, alacrity to employ physical capabilities for projected objectives and the ability to enlist aid of others. Information variables include long-term aspirations as well as presently pressing needs of systems, estimates of capabilities, awareness of goals-fulfilling means and the different ways in which others may react to its actions or independently pursue their aims. GST views information as the negative of entropy. Kaplan also regards it as an important causal factor in the success of actions of political and social systems, apart from being critical in the prediction of the likely doings of the system in the near future.

The equilibrium of these systems is of three types. The first is within the set of essential rules, since if behaviour contrary to the essential rules emerges, one or more of the essential rules will also undergo change. Second, changes in the set of essential rules will induce changes in at least one of the other system variables. Third, any changes in the parameters of the system will lead to changes in the system. The reverse is also true. Although not equilibrium models in the full Parsonian sense, Kaplan's models are still ultrastable or even multi-stable, in Ashby's sense, being not static but rather accommodative of change within specified limits. Equilibrium in the model is a dependent variable, to be explained with the help of the model.

Kaplan views the political system as distinctive in that 'its rules specify the areas of jurisdiction for other decision-making units and provide methods for settling conflicts of jurisdiction'. Political systems can however be either 'system dominant' (its essential rules serving as 'parametric "givens"' for any or all the sub-systems) or 'sub-system dominant' (when its essential rules lack that power or status). The international system as we have known it for the last several hundred years tilts or veers to the sub-system dominant pole but was never absolutely so; these two terms being rather end points in a scale. Kaplan also brands political systems as directive or non-directive, the terms not fully synonymous with democratic or dictatorial. A system tilts more towards directivity when (a) it is hierarchical in nature, (b) directives travel top-down rather than bottom-up along its hierarchy and (c) the higher one travels up the hierarchy the fewer role occupants one finds. Besides, since a system is an analytical entity, it is better described by roles than by concrete personalized holders, senders or receivers of them. Kaplan says that functional differences between the roles of systems and sub-systems are determined by whether they 'couple activity within the sub-systems of a larger system or between system levels'.[43]

Kaplan's Six Pure Models of International System

Balance of Power System Model

Within this general conceptual framework, Kaplan offers his initial list of six models of international systems or more accurately, 'six states of equilibrium of one ultrastable international system': (a) BOPS, (b) LBPS, (c) the tight bipolar system (TBPS), (d) the universal system (UVIS), (e) the hierarchical international system (HINS) in both its directive and non-directive varieties and (f) the unit veto system (UVTS). Ordered 'along a scale of integrative activity', these systems seem are the ones that can be devised, and 'the most representative'. Each has the five types of variables mentioned earlier.[44]

Apart from BOPS and LBPS, the other systems are non-historical, only 'heuristic' exercises, and important because: (a) the models having historical counterparts contain 'predictions' about new hypothetical types of systems if certain conditions obtain, which might provide helpful testing grounds for subjecting existing models to confirmation and (b) without benefits of testing against such hypothetical systems, 'predictions concerning the transformation of existing systems would be too loose for confirmation'. The models of BOPS or LBPS might be simpler and less complicated, says Kaplan, than their historical referents, for omitting some essential rules from oversight or ignorance. But such omissions are not debilitating. For, first, they would reappear when applying or engineering the models. Second, long before Waltz claimed that a model represents theory, by picturing reality 'by simplifying it' either 'through omission or through reduction of scale',[45] Kaplan said that simplicity in the two models importantly represent their system relations in the 'clearest and starkest forms', even though they 'necessarily abstract from a far richer historical context'.[46]

As a model, BOPS is avowedly different from others for possessing an international social system without an underpinning political sub-system. In its theory sketch, BOPS has the following characteristics: (a) the only actors in the system are nation states, even though certain periods of this historical pattern were marked by the existence of other organizational forms such as the Danube Authority and the League of Nations.[47] (b) The major actors of the system accord higher priority to 'optimization of security', meant as 'survival as major nations', than to maximization of chances of hegemony, sacrificing in the process 'a moderate probability of hegemony' attended by a moderate chance of 'elimination as a major actor', even though the examples of Napoleon's France and Hitler's Germany seem to have somewhat problematized this assumption. (c) The weaponry of the system is conventional and non-nuclear. (d) The presence of 'stochastic and unpredictable increases of productivity' in the system that may 'destabilize' it, if not recompensed timely, induces every actor to go for a 'margin of security' more than 'its proportionate share' in the system's total capabilities. (e) The benchmark for the number of actors of the system is five, the only number for which 'the argument for limitation in war' would apply. Two is unstable as number. Three seems able to turn it into an unstable two-nation system, if in a war between two and one the defeated nation is successfully eliminated. The logic of instability is not spelled out for a four-nation system. (f) Each actor needs the help of 'allies' to reach its goals, in spite of its 'great nation status'.

From these system characteristics emerge the essential rules of BOPS. All 'universalistic in character', they express the characteristic behaviour of BOPS, as in his own words.

1. Act to increase capabilities but negotiate rather than fight.
2. Fight rather than pass up an opportunity to increase capabilities.
3. Stop fighting rather than eliminate an essential national actor (henceforth ENA).
4. Act to oppose any coalition or single actor which tends to assume a position of predominance with respect to the rest of the system.
5. Act to constrain actors who subscribe to supranational organizing principles.
6. Permit defeated or constrained ENAs to re-enter the system as accepted role partners or act to bring some previously inessential actor within the ENA qualification. Treat all essential actors as acceptable role partners.

For smooth operation of BOPS, ENAs are important. Contrary to the widespread belief that the historical referent of BOPS is the international politics of Britain, France, Prussia, Austria and Russia, 'in the pre-First World War period, England, Germany, France, the Austro-Hungarian Empire, Italy and the USA fell within the essential actor category'. The first two essential rules stem from the need for an edge and an advantage of security over others in a world in which changes in capabilities are 'stochastically' unpredictable. Evidently, these rules are 'egoistic prescriptions' of Hobbesian provenance, although not violating 'classic philosophical standards' about 'the size of the just community' and 'practical limits' to it, because of seeking to reconcile the 'desirable' situation of a 'just ordering between communities' with 'the prudential necessity' of a community's strength to defend itself against potential enemies. The third rule, pertaining more to the 'classic standard' than Hobbes, warns the system about the dangers of expansion by ENA which might overshoot 'the optimal size of the just and lawful community' and recognizes the bonds between 'legitimate dynastic regimes' and 'modern national territorial states' arising in the system for ensuring the 'availability of future coalition partners'. The fourth and fifth rules are 'merely rational rules necessary to maintain the international action system', against potentially destabilizing actions of 'deviant actors' or 'of their followers or cohorts within other nations'. These two rules are also interlaced with the third, since limiting one's objectives and not eliminating other ENAs is necessary if one needs to align with them in the future. The sixth rule, also connected to 'the need for potential alliance partners' and cognizant of the dependence of membership in the system only upon behaviour which is in accord with its essential rules or norms, 'warns against restricting one's own choices unnecessarily'. For, keeping the number of ENAs 'above a critical lower bound' is an essential prerequisite of the stability of the system, which obviates reduction in number of essential actors.

No reduction in the number of essential rules is possible, because each one is in equilibrium with others in the set and is 'interdependent'. They are less 'descriptive' but rather 'prescriptive', which means that 'governing assumptions' being what they are, states will have sufficient motivation to abide by these rules, irrespective of other considerations to maximize their security, even though they are not required to do so. This will make the model both 'predictive and descriptive', showing some obvious as well as not-so-obvious consequences. Alliances are likely to be specific, short-lived and moved by advantages rather than ideologies. Even belligerents will not flout the rules of the system because they ensure the security of all including themselves. Apathy to 'intervention in the domestic affairs of another state, a rule violated on many occasions', also tends to be sustained under the conditions of the model. Fear of permanent alignments that may result from interventions either on the side of the rebels or of the government would incline states towards non-intervention. For similar reasons, recognition of new states would also follow objective considerations.

Loose Bipolar System Model

Structurally, unlike BOPS, LBPS is first populated by both supranational and national actors. Second, the supranational actors are further divided into 'bloc actors', exemplified by the NATO and the Communist bloc, and 'universal actors', as instantiated in the UN. The system being bipolar, a leading actor for each bloc constitutes a pole in the system. Third, the model is marked by role differentiation, caused by its norms. Unlike BOPS, where system norms are applied uniformly for all international actors, the norms of LBPS are 'specialized' leading to greater systemic complexity. Fourth, apart from blocs and bloc members, there are nations not aligned with either bloc, neutral actors.

The functioning of the system is shaped by the 'organizational characteristics of the supranational blocs'. If both are non-hierarchical in organization, it may look like BOPS, with the only change that 'shifting of alignment' occurs at 'two fixed points'. In spite of this, the bloc actors will remain comparatively loose organizations, allowing the system considerable flexibility. If one is hierarchical while the other is not, the resultant mixed hierarchical bloc will keep its membership undisturbed because its functional integration will make it hard for non-leading members to withdraw and maintain national integrity after withdrawal. The resulting constancy of membership will pose a sufficient threat to new members about joining it except when forced by military annexation or by political victory of a native political party already having 'associate membership in the bloc'. The unchangeable solidity of membership in the bloc will instil fear in the minds of other national actors, whether aligned with the rival bloc or independent. By contrast, in spite of loose control over members, the non-hierarchical bloc will have greater chances of forging 'cooperative pacts of one kind or another with non-bloc members'. However, the pressures generated by the hierarchically minded bloc will compel it to integrate more functionally or face instability. But if both blocs opt for hierarchical organizing principles, membership of both will become rigid, allowing alteration of existing alignments only with active support of uncommitted members to one of them. But if it happens, the flexibility of the system will be harmed by the disappearance of neutral actors. Non-bloc actors would accordingly desist from such total support for any one bloc, rather limiting themselves to support on specific issues.

Regarding capability variables, the weaponry in LBPS is nuclear, which in the contemporary times of 'efficient logistics and great organizational capacity' renders this feature 'an essential element of the system'. For, unless deterred by factors of scale resulting from their use, either of the blocs can be expected to go for the elimination of the other.

In *SAPIIP*, Kaplan stated 12 essential rules of LBPS, which are as follows:

1. All blocs subscribing to directive hierarchical or mixed hierarchical integrating principles for the international system are to eliminate the rival bloc.

2. All blocs subscribing to directive hierarchical or mixed hierarchical integrating principles for the international system are to negotiate rather than fight, to fight minor wars rather than major wars and to fight major wars—under given risk and cost factors—rather than to eliminate the rival bloc.
3. All bloc actors are to increase their capabilities in relation to those of the opposing bloc.
4. All blocs subscribing to non-hierarchical or non-directive hierarchical organizational principles for the international system are to negotiate rather than fight to increase capabilities, to fight minor wars rather than fail to increase capabilities, but to refrain from initiating major wars for this purpose.
5. All bloc actors are to engage in major wars rather than permit the rival bloc to attain a position of preponderant strength.
6. All bloc members are to subordinate objectives of universal actors to the objectives of their bloc but subordinate the objectives of the rival bloc to those of the universal actor.
7. All non-bloc member national actors are to coordinate their national objectives with those of the universal actor and to subordinate the objectives of bloc actors to those of the universal actor.
8. Bloc actors are to attempt to extend the membership of their bloc but to tolerate the non-member position of a given national actor if non-tolerance would force that national actor to support the objectives of the rival bloc or to join the rival bloc.
9. Non-bloc member national actors are to act to reduce danger of war between the bloc actors.
10. Non-bloc members are to refuse to support the policies of one bloc actor against the other except in their capacity as a member of a universal actor.
11. Universal actors are to reduce the incompatibility between rival blocs.
12. Universal actors are to mobilize non-bloc member national actors against cases of gross deviancy, for example, resort to force, by a bloc actor. This rule unless counteracted by other rules, would enable the universal actor to become the prototype of an international police system.

Although these dozen rules left greater scope to gear the functioning of LBPS to the organizational characteristics of the two blocs, Kaplan reduced them to leaner and sleeker eight in *SAIIP*, may be because he wanted the rules to operate at a higher level of generality. They are as follows:

1. Blocs strive to increase their relative capabilities.
2. Blocs tend to be willing to run at least some risks to eliminate rival blocs.
3. Blocs tend to engage in major war rather than to permit rival blocs to attain predominance.
4. Blocs tend to subordinate objectives of the universal actor to objectives of the bloc but subordinate objectives of rival blocs to [those of] the universal actor.
5. Non-bloc actors tend to support the universal actor generally and specifically against contrary objectives of blocs.
6. Non-bloc actors tend to act to reduce the danger of war between blocs.
7. Non-bloc actors tend to be neutral between blocs, except where important objectives of the universal actor are involved.

8. Blocs tend to extend membership but tend to tolerate the status of non-bloc actors.

The first three rules are avowedly indicative of the uncertainties of LBPS and the consequent need for an additional measure of security. The fourth rule states the need for 'mediatory' roles occasioned by the system, particularly in this nuclear age. While supporting such processes, against bloc leaders' lip service to such processes while seeking to utilize them to get favourable solutions, non-bloc actors find the greatest sources of succour in universal organizations and their 'universally applicable rules of conduct'. Since their interests in keeping objectives of the universal actor above those of rival blocs become hard to realize during times of major wars, Rule 6 suggests that non-bloc actors try to reduce the chances and possibilities of major wars. Again, since non-bloc or neutral states cannot perform this peace-promoting function without a measure of neutrality, Rule 7 enjoins it and Rule 8 shows bloc leaders desirous of extending bloc membership and yet valuing the mediatory role of uncommitted nations enough to suffer their independence and neutrality are called for.

For Kaplan, the first consequence of these rules is that alliances would be 'long term, based on permanent and not shifting interests', and would have strong 'ideological' factors. Wars would be 'unlimited' except when limited by fears of nuclear escalation. Universal organizations would be supportive of all 'mediatory and war-dampening' endeavours. International law would have 'few restrictions on intervention' except those prompted by fears of nuclear escalation. Regarding reasons of these consequences, alliances will be such not only because of the 'tendency' of the bloc members to support the 'leading member even on issues where there is a temporary divergence of interests' but also because of the 'tendency for ideological congruity in the bloc'. Wars will be extended and without limits because 'neither bloc would regard the other as a potential role partner'. Constraints on intervention through opposition from the other bloc would not be as quick and 'massive' as in BOPS. Still, 'fear of confrontation and escalation' would somewhat dampen the urge towards intervention. Some intervention would not be inconceivable in areas where one bloc had 'easy access' which the other did not. But in areas where both blocs had same ease of access, the area could either be kept insulated from 'bloc competition' or kept open for it, as demanded by the 'specifics of the situation', making general prediction difficult. But the 'fear that erosion of this particular rule of law' might gnaw at the 'general system of law' can be an inhibiting factor in attempts at intervention. So interventions that happen would be mostly 'indirect and covert'. Use of force would be permissible because of the same set of factors which tolerate intervention, in spite of the injunctions of the provisions of the UN Charter against it, as exemplified in the episodes of Palestine, the Congo, Cyprus, Greece, Korea, Vietnam, Suez, Hungary and so on. The ingrained bipolarity of the system itself will induce competition and encourage resort to force in situations in which one bloc has a 'clear preponderance of capabilities'. Bloc leaders have no interest in allowing prolongation of any war that none of them countenance because of its chances, however slight, of transformation into 'central confrontation' and none find any reason 'to risk even the lowest possibilities of nuclear war', particularly in situations in which benefits from use of force are not clear and there are convenient ways of avoiding it. Consequently, when universal organizations act to defuse armed confrontations and 'mediate conflicts' among non-leading nations, they serve the interests of bloc leaders. Unlike in BOPS, recognition is not based on the objective criteria of a state's control over a particular area or people's support of it but on the effects of such recognition for bloc policy, as suffered by East Germany, North Korea or Communist China at the height of the Cold War.

Kaplan says in *SAPIIP* that LBPS will have stability if six major conditions obtain to provide 'relatively constant bounds for the system':

1. Some mechanisms within the system are capable of conveying to all actors within the system the normative basis of the rules assigned for their role functions.
2. The rules of the system can 'integrate the role functions within the system'.
3. The rules of the system do not issue conflicting signals or instructions to any of the actors in important areas.
4. The blocs either keep within 'a similar capability range' or there are some other factors, internal or external, that 'prevent one bloc from taking advantage of its preponderant capabilities'.
5. Where LBPS accommodates more than two blocs, 'the additional blocs are minor' or of lesser capabilities than the polar blocs.
6. The blocs continue to augment their capabilities, since if any one of them is unable to defend itself, the capabilities hiatus cannot be filled up by neutral states or universal organizations. They might even 'defect to the opposed bloc' in such circumstances, and the bloc failing to preserve some degree of parity with the opposed directive hierarchical or mixed hierarchical bloc may go out of existence.

In the scenario depicted by the sixth condition, LBPS may change into HINS. Depending on whether the bloc in possession of greater capabilities is 'non-directive' or subscriber to supranational organizational objectives, LBPS may turn into BOPS or a universal or non-directive HINS.

LBPS be unstable under the following conditions:

1. Bloc actors are hierarchical in structure and national actors tend to disengage themselves from blocs, facilitating shift towards some kind of BOPS.
2. Hierarchy in structure and temperament, and animosity and discordance prevail between the blocs, heightening LBPS's tendency to change into TBPS or HINS.
3. Probability of war or surrender with greater degrees of dysfunctional tension in a system induces non-members to ignore their role function and join blocs, where LBPS will veer towards TBPS and persuades one bloc actor to succumb to a hierarchical or mixed hierarchical bloc, where LBPS will change into HINS; the tension leads to total war, where the outcome will be HINS if one side is victorious or 'international anarchy' if none wins and both sides are drained and prostrated.
4. If the war draws to a stalemate, the course of the war may usher in TBPS by forcing new alignments. If the role structure of LBPS expectedly heightens dysfunctional tension among bloc actors and lessens it within bloc actors, resultant simultaneous strong 'integrative tendencies within the bloc actor systems' and 'disintegrative tendencies between the two bloc actors' will breed instability.

5. If non-member actors fail to perform their role functions against the pressures of the blocs, LBPS may tilt towards TBPS or HINS and harm the universal actor in either case.
6. If internal political conditions inside non-leading national actors of a bloc do not contribute to the proper functioning of blocs, they may move towards instability. Where instability of one bloc is juxtaposed with stability of a hierarchical or mixed hierarchical bloc, it may be conducive to the emergence of HINS. Contrarily, if the stable bloc is non-hierarchical, LBPS may veer towards BOPS, UVIS or a mixed form of international organization. Where both blocs are unstable, reversion to BOPS or emergence of UVIS is likely.
7. Some system stability/instability/transformations may depend on the ease or otherwise of communicating rules to the leading national actor within a non-hierarchical bloc. If the leading actor utilizes its pre-eminence and strength within the bloc to arm-twist pursuit of ordained policy objectives, this may generate deviant tendencies in the non-leading members of the bloc. On the other hand, if the leading actor encourages formulation of policy objectives through consultation and compromise, bloc policy may prioritize maintenance of integrative propensities of the bloc over increasing relative capabilities of the bloc. In either situation, LBPS may veer towards HINS.
8. If a universal actor gets full success in the performance of its role functions, it may pulverize the bipolar system to usher in UVIS.
9. If the capabilities of one bloc actor increase or decrease disproportionately relative to the other, the system leans toward HINS. But if because of changes in technology, skills, economic facilities, discovery of resources and transformations in other logistic factors, the capabilities of both bloc actors increase disproportionately with respect to the rest of the international system of action, the system will veer towards TBPS. On the contrary, if capabilities of both sharply decline with respect to the rest of the international system of action, the system will tilt towards BOPS or UVIS.
10. Finally, LBPS suffers from a great amount of 'inherent instability'. Non-member actors' or universal actors' activities may seldom have potency to determine the contours of the policies of bloc actors. But their security cover is better than that of bloc actors, because encroachments on their sovereignty by one bloc actor would surely be resisted by another. However, bloc actors are 'considerably less secure' than them or than even the major actors of BOPS. Their 'strong strains' induce each to pre-emptively eliminate the other before it is itself wiped out by it. Amidst the unprecedented destructive power of modern weapon systems, such elimination becomes an unrealizable goal, and each bloc actor settles for 'some form of accommodation' by the other, to the extent permitted by 'the dysfunctional tension within the system and the insulating effects of the various national systems'. The 'vast changes in the international system of action' resulting from it may propel it towards UVS.[48]

Tight Bipolar System Model

TBPS, the first of the ahistorical systems, may experience some stability only when both bloc actors are hierarchically arranged, because when they are organized non-hierarchically, the desideratum of stability will induce it to turn into LBPS. The first noticeable change in TBPS is the removal of non-member national actors, universal actors and of their role functions because: (a) there are no uncommitted national actors for the universal actors to mobilize and (b) universal actors have left nothing to mediate. For, 'mediation always assumes a wider frame of reference within which differences are composed', which is no more available to universal actors after removal of uncommitted national actors. Even if universal actors have lingered, they remain 'microcosmic replica' of those of the LBPS era.

The second change is that all rules related to the functions of the uncommitted national actors and universal actor having disappeared, the rules under TBPS will comprise only instructions to the bloc actors concerning their goals and aspirations within the system and rules governing their relationship with each other, that is, only 'bloc-directed rules' of LBPS will survive. None of these rules will be able to control and limit dysfunctional tension within the system. Since both blocs will be nearing the hierarchical or mixed hierarchical forms, turning mutually incompatible, tension will pervade the system. The suppression of domestic interests and objectives of non-leading member states will cause 'deviant behaviour'; obsequious acceptance of directives of bloc leaders, but 'sabotage of agreed action'; and lessened sensitiveness to bloc communications. Organizational rigidities of blocs will be further ossified in the face of heightened external pressures. Lack of solidarity will permeate the system, marked by the absence of integrative devices and mechanisms. A system of this type can persist only when leading actors lack the capacity to change it. Such capacity can come in turn when due to technological or other developments one bloc actor gains a comparative advantage of sufficiently ample proportions over another. Although vast potential improvements in the retaliatory power of intercontinental ballistic missiles (ICBMs) and other weapons systems may deter even a bloc in such advantageous position from risking a combat, this tenuous 'factor of stability' can be neutralized by the mounting 'suspicions' let loose by TBPS and the perceived advantages of a surprise attack.

Universal International System Model

Arguably an offshoot of the elongation and acceleration of the activities of the universal actor in LBPS, UVIS, the second ahistorical system, bears the birthmarks of its genealogy. In contradistinction to the three alternative systems examined above, it possesses a political system as a sub-system, which 'with respect to some functions… will determine the jurisdictional boundaries of its members', although not for all decision-making functions, many of which will yet be left to the 'national sub-systems of the international system'. But if it starts affecting other political systems going beyond individual human beings, UVIS would fall in the category of 'confederated systems' and take the shape of 'an integrated and solidary system', endowed with integrative mechanisms that would perform functions with judicial, economic, political and administrative significances. Some national actors, normally habituated to seek attainment of their objectives 'only within the normal confines of the system', might band together informally under the organizational network of UVIS in the form of 'territorially based coalitions', 'ad hoc' coalitions or coalitions formed for exchanging favours or mutual voting support. But even under such informal groupings, recourse to the political rules of the system for settling conflicts of interest among them would be the normal pattern, overseen by a set of political officials and administrators owing allegiance to the international system itself rather than to its territorial sub-systems. The stability of otherwise UVIS would be determined by its 'direct access to resources or facilities' of the system or by the ratio of the capabilities of the general system and its national components.

The essential rules of UVIS would be as follows:

1. All national actors should attempt to increase their rewards and access to facilities.
2. All national actors should attempt to increase the resources and productive base of the international system.
3. When Rules 1 and 2 give rise to conflicting prescriptions, Rule 1 is to be subordinated to Rule 2. Likewise, if the operation of Rule 1 threatens the minimal standard of any national actor, it is to be submitted to considerations involving the ascriptive base of the total society.
4. All actors should use peaceful methods to obtain their objectives. They should not resort to force or to threat of force.
5. Human beings who have role functions within the organs of the international system should make decisions in these roles according to the requirements of the international system, not modifying their decisions by reference to national actors in which they also happen to hold membership.[49]

Hierarchical International System Model

The nature of HINS will differ according to its mode of formation: 'directive', when imposed by force on reluctant national actors in a bipolar or universal system, and 'non-directive', when evolved from UVIS; predominantly authoritarian in the former case and democratic in the latter. If HINS is formed as a result of 'world conquest by a national actor system like the Nazi system', the rewards system would be governed by 'ascriptive criteria' related to 'qualities of the actors like race or skin colour' and may not last long. But in its democratic avatar, HINS would comprise a political system in which functional lines of organization will dominate over geographical ones, thereby ensuring greater integration and stability, since the cross-cutting functional lines would be far more irreversible, even if the constitution of HINS allows such withdrawal. HINS would act directly upon human individuals, although intermediate levels of organization may exist as well. 'However, the national actors will lose their primary role function of transmitting the rules of the national systems', being 'territorial subdivisions of the international system' instead of 'independent political systems'. National rules would only be relatively uniform products of international rules, even if tailored 'to circumstances specific to individual localities'. Integration will span a range of functions wider than in UVIS. The rules of rewards and access to the facilities aimed at territorial actors in UVIS will be targeted primarily at 'functional actors such as unions, industrial organizations, police organizations and medical organizations' in HINS. The measure of territorial organization of these 'interest groupings' notwithstanding 'the functional lines across the territorial divisions will be more communicative than channels linking diverse functional activities within a given territory'. Coalitions formed for realization of 'political objectives' will also tend to be functional rather than territorial. The system accordingly would have considerable solidarity and nothing short of widespread destruction of communications facilities will spell its end.[50]

Unit Veto Systems Model

Sometimes wrongly confused with multipolarity, UVTS depicts a hypothetical situation in which 'some twenty odd nations have nuclear systems capable of a not incredible first strike', each possessing a nuclear arsenal which if the plan worked nicely, would wound enemy forces so grievously that a first strike would not be bad strategy. But even after a successful first strike, the attacking nation, just because its arsenal is emptied or vastly reduced, may be exposed to a possible attack by a third nation, whether because of the 'unprovoked' nature of its attack or simply due to the evil intention of the third nation. These calculations may dissuade a nation from a first strike except under grossly trying circumstances. Such a system will barely need 'specific' alliances, save 'pacts' enjoining an obligation against a nuclear 'aggressor' who has mounted a nuclear assault beyond certain specified proportions, although 'countervalue' (i.e., 'directed against cities or other non-combatant installations' possessing 'social importance') or 'counterforce' (i.e., directed against a nation's 'nuclear installations') assaults are unlikely. All the same, the system leaves chances for 'catalytic' or 'triggering' wars.

As a type of an international system, UVTS would show a Hobbesian condition of same-level horizontal existence of national or bloc actors, depending on the kind of organization obtaining when 'weapons of the indicated level of destruction are possessed universally', but having no universal actors. It would be a 'stand-off' system which, as long as functioning under existing rules, would preserve the existing state of affairs. If emanated from LBPS, it will probably sustain the non-member national actors, not if it has evolved from TBPS. Proportional to the present extent of hierarchical organization, it would sabotage bloc actors and render universal actors non-functional. If it stems from BOPS, it will introduce the greatest changes in its system of transitory and ever-changing coalitions. UVTS cannot succeed HINS unless that system has been experiencing 'internal decay'. It is equally implausible that UVTS would emerge out of UVIS.

UVTS can find stability only if all actors are ready to confront threats and seek retaliation in case of a first strike. If any actors turn out to be cowed down by military blackmails, they are likely to be wiped out and the system is likely to experience transformation. If successful transformation takes place in a national-actor-based UVTS, the change may be confined to reduction in the number of national actors or lead to the creation of more blocs. Contrarily, if one actor can successfully blackmail all others, the system will change from UVTS to HINS. UVTS 'requires that a surprise blow be technically impossible'. Actors endowed with relatively more territory and not possessing missile launching sites outside its territory would face total destruction. Finally, it is not implausible that an actor, through a combination of surprise first strike and far superior resources, would snuff out all other actors and install HINS. Or when in such a non-integrated and non-solidary system, dysfunctional tension soars to a point where human abilities of the actors buckle under the strain—making 'surrender to blackmail' increasingly likely and rendering the system chaotic—it may induce members to favour the formation of UVIS or HINS or negotiate 'joint agreements against any actor that attacks any one of the group'.[51]

Kaplan's Four Mixed Empirical System Models of International System

Apart from the above six models, Kaplan also offered a few mixed empirical system models later. Conceived as variations of LBPS or UVTS, these occur during situations when the two pure models do not enjoy maximum stability and, even if not 'genuinely equilibrium systems', depict conditions that might arguably prevail 'for critical periods of time', having in that sense a measure of local stability and meriting exploration as indicators of 'potential lines of development from the present situation'. The four models are very loose bipolar system (VLBS), détente system (DNTS), unstable bloc system (USBS) and incomplete nuclear diffusion system (INDS).

Very Loose Bipolar System

VLBS is marked by high, innate instability and is offered only because of its remarkable correspondence with contemporary international reality. It reifies the non-member actors of LBPS in terms of history, culture, economic growth, colour of skin and so on as economically straitened and lagging, modernization and development seeking, coloured ex-colonies of NATO. Here, increased nuclear stability has minimized the fear of a 'central' war except when caused by escalation. But the disappearance of classic military warfare (whether of movement or positions) has still left pockets of 'guerrilla and sublimited wars', as also 'rare limited wars', in sites where chances of escalation are low. Blocs continue despite debilitation. But spacious areas of concord and shared interests between the USA and the Soviet Union, the potential menace to them embodied by a rising and emerging Communist power in China and limited nuclear proliferation have shifted local stability to new loci. Blocs vie for support of uncommitted actors on issues of decolonization and racial justice inside the universal organization, but here the bloc that conservatively justifies the status quo is 'outbid' by the other, except where it can intervene militarily or financially. The blocs' struggle for the support of uncommitted actors may be hijacked by 'more or less radical wings of the revolutionary blocs'.

Other new tendencies visible in VLBS are: (a) 'quasi-legitimization of intervention against existing "conservative" governments by revolutionary governments (as evidenced in the 'announced support for the Congolese rebels by the Egyptian and Algerian governments')'; (b) quest for limitation of nuclear weapons sustained by inter-bloc accommodation; (c) interrogation of bloc policies by important bloc members resulting in 'a fragmentation or at least weakening of bloc structures'; (d) more frequent violations of the rule of non-intervention than in LBPS and (e) using the universal organization less as 'a mediatory instrument' and more as a means to 'control the path of political change'. Only great moderation on the part of the bloc leaders can save the system from going haywire.

Détente System Model

Prognostications of some welcome changes in the orientations and activities of the American and Soviet led blocs supplied the flesh of the hypothetical DNTS, although failing to predict developments from the mid-1960s up to the mid-1970s, Kaplan said that 'no responsible, reasonable and cautious social scientist' would risk forecasting such changes. The projected changes are: (a) opening up of the Soviet system and decrease of its aggressiveness; (b) lesser defensiveness of the USA in respect of the reigning international status quo; (c) taming of the Chinese system and chastening of its tendency to 'create difficulty' and (d) stabilization of much of the 'uncommitted' actors or of the so-called 'Third World'. Because of arms limitation pacts, countenancing of nuclear armament of 'finite deterrence' only by Russia and America and signs of reduction of existing stockpiles to only those needed for minimum deterrence, 'tensions are relaxed'. The workings of DNTS further loosen up the internal structures of the two blocs, as a result of which satellites of both the blocs take advantage of the emerging fissures within the blocs to take foreign policy stances consonant with those of the other. Even if most issues still generate groupings revolving around the two blocs, yet issue-specific variances in alignments are visible and some issues even find them concur against China or one or the other Western powers. With anti-colonialism finding its consummation, foreign polices of both the USA and the USSR favour 'liberal interventionism'. With the USA ceasing to support oligarchical but anti-communist regimes and the USSR learning to tolerate new non-communist nations and stopping 'support of national liberation movements within genuinely independent nations', the only source of trouble is the Chinese backing of national liberation movements.

In the domain of international law, the DNTS-induced changes are: (a) increased stress on 'non-intervention in the affairs of other states'; (b) new teeth acquired by rules of international law overseeing anti-expropriation in the governing of 'outer space', 'celestial bodies' and polar regions; and (c) activism of the universal organization regarding these, regarding eradication of colonialism, supervision of arms control measures and 'dampening of international breaches of peace'. So new breaches of peace no more involve direct confrontations between America and the Soviet Union and are likely to be local, circumscribed in objectives, confined to minor nations and strictly non-nuclear. Where these portend to be more, the USA and the USSR either 'cooperate within limits to prevent occurrences that might escalate' or at least do 'not seriously interfere with each other's action towards this end'. They involve the universal organization in all such endeavours.

Unstable Bloc System Model

USBS embodies the opposite projections that led us from LBPS to DNTS, displaying high mutual distrust between America and the Soviet Union; minimal arms control measures; extensive 'third area conflicts'; 'local outbreaks of violence'; lingering problems posed by 'national liberation movements', 'qualitative developments' rendering nuclear systems far more affordable and available; and greater conflict. Apart from the USA and the USSR, capable of 'incredible massive retaliation', four or five other states are in possession of nuclear systems fit for minimum deterrence only. Although all nuclear powers have 'strategies calling for limited strategic reprisal under appropriate circumstances', the USA and the USSR can far more easily and safely employ this strategy than the smaller nuclear powers not only against them but also against each other. It is not realistic and believable that smaller nuclear powers would employ 'limited strategic reprisal' against one of the larger holders for fear of fitting retaliation.

Alliance policy is determined by military might and strategy. Where the stance of America would not be matched by its capability for deterrence against retaliation targeting countries besides itself, the strains on its crisis-period alliances might be too onerous, except where the capabilities of allies combined with her own may be equally countervailing. The same considerations would apply for the Warsaw Pact powers, except that 'the organic relationships' among its members may, even if debatably, expose them less to such 'splitting tactics'. Generally, bloc alignments will be troubled by two 'conflicting pressures'. While endemic crisis in an essentially bipolar world would provide rationale for existence and greater cohesion to the blocs, their or their partners' repulsion to nuclear devastation of home ground would make them susceptible to nuclear blackmail, potent enough to 'shape expectations, attitudes and national policies'. How these contrary pressures will interact will depend on various calculations that cannot be forethought in the abstract. Foreign policy positions of both the blocs will be plainly 'interventionist' and reactive to basic clashes rather than concurrence of interests as in DNTS. Kaplan supplies details of the emergent situations and policy responses of the USA, the USSR and China.

Violations of peace stemming from face-to-face confrontations between the two superpowers, even though improbable, are not ruled out, and use of nuclear weapons in a limited manner, representing the 'limited reprisal variety' is allowed distinct chances. The universal organization remains preoccupied with its mediatory and mollifying role, siding with neither of the blocs. It would have no jurisdiction over issues relating to 'outer space, celestial bodies and arms control measures'. Interventions in USBS will be unchecked, limited only by the menace of nuclear escalation. Growth of international law will be at its tardiest.

Incomplete Nuclear Diffusion System Model

INDS has some similarities with USBS in that 15–20 odd nations other than traditional holders, the USA and the USSR, have nuclear forces, though not above the 'small, vulnerable variety'. Although it is a projection from UVTS, Kaplan stresses only on its dissimilarities with USBS. Here the USA and the USSR will possess nuclear weapons that would not suffice for first strike but would still provide significant advantage for the one employing them first. Smaller nuclear powers in possession of 'minimum deterrence' can expect only to deter assaults on the home country, though even that in highly provocative circumstances. Alliances between major or minor nuclear powers or between minor nuclear powers are not improbable, although the larger partner may fear being embroiled by the smaller partner's recourse to them. Of course, a general alliance among most of the nuclear-equipped small powers may ensure a 'reasonable deterrent'. But unless 'exceptional political or cultural circumstances' worked against it, the alliance may be prone to 'nuclear blackmail or splitting tactics'. Just as in USBS, wars are likely to be limited but would have greater tension and tendencies towards escalation. But owing to these factors, chances of a 'central confrontation' would decrease. The arbitrative mediatory roles of the universal organization would be greater than in USBS, and more emphasized, but other functions would lessen. Legal regimes would be weaker than in USBS, leading to more widespread interventions in other nations' internal lives. The 'conservative interventionist' tone of American foreign policy and the 'revolutionary' tone of Soviet foreign policy would be more marked. The disaffection and estrangement of some intellectuals and the counter trend of chauvinism of others will split informed opinion vertically within both blocs and their leaders. Lacking poise, governments and their defenders would vacillate between crippling caution and reckless adventurism.[52]

Kaplan: From Computerization to Engineering of the Models

Kaplan resolved to engineer the models from a realization that they were 'merely tools for investigating reality' and as per the forewarning in *SAPIIP*, they were merely 'hypothetical', 'quite crude' and 'based at best on plausible reasoning'. He admitted that the essential rules of some systems which enjoined increasing capabilities did not specify their extents, or permitting 'risk conditions', and general statements of the models contained unavoidable ambiguities. Differentiating between the behaviour of a nine-nation system and a seven-nation system just verbally, 'using words', also proved impossible. So he decided with co-researchers to 'play out realizations' of BOPS on a computer, through numerous simulations, to be able to 'link outcomes to the parameters that produce them'; test the susceptibility of the computer program to variances in the parameters; 'explore changes in the numbers of players, the battle exchange ratios, the motivations of the players' and so on; and find out what parametric changes would restore stability if the outcome was unstable. To ascertain if BOPS would function differently if the actors were 'hegemony oriented' instead of 'security oriented', they designed a 'pilot computer model' which revealed that while the presence of a hegemony-minded actor rendered the system unstable, initially a 'balance-oriented' actor was disadvantaged. But if the program was run to the end, the logic of the system ensured that the hegemony-oriented actor would lose in the end. Additionally, the program revealed that 'in a system of five states, wars will tend to be three against two and that wars of four against one will tend to destabilize the system'. Since in the initial pilot runs, wars were dominantly four against one, though still some of the systems continued to be stable through hundreds of war cycles, showing no indication that further runs will produce instability, Kaplan and his colleagues modified the program so as to make three against two wars dominant outcomes.[53]

The decision of engineering the models too was necessitated by some mismatches between these and real systems, arising from the fact that despite being 'closed systems', the models were being expected to apply to open systems. For example, while BOPS alliances were supposed to be 'transitory', interest driven, and oblivious of present or past alliance history in the models, the inflexible alliance pattern of Europe's great powers between 1871 and 1914 as well as the unlimited nature of the First World War belied the prescriptions. But since one cannot draw upon a separate systems model to examine 'every characteristically different state of the world', Kaplan pondered over how the underpinning theory of BOPS could be employed to explain the 'observed discrepancies', by diagnosing what other factors contributed to the 'specific sequence of events' and the 'general form' that they assumed, and by deciding under what conditions an existing theory can be 'extended' or a different theory has to be introduced. Since for Kaplan the six systems models offered in *SAPIIP* were 'equilibrium models' for explaining the corresponding phases through which the far more complex real world passes, he left undecided if these phases were to be regarded as 'real system changes or merely different equilibrium states of one ultrastable international system'. The discrepancies between the inflexible alliance system of the period 1871–1914 and the flexible and shifting alliance system postulated by BOPS could be explained by 'adjusting the theory for the change which French public opinion caused at the parameter'. He was aware that each historical system finds its incarnation in its distinctive and peculiar set of circumstances, that in some cases variances in these circumstances 'do not generate 'behavioural irregularities' calling explanations linked to 'variations at the parameter', but that in other cases such divergences facilitate 'either less or more stability in the system than would otherwise have been expected'. So Kaplan got ready to isolate causally unimportant or important parameters or such idiographic factors as the role of mercenaries in the Italian city–state system. In the Chicago workshops, they also decided 'to use historical studies to provide comparative material'. The parameters considered sensitized Kaplan and his team to the mistake of 'assuming the dominance of international factors in events of international importance' since in all these systems, 'the actors who threatened the stability of the system were sub-system dominant and directive'. In Kaplan's three historical examples, 'the Kuomintang roll-up of China, the Macedonian roll-up of Greece and the later Roman roll-up of Greece', it was not a central actor but a peripheral one who stacked up what is considered from some perspectives as a 'central system'. Since 'different combinations of parameters' may be compatible with equilibrium and a 'series of comparative studies of both regional and international systems' did help them 'fit the parameters of international systems' much more effectively than they can do at present, Kaplan advised that where behaviour is consonant with the model, we 'search more thoroughly for parameters that reinforce the result'.[54]

CONCLUSION

This chapter has till now traced the origins of the systems approach in IR to the developments led by Bertalanffy and Boulding in the POS in the mid-1950s that created GST. After defining the term systems, briefly introducing to readers different GST concepts and acquainting them with its application in sociology by Parsons, political science by Easton and comparative politics by Almond and Powell, it discussed the application of GST in IR by Kaplan. Together with Kaplan's general conceptual framework, it has analysed more or less comprehensively the six pure and four mixed empirical models of international systems offered by Kaplan, with their theory sketches and five types of variables. The chapter has also given a brief glimpse into Kaplan's engineering of his models. So my readers have now a fair idea of Kaplan's ambitious approach, which we will evaluate together with other variants of systems approaches in Chapters 9 (available on the companion website) and 10.

REVIEW QUESTIONS

1. Trace the origins of systems theory in IR in GST and its applications in specific social sciences.
2. Define systems as it would be suitable in IR and state the systems theoretic concepts relevant to it.
3. 'The emergence of systems theory in social sciences was intimately bound up with the fortunes of the battle of atomism and holism as modes of reflection in the natural sciences.' Discuss.
4. Give theory sketches of the six pure models of international systems offered by Kaplan.
5. Attempt theory sketches of four mixed empirical models of international systems offered by Kaplan.
6. After describing the models of international systems offered by Kaplan, show why he needed to engineer them.

NOTES AND REFERENCES

1. Steve Smith, 'Paradigm Dominance in International Relations: The Development of International Relations into a Social Science', in *The Study of International Relations: The State of the Art*, eds Hugh C. Dyer and Leon Mangasarian (New York, NY: Palgrave Macmillan in association with *Millennium Journal of International Studies*, 1989), 12.
2. See Ludwig von Bertalanffy, 'General Systems Theory', *Main Currents of Modern Thought* 11 (1955): 75–83, reprinted in *Yearbook of the Society for General Systems Research*, vol. 1 (1956), 1–10; Ludwig von Bertalanffy, 'General Systems Theory: A Critical Evaluation' (1962), in *Yearbook of the Society for General Systems Research* 7 (1962): 1–20; Kenneth E. Boulding, 'General Systems Theory—the Skeleton of Sciences', *Management Science* 2, no. 3 (April 1956): 197–208; Kenneth E. Boulding 'Political Implications of General Systems Theory', *General Systems* 6 (1961); and for subsequent publications, 'Introductory Literature on General Systems', *Background* 7, no. 3 (November 1963): 133–135, available at http://www.jstor.org/stable/3013675 (accessed on 6 December 2016).
3. Bertalanffy, 'General Systems Theory'.
4. Boulding, 'General Systems Theory'.
5. H. W. Spiegel, 'Adam Smith's Heavenly City', in *Adam Smith: Critical Assessments*, ed. John Cunningham Wood, vol. 1 (London: Routledge, 1984), 576; Adam Smith, *The Theory of Moral Sentiments: With an Introduction by Pat Moloney* (New York, NY: Barnes and Noble Books, 1759/2004), 242; Adam Smith, *An Inquiry into the Nature and Causes of the Wealth of Nations* (London: T. Nelson and Sons, 1852), pt. IV, Chapter I, para 10, p. 184.
6. Immanuel Kant, *To Perpetual Peace: A Philosophical Peace*, trans. Ted Humphrey (Cambridge: Hackett Publishing Company, 2003), 18.
7. For arguments about the philosophy of right, see Jeanne Morefield, *Covenants without Swords: Idealist Liberalism and the Spirit of Empire* (Princeton, NJ: Princeton University Press, 2009), 32.
8. Tim Delaney, *Classical and Contemporary Social Theory: Investigation and Application* (New York, NY: Routledge, 2016), 39–40.
9. Bronowski and Mazlish, *Western Intellectual Tradition*, 215–218; Stephen Gaukroger, *The Emergence of a Scientific Culture: Science and the Shaping of Modernity, 1210–1685* (Oxford: Oxford University Press, 2006), 253–317; Peter R. Anstey, *John Locke and Natural Philosophy* (Oxford: Oxford University Press, 2011), 14.

10. Norbert Wiener, *Cybernetics of Control and Communication in the Animal and the Machine* (New York, NY: MIT Press, 1948/1961), vii.
11. Erwin Schrödinger, *What Is Life? With Mind and Matter & Autobiographical Sketches*, (Cambridge: Cambridge University Press [1944] 2013), 68.
12. Ludwig von Bertalanffy, 'The Theory of Open Systems in Physics and Biology', *Sciences III* 23, no. 9 (1950), reprinted in F. E. Emery, ed., *Systems Thinking* (Harmondsworth: Penguin, 1969–1974), 70–83.
13. David Easton, *A Systems Analysis of Political Life* (New York, NY: John Wiley, 1965); Harry Howe Ransom, 'International Relations', *The Journal of Politics* 30, no. 2 (May 1968): 345–371.
14. John E. Gibson, William T. Scherer, and William F. Gibson, *How to Do Systems Analysis* (Hoboken, NJ: John Wiley & Sons, 2007), 11.
15. Oran Young, *Systems of Political Science* (Englewood Cliffs, NJ: Prentice Hall, 1968), 17–19, 109.
16. Gibson, Scherer, and Gibson, *How to Do Systems Analysis*, 1–2.
17. Patrick M. Morgan, *Theories and Approaches to International Politics: What Are We to Think?* (New Brunswick: Transaction Publishers, 1987), 130.
18. Lars Skyttner, *General Systems Theory: Ideas and Applications* (River Edge, NJ: World Scientific, 2001), 35–36.
19. Ibid., 86, 93–94.
20. Anatol Rapoport, *General Systems Theory: Essential Concepts and Applications* (Tunbridge Wells: Abacus Press, 1986), 108.
21. Schrödinger, *What Is Life*, 69–74.
22. See 'Propaganda and Social Control', *Psychiatry* 5, no. 4 (1942): 552; A. Javier Treviño, *Talcott Parsons Today: His Theory and Legacy in Contemporary Sociology* (Oxford: Rowman and Littlefield, 2001), 31–32.
23. Debora Hammond, *The Science of Synthesis: Exploring the Social Implications of General Systems* (Boulder, CO: University Press of Colorado, 2010), 94; Kenneth D. Bailey, *Sociology and the New Systems Theory: Toward a Theoretical Synthesis* (Albany, NY: State University of New York Press, 1994), 152.
24. David Easton, *The Political System*, 2nd ed. (New York, NY: Alfred A. Knopf, 1971), n. 16, 129.
25. David Easton, *The Political System: An Inquiry into the State of Political Science* (New York, NY: Alfred A. Knopf, 1953); David Easton, *A Systems Analysis of Political Life* (New York, NY: John Wiley, 1965); David Easton, *A Framework of Political Analysis* (Englewood Cliffs, NJ: Prentice Hall, 1965).
26. David Easton, 'Commentary on Robert E. Lane's Paper', in *Integration of the Social Sciences through Policy Analysis*, ed. James C. Charlesworth, Monograph 14 (Philadelphia, PA: AAPSS, 1972), 88–89; Easton, *Political System*, 2nd Indian ed. (Calcutta: Scientific Book Agency, 1971), 346.
27. See David Easton, 'An Approach to the Analysis of Political Systems', *World Politics* 9, no. 3 (April 1957): 383–400; Easton, *A Systems Analysis of Political Life*; Easton, *A Framework of Political Analysis* (Englewood Cliffs, NJ: Prentice Hall, 1965), 26, 32–34, 89 passim; Sarah Joseph, *Political Theory and Power* (Delhi: Foundation Books, 1988), 51–56.
28. G. A. Almond and G. B. Powell, Jr., *Comparative Politics: A Developmental Approach* (Boston, MA: Little Brown, 1965), 17–27.
29. Ibid., 21, 50, 73–298.
30. Marcel Hénaff, *Claude Lévi-Strauss and the Making of Structural Anthropology*, trans. Mary Baker (Minneapolis, MN: University of Minnesota Press, 1998), 120.
31. Nathan Rotenstreich, 'On Lévi-Strauss' Concept of Structure', in *The Review of Metaphysics* 25, no. 3 (March 1972): 489–526.

32. This point, along with the preceding section on the origins of systems theory in IR, has been inspired by Richard Little, 'A Systems Approach', in *Approaches and Theory in International Relations*, ed. Trevor Taylor (London: Longman), 184–189, though the author has his own reading list.
33. Robert J. Lieber, *Theory and World Politics* (London: Allen and Unwin, 1973), 129–131.
34. For the notion of Eastphalia, see David P. Fidler, Sun Won Kim, and Sumit Ganguly, 'Eastphalian Rising? Asian Influence and the Fate of Human Security', *World Policy* 26, no. 2 (Summer 2009): 53–64.
35. Lieber, *Theory and World Politics*, 130.
36. Little, 'Systems Approach', 188.
37. Morton Kaplan, *System and Process in International Politics* (New York, NY: John Wiley and Sons, 1957/Colchester: ECPR Press, 2005), henceforth *SAPIIP*.
38. Ibid., xviii.
39. For Morton A. Kaplan's statement of systems theory, I will be citing from Kaplan's 'Balance of Power, Bipolarity and Other Models of International System', *American Political Science Review* 51 (September 1957): 684–695; Kaplan, *System and Process*, xi-xviii, 3–20; Morton A. Kaplan, ed., 'The Systems Approach in International Politics' (SAIIP), in *New Approaches to International Relations* (*NATIR*; New York, NY: St. Martin's Press, 1968), 331–404; Morton A. Kaplan, *Macropolitics*: *Essays on the Philosophy and Science of Politics* (Chicago, IL: Aldine, 1969); Morton A. Kaplan, *Towards Professionalism in International Theory* (New York, NY: Free Press, 1979).
40. Kaplan, 'Balance of Power', 684.
41. See Hsi-Sheng Chi, *The Chinese Warlord System as an International System* (Washington DC: Center for Research in Social System); and Winfried Frankel, 'The Italian City-State System as an International System' in Kaplan, *New Approaches to International Relations* (New York, NY: St. Martin's Press, 1968), 405–458.
42. Kaplan, *Macropolitics*, 209–210; Kaplan, 'Systems Approach', 385.
43. Kaplan, *System and Process*, 3–20; Kaplan, 'Systems Approach', 387–388.
44. Kaplan, *System and Process*, 21.
45. Waltz, *Theory of International Politics*, 7.
46. Kaplan, 'Systems Approach', 388.
47. I would like to add the Central Commission for Navigation on the Rhine, founded in 1815 and continuing till date, and regarded by many as the world's oldest international organization.
48. Kaplan, *System and Process*, 21–52; Kaplan, 'Systems Approach', 389–396.
49. Kaplan, *System and Process* (2005), 54; Kaplan, *Macropolitics*, 223.
50. Kaplan, *System and Process* (2005), 55–57; Kaplan, *Macropolitics*, 223–224.
51. Kaplan, *System and Process* (2005), 57–58; Kaplan, *Macropolitics*, 224–225.
52. Kaplan, *Macropolitics*, 226–233.
53. Kaplan, 'Systems Approach', 385–386.
54. Ibid., 396–404; Kaplan, *Macropolitics*, 234–244.

CHAPTER

9

Systems Theory: From Modelski to Singer*

CHAPTER OUTLINE

* This chapter is available on the companion website.

CHAPTER

10

Critique and Evaluation of Formulations of Systems Theory

CHAPTER OUTLINE

- GST and Its Applications in Social Sciences
- Kaplan
- Other Theorists
  - *Modelski*
  - *Rosecrance*
  - *McClelland*
  - *Holsti*
  - *Singer*
- Conclusion

GST AND ITS APPLICATIONS IN SOCIAL SCIENCES

The critique and evaluation of systems theory in IR in this chapter will only very briefly touch upon GST and its applications in various other social sciences. I start by positing appreciatively that with its host of theoretical assumptions about systemic relationships and analytical method for specifying them, the merit of systems theoretic thinking is not just limited to its 'heuristic value' or capacity to incite 'new questions' and suggest 'adoption of different perspectives towards an old subject'. Beyond bringing about 'a major widening of the scope of scholarly enquiry',

GST has facilitated 'a certain emphasis on formalization as a self-conscious adoption of a more social-scientific approach', introduced 'a specialized vocabulary and classificatory scheme for the ordering of information' and promoted the conduct of 'scholarly enquiry at different systemic levels' without losing sight of interrelationship among them. With proven 'potential for generating hypotheses and for sharing in a process of stimulus, modification and reinforcement', GST has encouraged recent studies of political integration and has in turn been benefited by the 'empirical evidence of complex interrelationships between system levels'. Besides, its preoccupations about pattern maintenance draw attention to 'broad patterns of stability and change', and its stress on world-wide perspectives diverts our attention away from discrete foreign policy studies to facilitate a better focus on 'significant international interdependence'.[1] Tellis concedes even after his scathing critique that with all its limitations, viewed in the light of IR's 'evolution into a scientific theory', systems theory 'represents one of the first systematic attempts at objectivizing the traditional pragmatic understanding of international politics and presenting the same as a rationalist construction capable of further development'.[2]

Leaving aside an early charge by Buck in 1956 that it is 'a concept that applies to everything is logically empty',[3] systems theory faced little flak in the 1950s and 1960s. But from the 1970s, it attracted a barrage of criticisms, the most comprehensive of them being from Ida Hoos, David Berlinski and Robert Lilienfeld. Hoos critiqued what she termed interchangeably as systems analysis and systems approach as an offspring of operations research in public and corporate administration. For her, arguments forwarded by Bertalanffy in its support were grounded in 'a number of interrelated and nebulous postulates'. Hoos faults Bertalanffy's approach on three counts: (a) platitudinous acclamations about 'isomorphisms' and the 'universal applicability of mathematics'; (b) confusing 'superficial analogies' which hide 'crucial differences' and may generate 'erroneous conclusions'; and (c) hindrance from a dogged adherence to an '"irreducibility" doctrine' to 'analytic advances'. Hoos is undaunted by Bertalanffy's riposte that these isomorphisms go much beyond analogies, since his new organismic biology is not a rehash of old and discarded bio-organismic theories but is a step towards a new view of 'organized complexity', where the general model, relevant equally to physiological, neurophysiological, behavioural and social phenomena, is sustained by a feedback system, spelt out mathematically or as a quantitative scheme depending on the limits of the field.[4] Berlinski's fiercer but less substantial critique focused on the abuse of mathematics by systems researchers, for what he called 'the use of mathematical methods for largely ceremonial purposes'.[5] After discussing the historical origins and later developments of systems theory, Lilienfeld sought to unmask its true colours of an ideology favoured by the new scientific and technocratic elites.[6] Apart from him, 'a fascination for definitions, conceptualizations, and programmatic statements of a vaguely benevolent, vaguely moralizing nature, without concrete or specific references to historical, social and even scientific substance', other vices of systems thinkers were 'a fondness for abstract schematic formulae and diagrams, having little practical reference' and 'an unstated and presumably invisible shift from concrete world "systems" in their fullness and complexity to closed formal models based on convenient simplified assumptions'.[7]

The holistic nature and claims of GST have also come under criticism in the field of the POS, where Nagel has critiqued the pretensions of organismic biologists to the 'absolute autonomy of biology' on the specious plea of the 'inherent impossibility of physicochemical explanations of vital phenomena'. He has warned with sufficient examples that if organismic biologists want to contribute to 'the advancement of knowledge' and avoid 'mistaken unenlightening statements' profusely interspersed with 'locutions' such as 'wholeness', 'unifiedness' and 'indivisible unity' for expressions of genuine knowledge, they would have to follow the 'abstractive and analytical' path in their research programmes.[8]

Limitations of applications of GST in various social sciences have also come under scrutiny. For instance, Easton's theory has been charged with leaving too little scope for issues of major change, as also with soft-pedalling questions of power and influence. Young contends that the system perspective downplays questions of 'who gets what' and tends to foreground systemic processes and functions by ignoring goals and their formulation, thereby leaving out much that is crucial for politics. Thus, in spite of being in many respects the most compendious systems approach for political analysis, Easton's systems analysis is reduced to a framework for organizing data. Almond's structural functional analysis is pilloried not only for sharing with Easton's approach a readiness to sacrifice reality at the altar of conceptual elegance but also for being overly static and committed to justifying status quo patterns in its endeavours to show the functionality of existing arrangements. It suffered from an eternal Panglossian 'what is good bias'. Besides, Gregor found Easton's minimalist definition of a system as 'any set of variables regardless of the degree of interrelationship among them' so lax that it made diagnosis of the presence or absence of a system as impossible as immaterial. Referring to an individual, a family, a church, an army or a polity in the same breath as a system is nothing more than speaking metaphorically.[9] Moreover, in the absence of any straightforward definition of a system, the concept could be applied to almost all patterns of interaction, and its use in IR is nothing more than 'interrelation'. But if its meaning cannot be extended beyond this assumption, then the concept becomes not only 'irrefutable' but also 'useless', and the theory 'loses any claim to uniqueness as a method of analysis of social events'.[10]

It is not surprising that in spite of these limitations, systems theory was welcomed in a field teeming with bland descriptive studies of foreign policies of individual states, explications of key concepts ranging from non-alignment to arms control, and idiographic studies of individual events of crises and war. These never illumined the 'dynamic processes' characterizing the international system, produced concepts and ideas which would help us 'compare one pattern of events in the international system with another' or allowed us 'to relate international behaviour to behaviour at other system levels'. Systems theory was expected to address these desiderata, but the euphoria was evanescent, when even after dabbling for two decades with it, practitioners stayed put at 'expounding the virtues of systems thinking'.

KAPLAN

Being the first applier of systems thinking to IR, Kaplan naturally drew the greatest flak from critics who complained that apart from producing a plethora of mechanistic models that never were empirically verified, the introduction of systems failed to advance any scientific understanding of the international system. Vital charged that being distanced so far from diplomatic practice, these macro models were nothing but exercises in 'latter-day scholasticism'. He brought to fore a basic incompatibility between behaviouralism and systems thinking, claiming that 'no really convincing grounds' exist for hoping that Kaplan's macro models will ever receive empirical verification. Since social science is primarily preoccupied with human behaviour, it is hardly likely that macro-system analysis will ever be applicable at this level.[11]

The macro models were faulted on other grounds too. Weltman says, 'Few of Kaplan's "essential rules" for his six international systems have turned out on examination to flow in a logically necessary fashion from his regulatory hypotheses. Those that do, tend to be tautological or incapable of operational verification and falsification, or both.' Accordingly, 'Kaplan's conclusions concerning systemic stability and transformation are not compelling'.[12] First, Tellis says, 'Deductive systematization, as embodied in the essential rules, is faulty,' since nothing states why under BOPS, 'possessing the constitution defined for it in terms of the number of actors, states should act to increase their capabilities rather than merely maintain them', since neither their 'power-maximizing' nor their 'power-satisficing' drives are deducible from the properties of BOPS. Kaplan's argument that 'lines of organizational integration are much stronger within the internal systems of the national actors than they are in the international system' does not fully address the problem. Tellis reiterates Weltman's important point that of the six essential rules of BOPS, only the fourth rule is logically deducible from Kaplan's conception of 'regulatory capacity' and the numerical 'constitution' he has prescribed for BOPS. All the remaining essential rules are discretionary or inductive generalizations culled from history or this or other systemic universes.

Tellis secondly wonders whether the system or the units are the real determinants of system performance, change and stability. The knotty question is that where the systemic political universe is non-directive or sub-system dominant, why any component national unit would think it necessary to preserve it and abide by its essential rules. Kaplan resolved this tangle by providing an anthropomorphic reification of a basically hypothetical construct, turning it into a natural system 'invested with purpose, instincts and something akin to reason', so that while the system's needs are 'set' by its structure, its objectives are 'set' by its 'needs in the environment' as it interprets those which turn into systemic values, and by satisfying systemic needs become 'valuable' for it. Kaplan was aware that even this anthropomorphic transformation of the system cannot finally guarantee that the units will behave in terms of the essential rules needed to preserve systemic equilibrium. This explains why one system turns into another. But after all these provisos, component states rather than integral systems are the main movers in IP and to that extent retain theoretical primacy, which makes his systems approach less systemic than it appears.

Third, Tellis questions the adequacy of Kaplan's theoretical intentions and objectives. Given their inability to explain why a certain unit will act according to the essential rules, save hazarding that if 'certain step-level disturbances' occur, the existing universe will change from 'one formal operating state' into another, Kaplan's models at best serve the function of 'a mechanistic flow chart' that clarifies what happens when some variables unsettle others. But they are not theoretical models of the kind valued in science, which need 'conjectures' based on 'efficient causes' clothed by laws employable as hypotheses to explain why apparently formal transformations are occurring.[13]

This inability to provide theoretical explanations was worsened by the fourth problem of Kaplan's models, namely unavailability of 'evidentiary bases' for identifying 'what, if anything, entities he hypothesizes would do or actually did', stemming from 'the character of his explanations and the holistic nature of the entities'. This problem is common to all who choose 'methodological holism'. But the methodological variety of Kaplan's own explanations is also responsible for it. Tellis says that unless they were paired with 'observable predicates', explanations emanating from them amounted to 'little more than speculative guesses about a set of occult entities'. And Weltman adds that under such hollow holism,

> Systematic explanations become either metaphysical or meaningless: metaphysical insofar as they are cast in terms of disembodied purposes seen as immanent in patterns of concrete interaction. To identify certain activity by the statement that it forms part of a pattern leading to or maintaining a given state is not to explain it at all; it is merely to repeat the interpretation that such a state did in fact come into existence.[14]

Besides, the essential rules of the system are not only definitional, and out of sync with reality, but also not even always internally consistent. For example, the first rule in BOPS, 'Act to increase capabilities but negotiate rather than fight', is controverted by the second rule, 'Fight rather than pass up an opportunity to increase capabilities', unless the words 'an opportunity' are substituted by 'any major opportunity', or some such qualifier. If no national unit leaves any chance to increase capabilities, where is the scope for negotiation? Likewise, the third rule, which stipulates that member states stop fighting 'rather than eliminate an essential national actor', clearly runs athwart of the second part of the sixth rule, 'Bring some previously inessential actor within the essential national actor qualification'. If this can be done, then the very idea of 'essential national actor' becomes problematic. When any minor member of BOPS can be brought under this category, why limit war to maintain the status of essential national actors? Besides, in the backdrop of the crucial importance of increase of capabilities, the fifth rule, which advises constraining states that 'Subscribe to supranational organizing principles', is queered by the sixth rule, asking member states to consider 'all essential actors as acceptable role partners', just as Nazi Germany and the Soviet Union forged a non-aggression treaty in 1939.[15] To me, even the two clauses of the first sentence of the sixth rule appear contradictory. If any 'previously inessential actor' can be smuggled into the charmed circle of essential actors, where is the haste to allow 'constrained essential national actors to re-enter the system as accepted role partners'?

Joynt and Corbett find the claim that these rules can explain the behaviour of states under the BOPS of dubious merit. Even later efforts of Kaplan to 'engineer' his models represent adaptations of questionable significance, for instance, reconciling the inability of Germany and France to consider one another 'as potential allies after 1870', and the subsequent unlimited nature of German war aims to the persistence of 'revanchist opinion over Alsace Lorraine'. Kaplan's jargon-ridden 'relatively innocuous hypotheses' are also questioned. The conceptual grid of 'directive' and 'non-directive' systems qualified by categories of 'system-dominant' and 'sub-system-dominant' categories and the resultant description of the USA as a non-directive system-dominant national actor in the NATO is a suspect. While the USA was clearly 'directive' over withdrawal of Anglo-French forces from Egypt in 1956, it was generally 'non-directive' regarding NATO and was clearly not 'system-dominant' about issues concerning 'troop levels in the latter organization'. Kaplan's prediction that while the non-directive sub-system-dominant actor will 'devote its primary attention to external considerations', the non-directive system-dominant actor will reserve it for 'internal considerations in the formulation of policy' is similarly vacuous in the backdrop of superpowers' similarities regarding 'primacy of foreign policy considerations', as proven by the considerable importance given by Soviet policy to internal considerations in its 'wheat deal' in the late 1970s, and by American policy's imperviousness to internal considerations during the Vietnam War on strategic grounds.

Kaplan's differentiation between directive sub-system-dominant (e.g., the USSR) and non-directive actors (e.g., the USA), in terms of the primacy given to national interests and bloc interests, is similarly dicey for pretending that 'dominant actors can do pretty much what they like with their satellites'. The 'cases in which the USA subordinated its interests to those of its allies' are not only rare but the 'differences between the super powers' on this score are also 'small' in most instances. They cast doubts on Kaplan's statement that directive systems would be more attentive to 'external factors' than their non-directive counterparts, having 'a better division of labour' which allows each decision-maker to pay nuanced attention to unique, individualized and specialized aspects of the problem. How Kaplan knows that Soviet leaders pay closer attention to specialized aspects of problems is never cleared and is a 'dubious assertion' anyway, since American policymakers have traditionally reckoned and adjusted with 'a much larger range of external facts'.[16]

In the face of such criticisms, Kaplan frequently changed his positions about the models, first calling them 'tools for investigating reality', then 'hypothetical only' (in *System and Process*), as 'quite crude' in their initial version, and representing nothing more than 'plausible reasoning'.[17] Besides, the models failed to mediate between generality and reality. The moment details of significant economic, political, technological and personality-related inputs were introduced, they became cumbrous.[18] Even after Kaplan opted for playing out 'computer realizations, or simulations of the models, they led (as we have seen) to poor outcomes. It was difficult to salvage the models because of certain ingrained limitations of Kaplan's systems approach. The first was methodological inadequacy in the sense that a severe lack of operationalization makes the concepts unsuitable to empirical testing. Second, systemic relationships were often left undefined, and the mix-up between definitions and propositions was such that the principal function of a systems model became inextricable from its main attribute, that is, maintenance of order by minimization of coercion. Third, the unbridled import of concepts and terminology from other social sciences resulted in what James Gregor has described as a 'barbarous academic vocabulary', which dressed up 'reasonably well-confirmed or intuitively grasped low-order empirical generalizations'. Fourth, the approach and its models banished the study of political institutions, cultures, other important domestic variables, and historical and ideological factors in a way that the sanitized models became apolitical.[19] Considering all these points, Joynt and Corbett conclude that 'taken together ... the objections ... suggest ... the need for a new model rather than a mere adjustment in the existing theory'.[20]

It seems sad to end the critique of another grand theory of IR on such an anticlimactic note. But it is inescapable because of Kaplan's pretensions.

OTHER THEORISTS

Modelski

Modelski himself was critical of the initial version of systems theory and some of its exponents, for whom just mouthing the 'magic term "system" had become a ritual act of special potency', enabling 'the utterer instant admission not only to the circle of the initiated but also to a "sesame" of political wisdom'. He asked if despite doing the initial spadework for a 'geocentric approach' the usefulness of 'systems analysis' had not come to an end. In the new phase which the 'study of the politics of world societies' was entering, 'the simple "system" label' no more bore an additional significance.[21] 'System', said Modelski, 'is a concept of high generality, and what is true of all systems, while relevant to world politics, is not specific enough to add greatly to our understanding of that narrowly circumscribed field'.[22]

But Modelski's own geocentric approach, offered as a corrective to this problem, also did not pass criticism. His 'agraria system' and 'industria system', inspired by Fred Riggs's concepts of 'agraria' and 'industria' in the context of comparative development administration,[23] faced the same objections that arose regarding Riggs's models, with even greater force. Charges against Riggs were of: (a) visualizing development from an agrarian to an industrial in a unidirectional movement (despite postulating an intermediate stage, termed 'transitia'), which was not of much aid in the analysis of transitional societies, since modern industrial systems also possess agrarian attributes and (b) employing models of the analytic, not concrete type, that are too general and abstract to depict concrete reality. For example, categorized under industria, America has a huge agricultural production, and placed under agraria, India is an important industrial power.[24]

Modelski's theory of 'long cycles of world leadership' has also been criticized for its historical and geopolitical determinism, and its concept of power. As Bandyopadhyay puts it,

> The 'entropic decline characteristic of every order', which is supposed to be an explanation of the cycles, is a facile and unwarranted transference of one of the assumptions of physics to social science. It is in fact a pseudo-scientific camouflage for what in reality is an old cyclical theory of historical development, whose deterministic and faulty methodology was exploded long ago.[25]

This historical determinism creates other problems of analysis. As Flint points out, simply the existence of discoverable historical cycles of leadership in the past does not enable one to predict the USA's inescapable decline from its role of world leadership, since 'Portugal's sixteenth century history does not determine the US's twenty-first century future'. For example, as per the logic of 'structural determinism', America 'as world leader is a geopolitical agent', which can leverage its resources and 'freedom to choose its own actions' in a way that a 'drift towards global war' would, rather than being determined, at least 'partially' depend upon her actions. Flint not only criticizes Modelski's state-centric geopolitics which in its emphasis on rich and powerful countries neglects the impacts of the poorer states of the Global South but also faults Modelski's neglect of sea power.[26] He also reiterates the feminist criticism of Modelski's concept of power as 'strength and dominance' and 'the ability to exercise military force across the globe', which not only encourages 'an uncritical belief that the militarization of foreign policy is inevitable and beneficial' but also 'ignores gender relations within states and global economic iniquities'.[27] But as we will see in **Chapters 19 and 20,** the whole realist paradigm is subject to criticism from IPE and feminism, and Modelski is no special target. Rather, as Flint himself says, while 'a feminist critique of Modelski's power index is valid', we can 'yet still find value in the model'.[28]

To go back to the contours of Modelski's approach, Gills says in a neo-Marxist vein that Modelski's stress on the role of world leaders in the context of international order does not provide us any insight that is novel and not available in the writings of Carr, Aron, Bull or Waltz on the function of great powers in IR, 'except for the fact that Modelski seems to have reified the world system'. He does not try to explain the succession of world leadership in any way different from a traditional geopolitical one and leaves out any historical foray into the mode of production, although 'a strong association between the world power and the lead economy' is the fulcrum of his analysis. Besides, while his accent on sea power is clearly influenced by Alfred Mahan, his emphasis on 'capability concentration' strongly echoes Waltz's ideas.[29] Gills cites Aristide Zolberg's assault on Modelski's reification of the world system to show that the cycles which formed the basis of Modelski's theory are 'obtained from relating quite arbitrarily one feature common to widely different historical configurations for treatment as a formal property'. Modelski avoids describing empirically the economic components of the global macro structures which the world leaders temporarily dominated. This allows him to overstate the degree of influence powers like Portugal or the Netherlands exercised on the exiting historical inter-regional relationships, not only vis-à-vis the Asian empires including the Ottoman, Mughal and Ch'ing but also vis-à-vis other European counterparts such as the Hapsburg, French and British Empires. These confusions regarding units of analysis render Modelski's vociferous repudiation of the concept of states system as an overgeneralized concept to be of much value in social scientific explanation. Gills detects problems in his fixing of precise parameters for the units. Since even after admitting that the Ottoman Empire was creating pressure upon the Tordesillas order in both Mediterranean and Indian Oceans, Modelski downplayed its impact as a contender for world leadership; he could make the facile comment that as much as they knew, IP of modern times was little more than the regional politics of Europe. So in spite of his resolve to unearth world historical processes as the basis of his theory, Modelski could not traverse the full distance from mainstream traditional historical approach to the World System School of Historical Sociology. And his neglect of production processes in the purview of his empirical concerns makes 'any common ground with Historical Materialism extremely difficult'.[30]

Rosecrance

Dunne's is the most incisive analysis of the problems of the three stages or tiers in Rosecrance's analysis of systems. With the first stage of nine historical systems, the major problem from the viewpoint of explanatory theory is that 'formal analytical controls governing the selection of evidence' were absent. It is difficult to figure out from it how all the factors of decision-making spelt out in the systems could be assimilated into a coherent TIP, or how the international system can be viewed as relatively autonomous from all other aspects of the social and cultural environments is absent.

In the second stage, Rosecrance enumerated three primary components of international systems which helped account for changes in them, namely actor inputs, internal regulative influences and environmental constraints. While the first was the source of disturbances, the second and the third were limiting factors. But shortly afterwards, environmental constraints were left out as active factors and relegated to the status of a fixed constraint. This reduced the number of analytical ingredients to two. Moreover, the usefulness of this framework for the analysis of disturbances was diluted when Rosecrance conceded that determination of stability of the systems relies on whether 'outcomes fall within the limits generally "accepted" by the major participants in the system', although this factor was never tied to the ratio of actor disturbances and regulatory influences.

Dunne thinks that it was 'at this point that Rosecrance moved right to the brink of a theory of international politics as a distinct disciplinary field enterprise' via three concepts, namely resort to regulative influences as critical factors as in the Concert of Europe or shifting alliances; recognition that these diverse mechanisms might act differently in controlling national actor systems; and the perception that inputs stemming from these actor systems could constitute disturbances to the international regulatory system. If only Rosecrance constructed a typology and delineated ideal action patterns for each type of system, he could have designed a theory, but he desisted after only a peep into one and took acceptance by the major participants as the criterion of judging international stability, though that standard was indistinguishable from their national interests. Rosecrance's problems in explaining stability were compounded when to grapple with the problem of system change, he squarely interpreted it as a result of transformations in sub-systems. 'Thus', says Dunne, 'explanatory focus of the second stage shifted from explaining the transformations of outcomes to explaining the grounds for distinguishing among the nine systems.'

Drawing from Ashby's finding that the stability of a system is contingent on augmenting the proportion of the variety of regulatory responses to that of the variety of disturbances, Rosecrance claims that increase in the variety of regulatory influences accompanied by temporary decrease in that of disruptive influences achieved a far greater regulative impact in the post-war bipolar system than was previously seen, which generated a 'tenuous stability'. But in the absence of a major war, Rosecrance had no clue about the potential variety of disturbances to that of the regulator, and this made Ashby's mathematical tools largely ineffective. Since Rosecrance offered no compensatory qualitative coding scheme, it made the model doubly empty.

In the third tier, Rosecrance makes a still broader abstraction of four basic determinants of systemic stability and instability (namely direction, control, resources and capacity), although there was 'little analytical difference between this stage and the previous one, since these determinants were employed merely in the service of summation'.

Regarding the utility of Rosecrance's framework for capturing the dynamics of IP, Dunne thinks that Rosecrance gives inordinate weight to the actor framework of his analysis. All determinants of stability and instability are tied to individuated actors. International regulative factors, comprising only two subcomponents—institutional and alliance mechanism—have the status of mere constraints on actor disturbances. Consequently, Rosecrance's explication of international systems turns into 'an analysis of foreign policy formation' and its implications for the international system. Without denying the importance of both international and national actor-systems in the analysis of not just foreign policy but also IP, the question that Rosecrance leaves unresolved is which one to treat as system and which one as parameter. Because of these lacunae, instead of being 'explanatory', Rosecrance's approach was bogged down in an ambitious classification of initial conditions, resulting in 'a hornets' nest of complexity from which he could find no explanatory exit'.

Of course, while critiquing Rosecrance, it should be borne in mind that he never claimed that he had developed a theory. He humbly described his approach as 'systematic', purportedly establishing a link between 'general organizing concepts' and 'detailed empirical investigation' by providing a wealth of factual information to any theoretical approach which 'aims at a measure of comprehensiveness'. But in a book on IRT, he would be naturally judged from these lacunae.[31]

McClelland

The critique and evaluation of Charles McClelland would be limited to merits and demerits of EDI as a methodology and a focus on AIC in McClelland's conception of international system. To be fair, McClelland himself reiterated criticisms of the doubts and reservations of critics of the WEIP survey data, such as:

- Distortion of events by biases of reporters, editors and media proprietors through selection/suppression of stories
- Limited reflection of the real situations in world affairs in events reported publicly, a great part of the business of IP and relations being conducted in secrecy
- Introduction of interpretative distortions by 'partisan interests of reporters, editors and data set compilers', even where the representation in news media is objective, unbiased and exhaustive

Of course, even after admitting these weaknesses of EDI, McClelland did not consider global-scale news collection dispensable for several reasons. First, reports available in major newspapers and borne by wire services networks provided a raw version of international history. Second, participants in closed-door, confidential negotiations leaked information about themselves from diverse motives. Third, intelligence officers themselves obtained around 80–90 per cent of their information from unclassified sources; however, much later, revelations and historical research might modify the initial story and quite often the first selections, descriptions and interpretations survive later scrutiny to remain 'the conventional "truth" of history'.

But these self-critical observations did not cover all the points raised by critics, and sponsoring and use of events data declined sharply in the 1980s. Even existing programmes were abandoned midway. However, the continuous quantitative and qualitative spread of computer facilities and the growing muscle of online news sources motivated researchers to reconsider their options for exploring methods for exploiting news sources. The result was Data Development for International Research (DDIR) consortium, funded by the National Science Foundation in the USA; University of Maryland's Global Events Data System (GEDS) and so on.[32] And McClelland's innovative methodology, in moving away from 'born data' to make ones of his own, was praised by Singer for reminding us that a far larger part of social science has depended on data sets 'requisitioned' from other sources than is healthy for us, and for advising us that for access to difficult data, 'needed bodies of facts will have to be quarried by hand out of rock'.[33]

Efforts of McClelland along with others to engage in crisis analysis depended on outlining different types of activity at various stages of conflictive behaviour among states; measuring the direction and speed of behavioural change; locating shifts that betoken changes in interaction processes; evolving precisely defined concepts to refine these tasks; and constructing dynamic scales to rank the behavioural groups. These undoubtedly had some 'analytical shortcomings'. For example, the 'logic for designating the beginning and end of a crisis was not specified. Changes in process were not related to structure. Causes and effects of systemic crisis were not uncovered. The result was a group of essentially empirical studies of international crisis'.[34] Still a few words about the beneficial impact of McClelland's methodology and nature of crisis study in IRT are still in order. Although the events/interaction approach remains contentious, seeming quite distant from concerns of 'order' and anarchy, yet almost five decades after its first conceptualization it is still employed to analyse quite contemporary issues. The reason behind its resilience is that compared to less challenging but better known system models revolving around power attributes,

> This system artifice ... transcends the 'known': power and traditional structure images ... imagines a world of 'pure interactions', perhaps related to power but not necessarily, a sociometric analysis that finds beauty, interest and pattern solely in the interactions between units, and therefore addresses the 'order' questions indirectly through the patterning of interactions.

While power and balance systems were discerned though clear perceptions of conforming behaviour over long periods of time, only a few of these conceptualization being applied to a relatively brief time span, McClelland and his event survey chose a still more shorter temporal phenomenon, 'namely an AIC'.[35] The innovativeness of this approach drew kudos. Even Marxist critics gave kudos for this innovative approach for ignoring 'notions about the stability of the system in the historical long run...' and rightly paying attention to the impact of domestic politics on the international system. The only problem is that McClelland ignores or overlooks the 'socio-economic and political nature, character and content of this system', because of which his system betrays an 'extremely simplistic, distorted, mechanistic assumption of a structural-functional approach through the prism of behavioralism'.[36]

Holsti

Holsti funnily claims in a curiously self-acclamatory book that his systems formulation 'was the *first* to offer a review of non-European international systems ... described in terms of a common set of categories, thus inviting comparison'.[37] The claim is true, since Seyom Brown's description of five historical systems since 1648 not only came later but also ignored non-European systems.[38] Holsti's student Barry Buzan and Richard Little projected a 'new way of looking at international systems ... from a world historical perspective', and to take the study of IR back not only to at least 3500 BC, 'when the interaction among the Sumerian city-states constituted the first known fully fledged international system', in their resolve 'to investigate the pre-international systems that evolved several tens of thousands of years before the rise of city-states'. But that would come after a long time.[39]

But this is about all that is there to say about Holsti, who uses systems approach 'to classify an orderly treatment of historical material'. But in spite of his expanded notion of power,[40] he remains, as is evident from the high status of the structure and configuration of power and influence among the five defining aspects of systems firmly within the realist tradition, and merely dabbles a little with historical sociology.

Singer

Critiques of Singer's efforts to construct measures for the rankings of states, design indicators for the power capabilities of states and explain the variable impacts of the degree of power concentration in the international system during the 19th and 20th centuries are all captured in a critique of the COWP. But Singer did not singly implement it; rather, he contributed to only a part of the COWP, launched in 1963 via a Carnegie Corporation grant and later sustained by numerous grants from the National Science Foundation, for exploring the historical conditions linked to war. The first data set about indicators and recorded information on the commonness and chronicity, ferocity and magnitude of wars since 1815 was constructed by Singer with the help of Small. This was followed by data sets on alliances, diplomatic representations between states, density of intergovernmental organizations in the system and national capabilities of big powers in all their demographic, economic and military aspects, constructed by new recruits, graduate students or established IR scholars. Their new research interests inspired new measures for polarization, status inconsistency, concentration of power, arms spending and so on. The result was other well-known data sets affiliated with the COWP such as the COW international and civil war data set; Behavioral Correlates of War data sets; Militarized Interstate Dispute (MID) data sets; COW Dimensionality of Nations Project; 1914 Project; and Inter-Nation Simulation Project. In the beginning of the 21st century, they numbered 11.[41]

While the programme of research involved was 'immensely difficult and time consuming', the approach 'which applies systems to discrete phenomena, and in the end provides us with partial theories of how the international system actually operates', was judged by Joynt and Corbett to be 'the only feasible way of developing a general theory of international politics'.[42] But unfortunately, these partial theories have met with criticisms. For example, regarding the diplomatic ranking of states first conjoined with the COWP project, size and recognition were Singer's criteria for their inclusion in the interstate system.[43] But a commentator showed it 'possible that states existed in the world that are not included in the original or the revised versions of the Correlates of War list of members in the interstate system', even after meeting the prescribed criteria. The omission is sought to be justified by saying inter alia that political entities exhibiting attributes associated with statehood, yet fully autarkic, cannot be said to be members of the interstate system, because they do not interact with others. But even regarding recognition as criterion statehood, the pre-1920 yardstick employed by the COWP is problematic in relying exclusively on the establishment of British and French diplomatic missions because the resulting list is not only inexhaustive but also biased in excluding many European states, and virtually all Asian and African states. Even though sending of diplomatic personnel is a 'strong signal to the recipient and other states', its use as the sole measure of legitimacy of states before 1920 is also contentious for many reasons.

First, compared with other older diplomatic practices, exchange of permanent personnel with foreign courts was a relatively new mode in the 19th century. Second, it was not always easy to detect when and where diplomatic missions were founded, since quite a few European and precolonial states were wont to receive permanent delegates from Britain and/or France before coming up on the COW list. Third, the founding of diplomatic missions may have carried different imports for Europeans and non-Europeans, where, for example, permanent missions were assigned only to subject and 'inferior' states. Fourth, the condition of reception of diplomatic missions from Britain and France, as legitimizers, was not free from problems because their international relations, particularly in the Asian and African states were not always congruent.[44]

Similarly, the findings of Singer regarding capability concentration that alliances correlate fairly well with wars, against hypotheses of the 'peace-through-parity-and-fluidity model' for the 20th century, have been questioned by critics, since in the 19th century results were dissimilar, alliances not seeming to be highly correlated with wars. Some argued that a true BOPS was rarely in existence between 1815 and 1965. Others asserted that 'alliances may not restrict the flexibility of governments, particularly if they belong to more than one alliance at the same time'. Important scholars such as Organski and Jacek Kugler have showed from their churning of available data that alliances have not had much to do with the onset of wars. But other studies have found that alliances are not that irrelevant, only more restraining for lesser powers than great powers in affecting the possibility of war; and if alliances are significant additions to two rivals' military might, instead of being exclusively constraints as Singer and Small have contended, then BOP theorists are right in attributing some causal power to alliances, especially in situations where one side has a noticeable advantage over the other in breadth and depth of alliances.[45]

Some scholars have looked askance at Singer's efforts to construct a general theory of war. Suganami, for example, thinks that rather than being drawn in by Singer's efforts to find causes of war in general in terms of the regular chain of events which result in wars, we should rather try to develop understandable narratives of particular wars.[46] Houweling and Siccama have questioned Singer's real contribution in redefining the concepts of 'violence' and 'peace'. Dissatisfied with Johan Galtung's efforts in this regard 'to offer a promising path for the study of the phenomenon of war', and raising a plea for 'the compilation of rival hypotheses in relation to effect on war involvement of unequal distribution among states of economic capabilities', they looked up to Singer's COWP for useful insights in this regard, since he 'quite explicitly includes extra-systemic wars (principally colonial wars) in his analysis', only to be further disappointed in not detecting any contribution. They trace Singer's failure to his seeming assumption that the same 'causes' account for wars between established states and colonial wars. Since the COW variables are mostly 'defined exclusively for "states", or are derived from those units', for wars against non-state units, this generates 'the unacceptable situation that the predictors of violence relate solely to one of the warring parties', normally the European belligerent. Apparently, Singer thinks that in the event of expansionist moves of colonizing states, the resistance of non-state units will be automatic. As Houweling and Siccama put it,

> In the case of established states with professional fighting organizations such an assumption is not implausible, but from the research of primitive warfare reported by Wright ... it is evident that by no means all non-state units preside over a military organization of this kind. It therefore strikes us as desirable for variables for the territorial organization of 'states' and variables indicating the potential resistance by non-state units to be incorporated into Singer's research.[47]

Singer's and COW's methodology of detecting serious international disputes has also been questioned. The COW MID data set compiled by two later scholars contains an ordinal scale of 1 to 5 of the highest level of hostility (LOH) attained during the course of the dispute by each of the participants, ranging from military response aimed only at the target state (1), threat of military force (2), display of military force (3), use of military force (4) and full-scale war (5), and the scale has been further improved by others. Diehl and Goertz think that even the improved scales which have proceeded to construct 'a "rivalry" severity score for each dyad while using "the LOH scores for disputes with a time decay function", might capture the dynamics of disputes only when "rivalries or rivalry years are the units of analysis"'. This is because even after LOH variable was used as one input in a 'dispute severity indicator', the measure proved difficult to disaggregate to the dispute level. While the MID criterion restricts focus on events to only those that presuppose at least the possibility of military force, and consequently does not facilitate distinction between hostile and coercive actions that do not entail military force, the simple five-point LOH scale also suffers from many limitations in measuring severity:

- Being the only ordinal, it is unable to quantify the degree of differences among the categories.
- It misses the great differences between simple disputes and wars in terms of costs, duration and so on and treats wars merely as the most acute form of dispute.
- It contains 'little consideration of the relative symmetry of state behaviour' while adjudging dispute severity 'as the highest level of hostility achieved by *any one state in the dispute*'.
- The scale ignores differences between war severities, thereby registering little advance over the conventional war/no war distinction.

Diehl and Goertz find shortcomings even in the later revised 22-point scale for militarized action compiled by others with Singer in 1996. Although it makes some useful distinctions between actions that can be placed in the same category on the original five-stage scale, it does not make clear how a show of troops is necessarily 'less severe than a show of ships or planes'; threats of blockade are graver than threats to occupy territory, or go to war; or how a nuclear alert is much more serious than a conventional military alert but 'less severe than a mobilization or other action'.[48]

In his counting of wars since 1816, Singer with Small concentrated on combats with a minimum of 1,000 fatalities, which also attracted critiques. Two commentators railed at his arbitrary definition of wars by invoking a jurist's observation on pornography: 'I may not be able to define it, but I know it when I see it'.[49] Singer's response was that if industrial strikes in a decade can be distinguished in terms of man-days lost through them, there is no reason why wars would not be 'measured according to frequency as well as magnitude'. After drawing up their 'entire list of about 500 candidate wars', they adjudged that 'despite a temporal spread of a century and half and some dramatic changes in weapons technology and military medicine, very few of those cases with fewer than a thousand battle fatalities would be called serious international wars by qualified observers'. So it will be misleading to say that 'we treat a deadly quarrel with 900 battle deaths as a crisis and one with 1,000 as a war'.[50] I fully agree with Duvall's evaluation of Singer and his COWP:

> The tremendous care given to the gathering of information and the generation of data, the openness and honesty with which data and statistical reports have been reported, and the very real commitment ... to the task of untangling the causes of war make this project an admirable one. There is a real possibility that in the not too distant future we will arrive at some definitive answers about the occurrence, severity and duration of war through the efforts of the project.[51]

CONCLUSION

This chapter has just summarized the criticisms of the formulations of systems theory of Kaplan, Modelski, Rosecrance, McClelland, Holsti and Singer. I have shown that the critiques concentrated more on the methodological than on substantive aspects of these thinkers, although the two historical systems of Kaplan have had to be engineered to increase their match with reality. But not being abstracted models of reality, the nine historical systems of Rosecrance and the four of Holsti have not been questioned for factual inauthenticity. Unlike realists, the systems theorists have not criticized one another and merely employed the systems concept in various ways. So the criticisms also have no common kernel. For example, the problems of holism bedevil Kaplan's models only. With Rosecrance and Singer, criticisms concern mode of data collection. But for the *gotra* name, they could not be more alike each other.

REVIEW QUESTIONS

1. Identify the main strands of criticism against Bertalanffy's GST from Hoos, Berlinski, Lilienfeld and Nagel.
2. State the limitations of applications of GST in various social sciences identified by critics. Why was it welcomed in IR, although belatedly, even after these?
3. On what grounds were Kaplan's macro models faulted by Weltman and Tellis?
4. How do Joynt and Corbett critique Kaplan's essential rules of six international systems?
5. Summarize the criticisms of Modelski's 'agraria' and 'industria' and 'long cycles of world leadership' as system concepts.

6. Comment on Dunne's critique of the three stages or tiers of Rosecrance's analysis of systems.
7. Evaluate McClelland's methodology of diagnosing ACI through WEIP survey data.
8. Is there any originality in Holsti's conceptualization of historical systems? State with reasons.
9. What are the strengths and weaknesses of the measures and indicators used in Singer's COWP and its various data sets in providing a general TIP?

NOTES AND REFERENCES

1. Lieber, *Theory and World Politics*, 120, 140.
2. Tellis, 'Reconstructing Political Realism', 65.
3. Roger C. Buck, 'On the Logic of General System Behavior Systems Theory' (1956), 225, https://conservancy.umn.edu/bitstream/handle/11299/184257/1_09_Buck.pdf?sequence=1 (accessed on 31 March 2021).
4. Ida Russakoff Hoos, *Systems Analysis in Public Policy: A Critique* (Berkeley, CA: University of California Press, 1983), 39–41.
5. Berlinski cited in George J. Klir, *Facets of Systems Science*, 2nd ed. (New York, NY: Kluwer Academic/Plenum Publishers, 1991/2001), 194.
6. Ibid., 195–196.
7. Robert Lilienfeld, *The Rise of Systems Theory* (New York, NY: John Wiley and Sons, 1978), 191, 227.
8. Stuart Nagel, *The Structure of Science: Problems in the Logic of Scientific Explanations* (London: Routledge & Kegan Paul Ltd, 1961), 445–446.
9. Oran Young, *Systems of Political Science* (Englewood Cliffs, NJ: Prentice Hall, 1968), 19–20, 46–48 and 35–37; A. James Gregor, 'Political Theory and the Uses of Functional Analysis', *American Political Science Review* 62 (June 1968): 431; all cited and summarized in Lieber, *Theory and World Politics*, 126–128.
10. J. J. Weltman, *Systems Theory in International Relations: A Study in Metaphoric Hypertrophy* (Lexington, D.C. Heath: Lexington Books, 1973), 100, cited in Richard Little, 'A Systems Approach', 199–200.
11. D. Vital, 'Back to Machiavelli', in *Contending Approaches to International Politics*, eds K. Knorr and James Rosenau (Princeton, NJ: Princeton University Press, 1969), cited in ibid., 200.
12. Weltman, *Syetems Theory*, cited in Robert L. Flood and Ewart R. Carson, *Dealing with Complexity: An Introduction to the Theory and Application of Systems Science*, 2nd ed. (New York, NY: Plenum Press, 1988), 144–147, 161.
13. Tellis, 'Reconstructing Political Realism', 64.
14. Weltman, *Systems Theory*, cited in ibid., 65.
15. Joynt and Corbett, *Theory and Reality*, 72–73.
16. Ibid., 73–75.
17. Kaplan, *Macropolitics*, 210.
18. Kaplan, *New Approaches*, 389.
19. These points, as well as the citation from Gregor, 'Political Theory', 438, are taken from Lieber, *World Politics*, 142–143.
20. Joynt and Corbett, *Theory and Reality*, 73.
21. George Modelski, 'The Promise of Geocentric Politics', *World Politics* 22, no. 4 (July 1970): 633.

22. Ibid., 631.
23. Fred W. Riggs, 'Agraria and Industria: Towards a Typology of Comparative Public Administration', in *Toward A Comparative Study of Public Administration*, ed. William J. Siffin (Bloomington, IN: University of Indiana Press, 1957), 23–116.
24. See S. R. Maheswari, *Theories and Concepts in Public Administration* (New Delhi: Allied Publishers Limited, 1991), 174–175; V. Sivalinga Prasad and K. Murali Manohar, 'Fred W. Riggs', in *Administrative Thinkers*, eds D. Ravindra Prasad, V. Sivalinga Prasad, and P. Satyanarāyaṇa (New Delhi: Sterling Publishers Private Ltd, 1991), 237–238.
25. Bandyopadhyay, *General Theory*, 240–241.
26. Flint, *Introduction to Geopolitics*, 214–215.
27. Flint, *Introduction to Geopolitics*, 3rd ed. (London: Routledge, 2017), 221.
28. Ibid.
29. For this, see Waltz, *Theory of International Politics*, 131.
30. B. K. Gills, 'International Relations Theory and the Processes of World History: Three Approaches', in *The Study of International Relations: The State of the Art*, eds Hugh C. Dyer and Leon Mangasarian (New York, NY: Palgrave Macmillan in association with *Millennium: Journal of International Studies*, 1989), 115–116.
31. Andrew P. Dunne, *International Theory: To the Brink and Beyond* (Westport, CT: Greenwood Press, 1997), 55–59.
32. M. Sullivan, Jack Donnelly, and Jacqui True, *Theories of International Relations: Transition vs. Persistence* (New York, NY: Palgrave, 2001), 259; Arthur J. Alexander, *In the Shadow of the Miracle: The Japanese Economy since the End of High Speed Growth* (Lanham, MD: Lexington Books, 2003), 191–193.
33. Singer and Diehl, *Measuring the Correlates of War*, 10.
34. Michael Brecher, *Crises in World Politics: Theory and Reality* (Oxford: Pergamon Press, 1993), 21.
35. Sullivan, Donnelly, and True, *Theories of International Relations*, 100.
36. Allen Lynch, *The Soviet Study of International Relations* (Cambridge: Cambridge University Press, 1989), 76–77.
37. Kalevi Holsti, *Kalevi Holsti: A Pioneer in International Relations Theory, Foreign Policy Analysis, History of International Order, and Security Studies* (Cham: Springer, 2016), 6.
38. Seyom Brown, *New Forces, Old Forces, and the Future of World Politics* (Boston, MA: Little Brown, 1988), 14.
39. See Barry Buzan and Richard Little, 'International Systems in World History: Remaking the Study of International Relations', in *Historical Sociology of International Relations*, eds Stephen Hobden and John M. Hobson (New York, NY: Cambridge University Press, 2001), 200–201; Barry K. Gills, 'World System Analysis, Historical Sociology and International Relations: The Difference a Hyphen Makes', in *Historical Sociology of International Relations*, eds Stephen Hobden and John M. Hobson (New York, NY: Cambridge University Press, 2001), 141–161.
40. Holsti says that 'borrowing unabashedly from Robert Dahl's definition of power', he 'veered the reader away from thinking about power in terms of economy, geography and military strength, but concentrating instead on how governments attempt to wield influence in their mutual relations'. Holsti, *Kalevi Holsti: A Pioneer*, 6.
41. See Jeffrey Dixon and Meredith Reid Sarkees, *A Guide to Intra-state Wars: An Examination of Civil, Regional and Intercommunal Wars, 1816–2014* (Thousand Oaks, CA: SAGE Publications, 2015), 7–13; Paul Francis Diehl, 'Preface', in *The Scourge of War: New Dimensions of an Old Problem*, ed. Paul Francis Diehl (Ann Arbor, MI: University of Michigan Press, 2004), ix; Fred Chernoff, 'The Impact of Duhemian Principles on Social Science Testing and Progress', in *Oxford Handbook of Philosophy of Social Science*, ed. Harold Kincaid (Oxford: Oxford University Press, 2012), 242–243.
42. Joynt and Corbett, *Theory and Reality*, 77.

43. For these, see Singer and Small, 'The Composition'; Small and Singer, 'The Diplomatic Importance of the States'; Singer, Bremer, and Stuckey, 'Capability Distribution'.
44. Tanisha M. Fazal, *State Death: The Politics and Geography of Conquest, Occupation and Annexation* (Princeton, NJ: Princeton University Press, 2007), 15, 243–245.
45. Morgan, *Theories and Approaches*, 212.
46. Hidemi Suganami, *On the Causes of Wars* (Oxford: Clarendon Press, 1996), 42, 114–152.
47. Henk Houweling and Jan Geert Siccama, *Studies of War* (Dordrecht: M. Nijhoff, 1988), 81.
48. Paul F. Diehl and Gary Goertz, *War and Peace in International Rivalry* (Ann Arbor, MI: University of Michigan Press, 2000), 286.
49. David P. Barash and Charles P. Webel, 'The Meaning of Wars', in *Peace and Conflict Studies*, eds David P. Barash and Charles P. Webel (Thousand Oaks, CA: SAGE Publications, 2013), 37.
50. See R. Duvall, 'An Appraisal of the Methodological and Statistical Procedures of the Correlates of War Project', in *Quantitative International Politics: An Appraisal*, eds F. W. Hoole and D. A. Zinnes (New York, NY: Praeger, 1976), 67–98; J. D. Singer, 'The Historical Experiment as a Research Strategy in World Politics', in *Quantitative International Politics: An Appraisal*, eds F. W. Hoole and D. A. Zinnes (New York, NY: Praeger, 1976), cited in Houweling and Siccama, *Studies of War*, 76.
51. Duvall, 'An Appraisal', 68.

IC. GAME THEORY

CHAPTER

11

Game Theory or the Theory of Interdependent Decisions*

CHAPTER OUTLINE

* This chapter is available on the companion website.

SECTION 2

THEORIES OF THE PLURALIST PARADIGM

CHAPTER

12

Decision-making Theory: From Snyder to Allison and Beyond

CHAPTER OUTLINE

INTRODUCTION AND ORIGINS

This chapter will discuss the decision-making approach (henceforth DMA) of the pluralist paradigm and start with a seminal 1954 monograph about it.[1] Even today, no discussion of foreign policy decision-making (FPDM) can ignore this scheme where the situational and cognitive aspects of FPDM were presented as a combined focus, highlighting not only the *process* but also the protagonists of or participants in FPDM and their situation. We come to Snyder after a very brief excursus into pure theories of decision-making, the ideational sources of the DMA since all FPDM people undergo their common analytic processes.

PURE THEORIES OF DECISION-MAKING: DEWEY TO SIMON AND LINDBLOM

The 'rational', 'rational-deductive' or 'synoptic' approach to individual or group decision-making was first elaborated by pragmatic philosopher John Dewey, in a five-step standard agenda in 1910, involving '(i) a felt difficulty; (ii) its location and definition; (iii) suggestion of possible solution; (iv) development by reasoning of the bearings of the suggestion; (v) further observation and experiment lading to its acceptance and rejection, that is the conclusion of belief or disbelief'.[2] Later, scholars adapted these five steps as: 'definition and delineation of the problem, analysis of the problem, suggestion of solutions, reasoned development of the proposed solutions and further verification'.[3]

Although Dewey recognized the limitations of this linear stage model and its 'issue–goals–decision–action' sequence for encouraging 'an under-socialized understanding of the initial framing of issues and goals',[4] it was only Herbert Simon who exploded the myth of such rational decision-making through his twin concepts of 'bounded rationality' and 'satisficing'.[5] A rational-deductive model of decision-making centring on search, ends–means analysis and optimization[6] has been questioned by many psychologists, decision-theorists and organization theorists. They have instead offered various models of partial rationality, suboptimality and 'incrementalism'.[7]

Proceeding beyond Simon's 'bounded rationality' and 'satisficing', Lindblom suggested a model of 'marginal incrementalism' in which the time sequence of means and goals was discarded, and every 'good' decision was a consensual decision.[8] Even the modicum of rationality remaining in its skewed means–ends path vanished when he and Braybrooke showed how means were often used to choose goals, and problem-solving was never rational and one-stroke but involved repeated attacks and 'nibbling' from multiple centres.[9] The preposterousness of this disjointed incrementalism was later sought to be redressed by Etzioni's technique of meteorological observation to synthesize both the rationalistic and the incrementalist approaches, where 'a broad angle camera', covering 'all parts of the sky but not in great detail', is supplemented by 'a second one', presumably wide-angled, to 'zero in on those areas revealed by the first camera to require a more in-depth examination'.[10] This approach was welcomed by great decision thinkers, who were unhappy with incrementalism even of the marginal variety, not to speak of disjointed incrementalism, which is a far richer brew for FPDM people to welcome. Dror, for example, spurned Lindblom's claims for greater comprehensiveness of the incremental approach compared to rationalism. He charged it with political expediency, a conservative orientation to the status quo and imperviousness to pleas of technological and sociopolitical innovations.[11] Likewise, Lindblom's efforts at making America's pluralism, where 'every important value or interest has its watchdog', and a consensual decision is allowed chances of being a 'good' decision, a facilitator of this approach's comprehensiveness[12] was also questioned. Bachrach and Baratz showed how under pluralism 'power is also exercised' for 'creating or reinforcing social and political values and institutional practices that limit the scope of the political process to public consideration of only those issues which are comparatively innocuous'.[13] Schattsneider argued that in place of accommodating every single interest or issue, pluralism may organize certain issues out of politics and thereby limit comprehensiveness. Because the 'flaw in the pluralist heaven is that the heavenly chorus has a strong upper class accent'.[14] Schattsneider stopped short of calling American politics 'a meaningless stalemate' because of it, but Schlozman, Verba and Brady did not.[15]

THE SITUATIONAL AND COGNITIVE ASPECTS OF DECISION-MAKING CONJOINED: RICHARD SNYDER

The immediate disciplinary malaise motivating the original Snyder scheme was the contemporary 'state-centric', 'state-as-actor' or 'billiard-ball' model of IR (what much later Allison would call the rational actor model [RAM] of decision-making), to which it dealt a blow. Its impact and innovativeness can be gauged by comparison with the 'historical descriptive methodology' which characterized foreign policy studies before its publication, and which 'considered its task complete after explaining the external behaviour of the state in terms of what Ralph Pettman so felicitously called 'contextual imperatives',[16] associated with geography, history, economics and politics. In a context where state survival was the supreme goal, these 'contextual imperatives' provided a list of components of national power, the mechanical linking of which to state behaviour often generated an unrepentantly deterministic explanation. Statesmen supposedly helplessly adjusted these realities to external crises. In the backdrop of resultant discontents against this analytic realist orthodoxy, Snyder et al. helped 'crystallize the ferment and provide guidance—if not legitimacy—for those who had become disenchanted with a world composed of abstract states with a mystical quest for single-cause explanations of objective reality'.[17]

Both historically and methodologically true to the behavioural movement, which sought to reify the abstraction of the state and favoured small group analysis, Snyder momentously announced that 'State X as actor is translated into its decision-makers as actors'. Figure 12.1 details the internal and external settings of decision-making and how they influence the decision-maker's definition of the situation. In its famous box diagram summarizing the conceptual framework of Snyder, the most relevant decisional sources in the national and international systems were divided into these internal and external settings (boxes A and E), juxtaposed horizontally and linked by a two-way arrow. Three elements in box A were the (a) non-human environment; (b) society and (c) human environment, culture and population. Corresponding four elements of box B were the (a) non-human environment; (b) other cultures; (c) other societies and (d) societies functioning organized and functioning as states and government action. In the diagram, just below box A is box B of 'social structure and

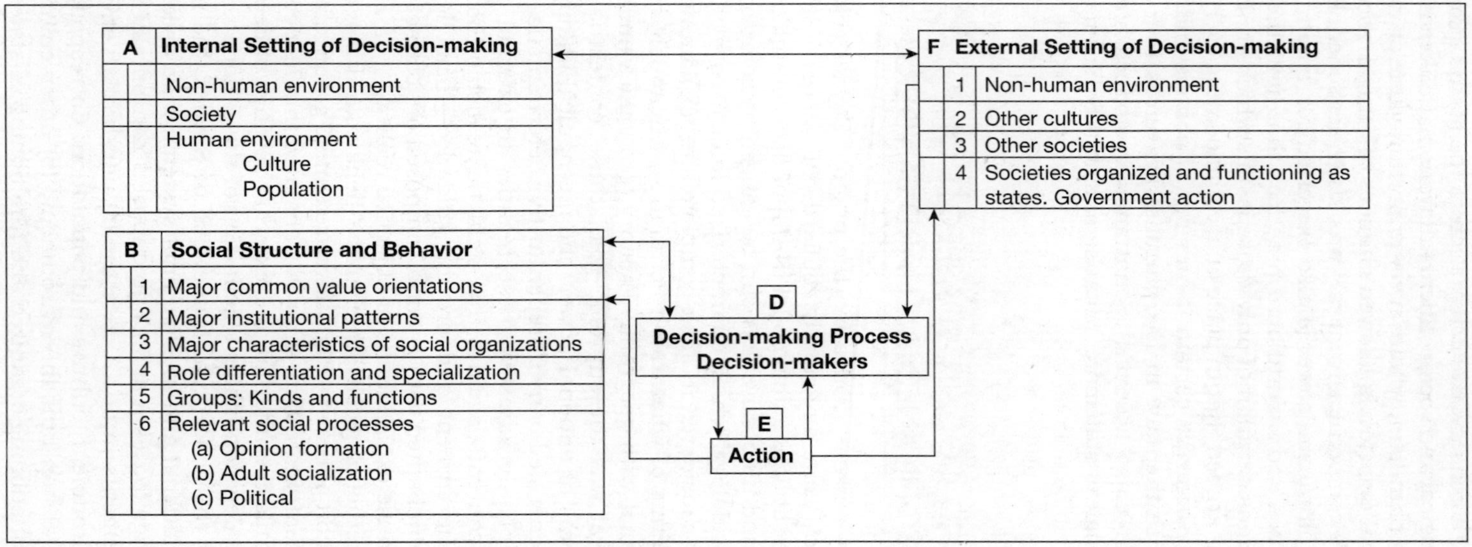

FIGURE 12.1 Snyder's Box Diagram of State X as a Situational Actor

Source: Adapted from R. C. Snyder, H. W. Bruck, and B. Sapin, The Decision-Making Approach to the Study of International Politics', 201, available at https://www.acsu.buffalo.edu/~fczagare/PSC%20346/SnyderBruckSapin.PDF (accessed on 23 August 2016).

behaviour', constituted by the major (a) value orientations, (b) institutional patterns, (c) characteristics of social organizations, (d) role differentiation and specialization, (e) groups: kinds and functions and (f) relevant social processes, further sub-divided into (i) opinion formation, (ii) adult socialization and (iii) political. Linking of box A and box B by two upward and downward arrows means that they influence and are influenced by each other. Box D, the decision-making process itself, is on the right side of box B, connected by a two-way arrow. Below box D is box E, which is 'action', connected by two upward and downward arrows with box D and also linked with box B by a two-way arrow.

Of course, in the 10 'commentaries' that Snyder provides on his concept of 'the state of actor in a situation' and the diagrammatic scheme of it, state-centricity is never frontally challenged. Rather, their first 'commentary' states that the best way of gaining 'perspective' on IP and the best means of 'grasping the complex determinants of state behaviour is fixing the analysis on the level of *any state*'. But this does not change the idea that theoretical progress in the study of IP would ultimately need a typology of actual states around their 'basic political organization, range of decision-making systems, strengths and weaknesses' of these, and 'types of foreign policy strategy employed'. The second 'commentary' claims the nation state to remain the most 'significant unit of political action for many years to come'. It makes action strategies and resource commitments operative only at the national level, rendering the collective action of the UN inexplicable without reference to actions in different capitals. The third 'commentary' describes the phrase 'state as actor in a situation' as a 'shorthand device', to sensitize readers to 'certain perspectives while still adhering to the notion of the state as a collectivity'. From the perspective of 'action analysis', wedded to the vocabulary of the 'Parsons–Shils scheme',[18] they posited that 'action exists when the following components can be ascertained: actor (or actors), goals, means and situation'. The ways in which the actor will relate himself to the situation will depend apart from these also on 'his definition of the situation'. In order to carry forward this 'actor–situation framework', avoiding the 'troublesome abstraction "State"', Snyder defines it in his fourth 'commentary' as 'its official decision makers—those whose authoritative acts are, to all intents and purposes, the acts of the state'. Thus reified, state becomes merely *'action taken by those acting in the name of the state'* (italics authors'). Coupled with the earlier stress on the actors' definition of the situation, this reification facilitates the desired 're-creation of the "world" of the decision-makers as they view it'. The fifth 'commentary' suggests analysing the actors' 'definition of the situation' for contemplated action in terms of their way of: (a) discriminating and relating objects, conditions and other actors; (b) perceiving and defining existing goals or setting up new ones as part of their expectations from the situation; (c) attaching 'significance to various courses of action suggested by the situation according to some criteria of estimation'; and (d) employing 'standards of acceptability' that (i) constrict the 'range of perceptions', (ii) circumscribe the range of things desired and (iii) compress the number of alternatives. Three major features of actors' orientations are 'perception, choice and expectation'. Although IP is only 'processes of state interaction at the governmental level', the sixth 'commentary' clarifies that any worthwhile analysis of it should take into reckoning all 'non-governmental factors and relationships', since state action has obvious non-governmental effects. Among these factors and relationships, 'domestic politics, the non-human environment, and cross-cultural and social relationships' are grouped together by Snyder under the analytic concept of setting, and divided in turn into two aspects, internal and external. These indicate that decision makers also 'act upon and respond to conditions and factors' that have existence 'outside themselves' and the governmental organization that they are a part of. The term 'setting' is preferred to environment because unlike environment, an excessively embracive word invested with technical significations in different other sciences, it suggests an ensemble of 'categories of potentially relevant factors and conditions which may affect the action of any state'. The external setting primarily signifies factors and conditions lying outside the territorial borders of the state, including not only 'the actions and reactions of other states' from their decision-makers, the societies for which they are taking actions and the physical world but also limiting the factors of environment, state of technology, morbidity rate and so on, which may either affect accomplishments of objectives or else become part of the conditions of action regardless of whether and how decision-makers perceive them. Whether these factors or conditions would be considered relevant generally or in particular cases would of course 'depend on the attitudes, perceptions, judgements and purposes of State X's decision-makers', and because the external setting is changing continually, what the decision-makers 'decide' about it would be important in its composition. The internal setting not only includes the factors or conditions loosely put together under domestic politics, public opinion and geographical position, but also less familiar and more intangible factors subsumed by the category 'social organization'. Snyder's seventh 'commentary' is exemplified in the line BD, which is a two-way arrow, illustrating 'an interaction between social organization and behaviour on the one hand and decision-making on the other'. The arrow and the line BD demonstrate the impact of domestic social forces on the execution of foreign policy plus the filtering continuing through the decision-making process. But this does not detract from the importance of line EB, which pinpoints how 'a nation experiences its own actions'. Even though state action aims primarily at altering factors and behaviour, or institutional changes in the external setting, its consequences may travel back to seriously affect its own society in various ways. The basic point of the diagram here is that 'the impact of domestic social factors (line BDE) must be viewed also as a part of a larger feedback process as indicated by line BDEBD'. The eighth 'commentary' uses the set of relationships manifest in line AB–F to indicate that 'the external and internal settings[s] are related to each other'. And instead of being confined to state interactions at the governmental level, it is about how societies also interact with each other in myriad ways, mediated by 'an intricate network of communications', including 'trade, family ties, professional associations, shared values, cultural exchanges, mass media and migration'. The analytical scheme of decision-making must offer some scope of understanding how such interactions induce or influence official action. Snyder shows how this can be diagrammed in the context of relations between two states (Figure 12.2).

The ninth 'commentary' not only points out that DE is a two-way arrow but also reminds us that 'in addition to the feedback relationship DEBD (that is, the two-way interactions between "social structure and behaviour", "decision-making process", "decision-makers" and "Action": AM) and DEF_3A_3 (that is, the loop between or rather *among* "decision-making process", "decision-makers", "Action", "human environment, culture and population" in the "internal" and "other societies" in the "external setting": AM), ED connotes a direct feedback from the awareness of decision-makers of their own action and from assessments of the progress of action'. Moreover, the tenth

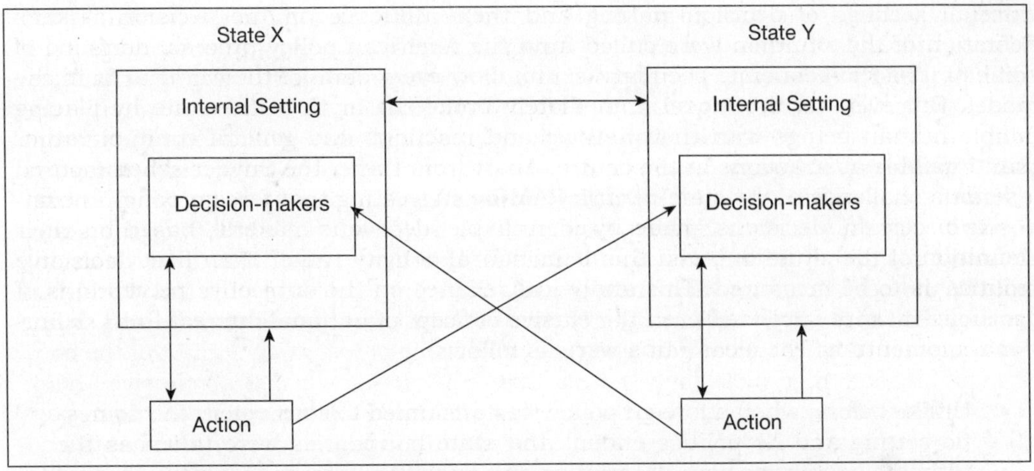

FIGURE 12.2 Snyder's Internal Setting in Interactions between Two Countries

Source: R. C. Snyder, H. W. Bruck, and B. Sapin, The Decision-Making Approach to the Study of International Politics', 205, available at https://www.acsu.buffalo.edu/~fczagare/PSC%20346/SnyderBruckSapin.PDF (accessed on 23 August 2016).

'commentary' clarifies that for purposes of this diagram, the greatest part of attention is directed to interactions represented by DEF$_4$DE. While DE stands for action(s), EF (especially EF$_4$) indicates their upshot for or impact upon the external setting and FD symbolizes new conditions or stimuli, that is, new actions or reactions lying on the line F$_4$D. So DEFDE captures the action–reaction–interaction chain.

Snyder did not hope that these few lines on a diagram would capture 'all the separate actions and reactions, all the combinations involved in the governmental relationships between one state and all others', unless these are conjoined with patterns or systems in such interactions: patterns pertaining to 'uniformities and persistence of actions and sets of relationships', exemplified by nationalism, imperialism, internationalism, aggression, isolationism, peace, war, conflict, cooperation and so on; and systems referring to 'the modes, rules and nature of reciprocal influence which structure the interaction between states'. Five kinds of such systems are: 'coalitions (temporary and permanent); supranational organization; bilateral; multilateral (unorganized); and ordination–subordination (imperial relationships and satellites)'. The diagram pointed to 'only two ways of scientifically studying IP: (a) the description and measurement of interaction and (b) decision-making—the formulation and execution of policy'. To that end, the diagram 'simultaneously invites attention to three interrelated, intersecting empirical processes—state interaction (DEFD) at the governmental level, inter-societal interaction (ABF) at the non-governmental level, and intra-societal interaction at both the governmental and the non-governmental level'.[19]

Critique and Evaluation of the Snyder Scheme

Critics objected that Snyder's state was nothing but a skeletonized essence of the policy framework of the American state, since the diagram's details of the internal and external settings of decision-making and their influence on the decision-maker's definition of the situation were culled from the American policy process, denuded of some of its socio-economic peculiarities, to allow every state of the world to fit in the model. But even so, the model immediately broke the myth of the state by placing fallible human beings with their actions and reactions and general conduct rather than infallible abstractions at the centre. Apart from these, the Snyder scheme posed a serious challenge to the state-centric RAM by suggesting that foreign policy is composed of certain 'decisions' made by identifiable 'decisions-makers', based on their 'definition of the situation', and this behavioural activity rather than fixed 'objective realities' is to be measured. This analytical reliance on the subjective perceptions of decisions-makers subjected even the elusive concept of national interest to its definitional momentum. The clear gains were as follows:

- Unlike before, when a foreign policy was presumed to start where the domestic setting and its politics ended, and state boundaries were taken as the ultimate barrier for both descriptive and analytical purposes, now it became imperative to look within and disaggregate the 'hard shell' of the billiard ball.
- Once attention shifted from the abstract state to its official decision-makers, both the external and internal factors became analysable, mutually interacting 'settings'. By redressing the neglect of the domestic sources by analysts, and treating the internal setting and the decision-making process as two sets of stimuli that provided structure and substance to the choices of decisions-makers, the diagram provided an intrastate dimension to foreign policy explanation which was hitherto neglected.

The diagram, however, has a few severe limitations. First, the domestic setting did not take into reckoning the impact of political parties, pressure groups, legislatures, the military–industrial complex and the domestic political system. Second, against all its tall claims, DMA could not tear itself away sufficiently from the state-centric model. Reference to the 'total relevant institutional environment' as a source of foreign policy decisions notwithstanding, it provides a rather restrictive view of the decision-making process, since contrary to its suggestion, many others apart from the persons who occupied 'duly constituted official positions' take part in the FPDM process. So reactions to the elements of Snyder scheme, rather than Snyder's own framework, became important for understanding FPDM. Although Snyder attempted to include both psychological and sociological variables in his scheme, the former was basically unspecified apart from references to 'perceptions' or 'definition of the situation' by decision-makers, and even the greater thrust on the situational context was essentially limited.[20] As Tanter and Ullman point out, the kind of rationality assumed by the scheme was a far more circumscribed one than the one posited by the comprehensive form of it adopted by the game theory, discussed in last chapter. But in the present scheme, the decision-makers were hamstrung by '(1) the lack of an explicit preference ordering; (2) incomplete information on alternatives; and (3) inadequate computational schemes to calculate the consequences of each option', all three of which flouted the requirements of comprehensive rationality.[21]

So the post-1954 thinking about how to comprehend the FPDM process set about subdividing the decision-making process into 'sub-processes' such as 'methodological', 'intellectual–cognitive psychological', 'social–organizational' and 'political'. It is where the theoretical impacts of the Snyder scheme are located and where they should be searched for.[22] In this sense, Vasquez's point that the limitations of the Snyder scheme are best manifest in the meagre research it produced is partly right and partly wrong. Apart from Snyder and Paige's study of the American decision to intervene militarily in Korea in 1950, directly influenced by Snyder, other studies of decision-making in international crises were also influenced by this pioneering attempt at regarding decisions as the stuff of IP.[23]

I first take up the intellectual sub-process of FPDM, breaking it down into cybernetic, psychological and cognitive aspects.

THE CYBERNETIC VIEWPOINT: DEUTSCH

For Deutsch, chief exponent of this viewpoint, states or their leaders pursue goals or interests depending on control of their behaviour through 'the continuous mixing, blending, analyzing, and selective use of three separate streams of information' or messages (a) 'from the outside world', (b) 'from the actor's own system and resources' and (c) 'from the memory'. Any autonomous or self-steering system possesses in itself fully 'operative information-processing structures' or 'channels' which will do the required task of combining and balancing these streams. Decision-making essentially involves combining new information with old memories, and unlike individuals' memories stored in their heads, state memories remain dispersed in the heads of heads of states, top officials, elites and the politically relevant strata; 'in the heads of the entire population, and in their culture and language', including their ingrained prejudices and predilections; and biases or predispositions held knowingly or unknowingly. These find their refuge in: 'maps, pictures, monuments and libraries'; 'diplomatic reports and policy memoranda'; 'organizations'; laws and treaties, and so on, resort to which for relevant information enhances quality of decision.

Deutsch gives a constructed list of what types of personal memories a typical assigned officer in the US State Department, faced with a message about an unforeseen political crisis in another country, will draw upon, and (where personal memories fall short) what kinds of files, earlier reports, memoranda of current policies and other written sources the officer would call upon; with whom at his level or higher in the bureaucratic hierarchy he will discuss the issue or report to, till it reaches the president and other key players, who may also search through their own memories and remembered images, prejudices and predilections, and the immense storehouse of the salient memories of the government and the society to reach a decision. Deutsch shows in the context of the Korean crisis of 1950 how all these memories may not point to the same direction and how incoming information may conflict with stored images. Besides, concrete decisions reached through such intermix of current messages and recalled memories may not be inevitable but contingent, 'probabilistic and combinatorial'. Apart from referring to the multiplicity of decision-makers and decision elements, Deutsch presents three images of the FPDM process to explain why it is so: (a) the 'pinball machine'; (b) the 'random walk model'; and (c) the 'gambler's ruin'.

In the pinball image, each interest group, agency, important official, legislator or national opinion leader is comparable to a pin, while the emerging decision matches the last leg of a steel ball bouncing down the board from pin to pin. Although some pins would be more strategically distributed than others and will have greater influence on the game, none of them can determine the outcome. Only the distribution of all the relevant pins on the board, sometimes predictable with a fair degree of certainty, will 'determine the distribution of the outcomes', but that too only after a large numbers of runs. Deutsch moves from the situational dynamics of the pinball board to the psychological by showing how a 'similar combinatorial process' goes on in the mind of any individual political leader or decision-maker. While he may receive diverse messages from the world outside, and may retrieve numerous 'items' from memory relating to facts and preferences that may have impacted his decision, he may be unable to say which single message, or recalled memory item, 'decisively influenced the way in which he finally made up his mind, and the course of action he chose'. The situation is similar to the dice game. Both show that even rough knowledge of the 'probability distribution of the decisions of a political leader, or of a political organization, a government, or a nation' provides some insights into their political 'character'; which could form 'the basis of a rational strategy' pursuable in regard to them.

Deutsch is aware that governments may pursue goals deliberately or in a machine-like manner, through simple trial and error, using information gained through both positive and negative feedback. Because in FPDM as in other areas, all the behaviour of governments, political leaders or interest groups are not necessarily purposive due to the finiteness of human faculties, or, in cybernetic parlance, to the limits of system capacities, captured in *Nerves of Government* in four sub-concepts of feedback: 'load' (or capacity of information intake at any given point of time, as determined by the number and types of channels available for the 'receptors' and 'effectors', and their 'responsiveness fidelity', 'background notice' and so on); 'lag' (or distance of the moving target), 'gain' (or extent of corrective action) and 'lead' (or extra speed for catching up with moving target). Deutsch shows how at all levels, from individual to international, apart from the communication channels and messages directing the decision-makers towards their goals, many other goals and 'several streams of messages from both without and within, may be competing for the limited available communication channels and for the time and the attention' of decision-makers', heightening 'the confusion within the decision-making system and the overload on its channels, facilities, and personnel', and possibly rendering the whole input–output cycle 'much less predictable in the distribution of its results'.

In the second image of 'random walk model', 'a drunken man is staggering around the broad, flat ledge of a cliff', observed by a non-interventionist mathematician who wonders what will happen if the drunkard oversteps the edge, employing stochastic processes and charts to predict his progress from distance. The intoxicated man can start a move only from where he stands and can take only one step at a time. The steps being random, they will frequently change directions and quite often reverse them, rather than going in the same direction. Deutsch draws pessimistic conclusions from the game for FPDM. Just like the drunkard and his fumbling steps, 'national policies and historical processes can only start at any one point of time, and from what is given then and there'; are susceptible to 'persistent influences, biases, and causal processes, ranging from economic conditions to political preferences to technical constraints and to the power and resources of particular actors, both within and among nations'; and despite being 'purposive' and results of 'deliberately chosen strategies of different participants' cannot banish 'random or nearly random elements'. This randomness results from decision-makers' reliance on: (a) components of decisions not entirely within their control, including 'unpredictable behaviour of many parts'; (b) environmental disturbances comprising the actions of their neighbours, partners and rivals, whose conflicts or discords may breed strategies that 'outdo one another and generate outcomes preferred by none'; and (c) occurrences within the 'larger suprasystem' in which their decisional unit is located, where 'the interaction among different system levels' is so high that 'the temper or headache of a leader in one country' gets connected with 'a national crop failure in another', and all of these are again embroiled with 'a worldwide business recession or monetary crisis'.

Word Help

'Stochastic' means having a random probability distribution or pattern which may be analysed statistically but may not be predicted precisely.

Deutsch's third image about 'gambler's ruin' deals the deadliest blow to rational FPDM by positing that contemporary IP partakes much of gamble, and in protracted games of chances 'gamblers who have small reserves are almost surely ruled out by changes in fortunes much before the game ends, and cannot avail of any future profitable run', since the greater are risks and the fluctuations of the game, the more are chances of the ruin of the smaller players. In the same vein, great powers, that is, gamblers with 'greater resources can afford more accidents and mistakes' and yet be in the game. But small countries, that is, gamblers with meagre resources, 'must be very skilful, and indeed very lucky, to survive'. So policymakers of small countries should 'work within these limitations' and not provide 'generous resources and reserves for expected and unforeseen contingencies', rather leaving them with broader margins of safety. Because the lesson of the 'random walk model' is that if the steps of an actor or decision-maker 'are likely to be random, he had better stay well away from the brink of the abyss'. And while responding to the moves of 'their adversaries, they had better stay mindful of the imperfect knowledge and control and probable random elements among the actions taken by the other side....'

With the help of cybernetic concepts of feedback and load put in the three images, Deutsch optimistically claims that models of 'probabilistic processes can do more for the understanding and making of foreign policy', by helping identify 'initial facts, relationships, probabilities, and rates of change' that we require knowing or estimating; identify the 'model of the process they imply'; and should the model be reasonably realistic, what most-likely consequences ought to be expected and what less-likely-but-still-quite-possible alternative outcomes ought to be provided for.[24]

COGNITIVE ASPECTS OF FPDM: IMAGE, BELIEF SYSTEM, OPERATIONAL CODE AND SCHEMA

While the first-generation studies in FPDM focused on the psychological traits of key decision-makers, the attention quickly shifted to their faculties of perception, cognition and information-processing. An early argument for a 'cognitive process model' of FPDM analysis was raised in as early as 1976 by Ole Holsti, mainly as a critique of Allison's bureaucratic politics model (BPM). Dissatisfied with lack of significant correlation between bureaucratic role and decision-making in Allison's work, Holsti said that whether a leader defines a situation as a 'crisis' partly depends on at least his 'basic beliefs about the political universe', not always corresponding to or predictable from his role. This called for a study of the 'mindsets' of key decision-makers. Addressing objections that much of the existing research on 'cognitive mapping' of the minds of elites as a model of FPDM concentrated on a single decision-maker, Holsti cited researches that dealt also with relatively larger samples of elites. Rebutting charges against the elusiveness of motives (as by Morgenthau in PAN) he referred to the importance given by Snyder to motivation for facilitating a better linking of the 'setting' and the 'unit', and highlighting such factors as personality, perception, values, learning and attitudes of the decision-makers, if at too general a level to show how to conduct this motivational analysis. Although the original decision-making framework drew both on the psychological and sociological variables, in its application to the Korean decision by Snyder and Page, the latter far outweighed the former.[25]

Even before the 'cognitive process model' appeared full-blown, some elements of it were used by earlier analysts. Boulding wrote on the role of 'image'[26] and Holsti on that of 'belief system' to indicate how perceptions of decision-makers were related to their foreign policy choices so that they respond not to the 'real' world but rather to 'images' of it, however discordant with reality.[27] Jervis showed how even logical thinking does not render decision-makers immune to misperception: 'The process of drawing inferences in light of logic and past experience that produces rational cognitive consistency also causes people to fit incoming information into preexisting beliefs and to perceive what they expect to be there.' The pitfall of the actor's ignorance about this process may tend 'to prematurely exclude alternative perceptions', rendering him too confident of his views....' And 'because people underestimate the impact of established beliefs and predispositions, they are slower to change their minds than they think they are.' They are also prone to magnifying 'both the degree to which they are sensitive to variations in others' behavior, and the ease with which they can influence others' images of them'.[28] President Bush Jr faced the weight of such perceptions when attempting a makeover of his democratic image after the Iraq invasion.

Two other allied concepts that predated the 'cognitive process model' are the concepts of 'psycho milieu' or psychological environment of individual decision-makers and 'operational milieu' or objective environment, associated primarily with the Sprouts. The former signified 'the milieu perceived and reacted to by a specified individual' and the latter 'the milieu in its total relations to that individual as this would appear to an individual who sees all and knows all'.[29] The Sprouts show how even if political decisions are grounded in statesmen's perceptions of the psycho-milieu, the outcomes of these decisions are shaped by the objective nature of the operational milieu.[30]

There have been other social–psychological attempts to observe and scrutinize the behaviour of decision-making individual or groups—ranging from quantitative and qualitative content analyses of decision-makers' statements and observations, or documents, in which their perceptions were reflected; experimental simulation of decision-making situations; intensive interview of key decision-makers; and close study of the psychology of key decision-makers.[31]

Belief System, Operational Code and Holsti

Ole Holsti studied the 'belief system' of John Foster Dulles, Secretary of State, architect of US foreign policy towards the USSR between 1953 and 1959, supplying more insights into America's Cold War foreign policy than many detailed histories. Quoting Quincy Wright, Holsti said, 'decision-makers act upon their definition of the situation and their images of states—others' as well as their own', which are in turn dependent upon the decision-maker's belief system', though 'these may or not be accurate representations of "reality"'. Accordingly, 'international conflict is not between states, but rather between distorted images of states'. So Holsti first of all construed Dulles's statements between 1953 and 1959 into 3,584 'evaluative assertions' and then classified them into four types: (a) '*Soviet Policy*: assessed on a friendship–hostility continuum (2,246 statements)'; (b) '*Soviet Capabilities*: assessed on a strength weakness continuum (732 statements)'; (c) '*Soviet Success*: assessed on a satisfaction–frustration continuum (290 statements); and (d) *General Evaluation of the Soviet Union*: assessed on a good–bad continuum (316). From a content analy[illegible] statements, Holsti constructed the Dullesian image of the Sovi[illegible] trinity of atheism, totalitarianism and communism, capped by [illegible] enduring social order could be erected upon such foundations[illegible]

Holsti's concept of 'operational code' (henceforth OC), used to [illegible] process of Dulles's decision-making, was coined by Robert K. Merton in 'Bureaucra[illegible] Structure and Personality' (1940), introduced into the field of political psychology by Nathan Leites in *The Operational Code of the Politburo* (1951) and *A Study of Bolshevism* (1953), and made current and simplified by Alexander George in 'The "Operational Code": A Neglected Approach to the Study of Political Leaders and Decision-making' (1969). Holsti refurbished the concept to show how apart from cognitive factors, situational characteristics would leave room for beliefs to influence FPDM behaviour. Since ambiguity, paucity and complexity of information, and the beliefs of a conveniently located key decision-maker in defining and selecting options, made situations liable to a multiplicity of interpretations, Holsti sought to construct an OC typology that would match a social–psychological theory of cognitive consistency. Its basic concepts are philosophical and instrumental beliefs, belief system, and foreign policy strategies and tactics; defining mode of inference is the principle of logical consistency; and two corollaries are: (a) beliefs are prone to confirm one another to gradually congeal into a belief system and (b) in defined circumstances, beliefs constrict the range of choices to shape the final decision.

Holsti synthesized the case studies in George's article of decision-making by eight key American decision-makers and defined new lines of enquiry into the cognitive consistency, psychodynamic origins and behavioural consequences of OC belief systems. Holsti analysed these case studies afresh to ascertain if the findings confirmed the existence of consistent belief systems that accorded with his OC typology. But since none of these case studies had used quantitative techniques of content analysis to an appreciable fashion, Holsti's attempt at validation had to rest content with indirect evidence.[33]

Falsely regarding beliefs and belief systems as fixed and invariant may provide one a distorted picture. Against lay and academic charge that the Carter administration lacked any stable and consistent image of the international system, Rosati showed that it had started with an 'optimistic worldview', only to become embittered and cynical with time, primarily in response to manifestations of 'Soviet expansionism'; and this belief system changed for the worse through the 'image dissensus' of the President, the National Security Advisor, Zbigniew Brzezinski, and the Secretary of State, Cyrus Vance.[34]

Schema and Deborah Larson

Even while political scientists were enthusiastic about Holsti's belief systems of elites as a new approach to FPDM analysis, some psychologists found schemas more fruitful, since they highlighted aspects of FPDM that a monomaniac focus on belief systems missed. Larson argued that schemas provide better lenses, since as a meta-construct, located 'at a higher level of analysis, schemas encompass belief systems as well as specific examples and analogies' and can help bridge the gap in research on [illegible] of [illegible]tures between political science and social psychology. [illegible]ysis of these evaluative [illegible] the broader definition as 'the total uni- [illegible]et Union, 'built on the [illegible] social world, and the self', and [illegible] the deep belief that no [illegible]set of beliefs about the political [illegible].[32] [illegible]re of politics and instrumental [illegible] unravel the cognitive [illegible]pite sharing some common fea[illegible] with them. Through containing [illegible]atic [illegible]ation of the world, a schema is rather a cognitive structure. Schemas includ[illegible]ific instances, exemplars, and analogies as well as the more abstract knowledge found in belief systems'. Its distinction lies in its recognition that 'people frequently approach problems not by applying abstract propositions but by drawing examples from their experience'. Larson showed as example how President Reagan 'liked to compare the Soviets to various Hollywood producers he had negotiated with as head of the Screen Actors Guild'. Larson considers historical analogies as important components of schemas, since even acknowledged experts sometimes resort to historical analogies or simplistic slogans, as Robert McNamara in simplifying the Vietnam War situation. Top academician-turned-decision-makers such as McGeorge Bundy, Dean Rusk, Walt Rostow, Arthur Schlesinger and James Thomson also often made inappropriate and confusing comparisons between Vietnam and Korea, and Munich and Malaya.[35]

Let us conclude this section by saying three things about the cognitive process model. First, it does not merely aim at delineating the process through which elite decision-makers arrived at their decisions but also aims at a policy orientation and some prediction. Bonham and Schapiro make this clear:

> The choice of a cognitive process approach … to foreign policy decision-making is based only partly on the expectation that it … will allow us to explain and predict decision makers' responses to international events, including crisis decision-making … might also yield predictive accuracy. The choice … is related to our long-range goal for research—namely, recommendations for policy planning and execution in international politics.[36]

Second, the inductive search for experience, which the model is rooted in, flows from the assumption that 'decision-makers, in the absence of firm beliefs about new events, tend to rely on past experience'. Even academicians-turned-decision-makers comparing Vietnam with Korea and Munich with Malaya are not excluded.

Third, research shows that cognitive complexity is positively correlated with 'the accuracy of an individual's predictions about people's behaviour'. This means that 'the more complex their perceptual discriminations, the better their prediction', and by implication 'to the extent ... an individual is more complex or differentiated in the way he views the power configuration in the international system, he is apt to consider a broader range of approaches to conflict management'.[37]

FOCUS ON BUREAUCRACY ON WAY TO ALLISON'S CRITIQUE OF THE SNYDER MODEL

Allison is known for the best and sympathetic critique of the Snyder scheme, as also for its most consummate development, where, besides correcting the bias in the Snyder scheme towards RAM, he pinpointed the role of the bureaucracy in FPDM. The pre-Allison first wave of empirical research on this role of bureaucracy in the early 1960s was spearheaded by Roger Hilsman, Samuel Huntington, Michel Crozier, Richard Neustadt and Warner Schilling, who provided 'crucial insights into how and in what ways process determined the content of policy', or how the manner in which decisions are made controls the types of decisions that are made. From their writings, Art teased out five distinct propositions that impinge on a bureaucratic perspective on FPDM:

- Political power is widely distributed at the national governmental level, leaving no single locus of sovereign power in Washington (Richard E. Neustadt).
- Inside these 'quasi-sovereign powers' are entrenched partners in the policy process whose divergent views on any policy issue emanate at least partially from their different positions (Warner R. Schilling).
- Political leadership within and among these institutions is exercised through the persuasive skill and the limited power afforded by the leader's position.
- So 'making of foreign policy in government ... is essentially a political process', either when happening in the entire government internally or when involving just one agency of the government (Roger Hilsman).
- The birthmark of this process is telltale in the upshot or outcome, reflecting in its content the requirements or conditions under which it was made and the prices paid for the agreement.

These crucial insights sensitized readers to the consequences of process for the substance of policy; re-impressed on them the significance of the political context of foreign policy inhering in reconciliation of conflicting goals through bargaining, negotiation, compromising and consensus construction; and reminded them that although 'politics stops at the water's edge', a lot occurs on the sandy road to it.

Art thinks however that what the scholars said was less significant and sonorous than their silences on the points that:

- Congress's impact on foreign policy is not ignorable, even if its role was reactive to executive initiatives.
- Perspectives and stances of the policy partners on different issues and ensuing conflicts over policy did not emerge exclusively from the institutional positions held by them.

- The nature of the policy process does not eclipse the images that participants possess of the international environment when weighing one policy choice against another.
- The upshot of the political policy process is never wholly unintended, despite its compromised nature. Rather, compromises are conscious and sought for.
- The processual aspect of policy cannot afford to oversee the impact of domestic factors on foreign policy, including the electoral constraints and accountabilities of the policymakers.[38]

Allison's Model

The 'second wave' of the processual, bureaucratic perspective on foreign policy has its best exemplar in Allison, who in a crucial paper and a book[39] analysed the famous Cuban Missile Crisis through three lenses that sensitize or desensitize us to certain types of data. The objective is to expose the limitations of RAM, which is a representative statement of the traditional, state-centric or state-as-actor approach to the study of foreign policy. Dissatisfied that many 'analysts and ordinary laymen attempt to understand happenings in foreign affairs as the more or less purposive acts of unified, national governments', 'personify and speak of their aims and choices', and see foreign policy as a 'governmental choice', Allison presents two other alternative models that drastically alter the analytical focus. Conceding the limited uses it has, the traditional approach must be supplemented if not replaced by a Model 2 or the organizational process model (OPM), and a Model 3 or BPM. In the latter two models the frames of reference have shifted to the governmental machine, and to the organizational–political actors active in the policy process, in a refashioning of Snyder's decision-making framework. The second model starts from the assumption that 'government consists of a conglomerate of semi-feudal, loosely allied organizations, each with a substantial life of its own'. Seen as this, foreign policy is just 'outputs of large organizations, functioning according to standard patterns of behaviour', instead of being reasoned choices of unified governmental actors. When critics objected to the demarcation by saying that Models 2 and 3 were not all that different, OPM was merged by Allison with BPM in a later article written with Morton Halperin.[40]

While organizational theory and sociology provided the moorings and insights of Model 2, Allison's Model 3, alternatively called as governmental politics model (GPM) or BPM, was anchored in political science. Unlike RAM, BPM does not focus on just one unitary rational actor but on many actors or players, who 'focus not on a single strategic issue, but on many diverse international problems as well'; 'act in terms of no consistent set of objectives but rather according to various conceptions of national, organizational and personal goals'; and 'make government decisions not by a single, rational choice but by the pulling and hauling that is politics'. BPM eschews the conventional distinction between domestic and foreign politics and claims that the latter shares many of the identifying characteristics of domestic politics, making many tools and approaches of political science applicable here. Predictably, foreign policy is seen here neither as governmental choice nor as organizational output but as a 'resultant' of various bargaining games among the players. Allison would consider foreign policy 'explained' by a 'Model 3 analyst', only when he has found out that 'who did what to whom that yielded the action in question'.

BPM involves a large conglomerate of large bureaucratic organizations plus a number of foreign policymaking actors. The former's role is important for the following reasons:

- Outputs produced by bureaucracies that shape the situations in which policymakers engage in decisional games, including information supplied to governments; foreign policy options placed before the government as a menu for choice; and the standard operating procedures (SOPs) developed, which structure the mode of implementation of foreign policy decisions.
- Common attitudes and shared images developed by bureaucracies, which organize how a specific foreign policy question or happening is perceived by foreign policy makers, and the prism of shared attitudes and images imposed by bureaucracies on a foreign policy event while studying it for policy framing. For example, the same event will be judged by the treasury from the budgetary angle, by the Department of Defence from the national security angle and by the Foreign Office from the point of view of intentional relations.

Besides, true to the tautological aphorism, 'where do you stand depends on where you sit', current during the Truman administration and famous as Mile's law, bureaucracies borrow their influence on foreign policy from their positions in the power structure of the state and government. These positions also have ingrained interests. While serving the organizational well-being of bureaucracies qua bureaucracies, these may not only not coincide with national interests but may also even undercut and override them.[41]

Preston and 't Hart deduce an operational definition of BPM from these features, comprising first three structural and then last three processual properties: (a) 'multiple bureaucratic actors in the policy making arena'; (b) their 'diverging and conflicting interests' and 'multiple-n game contexts with one another, requiring cooperation in areas of disagreement for the sake of future policy interaction'; (c) diffuse power relationships between these actors; (d) 'continuous "pulling and hauling" and bargaining' between these '(clusters of) actors'; (e) reaching decisions by 'bargaining, coalition formation, and compromise building between different parties'; and (f) sensitivity of decisional outcomes to temporal slippage (e.g., time gaps and delays between decision-making and actual implementation) and content slippage (e.g., post-decisional modification of the content of the policy).[42]

Allison's Model: Critique

Despite being the most dominant framework of bureaucratic politics in FPDM, BPM was subjected to a barrage of criticisms. The main charges of academic detractors not only questioned 'the deficiencies, including the descriptive inaccuracies' of the model but also its explanatory power. The model was avowedly: (a) excessively complex, 'too thick' and accommodative of too many variables turning it into 'an analytical kitchen sink'; (b) 'too ambiguous and imprecise', some undergirding assumptions of Models 2 and 3 being 'difficult to separate analytically', and the scope of pure versus bounded rationality in Model 3 being left unclear; (c) not genuinely social-scientific, containing 'relatively few if–then propositions which link independent and dependent variables'; (d) neglectful of 'the roles of the Congress, interest groups, and other actors outside the executive branch' and providing 'a distorted view of policy from the perspective of public government process'; (e) lacking clarity about whether 'an actor's policy stand is determined by governmental position', since frequently decision-makers are found not standing where they sit, and sometimes not sitting anywhere, as manifest in the positions chosen by members of the Executive Committee of the National Security Council during the Cuban Missile Crisis; (f) neglectful of the role of 'idiosyncratic factors in FPDM'; (g) where accurate, undercutting 'accountability and democratic responsibility'; and (h) 'unduly' dismissive of the 'considerable position and power of the President in U.S. foreign policy making'.[43]

Art's devastating criticism of BPM revolves round three propositions from Allison's Model 3: (a) 'Organizational position determines policy stance', (b) 'The sum of behaviour of representatives of a government relevant to an issue is rarely intended by any individual or group' and (c) 'Organizational routine, SOPs and vested interests can affect the presidential implementation of policy much more than they can its formulation'.

Art's most fundamental question regarding the first proposition is: 'Do different men who occupy the same seat over time see the responsibilities of the office in the same way? If not, then what is the relative weight of position in policy stance?' To Art, the bureaucratic paradigm can help explaining FPDM only if it can start with the assumption that presidential choices do not significantly bind the hands of senior executive players in pursuing their own preferences. But the paradigm can achieve little if it has to accommodate such amendments as: (a) when senior executive players are disunited in their policy positions, the president can make use of this division to have considerable leverage in carrying out his resolve and (b) when they are so divided, the president might choose to respond only to those demands that he thinks will hurt him politically if not accommodated. Both corollaries make presidential deliberation more causal than bureaucrats' hauling and pulling, and render them overdependent on president's indulgence.

Some questions about the second proposition compel us to look away from the 'internal mechanics of government' to external constraints perceived by the president. These are: How often and over what issues partners disagree in their policy stances? Are they in one voice against presidential preferences? Do they not disagree over the direction of action to be taken? Where organizational commitments fail to draw players apart, and shared images 'dominate senior players' outlooks', and additionally 'pull them in one direction', then a 'unitary purposive actor' is more apt than Allison's multiple players.

Art wonders where the third proposition about the impact of organizational routine and vested interests on presidential 'implementation of policy more than its formulation' takes us to. Assuming that 'Presidential intent can be subverted by bureaucratic implementation', the difference that the initial decision makes becomes problematic. If bureaucracies can really control the 'detail and nuance' of policy, then it follows that the bureaucratic paradigm is equally effective if 'its validity with respect to policy formulation is close to nil'. The questions that arise here are: (a) Whether acceptance of the third proposition nullifies the criticisms of the first and second propositions? and (b) Whether our understanding of the third proposition hangs heavily on how we answer three additional questions? (i) How important are the initial acts of presidential choice? (ii) How much slippage is there between intent and output? and (iii) How detrimental is the slippage to the success of policy?

Art makes three general points that take away the edge off the third proposition and its logical consequence that 'organizational procedures can cause slippage'. First, 'the initial act of choice is crucial, no matter how the choice is implemented'. Second, 'the slippage' between presidential preference and organizational output is substantial in only those issues that president deems least important, as proven by Allison's own study of presidential control in the Cuban Missile Crisis blockade. That slippage is not equally consequential or harmful in all types of policy issues is proven in Lyndon Johnson's decision to deploy an ABM system in 1967, where given the president's desire of a positive choice, the details of implementation were of secondary importance and slippage was irrelevant. In certain other decisions, slippage can be detrimental, unless presidential commitment pre-empts it. But in a third type of decisions, the president can be perceived as welcoming slippage and existence of ambiguities in his decision to that end as deliberate, as in the multilateral nuclear force decision by Kennedy in 1963 and continued by Johnson in 1964.

Not content with exposing serious chinks in 'the internal consistency and logical implications' of BPM, and seeking to test the theory against 'the record of American foreign policy by issue area in order to determine the fit of the paradigm to the record', Art identifies three issue types, involving: (a) 'decisions to intervene with military force'; (b) 'decisions marking major policy shifts'; and (c) 'decisions revolving primarily around institutionally-grounded matters'. In the first type, such as in Korea (June 1950), Vietnam (1961–1965), Cuba (October 1962) and Dominican Republic (April 1965), the importance of presidential decision to intervene and the favourable mentality of the bureaucrats rendered them 'non-decisions'. In the second group, involving fundamental departures and transformations of American foreign policy, that is, decisions like 'the Truman Doctrine, the Marshall Plan, the NATO alliance, massive retaliation, flexible response, the 1972 detente with Russia and China, and the SALT I treaty' too, presidential preference and kindred bureaucratic mindsets rendered BPM insignificant. But even in the third group of decisions, entailing 'immediate, clearly predictable results for the structural set-up of institutions' and various degrees of shared power—like in decisions involving 'the roles and missions of the military services ... career advancement in the foreign service or in the uniformed military, budgetary allocation decisions, or those regulating the instruments by which institutions will carry out the tasks assigned to them (like weapon systems for the services)—the results of pulling and hauling cannot be predicted for all cases. 'Too much depends on Presidential predispositions, on senior players' conceptions of the institutional responsibilities ... and on the Congressional climate for any analyst to state what the probable outcome will be before someone specifies to him the personal and situational constraints'. So 'too many constraints of a non-bureaucratic nature' have to be taken into reckoning before the paradigm can start functioning and, even after this, the paradigm reveals precious little.[44]

Krasner considers BPM's 'vision' as

> Misleading, dangerous, and compelling: misleading because it obscures the power of the President; dangerous because it undermines the assumptions of democratic politics by relieving high officials of responsibility; and compelling because it offers leaders an excuse for their failures and scholars an opportunity for innumerable reinterpretations and publications.[45]

Lawrence Freedman questions the model on methodological considerations for making a false distinction between RAM and BPM through an overdrawn dichotomy between logic and politics.[46]

Wallace contends that outside American FPDM process, the applicability of the model is even more suspect. Comparing British, French and German FPDM in the late 1970s, in no case can an observer 'safely ascribe the outcome to bureaucratic politics *alone*' (italics mine), since it is an upshot of 'the continuous interaction between political direction and administrative habit, against the background provided by cultural tradition and constitutional authority'.[47] This does not mean that bureaucracy is unimportant, considering 'the high morale and prestige of the British Civil Service, and its successful resistance to the by-passing of its regular procedures by political channels', which 'makes the problem of organizational inertia particularly acute for policy-makers in Britain'.[48]

BEYOND ALLISON

Amid growing critiques of relevance of BPM and Allison, Halperin and associates' desperate attempts to silence these critiques through rebuttals or corrections, a small group of scholars used the model as a 'point of departure'. Notable attempts are Rosati's design of a systematic decision-making framework embracing 'decision context, structure, participants, process, and outcome'[49]; Kellerman's efforts to extend Allison's 1971 scheme by constructing Models 4, 5 and 6 around the role of small groups, the dominant leader, and the cognitive process in shaping decisions[50]; Hammond's set of propositions pertaining to the impact of organizational structure on bureaucratic politics and policymaking culled from the agenda-control literature[51]; Hollis and Smith's examination of the relationship between bureaucratic roles and decision-makers' individual perceptions[52]; and Kozak's defence of Allison and Halperin with insights from others to construct a more embracive and loose-fitting model of bureaucratic politics for exploring the US national security policy.[53]

Some scholars simply tested the model. Smith showed the applicability of the model even for crisis decision-making in the context of the American hostage rescue mission in Tehran under the Carter administration, after student revolutionaries took the American Embassy under siege in November 1979. There, decisions taken at three meetings on 22 March, 11 April and 15 April 1980, 'participants adopted positions that reflected their location in the bureaucratic structure'.[54] Preston and 't Hart applied the model to President Truman's decision to intervene in the Korean crisis in 1950 and attributed the lack of theoretical progress of BPM and its stagnation mainly to treating bureaucratic politics as an independent variable, instead of as a dependent variable, where one would search for the 'impact of leader characteristics (need for control and sensitivity to the context) on the nature of bureaucratic politics within particular administrations'. They showed how to some extent his 'measurable personal characteristics' helped shape the 'advisory systems structures and processes' that deeply influenced the 'nature of information processing, advising and decision-making on Vietnam between 1965 and 1968'.[55] Applying the model to US technology transfer to Iraq in the pre-war period and to production of V-22 Osprey aircraft, Jones not only found that 'bureaucratic organizations' may function as 'single-policy players', where their policy choices became predictable from their 'institutional missions and interests', but also that the central assumptions of BPM can apply for actors outside the executive branch.[56] But after employing BPM to the Iran–Contra affair, Operation Desert Shield and Operation Desert Storm, Hicks and Holland found it unworkable.[57]

NON-PARADIGMATIC THIRD GENERATION

Amid continuing criticism of the deficiencies of BPM, neither the second edition of Allison's book with Zelikow in 1999 nor a new edition of Halperin and Clapp's 1974 book added anything theoretically except adding new data from Soviet sources and examples and developments in the Carter, Regan, Bush I, Clinton and Bush II administrations.[58] This started a third generation of FPDM, in which Carlsnaes saw some potential, because 'although earlier claimed to be excessively US-centred in its empirical applicability, it is slowly finding its way to Europe and elsewhere'.[59] Jones cites scholars attempting adaptations and modifications or making new proposals for: (a) giving a positive scientific turn to BPM for increasing its potential for cumulative knowledge, with a 'menu' for BPM; (b) updating BPM through a social psychological path; (c) using public administrative knowledge for empirical investigation of the sources of bureaucratic politics with a normative enquiry into its implications; (d) restating Mile's law in a 'neopluralist approach' to explain actors' diverse and often conflicting roles, to show how organizational culture conditions them; (e) probing the political psychology of bureaucratic politics to explain the 'bureaupolitical dynamics' resulting from the 'interaction between leaders and their advisory groups'; (f) offering 'new governmental politics paradigm encompassing multiple analytical models'; (g) melding Allison and Zelikow's renovated Model 3 with Lemieux's 'structuration of power', to study beyond the players' 'pulling and hauling' the power they exercise to ensure that their preferred choices finally win over; (h) combining Allison with ethnographic researches to focus on the political behaviour of low-level officials in search for identity, complementing high-level players' pulling and hauling, to compare 'politics from below' with Allisonian 'politics from above'; (i) using the literature in political science, public administration and social psychology that prioritize the process of policymaking (involving elements of bargaining, pulling and hauling) over its structure, supposedly overstressed by Allison; (j) comparing the explanatory potentials of BPM with 'poliheuristic theory' to show how decision-makers judge alternatives through political evaluations, heeding inputs from numerous advisers from various foreign policy bureaucracies; (k) statistics-based analyses of the US navy of players' ideas and images explaining bureaucratic outcomes better than their structures and roles (as by Rhodes), and navy service unions impacting bureaucratic outcomes through their ideas and interests (as by Mitchell); and finally (l) an ideational approach that fills research gaps in bureaucratic politics literature by compelling attention to the wellsprings of bureaucratic preferences and the vital role of ideas in sustaining final outcomes.[60]

CONCLUSION

This chapter has traced the disciplinary origins of the Snyder scheme of FPDM in pure theories of decision-making and its contextual origins in the disaffection with state-centric and contextual-imperatives-oriented analyses of foreign policy analysis, and has showed its strengths and limitations. After a brief excursus into the informational and cybernetic perspective on FPDM by Deutsch, and the cognitive process model of FPDM enriched by Holsti, Jervis, Larson and so on, it has accounted for the emergence of the anti-rationalist BPM of Allison and his associates and followers, and has summarized critiques of Allison, applications of his BPM, and adaptations and emendations of it in a third generation of FPDM analysis. These menus for improvements of Allison's BPM might give my readers the wrong impression that bureaucratic politics has become a standing analytical perspective on FPDM analysis. But to dispel this misperception, I point out that Gvosdev et al. have in their recent book analysed FPDM in the American context through seven perspectives: the unitary state, cognitive, organizational process, bureaucratic politics, palace politics, sub-bureaucratic politics and domestic politics.[61] The first mirrors Snyder scheme and Allison's RAM; the second is represented in my analysis by Holsti, Jervis, Larson and so on; the third, fourth and partly the sixth relate to Allison, Halperin and so on; and the seventh reminds us of Rosenau and other spokespersons of *Innenpolitik*. The fifth has not been covered in the discussion. After explication of them, I feel tempted to express my appreciation for Christopher Hill's following words:

> Understanding how foreign policy decisions are arrived at, implemented, and eventually changed is not a matter of a single theory, even less of generalizing on the basis of an individual case ... there are two sides to the politics of foreign policy [the international system and bureaucratic-domestic politics impacting on policymakers].... It is the interplay between the two which constitutes our large, elusive but fascinating subject.[62]

I would just sprinkle elements of the cognitive process approach in the brew, because policymakers do and will create their own realities for FPDM that scholars would ignore to their detriment.

REVIEW QUESTIONS

1. Describe the contextual and disciplinary factors operative behind the emergence of Snyder et al.'s DMA.
2. Discuss Snyder et al.'s DMA, mentioning its strengths and limitations.
3. Comment on Karl Deutsch's informational or cybernetic viewpoint of FPDM.
4. Discuss image, belief system and schema as components of foreign policy decision-making.
5. Comment on the belief system and OC as tools of decision-making analysis after Holsti.
6. Write a short note on Deborah Larson's view of schema as an important aid in FPDM.

7. Write a short note on the pre-Allison first wave of empirical research on the role of bureaucracy in foreign policy decision-making in the early 1960s.
8. Analyse Allison's three models of foreign policy decision-making critically.
9. Comment on later scholarly attempts to use Allison's BPM as a 'point of departure', leading to a non-paradigmatic third generation on BPM.

NOTES AND REFERENCES

1. R. C. Snyder, H. W. Bruck, and B. Sapin, *Foreign Policy Decision-Making: An Approach to the Study of International Politics*, Monograph No. 3 of the Foreign Policy Analysis Project Series, 1954 (New York, NY: Free Press, 1962).
2. John Dewey, 'The Analysis of a Complete Act of Thought', in *How We Think* (Mineola, New York, NY: Dover Publications, 1910/1997), 68–78.
3. H. McBurney and K. G. Hance, *The Principles and Methods of Discussion* (New York, NY: Harper & Bros, 1939), cited in John F. Cragan, Chris R. Kasch, and David W. Wright, *Communication in Small Groups: Theory, Process, Skills* (Boston, MA: Wadsworth Cengage Learning, 2009), 34.
4. Peter Edward, 'Decision-making: Coping with Madness beyond Reason', in *The Routledge Companion to Philosophy in Organization Studies*, eds Raza Mir, Hugh Willmott, and Michelle Greenwood (Abingdon: Routledge, 2016), 353
5. See Herbert A. Simon, *Administrative Behavior* (New York, NY: The Free Press, 1945/1997), ix, 20, 88–89, 118, 120–123, 158 and passim; Herbert A. Simon, 'A Behavioral Model of Rational Choice', *Quarterly Journal of Economics* 69 (February 1955): 129–138; Herbert A. Simon, *Models of Man: Social and Rational* (New York, NY: John Wiley, 1957), 196–206.
6. For a formulation of this optimization-based concept of decision-making, see Richard A. Zeckhauser and Elmer Schaefer, 'Public Policy and Normative Economic Theory, in *The Study of Policy Making*, eds Raymond Bauer and Kenneth J. Gergen (New York, NY: The Free Press, 1968), 27–101; Charles E. Lindblom, *The Policy Making Process* (Englewood Cliffs, NJ: Prentice-Hall, 1968), 13.
7. R. J. Audley, 'What Makes Up a Mind', in *Decisions, Organization and Society*, eds F. G. Castles, D. J. Murray, D. C. Potter, and C. J. Pollitt (Harmondsworth: Penguin Books in association with the Open University, 1976), 49–58; James G. March and Herbert A. Simon, *Organizations* (New York, NY: John Wiley and Sons, 1958), 47–52, 136–149, 173–177; Charles E. Lindblom, 'The Science of Muddling Through' (1959), in *Perspectives on Public Bureaucracy*, ed. Fred A. Kramer, 2nd ed. (Cambridge, MA: Winthrop Publishers, 1977), 132–150; A. O. Hirschman and C. E. Lindblom, 'Economic Development, Research and Development, Policy Making: Some Converging Views', in *Systems Thinking*, ed. F. E. Emery (Harmondsworth: Penguin Education, 1969), 357–359; D. Braybrooke and C. E. Lindblom, *A Strategy of Decision* (New York, NY: The Free Press, 1963), 71–143; Herbert A. Simon, 'Theories of Decision Making in Economics and Behavioral Sciences', in *Decisions, Organization and Society*, eds F. G. Castles, D. J. Murray, D. C. Potter, and C. J. Pollitt (Harmondsworth: Penguin Books in association with the Open University, 1976), 30–48; Anthony Downs, *Inside Bureaucracy* (Boston, MA: Little Brown, 1967) excerpted in n *Decisions, Organization and Society*, eds F. G. Castles, D. J. Murray, D. C. Potter, and C. J. Pollitt (Harmondsworth: Penguin Books in association with the Open University, 1976), 50–78. Also see C. E. Lindblom, 'Still Muddling, Not yet through', *Public Administration Review* 39 (1979): 517–526.
8. Lindblom, *Policy Making Process*, 26–27.
9. Braybrooke and Lindblom, *Strategy of Decision*.

10. Amitai Etzioni, 'Mixed-Scanning: A "Third" Approach to Decision-Making', *Public Administration Review* 27 (December 1967): 385–392, esp. 388–389.
11. Yehezkel Dror, 'Muddling through—Science or Inertia', *Public Administration Review* 24 (September 1964): 153–157.
12. Lindblom, 'Muddling through', 135, 143.
13. Peter Bachrach and Morton S. Baratz, 'The Two Faces of Power', *American Political Science Review* 56, no. 4 (December 1962): 947–952, esp. 948; Peter Bachrach and Morton S. Baratz, 'Decisions and Nondecisions: An Analytical Framework', *American Political Science Review* 57, no. 3 (September 1963): 632–642.
14. Elmer Eric Schattsneider, *Semi Sovereign People: A Realist's View of Democracy in America* (New York, NY: Holt, Rinehart & Winston, 1960), 34–35.
15. Kay Lehman Schlozman, Sidney Verba, and Henry E. Brady, *The Unheavenly Chorus: Unequal Political Voice and the Broken Promise of American Democracy* (Princeton, NJ: Oxford University Press, 2012).
16. Ralph Pettman, *Human Behaviour and World Politics: A Transdisciplinary Introduction* (London: Macmillan, 1975), 34, cited in B. P. White, 'Decision-making Analysis', in *Approaches and Theory in International Relations*, ed. Trevor Taylor (London: Longman, 1978/1984), 143.
17. James N. Rosenau, *Domestic Sources of Foreign Policy* (New York, NY: Free Press, 1967), 202, cited in B. P. White, 'Decision-making Analysis', in *Approaches and Theory in International Relations, ed. Trevor Taylor* (London: Longman, 1978/1984).
18. Talcott Parsons, The Social System, with a New Preface by Bryan S. Turner (New York, NY: Routledge: 1991), 1–14; Richard W. Moodey, 'Tradition: Why Shils and Polanyi Abandoned the Action Frame of Reference1', *Preface to Tradition and Discovery* 39, no. 3 (2013): 5.
19. R. C. Snyder, H. W. Bruck, and B. Sapin, 'Foreign Policy Decision-Making', in *International Relations and Foreign policy: A Reader in Research and Theory,* in ed. James N. Rosenau (New York, NY: The Free Press, 1968), 34–39, 57–58, 50–66 and 118–120; R. C. Snyder, H. W. Bruck, and B. Sapin, The Decision-Making Approach to the Study of International Politics', 60–74, available at *https://www.acsu.buffalo.edu/~fczagare/PSC%20346/SnyderBruckSapin.PDF* (accessed on 23 August 2016).
20. The critique of the Snyder scheme here draws from White, 'Decision-making Analysis' and his citations, 152.
21. Raymond Tanter and Richard H. Ullman, 'Introduction: Theory and Policy in International Relations', in *Theory and Policy in International Relations*, eds Raymond Tanter and Richard H. Ullman (Princeton, NJ: Princeton University Press, 1972), 10.
22. Vasquez, *The Power of Power Politics: A Critique* (New Brunswick, NJ: Rutgers University Press, 1983), 66.
23. See R. C. Snyder and Glenn D. Paige, 'The United States Decision to Resist Aggression in Korea: The Application of an Analytical Scheme', *Administrative Science Quarterly* 3 (December 1958): 342–378; A. S. Whiting, *China Crosses Yalu: The Decision to Enter the Korean War* (New York, NY: Macmillan, 1960); E. Abel, The Missile Crisis (Philadelphia: Lippincott, 1966); H. Thomas, *Suez* (New York, NY: Harper and Row, 1966); G. Paige, *The Korean Decision* (New York, NY: Free Press, 1968); Graham T. Allison, 'Conceptual Models and the Cuban Missile Crisis', *American Political Science Review* LXIII (September 1969); Graham T. Allison, *Essence of Decision: Explaining the Cuban Missile Crisis* (Boston, MA: Little, Brown, 1971).
24. Karl, W. Deutsch, *The Analysis of International Relations* (New Delhi: Prentice-Hall of India Private Limited, 1989), 81–96.
25. See Snyder, cited in Rosenau, *Domestic Sources*, 247–253; Ole Holsti, 'Foreign Policy Making Viewed Cognitively', in *The Structure of Decision: The Cognitive Maps of Political Elites*, ed. Robert Axelrod (Princeton, NJ: Princeton University Press, 1976), 24.

26. Kenneth E. Boulding, *The Image: Knowledge in Life and Society* (Ann Arbor, MI: University of Michigan Press, 1969).
27. Ole Holsti, 'The Belief System and National Images: A Case Study', *Journal of Conflict Resolution* 6 (September 1962): 244–252.
28. Robert Jervis, *Perception and Misperception in International Politics* (Princeton, NJ: Princeton University Press, 1976), 143, 410.
29. Harold Sprout and Margaret Sprout, *The Ecological Perspective on Human Affairs: With Special Reference to International Politics* (Princeton, NJ: Princeton University Press, 1965), 136, 118.
30. See Kautilya, *Arthashastra*, Rangarajan, 56; Shamasastry, *Arthashastra*, 269.
31. For citations of these attempts, see White, 'Decision-making Analysis', 148–149.
32. Holsti, 'The Belief System', 244, 246–247, passim.
33. Stephen G. Walker, 'The Evolution of Operational Code Analysis', *Political Psychology* 11, no. 1 (June 1990): 403–418.
34. Jerel A. Rosati, 'Continuity and Change in the Foreign Policy Beliefs of Political Leaders: Addressing the Controversy over the Carter Administration', *Political Psychology* 9, no. 3 (September 1988): 471–505.
35. Deborah Welch Larson, 'The Role of Belief Systems and Schemas in Foreign Policy Decision Making', *Political Psychology*, Special issue, Political Psychology and the Work of Alexander L. George (March 1999): 17–33.
36. Michael J. Bonham and G. Matthew Shapiro, 'Cognitive Process and Foreign Policy Decision-making', *International Studies Quarterly* 17, no. 2 (June 1973): 147–174.
37. Ibid.
38. For citations of the views of Neustadt, Schilling, Hilsman and Samuel P. Huntington, see Robert J. Art, 'Bureaucratic Politics and American Foreign Policy: A Critique', *Policy Sciences* 4, no. 1 (December 1973): 467–472.
39. Allison, 'Conceptual Models'; Allison, *Essence of Decision*.
40. Morton Halperin, 'Bureaucratic Politics: A Paradigm and Some Policy Implications', in *Theory and Policy in International Relations*, eds Raymond Tanter and Richard H. Ullman (Princeton, NJ: Princeton University Press, 1972), 40.
41. White, 'Decision-making Analysis', 153–155; Chris Alden and Aran Amnon, *Foreign Policy Analysis: New Approaches* (Abingdon: Routledge, 2012), 31–33.
42. Thomas Preston and Paul 't Hart, 'Understanding and Evaluating Bureaucratic Politics: The Nexus between Political Leaders and Advisory Systems', *Political Psychology* 20, no. 1 (March 1999): 49–98, here 55.
43. For citations of and from critics who raised these points, see Christopher M. Jones, 'Bureaucratic Politics', in *Routledge Handbook of American Foreign Policy*, eds Steven W. Hook and Christopher M. Jones (New York, NY: 2012), 122–123. Words within quotes are of critics.
44. Art, 'Bureaucratic Politics', 467–490.
45. Stephen D. Krasner, 'Are Bureaucracies Important (or Allison Wonderland)', *Foreign Policy* 7 (Summer 1972), 159–179, esp. 160, available at http://www.jstor.org/stable/1147761 (accessed on 11 February 2010).
46. Lawrence Freedman, 'Logic, Politics and Foreign Policy Processes: A Critique of the Bureaucratic Politics Model', *International Affairs* 52, no. 3 (1976): 434–439.
47. William Wallace, 'Old States and New Circumstances: The International Predicament for Britain, France and West Germany', in *Foreign Policy in Western Europe*, eds William Wallace and William E. Paterson (Farnborough: Saxon House, 1978), 48.
48. William Wallace, *The Foreign Policy Process in Britain* (London: Royal Institute of International Affairs, 1975), 8.
49. Jerel A. Rosati, 'Developing a Systematic Decision-Making Framework: Bureaucratic Politics in Perspective', *World Politics* 33, no. 2 (1981): 234–252.

50. Barbara Kellerman, 'Allison Redux: Three More Decision-Making Models', *Polity* 15, no. 3 (1983): 351–367.
51. Thomas H. Hammond, 'Agenda Control, Organizational Control, and Bureaucratic Politics', *American Journal of Political Science* 30, no. 2 (1986): 379–420.
52. Martin Hollis and Steve Smith, 'Role and Reasons in Foreign Policy Decision Making', *British Journal of Political Science* 16 (July 1986): 269–286.
53. David C. Kozak, 'The Bureaucratic Politics Approach: The Evolution of the Paradigm', in *Bureaucratic Politics and National Security: Theory and Practice*, eds David C. Kozak and James M. Keagle (Boulder, CO: Lynne Reinner, 1988).
54. Steve Smith, 'Policy Preferences and Bureaucratic Position', *International Affairs* 61, no. 1 (Winter 1984–1985): 9–25.
55. Preston and Hart, 'Understanding and Evaluating', 53–98.
56. See Jones, 'Bureaucratic Politics', 123.
57. Bruce D. Hicks, 'Internal Competition over Foreign Policy Making: The Case of the U.S. Arms Sales to Iran', *Policy Studies Review* 9, no. 3 (1990): 471–484; Lauren Holland, 'The U.S. Decision to Launch Operation Desert Storm: A Bureaucratic Political Analysis', *Armed Forces & Society* 25, no. 2 (1999): 219–242.
58. Graham T. Allison and Philip D. Zelikow, *Essence of Decision: Explaining the Cuban Missile Crisis*, 2nd ed. (New York, NY: Longman, 1999); Morton Halperin and Priscilla A. Clapp, *Bureaucratic Politics and Foreign Policy*, 2nd ed. (Washington DC: The Brookings Institution Press, 2006).
59. Walter Carlsnaes, 'Foreign Policy', in *Handbook of International Relations*, eds Walter Carlsnaes, Thomas Risse, and Beth A. Simmons, 2nd ed. (London: SAGE Publications, 2013), 311–312.
60. For citations for each of the adaptations, modifications and new proposals, including those of Edward Rhodes, 'Do Bureaucratic Politics Matter?': Some Disconfirming Findings from the Case of the U.S. Navy', *World Politics* 47 (October 1994): 1–41 and Paul T. Mitchell, 'Ideas, Interests and Strategy: Bureaucratic Politics and the United States Navy', *Armed Forces & Society* 25, no. 2 (1999): 243–65, see Jones, 'Bureaucratic Politics', 124–126.
61. Nikolas K. Gvosdev, Jessica D. Blankshain, and David A. Cooper, *Decision-Making in American Foreign Policy: Translating Theory into Practice* (Cambridge: Cambridge University Press, 2019), passim.
62. Christopher Hill, *The Changing Politics of Foreign Policy* (Hampshire: Palgrave Macmillan, 2003), xix–xx.

CHAPTER 13A

Integration Theory: The Four Schools and Beyond

INTRODUCTION AND ORIGINS

As a modern European wing of the broader theory of regionalism, integration theory addresses an old problem relating to the political structure of the world through a social scientific methodology and sophisticated concepts, learning from the process of European integration, guiding it, in turn, and providing one of the best examples of living exchange between theory and praxis. However, despite having acquired a new self-awareness and terminology as a field in IR, its thought structure can be traced far back in the history of political thought. Pentland saw advocacy and 'prophecy of world government or regional (usually European) unity' as 'an ancient tradition of Western political thinking', together with 'a closely related analytical literature on the unification of states, the rise and fall of empires and the maintenance of peace'. But from my earlier distinction between the 'analytic tradition' and historic tradition'[1] and agreeing with Pentland and Hodges,[2] I would say that despite not being the brainchild of modern American and European scholars, the study of political integration did not emerge as a systematic search for empirically based theory before the early 1940s and 1950s.

But can the new body of researches form an integrated theory? Great differences prevail between the strands of thought that jostle under the umbrella of integration theory regarding the meaning and nature of integration, its status as a dependent or an independent variable, its nature as a process or a condition (state) or both, the relative status of normative social engineering and dispassionate observation of integrative trends and the question whether a group of states can be 'integrated' into a supranational entity without relinquishing their sovereignty and identity.[3]

DIFFERENT DEFINITIONS OF INTEGRATION AND DIFFERENCES IN ITS PERCEPTIONS

Definitions of integration differ. To Haas, the doyen of the 'neofunctionalist' approach, integration was an independent and a dependent variable: 'a process whereby political actors in several distinct national settings are persuaded to shift their national loyalties, expectations and political activities to a new centre, institutions of which possess and demand jurisdiction over pre-existing national states', and a product, 'a new political community, superimposed over the pre-existing ones'.[4] Lindberg's neofunctionalist definition, as follows, also stresses the processual element but without suggesting, unlike Haas, any terminal point, thereby insinuating that integration, both in its depth and breadth might remain in a constant flux:

> (1) The process whereby nations forgo the desire and ability to conduct foreign and domestic policies independently of each other, seeking instead to make joint decisions or to delegate the decision-making process to new central organs; and (2) the process whereby political actors in several distinct settings are persuaded to shift their expectations and activities to a new centre.[5]

By contrast, Deutsch, a colossus of the 'transactionalist' school, defines integration both as a condition or state, a dependent variable, and as a process, '... a relationship among units in which they are mutually interdependent and jointly produce system properties which they would separately lack'. The aim being the construction of a supranational entity, the underlying *tasks* involve '1) maintaining peace; 2) attaining greater multipurpose capabilities; 3) accomplishing some specific tasks; and 4) gaining a new self-image and role identity'. Regardless of whether the end product is a new state-like institution or not, integration signifies 'the attainment, within a territory, of a "sense of community" and of institutions and practices strong enough and widespread enough to assure, for a "long" time, dependable expectations of "peaceful change" among its population'.[6]

The point where the divergent definitions converge is that regional integration denotes peaceful change and unlike cooperation, cannot afford to be conflictual. Keohane famously said that 'Cooperation should not be viewed as the absence of conflict ... Without the specter of conflict there is no need to cooperate'.[7] Besides, cooperation never implies the creation of supranational loyalties or arrangements, though integration necessarily does.

But perspectives differ on how this peaceful process of change comes about, resulting in the emergence of four dominant schools of integration, variously and confusingly ordered and christened.[8] I would discuss them as follows.

Federalism

Among these perspectives, federalism has the oldest history, being part of the literature on pacifism concerned with banishing war through the formation of a supranational authority that could reform the behaviour of states by relieving them of many of their sovereign powers, privileges and tasks. Its plea that nothing short of a merger of existing states through federal institutions, including military and police forces and a common legal system into a world federation, can ensure peace has risen since the early 17th-century European wars up to the Second World War.

There were three principal historical sources of the federalist ideas in Europe: (a) projects for the preservation of peace and restructuring of IR from ancient leagues of Greek city-states to the US model, (b) experiences of the small number of existing federal states of the world and (c) more abstract ideas not tied to the 'legal constitution of a territorial state' flowing down from medieval to modern Western thought.[9] The third source comprised: (a) rich heritage of federal ideas starting from the Biblical covenant, which addressed many of Europe's problems of internal unity, before travelling to America,[10] (b) Althusius's construction of a whole system of polities (only once called federal) around the three principles of 'pluralization of governance', 'a general consent requirement' and 'a normative commitment to social solidarity' and related concepts of consociation and subsidiarity,[11] (c) the correspondences between Leibniz and l'Abbé de Saint-Pierre around the idea of a federal union in Europe based on the contractual tradition[12] and (d) Proudhon's enrichment of the tradition set by Althusius and Rousseau that leavened, in the late 19th and early 20th centuries, such diverse theoretical developments as guild socialism, functionalism and pluralism, spearheaded by thinkers, including Otto von Gierke, Frederic William Maitland, G. D. H. Cole, Léon Duguit and Harold Laski. These, again, mingled with syndicalism, left-wing Catholicism and so on to create an 'eclectic' brew, known as the intellectually, though not politically, impactful 'integral federalist movement' in the 1930s.

True to the conviction shared by Harold Laski, Carl Friedrich and so on that the utility of the federal idea transcends the domestic political domain of the state because integrative process operates at systemic, sub-systemic or state and individual levels; many federalists put federalism above other types of the supranational state as a stable solution to the problem of power in the international sphere. It reconciles the 'centralizing' norms of 'security, order, authority, administrative rationality, constitutionalism and unity' with the decentralist principles of 'liberty, local autonomy, representation, pluralism, flexibility and diversity' at the international systemic level, shifting from the legalism and static description of the early federalist scholars to the dynamic thinking of modernists, such as C. Friedrich and Amitai Etzioni, who concentrate on a processual explanation of how international anarchy and disorder slowly move towards federal order. Federalists abjure systemic qualities like 'economic and technological interdependence or other such "background conditions" as potent propellers towards greater political integration since, in the ultimate instance, trade pursues politics than otherwise.' Integration can be initiated only by the states themselves, reified as their foreign policy elites when they are persuaded that the sheer magnitude of their problems necessitates a dramatic revamping of the system beyond the capacity of incremental tinkering towards a supranational state. Federalists downplay the level of individual attitudes or behaviour impacting integration, departing from many assumptions and premises of the old federalists who subscribed to the Wilsonian faith in the popular initiative. Anyway, this clearly insinuates that the shift in allegiances towards the centre, which integration takes to be inexorable and total, is not always present.[13]

Federalism found favour in the post-First World War practice after the failure of the League of Nations to tide over the twin principles of sovereign equality of nations and national self-determination for ensuring peace. It deflected scholarly and political attention to pacifist schemes not revolving around sovereign states, such as (a) Richard von Coudenhouve-Kalergi's *Pan-Europe* (1923), (b) Pan-European manifesto (1924) and (c) a Pan-European Congress (1926), all of which presented the outlines of a future European federation. The federalist strain was carried forward by both political elites and participants in anti-fascist resistance movements in continental Europe after European BOP had ushered in the Second World War. Having called for a union of Britain and France in 1940 on the advice of British civil servants and French partisan Jean Monnet, Winston Churchill reverted to his idea of a federal European unification after his defeat in the post-war election, urging in his September 1946 Zurich speech the formation of a 'United States of Europe'. This plea fired up enthusiasts for federalism in the resistance movements after the defeat of Germany. The apical points of enthusiasts' zeal for these pleas were the post-war 1948 Hague Congress (1948) and the Council of Europe (1949, henceforth COE).

The Hague Congress witnessed the convergence of three strands of federalist thinking on post-war European reconstruction. The first recoiled from the shocks of war and placed hopes for lasting European peace after Hitler's defeat in the path charted by Churchill's Zurich speech and the activities of the pan-European movement. The second, reflected in a contemporary key federalist tract, *Manifesto di Ventotene* (1944), was a host of assumptions, attitudes and conceptions about a federalist shape of European integration. It was drafted by Ernesto Rossi, Eugenio Colorni and, most importantly, Altiero Spinelli, a member of the European Parliament, adviser to the Italian government and general secretary of the Italian Federalist Movement, who authored two abortive projects, the European Defence Community (EDC) and the European Political Community (EPC). After EDC and its parallel EPC became non-starters, Spinelli's idea of European Parliament survived. The second integrative process was initiated by the Anglo-French wing of federalists after the COE stumbled under the leadership of Jean Monnet and revolved around the 'community method' of integration. The third strand of federalist thinking emerged after the initiation of ideologically diverse individual national-level federalist movements as part of the European movement, which sought to decentralize the decision-making process further, rope in civil society in the management of European affairs and the formation of a truly federal EU, endowed with a federal system of governance.

The failure of the COE, caused partly by British opposition to federalism following Churchill's disillusionment after his return to power in 1951[14] and by the French

Assembly's rejection of proposals for EDC in 1954, signalled the end of Europe's federalist phase. Academically also, federalism was facing critiques. Its preoccupation with political solutions, institutional arrangements and institutional politics was anathema among the older functionalists who were bent on substituting the harmful and war-prone state system with a welfare-minded world society. As we will shortly see, to functionalists, the federalist vision of integration around superimposition of a global or regional superstate to oversee order among the old states and later replace them at an opportune time not only retained 'the old political divisions' that caused the 'present discontents' but also complicated them by proposing 'larger states on a new level'. And despite accommodating some kind of supranational body, including state among the end products of integration, neofunctionalists tend to focus more on the process than on the outcome. So while the neofunctionalist keeps on reckoning both the economics and the politics of scale, 'the federalist is more concerned to balance the advantages of size and uniformity with those of smallness and diversity'.[15]

Europe's federalist phase, however, overcame a period of ignominy and relative oblivion to experience a revival in the 1990s through reflections on the ongoing project of European unification around the Maastricht Treaty, generating thereby more sophisticated and variegated federalist approaches, which fertilized and integrated with other concepts and theories of integration, including the new writings on governance and liberal intergovernmentalism, apart from linking reflections on the EU with the concepts and methods of political science. This, in turn, generated new comparative approaches to federalism, which differed from the older federalisms in eschewing the one best way of governing a multi-state body like the EU. Drawing sustenance from German Foreign Affairs Minister Joschka Fischer's federalism speech of May 2000 and the convening of the 2002–2003 European Convention on the Future of the EU, comparative federalism brought back into currency the concepts of devolution, decentralization and subsidiarity from earlier studies of federalism. Three distinguishable areas of it were (a) polity- and democracy-related aspects, concerning the structure and constitutional characteristics of the EU, (b) policy frames and (c) studies of the political features of the EU, including parties and elections and other important aspects of its politics.

The first area of post-1990s comparative federalism was interested in questions of 'democracy and democratic deficit'; the 'origins of various forms of legitimacy in a political context in which diverse levels of government and governance interact'; the nature of 'democratic representation in federal states' and political accountability, and comparison of the relationship between territorial representation and political organization in national federal systems and the EU, reflected in territorial representation in both the Council of Ministers (henceforth COM) and also 'in some sense' in the European Council. Comparative federalism also seeks to explain the Euroscepticism of citizens and the system's deficit of legitimacy emerging from the expansion of the federal powers of the EU to rubbish the claim of some scholars from both rationalist and constructivist planes that the increasing opportunities that federal institutions offer can best explain why the transfer of authority from the national to the federal level will be automatic. With the sharp increase in the variety of state interests and the new methods of decision-making in the EU, exemplified in the open method of coordination, it was difficult for the EU to assure the degree of accountability that European citizens may consider guaranteed.

The second emerging area of policy frames in comparative federalism, in the context of the EU, concerned European public policy. Here, some scholars concentrated on how in systems where member governments take part in unanimous decision-making, tensions (joint decision traps) and resultant suboptimal decisional outcomes can be avoided. Others contend that the evolution of the EU regulatory policy can be properly grasped only if the EU is seen as a federal system that 'mediates conflicts and imposes common regulations aimed at harmonizing standards and practices'.

In the third area of political features of the EU, comparative federalists analyse if and how the emerging party system at the EU level can be constructed in a confederal manner, managing the resultant heterogeneity in the party system where 'a large number of national political parties operating outside the strict ideological logic of the main families of European political parties' coexist with other parties that 'have emerged within the framework of European elections alone'. They have used their toolkit of federalism to focus on the principal challenges of designing 'a system of integrated parties at the supranational level'.

Finally, the approach of 'consociative democracy', stemming from Arend Lijphart's theory and other comparative researches carried out on the consociative federal democracies of the Netherlands, Austria and Switzerland, has been applied to the EU on the analogy of segments with states. The EU system is supposedly populated by sovereign nations, each with its distinctive 'national identity, political traditions, social structure and national culture'. The consociational approach aims to find out the resultant dilemmas of the EU member states, who 'cooperate either on a unanimous or proportional basis to take decisions'. Apart from making a plea for a 'non-contentious mode of politicizing the EU', this approach eschews 'fostering the role of mass, competitive and partisan politics in the EU' as facilitators of its democratic character to focus more on its consensual decision-making processes', which stress 'compromises and cooperation and permit integration of 'globalization losers' such as 'acutely Eurosceptic citizens and anti-system political entrepreneurs'.

Federalism: Critique and Evaluation

Even with all this reincarnation of federalism through the EU and despite being one of the earliest theories of European integration, federalist approaches are, according to Saurugger, generally found on the margins of the EU studies, 'replaced instead by multi-level governance agendas' because of three problems persisting even with this broad-based image of Europe as an 'asymmetric federation'. First, due to the high normative overtones of federalism, its employment to defend national and international integration projects taints and delegitimizes them. Second, the extreme heterogeneity of the current federalist approaches implies that despite being touted as a theory, most applications of federalism do not offer a set of verifiable or refutable hypotheses, harbouring instead variegated and contradictory approaches to a political entity, interstate in character. Third, empirically, even the latest European treaties have tended to fortify the member states against the European Commission so that members remain stronger than the supranational entity and its institutions, the COM being able to stall policy developments in areas not favoured by the member states. So although it is possible to regard the EU as 'a club of states with federal characteristics', and conceptual tools fashioned by federalist scholars have enabled a better understanding of the power game in which member states of EU, subnational actors and European institutions remain embroiled, the EU cannot be placed on par with other national federations. There is no superordinate European government with an exclusive sphere of constitutional jurisdiction flaunting a distinct or superior political legitimacy before the member states. The EU rather shares legal competencies with national judicial systems since its emergence.[16]

Despite these pitfalls, federalism is not wholly marginalized as an approach to European integration. A 1994 research project aimed at testing 'the applicability of the federative model in relations between states in post-communist Europe' explored how Middle Europe, comprising states located between the EU and the erstwhile Soviet Union, could associate with one another before their coveted 'eventual absorption into the EU'. Then, researchers of the project extended their horizons to the historical experiences of federalism in Eastern and Central Europe—Austria, Germany, Italy, Spain and Belgium—and Western Europe to explore the possibilities of an all-European federal integration from 'a common expectation that the future of Europe is and ought to be profoundly federal', even if this would be what Ortino says in the concluding chapter a 'functional federalism, that is, a federalism in which the territorial extension, as well as the jurisdictions of the supranational, national and local authorities, is subject to change according to the situation.'[17]

Functionalism

Inside the first wave of theoretical reflections on European integration, functionalism offered a substitutive picture of future IR. Developing since the 19th century as part of the liberal movement from Kant to Wilson and building its conceptual framework as a definitive response to the realist, 'state-centric', 'state-as-actor' or 'billiard ball' models of IP, the dynamics of the type of peaceful international change diagnosed by 'the functional approach' were not first recognized by David Mitrany. Vestiges of it are found in the writings of P. S. Reinsch (*Public International Unions*, 1911) and L. S. Woolf (*International Government*, 1916). But the germ of the most vigorous statement of what a small but varied group of scholars, led by Mitrany, called 'the functional development of international organization' was given in *The Progress of International Government* (1933), to be developed more fully in *A Working Peace System* (1943) and much later in *Functional Theory of Politics* (1975). Frankel says Mitrany's views constitute more creed or philosophy than a theory. It seeks to link 'authority to a specific activity' so as 'to break away from the traditional link between authority and territory'. Mitrany pleaded for the formation of separate bodies invested with authority over functionally specified areas, such as security, transport and communication, to enthuse international cooperation faster and more effectively than grandiose territory-based schemes. The scales and structures of these international organizations were to be determined by the requirements of their functions. The emerging community was also to be built function by function, with adaptive structures, true to Mitrany's maxim, 'form follows function'. Less concerned to present an irrefutable theory than a conceptual framework that would promote conditions that discourage wars, Mitrany searched for specific factors that would assist in the establishment of permanent international organizations that will assure peace and yet not urge a retreat to the 'quick fix' and over-zealous idealism of the interwar era. Naturally, functionalists were strongly convinced about the inadequacies of the realist assumption that the state was the basic unit of international society.

Even though never adequately codified, the core logic of functionalism revolves around a 'threefold distinction between contextual conditions, process conditions and the conditions necessary for task expansion (or spillover)'. From its core belief that the typical game of politics is a stumbling block to the creation of common welfare, and nation-states are the least well-equipped for nurturing the most fundamental development of the nationals because public policies are distorted by the politicians' self-seeking, functionalism regards the traditional view of problem-solving by authoritative territorial structures, created through 'political amputations', as neither the only nor the best way to cope with practical problems facing countries.[18] The management of navigation on the Rhine or Danube, the control of pollution in the Mediterranean and regulation of air traffic across several countries do not automatically demand that there should be a territorial state with national elections, voting rights, armies and state control to cope with them. So functionalists urged for the inclusion of supranational organizations in IR to perform, aided by their experts and civil servants, functions wrongly attributed to states.

The contextual or background conditions that filliped functionalism included the muffling of ideological conflict among prominent social groups (workers and capitalists, religious and ethnonational groups, etc.) amid the articulated structures of late capitalism, making society veer away from cleavages towards collective gains through cooperation, and the 'economic problem' to be concerned more about productivity than distribution. The venue of thick economic exchange comprising trade, capital flows, tourism, communication and so on that Europe had become generated international processes which were unspectacular and mundane but proved highly conducive to further cooperative initiatives. These made the creation of a coal and steel community and later a free trade area and customs union look like normal policy responses rather than novel turnarounds. Last, the task expansion or spillover stipulated by functionalism suggested that the process of integration will be cumulative and multi-sectoral, undergoing a learning process that will ultimately change the very core of the present international system, inhering in state sovereignty. The supranational organizations will begin with relatively mundane and non-contentious socio-economic fields to venture later into bigger and more controversial areas.[19]

In the initial formulation by Mitrany, redolent of the Marxist emphasis upon the primacy of economics together with social needs, politics would cede place to the socio-economic determination, and if and when international society is arranged in functionalist terms with a network of organizations gratifying its diverse needs, the inclination to and ultimately the very likelihood of war would be overcome, and mankind would be launched on the road to abiding peace. This style of thinking sprang from the early functionalist assumption that war is caused by human nature not as pristine but warped by the present system. So fresh and novel institutions, traditions and ideas can usher in a Manichean reversal in human behaviour towards pacifism. Later, more refined and softened functionalism posited that the experience of smooth and effective cooperation in a broad range of welfare areas and their management under international administration in modern industrial states would eventually lessen the chances of violent conflicts between national objectives and would invigorate the ethos of cooperation further. Mitrany contended that once these functional organizations were put in place, they had no choice but to work with one another. For instance, road, rail and air agencies would have to cooperate technically in areas of timetable coordination and the creation of infrastructure for managing different volumes of passenger and freight traffic. After different groups of functional agencies are pitted against or juxtaposed with one another in their work, the resultant coordinated planning will come not as much from the origination of a new system as from the restructuring of existing systems through a process of adaptation and evolution. Amid states entering/exiting existing and new organizations, this would ultimately culminate in a 'rounded political system ... the functional arrangements might indeed be regarded as organic elements of federalism by instalments'.[20]

Avowedly, this shift in the centre of political gravity from the national to the regional would substitute the 'divisive subjective allegiances' to national units that caused wars by 'new loyalties fostered by the new cross-national units' that neutralized pernicious national attitudes. Seeing the proficiency with which these new supranational organizations met all the needs that states found impossible to cater for and solved the most chronic and nagging problems of mankind, including poverty, underdevelopment and inequality, 'people would willingly transfer their allegiance to a new functional international community woven around function rather than territory.[21] In Mitrany's words, functionalism would accordingly 'overlay political divisions with a spreading web of international relations and agencies in which and through which the interests and life of all nations would be gradually integrated'.[22]

Mitrany had little love lost for either regional unification, which he thought would merely replicate the problems of the state system at a bigger level, with interregional tensions substituting interstate tensions; or for the idea of world government, which would be deleterious for human freedom. The federalist solution was unnecessary in requiring categorical consent on the part of state or provincial governments to an enduring but constitutionally circumscribed arrangement. Because for functionalism, the disposition of living peacefully in a global community can be created simply through a chain of small incremental steps without the implication of any 'knowing consent' to the global community. While federating 'partakes of high public drama', achievement of community through functional dynamics demands nothing more than 'low public awareness, if not sustained public sleepwalking'.[23]

Mitrany's ideas deeply appealed to those who found the unavoidable association of the federalist idea with nation-states with its baggage of nationalism, militarism, bilateral deals, BOP and so on repellent. Contrarily, beyond 'functionalism's preoccupation with details of production and commerce' lurked a definite normative change that provided 'opportunity to think and talk in terms of transnational economic ties, mutual cooperation, the taming of nationalism, spillover and community spirit'. These non-institutionalist solutions touched Jean Monnet and Robert Schuman, putative architects of the EU. Borrowing from Mitrany, Monnet showed how 'the most mundane facts, smallest acts of everyday life of production, commerce and voluntary associations could lay the groundwork of new ways of organizing relations among countries'. So what is the signature argument of functionalism? To Caporaso and Keeler, it is 'preoccupation with the technical and the forestalling of the political', its pathway or programme being, '(a)void comprehensive plans for integration, and minimize the political, at least initially. Take advantage of social differentiation and carve society into sectors, the more specialized and autonomous the better. Beginning with piecemeal cooperation, allow the chief dynamic mechanism—spillover—to do its work'.[24]

Critique of Functionalism

The optimistic functionalist logic was faulted on many grounds. First is its basic contradiction as a 'sociological theory of modern industrial capitalism'. By differentiating various subsystems in society, particularly sectoral ones, functionalism provided the expert with a greater role and space for autonomous expert action which was never adequately theorized. The conditions under which political integration could be resisted by experts were also never sufficiently spelt out. The contingency that the crucial process of spillover could move in different directions, as implied by the terms *spillback* and *spillaround*, was ignored. So the most critical variable in the theoretical dynamics of integration was kept 'indeterminate, adaptable to any outcome' but shorn of predictive potential.

Second, insights of modern rational choice theory controvert claims of functionalism as an articulate theory of political choice. Its plea to focus on 'changing constraints and preferences' caused by exogenously specified social and economic cooperation' did not reckon with the fact that 'incentive structure alone cannot explain outcomes. In a world of strategic indeterminacy, even with preferences specified, many outcomes are usually possible'.[25]

Third, critique of functionalism for its normative and teleological limitations focuses on the insufficient explication of (a) the notion of human needs, which are 'legion and often contradictory', while the notion of rationality is contextually determined; (b) why supranational institutions will necessarily employ a more rational approach, or (c) why individuals will accord greater credence to functionalists' interpretations of human needs than those of states.

Fourth, functionalism's inattention to the political nature of decision-making stemming from its overemphasis on the technocratic character of the emerging supranational organizations and Mitrany's oversight of the permanent and ubiquitous presence of politics even in public policy management are also pilloried.[26]

Fifth, the force of the above arguments in the context of community building makes even an innocuous concept like development unable to free itself from political debates and makes the global consensus on the definition of welfare assumed by functionalists chimerical. Far from being independent of 'prior political consensus,' smooth welfare expenditure presupposes it. Neofunctionalists showed from their case studies that the assumption that functional cooperation can be isolated from its political context and especially from the political objectives of national elites and yet assure long-term shifts in political allegiance from the national to the global community is unfounded.[27]

Sixth, functionalism (including Mitrany as its spokesman) is faulted for the severe lack of sociological analysis of the character of actors operating within functionalist transnational and supranational institutions and of the bases and criteria of their selection. Despite 'experts' being an abstract and imprecise category resisting operationalization in empirical research, functionalists have constructed the following contestable hypotheses for 'experts': (a) international institutions exorcize national loyalties among them, (b) international officials' conceptualization of national interests significantly differs from that of state officials and thereby better facilitates international unity and (c) non-governmental or NSAs endorse views of experts more than those of state officials. But Harold Guetzkow's empirical psychological investigations did not find any appreciable clash between these two types of officials, although this differentiation brings to mind Gouldner's organizational typology of 'cosmopolitans'/'experts' and 'locals'/'home-guards' and his empirical finding that 'cosmopolitans' are always more 'outward looking', more of an 'outsider' and less loyal than 'locals'.[28] Rather, in Frankel's words, 'the best international civil servants are recruited among individuals loyal to their own countries than convinced 'internationalists' who are rootless and lack the habit of loyalty'.[29]

Seventh, I mention Claude's rejection of the following theses and assumptions of functionalism:

1. Thesis that 'war is a product of unsatisfactory social and economic conditions in the global community.'
2. The 'separability assumption' revolving around the misperception that among the needs met, purposes served and claims of members satisfied by a successful state in a society, we can segregate governmental functions between political and non-political groups.
3. Even when these are separable, one should give priority to cooperation in non-political sectors, since the government's task is 'to practice the "political art" of accommodation, negotiating acceptable arrangements among groups'.
4. Even where the separability and prioritization are granted, there is a belief that this is the only way to solve political problems and the resultant 'doctrinaire quality of functionalist pragmatism.[30]
5. The bonds of individuals with their nation states are rational.

The legacy of functionalism survived even after these critiques, proven in the functionalist reincarnation of the League of Nations that saved it from the ignominy of total failure and passed on to its successor, the UN. The survival of Mitrany's maxim of 'federalism by instalments' is proven by Nye's famous concept of 'peace in parts'.[31] But functionalism survived mostly in its academic successor, neofunctionalism.

Neofunctionalism

Haas laid the foundations of this prominent paradigm of regional integration in the context of his doctoral research on the European Coal and Steel Community (ECSC) at the end of the 1950s, from which grew *The Uniting of Europe* (*UOE*). It employed inductive theorizing to capture the inner dynamics of the European integration process that followed from the Treaty of Paris (1951) to the Treaty of Rome (1957). Essentially, neofunctionalism is a carryover from functionalism, which retains and develops some of the most crucial concerns and ideas of functionalism but drops others. Retained elements are heightened importance of social and economic actors, vital role of issue linkages and spillover and impact of initial cooperative probes in changing the incentives facing political elites. Dropped ones are severability of technical, non-controversial, economic issues from political issues since 'economic integration, however defined, may be based on political motives and frequently begets political consequences'.[32] Three new characteristics acquired by neofunctionalism are (a) 'a methodological reorientation', aimed at systematizing and articulating the process of integration through social scientific concepts and terminology drawn from 'interest group theory, systems theory and to a lesser extent economics', (b) an attempt to integrate into architectonic model fragments of theory relating to 'background conditions, conditions at the time of union, process conditions and outcomes'—'a comprehensive account', where the fragments would fit together and (c) provision, beyond mere recognition of the role of supranational institutions, of a theory of politics.[33] That is why neofunctionalism is sometimes taken to be 'a case of mistaken identity'[34] or 'conceptually or otherwise in limbo between functionalist or federalist approaches', sharing with functionalism 'the centrality of transnational actors' and with federalism 'that of the central institutions'.[35]

For explaining why states go for surrendering decisional autonomy to international or supranational organizations, Haas looks at Western Europe's wide spectrum of organizations requiring collaboration of European governments as a 'living laboratory'. Since 'detailed data on how—if at all—cohesion is obtained through these processes is lacking',[36] neofunctionalism set about unravelling this process.

While Haas's other writings and works of Lindberg, Scheingold and so on enriched neofunctionalism,[37] it was continually 'refined, adapted and retested and cyclically challenged and reinforced' in the works of Nye, Puchala and Schmitter in the early and mid-1970s and 1980s. One contextual reason behind neofunctionalism's emergence was the acceptance of functionalism's major tenets by political-administrative actors such as Monnet and Schuman during the appearance and consolidation of the behaviourist movement between the 1940s and 1950, popularizing attempts to render the study of social phenomena more scientific through verifiable or refutable by empirical observation of facts.

Accordingly, neofunctionalists set about clarifying the dependent variable of regional integration and demarcating it from allied terms such as regional cooperation and regional systems. They departed from functionalists' downplaying of domestic factors. Through a searching probe into the political systems and administrative structures of the European Communities' (EC) founder states and the activities and tendencies of the political elites operative in parties, governments and interest groups, employers' associations and trade unions, neofunctionalism sought to explain 'how and why they (states) voluntarily mingle, merge and mix with their neighbours so as to lose the factual attributes of sovereignty while acquiring new techniques for resolving conflicts between themselves.'[38] This stance was clearly opposed to the current neorealist explanation of regional integration, as something caused by the threat from an external enemy and smaller states banding against it.

For neofunctionalists the basic element inducing actors to forge supranational communities was not Mitrany's 'technocratic automatism' but the rational initiative on the part of a political or administrative elite, whose decision to persist with or resist integration 'rests on the perception of interests and the articulation of specific values'. Haas contends that instead of 'relying on a scheme of integration which posits "altruistic" or "idealist" motives as the conditions of conduct, it seems more reasonable to focus on the interests and values defended by the major groups involved in the process, experience showing that these are far too complex to be described in such simple terms as the "desire for Franco-German peace" or the "will to a united Europe"'. However, with the broadening and expansion of integration, the perceptions and views of the political elites will also alter, 'values will undergo change; interests will be redefined in terms of a regional rather than a purely national orientation, and the erstwhile set of separate national group values will gradually be superseded by a new and geographically larger set of beliefs'.[39] While stressing the perceptions of the elites of their self-interests as motivators of integration, Haas points to the myopia of the elites. According to him, 'neo-functionalists rely on the primacy of incremental decision-making over grand designs' since the elites are 'incapable of long-range purposive behaviour'.[40]

Although he conceded that functional necessities furthered integration no less than the ideologies and politics of actors, Haas and other neofunctionalists focused more on political elites' perceptions of supranational institutions as the most effective way of gratifying their pragmatic interests on how processes of collective decision-making develop and how both the governing and non-governing elites adjust their plans and organization to cope with the shift of the decisional processes from the national to the supranational plane. Despite accepting the functionalists' notion of incremental change implicit in the concept of spillover, neofunctionalists reject their view that welfare is a non-contentious affair that can be segregated from political strife. Power is not isolable from welfare because welfare involves reallocation and redistribution of limited resources, rendering progress of integration contingent on not only the size of the developmental pie but also the clout of the national participants distributing it. This confers greater integrative potentiality on regional bodies compared to global entities which represent a greater mix of cultural values.[41]

But in contradistinction to the stress on exchanges and transactions by Deutsch and transactionalists/interactionists, coming later below, Haas and neofunctionalists also considered institutions and attitudes important. As Caporaso and Keeler put it: 'With regard to institutions, decision-making patterns were critical. With regard to attitudes, the learning of integrative habits was important'. While institutional loyalties, orientations and lobbying activities had to shift to EC institutions as 'practical problems were addressed, and perhaps solved', Haas made these 'authority-legitimacy transfers' his central concern and a 'highly general, continuous variable, not confined to discrete, holistic outcomes (confederation, federation)'.[42]

The main analytical attributes of neofunctionalism can be spelt out in terms of major actors, motives, process and context of integration. Among *actors*, below the state are interest groups and political parties, and above are supranational regional institutions. They nurture the development of interest groups, develop close relations with them as with fellow technocrats in the national civil services and manoeuvre them into promoting integration. The role of the governments has to be 'creatively responsive'. Concerning *motives*, functionalists' invocation of the innate goodness of will, the community of interests or commitment to the common good as basic motivators is substituted by the unalloyed utilitarian notion of interest-based politics. In Haas's own words: '(T)he "good Europeans" are not the main creators of the community; the process of community formation is dominated by rationally constituted groups with specific interests and aims, willing and able to adjust their aspirations by turning to supranational means when this course appears profitable.'[43]

Process-wise, key elements are spillover and upgrading of common interests, domains, directions and depths of which are left undefined. For example, Lindberg terms it as 'a situation in which a given action, related to a specific goal, creates a situation in which the original goal can be assured only by taking further actions, which, in turn, create a further condition and a need for more action and so forth'.[44] Haas retains Mitrany's concept of spillovers as sectoral, related to integrative activities or impulses from one sector to another.[45] But he breaks down the concept further into functional, technical and political types. Functional spillover, akin to the sectoral, suggests that national economies are so interlinked that if integration happens in one sector, integration in other sectors would necessarily follow. The multitude of functional bodies created to monitor the process and bonds and ties created between them will get the power of national government institutions eroded. Technical spillover stems from the functionalist contention that '"technical self-determination" increasingly replaces politics as we know it'. Under this, discrepancies/divergences in national standards will impel states to come up or go down to the level of the state(s) having the strictest or laxest standards, as when Bulgaria and Romania, which had the laxest environmental laws before they joined EU had to meet requirements of EU law, fashioned by pressures from Germany and Netherlands which had the strictest. Finally, political spillover, entailing increased politicization of sectoral impulses, assumes that after the integration of different functional sectors is completed, interest groups will move on from influencing national governments to trying to influence regional organizations; resist any attempt at downsizing integration, and lift politics from the national to the regional level.[46] Upgradation of common interests takes place when, after experiencing problems in reaching a common policy, even while recognizing the need for a joint stand to conserve other aspects of interdependence, member-states trade concessions in other cognate fields, which again shores up the power base of the central institutions.[47]

Regarding the context of integration, Haas accepted the key premise of Mitrany and functionalists that functional cooperation would start on comparatively low-key economic and social levels but rejected the dichotomous insulation between the economic and the political posited by functionalists: 'The supranational style stresses the indirect penetration of the political by way of the economic because the "purely" economic decisions always acquire political significance in the minds of participants.'[48] But rather than economic nature of tasks, it is the 'degree' of their 'functional specificity' in non-trivial matters that is 'causally related to the intensity of integration,' which, however, 'may be so trivial as to remain outside the stream of expectations and actions vital for integration'.[49]

But the key concept of spillover in the context of the ECSC also brought the first theoretical jolt for neofunctionalism. The High Authority and the Commission of the ECSC did provide the transnational institutional mediation necessary for integration with some initial success, which emboldened Haas in 1965 to claim prematurely that the community's progress made the dream of 'voiding the power of the national state' in all domains except 'defence, education and foreign policy' seem quite achievable, proving the worth of the functionalist belief in progress from a common market to political unification. But the rudest empirical jolt to neofunctionalism was provided by Charles de Gaulle's initiation of the Empty Chair Policy in July 1965 over the dispute about the financing of the common agricultural policy, after which Gaullist France recalled the permanent representative in Brussels and announced France's intention not to take its seat in the COM until it had its way. De Gaulle's insistence that governments are and should be the real engines of integration and his cynicism about the Commission's zeal for supranationalism indicated that neofunctionalism had overestimated ramifying potentials of increments in the economic domain and the possibility of a shift from sectoral/functional spillover to political spillover.

This turn of events, particularly the Empty Chair Crisis, only partly resolved by the 1966 Luxembourg Compromise and giving member states veto power on issues that they thought pernicious for their national interests, rattled neofunctionalists. Haas,

Lindberg and Scheingold, Nye, Schmitter and so on resorted to a reappraisal of their analytical framework and conceded that integration was not an unstoppable process. Especially, Schmitter coined a host of terms denoting alternatives to spillover, such as 'spill-around' (spread of integration to new domains without adding to the competences of the High Authority), 'build up' (augmenting the competencies of supranational authorities but holding them in reserve), 'retrench' (raising the level of joint deliberations but outside the purview of institutions), 'muddle about' (permitting debates but not decision-making at the supranational plane) and 'spill-back' or 'encapsulate' (non-reaction or delayed response to a crisis). With such radical modifications, neofunctionalism became so much a discredited doctrine in the late 1960s and the early 1970s that after ruminating over the 'joys and anguish of pre-theorizing' in 1970, Haas somewhat prematurely announced its 'obsolescence'. Four factors explained the predictive failure of neofunctionalism: (a) soft-pedalling changes in member states' preferences from the time integration starts to the emergence of new expectations after membership, (b) a misplaced 'end of ideology' assumption which encouraged marginalizing national political aspirations, (c) lack of knowledge regarding actors' external relations with states existing outside the integration scheme and (d) imperviousness to colossal changes happening in European societies and also to diverse political cultures and idioms across the political systems. But the epitaph was written a little too soon. As European integration acquired momentum in the mid-1980s, neofunctionalism also got back its popularity and prestige. In the 1990s, it bounced back into relevance with reformulated hypotheses after the European integration gathered new momentum.[50]

Critique of Neofunctionalism

However, neofunctionalism had problems and weaknesses both in its 'doldrums period' and the period of revival. The first arose from the point that the EC–ECSC conflation, the subject of Haas's great book, had a sample universe of just one. So attempted empirical generalizations failed to meet the requirements of theory for two reasons: (a) not resulting from an 'intellectual structure that explains regularities' and (b) unable to sustain 'counterfactual claims about what "would happen if ..."'.

The second problem or weakness related to an inane theory of politics which drew our attention to elites, political parties, interest groups, domestic affairs and bargaining going on between Brussels and state capitals, without any backing from a theory of bargaining or political choice, in which successes and failures were inevitably accounted for by presence or absence of political will.[51]

Third, despite its relentless harping on supranationality as the only option before states striving for maximization of welfare, neofunctionalism was never able to provide a theoretical connection between welfare optimization and regional integration. While pinpointing the institutional formulas in a region that facilitate transactions, it leaves the nature and content of the transactions unspecified, as well as the circumstances in which societal demands for integration find acceptance at the national political level. All this owes to the naive assumption that where an issue with cross-border implications and a felt desideratum exist, both subnational and supranational players will marshal resources to resolve the crisis. This simplistic belief comes from the scant attention paid to the preferences of governments and inadequate comprehension of the 'nature of collective action problems' that may run athwart efforts towards integration. Consequently, neofunctionalism keeps mum about: (a) what makes supranational-level decision-making efficient; (b) what makes some integration schemes grounded fliers; (c) what is the reason that a state decides to join an existing combine and (d) what causes the timing of the decision?[52] Without convincing answers to these questions neofunctionalism remains a poor theory.

Many of neofunctionalism's assumptions about interest group activity have also been questioned. Studies of interest group operations in the EC indicate that despite minor reorientations, the major part of their efforts remained fixated on national goals, and very few of them wanted a transnational consensus on general policy concerns, rather than arriving at COM's meetings ready with a national negotiating strategy more or less inflexible about all importunities from supranational-level interest groups. Besides, the weakness of the neofunctionalist arguments about an automatic transition from the economic to the political spillover stems not just from the inattention to the contingencies pointed above or from the failure of EC member states to move from the 'low politics' of economic issues to the 'high politics' of general policy concerns due to differences of their national objectives and situations and the lack of consensus on what are the 'unifying' elements of 'European' issues. It is more fundamental. Actually, the very rapid and tangible benefits accruing to member states from the economic integration achieved by the EC enabled them to pursue more autonomous courses in these 'high' areas of foreign policy. General de Gaulle's foreign policy dramatized the considerable extent of independence exercisable by member states without endangering the interlocking pyramid of bargains constituting the ECs. Once the major pragmatic interests of the politically relevant groups were satisfied by a relatively modest degree of integration, sometimes the ideological commitment to go any further was lacking. This obvious disjuncture and disconnect between economic and political integration has induced Nye to suggest keeping the economic, political and social components of integration in separate boxes with pertinent tools and indicators (such as mail flows for the social component) to assess them.[53]

Finally, the constantly, though subtly, evolving nature of the integrating political community and its undergirding supranationality was never free from ambiguity. In *UOE*, Haas regarded it as 'a process whereby political actors in several distinct national settings shift their national loyalties, expectations and political activities to a new centre, institutions of which possess and demand jurisdiction over pre-existing national states', the emerging 'political community', being *'superimposed over the pre-existing ones'* [italics mine]. Its exacting nature and rigour remind us of the political community envisioned by federalists. But shortly thereafter, a broadened definition of the political community made it 'compatible' with a 'variety of constitutional and structural factors,' the only requirement being that 'there is a likelihood of internal peaceful change in a setting of contending groups with mutually antagonistic aims'. But now, the 'institutions' of the 'new and larger centre' either 'possess *or demand* jurisdiction over the pre-existing national states [italics mine].'[54] While it will be seen below that this closely resembled Deutsch's transactionalism and 'pluralistic security community', only three years later Haas and Schmitter defined 'Political union' as 'any arrangement under which existing nation states cease to act as *autonomous* decision-making units with respect to an important range of policies'. Really inclusive, 'the constitutional features which can be accommodated under this label range from the unitary state to the principle of shared-but-not-sharply-divided powers which is typical of the European supranational approach', allowing even confederal arrangements to 'qualify for inclusion, depending on whether any actual delegation of national power to a central agency has taken place'.[55]

Unable to specify the exact nature of the post-regional integration political community from the early to the mid-1960s, Haas merely defined it around the idea of supranationality. Its uniqueness as a 'style of making international decisions' consists in the type of participants involved, as well as the context and quality of decision-making. Haas considers it, 'not federation, confederation or intergovernmental organization,' as 'the appropriate regional counterpart to the national state which no longer feels capable of realizing welfare aims within its narrow borders, which has made its peace with the fact of interdependence in an industrial and egalitarian state'.[56] Lindberg advised an even 'more cautious' view of the end product of integration, 'limited to the development of devices and processes for arriving at collective decisions by means other than autonomous action by national parliaments'.[57] In transactionalism, however, which Haas called a pre-theory of integration, we find an alternative conception of not only the process of integration but also of the end product.

Transactionalism

Essentially an application of communications theory and cybernetics to the integration concept by Deutsch and fellow scholars in the 1950s, the transactionalist approach, did neither postulate any particular legal or institutional framework, like federalism, nor presuppose gratification of social welfare needs like functionalism. Instead, it focused on 'the conditions necessary to create and maintain a sense of community among populations of different countries' and looked upon integration 'as a process of cultural assimilation'.[58] Because it arose from Deutsch's concern, in the aftermath of the Second World War, with how to avert future conflict between nations through their integration, transactionalism thought basically about transactions that brought about security communities or groups of people marked by 'the attainment, within a territory, of a "sense of community" and of institutions and practices strong enough and widespread enough to assure, for a "long" time, dependable expectations of "peaceful change" among its population'. Security communities are basically of two types determined by the principle of their composition: amalgamation or pluralism. Amalgamation means 'the formal merger between two or more previously independent units into a single larger unit with some type of common government after amalgamation, unitary or federal' and having 'one supreme decision-making centre', like the USA. Contrarily, the pluralistic security community (henceforth, PSC) 'retains the legal independence of separate governments' as with the USA and Canada, 'whose two separate governmental units form a security community without being merged'.[59]

Deutsch's originality lies in regarding even some existing states, that too not just federal but even unitary ones[60] as outcomes of integration and in giving us four types of political units using both integration and amalgamation as constituent principles: state, empire, pluralistic PSCs and amalgamated security communities (henceforth ASCs). States betoken integration but not amalgamation, although some (such as the USA and the UK) do both. Empires indicate amalgamation but not integration. PSCs possess integration but not amalgamation. ASCs possess both. Apart from Canada and the USA, Deutsch also cites Norway and Sweden as examples of PSCs because neither of them has resorted to force for a long time. Much like power, integration has four dimensions: 'domain', 'scope', 'range' and 'weight', the last measured in terms of 'cohesion or cohesiveness'.[61]

Contrary to federalist, functionalist and neofunctionalist approaches, Deutsch regards states also as results of integration because his extensive research on nation-building taught him that communication is the secular glue that holds social groups and political communities together, missed by the power-monism of political science. Accordingly, while describing 'laws and institutions of states, much as anatomists describe the skeletons and organs of body', political scientists miss 'the nerves of government' and 'the channels of communication and decisions' through which governments wield their power.[62] But communications help in community-building by enabling 'a group to think together, to see together and to act together'. Communication processes and transaction flows between nations are not only 'facilities for attention' but also workshops of shared identification. For, the cementing factors of existing national communities are high amounts of cohesion, mutual trust and sentiments of shared identity, released by social, political and economic transactions on both elite and mass levels. To that extent, a nation is a 'community of social communication'.

Assuming that what will bind people within nations should also draw them together across nations, Deutsch and his associates sought to apply the same mechanisms of communication and interaction to the international level.[63] Concentrating on the volumes of transactions among nations or peoples as the most revealing indicators of integration and taking cohesiveness among individuals, fostered by 'the extent of mutual relationship or interaction among them', as measurable objectively and impartially, they employed a statistical tool named 'the index of relative acceptance'. It measures the ratio of extra-regional relative to intra-regional communication and transactions, taking higher volume and range of communications between members of communication-communities than with others as quantitative indicators of ongoing integration. The indicators commonly used are mail flows, telephone traffic, imports/exports, travel and transportation patterns, migration, student exchanges, transnational currency transfers, translations of books and so on. For a certain country, domestic/foreign ratios of such transaction flows are calculated, and statistical and content analyses for them are employed. Depending on how more or less varied and numerous transactions are, the international community will be more visible and robust or less.

Reservations about making judgements about IP from data of apparently trifling things such as mail flows, telephone calls and trade figures can be addressed if we remember that (a) not a single index but a set is needed; (b) not raw volumes of transactions but ratios and proportions of total volumes are to be counted, and (c) beyond the counting of proportions, determination of integration is to be done through 'covariance' or the study of joint rewards and penalties in these transactions. The actual likelihood of a joint reward can be termed 'interest' in an objective sense, which induces people to say that they belong together; conceive of themselves as members of the community; refer to it as 'we' when speaking of it as a group, and call it home when talking about a territory. Deutsch culls two hypotheses from these abovementioned assumptions: (a) Having experienced a high level of transactions accompanied by considerable joint rewards at one time, people may bear with later joint deprivations, if joint rewards assuredly succeed them and (b) a group of people who have learnt to identify with each other through initial joint rewards followed by such a probabilistic mixture of joint deprivations will be characterized by greater connectedness and strength of habit than a group of people who have expected and received only joint rewards.[64]

After identifying the conditions necessary for fostering and preserving a sense of community among the residents of a given region and delineating the role of social communication in fuelling the engine of nationalism, Deutsch proceeded with his team to analyse the formation of such integrated communities and the processes of their disintegration in 10 historical cases, including the English–Scottish union, the union between Ireland and the UK, Germany from the middle ages to 1871, Italy during the 18th and 19th centuries, the Hapsburg Empire, the union of Norway and Sweden, Switzerland before 1848, English–Welsh union after 1485, England itself and finally, American colonies after 1789, the Civil War and the final reunion. The objective of this study (*Political Community and the North Atlantic Area*) was to learn from these integrating efforts in the past if the 'Atlantic community' was an incipient integrating region or not. In Deutsch's view, although nation states became more relevant to each other as they interacted with one another, just an increase in mutual relevance was not sufficient for integration unless it was coupled with mutual responsiveness since transactions alone are no sure recipes for the birth of a community. Communication can also beget tension if they stress divergent values and expectations in place of the identity of values and interests.[65]

Regarding security communities, the destination points of integration, the general findings of Deutsch and his fellow researchers from these historical cases are as follows:

- PSCs proved easier to build, and they survive longer than ASCs, though the latter respond to challenges more decisively.
- Rather than being narrow as expected, the 'threshold of integration' had surprisingly a much wider 'zone of transition'.[66]
- The type of sense of community apposite for the study integration,

> Tuned out to be rather a matter of mutual sympathy and loyalties; of 'we-feeling', trust and mutual consideration; of partial identification in terms of self-images and interests, of mutually successful predictions of behaviour; and of cooperative action along with it—in short, a matter of perpetual dynamic process of mutual attention, communication, perception of needs, and responsiveness in the process of decision-making.[67]

- 'Larger, stronger, more politically, administratively and educationally advanced political units were found to form the cores of strength around which in most cases the integrative process developed'.[68]
- The integrating capacity of the participating units was composed of two broad groups of capabilities: (a) a political unit's capacity to act, coming from its 'size, power, economic strength, administrative efficiency and the like' and (b) the cybernetic ability of a unit 'to control its behaviour and to redirect its attention'.
- The attainment or loss of amalgamation was determined to a great extent by 'the relationship of two rates of exchange: the growing rate of claims and

> burdens upon central governments as against the growing—in some instances, insufficiently growing—level of capabilities of the governmental institutions of the amalgamated political community'.[69]

The 'essential requirements' for the formation of ASCs are nine, with three more that might acquire essentiality later. The original nine include '(1) mutual compatibility of main values; (2) a distinctive way of life; (3) expectations of strong economic gains; (4) a marked increase in political and administrative capabilities; (5) superior economic growth on the part of at least some participating units; (6) unbroken links of social communications, both geographically between territories and sociologically between different social strata; (7) a broadening of the political elite; (8) mobility of persons, at least among the politically relevant strata; and, (9) a multiplicity of ranges of communication and transactions'. The additional potential ones are (a) the compensation of flows of communication and transactions, (b) a not too infrequent interchange of group roles and (c) considerable mutual predictability'.[70]

On the basis of their studies of failures of integration of England–Ireland, Norway–Sweden and three instances in Austria, the Deutsch team diagnosed some 'background conditions conducive to disintegration', which could be categorized into two groups: (a) those which increased the burdens on amalgamated governments and (b) those which weakened the capabilities of governments or political elites regarding timely response. Under the first group fell enormous 'military burdens' and participation of many members new to politics and the consequent strains on the political system, particularly where such participation has heightened 'ethnic or linguistic differentiation'. Under the second were placed prolonged economic decline; compulsion of political elites 'to be open to new members and to be able to adjust to new circumstances' or the emergence of 'counter elites'; gaps in expectations left by 'social, economic or political reforms', and disintegrative consequences of any failure on the part of a formerly strong or privileged state, group or region', to cope 'psychologically or politically' with 'its loss of dominance' due to changed circumstances.[71] Directing their attention to PSCs, Deutsch et al. found that while both ASCs and PSCs were viable means to integration, PSCs had two advantages. First, they were easier to achieve since only a few of the essential requirements for ASCs suffice for their formation. Second, against numerous examples of failures of ASCs (e.g., the USA in 1861, Norway–Sweden in 1905, Austria–Hungary in 1917, England–Ireland in 1918, Metropolitan France from 1789 to 1871, due to many wars and revolutions), there was only one for PSCs (that of Austria and Prussia in the German Confederation).[72] So Deutsch considered them superior to prematurely conceived political unions.

Critique of Transactionalism

Enriched by contributors such as Bruce Russett, Helen Feldstein, Theodore Caplow and Kurt Finsterbusch and Donald Puchala, the transactionalist approach won wide recognition from American political scientists from the 1950s to 1970s because of its 'scientific' tone, openness to the newest technological breakthroughs in data collection and analysis, the portrayal of integration as a directly observable and measurable quantitative concept and belief that states can learn how to conduct mutual relations between them without surrendering their sovereignty to supranational institutions.[73] But the points of criticism against this approach are many and varied.

First, the choice of the North Atlantic area was questioned because the study mainly considered societies that were pre-industrial or at an early stage of industrial development and consequently of doubtful applicability for fully industrialized societies.

Second, transactions are inadequate indicators of integration because 'the content of messages' in transactions flows not being specified, 'the attention to transactions is far too crude and non-political.' Deutsch tried to silence this criticism by saying that the focus is not on indicators of transactions individually but as parts of an ensemble, highlighting the relationship between all the components, as is done by a doctor using a patient's blood count in making a diagnosis, where the blood count is judged against the patient's past medical diagnoses and present symptoms.[74]

But criticisms against the evidence of increasing transactions may add points, such as (a) 'it does not directly measure the growth of community or sense of mutual obligation, which may lag far behind interactions' and (b) the focus should be on transactions which are more revealing of mutual relevance and incipient cohesion within a given region since, amid cross-pressures, contrary readings or divergences among different components of the ensemble are possible. Some studies emphasize the second point: (a) Russet showed that in Anglo-American relations between 1890 and 1954, amid the decline of the relative intensity of economic transactions between these two countries during the period, a little increase in political and military exchanges of views occurred; (b) Deutsch with Edinger and others linked transactions flows measured by trade, mail and telephone traffic, student exchanges and tourist flows with mass and elite attitudes assessed through interviews, opinion polls and newspaper editorials, to find that European integration had slowed down since the mid-1950s to finally reach a tableland in 1958 and would not pick up in the foreseeable future; (c) later, Cobb and Elder established that although transactions might foster relevance, changes in transactions flows either affects less mutual responsiveness or does that with significant time lags; and (d) Inglehart used a different approach based on study of public opinion in Western Europe to question the stress Deutsch laid on the above types of transactions flows in place of the changes in the attitudes of the relevant groups since in these might lie a threshold of structural integration. So the vital factor was not transactions but rather the attitudes that sustained them. Inglehart's contention was that, by far, the most transformative change came in the relatively steadier and abiding pro-European mindset of the generation that became socialized since 1945, compared with the earlier generations which held nationalistic attitudes. Starting from the premise that the fundamental and abiding political attitudes are formed in adolescence, Inglehart guessed that generational attitude changes would make European integration run full throttle in the 1980s.[75]

There are chinks in these critiques. Inglehart's one is that Deutsch himself had found that younger members of French and German administrative elites were more pro-European than their seniors. But he was not ready to read in it anything more than a reaction against earlier chauvinism, surely not an endorsement of the strengthening of the European community. For others, Deutsch's own empirical research had showed that in the backdrop of decreased flows of trade and mail national societies and economies looked actually less integrated than before, and in the context of Eurosclerosis and the Luxembourg compromise, he adjudged that European integration had reached a halt.[76] Yet he had high hopes for it in the middle term just because of the new generation's attitudes. After 1975, 'a new generation, which was young when integration was first proposed after the Second World War, will come to power in Europe'. If and when they do come to power, they may then take Europe to another substantial step towards integration.[77]

However, a study by Puchala corroborated Inglehart's reasoning that contrary to Deutsch's diagnosis, European integration did not stop or slow down after 1958. Inglehart claimed that since transaction flow indices are available for only a limited range of quantitative data, they would perforce exclude transactions that elude quantification, such as informal political deliberations between and coordination by national governments. Besides, Puchala contended that transactions *reflect* political integration more than *cause* it and are useful for monitoring integration, not for predicting it. Still, Puchala's own findings suggested that since the EEC came into being, convergence in attitudes and a moderate increase in transactions continued, which belied Deutsch's pessimistic diagnosis of a halt in European integration.[78]

The concession that transactions might reflect rather than induce integration points to a deeper epistemological problem of transactionalism, namely 'the failure to specify a theoretical relationship between transaction flow and social assimilation on the one hand and political change on the other'. Sangiovanni judges that the approach cannot show the relationship between social assimilation and political change because 'social assimilation is a psychological variable relating to the attributes of mass publics', while political integration, both as PSC or ASC, is 'a variable relating to the behaviour of political elites'.[79] Hodges says that since 'much of the regional dispute settlement' implies that 'supranational decision-making procedures are a function of high diplomacy, there are formidable problems in devising appropriate indicators'.[80] Another point about transactions is that since the communication pattern established by them is so loosely correlated with the formation of political community, the two phenomena do not rise and fall together and do not necessarily covary.

Intergovernmentalism

Precursor: Hoffmann and His High and Low Politics

Initiated by Stanley Hoffman in the early 1960s, intergovernmentalism is a major theoretical critique of neofunctionalism and a new approach to European regional integration. Hoffman thought that the recent neofunctionalist accent on spillover and allegiance transfer soft-pedalled the crucial importance of states and their interests in the integration process because it missed the distinction between high and low politics,[81] although later Hoffmann clarified that what constitutes 'high' and 'low' politics alters over time.[82] Anyway, Hoffmann told Haas that national governments had more resilience than he thought, setting not only clear limits on the process of spillover but even employing it to their benefit. He judged the post-Second World War devastation and 'political collapse' in Europe, her loss of 'power and wealth', her subjection to what de Gaulle had so infelicitously called the 'two hegemonies' and the national interests and national situations of states as key conditions that motivated the key states to get busy with institutionalized economic cooperation that begot EEC. In no way, it signalled the end of national states as gatekeepers to integration.[83]

Prelude: Domestic Political Approach

Midway between neofunctionalism and intergovernmentalism, a 'domestic political approach' championed by Wallace and Bulmer pointed out the importance of domestic politics and national governments in decisions about partial surrenders of sovereignty. To Wallace, the domestic factors that shaped national differences in the coherence of responses to community matters included varied administrative traditions and national objectives of the member states, such as the centralized administrative systems of Britain and France that had enabled these governments to pursue a 'relatively consistent line in community negotiations' and the internal balance of governments and the constitutional role of their political leaders'. Bulmer faulted existing theories for their overemphasis on the 'upper tier' of the EC policy elite that desensitized them to the domestic sources of national negotiation games. He blamed the myopia of neofunctionalism for overstressing the role of interest groups and political elites in sustaining the momentum of integration and the myopia of intergovernmentalism for recognizing the key role of the national governments but underemphasizing member states' attitudes towards the EC because of taking them as monolithic structures. Bulmer emphasized national polities as the fundamental units in the EC and their different sets of social and economic situations as sources of their national interests and policy contents; warned that European policy was but one aspect of a national system's substantial concerns, and introduced the concept of policy style to explicate the relationship between governments and other domestic political forces vis-à-vis European policy.[84]

Culmination: Andrew Moravcsik—Intergovernmental Institutionalism to Liberal Intergovernmentalism

A full theory of liberal intergovernmentalism (henceforth, LI) had to wait till the arrival of Andrew Moravcsik, addressing 'the most fundamental puzzle for those who seek to understand European integration', namely 'why sovereign governments in Europe have chosen repeatedly to coordinate their core economic policies and surrender sovereign prerogatives within an international institution'[85] in *The Choice for Europe* (*CFE*) and a chain of articles from 1993 to 1997.[86]

In 'Negotiating the Single European Act' (1991), Moravcsik sets out a theory of 'intergovernmental institutionalism', comprising three strands. Intergovernmentalism, the first, shows that interstate bargains between its leading member states have always been the fulcrum of the EC since each government assesses the EC through 'the lens of its own policy preferences'. 'Lowest-common-denominator bargaining', the second, signifies that in the absence of a European hegemon powerful enough to provide 'universal incentives or threats to promote regime formation', the bargains made in the EC 'reflect the relative power position of the member states', which entice small states with 'side payments' but allow larger ones to veto all 'fundamental changes in the scope or rules of the core element of the EC'. Protection of sovereignty, the third, implies that policymakers 'safeguard their countries against the future erosion of their sovereignty' by imposing the condition of 'unanimous consent of regime members to sovereignty-related reforms'. By Moravcsik's own admission, intergovernmental institutionalism endorses Keohane's 'modified structural realist' explanation of 'regime formation and maintenance', in which states are the major actors in the international system; interstate bargains 'reflect national interests and relative power', and international regimes structure 'interstate politics by providing a common framework that reduces the uncertainty and transaction costs interstate interactions'.[87]

In 'Preferences and Power in the European Community: A Liberal Intergovernmentalist Approach' (1993), Moravcsik moved over to offer a theory of LI, coupled with a straightforward theory of national preference formation around a liberal conceptualization of domestic politics and a systemic level exposition of interstate bargaining. To do it, he first summarized the self-criticisms of neofunctionalism, which are as follows:

1. Theories of European integration 'should be supplemented, perhaps supplanted, by a general theory of national policy responses to international interdependence'.
2. Explanations of integration 'require stronger underlying theories of variation in substantive, as well as institutional, outcomes' that would not overlook 'distributional conflicts in the EC over issues such as the level of external tariffs, agricultural prices and regulatory harmonization, which require attention to the substantive measures of policy coordination'. A broader definition of European integration should ideally consider 'four dimensions of policy coordination: (a) the geographical scope of the regime; (b) the range of issues in which policies are coordinated; (c) the institutions of joint decision-making, implementation and enforcement, and (d) the direction and magnitude of substantive domestic policy adjustment'. Overstressing formal transfers of authority to the EC has often shifted attention from a failure to manage a real transfer of sovereignty.
3. Univariate or unicausal theories cannot capture the dynamics of EC policy-making. 'More than one theory is required'.

But in place of retrieving neofunctionalism by tinkering with these self-criticisms, Moravcsik opted for constructing a new theory because they 'point towards a conception of the EC more closely in line with contemporary theories of IPE'. These theories suggest that the EC is best viewed as 'an international regime for policy coordination, the substantive and institutional development of which may be explained through the sequential analysis of national preference formation and intergovernmental strategic interaction'. If the stress on the 'three essential elements—the assumption of rational state behaviour, a liberal theory of national preference formation and an intergovernmentalist analysis of interstate negotiation'—leaves one wondering that as not much seems different from structural realism, one may remember that, here, unlike neorealists, Moravcsik does not treat the state as 'billiard balls' or 'black boxes' 'with fixed preferences for wealth, security or power'. In its place, 'governments are assumed to act purposively in the international arena but on the basis of goals that are defined domestically'.[88]

Brushing aside criticisms that Moravcsik's exposition of the process of domestic definition of foreign policy goals is much less refined than Hoffmann's,[89] I would show the length he has taken gone to delineate the process in 'Taking Preferences Seriously' (1997) through differentiation of three major versions of liberal theory, each springing from a distinctive causal logic of 'social preferences and state behaviour'. The first, 'ideational liberalism', emphasizes the impact on 'state behaviour of conflict and compatibility among collective social values or identities concerning the scope and nature of public goods provision'. The second, 'commercial liberalism', foregrounds 'the impact on state behaviour of gains and losses to individuals and groups in society from transnational economic interchange'. The third, 'republican liberalism', underscores the impact on state behaviour of varying forms of domestic representation and the resulting incentives for social groups to engage in rent seeking'. The 'fundamental premise' of the liberal theory of IR—'that the relationship between states and the surrounding domestic and transnational society in which they are embedded critically shapes state behaviour by influencing the social purposes underlying state preference'—follows from its three core assumptions. First, the 'primacy of social actors', comprising 'individuals and private groups, who are on the average rational and risk-averse and who organize exchange and collective action to promote differentiated interests under constraints imposed by material scarcity, conflicting values and variations in societal influence'. Second, 'representation and state preferences', which posits that 'States (or other political institutions) represent some subset of domestic society, on the basis of whose interests state officials define state preferences and act purposively in world politics'. Third, and finally, 'interdependence and the international system', signifying that the 'configuration of interdependent state preferences determines state behaviour'.[90]

In Moravcsik's model of rational state behaviour, the 'foreign policy goals of national governments are viewed as varying in response to shifting pressure from domestic social groups, whose preferences are aggregated through political institutions'. This 'domestically constrained preferences' model suggests that international conflict and co-operation can be viewed analogically as what Robert Putnam called 'two-level games' of demand and supply function for interactional co-operation, in Moravcsik's words a 'two-stage process of constrained social choice', where, first, a 'domestic preference formation process identifies the potential benefits of policy coordination perceived by national governments (demand), while a process of interstate strategic interaction defines the possible political responses of the EC political system to pressures from those governments (supply)'.[91]

This expanded liberal framework was applied by Moravcsik in *CFE* to five key moments in the construction of the EU: (a) the negotiation of the Treaty of Rome (1955–1958), (b) the consolidation of the common market and the common agricultural policy (1958–1969), (c) monetary cooperation and the founding of the European Monetary System (1959–1963), (d) the negotiation of the Single European Act (SEA, 1984–1988) and (e) the negotiation of the Treaty of EU or the Maastricht Treaty.[92] To explain these five episodes of success, he first started with his 'tripartite rationalist formula', which suggests that in their collective decisions each of thc concerned national governments, 'the first formulates national preferences, then engages in interstate bargaining and finally decides whether to delegate or pool sovereignty'. Within each stage, he tested the applicability of more specific propositions about the sway of economic incentives emanating from increasing trade and capital flows, 'relative bargaining power' stemming from 'asymmetrical policy interdependence' and the requirement of 'credible commitments against defection from particular agreements'. Since in all the five case studies this theoretical formula and rejoinder were borne out, Moravcsik relegated all the most widely mentioned alternative explanations—'geopolitical threats, European federalist ideas, technocratic imperatives to delegate and intervention by supranational political entrepreneurs'—to secondary importance.[93]

Among these episodes, Moravcsik picked out German, French and British preferences relating to the most significant policy involvement in each of the agreements to get a tally of 15 positions. He found that:

- In regard to national preferences, in seven of these positions, there was no 'hard evidence' indicating that geopolitical ideas or interests were used as more than *post-factum* overt justifications for national positions. In the other eight cases (including Germany and France in the Treaty of Rome and the 1960s, France during discussions of the SEA and all three countries in the Maastricht negotiations), geopolitical ideology was seen to have figured in 'a secondary or parallel role'. In not more than four of these instances—Germany in the Treaty of Rome and the 1960s, France and Germany in the Maastricht negotiations—geopolitical considerations significantly changed final choices in economic matters. Just in two or three of these (Germany in the Treaty of Rome, the 1960s and probably in the Maastricht negotiations), there is solid evidence for geopolitical motivations significantly affecting national stances. So in 12–13 of the 15 key episodes politico-economic calculations appeared adequate explanations of national motivations, and 'in all 15, the predominant influence on national preferences was economic interest'.[94]
- As for interstate bargaining, concerned member governments or private individuals rather than supranational officials initiated and mediated major EC negotiations, and wherever mediators were enlisted, 'they tended to be third governments, as in the case of the Maastricht'. Unsurprisingly, 'with a few minor exceptions, supranational actors generally failed to influence the distribution of gains'. Besides, distributional outcomes always 'mirrored the bargaining power of governments'. Further, governments 'also employed explicit threats of exit and exclusion, which altered the negotiated outcomes to the extent those threats were credible and costly'. So for Moravcsik, generally speaking, 'intergovernmental barging theory is clearly confirmed. Supranational entrepreneurs have only a rare and secondary impact on the efficiency of negotiations'.[95]
- In the sphere of institutional delegation, '*deliberate triumphs* of European integration, not its unintended side effects appear to have increased support for further integration'. Moravcsik found the historical record to reveal that 'the consequences of major decisions were, in fact, foreseen and desired by national governments to a much greater extent than most analysts have been aware'. Scrutiny of major bargains also demonstrated that 'the construction of an international regime in which legislation was voted over the opposition of minorities, and rules are enforced against the obstruction of the recalcitrant—in short, the transfer of sovereignty and autonomy to supranational institutions was not an unintended consequence of major EC decisions; it was *their primary purpose*.[96]

Critique of Intergovernmentalism

Predictably, a clear, unaccommodative and intransigent framework, like LI, drew some flak. First, LI did not supposedly fit the facts 'in an era of multiple international actors and complex interdependence between the states' and the lack of fit owed to Moravcsik's extreme selectiveness about empirical references demonstrating the applicability of his framework. Since he concentrated overly on 'historic decisions' and insufficiently on 'more commonplace and routine decisions', it inevitably introduced distortions in analysis. 'Historic decisions' are not only essentially atypical but 'being channelled via the European Council' they 'necessarily emphasize the role of national governments'.[97] One inevitable vice of selectivity about empirical referents was tautological corroboration of hypotheses. Scharpf viciously asked,

> Since only intergovernmental decisions are being considered, why shouldn't the preferences of national governments have shaped the outcomes? Since all case studies have issues of economic integration as their focus, why shouldn't economic concerns have shaped the negotiating positions of governments? And since only decisions requiring unanimous agreements are being analysed, why shouldn't the outcomes be affected by the relative bargaining power of the governments involved?[98]

On the same lines, Wincott says that after this type of selective attention, it hardly surprises one to see Moravcsik viewing the EC as 'primarily motivated by aggregation and conciliation of interests'. The implication is that had Moravcsik focused on quotidian decisions of much smaller dimensions inside the EU and not on formal and end-point decisions, the picture would have been different, as supranational actors might then have been seen to be exerting more influence and national preferences less clearly articulated and fiercely defended.[99]

Second, critics contend that LI has constricted the conception of the state, and that is not just because it pays less attention to 'the black box of the state and more especially to disaggregating different parts of the government'. While viewing socio-economic interests as the primary determinant of domestic politics, LI ignores other factors that may impact preference formation, like domestic political or economic structures.

Third, an oft-repeated criticism of LI is that it severely downgrades the influence exercised by supranational players such as the Commission and the European Court of Justice and transnational actors such as European firms and interest groups. Nugent cites several scholars who refer to many cases where supranational bodies endeavouring to increase their autonomy and influence found substantial success, problematizing Moravcsik's depiction of the role of the Commission as a mere facilitator of momentous decisions taken by the national governments. A host of empirical studies have shown the Commission exercising an 'independent and influential decision-making role' whether as 'an *animateur*, policy entrepreneur or a motor force'.[100]

Apart from these lacunae are others pointed out by all the three branches of institutionalism—historical, rational choice and sociological. In *CFE*, Moravcsik sought to refute the position of historical institutionalism (termed as historical institutionalism theory by him), which claimed that institutions shape a nation's response to new challenges and opportunities as an approach to integration. But sociological institutionalism, a branch of generic institutionalism, raised a few pertinent points. It is that apart from EU-level actors participating in different ways in the treaty reform process, 'the role of EU institutions (such as the Commission and the European Parliament) and transnational actors (such as the European Party federations, private lobby groups, citizen action groups, transnational labour–employer alliances) should not be assumed away'. By not considering them, LI 'tends to exclude what are potentially important aspects of the subject'. Besides, in any study of structures that shape integration, Moravcsik can be ignored since 'the very ontology of treaty reform as conceived of by liberal intergovernmentalism is actional.' They concede Moravcsik's claim in 'Why the European Union Strengthens the State' that European integration does really create opportunities for national executives by ushering in 'an extraordinary centralization of domestic power' in their hands.[101] But this leeway does not apply for 'factors such as public opinion on deeply engrained policy issues that cannot easily be circumvented by governments forming their negotiating positions for intergovernmental conferences.[102]

CONCLUSION: GLIMPSE OF NEW SYNTHESES

This chapter has already described and evaluated four traditional approaches to regional integration (federalism, functionalism, neofunctionalism and transactionalism) and intergovernmentalism, which started as critique and became a fifth substantive approach itself. Since each of the individual approaches has many shortcomings, there has been a recent trend towards synthesis. We would just mention a few here. Arguing that 'intergovernmentalism hardly displaces neofunctionalism but rather relies on a causal argument developed by the neofunctionalists', Stone Sweet and Sandholtz propose a theory of European integration, 'focusing on the process through which supranational governance—the competence of the EC to make binding rules in any given policy sector—has been constructed'.[103] Hooghe and Marks offered a post-functionalist research programme that sought to interpret new developments in the politics of the EU through appropriate middle-range theories 'by using the building blocks of the multi-level governance approach to European integration' to arrive at the finding that the EU is 'part of a system of multi-level governance which is driven by identity politics as well as by functional and distributional pressures'.[104] Further, Bickerton, Hodson and Puetter clarify that although, as intergovernmentalists, they accept national governments as key players, their new synthesis does not belittle the role of supranational institutions, only 'seeks to recast it in a new mould'. Aware of the instability of existing institutional arrangements', it warns that 'the existing institutional framework may fall victim to the self-destructive tendencies which it undoubtedly contains'. Finally, it is willing to open the black box of the state in order to grasp the logic of support or opposition of national governments to European integration.[105]

Another bold synthesis seeks to reconcile the legacy of rational choice institutionalists who were, particularly in their 'initial applications', deeply critical of both neofunctionalism for its inattention to 'microfoundations' and Moravcsik's 'minimalist accounts of EU institutions'. Pollack finds this possible because although LI was 'widely considered as a rival to rational choice institutionalism', it, 'in fact, shares most of its basic assumptions, including the notion that states aggregate interests and act rationally to advance their preferences at the EU level, and member governments rationally select institutions that are designed to maximize their utility'. On the other hand, Moravcsik has amply clarified, at least in *CFE*, that his cynicism about supranational influence is confined to its facile 'claims about informal agenda setting or entrepreneurship in unanimous treaty amending decisions' and does not extend to 'the day-to-day policymaking within the treaties that is the bread and butter of rational choice intuitionalists'. So LI, rational choice institutionalism and 'even Grieco's purportedly neorealist voice opportunities' are made all part of an emerging rationalist research programme.[106] Pollack sees that 'the meta-theoretical gulf separating rationalists and constructivists appears to have narrowed considerably, and EU scholars have arguably led the way in confronting and possibly reconciling the two theoretical approaches'. New scholars are putting forward 'a framework for promoting the integration of—or at least a fruitful dialogue between—rationalist and constructivist approaches'. But compared to the 1970s, 'the 1990s and early 2000s have witnessed a partial retreat from grand theorizing about the integration process in favour of a series of mid-range theories addressing a variety of topics, including inter alia the workings of the EU's legislative, executive and judicial processes, the prospects of socialization or deliberation in EU institutions, the effects of European integration on national institutions and policies and a wide range of other questions'.[107] The times of competing theories are over.

REVIEW QUESTIONS

1. After mentioning the three principal historical sources of the federalist ideas in Europe, comment on its rise and fall as an approach to regional integration in Europe.
2. Give a critical estimate of the federalist approach to regional integration in Europe.
3. Comment on the strengths and weaknesses of the functionalist logic of European integration.
4. Bring out the central tenets and analytical attributes of the neofunctionalist theory of regional integration. What are its main problems?
5. Why is Deutsch's transactionalism built around an IRA index and the concept of PSCs and ASCs important as an approach to regional integration in Europe? What are its main weaknesses?
6. Show how Moravcsik's intergovernmentalist critique of neofunctionalism itself became a substantive approach to regional integration in Europe.
7. Show how Moravcsik's intergovernmentalism has done the full journey from intergovernmental institutionalism to liberal intergovernmentalism in the context of regional integration in Europe.
8. Attempt a sketch of the main individual approaches to regional integration in Europe, their central propositions and their replacement by new syntheses.

NOTES AND REFERENCES

1. See notes 13 and 14 of 'Chapter 1'.
2. Charles Pentland, *International Theory and European Integration* (London: Faber and Faber Limited, 1973), 13–14; Michael Hodges, 'Integration Theory,' in *Approaches and Theory*, ed. Trevor Taylor (London: Longman, 1978), 237.
3. Hodges, 'Integration,' 237; Pentland, *European Integration*, 18–19.
4. For the definitions, see Ernst B. Haas, *The Uniting of Europe: Political, Social and Economic Forces, 1950–1957* (Notre Dame, IN: University of Notre Dame Press, 1958), 16.
5. Leon Lindberg, *The Political Dynamics of European Economic Integration* (Stanford, CA: Stanford University Press, 1963), 6.
6. Karl W. Deutsch, *Analysis of International Relations* (Hoboken, NJ: Prentice Hall, 1988), 212, 271; Karl W. Deutsch, *Political Community and the North Atlantic Area: International Organization in the Light of Historical Experience* (Princeton, NJ: Princeton University Press, 1957/1968), 5.
7. Robert O. Keohane, *After Hegemony: Cooperation and Discord in the World Political Economy* (Princeton, NJ: Princeton University Press, 1984), 53–54.
8. Pentland lists them as (a) the pluralist approach, (b) functionalism, (c) neofunctionalism and (d) federalist theory; Hodges as (a) federalism, (b) functionalism, (c) neofunctionalism and (d) transactionalism, and Lieber as (a) federalism, (b) functionalism, neofunctionalism subsumed within it and (c) communications theory (synonymous with Pentland's Pluralist Approach and Hodges's transactionalism). Pentland, *European Integration*, 29–186; Hodges, 'Integration Theory,' 239–247; Lieber, *Theory* and World Politics, 38–59.
9. Pentland, *European Integration*, 147–148, 158–160.
10. See Daniel J. Elazar, 'From Biblical Covenant to Modern Federalism: The Federal Theology Bridge,' in *The Covenant Connection: From Federal Theology to Modern Federalism*, eds. Daniel Judah Elazar and John Kincaid (Lanham, MD: Lexington Books, 2000), 1–13.
11. Thomas O. Hueglin, *Early Modern Concepts for a Late Modern World: Althusius on Community and Federalism* (Waterloo: Wilfrid Laurier University Press, 1999), 2–3, 85–168.
12. Lukas K. Sosoe, 'Leibnitz and European Cosmopolitanism,' in *Join or Die—Philosophical Foundations of Federalism*, eds. Dietmar Heidemann and Katja Stoppenbrink (Berlin: De Gruyter, 2016), 54–59.
13. Pentland, *European Integration*, 155–174.
14. David Mutimer, 'Theories of Political Integration,' in *European Integration: Theories and Approaches*, eds. Hans J. Michelmann and Panayotis Soldatos (Lanham, MD: University Press of America, 1991), 15–16; Sabine Saurugger, *Theoretical Approaches to European Integration* (Basingstoke: Palgrave Macmillan, 2014), 4–25.
15. Pentland, *European Integration*, 148–149.
16. Saurugger, *Theoretical Approaches*, 25–33.
17. Sergio Ortino, Mitja Zagar, and Vojtech Mastny, 'Introduction'; Peter H. Russell, 'The Future of Europe in an Era of Globalization,' and Sergio Ortino, 'Functional Federalism between Geopolitics and Geoeconomics' in *The Changing Faces of Federalism: Institutional Reconfiguration of Europe from East to West*, eds. Sergio Ortino, Mitja Zagar, and Vojtech Mastny (Manchester, NY: Manchester University Press, 2005), 274–298, especially 1–2, 4, 284, 290.
18. Saurugger, *Theoretical Approaches*, 17; Joseph Frankel, *Contemporary Theory of International Relations and the Behaviour of States* (Oxford: Oxford University Press, 1973), 50–51; David Mitrany, *A Working Peace System* (Chicago, IL: Quadrangle Books, 1966), 82.

19. James A. Caporaso and John T. S. Keeler, 'The European Union and Regional Integration Theory,' in *Building a European Polity?* eds. Carolyn Rhodes and Sonia Mazey (Boulder, CO: Rienner, 1995), 30–32.
20. Mitrany, *A Working Peace System*, 83.
21. Frankel, *Contemporary Theory*, 50–51.
22. Mitrany, *A Working Peace System*, 72–73.
23. James Patrick Sewell, 'Functionalism,' in *Routledge Encyclopaedia of International Political Economy*, ed. R. J. Barry Jones (Volume 1, Entries A–F, London: Routledge, 2001), 580.
24. Caporaso and Keeler, 'European Union,' 31–32. Also see, Pentland, *European Integration*, 64–99.
25. Caporaso and Keeler, 'European Union,' 32.
26. Saurugger, *Theoretical Approaches*, 19–20.
27. For citations on these points, see Hodges, 'Integration Theory,' 240.
28. Alvin Ward Gouldner, 'Organizational Analysis,' in *Sociology Today: Problems and Prospects*, eds. Robert K. Merton, Leonard Broom, and Leonard S. Cottrell, Jr. (New York, NY: Harper and Row, 1965), 400–427; Alvin Wald Gouldner, 'Cosmopolitans and Locals: Toward an Analysis of Latent Social Roles I,' *Administrative Science Quarterly* 2, no. 4 (1957): 281–306.
29. Frankel, *Contemporary Theory*, 51; Saurugger, *Theoretical Approaches*, 20.
30. Inis L. Claude, Jr., *Swords into Ploughshares: The Problems and Progress of International Organization* (4th ed., New York, NY: Random House, 1971), 387–390, cited in Nejat Dogan, *Pragmatic Liberal Approach to World Order: The Scholarship of Inis L. Claude, Jr.* (Lanham, MD: University Press of America, 2012), 70–71.
31. Joseph Nye, *Peace in Parts: Integration and Conflict in Regional Organization* (Boston: Little, Brown & Co., 1971).
32. Haas, *The Uniting of Europe*, 12.
33. Caporaso and Keeler, 'European Union,' 32–33.
34. A. J. R. Groom, 'Neofunctionalism: A Case of Mistaken Identity,' *Political Science* 30, no. 1 (1978): 15–28.
35. Dimitris N. Chryssochoou, *Theorizing European Integration* (New Delhi: SAGE Publications, 2001), 54.
36. Haas, *The Uniting of Europe*, 4.
37. Ernst B. Haas, *Beyond the Nation State: Functionalism and International Organizations* (Stanford, CA: Stanford University Press, 1964); Lindberg, *Political Dynamics*; Stuart A. Scheingold, *The Rule of Law in European Integration: The Path of the Schuman Plan* (New Haven, CT: Yale University Press, 1965); Leon N. Lindberg and Stuart A. Scheingold, eds., *Regional Integration: Theory and Research* (Cambridge, MA: Harvard University Press, 1971).
38. Haas, *The Uniting of Europe*, 13–14; E. B. Haas, 'The Study of Regional Integration: Reflections on the Joy and Anguish of Pretheorizing,' in *Regional Integration*, eds. Leon N. Lindberg and Stuart A. Scheingold (Cambridge, MA: Harvard University Press, 1971), 6; Saurugger, *Theoretical Approaches*, 34–36.
39. Haas, 'Study of Regional Integration,' 627.
40. Ibid.
41. Haas, *Beyond the Nation State*, cited in Hodges, 'Integration Theory,' 245–246.
42. Caporaso and Keeler, 'European Union,' 32–33.
43. Haas, *The Uniting of Europe*, xxxiv.
44. Lindberg, *Political Dynamics*, 10.
45. Haas, *The Uniting of Europe*, 297.
46. Sewell, 'Functionalism,' 580–581; John McCormick, *European Union Politics* (New York, NY: Palgrave, 2011/2015), 302.

47. Walter Mattli, *The Logic of Regional Integration: Europe and Beyond* (Cambridge: Cambridge University Press, 1999), 26.
48. E. B. Haas, 'Technocracy, Pluralism and the New Europe (1964),' in *International Regionalism*, ed. J. S. Nye (Boston, MA: Little Brown, 1968), 159.
49. E. B. Haas, 'International Integration: The European and the Universal Process,' *International Organization* 15, no. 3 (1961): 366–392, here 372–373.
50. Saurugger, *Theoretical Approaches*, 39–42; Mattli, *Logic*, 27–28; Laura Cram, *Policy-making in the European Union: Conceptual Lenses and the Integration Process* (London: Routledge, 1997), 20–22.
51. Caporaso and Keeler, 'European Union,' 36.
52. Mattli, *Logic*, 28.
53. Lindberg, *Political Dynamics*, 287; relevant citations in Hodges, 'Integration Theory,' 250–252.
54. Haas, 'International Integration: The European,' 366–367.
55. E. B. Haas and P. C. Schmitter, 'Economics and Differential Patterns of Political Integration: Projections about Unity in Latin America,' *International Organization* 18, no. 4 (1964): 705–737, here, 709–710.
56. Haas, 'Technocracy, Pluralism,' 151, 159.
57. Lindberg, *Political Dynamics*; cited in Pentland, *European Integration*, 103–104.
58. Mette Sangiovanni, ed., 'Introduction,' in *Debates on European Integration: A Reader* (Basingstoke: Palgrave Macmillan, 2006), 29.
59. Deutsch, *Political Community and the North Atlantic Area*, 6.
60. Deutsch shows that England and Wales 'are integrated not only politically by means of all the many policies of a welfare state, but they were integrated until the early twentieth century also in regard to religion through the Church of England.' Deutsch, *Analysis*, 213.
61. Ibid., 213–214.
62. Karl W. Deutsch, *The Nerves of Government: Models of Political Communication and Control* (New York, NY: Free Press of Glencoe, 1963), xxvii.
63. Karl W. Deutsch, *Nationalism and Social Communication: An Inquiry into the Foundations of Nationality* (New York, NY: John Wiley and Sons, 1953), 70; cited in and commented on Theresa Kuhn, *Experiencing European Integration: Transnational Lives and European Identity* (Oxford: Oxford University Press, 2015), 43.
64. See Karl W. Deutsch, 'Transaction Flows as Indicators of Political Cohesion,' in *The Integration of Political Communities*, eds. Philip E. Jacob, James V. Toscano, Karl W. Deutsch, Henry Teune, and William L. C. Wheaton (New York, NY: Lippincott, 1964), cited in Lieber, *Theory* and World Politics, 51–52, and W. J. Feld, 'Sociological Theories of European Integration,' in *European Integration*, ed. H. J. Michelmann and P. Soldatos (Lanham, MD: University Press of America, 1994), 467.
65. Lieber, *Theory and World Politics*, 53–54; Hodges, 'Integration Theory,' 243–245.
66. Deutsch, *Political Community and the North Atlantic Area*, 33.
67. Ibid., 36.
68. Ibid., 38.
69. Ibid., 42.
70. Ibid., 58.
71. Ibid., 64.
72. Ibid., 66–67.
73. Sangiovanni, 'Introduction,' 31–32.
74. Lieber, *Theory and World Politics*, 57–58.
75. Bruce M. Russet, *Community and Contention: Britain and America in the Twentieth Century* (Cambridge, MA: MIT Press, 1963); K. W. Deutsch and I. Edinger, R. C. Macridis, and R. L. Meritt, *France, Germany and the Western Alliance* (New York, NY: Scribner,

1967); R. W. Cobb and C. Elder, *International Community: A Regional and Global Study* (New York, NY: Holt McDougal, 1970); R. Inglehart, 'An End to European Integration?' *The American Political Science Review* 61, no. 1 (1967): 91–105; R. Inglehart, 'Public Opinion and Regional Integration' International Organization 24, no. 4 (1970): 764–795; D. J. Puchala, 'International Transactions and Regional Integration,' *International Organization* 24, no. 4 (1970): 732–762; all cited in Hodges, 'Integration Theory,' 247–249.

76. Deutsch, *Political Community and the North Atlantic Area*, 120, 206; Karl W. Deutsch, *Nationalism and its Alternatives* (New York, NY: Alfred Knopf, 1969), 34, cited in Kuhn, *Experiencing European*, 44.
77. Deutsch, *Nationalism Alternatives*, 35, 45.
78. Puchala, 'International Transactions and Regional Integration,' cited in Sangiovanni, *Debates*, 32.
79. Ibid.
80. Hodges, 'Integration Theory,' 249.
81. Stanley Hoffmann, 'Obstinate or Obsolete? The Fate of the Nation State and the Future or Western Europe,' *Daedalus* 95, no. 4 (1966): 861–898.
82. Stanley Hoffmann, *The European Sisyphus: Essays on Europe, 1964–1994* (Boulder, CO: Westview, 1995), 218.
83. Hoffmann, 'Obstinate?' 869, 872, 901.
84. Helen Wallace, 'National Bulls in the Community China Shop: The Role of National Governments in Community Policy-Making,' in *Policy Making in the European Community*, eds. Helen Wallace, William Wallace, and Carol Webb (New York, NY: Wiley, 1977), 33–68; Simon Bulmer, 'Domestic Politics and European Policy Making,' *Journal of Common Market Studies* 21, no. 4 (1983): 349–363, cited in Ian Bache, *Politics of European Union Regional Policy: Multi-Level Governance or Flexible Gate-Keeping* (Sheffield: Sheffield Academic Press, 1998), 20–21.
85. Andrew Moravcsik, *The Choice for Europe: Social Purpose and State Power from Messina to Maastricht* (Ithaca, NY: Cornel University Press, 1998), 1.
86. Andrew Moravcsik, 'Negotiating the Single European Act: National Interests and Conventional Statecraft in the European Community,' *International Organization* 45, no. 1 (1991): 19–56; Andrew Moravcsik, 'Preferences and Power in the European Community: A Liberal Intergovernmentalist Approach,' *Journal of Common Market Studies* 31, no. 4 (1993): 473–524; Andrew Moravcsik, 'Why the European Union Strengthens the State: Domestic Politics and International Cooperation,' Centre for European Studies CES Working Paper Series 52, presented at Annual Meeting of APSA, 1994; Andrew Moravcsik, 'Taking Preferences Seriously: A Liberal Theory of International Politics,' *International Organization* 51, no. 4 (1997): 513–553.
87. Moravcsik, 'Negotiating the Single European Act,' 25–27.
88. Moravcsik, 'Preferences and Power in the European Community,' 474, 478–481.
89. Rhodes and Mazey, *Building a European Polity?* 180.
90. Moravcsik, 'Taking Preferences Seriously,' 515–533, passim.
91. Ibid., 544; Moravcsik, 'Preferences and Power in the European Community,' 481.
92. Moravcsik, *The Choice for Europe*, Chapters 2–6.
93. Ibid., 473.
94. Ibid., 474.
95. Ibid., 480, 482, 485.
96. Ibid., 491, 492.
97. Neill Nugent, *The Government and Politics of the European Union* (6th ed., Durham: Duke University Press, 2006), 566.
98. F. Scharpf, 'Selecting Cases and Testing Hypotheses,' in Helen Wallace, James A. Caporaso, Fritz W. Scharpf, Andrew Moravcsik, 'Review Section Symposium: The Choice

for Europe: Social Purpose and State Power from Messina to Maastricht, *Journal of European Public Policy* 6:1 (March 1999): 155–179, especially 165, Abstract.

99. D. Wincott, 'Institutional Interaction and European Integration: Towards an Everyday Critique of Liberal Intergovernmentalism,' *Journal of Common Market Studies* 33, no. 4 (1995): 597–609.
100. For these criticisms, relevant citations and comments, see Nugent, *The Government and Politics*, 566–567.
101. Moravcsik, 'Why the European Union Strengthens the State,' 3.
102. Thomas Christiansen, Gerda Falkner, and Knud Erik Jørgensen, 'Theorizing EU Treaty Reform: Beyond Diplomacy and Bargaining,' *Journal of European Public Policy* 9, no. 1 (2002): 12–32, here 12–14, doi: https://doi.org/10.1080/13501760110104154 (accessed on 5 April 2021).
103. A. Stone Sweet and W. Sandholtz, 'European Integration and Supranational Governance,' *Journal of European Public Policy* 4, no. 3 (1997): 297–317.
104. L. Hooghe and G. Marks, 'A Postfunctionalist Theory of European Integration: From Permissive Consensus to Constraining Dissensus,' *British Journal of Political Science* 39 (2009): 1–23, doi: https://doi.org/10.1017/S0007123408000409 (accessed on 5 April 2021).
105. Christopher J. Bickerton, Dermot Hodson, and Uwe Puetter, eds., 'The New Intergovernmentalism and the Study of European Integration,' in *The New Intergovernmentalism: States and Supranational Actors in the Post-Maastricht Era* (Oxford: Oxford University Press, 2015), 39–41.
106. M. A. Pollack, 'International Relations Theory and European Integration,' Robert Schuman Centre for Advanced Studies, EUI Working Papers RSC No. 2000/55, 2000, 7 and 13–14.
107. M. A. Pollack, 'Theorizing the European Union: International Organization, Domestic Polity, or Experiment in New Governance?' *Annual Review of Political Science* 8 (2005): 357–398, here, 367, 391, doi: https://doi.org/10.1146/annurev.polisci.8.082103.104858 (accessed on 5 April 2021).

CHAPTER

13B

Theories of Regionalism: Early, Old and New*

CHAPTER OUTLINE

*This chapter is available on the companion website.

CHAPTER

14

Theories of Interdependence

CHAPTER OUTLINE

INTRODUCTION

This chapter and the next, which will broach theories of interdependence and regime formation, share three common features: (a) both are expressions of liberalism/pluralism in IR; (b) Robert Keohane figures prominently in both and (c) both are linked with the falling fortunes of integration theory, treated in **Chapter 13A**. At a time when neofunctionalism was losing its charm and appeal, and Haas was frantically revising his earlier pronouncements on the inexorability of the spillover process, a new theoretical flurry was set in motion, driving attention away from regional integration as such to the more general phenomenon of international cooperation, analysed by confederalism, regime theory, interdependence theory and the concordance systems approach. Among them, regime theory brought into focus 'the question of whether institutions matter in processes of internationalized governance', as exemplified by the 'proliferation of extra-treaty arrangements since the early 1970s, alongside the preferred pattern of policy interaction for greater coordination but not harmonization'. The interdependence school depicted the phenomenon and possibility of 'a more dynamic system of increased connectedness, which sets the pace and limits of integration'.[1]

DEFINITIONS OF INTERDEPENDENCE AND ITS RESULTANT TYPES

Even after all scholarly attention to it, interdependence still remains an imprecise though potent analytical concept. Treating it as synonymous with interconnectedness among people, diagnosable 'simply in the patterns of association and interaction among actors of various kinds' and measurable in terms of 'numbers of telephone calls, flow of goods and services, and correlations among such indicators as the rates of interest paid within separate national economies' creates two problems: (a) it runs athwart common usages and understandings of these terms; (b) such patterns, even when intense, are not automatically of great significance. An alternative, if conventional, approach defines interdependence as 'the existence of significant dependencies between or among those who experience the phenomenon'. Here dependence characterizes an actor's situation 'when a satisfactory outcome on any matter of significance for that actor requires an appropriate situation or development elsewhere', whereas interdependence characterizes 'a grouping of two or more actors when each is dependent on at least one member of that group for satisfactory outcomes on any issue(s) of concern'. In the sense of the above definition, diverse patterns of dependence and 'imbalanced levels of interdependence', stemming from uneven distribution of power and influence, advantage and disadvantage are common characteristics of the present international system, and many if not most of the present international discords owe to them.[2]

Different forms of international interdependence have gained salience at different times. In the 1970s, the focus was more on economic interdependence, although whether it will be an instrument for peace or conflict was a contentious issue in IR. Liberals thought yes, since interdependence convinces states that trading is a superior alternative to aggression. Realists' counterargument was that high interdependence heightens the probability of war, since dependent states compete for 'continued access to vital goods'. These contrary perceptions emanate from liberals' and realists' emphasis on different elements of interdependence. Liberals laid stress on sensitivity and vulnerability as its criteria. Sensitivity interdependence signifies 'mutual effects' or costs for the state resulting from ongoing trading and commercial activities, such as decrease in state autonomy and repercussions of price changes in one country or the other. Vulnerability interdependence on the other hand implies not only the costs a nation has to bear even after policy adjustments to cope with external shocks but also opportunity costs of a complete cessation of trade and commerce. Realists too emphasize the vulnerability element in interdependence, but in a different way. Liberals keep in mind only the 'loss of the original benefits or "gains from the trade"' coming from shift to autarky. For realists, however, the resolve to trade is essentially a choice for specializing in certain goods to the exclusion of others, because of the fear of the huge 'costs of adjustment' for the restructured economy in the event of severance of trade in a situation of the state's dependence on others for vital goods such as oil and raw materials. So realists would not be attracted by the liberal argument, best stated by Richard Rosecrance that in highly interdependent systems incentives to war are wanting, because trading states come to realize that they can achieve more by trade 'than by trying to conquer and assimilate large tracts of land'. They would rather consider the shattering effects of possible cut-offs in imported goods in an anarchic system lacking any central authority that could guarantee long-term trade and would repeat the traditional mercantilist argument that states requiring supplies and markets will seek to reduce their dependence drastically through colonial imperialism.[3]

In political science, interdependence refers to 'independent social actors who wish to preserve their identity, but who are structurally affected by one another's behaviour' regardless of their wishes. The actors may either be involved in each other's affairs, leading to 'functional or integrative interdependence', or in interdependence emanating from their membership in the same system, generating 'systemic interdependence'. These are not mutually exclusive, since actors who are part of the same system are indirectly involved in each other's affairs. Contrariwise, social systems presuppose involvement of actors with one another. However, from the perspective of the structure–agency debate, distinction between systemic, functional and integrative interdependence is still meaningful. The structural effect can be studied by breaking them into three qualitative depictions of how given actors may be 'mutually affected by one another's behaviour'. The first depiction relates to the degree of mutual involvement, including both the quantitative aspect of the 'intertwinement' and the 'existential value of the relationship for the actors'. The second depiction, dealing with the character of the mutual involvement, gives us two types of interdependence: 'constructional' and 'confrontational', their difference stemming from two connotations of the term dependence, 'subordination, and need or want'. The second connotation is captured by idealist visions of interdependence, based on either a mutually perceived necessity or benefits of symbiosis. Also termed as 'positive interdependence', constructional interdependence is also seen in vistas of economic interdependence. Confrontational interdependence is present when it is the result of a 'mutually perceived necessity of obstruction or competition', as exemplified in BOP or in the Cold War deterrence situation of mutually assured destruction (MAD) between the USA and the then USSR. The third depiction relates to the (a)symmetry of mutual involvement, stemming from distribution of costs and benefits and resulting whether from the disputes about the costs to be paid for a surplus value, structural asymmetries in the world economy or the asymmetry of the existential value of the relationship to the actors.[4]

It is in this sense that scholars speak of 'imbalanced interdependence' and/or 'asymmetrical interdependence', almost interchangeably, despite a subtle difference between them. Imbalanced interdependence represents 'a situation in which one side is more dependent than the other(s), because the costs involved in maintaining and disrupting an alliance are greater for them'. Balance is still achievable, but that would require an asymmetric relationship in which the composition of costs would be variable, such as changing importance of economic costs vis-à-vis security costs. Yet an asymmetric relationship is frequently an imbalanced relationship in which the total level of costs is greater for one side'.[5] 'Moral interdependence' is another concept, arising from the Kantian postulate that international economic interdependence only meant extension of cosmopolitan rights abroad, and communitarian argument (as Charles Beitz's) that moral justice and duty are destined to cross national borders, just because interdependence presupposes social cooperation and distribution of significant benefits and burdens that would be inconceivable if states remained autarkic.[6]

INTELLECTUAL AND SITUATIONAL BACKGROUND OF INTERDEPENDENCE THEORY

The concept of interdependence was first set in currency by Sir Norman Angel, who wrote in 1909 that the 'contemporary rivalry in armaments...cannot go on in its present form indefinitely', because of the 'delicate interdependence of the financial world (an outcome of our credit and banking systems)' and the 'credit-built finance and industry', and of the 'vital interdependence' from this that cut 'across frontiers'. Angell applied increasingly stronger adjectives to it, such as 'extraordinary', 'real' and 'necessary' to sensitize us to 'the unity and interdependence of the modern world',[7] and was attacked by Carr during the idealism–realism debate.[8] Among other precursors, French Left-syndicalist Francis Delaisi argued somewhat like functionalists later that economic interdependence will usher in a world structure that will explode political myths about the essentiality of the nation state and showed the need for stable institutions to manage interdependence. English historian and Liberal leader Ramsay Muir discussed interdependence as an analytical concept.[9]

Predictably, the modern theory of interdependence also arose in response to the visible inadequacies of realism. The concept appeared in the field of IR in the 1960s in the context of the North–South and the East–West conflicts. And the idea that global interdependence was the keystone of world peace struck firm roots after the drastic shortening of distances caused by new intercontinental ballistic missiles, which led Morse to argue that a state can neither 'move towards isolation' nor 'increase its autonomy so far as security is concerned' by its solitary efforts. This 'security-related or military-strategic interdependence' was the upshot of the realist dystopia of an enduring global relationship generated by the conflict between two mutually exclusive conceptions of world politics and the existence of nuclear weapons as the menacing means of resolving this conflict.[10]

Yet it was not until academic writings on interdependence started in the late 1960s and especially the 1970s, in the backdrop of crisis moments in the world economy traceable directly or indirectly to the USA's policy stances and conflicts between countries in the industrialized West over these crises, exemplified by the collapse of the Bretton Woods monetary system in August 1971 and the First Oil Shock in 1973, that interdependence was taken seriously in IR. America's unilateral decision to end gold–dollar convertibility crippled the Bretton Woods system. OPEC's oil embargo retaliated this, and USA's and other Western economies' support for Israel in the Arab-Israeli conflict, culminating in the Yom Kippur War. The overheating and decline of the American and other Western economies, caused first by the steep hike in oil prices and the resulting stagflation and second by the costs of the Vietnam imbroglio heavily undermined the credibility of the concerned governments. So when occasions arose for changes of the heads of states and governments of the USA, West Germany, Japan and France, the new incumbents decided to coordinate their strategies to cope with the new crises. Since the 1975 World Economic Summit and the formation of the G7 (Group of Seven)/G8 (Group of Eight) thereafter, leaders sought to dispel the perceptions of citizens that the post-crises costs of adaptation and stabilization were caused by mistakes of individual regimes by employing the new rhetoric that it was the 'worldwide interconnections and dependencies' that were hindering their genuine attempts to tackle the crises and necessitated international coordination. This rhetoric of interdependence facilitated passing off the responsibility of individual or group national-level failures on to the world economy and presenting the causes and costs of adjustment as international. Interdependence aided political elites in America and elsewhere in shrouding the declining competence of individual governments to control national contingencies and in pleading for multilateral cooperation. In the context of the East–West détente, 'problems were politicized beyond military security issues' to accommodate new concerns about ways to maintain prosperity and resource availability and avoid environmental degradation. In the new situation, a posse of economists and political scientists started questioning the explanatory adequacy of the prevailing realist orthodoxy, rooted in the pre-eminence of 'high politics' and the vital importance of military power as an instrument of policy. The new approach of PE came to the forefront to bring out the links between economics and politics.[11]

Heralding this approach, Keynesian economist Cooper detected a strong tendency towards economic interdependence in the 1960s, which had made the 'the successful pursuit of national economic objectives much more difficult'. For, 'it complicated the successful pursuit of national economic objectives' in three different ways: (a) by increasing 'the number and magnitude of the disturbances to which each country's balance of payments is subjected', thus reorienting policymaking and its instruments of policy to 'the restoration of external balance'; (b) by slowing down 'the process by which national authorities, each acting on its own, are able to reach domestic objectives' and (c) while responding to greater integration, involving 'the community of nations in counteracting motions which leave all countries worse off than they need be'.[12] Edward Morse asserted that by its own strength, economic interdependence increases the desirability of peace between states which rationally calculate their interests, thereby reducing the chances of war between them.[13] For operating through interdependence modernity has changed the nature of the international system so profoundly that the 'anarchy' model of sovereign nation states is outmoded. Rather, in contexts of interdependence, all modern societies share greatly similar political experiences of strong welfare pressures, bureaucratization and legitimation crises which increase the salience of domestic politics in foreign policymaking. Structured linkages among states render obsolete the traditional models of the system centred on anarchy, and the linkages of diverse elements of the domestic society through international forces reduces the sharp distinction between foreign and domestic politics.[14]

KEOHANE AND NYE ON INTERDEPENDENCE

The social scientific version of interdependence that attracted most attention in the late 1970s was stated in Keohane and Nye's books, *Transnational Relations and World Politics* (1972, henceforth *TRAWP*); *Power and Interdependence: World Politics in*

Transition (1977, henceforth *PAIWPIT*); *After Hegemony: Cooperation and Conflict in World Political Economy* (1984, henceforth *AH*), and a bunch of articles. *PAIWPIT*, the iconic IR book of the 1970s, was rated by Holsti as 'one of the most significant writings in international relations theory of the past two decades'.[15] Michalak prognosticated that *PAIWPIT* may turn out *PAN* of the 1970s, a 'groundbreaking work…that will for a long time impact on the ways in which teachers and scholars conceptualize international phenomena'.[16]

According to Moravcsik, Keohane and Nye's essential contributions to IRT between 1970 and 1985[17] lie in their focus on 'new issues' (IPE in place of international security), 'new actors' (transnational actors instead of states), 'new forms of interaction' (transnational and transgovernmental relations in preference to interstate relations), 'new outcomes' (international cooperation in contradistinction to international conflict) and 'new structures' (international institutions instead of 'pure' anarchy). Their central, challenging hypothesis is avowedly that institutionalized cooperation continued even after the end of the post-war American hegemony. It springs from Keohane's three 'basic causal premises' regarding international politics, woven around a simple model of rationalist international cooperation. It is divisible into three ascending steps: '(a) the formation of state preferences, (b) interstate bargaining and strategic interaction; and (c) institutionalization of the bargain'. Keohane's three books of the period too, in that chronological order, can be seen as highlighting three 'fundamental theoretical causes of state behaviour'. While *TRAWP* launches 'state preferences, driven by globalization' as the basic variable, *PAIWPIT* floats a new view of 'interstate bargaining power', flowing from asymmetric interdependence as the primary variable impacting on state behaviour, and *AH* foregrounds the concept of international regimes to explain how bargains are preserved via their institutionalization. Clubbed together, they constitute the fundaments of Keohane's gestalt of state cooperation and, aided by supplementary theoretical ideas and assumptions, the core assumptions of the modern theoretical IPE.

At its basics, *TRAWIP* seeks to probe the importance of the politics of interaction among non-state actors, as distinct from that among states and international organizations for world politics. Transnational relations, classifiable in terms of the elements transported across borders by private actors—information, goods, money or people—that are the crux of this politics, lead to 'societal interdependence', which not only makes countries more 'sensitive' to one another but render policy processes more 'pluralistic', 'complex' and 'fragmented' by bringing in new actors, issues and processes. The examples of these processes, issues and actors are economic in character, including international trade and monetary policies, farm policies, international trade union federations, interstate airline regulation, global inequality, newspaper sales offices, multinational firms and so on; the motley further enriched by a residual category of transnational non-governmental groups (whether reformist or revolutionary), religious groups and mass communication. But at a deeper level, *TRAWP* moves beyond this focus on new issues and actors to suggest that the most profound implication of the prevalence of these transnational relations is that contrary to claims of realists, state preferences about the conduct of world politics are not a 'zero-sum constant' but rather a 'positive-sum variable'. In the realms of trade and other forms of economic cooperation, domestic interest groups have great stakes in the transnational social relations (henceforth, TSRs) in which they have invested. So governments do not always thwart the interests of transnational actors, even when engaged with security interests and in wartime. To that extent, TSRs not only divert basic state preferences, but place new constraints on and opportunities for state behaviour, modify the nature of relative interstate power and leave lesser roles of traditional statecraft and the military. This makes TSRs constituents of the basic structure of the international system in which states are rooted and give them limited control over it. Its corollary is that states reap some mutual benefits by managing their affairs in concert with others, although this may not render interstate conflict over control over these activities impossible.

So contrary to realists' claims again, far from being autonomous, international politics is deeply influenced by its transnational social context, which not only disallows maintenance of the realist issue hierarchy with predominance of military issues but begs the question about state preferences by saying that with interests, beliefs and so on, they are epiphenomenal. Examples of this are: markets and communications that operate beyond the ken of foreign ministries; internal tensions between competing policy options, between, for example, the US multinational firms and the national interest in promoting economic development and stabilizing the IPE; and tensions resulting from the gamut of choices faced by governments in their economic policy, including defensive protectionism, affirmation of national jurisdiction and facilitation of policy coordination through international institutions. The implications are that conflict and cooperation are not predetermined conclusions but choices in a variable sum environment, and this leads to a thinning between the Angellian lines of 'high' and 'low' politics.

According to Moravcsik, another corollary of the variations of societal interdependence and state preferences is the increasing salience of domestic politics, although individuals and groups inside these societies are conceded to have differential links to global society and consequently possess different interests about the way it is to be managed. This runs athwart realist expectations of more homogeneous preferences for security as some public good. Keohane and Nye demonstrate the interdigitation of domestic and transnational forces by tracing the increasing 'politicization' of international economics to the concomitance of 'secular trends' towards heightening of governmental accountability for economic welfare and economic internationalization, which render governments 'more sensitive to external disturbances that may affect developments within their own societies'. Keohane and Nye also pointed to the fragmentation of bureaucratic politics (instantiated in 44 American federal bureaucracies represented in the London embassy in the 1960s) and strategy of private groups to act through domestic politics, construct transnational alliances and bring on international organizations to evade or bypass the designs of their national governments as other indicators of this interdigitation.[18]

In *PAIWPIT*, Keohane and Nye start with the statement that since one's assumptions about world politics deeply influence what one detects in it, the assumptions of the realist orthodoxy, which dominated the post-war theoretical scene, not only provide an inadequate basis for understanding the current situation of interdependence but at best 'define an extreme set of conditions or ideal type'. So they decide to start by constructing 'another ideal type, the opposite of realism', and term it as 'complex interdependence'. They rephrase what is termed as the 'signature argument' of realism,[19] based on primacy of states in IR, pre-eminence of power as state policy in it, and graded and hierarchical nature of the international agenda, to endow their anti-realist ideal type of complex interdependence with the following features:

1. All societies are linked by *multiple channels*, which comprehend 'informal ties', between not just 'governmental elites and formal foreign office arrangements' but 'non-governmental elites' (whether in personal presence or telephonic) and transnational organizations (including multinational banks or corporations). These channels exemplify interstate, transgovernmental and transnational relations, each of which has differential distances from the realist ideal type: interstate reactions being the closest and the favourites; transgovernmental ones getting salience when the realist assumptions about states behaving coherently as units are slackened and the epithet transnational applying when the assumption that states are the only units is loosened.
2. Even the realist-friendly agenda of interstate relationships comprise *multiple issues* that are not clearly or distinctly ranked or graded, so that 'military security does not dominate the agenda'. Rather, numerous pertinent issues spring from the welter that was loosely labelled as domestic politics, which make the demarcation between domestic and foreign issues fuzzy, are deliberated on in diverse governmental settings, entailing different amounts of costs arising from insufficient policy coordination, and 'generate different coalitions, both within and across governments'.
3. When *complex interdependence* prevails, governments shun employing military force against governments within the regions or about some issues, though do not desist from it against governments outside the regions or about others. It may be avoided for settling differences on economic issues among alliance partners, but employed against governments outside the region or against both on other issues.

Even though realists may deny the validity of these three assumptions, they are 'fairly well approximated on some global issues of economic and ecological interdependence', besides coming close to 'characterizing the entire relationship between some countries'. After demonstrating the empirical validity of these three assumptions, Keohane and Nye provide two qualifiers or riders about the third reduced role of military force. These are: '(a) drastic social and political change could cause force again to become an important direct instrument of policy and (b) even when elites' interests are complementary, a country that uses military force to protect another may have significant political influence over the other country'. Besides, military force has considerable salience in North–South relations, as well as East–West relations, though even for these conflict-prone contexts, employment of force had become 'less likely' in 1977, compared to the times before 1945. But the fact that changes in the role of force have uneven distributions does not render the change 'less important', only makes the situation 'more complex'.

These three characteristics of complex interdependence have diverse repercussions for its underlying political processes. First, while in the realist vision, military security, the dominant goal of states, will colour even non-military issues, such as balance of payments, teasing out their politico-military significances, as per the insight of complex interdependence, a diversity of even unrelated goals will be pursued by at least the lower echelons of bureaucracy. Second, these variances of goals in terms of issue areas and the resultant changes in the 'distribution of power and the typical political processes' will weaken the old realist assumption that militarily and economically strong states can overpower a variety of organizations and control a variety of issues by 'linking their own policies on some issues to other states' policies on other issues' and, thus, effect 'a congruence between the overall structure of military and economic power and the pattern of outcomes in any issue area'. This 'congruence', which made world politics look a 'seamless web', would no more hold under complex interdependence. For in the devaluation of military force, states of superior military strength may not find it easy to extend their 'overall dominance to control outcomes on issues on which they are weak'. And when 'distribution of power resources', as for example in trade, shipping or oil, are incongruent, the nature of outcomes and their underpinning political processes are also likely to be different from one bunch of issues to another. Since this divergence among issue areas will problematize and weaken the international issue hierarchy, linkage strategies will assume additional importance for states, posing problems about whether to pack together or disaggregate the distinct issues. The reduced role of force will compel states to search for other instruments to exercise power and the scenario will be as summarized below:

- States 'will try to use asymmetrical interdependence in particular groups of issues as a source of power.'
- They 'will also try to use international organizations and transnational actors and flows.'
- States will resort to economic interdependence not only in terms of power but also 'its effects on citizens' welfare', even though thoughts about welfare considerations will modify their quest for maximization of power.
- Since most instances of economic and ecological interdependence entail potential joint gains or losses, shared perceptions of them, and awareness of the possibility of weakening each other's position through unyielding competition over distribution of gains, can hold down the pursuit of asymmetrical interdependence.

Third, contrary to the myopia of traditional realist analysis about the broader politics of agenda setting and control stemming from their monomania with politico-military issues, the want of a 'clear hierarchy among multiple issues will endow the politics of agenda formation with greater importance. This is partly because under complex interdependence, due to the blurring of the distinction between 'high' and 'low politics', there will be multiple agendas, and they will be 'affected by international and domestic problems created by economic growth and increasing sensitivity interdependence'. This will lead disaffected domestic groups to politicize issues and place problems, deemed domestic before, into the interstate agenda. The agendas will also be influenced by changes in the disposal of resources within clusters of issues, as in the early 1970s, when the greater clout of the oil-producing powers over TNCs and the consumer countries remarkably changed the international policy agenda. Besides, agendas for one cluster of issues may be altered because of linkages from other clusters that are experiencing changes in power resources, as when the configuration and architecture of the North–South trade issues underwent modifications after the OPEC price hike and the oil embargo of 1973–1974. Even in situations where distribution of capabilities among states has remained unchanged, 'agendas may be affected by shifts in the importance of transnational actors', as seen by the greater attention to regulations about MNCs in the UN agenda, after their adverse publicity in the 1970s. The politicization of an issue, comprising agitation and controversy, that boosts its rise to the top of the agenda may stem from many sources, at the top or below: (a) governments whose powers are on the rise may do it by linking an issue to others, (b) discontented governments may insist on changing a non-functional regime[20] and (c) domestic public may also become impatient about reviving a dormant issue or intervening in instances of high-level international bargaining, exemplified in 1974 when the success of domestic American groups working with the Congress in linking a trade agreement with Soviet policies on emigration queered the pitch of 'the American Secretary of State's tacit linkage of a Soviet-American trade pact with progress in détente'.

Besides, according to Keohane and Nye, the third characteristic of complex interdependence, that 'multiple channels of contact among societies further obfuscate the distinction between domestic and international politics', arises from the fact that contrary to what realists claim, the availability of partners in coalitions is no more restricted by national boundaries and 'the outcomes of bargaining come to be affected by transnational relations'. While MNCs may act both as independent agents and as instruments that governments exploit, both institutionalized and unorganized communications between them and their counterparts abroad influence the orientations and policy stances of the domestic groups. Consequently, the expected limits on the ability of statesmen to compute the costs of interdependence and pursue a coherent linkage strategy travel beyond the confines of domestic politics, as statesmen have to keep in reckoning the 'differential as well as aggregate effects of interdependence strategies' and their likely effects on politicization and agenda control. The multiplicity of channels of contact is not confined to non-governmental actors but is extended to government bureaucracies, who in course of their performance of similar tasks form transnational coalitions. The presence of transgovernmental policy networks problematizes the standard realist dictum on international politics, that states act only in their self-interest. Complex interdependence not only underscores that a 'government agency may pursue its own interests under the guise of national interests and recurrent interactions can change official perceptions of their interests' but shows how the vagueness of national interests befuddles apex-level government leaders. Bureaucracies meeting unmediated across national borders make assertion of central control over interpretation of national interests difficult and decrease chances of states offering a unified position when confronting foreign governments or its constituent parts interpreting national interest in one voice, when bargaining with foreigners. As a result, in a 'multifaceted, even schizophrenic' state, national interest will no more be an abstraction and will rather be interpreted 'differently, on different issues, at different times and by different governmental units'.

Finally, the presence of multiple channels will entail a role for international organizations in world politics that realists, in their vision of congruence of issues around security, never perceived. For 'in a world of multiple issues imperfectly linked, in which coalitions are formed transnationally and transgovernmentally, the potential role of international organizations is greatly increased', whether in assisting to help shape the international agenda or in acting as 'catalysts for coalition formation and as arenas for political initiatives and linkage by weak states'.[21]

Against the conventional naïve equation between interconnectedness and interdependence, Keohane and Nye rightly differentiate between them via the yardstick of costs, taking interdependence to prevail only in situations of reciprocal costs of interactions, whether or not distributed evenly among the actors concerned. From this presumption of the invariable costliness of interdependence, they also introduce a finer distinction between two types of cost outcomes and responsiveness to them, revolving around 'sensitivity' and 'vulnerability'. Sensitivity signifies 'degrees of responsiveness within a policy framework', demonstrated by how soon changes in one country induce 'costly changes' in another, and how costly are the effects, even in the absence of any political responses by the state harmed or benefited. It also depicts situations where costs induced by another state can be drastically reduced by a change in existing policy. By contrast, vulnerability signifies a state's ability, or lack of it, to compensate and bounce back from costs initiated by policy changes by another state, and to that extent 'an actor's liability to suffer costs imposed by external events' even after its policies have been changed significantly. The vulnerability aspect of interdependence, or the degree of availability and cost consequences of various policy measures for the actors, will however vary from one issue area to another. For example, a state may be less vulnerable to vicissitudes in the supply of certain strategic mineral resources by other countries than to those in supply and pricing of oil. For Keohane and Nye, the vulnerability dimension of interdependence is more crucially relevant to the analysis of the 'structure of relations' than its sensitivity aspect.

In *PAIWPIT*, interdependence is not viewed from a teleological perspective, but 'simply as a condition', an empirical, intervening variable that mediates between the independent variable of power and the dependent variables of outcomes of political processes. It alters the context and structure of international negotiations and, thus, circumscribes the capacity of states for autonomous political action. The problem for politics emanates from the costs of interdependence and how they are borne, since the costs of the states' adaptation to changed circumstances are always sought to be evaded or passed on to others. So the crux of the politics of individual states will be to determine how the distribution of costs and benefits can be turned to their advantage. They would do so egoistically from their cost–benefit calculus, in a context of asymmetric interdependence, because unilateral pursuit of gains always leads to suboptimal results and states are locked in conditions of vulnerability relative to other entities and units involved in the interrelationship. In this situation, individual governments are faced with problems from two perspectives: problem of how to derive maximum benefit from international exchanges with the minimal cession of autonomy (from the foreign policy angle) and 'how to generate and maintain a mutual beneficial pattern of cooperation' in the backdrop of 'competing efforts by governments (and non-governmental actors) to manipulate the system for their own benefit (from the international systemic viewpoint).

In all this, the academic-political objective of Keohane and Nye was showing that the American quest for unilateral leadership being untenable in conditions of complex interdependence and the possibilities of a 'neo-isolationist strategy' being unavailable in the backdrop of the costs of interdependence, a better option for vulnerability reduction would be 'a strategy of policy coordination and international leadership'. International leadership again can be of three types: hegemonic, unilateralist and multilateralist. In conditions of emaciation of American hegemony, and the resultant impracticability of unilateralism, the wisest way to approach interdependence would be to adopt a policy of multilateralism based on 'action to induce the states to help stabilize an international regime'.[22] Here, potential gains achievable from international cooperation would be the signpost. Spindler sums up the lesson of *PAIWPT* as provision of 'a political scientific foundation for the efforts by Western industrialized states, under the leadership of the USA, to achieve policy coordination through multilateral coordination in the 1970s and the 1980s'.[23]

Admittedly, the theoretical underpinnings of *PAIWPIT* rejected the complacency of 'modernist' commentators that at present 'the territorial state, which has been dominant in world politics for the four centuries since feudal times ended, is being eclipsed by non-territorial actors and international organizations', as well as the equally simplistic view that military force has been obsolescent and economic interdependence is always benign, both predestining an observer to 'equally grave, though different, errors'. Truly four factors had made the use of force 'increasingly costly for major states': 'risks of nuclear escalation, resistance by people in poor or weak countries, uncertain and possibly negative effects on the achievement of economic goals, and domestic opinion opposed to the human costs of the use of force'; although the fourth factor had less salience for totalitarian or authoritarian governments, and 'lesser states involved in regional rivalries and non-state terrorist groups' might find resort to force 'easier than before'. Still, all 'these contrary trends in the role of force' have irretrievably weakened the hierarchy revolving around military power'.[24] But revisiting *PAIWPIT* after 10 years, Keohane and Nye found that contrary to the opinion of detractors that unlike the decade of the 1970s which looked congenial for interdependence, the 1980s were characterized more by 'the use of force and concern for security', which made *PAN* more appropriate than *PAIWPIT* for the times, 'the general argument' they had made there about the 'systemic constraints on the use of force' still held ground due to the following similarities between the 1970s and the 1980s, despite their apparent differences.

Two similarities were that the relevance of nuclear weapons was still mainly for deterrence and the 'social mobilization of populations' still restrained the superpowers, as evidenced by the failure of Soviet intervention in Afghanistan and by the low-key American response to hostage taking by Iran in 1979. Also, the Reagan administration was still cautious, despite its rhetoric, in deploying US ground forces even in Central America. The more recent problems faced by the USA in the use of force in Iran, Nicaragua and Lebanon during the 1980s, and even in tiny Grenada, compare unfavourably with the ease, lower cost implications and efficaciousness of the Eisenhower administration's interventions in Iran (1953), Guatemala (1954) and Lebanon (1958). The only exceptions were the US success in dealing with force with tiny Grenada and with Libya for which the USA refrained from deploying ground troops. Besides, according to Keohane and Nye, the success of smaller states and terrorists in the use of force and the limited nature of American response to terrorism buttress their arguments for the existence of constraints on Amcrican use of force.[25]

Walker deplores the fact that Keohane and Nye later sought to 'graft' *PAIWPIT* 'onto neorealist theory'. Instead of tracing out 'the linkages between complex interdependence and liberal internationalism', they made a consistent attempt to develop 'potentially complementary models' to political realism. This prevented them from 'highlighting how their ideas challenge realist expectations' and obscured the 'close relationship' between the themes of *PAIWPIT*, 'a work seeped in the tradition of liberal internationalism', and those of liberal internationalist theory.[26] Truly, they conceded in 'PAIR' that while conjoining neorealist analysis and liberals' concerns with interdependence, instead of 'viewing realist theory as an alternative to liberal "interdependence theory"', they 'regarded the two as necessary complements to one another'. The justification was that both realism and liberalism are firmly rooted in 'a utilitarian view of the world, in which individual actors pursue their own interests by responding to incentives', and both 'view politics as a process of political and economic exchange, characterized by bargaining'.[27]

COMPLEX INTERDEPENDENCE IN THE INTERNET AGE AND UNDER GLOBALIZATION

Eleven years later,[28] Keohane and Nye talked about how the early phase of the Internet Age has changed one important feature of the 'complex interdependence' they first described in *PAIWPIT*, characterized by the lessening importance of security and force in a situation of countries 'connected by multiple political and social relationships'. In a scenario where 'anyone with a computer can be a desktop publisher and anyone with a modem can connect with distant parts of the globe at a trivial cost', the earlier mediation and control by large bureaucracies like MNCs or the Catholic Church have weakened. The 'dramatic cheapening of information transmission has opened the field to loosely structured organizations' like NGOs and even to individuals, so that the latter can penetrate states regardless of borders and influence 'domestic constituencies' to compel attention of political leaders to their chosen agendas. The third feature of complex interdependence has been irrevocably altered by the resultant numerical increase in channels of contact between societies.

But the effect of the information revolution on two other defining characteristics of complex interdependence has been much less pronounced. Relations between states are still defined and determined by military force, and security tops the list of issues in foreign policy. One reason behind this stunted effect of information revolution on complex interdependence is that 'information does not flow in a vacuum but in a political space that is already occupied'. Another is that outside the limited reach and sway of the 'democratic zone of peace', the domain of states is infected less by values of and belief in complex interdependence than by realist faith in the primacy of military force and security. The lingering influence of these realist assumptions on states owe to the legacy of the last four centuries of nearly exclusive information flow across the borders of political structures created by them, more so as the information revolution is understandable only in the context of the deliberate US policy during the half century since the end of the Second World War to fashion an open IPE to avert another depression and keep communism at bay. But because of its genealogy, and its existence in a political structure, the cyberspace cannot assure the same free flow for all types of information. 'Free information will flow faster without regulation. Strategic information will be protected as much as possible, for example, by encryption technologies. The flow of commercial information will depend on whether property rights are established in cyberspace'.

From this, Keohane and Nye make the prediction that the information revolution will be as much shaped by politics as would be politics by it.[29] Of course, the information revolution has affected 'power measured in terms of resources rather than behaviour' and has made soft power more important, although without removing the salience of hard power. It has made maintenance of closed systems more costly. But in spite of its acclaimed levelling effect, it has not 'greatly decentralized or equalized power among states' and has not benefited small states at the cost of large states uniformly. In the information warfare, credibility plays a crucial role, so that contrasted with asymmetric interdependence in trade, where power accrues to those 'who can afford to hold back or break trade ties, information power flows to those who can edit and credibly validate information to sort out what is both correct and information' from distracting 'noise'. Here, democratic states have an advantage over non-democratic ones, because they are reputed for 'free exchange of information and their institutions of governance are not threatened by it'. Closed systems suffer because their 'opaque' decision-making systems discourage foreign investments.

But while cheapness of information flows has greatly augmented and deepened the transnational channels of contact, enabling non-governmental actors 'to organize and propagate their views', and has made states penetrable with their political leaders less able to 'maintain a coherent ordering of foreign policy issues', states, especially the democratic ones, remain supple and well positioned enough to reap maximum advantages from the information society. While their policy coherence may suffer in the permeable and pluralistic scenario, the credibility of their contentions and their felicity in using soft power to attain their goals will ensure that the future does not belong exclusively to transnational relations, if not to them. So 'geographically based states will continue to structure politics in the Information Age', even if depending 'less on material resources and more on their ability to remain credible to a public with increasingly diverse sources of information.[30] The upshot of all this was that complex interdependence remained a complementary vision of world politics with realism.

But three years later, while adapting their flexible model to advanced globalization, Keohane and Nye pondered on how this realist influence will be eroded by growth of networks among individuals (including scientists, professionals in various fields) and NGOs (including human rights and environmental activists) 'aided greatly by the fax machine and the Internet and by institutional arrangements that incorporate these networks into decision-making'. To show that this is already happening, Keohane and Nye showed how it was natural and social scientists who created, without answering to any governments, the underpinning consensus of the Kyoto Protocol through the Intergovernmental Panel on Climate Change in a way that hostile governments were left with no scope of renegotiating its scientific guidelines. They hoped that the steep fall in the cost of long-distance communication will encourage the growth of a large number of similar transnational networks, owing to which 'wealthy hierarchical organizations, MNCs as well as states', would find it hard to corner transnational communications. The optimistic note is so clearly visible and infectious in a passage that we quote it whole:

> Therefore, the future accountability of international institutions to their publics may rest only partly on delegation through formal democratic institutions. Its other pillar may be voluntary pluralism under conditions of maximum transparency. International policies may increasingly be monitored by loose groupings of scientists or other professionals, or by issue advocacy networks such as Amnesty International and Greenpeace, whose members, scattered around the world, will be linked even more closely by modern information technology. Accountability will be enhanced not only by chains of official responsibility, but by the requirement of transparency. Official actions, negotiated among state representatives in international organizations, will be subjected to scrutiny by transnational networks.[31]

CRITIQUE AND EVALUATION

A critique of interdependence theory, *PAIWPIT*, and Keohane and Nye as authors, cannot afford to start without first assessing their impacts. Asked in a survey about 'whose work had the greatest impact in the past 20 years', IR scholars from a large number of countries graded Keohane as first and Nye as sixth, largely because of *PAIWPIT*. The book was written at a time when the smarting failures of the USA to chastise North Vietnam and prevent OPEC from imposing its oil embargo revealed the non-exchangeability of military power and yet as demonstrated by Vasquez, 40 per cent of the hypotheses tested by IR scholars up to the 1970s were generated by realism. As Walker rightly points out, before *PAIWPIT* invaded the IR theoretical scene, 'questions concerning the fungible aspects of power, the interplay between domestic and international politics, the roles of international organization and the importance of international regimes' were moved to the periphery of international politics, smacking of interwar idealism or utopianism. It was Keohane and Nye who strung together these peripheralized aspects of world politics in their book and its theoretical grid.[32]

But Spindler mentions a number of problems of the interdependence approach and *PAIWPIT* as their best statement, the general source of which is that 'the conceptualization of interdependence was not just the jumping-off point for further developments in theories of cooperation and institutions but also for studies on the relationship between mutual dependence and conflicts, as well as the increased potential for conflict and violence within the international system as a result of mutual dependencies more generally'. As it is shown by numerous scholars, it is from such reflections that the impetus for empirical research on the old liberal thesis on the pacifying effects of 'international trade relations' or *pax mercatoria* draws sustenance. The same argument holds for studies concerning the contribution of international institutions to peace. Scholars who talk of the civilizing effects of international institutions on IR fail to notice that the civilizing effects are restricted to relations between 'civilized' Western industrialized states, already caught in the web of complex interdependence, characterized by a 'high degree of regulation' nurtured by a multitude of institutions. So studies on them necessarily touch on research exploring the 'democratic peace' hypothesis. In this context, the study of complex interdependence should have been more enriched by 'an adequate theory of the role of transnational actors such as MNCs and other actors operating across borders'. But while developing such a theory, Keohane and Nye could not afford to be glued to the level of international system and a state-centric approach that much like realism views states as the pre-eminent actors and enclosed, free-standing units looking upon international institutions or organizations as the only relevant non-state actors.

This systemic, state-centred orientation has other tragic consequences. Keohane and Nye desist from depicting how states are differentiated inside, even while taking into reckoning transnational relations together with actions taken by social actors, since they are definitional of the character of international interdependence. But they miss the contradiction that the conceptual components of complex interdependence leave no room for a strict separation between 'the internal sphere of a state and the systemic dimension'. Yet researches on interdependence have borne empirical fruits only when they have analysed, away from the systemic level, 'the mutual dependency of a limited number of states in specific political fields', through the lens of the 'interplay of domestic, transnational and international processes' or when they have focused on this problem and stretched this focus of analysis to the level of the state.

Another lacuna of the book is that while contending that a high degree of mutual dependence transforms both foreign policy goals and choice of political means for them, and that welfare issues acquire greater salience than security goals or military force because of it, *PAIWPIT* treats these changes as 'already...givens in their characterization of the international system', as '*both* characteristics and consequences of complex interdependence'. Spindler quotes 'PAIR' to show that Keohane himself was aware of this tautology: 'Since we define complex interdependence in terms of the goals and instruments of state policy, any general arguments about how goals and instruments are affected by the degree to which a situation approximates complex interdependence or realism will be tautological'. Of course, Spindler does not quote the remainder of the admission, which could take the edge of this piece of critique, since Keohane and Nye themselves concede that due to it they limited their propositions concerning political processes to 'issue-linkage, agenda formation and the roles of international organizations'; and because reflections on linkage are germane both to the world of realism and to complex interdependence, in effect they had to make do with 'two dependent variables: changes in agenda and in the roles of international organizations'.[33] But more fundamental is Spindler's point that they do not explain how interdependence appears; first, because the focus on the systemic level is bound to miss 'how state interests come about', through the churning done by 'social actors, transgovernmental networks and policy communities', and ipso facto cannot tease out 'the implications of an international politics of interdependence for the internal life of states'. Second, even though they make vague references to the impersonal 'forces of modernization' as the engines of this interdependence, they do not engage with the wider debate of modernity to spell out how these forces work and do not show if in place of these impersonal forces, some 'instrumental, goal-directed action by human actors' is not giving shape to this interdependence.

Ironically, Keohane and Nye took pains to humour realism as a complementary vision in *PAIPWPIT*. But (neo)realists attack them as much for their failure to provide an alternative as for their inability to make a fundamental critique of realism, because of their 'straw man' account of realism. Both Waltz and Mearsheimer have termed interdependence as 'myth', in an international system which does not allow any division of labour or specialization among the component units. In 'The Myth of National Interdependence' (1970), Waltz claims that 'high inequality among like units is low interdependence', which means that in a system of high inequality between states' interdependence is not conceivable. The stronger states can shift towards economic autarchy anytime, rendering interdependence vulnerable.[34]

Keohane and Nye could neither please the (neo)realists nor could they satisfy the proponents of liberal internationalist theory. I remind my readers of Walker's charge of Keohane's missed opportunity of revealing the 'close relationship' between the themes dealt with in *PAIWPIT* and those in liberal internationalist theory. Probing the question of why a safe distance was kept by *PAIWPIT* with liberal internationalism, Walker ventures that the reason might have been strategic. In the 1970s, any frontal attack on the traditional realist orthodoxy might have brought a 'quick dismissal of their ideas'. But Walker also imagines what would have happened if in place of this expedient move, they had located *PAIWPIT* into classical liberal theory. First, the focus on how the 'causal processes of complex interdependence might foster peaceful relations and change the nature of global politics', presently neglected, would have helped them find out whether Kant's insight that 'peace through interdependence results from the efforts of states' was right, or was Paine's that it results 'from the multi-layered societal exchanges and learning'. Second, a more probing look at liberal internationalist theory might have compelled some discussion on the role of democratic governance, the new avatar of liberal internationalism. With their thorough case studies on Australia, Canada and the USA (all democratic states), Keohane and Nye would have been able to provide real insights into this. We have already pointed out how their work had an affinity with the democratic peace hypothesis that was not explored. Third, had they taken on realism more directly, they would have been able to shed similar light on the relation between trade and peace that both Morgenthau and Waltz had denied.[35]

CONCLUSION

This chapter has discussed the origins of the concept of interdependence, one of the late-1970s solvents of the realist view of IR; it has traced the development of the idea since the times of Angell, Cooper and Morse but has concentrated on its most famous formulation and development by Keohane and Nye, before moving on to how these great collaborators developed their joint insights in separate ways. But how do they stand theoretically? Walker, one of the hard sympathetic critics of Keohane and *PAIWPIT*, gives the best answer. He still brands it as a substantial book that has resuscitated many peripheralized aspects of liberal internationalism, with its curious blend, writ large in the title itself, of the realist aspects of power and the liberal aspects of interdependence. Consistently asking, in the 'Afterword' of the 1989 edition of *PAIWPIT*, under what conditions liberal or realist approaches will offer better clues to the realities of world politics, the book offered a new research programme. The best example of this is how the authors pursued their different lines of enquiry from the insights of the book. While Nye moved on to fine-tune the concept of soft power in *Bound to Lead*, Keohane went on to hone the concept of regimes first put forth in his own *After Hegemony* (1984),[36] which I will discuss at length in the next chapter.

REVIEW QUESTIONS

1. Define interdependence. Differentiate it from interconnectedness and cooperation in IR and comment on its identified types with suitable examples from the realities of IR.
2. Analyse how Keohane and Nye have theorized complex interdependence as the dominant reality of IR and show the lacunae of their theory.
3. Attempt a critical evaluation of the paradigm of complex interdependence as a critique of the realist view of IR.

NOTES AND REFERENCES

1. Dimitris N. Chryssochoou, *Theorizing European Integration*, 2nd ed. (London: Routledge, 2009), 33.
2. See R. J. Barry Jones, *'Interdependence', in Routledge Encyclopedia of International Political Economy, ed.* Barry Jones, vol. 1, Entries A–F, p. 788 (London: Routledge, 2001); Barry Jones, *Globalisation and Interdependence in the International Political Economy: Rhetoric and Reality* (London: Bloomsbury, 1995/2013), 6–32.
3. Dale C. Copeland, 'Economic Interdependence', in *Routledge Encyclopedia of International Political Economy*, ed. Barry Jones, vol. 1 (London: Routledge, 2001), 403–404; Dale C. Copeland, *Economic Interdependence and War* (Princeton, NJ: Princeton University Press, 2015), 33–35.
4. Jaap de Wilde, 'Interdependence', in *International Encyclopedia of Political Science*, eds Bertrand Badie, Dirk Berg-Schlosser, and Leonardo Morlino, vol. 1 (Los Angeles, CA: SAGE Publications, 2021), 1216–1217.
5. Amanda Dickins, 'Interdependence, Asymmetrical', 'Interdependence, Imbalanced', in *Routledge Encyclopedia of International Political Economy*, ed. Barry Jones (London: Routledge, 2001), 791, 793.
6. Paul G. Harris, 'Interdependence, Moral', in *Routledge Encyclopedia of International Political Economy*, ed. Barry Jones (London: Routledge, 2001), 794.
7. Norman Angell, *The Great Illusion* (New York, NY: Cosimo Classics, 2010), 3, 28, 32, 50, 53, 141, 157, 360 and passim, available at https://books.google.co.in/books?isbn=1616402563 (accessed on 3 April 2021).
8. See Molloy, *The Hidden Hand of Realism*.
9. Delaisi, *Les Contradictions du monde moderne* (1925) and Muir, *The Interdependent World and Its Problems* (1932) cited in de Wilde, 'Interdependence', in *International Encyclopedia of Political Science*, eds Bertrand Badie, Dirk Berg-Schlosser, and Leonardo Morlino, vol. 1 (Los Angeles, CA: SAGE Publications, 2021), 1217.
10. For citation of Edward L. Morse, 'Crisis Diplomacy, Interdependence, and the Politics of International Economic Relations', *World Politics* 24, Supple. (1972): 138–139 and comments, see Manuela Spindler, 'Interdependence', in *Theories of International Relations*, eds Siegfried Schieder and Manuela Spindler, trans. Alex Skinner (London: Routledge, 2014), 57.
11. Spindler, 'Interdependence', 57–8.
12. Richard Cooper, 'National Economic Policy in an Interdependent World Economy', reprinted from Cooper, *The Economics of Interdependence: Economic Policy in the Atlantic Community* (New York, NY: McGraw-Hill, 1968), in *The Theoretical Evolution of International Political Economy: A Reader*, eds George T. Crane and Abla Amawi, 2nd ed. (New York, NY: Oxford University Press, 1996), 110–132, esp. 110.
13. Edward Morse, 'The Transformation of Foreign Policies: Modernization, Interdependence, and Externalization', *World Politics* 22, no. 3 (1970): 371–392.
14. Edward Morse, *Modernization and the Transformation of International Relations* (New York, NY: The Free Press, 1976), cited in Peter Gourevitch, 'The Second Image Reversed: The International Sources of Domestic Politics', in *The State: Critical Concepts*, ed. John A. Hall (London: Routledge, 1994), 213–214, 226–227.
15. K. J. Holsti, 'A New International Politics?', *International Organization* 32, no. 2 (Spring 1978): 513–530, esp. 524.
16. Stanley J. Michalak, 'Theoretical Perspectives for Understanding International Interdependence', *World Politics* 32, no. 1 (1979): 136–150, esp. 136.

17. Andrew Moravcsik, 'Robert Keohane: Political Theorist', in *Power, Interdependence, and Nonstate Actors in World Politics*, eds Helen V. Milner and Andrew Moravcsik (Princeton, NJ: Princeton University Press, 2009), 243–264.
18. See Robert O. Keohane and Joseph S. Nye Jr., 'Transnational Relations and World Politics: An Introduction', *International Organization* 25 (1971): 329–349, esp. 332–336; Robert O. Keohane and Joseph S. Nye Jr., 'Transnational Relations and World Politics: Conclusion', *International Organization* 25 (1971): 721–748, esp. 721, 724, 741–742, 744; Robert O. Keohane and Joseph S. Nye Jr., 'International Interdependence and Integration', in *Handbook of Political Science*, eds Fred I. Greenstein and Nelson W. Polsby (Reading, MA: Addison-Wesley, 1975), 384–401, esp. 397–398; all as cited in Moravcsik, 'Robert Keohane', 244–248. There is, however, no reference to the 1972 book (*TRAWP*) here.
19. See Wohlforth, 'Realism', 132–135.
20. The concept of regime will be defined in Chapter 12.
21. Robert O. Keohane and Joseph S. Nye Jr., *Power and Interdependence, 2nd* ed. (New York, NY: HarperCollins Publishers, 1989), 24–37.
22. Ibid, 9–16, 32, 229–231.
23. Spindler, 'Interdependence', 64.
24. Robert O. Keohane and Joseph S. Nye Jr., 'Power and Interdependence Revisited', *International Organization* 41, no. 4 (1987): 725–753, esp. 730, henceforth 'PAIR'.
25. Robert O. Keohane and Joseph S. Nye Jr., *Power and Interdependence: World Politics in Transition* (Boston, MA: Little, Brown, and Company, 1987), 3, 5, 228, cited with comments in Keohane and Nye, 'Power and Interdependence Revisited', 727–728.
26. Thomas C. Walker, 'A Circumspect Revival of Liberalism: Robert O. Keohane and Joseph S. Nye's Power and Independence', in *Classics of International Relations: Essays in Criticism and Appreciation*, eds Henrik Bliddal, Casper Sylvest, and Peter Wilson (Abingdon: Routledge, 2013), 149, 152–153.
27. Keohane and Nye, 'Power and Interdependence Revisited', 728.
28. Keohane and Nye, 'Power and Independence in the Information Age', *Foreign Affairs* 77, no. 5 (1998): 81–91.
29. Ibid., 81–85.
30. Ibid., 85–91.
31. Robert O. Keohane, *Power and Governance in a Partially Globalized World* (London: Routledge, 2002), 36.
32. Walker, 'A Circumspect Revival', 150.
33. Keohane and Nye, 'Power and Interdependence Revisited', 738.
34. Spindler, 'Interdependence', 65–68.
35. Walker, 'A Circumspect Revival', 152–154.
36. Ibid., 154–155; also see Joseph S. Nye Jr., *Bound to Lead: The Changing Nature of American Power* (New York, NY: Basic Books, 1990).

CHAPTER 15

Regime Theory

CHAPTER OUTLINE

INTRODUCTION, ORIGINS AND LOCATION

Like interdependence theory, regime theory is also a derivative of liberalism/pluralism in IR, owing its rise to the decline of integration theory (treated in **Chapter 13A**). Keohane is its earliest and prominent exponent. Regarding the disciplinary context of its emergence, I remind that in the 1970s, intellectual traditions focusing on the societal dimension of IR bore the academic stigma of idealist provenance. Besides, realism's detestation of international law as a restraining influence on state behaviour made a serious study of it unfashionable. Despite the rich theoretical harvests in the sub-area of international organization and in studies of regional integration, the monomania with formal international organizations lost sight of 'a range of state behaviour that nonetheless appeared regularized or organized in a broader sense'. Even the insight of scholars like John Ruggie about international behaviour being institutionalized could not generate much theoretical dividends. In such a situation, regime analysis bridged the theoretical hiatus by 'defining a focus that was neither as broad as international structure nor as narrow as the study of formal organizations'. Since regime theory arose as a critique of realism/neorealism and upheld the value and validity of institutions in IR, paradigmatically, it is best located in the group of neo-institutionalism, away from either pure neorealism or liberalism. It shares with neorealism its beliefs about the pre-eminence of states as actors in international politics, tracing their existence in the anarchical structures of world politics, and their rational pursuit of selfishly conceived goals. But regime theory also contains ideas that have the stamp of the liberal paradigm on them. Athwart the advocacy of hegemonic stability, inspired by neorealists' contention that lasting international cooperation is inconceivable without a hegemonic power forcibly imposing it on other states, regime theory contends that international cooperation can happen even when hegemonic structures are absent and can circumvent them when they are not. This is because, as argued by the concept of complex interdependence, international cooperation serves the interests of all states concerned. Against another corollary of neorealists derived from these premises that international institutions are nothing but instruments in the hands of hegemonic powers, regime theory demonstrates that these institutions are important in their own right, as mechanisms that assist the society of states to resolve their problems of cooperation arising from this very interdependence, when such cooperation is congenial for their pursuit of interests.

No theory of international cooperation can, however, emerge solely from academic debates without the push of contextual imperatives. Like interdependence theory before it, regime theory also claims its descent from debates on the perceived decline of America's hegemonic position since the 1970s, and the resultant predictions of neorealists that this decline will render present international institutions such as GATT and the International Monetary Fund (IMF) moribund in a short time and will harm the tempo of cooperation in international trade and monetary affairs. Actually, there were early signs of the diminution of such cooperation: for GATT facing resurfacing protectionism and for IMF, forced to bid adieu to the fixed exchange rates for a consensual pegged regime of 1944 and compelled to go for flexible rates. But belying early hiccups, these institutions remained operational, if not vibrant, in the 1970s and the 1980s, and protected international cooperation and safeguarded trade relations from competitive protectionism. Declining clout of the USA did not hamstring a mostly liberal world from maintaining the upswing of economic integration. Further embarrassing neorealists, new international institutions continued to emerge in the backdrop of the East–West conflict, led by CSCE and the Treaty on the Non-Proliferation of Nuclear Weapons, as did a few arms control regimes that bred cooperative relations, even though neither the USA nor the USSR enjoyed hegemonic positions any more. These new institutionalized accords were the sources of the optimistic view of international institutions that characterized regime theory. While the pre-1970s traditional institutionalism analysed international institutions—rather organizations—mainly from the vantage point of their capacities or proficiencies, neo-institutionalism incited researches rather on the international impacts of a number of institutions, beyond organizations. Scholars of regime theory focused on particular institutions—renamed international regimes—in the fields of international trade, currency, arms control, environment or human rights.

MEANINGS AND DEFINITIONS OF REGIME IN REGIME THEORY

The word regime is derived from the Latin word *regimen* and signifies 'rule, guidance, government, means of government, rudder', the last again derived from another Latin word *regere*, meaning 'to direct, to guide'. Flowing unaltered in the 14th century in Old French to become *régime*, generating 'regime' in English, it implied: (a) a certain government or method or system of government (*ancient régime* in France); (b) a past or present government in power (like the Trump, May or Modi regime) and (c) a system or a particular ordered way of doing things, operating a business and so on. The Latin origin also survives in a fourth meaning of the word of a coordinated programme aimed at the promotion or restoration of health, and in a modern fifth connotation, meaning conditions under which a scientific or industrial process takes place.

Regimes are to be differentiated from international organizations, not being actors like them but focused on particular issue areas in international politics. The concept's main concern in its first emergence in the USA in the 1970s was the international political economy (IPE). But since then, it has been taken to other areas by Keohane (1977, 1984 and 1989), Stephen Krasner (1983), Kenneth Oye (1986) and John D. Ruggie (1998). In Europe, however, even after its belated entry in the 1980s, regime theory remained confined to the efficaciousness of regimes in stabilizing security, as in the writings of German scholars such as Volker Rittberger and Michael Zürn (1990).[1]

The diverse definitions of regime in IRT induced Strange to describe it as 'one more woolly concept'.[2] Ruggie thought it 'refers to a set of mutual expectations, rules and regulations, plans, organizational energies and financial commitments, which have been accepted by a group of states'.[3] Keohane and Nye defined regimes as 'sets of governing arrangements' that include 'networks of rules, norms, and procedures that regularize behavior and control its effects'.[4] As per a more inclusive and widely accepted definition offered by Krasner:

> Regimes can be defined as sets of implicit or explicit principles, norms, rules and decision-making procedures, around which actors' expectations converge in a given area of international relations. Principles are beliefs of fact, causation, and rectitude. Norms are standards of behavior, defined in terms of rights and obligations. Rules are specific prescriptions and proscriptions for action. Decision-making procedures are prevailing practices for maintaining and implementing collective choice.[5]

Krasner's definition, which has survived till now, went beyond a bare legal and formalistic study of international accords and organizations to look at implicit rules and norms. It enthused researchers to focus on instances of cooperation that were not accommodated by formal organizations or treaties, bidding adieu to overly realist structural analyses that underscored conflict more than cooperation. But this consensual definition was found inadequate shortly. For Young, first, 'it does not allow us to identify regimes with precision or to separate regimes easily from the rest of IR', being nothing more than 'a list of elements that are hard to differentiate conceptually and that often overlap in real-world situations'. Second, it would compel us to 'now cope with another set of ambiguous terms in the form of beliefs, standards, prescriptions and practices, in addition to the original set consisting of principles, norms, rules and procedures'. So there was 'a disconcerting elasticity' in the consensual definition 'when applied to the real world of IR'.[6] The weakness of the definition avowedly stemmed from its problems of operationalization. Of two remedial procedures for operationalization, one enjoins looking for 'explicit rules or injunctions (with an embodiment independent of the actors)'. The second 'suggests adding an element of observable behaviour to the definition'. Both procedures have serious pitfalls when driven to extremes. The substantive procedure suffers from 'the danger of circular reasoning—identifying regimes on the basis of observed behaviour and then using regimes to explain this behaviour'. Additionally, this approach needs 'difficult causal inferences about regimes in order to identify them'. Contrarily, a purely formal operationalization introduces numerous 'paper regimes', more frequently 'an inflated universe of cases'. Of course, as Levy, Young and Zürn point out, these two do not exhaust all options, since the debate involves two separable dimensions, the first of which 'highlights the degree of formality of the rules', while the second underscores 'the degree to which the expectations of actors converge'.[7] These defects of Krasner's definition led Keohane to suggest that regimes are 'institutions with explicit rules, agreed upon by governments, that pertain to particular sets of issues in IR'.[8]

But while this definition retained the elasticity of Krasner's definition by emphasizing explicit rules and regulations discoverable in international treaties or other international public announcements and banishing implicit rules and regimes from the theoretical scope of regime theory, it was criticized by some scholars as overly contract minded and oblivious of the fact that the question of implementation was the lifeblood of regimes. So a behavioural approach to definition emerged, which chose to diagnose the presence of regimes through 'observable regularities in the behaviour' of actors.[9] Here, 'a stable pattern of collective behaviour, coupled with statements by at least the most powerful actors in a system that they support certain rights and obligations, provides strong evidence for the existence of regime injunctions' in an issue area. But this does not mean that all behaviours always comply with the dos and don'ts suggested by the regime, although 'occurrences of major or long-term noncompliance, particularly involving participation of or support by major actors in the system, bring into question the efficacy of regime injunctions'. Thus, for Zacher, 'effectiveness of behavioural guidelines' is an integral part of regimes beyond their contingent properties.[10] There are others who think on these lines.[11] For them, 'a regime exists in every substantive issue area in IR where there is discernible patterned behaviour. Wherever there is regularity in behaviour, some kinds of principles, norms or rules must exist to account for it'.[12]

Due to limitations of the behavioural definition based on 'overt behaviour', a self-proclaimed 'cognitive' approach turned attention to intersubjective meanings of Weberian vintage and shared understandings and relaxed the requirement of rule compliance in judging the presence and influence of norms and rules on the ground that 'norms are counterfactually valid'. It defined regimes as 'governing arrangements constructed by states to coordinate their expectations and organize aspects of international behaviour in specific issue areas', thus combining 'a normative element, state practice and organizational roles'. For cognitivists, far more important than the actual violation/observance of any rule is how it is interpreted by the community of states and what kind of communicative steps, including chastisements, pretexts and rationalizations, it engenders. Accordingly, Kratochwil and Ruggie suggest changes in Krasner's consensual definition, which replace the positivist methodology of mainstream regime analysis with an epistemology wedded to *verstehen*-based meta-theory on these lines:

> International regimes are commonly defined as social institutions around which expectations converge in international issue-areas. The emphasis on convergent expectations as the constitutive basis of regimes gives regimes an inescapable intersubjective quality...we know regimes by their principled and shared understandings of desirable and acceptable forms of social behavior.[13]

But the cognitive approach too had some weaknesses. First, it might prove 'enormously difficult', even 'ultimately impossible', to assess to what extent these 'principled and shared understandings' are principled and shared. Apart from having 'to enter into the minds of human beings to determine this', one would have to decide 'which human beings will count'. Besides, even if it were possible to 'devise a way to assess convergent expectations intersubjectively', one would still have to fix what 'standard of convergence' would be needed to ascertain 'that a regime existed'.[14] To set the stage clear, a revised consensus definition emerged in the 1990s, which retained the formal thin definition offered by Keohane, but melded it with two behavioural requirements: (a) the existence of explicit rules in an issue area as demanded by Rittberger and Keohane and (b) actors' obligation to provide recognition to them as valid and often invoke them in a positive vein.[15] We accept it for our purposes and then move on to the thoughts of individual regime theorists in its light, starting with Keohane.

Keohane on Regimes

Along with 'the relationship between power and interdependence' and 'the ideal type of complex interdependence', 'explanations of changes in international regimes' were the third most important theme in *PAIWPIT*. After defining regimes as 'sets of governing arrangements that affect relationships of interdependence', Keohane and Nye presented 'four roughly sketched models' that could explain changes in those regimes. The first model took account of economic and technological change. The second and third were structural. The second resorted to 'overall power structure to predict outcomes'. The third relied on 'the distribution of power within issue areas'. The fourth was an 'international organization model', wherein 'networks of relationships, norms and institutions' were treated as 'important, independent factors helping to explain international regime change'.[16] Since Keohane and Nye did not part with realism while discussing interdependence in *PAIWPIT*,[17] their thoughts on regimes do not avoid the role of governments, arguing that By 'creating or accepting procedures, rules or institutions for certain kinds of activity, governments regulate and control transnational and interstate relations.' We refer to those governing arrangements as international regimes.[18]

The four models apply according to contextual requirements. Where the underpinning springs of power are inexpensively translatable into changes in international regimes, a power structure based explanation is apposite. Where resources of power are not substitutable across issues, an issue structure model best applies. Where power over outcomes emanates from 'organizationally dependent capabilities, such as voting power, ability to form coalitions and control of elite networks, that is, by capabilities that are generated by the norms, networks and institutions', Keohane's fourth model would be an obvious candidate. But whenever the economic costs of disturbing the configurations of complex interdependence soar, the economic process explanation, that is, Keohane's first model, would be pertinent. The models are not timeless either, since 'one model may apply quite well for one period, but poorly for another'.[19] Suhr says quite insightfully that 'with this situationology they seemed to distance themselves from the view that the international system was undergoing a gradual, but fairly linear, modernization, which was characterized by complex interdependence'. So Keohane and Nye effectively undermined the basis for the binary division of world politics into a traditional one where realism was apposite and a modernized one, where the 'world politics paradigm' was relevant. Rather, thinks Suhr, through the presentation of 'this more nuanced view of the possibility of combining various models depending on the situation', they attempted to carve out a middle ground between realism/moderated realism and bland modernism, and strike out 'a differentiated approach that distinguishes among dimensions and areas of world politics'.[20]

But despite the attention to the 'overall power structure to predict outcomes' in the second model, Keohane and Nye never supported purely power-based or structural accounts of regime building and regime change, particularly when dealing with the management of the global economy. For them, military power provided only partial and insufficient explanation. For, even as powerful states continue to frame rules, a fuller comprehension of international regimes is not possible without an adequate investigation of the salient issues. A world marked by complex interdependence was understandable through a model of 'issue structuralism', where, in the absence of any clear issue hierarchy, outcomes are not dictated by conventional power relationships. In consequence, both regime effectiveness and distribution of power change across issues. Inspired by the experiences of the oil resource issue and the clout of OPEC, this model does not contend that distributions of power are irrelevant for international regimes. They only suggest that as time passes and interdependence increases, importance of military power slowly decreases. For, even though regimes 'are established and organized in conformity with distribution of capabilities...subsequently the relevant networks, rules, norms and institutions will themselves influence the actors' abilities to use these capabilities'. Finally, their treatment of international regimes bears out the propriety of the title of their book, because in spite of power remaining an important determinant of the formation and maintenance of regimes, 'it must be complemented with an appreciation of the variety of issues facing states in a world of *interdependence*'.[21]

Moravcsik says that even though both in *TRAWP* and *PAIWPIT*, Keohane raised the question of 'how and why institutions alter the behaviour of states', he left the explanation of it to a 'broadening inductive mode' rather than to a 'micro-foundationally grounded' one. But in *AH*,[22] he remained 'tightly focused on developing a rigorous theoretical answer to this question, even if it means setting aside other factors that might be relevant in explaining international cooperation', only to formulate 'the problem of cooperation in a more tractable form'.[23] He starts with how 'dismal' seem efforts to write about international cooperation in books of political studies, and how even the clarification that the 'book would also discuss discord, a much more common feature of world politics' failed to change the advice of a former teacher to make it 'short'. Keohane says justifying the advice that in spite of the record of extensive international cooperation among the advanced industrialized countries since the end of the Second World War, unparalleled by 'any period of comparable length in history', 'cooperation remains scarce relative to discord'. For, despite 'the rapid growth of international economic interdependence since 1945, and the increasing involvement of governments in the operation of modern capitalist economies', sources of 'potential friction' remain if do not increase. This is because interdependence 'can transmit bad influences as well as good ones'.[24] Anyway, since Keohane actually wrote a 290-page book even without large fonts or wide margins, we have to summarize his central arguments in *AH*.

To point out how difficult it is to stabilize international cooperation even in the backdrop of shared interests of states in the context of interdependence, Keohane referred to the game-theoretic concept of PD and the arguments of Mancur Olson Jr. regarding the logic of collective action, which is similar in its essentials to this logic of PD.[25] Having discussed it before,[26] I skip it, save stating the moral and the lesson that in the resultant array of interests, none of the superpowers will desist from clandestine nuclear arms stockpiling even after knowing that it will be mutually counterproductive, representing the so-called Nash equilibrium. But Keohane reminds us that 'the apparently compelling conclusion—that defecting is a dominant strategy—depends on the assumption that the game is only played once, or at most a small number of times'. So if and when 'the game is played repeatedly by the same players', that is, 'iterated', it might look different and 'players may rationally cooperate' for two reasons. First, in 'multiple-play' versions of the game, 'defection is in the long run unrewarding, since the short-run gains thus obtained will normally be outweighed by the mutual punishment that will ensue over the long run'.[27] Second, as Olson deduced from his studies on provision of collective (public) goods, for large groups aiming at these, stringing themselves together is very difficult 'since each member would have an incentive not to contribute to provision of the good'. But small groups would not be similarly hamstrung. And while current IR are similarly marked by dilemmas of collective action, they 'are rendered less intractable by the small number of states involved' (not more than 150 states even global negotiations). Besides, finding themselves repeatedly in the same band of interests in such less-than-large groups, the major actors know that 'when decisions to contribute are not made only once but are taken frequently over time, it may pay to cooperate because otherwise one's partners may defect, leaving oneself worse off'. This proves that even in situations marked by the Olsonian logic of free riding on collective goods or PD, strategic interaction permits cooperation.[28]

Accordingly, to Keohane, the rational choice analysis forming the epistemological core of *AH* does not accept that 'cooperation must be rare in world politics' and shows instead that 'it can be pursued even by purely rational, narrowly self-interested governments, unmoved by idealistic concern for the common good or by ideological commitment to a certain pattern of IR'. But still the truth remains that cooperation is facilitated by regimes, not always created by hegemonic powers. Both in the presence and absence of hegemons, 'international regimes depend on the existence of patterns of common or complementary interests that are perceived or capable of being perceived by political actors', and the intensive cooperation born of this perception among a few actors may substitute for the initiatives of a hegemon. This is why when a hegemon's clout weakens, we witness post-hegemonic cooperation. Here, incentives to construct international regimes may emanate from the propulsion of shared interests that may help actors envision the gains to be secured by pursuing others more vigorously.[29] Regimes being so important, the issues of their effects and the conditions of their successful formation are also pertinent. Let us first move to Keohane's views on regime effects.

Regime Effects

Keohane says that much like 'oligopolistic quasi-agreements', the general effect of regimes is reduction of costs of transactions related to the negotiation, monitoring and enforcement of cooperative agreements.[30] These effects materialize via the following processes:

1. Regularization of international politics and issues into an inclusive framework of bargaining and the resultant reduction of transaction costs. By forbidding certain agreements (as GATT does for 'discriminating trade arrangements except under certain specific conditions'), regimes exalt 'injunctions to the level of principles and rules' and, thus, 'construct linkages between issues', so that no discriminatory agreement remains a 'particular act, without general significance'. In game-theoretic terms, the situation has been changed from single play to iterative, while in the language of market failure, 'transaction costs of certain possible bargains' rise, while the costs of others get lower.[31] International economic regimes reduce transaction costs by 'making it cheaper for governments to get together to negotiate agreements' through their ingrained tendency to 'incorporate international organizations that provide forums for meetings and secretariats that can act as catalysts for agreement'. As a corollary to this, international regimes help governments to utilize potential economies of scale, partly by reducing the 'marginal cost of dealing with each additional issue'. So unsurprisingly, 'specific agreements tend to be "nested" within regimes', which in turn 'affect transaction costs by making it easier or more difficult to link particular issues and to arrange side payments, giving someone something on one issue in return for her help on another'. The bunching of issues under a regime facilitates or incommodes the linking of particular issues to organize side payments among them. Even bureaucratic costs of transactions are brought down by regimes, because 'successful regimes organize issue areas' in a way that encourages 'agreements consistent with the principles of the regime' and discourages others.[32]
2. Facilitation of cooperative international agreements by increasing information and thereby reducing uncertainty. Market failure literature provides the key insight that due to the desideratum of appropriate institutions, some mutually beneficial bargains are never made. The crucial limiting factors are 'uncertainty, asymmetrical information, moral hazard and irresponsibility',[33]

all addressed by regimes' supply of information to members, as brought out by studies and researches on market failure. Against these, the norms and regulations of a regime 'reduce the range of expected behaviour and uncertainty declines, and as information becomes more widely available, the asymmetry of its distribution is likely to lessen'. The concatenation of issues brought about by regimes heightens 'the costs of deception and irresponsibility', because the derivative effects of such behaviour are prone to travel beyond the immediate issue of their expression to others.

3. Reduction of distrust between governments, which is an integral part of the anarchy problematique, also a result of the informational change. In Keohane's terms, 'Close ties among officials involved in managing international regimes increase the ability of governments to make mutually beneficial agreements, because intergovernmental relationships characterized by ongoing communication among working-level officials, informal as well as formal, are inherently more conducive to exchange of information than are traditional relationships between closed bureaucracies'. In a situation where the fear of 'being double-crossed' decreases, cooperation increasingly seems sensible.
4. Regimes are of great use to governments because of the above-mentioned effects. Let alone posing 'threats to governments (in which case it would be hard to understand why they exist at all), they permit governments to attain objectives that would otherwise be unattainable'. They facilitate 'intergovernmental agreements...by raising the anticipated costs of violating others' property rights, by altering transaction costs through the clustering of issues and by providing reliable information to members.[34]

But from his close study of the politics of oil and energy, Keohane was loth to 'view regimes and their international organizations' in a post-hegemonic world as kinds of 'hierarchies or quasi-governments' equipped with enforceable rules and decision-making powers. He rather preferred to give priority to the rules contained in them that 'legitimize cooperation' or act 'as guidelines for it' through their symbolic character. This is because 'cooperation, which involves mutual adjustment of the policies of independent actors, is not enforced by hierarchical authority'.[35] The coordinating and 'information-producing patterns of action...embedded in international regimes' largely explains why 'the erosion of American hegemony during the 1970s was not accompanied by an immediate collapse of cooperation, as the crude theory of hegemonic stability would have predicted'. The 'level of institutionalization of post-war regimes' being much higher than their historical predecessors, 'with intricate and extensive networks of communication among working-level officials', it was legitimate to expect 'the time lag between the decline of American hegemony and the disruption of international regimes to be quite long and the "inertia" of the existing regimes relatively great'.[36]

Regime Formation

Having done with regime effects, Keohane turned to the situational requirements of regime formation, since the functionality of regimes does not ease their formation. The factors of transaction costs and uncertainty only imply that 'regimes are easier to maintain than they are to create. Complementary interests are necessary but not sufficient conditions for their emergence'. The incentives to their construction range from proactive efforts by a hegemon, as was the case historically for the IMF and GATT after the Second World War, to 'the pressures of a sudden and severe crisis', as in the case of the International Energy Agency. But after a regime gets established, the benefits it begets of 'the relatively high and symmetrical level of information' and the easier conduct of 'regime-supporting bargains' help its survival.[37]

The cost factor and the insufficiency of shared interests generate other requirements of regime formation. While lesser costs and greater associated benefits make regimes easier to build, the cost–benefit ratio itself is deeply dependent on the degree of interdependence in an issue area. See how the factor of interdependence is only indirectly illustrated by Keohane in terms of 'issue density':

> The incentives to form international regimes will be greater in dense policy spaces than in areas with lower issue density, owing to the fact that ad hoc agreements in a dense policy space will tend to interfere with one another, unless they are based on a common set of principles and rules. Where issue density is low, ad hoc agreements may well be sufficient; but where it is high, regimes will reduce the costs of continually taking into account the effect of one set of agreements on others.[38]

The interdependence logic gains importance also from another fact. As Keohane shows, 'Regimes rarely emerge from chaos; on the contrary, they are built on one another'.[39] But Keohane also makes the very perceptive point that if regimes were costless to build, there would be little point in constructing them'. For, then 'agreements would also be costless' and, waiting till specific problems appeared, necessitating agreements to deal with them, governments would have no incentives to build international regimes to smoothen cooperative agreements. 'It is precisely the costliness of agreements, and of regimes themselves, that make them important. The high costs of regime building also help existing regimes to persist'.[40]

Other Theorists of Regimes

Krasner's view of international regimes too does not forsake realist perspectives. He identifies two distinct structural realist strands of it: (a) 'the billiard ball version, focuses purely on interaction among states', and (b) 'the tectonic plates version (which he labelled as "modified structural" viewpoint), focuses on the relationship between the distribution of power and various international environments'. It is the latter strand that shows the importance and relevance of regimes even in a realist framework and 'also opens the possibility for viewing regimes as autonomous, not just as intervening, variables'. In the backdrop of possible 'lags between changes in basic causal variables and regime change', and 'feedback from regimes to basic causal variables', both 'lags and feedback suggest importance for regimes that would be rejected by conventional structural arguments'.[41] Remarkably, apart from Young, Hopkins, and Puchala (who view regimes from a Groatian perspective as 'a pervasive characteristic of the international system', since it is not possible for any 'patterned behaviour' to 'sustain itself for any length of time without generating a congruent regime'), and

Strange (already cited as a critic of regimes as a fuzzy and woolly concept), the majority of contributors in Krasner's edited volume have written from a 'modified structural' viewpoint. Krasner's project started with this basic assumption that as 'intervening variables standing between basic causal variables (most prominently power and interests) and outcomes and behaviour, regimes 'do not rise of their own accord', are not viewed 'as ends in themselves', are not 'merely epiphenomenal' and once founded, 'affect related behaviour and outcomes'. The five causal variables that account for or help the rise of regimes are: (a) egoistic self-interest; (b) political power, understood less as power 'in the service of the common good' and more as facilitator of 'particular interests'; (c) norms and principles that are not necessarily 'endogenous' but are also exogenous or existing outside the regime being contemplated for creation; (d) usage and custom, also exogenous and (e) knowledge.[42]

CONTESTATIONS OF KEOHANE, OTHER APPROACHES/ ALTERNATIVES TO REGIME ANALYSIS

Expectedly, the Groatian, modified structural realist, and functional perspectives (Keohane figures in both) on the explanation of regime development and regime consequences left many scholars dissatisfied and in the 1980s, a vibrant debate on Keohane's version of regime theory generated a slew of competing theories, grouped together differently by different commentators. Zangl has identified them as (a) the theory of hegemonic stability, (b) the situational structure theory, (c) the two-level approach, (d) the problem structure approach (e) approaches built around epistemic communities. While stating them in the order set by him,[43] I will add a few points from the extant literature.

1. All through *AH*, Keohane has sought to keep the *theory of hegemonic stability* as an explanation of regime formation at a far remove,[44] because of the weak empirical evidence for its general validity, its 'simplistic starting point for an analysis of changes in international cooperation and discord',[45] its 'unsatisfactory explanation of regime change in international monetary relations', its failure 'to explain recent changes in international trade regimes' compared with its relative success in explaining changes in oil regimes[46] and many other reasons. Yet proponents of HST itself claim to provide a form of regime theory, and they quote Kindleberger and Krasner to point out that while this theory 'ascribes no independent effect to international regimes, it can still help analyse their formation. For, it claims that 'international regimes can be maintained only as long as the hegemon is able to maintain his/her superior power position'.[47]

   Truly, all through 'State Power', Krasner never so much as mentions regimes but argues that just as 'a system composed of a large number of small, highly developed states...is likely to lead to an open international trading structure', a hegemonic system too favours an open structure, since the hegemon 'will have a preference' for it, and at a 'symbolic level, the hegemonic state stands as an example of how economic development can be achieved. Its policies may be emulated even if they are inappropriate for other states'. And he says that more 'importantly, the hegemonic state can use its economic resources to create an open structure'.[48]

2. The *situation structure* or *game theory* offers a competing theory of regimes that moves beyond Keohane's clever employment of its PD logic to argue that international regimes can emanate from a diverse bunch of interests that exemplify both a common interest in cooperation and an individual concern for self-help. This approach discusses many of these 'mixed motive constellations' that allow the emergence of regimes to various extents. These arrays of interest typify both 'coordination' games and 'dilemma' games. While 'dilemma' games try to show that their cooperation would be rewarded only by deceit and deception by others, all the concerned states consider reneging on existing cooperation agreements beneficial, in 'coordination' games, the concerned actors have no such incentive and no such fear. Here, the formation of regimes is incommoded only by different states' preference for different cooperative agreements, even regimes.
3. The 'two-level approach' is still another approach that fine-tunes Keohane's conception of regimes. The core idea of this approach is that 'the interplay between the constellations of interests *among* states and *within* states' facilitates the rise of international regimes in different issue areas of international politics. This compels national leaders to take simultaneous initiatives both at the national and international planes, bargain externally with other states from the perspectives of national interests but ascertain internally if the proposed regimes are congruent with these interests. To show how statesmen do so, Moravcsik cited the experiences of the 1933 World Economic Conference in London, the European Commission meeting in 1986 in the context of the US threat to block agricultural imports from Europe, the efforts by Gorbachev in post-liberalization Russia to 'use massive unilateral concessions' worldwide 'to gain Western aid needed to carry out *glasnost* and *perestroika*' in Russia as a modification of Brezhnev's 'inconsistent policy of reconciliation in Europe and rivalry in the Third World' and eight other case studies. With insights derived from Robert Putnam's metaphor of 'two-level games', applied to these 11 case studies, Moravcsik says that the 'question facing IR theorists today is not *whether* to combine domestic and international explanations into a theory of "double-edged diplomacy" but *how* to do so'.[49]
4. The *problem structure approach* represents the core belief that 'regimes are instruments for the cooperative processing of conflicts' and the chance of their formation 'varies depending on the prevailing object of conflict within a given issue area of international conflict'. In cases where conflicts involve divergent values so that 'states cannot identify common goals' regarding them, the probability of regime formation is very weak. But in situations where conflicts involve means, regime formation is far more likely. Where conflicts concern interests, 'the probability of regime formation depends on how a given object of conflict is evaluated'. If it is assessed in light of 'the proportion of the object of conflict accounted for by other states' (as seen in an arms race), then probability is nearly as bleak as in the case of value-based conflicts. But where the conflict is evaluated in absolute terms, in the

sense that states bother only about the share of the pie they get, regardless of how much other states obtain (as exemplified by the environmental benefit of clean air), the chances of regime formation are even greater than in conflicts over means.[50]

5. At the farthest from Keohane's formulation of regime theory is the approach based on *epistemic communities*, which traces the formation of regimes predominantly in the distribution of knowledge systems within the particular issue context. Epistemic communities are usually transnational 'coalitions of scientists and policymakers', sharing 'a common understanding of the nature of the problem and appropriate solutions' and making 'a concerted effort to inject their point of view into the process of regime formation'. Young says 'such communities regularly constitute important presence in cases of success'.[51] Haas finds these communities 'causally implicated in the form and persistence of regimes', as evidenced in the 19th-century free trade, Bretton Woods, the New International Economic Order, a liberal post-post-Second World War trading Order and international environmental regimes. He claims, citing considerable researches, that ever since the 1970s, regimes that have proliferated arrived only through a process of social learning, which is why 'regimes negotiated in the shadow of epistemic communities and strong international institutions' alone 'have yielded patterns of comprehensive environmental management through a process of social learning'.[52] But the fact remains that this approach is the weakest in the sphere of regime effects. As Ward, Grundig, and Zorick complain, it is on the basis of simple deduction from a relatively small number of cases that scholars of this field claim that the influence of the academics who have coalesced will be at its greatest when 'the problem is complex and uncertainty is high, there is a perception of crisis and politicians are looking for new solutions, the internal consensus in the community is great and its members are highly regarded within their professions and members of the community come to occupy important bureaucratic roles within states'. But empirical researchers have identified a 'significant minority of regimes', which 'exists even in situations where the regime has failed to serve as an arena for learning'.[53]

Haggard and Simmons look at theories on regimes in the light of their dimensions of: (a) strength as 'measured by the degree of compliance with regime injunctions', against 'short-term or myopic self-interests'; (b) organizational form, meant as 'at least some minimal administrative apparatus' for settling disputes, gathering or sharing information and maintaining surveillance; (c) scope, signifying 'the range of issues the regime covers' and (d) allocation mode, referring to whether the 'social mechanisms of resource allocation' are 'private', as in 'market-oriented' regimes, or 'authoritative', as in 'more extensive, and potentially autonomous, organizational structures'. From this perspective, the writings on regime development and change can, according to them, be classified into four overlapping 'families': structural, game theoretic, functional and cognitive'.

The first three theory families are 'state centred', presupposing 'unified rational actors', the assumption sometimes 'relaxed only to gain explanatory leverage'. Of them, structural analyses seek to underline how international conditions set the limits for cooperation, and especially in its aspect of HST 'links regime creation and maintenance to a dominant power's existence', and regimes' weakening to its loss of clout. Here, national policies are not deducible from intentions since structures shape and control state behaviour. I have already touched upon it above, among game-theoretic explanations. Functional theories, of which Keohane's *AH* is the most famous statement, have also been covered. So I concentrate on the cognitive approach, touched upon only in the definition of regimes, focusing on intersubjective meaning structures of Weberian vintage as factors that bind actors. Cognitivists contend that even seemingly 'determinative structural constraints' must be assessed 'in terms of historically conditioned interpretative frameworks'. For, the urge for and possibility of cooperation cannot be adequately explained without referring to the actors' ideologies, values and beliefs regarding the interdependence of issues, knowledge of ways to achieve selected goals, perceptions and misperceptions, ability to process information and social learning. Since cognitivists consider a given issue area not as unambiguously given but as open and interpretable, their approach is especially helpful in 'explaining the substantive content of regime' rules and the ways they evolve. The emphasis on actor learning is claimed to provide a new dynamism to regime analysis.[54]

PROPOSED SYNTHESES

After examining these four approaches, Haggard and Simmons make no effort to combine them into a synthetic framework, save suggesting inclusion of 'domestic political processes' in them to facilitate a better understanding of their effect on domestic political determinants of international cooperation'.[55] But having evaluated neoliberalist, realist and cognitivist approaches to regime formation, Hasenclever, Mayer, and Rittberger think 'the possibilities of a synthesis or division of labour among the three schools of thought' to be high and necessary. For, while each of the three schools provides 'a coherent and plausible vision of international regimes' and is able to fortify 'its preferred interpretation with considerable empirical support', there is no empirical evidence 'compelling or strong enough' to declare any one school as a clear victor. The possibilities of a synthesis avowedly arise from the fact that the central variables of these three schools, *interests* (neorealism), *power* (realism) and *knowledge* (cognitivism), 'somehow interact in bringing about and shaping international regimes'. And if they can be 'integrated, with their mutual relationship clearly specified', instead of being 'lumped together', they can form a more complex theory. The first phase of this two-stage synthesis, between principal formulations of neoliberalism and realism, is easier. For, they 'not only share a commitment to rationalism as a metatheoretical stance but may fruitfully work together when it comes to explaining international regimes, thus offering the prospect of a more unified rationalist theory of international institutions' through a kind of 'contextualized' theory. In the second stage, a distinct strand within the cognitivist school, identified as 'weak cognitivism', can be a supplement to, and be incorporated into, a rationalist analysis of international regimes. Here, realism and neoliberalism's view of exogenously given actors' interests might be complemented with weak cognitivism's focus on how interests are internally interpreted. So the second stage of the synthesis will be grounded in the assumption that 'rationalist and cognitive variables represent different links in a causal chain (with cognitive variables either preceding or following rationalist ones).[56]

CRITICISMS OF REGIME THEORY

The sharpest barbs against regime theory came expectedly from neorealism. Grieco contended that neoliberal institutionalism (of which regime theory is a part) 'misconstrues' the realist engagement with the anarchical structures of international politics and overlooks realist insights into the 'impact of anarchy on the preferences and actions of states' due to the misconception about states as 'atomistic' maximizers of their 'individual absolute gains', unconcerned about 'the gains achieved by others' and incommoded in cooperation under anarchy only by cheating. Its removal by international institutions makes cooperation between these atomistic actors likelier. But Grieco argues that for realists even while aiming at absolute gains and worrying about compliance, states are 'positional, not atomistic, in character', and besides 'concerns about cheating', are also anxious if 'their partners might gain more from cooperation than they do'. So a realist state, even when 'satisfied with a partner's compliance in a joint arrangement might nevertheless exit from it because the partner is achieving relatively greater gains'. While realism addresses both the 'major barriers to international cooperation', neoliberal institutionalism 'pays attention exclusively to the former and is unable to identify, analyse or account for the latter'. Realists are lukewarm to joint relative gains as a basis for cooperation from the two fears that 'today's friend may be tomorrow's enemy in war', and 'achievements of joint gains that advantage a friend in the present might produce a more dangerous potential foe in the future'.[57]

From an opposite direction, social constructivists contend that regime theory considers the identities and interests of states as preconceived and a large body of regime theory overlooks 'the crucial link between the costs and benefits of specific legal rules and the role of international law as constitutive of the structure of the state system itself'.[58] From this instrumentalist view, regimes are seen as instrumentalities deployed by states to promote their interests, ignoring the fact that beyond passively reflecting their interests, these regimes are also active agents in their reconfiguration. Although regime theory overlooks this constitutive role of institutions because of visualizing states as pursuers of pre-existing interests in rational ways, rather than unceasingly prosecuting pre-given interests rationally, states sometimes explore in an argumentative mode, together with other states, interests that are congruent with norms embedded in the international system. Neorealist and neoliberal regime theories fail to recognize this because they soft-pedal the role of ideas as solvents of identities and interests. If we start from the neorealist contention that state interests emerge from the material structure of anarchy, then ideas receive a secondary role. This conceptual mistake was repeated by neoliberal regime theory in the 1980s, when it restated the theoretical problem as demonstrating how 'international institutions (which are shared ideas) explained [the] additional variance beyond that explained by material power and interest alone—as if institutions did not also constitute power and interest'. Wendt complains that the mistake is being repeated in recent neoliberal literature about ideas too.[59]

Foucauldian critique of the liberal version of regime theory blames it for the perception of regimes as 'benevolent, voluntary, cooperative and, thus, legitimate associations' and regards it as doubly faulted. First, analytically, however theoretically useful its assumptions might be, they circumscribe the concept of regime in ways that miss 'a full sense of the world as contestable and contested'. Second, ideologically, the approach hides in its assumptions and prescriptions, a 'language of apology or justification, a form of special pleading by and for the powerful and satisfied'.[60] Keeley quotes Strange's contention that the concept of regime 'tends to exclude hidden agendas and to leave unheard or unheeded complaints, whether they come from the underprivileged, the disenfranchised or the unborn, about the way the system works'; that 'government, rulership and authority are the essence of the word, not consensus, nor justice, nor efficiency in administration'; and is mainly an American academic fashion that reflects 'somewhat subjective perceptions in many American minds'.[61]

From this perspective, Keeley berates Krasner's definition of international regimes, which, despite being apparently linked with a 'specific complex of liberal idea' in its exposition, is perusable and pursuable in other non-liberal directions, for example, to depict the formation and operation of the historical Mongol and Athenian Empires, or even to instantiate the theory of hegemonic stability by contending that they supplied a few normal benefits associated with functional explanations of regimes. It purportedly included: 'a system of liabilities, reduced transaction costs, improved information, a stable and predictable environment with less need to hedge and an enforcement mechanism', even if 'these claims of benefits' might 'stick in our throats', partly because it 'offends our sense of what communities are'.

To tease out the non-liberal possibilities of the seemingly liberal approach of Krasner, Keeley shows how couched in a discourse/discipline set, a regime just does not provide shape and order to an Arendtian public realm of action; identify a politicized issue area involving public interest; specify the traits of the occupiers of this realm and delineate the relations in the context of which they judge one another and are judged as providers/recipients of benefits or as 'free riders' while conducting the relevant public business. Also, through a Foucauldian lens, these actors are sorted out and made panoptically 'visible as targets of observation and control...open to inspection and action and, thus, are no longer private'. They are subjected to 'ordering techniques' that render them amenable 'for observing, documenting, classifying, comparing, assessing and individualizing target actors as well as for correcting behaviour, punishing or repressing undesired behaviour and producing desired behaviour'. Where this discourse/discipline set is internalized by actors, pliant conduct with lower enforcement costs results, a situation also captured by 'both Gramscian notions of hegemony and "ideological structuring" in theories of meta-power'. Since regimes are thus foci or loci of struggle, the key question is not only how order is engendered or preserved but also how 'disorder' and resistance can flourish even in the presence of ordering efforts and can even be nurtured by them through rival knowledge not absorbed, subjugated or snuffed out by the hegemonic discourse and its supporting disciplines.

Again, Foucault's concept of sexuality may explain how regimes can lose coherence. Just as regimes and their issue areas can nest and be 'nested' within other regimes through cross-regime linkage patterns and can 'overlap, spread and compete along these connections' to merge with, absorb or be absorbed by other regimes', they can be destabilized by the same forces. Because of the resultant pressures on all-inclusive discourses and orders, the total network may not exhibit a neat and congruent issue ordering. This factor problematizes contentions that single regimes might even order the entire system, where their issue areas and mechanisms are weightier than others.

Foucauldian power/knowledge equation, which systematizes the insights of disciplines and discourses into a capillary network of relations, allows us to see regimes as 'localized power/knowledge—specific arrays of analyses, issue areas and disciplinary devices—in this network'. It would be as misleading to view the order/regime fashioned in this way as a phenomenon of 'framing texts and formal organizations', as to regard international law as 'simply a matter of multilateral conventions'. Leaving deconstruction aside, while constructing a Foucauldian alternative to regime analysis in light of the above-mentioned concepts, the first path-clearing task would be 'to identify contending discourses and techniques and to see how they stand at any one time and how they change over time'.[62]

CONCLUSION

This chapter has discussed the disciplinary context of the emergence of regime theory in the decline of integration theory and the situational context in the debates on the perceived decline of America's hegemonic position since the 1970s. It has shown how different definitions of regimes, and controversies even about Krasner's 1983 consensus definition led by the cognitivists culminated into a revised consensus definition of regimes in the 1990s. It was based on existence of explicit rules in an issue area and actors' recognition to and invocation of them in a positive vein as valid criteria. This chapter has also presented the standard mainstream theories of Keohane and Krasner on regime effects and regime formation and its contestation by Young, Hopkins, and Puchala. But how are we to find a balanced and comprehensive position on regime theory?

In their comprehensive literature survey of regime theory, Levy, Young, and Zürn suggest mainstreaming of the following side-stream traditions of regime analysis: 'the historicism of those who have looked at regimes as path-dependent constructs, the linguistic and legal analyses of those who have endeavoured to sort out different types of rules and the CT of those who see regimes as expressions of larger social forces at work in human affairs'. They suggest that the challenge before regime theorists is 'to devise methods for drawing on both of these streams of analysis (the neo-positivist and the postpositivist)' for 'developing a deeper understanding of international regimes than either body of work alone can support'. Despite the intimidating difficulties of the task, owing to the incongruities of the findings of the rationalists and the reflexivists, and the proneness of 'both groups to disparage the contributions of the other', the future potentials of regime analysis may well depend greatly on our ingeniousness 'to find the language and analytic procedures needed to bridge this gap'.[63]

REVIEW QUESTIONS

1. Trace out the disciplinary and contextual factors operative behind the emergence of regime theory.
2. Comment on the different definitions of regime in different approaches and the possibilities of a consensus definition.
3. Delineate Keohane and Krasner's versions of regime theory and their shortcomings.
4. Summarize the neorealist, social constructivist and Foucauldian critiques of regime theory and comment on the need to incorporate the reflexivist insights into regime analysis in its mainstream.

NOTES AND REFERENCES

1. Stephen Haggard and Beth A. Simmons, 'Theories of International Regimes', *International Organization* 41, no. 3 (Summer 1987): 491–517, esp. 492; Bernhard Zangl, 'Regime Theory', in *Theories of International Relations*, eds Siegfried Schieder and Manuela Spindler (Abingdon: Routledge, 2014), 76–77.
2. Susan Strange, 'Cave! *hic dragones*: A Critique of Regime Analysis', *International Organization* 36, no. 2 (Spring 1982): 479–496, esp. 484–485, available at http://www.jstor.org/stable/2706530 (accessed on 8 August 2018).
3. See J. G. Ruggie, 'International Responses to Technology: Concepts and Trends', *International Organization*' 29, no. 3 (1975): 557–583, here 570, available at https://www.jstor.org/stable/2706342 (accessed on 20 June 2020).
4. Keohane and Nye, *Power and Interdependence* (1977), 19.
5. Stephen D. Krasner, 'Structural Causes and Regime Consequences: Regimes as Intervening Variables', *International Organization* 36, no. 2 (1982): 185–205, esp. 186, available at www.jstor.org/stable/2706520 (accessed 21 June 2020).
6. Oran Young, 'International Regimes: Toward a New Theory of Institutions', *World Politics* 39, no. 1 (1986): 105–106.
7. Marc A. Levy, Oran R. Young, and Michael Zürn, 'The Study of International Regimes', *European Journal of International Relations* 1, no. 3 (September 1995): 267–330 esp. 271–272.
8. Robert Keohane, *International Institutions and State Power* (Boulder, CO: Westview Press, 1989), 4, cited in Andreas Hasenclever, Peter Mayer, and Volker Rittberger, 'Interests, Power, Knowledge: The Study of International Regimes', *Mershon International Studies Review* 40, no. 2 (October 1996): 177–228, esp. 180.
9. O. Young, *International Cooperation: Building Regimes for Natural Resources and the Environment* (Ithaca, NY: Cornell University Press, 1989), 13–15.
10. M. Zacher, 'Trade Gaps, Analytical Gaps, Regime Analysis and International Commodity Trade Regulation', *International Organization* 41, no. 2 (1987): 173–202, esp. 174.
11. For these citations, see Andreas Hasenclever, Peter Mayer, and Volker Rittberger, *Theories of International Regimes* (Cambridge: Cambridge University Press, 2006), 15–16.
12. Donald Puchala and Raymond Hopkins, 'International Regimes: Lessons from Inductive Analysis', in *International Regimes*, ed. Stephen D. Krasner (Ithaca, NY: Cornell University Press, 1985), 63.
13. Friedrich Kratochwil and John Gerard Ruggie, 'International Organization: A State of the Art or an Art of the State', *International Organization* 40, no. 4 (Autumn 1986): 759, 764–767.

14. R. Keohane, 'The Analysis of International Regimes: Towards a European-American Research Programme', in *Regime Theory and International Relations*, ed. Volker Rittberger (Oxford: Clarendon Press, 1993), 27, cited in Hasenclever, Mayer, and Rittberger, *Theories of*, 17–18.
15. Volker Rittberger, 'Introduction', in *Regime Theory and International Relations*, ed. Volker Rittberger (Oxford: Clarendon Press, 1993), 10–11; R. Keohane, 'The Analysis', in *Regime Theory and International Relations*, ed. Volker Rittberger (Oxford: Clarendon Press, 1993), 28, cited by Dimitrios Anagnostakis, *EC-US Cooperation on Internal Security: Building a Transatlantic Regime* (London: Routledge, 2017), 24.
16. Keohane and Nye, *Power and Interdependence*, 38–58; Keohane and Nye, 'Power and Interdependence Revisited', 732–733.
17. See Walker, 'A Circumspect Revival' and Keohane and Nye, 'Power and Interdependence Revisited' on 'theories of interdependence'.
18. Keohane and Nye, *Power and Interdependence*, 5.
19. Ibid., 58–60.
20. Michael Suhr, 'Robert O. Keohane: A Contemporary Classic', in *The Future of International Relations: Masters in the Making?* eds Iver B. Neumann and Ole Waever (London: Routledge, 1997), 94.
21. Walker, 'A Circumspect Revival', 151.
22. Keohane, *After Hegemony*.
23. Moravcsik, 'Robert Keohane', 251.
24. Keohane, *After Hegemony*, 5.
25. Ibid., 67–69.
26. See Allan and Dupont, 'International Relations'; Duncan Luce and Raiffa, *Games and Decisions*; Peterson, 'Introduction'; Campbell, 'Introduction'; Morrow, 'The Strategic Choice'; Brams, *Negotiation Games* on game theory; All referred to in Chapter 11 (Game Theory) and Waltz's reference to Rousseau's tale of the stag hunters, which echoes the logic of PD in Jervis, 'Cooperation under the Security Dilemma'; All referred to in Chapter 5 (Neorealism).
27. Keohane, *After Hegemony*, 75.
28. Ibid., 76–77.
29. Ibid., Chapter 3, 31–46, 78–79.
30. Ibid., 89.
31. Ibid.
32. Ibid., 90–92.
33. Ibid., 94.
34. Ibid., 97.
35. Ibid., 237.
36. Ibid., 101.
37. Ibid., 100.
38. Ibid., 79
39. Ibid., 80.
40. Ibid., 101–102.
41. S. Krasner, 'Regimes and the Limits of Realism: Regimes as Autonomous Variables', *International Organization* 36, no. 2 (1982): 497–510, available at https://doi.org/10.1017/S0020818300019032 (accessed on 6 August 2018).
42. S. Krasner, 'Structural Causes and Regime Consequences', in *International Regimes*, ed. Stephen D. Krasner (Ithaca, NY: Cornell University Press, 1985), 1–2, 5–6, 10–21.
43. Zangl, 'Regime Theory', 82–84.
44. Keohane, *After Hegemony*, 34–41, 184, 198, 201–202, 207–209, 213.
45. Ibid., 38–39.
46. Ibid., 213.

47. Charles P. Kindleberger, 'Systems of International Economic Organization', in *Money and the Coming World Order*, eds David P. Calleo and Harold B. van Cleveland (New York, NY: New York University Press, 1976); Steven B. Krasner, 'State Power and the Structure of International Trade', *World Politics* 28, no. 3 (1976), 317–347.
48. See Krasner, 'State Power', 321–323.
49. See Zangl, 'Regime Theory', 83; A. Moravcsik, 'Introduction: Integrating International and Domestic Theories of International Bargaining', in *Double-Edged Diplomacy: International Bargaining and Domestic Politics*, eds Peter B. Evan, Harold K. Jacobson, and Robert D Putnam (Berkeley, CA: University of California Press, 1993), 3–9.
50. V. Rittberger and M. Zürn, 'Towards Regulated Anarchy in East-West Relations: Causes and Consequences of East-West Regimes', in *International Regimes in East-West Politics*, ed. V. Rittberger (London: Pinter, 1990), 9–63, cited in Zangl, 'Regime Theory', 83.
51. Oran R. Young, *International Governance: Protecting the Environment in a Stateless Society* (Ithaca, NY: Cornell University Press, 1994), 96.
52. Peter M. Haas, *Epistemic Communities, Constructivism, and International Environmental Politics* (London: Routledge, 2016), 17, 175.
53. Hugh Ward, Grank Grundig, and Ethan Zorick, 'Formal Theory and Regime Effectiveness', in *Regime Consequences: Methodological Challenges and Research Strategies*, eds A. Underdal and Oran R. Young (New York, NY: Kluwer Academic Publishers, 2004), 171.
54. Haggard and Simmons, 'Theories of International Regimes', 499–500, 509–511; Kratochwil and Ruggie, 'International Organization'.
55. Ibid., 513.
56. Andreas Hasenclever, Peter Mayer, and Volker Rittberger, 'Integrating Theories of International Regimes', 26, no. 1 (January 2000): 3–33, esp. 5–6 and 33.
57. Joseph M. Grieco, 'Anarchy and the Limits of Cooperation: A Realist Critique of the Newest Liberal Institutionalism', *International Organization* 42, no. 3 (1988): 485–507, esp. 486.
58. Andrew Hurrell, 'International Society and the Study of Regimes: A Reflective Approach', in *Regime Theory in International Relations*, ed. Volker Rittberger (Oxford: Clarendon Press, 1993), 49–72, cited in Levy, Young, and Zürn, 'Study of International Regimes', 271.
59. Alexander Wendt, *Social Theory of International Politics* (Cambridge: Cambridge University Press, 1999), 10.
60. James F. Keeley, 'Toward a Foucauldian Analysis of International Regimes', *International Organization* 44, no. 1 (Winter 1990): 83–105.
61. See Strange, 'Cave! *hic dragones*', 480–481, 486.
62. Keeley, 'Foucauldian Analysis', 95–98.
63. Levy, Young, and Zürn, 'Study of International Regimes', 318.

SECTION 3

THEORIES OF THE GLOBALIST PARADIGM

CHAPTER

16

Marxism and Its Variants in International Relations Theory

INTERROGATING AVOIDANCE OF MARXISM IN IR

The ambivalence about Marxism in IRT is unmatched by any other theory or approach. Actually, apart from an indirect entry through neo-Marxist historian Carr's writing during the interwar First Great Debate,[1] Marxism suffered a silence here that was only partly broken by the onset of the triangular 'interparadigm debate' or the Third Great Debate of the late 1970s–1980s. For, even there, Marxism remained relatively subdued, since the debate was not really triangular, most of the parleys having had been between realism and liberalism.[2] Things again worsened after the collapse of the Soviet Union and the East European satellite socialist regimes in the late 1980s, which brought official Soviet Bolshevism into disrepute, but whose stigma stuck with theoretical Marxism too. The global triumph of 'free-market' capitalism, signified by the end of the Cold War, put paid to the hopes of Marxists for the end of international capitalism and fed fuel to the common-sense belief about the *fin de siècle* of the 19th-century radical optimism. The talk about the 'end of history' suggested that the ideas of Marx and other Marxist thinkers could now be safely dumped in the garbage can of history. Despite holding on to political power in China, Vietnam and Cuba, let alone posing a threat to the smug triumph of the global capitalist system, communist parties, particularly the CPC, was adopting the market logic under oxymoronic slogans like the 'socialist market economy'.

But even before this contextual, practical-level rejection, Marxism was largely kept aside from the English-American academic domain. So unlike the pattern followed throughout this book of presenting the critique of a theory after its statement, I would, in this chapter, state the critique first. Marxism's banishment from the English-American academic domain was sought to be legitimated on the following grounds. First, it was avowedly difficult to fit Marx's and Engels's thoughts in the entrenched habits of thought and theoretical traditions of IR. Having never given primacy to interstate relations in their analyses and having differentiated human societies from one another on the basis of labour relations and production relations, Marxism was kind of incongruous in IR. Kaldor says that there is no explicit Marxist theory of IR because there is no undergirding Marxist theory of the state.[3] Second, in arguing that production relations and mode of production were the most important in the shaping of a socio-historical formation, Marxism questioned the very basis of IR. Third, giving overemphasis on economic factors even at the international level, it ignored those political and security-related issues which were central to the scope and subject matter of IR. It had no contribution in the three great debates either, silence on the third debate being more damning, because it was Marx who first showed how capitalism created a global market and class forces operative at the global level. Fourth, Marxism underestimated the impact of nationalism, war, BOP, international law and the structure of world politics, which are the most conventional issues in IR. Fifth, Marx was said to be never much interested in IR. Kubálková and Cruickshank say that the 'main difficulty in studying Marx's ideas on international relations seems to be that he paid such small *explicit* attention to them'.[4] Brown says less dismissively that the 'celebrated—if controversial—metaphor of "base" and "superstructure", outlined most effectively in the preface to *A Critiques of Political Economy*, posits the state as part of the superstructure and implies that IR, defined here as interstate relations, are even further away from the base, "the economic structure of society, the real foundation"'. However, this betokened no disinterest in either the State or IR. Both Marx and Engels 'were deeply involved in foreign affairs and wrote extensively about them'. Only they did so 'mainly as journalists' and 'produced no "Marxist theory" of the state or IR'. And when their immediate successors 'did create such a theory, it was one-sided and positivist, imbued with "economism" and shorn of all ethical overtones'.[5] So the consensus of the detractors is that there is no point in dragging either Marx (or Engels) into an alien, inhospitable field.

Detractors' aversion was 'compounded by the dogmatisms, polemics and simplifications' of Marxist ideas forcefully propagated by official Marxists seeking or clinging to political power,[6] even as one commentator speaks of the lack of a 'significant body of literature which has integrated Marxist insights with the IR literature in English', save two exceptional endeavours by Linklater and Rosenberg.[7]

Yet the spectre of Marxism refused to disappear from the precincts of academic IR, this again for many reasons. First, in spite of its apparent threat to academic orthodoxies, Marxism was also one of the proud legatees of the radical liberating ethic bequeathed by Enlightenment. Besides, together with other social sciences beyond economics, Marxism was a sophisticated response to the problems of the social life generated by the Industrial Revolution. So some of its insights and ideas not only created a Marxist countertrend in these disciplines but found universal acceptance there and a broader process of diffusion of its ideas made Marxism what Gramsci so aptly described, 'the common sense of our epoch'.

Second, although during the Stalinist phase of Soviet Bolshevism, communist rule was as distant from the historical-teleological and messianic content of Marxism as was the Sermon on the Mount from the Vatican, after the break-up of the Soviet state and the breakdown of its communist model, the historical-teleological and emancipatory content of Marxist thought could be resurrected as the Sermon. It rid Marxists of a major and nagging source of moral embarrassment. They could now argue that Marxism need not be equated with the politics and policies of communist party states. With a new clean slate or *tabula rasa*, it became again conceivable to speak about the application of Marx's ideas without having been burdened by lapses of erring governments and parties distorting them for their aggrandizement. As Halliday puts it boldly, 'If realism can detach itself from its cousins—social Darwinism, racism and *Machtpolitik*—so can an interpretive Marxism be distinguished from instrumental companion'.[8] This is more so because as Hobden and Jones point out, 'Marx's social theory retains formidable analytical purchase on the world we inhabit'. At a time when the globalizing tentacles of the market mechanism are invading all aspects of our lives, Marx's 'forensic examination of both the extraordinary dynamism and the inherent contradictions of capitalism' acquires even greater salience than in his times. And particularly important now are Marx's insights into the crises of capitalism, which, against liberal hopes of the automatic movement of the free market towards equilibrium and of its quintessential stability, have now faced us with the stock market crash of 1987, the Asian Financial Crisis of the late 1990s, and the 'credit crunch' and global meltdown of 2008–2009, whose effects are felt even now.[9]

But to distinguish Marxism from deviant socialist state practices, we need to foreground the original ideas/words of Marx and Engels themselves, and to a lesser extent of independent Marxists who wanted to keep intact the integrity of their ideas even while creatively applying them (such as Lenin and Gramsci). Besides, while exploring the ways these ideas help reconstruct/reconstitute IR theoretically, we have to remember that this exercise generates, as Thorndike says, 'a problem and a puzzle'. The problem, stated empirically, is the prevalence of a state-centric international system, where, against the clear Marxist prophecy about an eventual post-capitalist stateless society, both socialist and capitalist states coexisted and socialist states enthusiastically acquiesce in this juxtaposition, till some of them did kind of 'wither away'. Until then, both the types of states were mainly differentiated by ideology, although viewed in original Marxist terms, ideology emanates from the material conditions of life and to that extent, involves 'false consciousness', apart from being a 'screen for reality'. The puzzle following from this is that 'despite its significance, the study of IR has rarely been framed in a true Marxist manner', both as a methodology and as a conceptual framework, although in both cases it could be far more profitably used. The attacks on state centricity came from the writings of interdependence, pluralist and even systems theorists such as Keohane and Nye, Rosenau and Burton (whom I have referred to before in and different contexts of interdependence/pluralism). Even the resurgence of interest in issues of IPE and in the economic aspects of foreign policy as in the writings of Gardner, Strange, Knorr and Kindleberger does not have a strictly Marxist provenance.[10] To posit that in the world out there 'economic and political factors are constantly interacting and are extremely hard to disentangle from each other', Strange did not need to embrace Marxism.[11] So what was the utility of Marxism in theorizing IR in the 1970s or is even now?

Some would argue that the utilization of the Marxist methodology still 'makes for a deeper degree of scrutiny—and for a greater relevance—in pursuit of such alternative and non-traditional *Gestalen*'. Its criticism for overemphasis on the economic system as the determinant element of the structure of IPE, making the political as the short-term epiphenomenal process, overlooks that the methodological foundations of Marxist studies can provide a sense of unity, direction and purpose to the study of the interdigitations of economic and political elements, apart from throwing up new paradigmatic lines of enquiry into 'major concerns of IR such as war and peace, nationalism, international law and morality, and the state'.[12] And just as an independent Marxist leaven has fermented a new and analytically fruitful body of work in sociology, history and other social sciences, it possesses the potential to fertilize new areas of thoughts in IR too. But to unearth this unexplored potential, we should focus more on its main theoretical plank, the materialistic interpretation of history, shortly called historical materialism.

INTERROGATING PARTIAL AND REDUCTIONIST ACCOMMODATION OF MARXISM IN IR THROUGH CT AND STRUCTURALISM

In spite of the manifold potentialities of the interaction of historical materialism with the discipline of IR, the fault for scanty work on it is as much of the discipline as of Marxism. Speaking disciplinarily, since the 1970s, writers who have wanted to discover possible points of contact between the two, whether for a general Marxist tingeing of IR or for identification of discrete domains where IR as presently formatted as an analytical discipline can accommodate it, have sought to cull select elements within historical materialism. For example, Linklater (mentioned above) explored the implications of developing a 'critical' Marxism for IR. But as I will show in **Chapter 24**, CT, in caps, does not differ just from Soviet Marxism. It has points of departure from classical Marxism too.[13]

Regarding structuralism, when in the 1970s and early 1980s, academic IR opened the door slightly for Marxism in course of the interparadigm debate through a reduction of historical materialism to it, this limited the scope of Marxism due to three reasons. First, as a concept that originated in linguistics and anthropology before travelling to IR, structuralism is more deterministic, because of leaving no scope for freedom of action or agency against the structure.[14] Of course, Marxism shares some common features with structuralism as a concept of causality opposed to empiricism and the Althusserian version of Marxism is structural. As Godelier contends, while comparing Marx's and Lévi-Strauss's versions of structuralism, that 'for Marx, as for Claude Lévi-Strauss…"Structures" should not be confused with visible "social relations" but constitute a level of reality invisible but present behind the visible social relations'. To this extent, Marx 'inaugurates the modern structuralist tradition. And he is fully in accord with this tradition when he proposes the priority of the study of structures over that of their genesis and evolution'.[15] But despite its apparent concession to structuralism because of its concern with 'iron laws' of history and the primacy of socio-economic components it posits, Marxism allows some scope for freedom of action and even some voluntarism, inasmuch as it envisions a specific moment of the struggle between the forces and relations of production in which workers will unite to overthrow the moribund structure. Even Godelier admits that there are 'two notions of contradiction' in Marx's capital. The first is 'between the capitalist class and the working class' and the second is 'between the conditions of production of value and surplus value and the conditions of their realization, and basically between productive forces and relations of production'. As 'an internal condition of a structure', the first 'contradiction is specific…to the capitalist mode of production', characterizing 'the system from the beginning' and remaining 'until the disappearance of a system'. The second and basic 'contradiction between the development and the socialization of the productive forces and the private ownership of the means of production', visible 'partly in periodical crises', is 'not a contradiction within a structure but between the above-mentioned two structures', the 'structure of the productive forces' and 'the structure of the relations of production'. Paradoxically, despite being basic in explaining the 'evolution of capitalism and its inevitable disappearance', this contradiction is 'not original' but appears at 'a certain stage', at a 'certain stage of maturity', the 'stage of large-scale industry' of the system.

Because he identifies two contradictions, even though one of them is basic, Godelier thinks that the Althusserian notion of structural overdetermination does not 'grasp the essential point' of the relationship of the two contradictions. Although the first contradiction is prior in time and its appearance and disappearance are contingent on modes of production' and the second 'appears with the development of the system as an effect of the functioning of the first contradiction', it is the 'second one which creates the material conditions for the disappearance of the system' and is 'the fundamental contradiction'.[16] But this does not make the first contradiction as inconsequential as structuralists think. Marx's radical criticism of the capitalistic mode of production was mainly intended as a way of making the proletariat aware of understanding its historical role, of the irreconcilable nature of the clash of interests between them and the bourgeoisie, and of the dangers of its false consciousness. In an impassioned passage, Marx wrote:

> As philosophy finds in the proletariat its material weapon, so the proletariat finds in philosophy its intellectual weapons. The *head* of this emancipation is *philosophy*, its *heart* the *proletariat*. Philosophy cannot realize itself without the transcendence [Aufhebung] of the proletariat, and the proletariat cannot transcend itself without the realization [Verwirklichung] of philosophy.[17]

Equating structuralism with historical materialism is, second, inappropriate because in its generic form, structuralism shows how a host of relations may affect only any single element in the system. But even though it recognizes a diversity of influences and highlights the possibilities of multiple 'determinations of class, nation, gender, place, culture and historical context', historical materialism just affirms the primacy or pre-eminence of the substructural (class-based) socio-economic level. Such multi-faceted determinations in IRT are exemplified by Strange's elaboration of 'four structures' of power relationships and Galtung's 'structural' theory of imperialism. Strange's 'image' of IR is a 'four-faceted triangular pyramid or tetrahedron', each touching the other three and being 'held in place by them', while each facet represents one of the four structures' of 'security, production, finance and knowledge'.[18] Galtung's 'famous structural theory of imperialism' is essentially a 'centre–periphery' model, in which the world is composed of 'Center and Periphery' nations. But every nation has a centre and periphery. Imperialism is a process of unequal exchange of value, where the centre of the 'periphery' is used by the centre of the centre as a base or foothold to bring about a 'harmony of interests' between both that would leave the periphery of the 'Center nation' and the periphery of the 'Periphery nation' with a disharmony of interests concerning material and non-material living conditions. This imperialism again can take economic, political, military and communicational forms.[19] In these examples, the economic element stressed by historical materialism—exploitation and resultant alienation—is present but on equal footing with other determinants of domination, so that the Althusserian 'structure in dominance' is substituted by indeterminacy in determination. A structuralist solution will distort the picture.

The third reason why a structuralist turn to IR was constricting is that in IRT the structuralist paradigm stands for a general theory of North–South relations, accounting for its two limitations. (a) Despite its claims of a novel lens, the structuralist theoretical account of North–South relations presents a narrower and more one-sided account of the subject. While it predominantly highlights the exploitative, hegemonic nature of imperialism, another current within Marxism, closer to Marx's and Engels's perceptions, finds that imperialism had both destructive and regenerative impacts, simultaneously subverting entrenched forms of economic and social activity while creating new ones. The second interpretation draws upon Marx and Engels to portray a similar dual nature of capitalism. While lashing at the dehumanizing impact on humanity of capitalism's spread both in the first and the third colonial world, Marx does not lose sight of its positive effects in introducing a universal realm of material and mental artefacts, needs, satisfactions and progress, and never gets nostalgic about pre-capitalist socio-economic formations. Even Lenin does not greatly depart from this reading while assessing the situation in Russia. Actually, it was not before the rise of the dependency approach and before a strictly Third-World reading of Marx that capitalist imperialism was painted in a wholly black brush. (b) Besides this one-dimensional portrayal of capitalist imperialism, structuralism confers on North–South relations a constitutive role for IR that is unwarranted because it ignores the vicissitudes of the relations between the countries of the North and the countries of the South, conflicts and wars. Accordingly, structuralists cast even Lenin's *Imperialism* in a North–South relations mould, oblivious of the fact that Lenin wrote the booklet to show why the imperialist European powers waged wars with each other in 1914, which led to the First World War, and what are its lessons for the socialists.

So to qualify as a comprehensive, alternative Marxist paradigm of IR, structuralism should ponder on how to accommodate the missing elements of classical Marxism in its broadened contours. But how better a candidate is historical materialism?[20]

POSSIBILITIES OF HISTORICAL MATERIALISM IN IR

Historical Materialism Summarized

While presenting the main tenets of historical materialism and arguing their acceptability to IR, I would sometimes recast them in the familiar parlance of IR to set in better relief the points of their relevance and applicability. To ward off the perception that I am deviating from Marxism, I would frequently quote Marx and occasionally Engels and Lenin.[21]

Man, Production and Dialectic, and Class

Conventional social or political theories have their undergirding concepts of man, such as: Aristotle's political man; Machiavelli's bestial man; Hobbes's fearful, egotist, aggressive man; Adam Smith's bartering/trading man; Comte's social man; Hegel's rational 'burgher'; Bentham's calculative utilitarian man (consumer, appropriator and a sum of appetites); John Stuart Mill's man as an 'exerter and developer and enjoyer of his capacities'.[22] Even though the concepts of human nature relevant to realism have attracted the maximum attention in recent years, other IR theoretical perspectives too have concepts of man implicit in and lurking behind them.[23] What does Marx, whose 'Sixth Thesis on Feuerbach' is widely interpreted to brush aside a timeless human nature or a human essence, say about it?[24] Marx described it in his writing as variable, never immutable,[25] neither perennially 'horrifying'/reassuring nor fixed as of *men of nature*,[26] and thought a universal 'natural man', invested with 'natural' rights and governed by or following natural laws, to be chimerical. Men 'begin to distinguish themselves from animals as soon as they begin to produce their means of subsistence', and through that start 'indirectly producing their material life'. To that extent, man 'is not only a social animal but an animal who can individualize himself only within society'. Production 'by an isolated individual outside society' is 'a rare event'.[27] However, a passage in *Holy Family*, echoed in *German Ideology*, describes the proletariat as indignant at its 'abasement', caused by 'the contradiction between its human nature and its condition of life, which is the outright, decisive and comprehensive negation of that nature'[28]; and another in *German Ideology* defines the proletariat in bourgeois society as one whose 'position does not even allow him to satisfy the needs arising directly from his human nature'.[29]

So fitting *The Theses on Feuerbach* chronologically between *Holy Family* (late 1844) and *German Ideology* (1845–1846), Geras rightly concludes that the Sixth Thesis does not provide a definitive proof of Marx's rejection of an essential human nature.[30] I mention these debates only to help my readers situate historical materialism in Marx's view of the making of human nature and comprehend Marx's statement that 'for a socialist man what is called world history is nothing but the creation of man by human labour and the development of nature for man'.[31] So human history is nothing but a gruesome struggle of human beings to satisfy their basic material needs and for that, to 'participate in', confront and control the natural world.[32] Human beings' production of their means of subsistence is focal. But since this necessarily takes place in a social milieu, social relationships are implicit in them, as is also partial historical constraint, as seen in this famous quote from *Eighteenth Brumaire*: 'Men make their own history, but they do not make it just as they please, they do not make it in circumstances chosen by themselves, but under circumstances directly encountered, given, and transmitted from the past'.[33] It implies that while making their own history, human beings are constantly transformed, and working on nature, they not only alter nature but have their needs changed too.

But a crucial question regarding the fulfilment of these needs is whether, when and how the existent and *synchronic* 'mode of production' (understood as the totality of the forces and relations of production) gives free scope to or deforms man's nature as 'species being'. In other words, is this 'mode of production', characterizing certain social, political, legal and economic processes of an epoch, congenial or is it harmful for humans in their society, generating their alienation. It is in this sense that the process of human development was understandable only through the emergence and dissolution of *diachronic* modes of production, giving rise in the West to primitive communism, serf or slave societies, feudalism and capitalism, and in the East to what Marx called the 'Asiatic mode of production', and Weber called more disparagingly as 'Oriental despotism'.[34] The argument that the nature, condition and critical practical thought of human beings are shaped by their relationship to the existent mode of production rather than by their belongings to state and nation, inevitably generates what in modern IR parlance would be called 'domestic conflicts' with transnational overtones. In these 'earlier epochs of history', one would 'find almost everywhere a complicated arrangement of society into various orders, a manifold gradation of social rank', locked in 'an uninterrupted, now hidden, now open fight that each time ended in a revolutionary reconstitution of society at large, or in the common ruin of the contending classes'. The classes changed—'patricians, knights, plebeians, slaves' in Rome; 'feudal lords, vassals, guild masters, journeymen, apprentices, serfs' in the Middle Ages, and subordinate fractions of these classes—but the conflict remained, leading Marx to utter perhaps his most famous words: 'The history of all hitherto existing societies is the history of the class struggle'. The heart of the concept of historical materialism is contained in these words.

Among these societies, all of them riven by class conflicts, capitalism was initially the most progressive in that most of the major achievements of human history, manifested in human beings' control of adversarial natural forces, came during the capitalist epoch of development, wherein bourgeoisie played a progressive social role. It also replaced the intangible social ties under feudalism with a more transparent 'callous cash nexus', and even global expansionism of capitalism had a positive side: its universalist logic ushered in a universalist history. But the inevitable contradiction between socialization of the forces of production and the private ownership of the means of production turned capitalism into a stinking, reactionary and exploitative system.[35]

This system, however, could not be permanent. For, contrary to the liberal Smithian or Benthamian view of self-interested individuals, Marx offered what Rupert calls 'a *relational* and *process-oriented* view of human beings'. According to this view, humans become what they are not because it is teleologically ingrained in them to be such. It is because they operated 'at the intersection of a three-sided relation encompassing the natural world, social relations and institutions, and human persons'. These relations are organically related and cannot be understood in isolation. And since human beings constantly reconstitute the world they live in, should contemporary human beings appear egotistical, then it is not due to their essential nature, but owing to the particular ways in which they have reproduced their social lives and themselves. By implication, human persons should be collectively able to remake their world and themselves in new and better ways if they critically ponder on the ways to alter the historically evolving social relations which constrain them.[36] But that does not, unlike in structuralist overdetermination, inevitably mean that it will bring forward a socialist society in the very first instance. As Hobsbawm so incisively said,

> This does not mean that we are obliged to accept Marx's list of historical epochs as given in the Preface, or in the *Formen*. The general theory of historical materialism requires only that there should be a succession of modes of production, though not necessarily any particular modes, and perhaps not in any particular order.[37]

Critique of Capital and State

Noted Marxologists such as Nicos Poulantzas, I. I. Rubin and Godelier and other Anglo-American commentators accept that 'historical materialism is a general theory of history and that *Capital* is a specialized application of that theory to capitalist society'. A detractor's complaint about it under what he calls 'subsumption theory' is that it 'obscures the scientific merits of Marx's economic analysis by assimilating it to the less rigorous hypotheses of historical materialism. *Capital* goes significantly beyond Marx's earlier achievements in its standing as a work of social science'. But still a discussion of historical materialism will not be complete without a Marxian critique of capitalism for a number of reasons. First, Marx's critique of capitalism is not first presented in *Capital*. Second, Little himself admitted that 'there is an ancestral relationship between historical materialism and *Capital*. Historical materialism provided Marx with the general problem of research for *Capital*....'[38] Third, in this chapter, arguing for the relevance of historical materialism for IR, we are not concerned with the trajectories of Marx's ratiocination in *Capital* but with simply mentioning the negative features of this form of socio-economic life in Marx's view.

Marx introduced the concept of 'primitive accumulation' to explain how necessary assets accumulated in the hands of the capitalists.[39] Unlike what classical political economy taught, capital was not one of the elements of production brought from the outside by capitalists but was immanent in the production process.[40] The process was described by Marx as follows:

> By turning his money [i.e., past expropriated surplus value] into commodities that serve as the material elements of a new product, and as factors in the labour-process, by incorporating living labour with their dead substance, the capitalist at the same time converts value, i.e., past, materialized, and dead labour into capital, into value big with value, a live monster that is fruitful and multiplies.
>
> So capital is 'dead labour that vampire like, only lives by sucking living labour'. After being converted into 'an automaton, the instruments of production confront the labourer during

the labour process in the shape of capital, of dead labour, that dominates and pumps dry, living labour power'.[41]

As a socio-economic formation, capitalism is not to be equated with market or exchange, both of which predate it. It is rather a situation where commodification of human labour has reached such proportions that human labour is bought and sold in the marketplace, crippling the possibilities of social self-determination of humans. It is not only exploitative in a unique and unprecedented way but creates a niche for '*private social powers* located in a separate "economic" sphere', which is presented as both 'privatized and depoliticized'.[42]

Regarding the state, materialism rather than nationalism being the central theoretical concern of Marxism, the state in every epoch of dialectical history was part of the superstructure and to that extent changeable. In his words:

> At a certain stage of development, the material productive forces of society come into existing relations of production or...with the property relations within the framework of which they have operated hitherto. From forms of development of the productive forces these relations turn into their fetters...The changes in the economic foundation lead sooner or later to the transformation of the whole immense superstructure...it is always necessary to distinguish between the material transformation of the economic conditions of production, which can be determined with the precision of natural science, and the legal, political, religious, artistic or philosophic—in short, ideological forms in which men become conscious of the conflict and fight it out.[43]

On the complex nexus between capital and the state, Marx first points out that the bourgeoisie, the protagonist of capital accumulation, is goaded by the 'need of a constantly expanding product' to traverse 'the whole surface of the globe' to 'nestle everywhere, settle everywhere, establish connexions everywhere', and that it has 'through its exploitation of the world market given a cosmopolitan character to production and consumption in every country'. As a result, the 'old local and national seclusion and self-sufficiency' have been substituted by 'intercourse in every direction, universal interdependence of nations', and that 'as in material, so also in mental production'.[44] Second, he asks whether 'the whole organization of nations, and all their international relations', is anything but 'the expression of a particular division of labour', which must 'change when the division of labour changes', and obviously answers this question in the negative.[45] What is the role of even an epiphenomenal national state in this?

The answer to the question can be found in Marx's contention that as the 'executive of the modern state', which is nothing but 'a committee for managing the common affairs of the whole bourgeoisie',[46] its pursuit of the capitalist general interest pertains not only to the national level but to the international level as well. The position does not basically change whether Marxists adopt the 'instrumentalist' or the 'structural constraint' thesis on the role of the state.[47] It does not matter that sovereignty of states does not extend externally because for a long time, capitalist states have forged networks of bilateral and even multilateral arrangements 'for the mutual support of national jurisdiction (e.g., extradition), as well as of specific functional multinational organizations for the coordination of state functions (e.g., the Universal Postal Union)'.[48] This has been shown in Chapters 14 and 15 dealing with interdependence and regime theories. But for Marxists, the issue of the states' pursuit of capitalist general interest internationally brought to the fore the theme of imperialism.

Marxian Theories of Imperialism

It is conventional to argue that Marx himself did not provide us any articulate theory of imperialism. Brewer famously said, he 'did not use the word "imperialism". Nor is there anything in his work that corresponds at all exactly to the concepts of imperialism advanced by later Marxist writers'.[49] But Barone contends short of writing his projected book about capitalism and world markets in his lifetime, Marx spared no words to point out the innate expansionism of capital and how while expanding it changes the non-capitalist world 'in its own image'. He demonstrated even in the first volume of *Capital* how the 'foreign sector' played a role in primitive accumulation, diagnosed the need for world markets as a bulwark against the inevitable tendency of the rate of profit to fall and mentioned how the 'furious combat' for market shares incited rapid technological changes. Finally, the transition from competitive capitalism to monopoly capitalism, which is the germinal seed of Leninist theory of imperialism, is presaged and portended in these lines of Marx:

> In practical life we find not competition, monopoly, and the antagonism between them, but also synthesis of the two, which is not a formula but a movement. Monopoly produces competition, competition produces monopoly. Monopolists compete among themselves; competitors become monopolists...and the more the mass of the proletarians grows as against monopolists of one nation, the more desperate competition becomes between monopolists of different nations. The synthesis is of such a character that monopoly can only maintain itself by continually entering into the struggle for competition.[50]

It was in the context of the looming First World War that a host of Left-liberal and Marxist thinkers, including John A. Hobson, Luxemburg, Rudolf Hilferding, Nikolai Bukharin, Karl Kautsky and most memorably Lenin, started developing their separate but related theories of imperialism. Lenin's theory, much influenced by Hobson, and Marx's prognosis of transition from competitive capitalism to monopoly capitalism argued that a constantly increasing number of industrial firms are being dominated by a few enterprises that have merged with the largest banks. As a result, a few monopolists and financial tycoons are dominating not only the international economy but also exercising decisive influence over the state. Fed up with decreasing profit rates in their home states, these monopolies are now exporting not only commodities but capital to other states, thereby pocketing a large portion of the surplus value of these other lands and acquiring a 'parasitic' character. First losing vitality and then enlivening technological progress, imperialist capitalism becomes stagnating, 'decaying' and 'dying'. Lenin found this 'inter-imperialist rivalry' as one of the most potent causes of the First World War.[51]

For historical materialism, imperialism is significant because it transfers the acute confrontation between the bourgeoisie and the proletariat under capitalism to the international level, which comes out in this apt statement by Lenin:

> The enormous dimensions of finance capital concentrated in a few hands and creating an extraordinarily dense and widespread network of relationships and connections which subordinate not only the small and the medium, but the very small capitalists and small masters, on the one hand, and the increasingly intense struggle waged against other national state groups of financiers for the division of the world and domination over other countries, on the other hand, cause the propertied classes to go over entirely to the side of imperialism.[52]

The discussion supports Halliday's apt identification of four general and constitutive themes of historical materialism: (a) material determination, which has already been discussed and would not be repeated; (b) historicism, since historical determination arraigns a presentism which does not see the developments in and the nature of a society in its historical context; (c) the centrality of classes, defined by ownership or non-ownership of the means of production, as the prime actors in politics at the intra-state or transnational levels; and (d) the centrality of conflict and its inevitable culmination into social revolution.[53]

Implications of the Four Themes of Historical Materialism for IR

Halliday asserts that against any crude appraisal of Marxism, application of these four themes to IR does not entail mechanical reduction of everything to economic reasons or determinants. For example, as regards *material determination*, Marx's own analyses of national and international events of his time in the 1840s and the 1870s, as seen in *The Class Struggles in France, 1848–1850*, *The Eighteenth Brumaire*, *The Civil War in France* and so on do not betray any such unbridled economic determinism. Besides, by capitalism he does not mean just concrete and distinct forces of production with capitalists' ownership of means of production but subsumes under the concept a broad array of related and interacting political, legal and cultural institutions. But still the first theme could change the face of IR if applied, because the real significance of generic concepts like 'mode of production' or 'social formation' for IR is that under it any field of human activity would have to be seen in its socio-economic setting than outside it. Consequently, no state, belief, conflict or power can be seen as independent of this context, and any international system or its constituent processes, such as war or diplomacy, cannot be properly understood in abstraction from the mode of production. Its deeper implication would be that the discipline of IR would no more be about relations between states. Its main point of reference would be social formations, which could cause a change of focus from the national interest or juridical objectivity of states to the interests of the social formation as constituted by its socio-economic structure. The questions that would be raised in this context are what classes, to what extent, control the state or are segregated from/by it. The concept of sovereignty would also lose its halo to become nothing but prerogatives of specific social forces, and its history would be read as legitimation of a form of social power in a specific formation. State security would also signify nothing more than security of the dominant social groups in their pursuit of special and exclusive socio-economic privileges. The history of the state system too would be seen through the global spread and sway of capitalism through suppression and triumph over pre-capitalist modes of production and social arrangements.

Much modification of the contours of the discipline would be effected by the second theme of historical determination too, since it would sensitize persons to capitalists' attempts at 'ideological suppression of the origins of the system' steeped in 'the violence involved in its creation' and attempts at hiding the masquerade of forces in IR in the garb of nationalism and other irrational creeds. Marx's general theory of history would be applicable also to the situation of a particular country, including its domestic and foreign policies; the biases, inclinations and preferences of its leaders; expectations, hopes, fears and grievances of its public; the institutional structure of policy implementation and delivery, and would reveal to what extent all these were conditioned by past conventions, habits, memories and practices. Additionally, historical materialism lays bare how all social events that are at the best contingent, if not accidental, are made to look 'natural' or 'eternal'. Actually, one of the major functions that political sociology performs in any liberal (read capitalist) political society is making even the contingent, evanescent and temporary aspects of social life perennial or ineluctable, and historical materialism tears these veils off them,[54] a little like post-structuralist 'deconstruction'.[55] It places the apparently unchanging features of the international system, such as nation, state and sovereignty, and shows how they are also anything but immutable. It acts as a corrective to the instrumental use of history in IR, a charge which, according to Halliday, applies even to Der Derian or Martin Wight, and for me to Morgenthau.[56] Besides, the tendency of non-Marxist scholars of IR to treat important issues in the field away from their historical context is not confined to the behaviouralists or IR. Ahistoricism is writ large in scholars' claim that compared to the non-West, Western nations are instances of peaceful and non-revolutionary paths of development, well captured by the slogan 'ours is patriotism, theirs is nationalism'.[57] It ignores stark facts of colonial subordination, plunder and even decimation of populations in the expansion of Western society into their non-Western counterparts which brought the international society into being. Historical materialism wrenches off this conceptual blinder.

Application of class centrality to IR shows how inside a state, specific classes, in their bid to control and subjugate other contending classes, resort to the international sphere or level to forge alliances with similar groups in other states, or seek competition with them through peaceful or forceful means, depending on whether peace or rivalry is preferred. Conflicts between groups at par in status and power or groups occupying different positions in different states naturally transfer domestic conflicts to the international level. The accordance of analytical primacy to classes breeds two consequences for IR: (a) all major conflicts come under a distinct socio-economic lens and (b) the debates that have racked the theoretical field of IR to seem even constitutive of it seem to have depended on flimsy foundations. As for the first, even if all the signal conflicts of IR are not tokens of class struggles, they have often contained crucial components of them, right from the pre-Cold-War period to the post-Cold-War one. Cases in point would be the onset of the First and Second World Wars, the Gold Standard Crisis of 1931, the crisis stemming from the first oil shock from OPEC of 1971–1973, the disputes concerning trade and interest rates within the Atlantic Alliance in the early 1980s, the stock market crash of 1987, US-Japanese trade disputes in the 1990s, the Asian Financial Crisis of the late 1990s, the Gulf War of 1990–1991 led by America against Iraq, American War on Iraq that started in 2003 and lasted till 2011, the 'credit crunch' and global meltdown of 2008–2009 and so on. In all these conflicts between capitalist ruling classes, between entrenched and ascendant capitalists, economic interests played the role of basic motivators.

As for the second impact, the debates on the continuing or lessening powers of the states between realist paradigm (discussed in Chapter 2) and their pluralist counterparts (discussed in Chapters 12–15), that have the theory field of IR what it is today, would change in character. The state not being an independent entity but the product of wider historical forces, the question would no more be if the state has been greatly affected by NSAs recently (i.e., in 1945 or 1970), since it has always been so, but how have classes masquerading as NSAs exerted their power through and outside the state. This would not only problematize the immutability of nation states but expose the alleged 'impermeability of domestic politics' as a camouflage for an ongoing, subterranean internationalization of power, resources and initiatives. Marx was concerned about this problem, since despite his conviction and hope about the international character of the proletariat, his theoretical insight was that by education, culture and the nature of their economic interests, the bourgeoisie were potentially the class best poised to act internationally. The subsequent history of capitalism has unfortunately vindicated Marx's theory against his inclination in showing how internationalization of the ruling class has proceeded much faster than that of the proletariat. Not only were the European Communities (1958, Community since 1993), the Trilateral Commission (1973), but subsequently the G8 (1975, reformatted G7 from 2014), G20 (Group of Twenty; 1999), the World Economic Forum (1971 till date) are living instances of transnational elite coordination. The domination and power of such 'informal' and private 'transnational elite clubs', or internationally 'connected executives and their companies' have been a subject of academic research for a long time.[58]

The fourth theme of centrality of conflict also may accord well with the agenda of IR, even though the discussions on conflict within Marxism, at the epistemological and axiological levels, are heavily influenced by Hegel's thought and by the 19th-century positivist view of the methodological unity of the human and natural sciences. In the sense of being primarily generated among the classes by their inequalities arising from relationship with the means of production, conflicts according to historical materialism are ineluctable characteristics of not only relations within societies but also across them. They can culminate either into revolution or war, or in a mixture of both. Wars happen in conflicts between comparable social classes, contenders for control over markets, means of production, lands and resources very often across states. However, revolutions—not political but social—occur between dissimilar social classes mainly within states and introduce changes in the social character of states. To that extent, they lead to discontinuances and dislocations in the character of international politics. Its major implication for IR would be that its central preoccupation would not be any more security or the actions and problems of states in facing what Hertz called the 'security dilemma',[59] but conflict, including the ways of its generation, management, resolution and effects. Since the kaleidoscopic events of international politics are all undergirded by social conflicts both inside and outside states, stemming from divergent pursuits of wealth and power, historical materialism can delve into the insides of states to unearth their historical roots and trajectories to expose how the seemingly most pacifist states at present (such as Austria, Netherlands or Japan) had gory pasts of blood and iron. IR can also use with benefit Marx's insight about the mid-19th-century European politics that behind BOP sustained by five powers lurked a sixth great power in revolution, to show how behind the conventional reading of search for security in IR hides the stark reality of 'containing the inter-capitalist conflict on the one hand and social revolution on the other'. So whenever a historical materialist hears the quip that the sole preoccupation of present-day international politics is 'order', he/she can ask 'order' for whom and sustained by whom.[60]

Already Realized Potentialities of Historical Materialism in IR

Even with the inadequacies of historical materialism for IRT, stemming from lack of theoretical foray, it has directly or indirectly inspired some theories that have radically questioned the field's reigning orthodoxies of liberalism/realism/pluralism.[61] Even not counting the efforts by Marxist writers during the first two decades of the 20th century to theorize the international system around the concept of 'imperialism', understood as strategic rivalry among capitalist states to control the non-capitalist world, we have seen other theoretical offshoots. These are dependency theory, WST and Marxist strands within the IPE approach (all three discussed in Chapters 17, 18 and 19). Many of the revisionist accounts of the origins and development of the Cold War, up till recent times, have been indebted to insights from Marxism/Leninism/historical materialism.[62] Influences have also been insidious and subtle. The works of Keohane, Gilpin and Strange in the context of 'decline' of the USA and its implications for inter-capitalist relations have recognized the debt to the pre-First World War literature on it produced by Marxist writers.

Moreover, the leaven provided by Marxism fermented a field which runs parallel to IRT in many ways, namely international history, where scholars such as Eric Wolf, Perry Anderson and Eric Hobsbawm produced commendable research. While showing how European expansion not only transformed the historical trajectory of non-European societies but also reconstituted the historical accounts of these societies before European intervention, Wolf acknowledged his 'debt to Marxian thought without apology'. Addressing critics on the affinity of his book with 'systems Marxism' or 'Promethean Marxism', he said he used Marxian (not Marxist) ideas, 'not as foundational notions for a science aimed at developing laws of universal generality'.[63] While tracing the lineages of the absolutist state till its democratic transformation, propelled by social and political development inside and competition coming from outside, Anderson's 1974 study of it was conceived as 'a Marxist study of absolutism' and employed Marx's concept of the Asiatic mode of production,[64] and his long-range, sequel study of the transition from 'antiquity' to feudalism...squarely places the discussions of them 'primarily...within the field of historical materialism'.[65]

Mention can also be made about the comparative international historicist oeuvre of Hobsbawm, highly relevant for the issues and concerns of IR, including the appearance/arrival of nations and states, markets, the nature of economic, political and strategic factors operative in international affairs, sources of conflict within and across societies. These studies are unmatched in breadth and depth by anything written within conventional international history or the discourses on international society in IR (say in ES, which I shall take up in **Chapter 23**). In spite of being firmly rooted in chronology, empiricism and devotion to idiographic details, and dazzling in its careful avoidance of reductionism, the Hobsbawm oeuvre is firmly located in historical materialism and the repertoire of its concepts.[66]

CONCLUSION: ABOUT THE DETRACTORS OR CRITIQUES OF CRITICS

Regarding the first critique of detractors in the second paragraph of the essay, that is, difficulty to fit Marxism in IR, I anticipate **Chapter 24** of this book to introduce

Jürgen Habermas's subtle point about three kinds of 'knowledge interests'—'empirical analytical, historical hermeneutic, and critical emancipatory'—and the resultant classification by Max Horkheimer of traditional and critical theories, and of Robert Cox into problem-solving and critical theories.[67] I argue that since Marxism is a representative of critical-emancipatory knowledge-interest and critical-emancipatory theory, fitting it within the IRT field would require the kinds of overhauling and adjustments that have been suggested in the sections on implications of the four themes of historical materialism for IR, and its partly realized potentialities here. This answer seems to fully cover the second point of questioning the basis of IR as a problem-solving science (sure it does), and the third and the fourth points that by overemphasizing economic factors, it downplays security-related issues of BOP and war. This is not only because how Marx showed the relationship between the five-player BOP and the sixth kibitzer of revolution but also because shifts in BOP always had strong economic motivations. Further, if we remember David Keen's famous utterance that 'war may be a continuation of economics by other means,'[68] then BOP also may be such a means. Actually, critics of realist theories of BOP have commented on their failure 'to integrate fully the effects of economic competition and cooperation into their theoretical framework'. Their complaint is that the 'economic components of balancing, bandwagoning or buck passing—key concepts used to describe balance of power politics—have not been described by existing theory.[69]

The final point that Marx (or Engels) was not seriously interested in IR or paid insufficient attention to it seems not a little out of the blue in the backdrop of Comintern slogans of 'Weltklasse, Weltpartei, Wetrevolution' (world class, world party, world revolution). True that Marx did not speak of IR in the way IR pundits of realist, liberal or pluralist persuasions do. But he could not, without belying the theoretical foundations of Marxism. In *German Ideology*, Marx says:

> The relations of different nations among themselves depend upon the extent to which each has developed its productive forces, the division of labour and international intercourse. ...But not only the relation of one nation to others, but also the whole internal structure of the nation itself, depends on the stage of development reached by its production and its internal and external intercourse.[70]

This quote provides significant insights into the relations between the First-World and the Third or even the Fourth-World countries, despite its element of *determinism*, which can be softened down, in the way of Western Marxists, who did not rob 'all non-material phenomena of any meaning' or belittle the 'individual capacity for action and change' but rather viewed it 'as providing a context, a set of limits and significances within which these factors can be assessed'.[71]

The possibilities of the insights in the last quote for a new, fruitful approach to IR have been provided by Gramsci's concepts of hegemony and resistance, and neo-Gramscians' application of these concepts in productive ways. Even now, as Cox says, the 'corporatist process' undergirding 'state-capitalist development', which covers in its folds 'business and labour in the world market oriented sector and workers in the tertiary welfare services sector, necessarily keeps out 'certain marginal groups'. They are frequently at the passive and helpless receiving end of the welfare services because of their powerlessness to influence the policymakers and are overwhelmingly found among the young, women, immigrant or minority groups and the unemployed, mostly in the countries where, as said in *German Ideology*, 'productive forces, the division of labour and international intercourse' are backward and undeveloped, and their numbers tend to increase with each restructuring of the production process. While the new marginalized and proletarian classes are being 'fragmented and relatively powerless', their exclusion has gone unnoticed and unchallenged, even though collectively they constitute a 'latent threat to the corporatist processes'. When they break out into 'anomic explosions of violence' or start political mobilization to flaunt the demands of democratic inclusiveness and legitimacy against the propagators of corporatist efficiency, their demands are sought to be drowned in the neoliberal shibboleth of 'ungovernability'.[72] Gramsci may now represent Marxism of our times. For, it is through his influence that neo-Gramscian IPE has brought to the fore 'the interrelations among social forces, state forms and world orders' to confront liberal IR and 'IPE's failure to develop compelling accounts of class, power and hegemonic relations within the economic and political arrangements of the capitalist world system'.[73] But could there be a Gramsci without Marx's brilliant insights?

REVIEW QUESTIONS

1. Why was Marxism avoided in IR for so long? Was the avoidance unavoidable? State your case.
2. Comment on partial and reductionist accommodation of Marxism in IR and its limitations.
3. Summarize historical materialism for IR and its implications for IR.
4. Show to what extent the possibilities of historical materialism in IR have been realized. What can increase these possibilities?

NOTES AND REFERENCES

1. See Note 31 of Chapter 1.
2. See Notes 51 and 55 of Chapter 1.
3. Mary Kaldor, *The Imaginary War: Understanding the East-West Conflict* (Oxford: Basil Blackwell, 1990), cited in Hazel Smith, 'Marxism and International Relations Theory', in *Contemporary International Relations: A Guide to Theory*, eds A. J. R. Groom and Margot Light (London: Pinter, 1994/1999), 143.
4. V. Kubálková and A. A. Cruickshank, *Marxism-Leninism and Theory of International Relations* (London: Routledge, 1980/2016), 12.
5. Chris Brown, 'Marxism and International Ethics', in *Traditions of International Ethics*, eds Terry Nardin and David R. Mapel (Cambridge: Cambridge University Press, 1992/2002), 235.
6. See Stephen Hobden and Richard Wyn Jones, 'Marxist Theories of International Relations', in *The Globalization of World Politics: An Introduction to International Relations*, eds John Baylis, Steve Smith, and Patricia Owens, revised ed. (Oxford: Oxford University Press, 2016), 142–143; Fred Halliday, 'A Necessary Encounter: Historical Materialism and International Relations', in *Rethinking International Relations* (Basingstoke: Macmillan, 1994), 49.

7. Smith, 'Marxism and International Relations Theory', 142. Smith is referring to Andrew Linklater, *Beyond Realism and Marxism: Critical Theory and International Relations* (London: Macmillan, 1990), and Justin Rosenberg, *The Empire of Civil Society: A Critique of the Realist Theory of International Relations* (London: Verso, 1994).
8. Halliday, 'Necessary Encounter', 47–48.
9. Hobden and Jones, 'Marxist Theories', 142–143.
10. For these points and relevant citations of Keohane and Nye, Burton, Rosenau, Gardner, Strange, Knorr and Kindleberger, see T. Thorndike, 'The Revolutionary Approach: The Marxist Perspective', in *Approach and Theory International Relations*, ed. Trevor Taylor (London: Longman, 1978/1984), 55–99, here 55–56.
11. Susan Strange, 'The Study of International Relations', *International Affairs* 52, no. 3 (July 1976): 337, cited in Thorndike, 'Revolutionary Approach', 55.
12. Ibid., 55–58.
13. I skip discussion of 'critical Marxism' as part of critical theory here because it will be taken up in Chapter 24.
14. Halliday, 'Necessary Encounter', 48, 52.
15. See Maurice Godelier, 'System, Structure and Contradiction in Capital', *The Socialist Register* 4 (1967): 91–119, here 92–94, available at socialistregister.com (accessed on 14 August 2018); also see Godelier *Rationality and Irrationality in Economics* (London: New Left Books, 1974), xix for a largely similar assertion, 'For Marx, as for Lévi-Strauss, a structure is not a reality that is directly visible, and so directly observable, but a level of reality that exists beyond the visible relations of men, and the functioning of which constitutes the underlying logic of the system, the subjacent order by which the apparent order is to be explained'.
16. Godelier, 'System, Structure', 102–108, and passim.
17. Karl Marx, 'A Contribution to the Critique of Hegel's Philosophy of Right: Introduction', first published in *Deutsch–Französische Jahrbücher* 7 and 10 February 1844, available at https://www.marxists.org/archive/marx/works/1843/critique-hpr/intro.htm (accessed on 4 July 2020).
18. Susan Strange, *States and Markets*, 2nd ed. (London: Continuum, 1988/1994), 26–8, 139, 183, 209.
19. Johan Galtung, 'A Structural Theory of Imperialism', in *Perspectives on World Politics*, eds Richard Little and Michael Smith, 3rd ed. (London: Routledge, 1980/2006), 233–241.
20. Halliday, 'Necessary Encounter', 49.
21. Except where indicated otherwise, this section draws largely on Halliday, 'Necessary Encounter', 52–55.
22. For the most competent, critical and current expositions of these concepts of man, see Eugene Garver, *Aristotle's Politics: Living Well and Living Together* (Chicago, IL: University of Chicago Press, 2011), passim; Erica Benner, *Machiavelli's Ethics* (Princeton, NJ: Princeton University Press, 2009), 190–197; Alison McQueen, *Political Realism in Apocalyptic Times* (Cambridge: Cambridge University Press, 2018), 138, 145; Wesley C. Mitchell, 'Bentham's Felific Calculus', in *Jeremy Bentham: Ten Critical Essays*, ed. Bhikhu Parekh (London: Frank Cass, 1974), 168; C. B. Macpherson, *The Life and Times of Liberal Democracy* (Oxford: Oxford University Press, 1977), 5, 33, 47–48.
23. Daniel Jacobi and Annette Freyberg-Inan, 'Introduction: Human Being(s) in International Relations', in *Human Beings in International Relations*, eds Daniel Jacobi and Annette Freyberg-Inan (Cambridge: Cambridge University Press, 2015), 9.
24. See Norman Geras, *Marx and Human Nature: Refutation of a Legend* (London: Verso Editions and NLB, 1983), 50–51; Karl Marx, 'Debates on Freedom of the Press', in *Marx Engels Collected Works*, vol. 1 (Lawrence: Electric Book, 2010), 152.
25. Geras, *Marx and Human Nature*, 24.

26. Marx, 'Debates', 169; Karl Marx, 'The Philosophical Manifesto of the Historical School of Law', first published in *Rheinische Zeitung* (1842, August 9), reproduced in *Marx Engels Collected Works*, vol. 1 (Lawrence: Electric Book, 2010), 203.
27. Karl Marx and Fredrich Engels, *The German Ideology, Part One, with Selections from Parts Two and Three and Supplementary Texts*, ed. C. J. Arthur (New York, NY: International Publishers, 1847/1996), 42, 125.
28. Karl Marx and Fredrich Engels, *The Holy Family: Critique of Critical Critique* (Moscow: Foreign Language Publishing House, 1956), 51, available at https://books.google.co.in/books?isbn=5880260437 (accessed on 18 August 2018).
29. Marx and Engels, *German Ideology*, 31; both the quotes were suggested to me by Geras, *Marx*, 63.
30. Ibid., 63–86.
31. Karl Marx, 'Early Texts', 156, cited in David McLellan, *Karl Marx: His Life and Thought* (London: Macmillan, 1973/1985), 122; David McLellan, ed., *Marx: Selected Writings* (Oxford: Oxford University Press, 2000), 104.
32. Karl Marx, *Capital: A Critique of Political Economy*, ed. F. Engels, vol. 1 (New York, NY: Modern Library, 2006), 197–200.
33. Karl Marx, *The Eighteenth Brumaire of Louis Bonaparte*, cited in McLellan, *Karl Marx: His Life and Thought* (London: Macmillan, 1973/1985), 329.
34. See for example, James Morris Blaut, 'Max Weber: Western Rationality', in *Eight Eurocentric Historians* (New York, NY: The Guilford Press, 2000), 21–22; Alan Sica, *Max Weber: The New Century* (New Brunswick: Transaction Publishers, 2004), 105.
35. Karl Marx and Fredrich Engels, *Manifesto of the Communist Party*, 2nd revised ed. (Moscow: Progress Publishers, 1977), 35–48.
36. This modern rephrasing of Marx's ideas largely draws on Mark Rupert, 'Marxism and Critical Theory', in *International Relations Theories: Discipline and Diversity*, eds Tim Dunne, Milja Kurki and Steve Smith (Oxford: Oxford University Press, 2007), 150.
37. 'Preface' refers to Preface to *Contribution to the Critique of Political Economy*, and *Formen* to the sections of *Grundrisse* dealing with pre-capitalist societies. Eric Hobsbawm, 'Introduction', in Karl Marx, *Pre-Capitalist Economic Formations* (London: Lawrence and Wishart, 1964), 20.
38. See Daniel Little, *The Scientific Marx* (Minneapolis, MN: University of Minnesota Press, 1986), 59–61.
39. Later Marxists, including Rosa Luxemburg, however, thought that primitive accumulation should not be relegated to the prehistories of capitalism but should be seen as a permanent feature of it. See Julian Francis Park, 'On the Historical Conditions of Accumulation', in *Rosa Luxemburg: A Permanent Challenge to Political Economy: On the History and Present of Luxemburg's Accumulation of Capital*, eds Judith Dellheim and Frieder Otto Wolf (London: Springer Nature, 2016), 2–22; David Harvey, *A Companion to Marx's Capital: Volume 1* (London: Verso, 2010), 292, 305–306.
40. On this point, see how Althusser compares the immanence of capital in the production process with the mistaking of a phologistic element that helped burning of something in the phologistic theory of chemistry, which was corrected by the discovery of oxygen whose influx from outside caused it. See Louis Althusser and Étienne Balibar, *Reading Capital*, trans. Ken Brewster (London: New Left Books, 1970), 22–26, 150–54, 181, 316.
41. See Karl Marx, *Capital: A Critique of Political Economy*, vol. 1, pp. 217, 238, 257 and 462.
42. Rupert, 'Marxism', 152–154.
43. Karl Marx, 'Preface', in Karl Marx, *A Contribution to the Critique of Political Economy* (Moscow: Progress Publishers, 1970/1989), 25.
44. Marx and Engels, *Manifesto*, 39.
45. Karl Marx, *Poverty of Philosophy* (Moscow: Foreign Language Publishing House, 1966), cited in Rupert, 'Marxism', 135.

46. Marx and Engels, *Manifesto,* 38.
47. See for these P. Wetherly, *Marxism and the State: An Analytical Approach* (Basingstoke: Palgrave Macmillan, 2005), Chapters 3, 4 and 6.
48. Sol Picciotto, 'The International Capital and the International State System', in *The State Debate*, ed. Simon Clarke (Basingstoke: Macmillan, 1991), 219–220.
49. Anthony Brewer, *Marxist Theories of Imperialism: A Critical Survey*, 2nd ed. (London: Routledge, 1990), 25.
50. Karl Marx, *Poverty of Philosophy* (Moscow: Progress Publishers, 1966), 132; Marx, *Capital,* vol. III, pp. 237–239; Marx, *Capital,* vol. I, pp. 450–451; Marx, *Poverty of Philosophy* as quoted by Charles Barone, *Marxist Thought on Imperialism: Survey and Critique* (London: Routledge, 1985), 11–12.
51. This bare summary of Vladimir Lenin's *Imperialism: The Highest Stage of Capitalism* (Moscow: Progress Publishers, 1917); Michael Heinrich, *An Introduction to the Three Volumes of Marx's Capital*, trans. Alexander Locascio (New York, NY: Monthly Review Press, 2004), 213–215.
52. Lenin, *Imperialism,* 104–105.
53. Elucidation of these four themes and their pay-offs for a richer theoretical study of IR builds on Halliday, 'Necessary Encounter', 59–67; I would, however, add new sources in citations and points, not just summarize him.
54. Ibid., 60–62. For example, Raymond Williams tears the veil off the symbol of the Hyde Park in London as an iconic example of the perennial nature of freedom of expression in England. See Raymond Williams, 'A Hundred Years of Culture and Anarchy', in *Problems in Materialism and Culture* (London: Verso, 1980), 4–8.
55. See Notes 33–40 of Chapter 26.
56. For Morgenthau's and Wight's treatment of history, see Chapters 4 and 23 of this book.
57. See Michael Billig, *Banal Nationalism* (London: SAGE Publications, 1995), 37–38, 55.
58. See Jean-Christophe Graz, 'How Powerful Are Transnational Elite Clubs: The Social Myth of the World Economic Forum', *New Political Economy* 8, no. 3 (November 2003): 321–340; S. Gill, *American Hegemony and the Trilateral Commission* (Cambridge: Cambridge University Press, 1990); Michael C. Dreiling and Derek Y. Darves, *Agents of Neoliberal Globalization: Corporate Networks, State Structures and Trade Policy* (New York, NY: Cambridge University Press, 2016), 49–51.
59. John A. Hertz, 'Idealist Internationalism and the Security Dilemma', *World Politics* 2 (January 1950): 157–180.
60. Halliday, 'Necessary Encounter', 59–67.
61. As in Note 53 above, I will develop on Halliday's summary in 'Necessary Encounter', 55–58.
62. See for example, Richard Saull, *Rethinking Theory and History in the Cold War: The State, Military Power and Social Revolution*, with a 'Foreword' by Fred Halliday (London: Frank Cass, 2001), 16–24, 104–140.
63. Eric Wolf, 'Preface', *Europe and the People without History* (Berkeley, CA: University of California Press, 1997), xxi–xxii.
64. Perry Anderson, *Lineages of the Absolutist State* (London: New Left Books, 1974/2013), 7, 478–487.
65. Perry Anderson, *Passages from Antiquity to Feudalism* (London: New Left Books, 1974/2013), 9.
66. Halliday mentions E. J. Hobsbawm's *The Age of Revolutions, 1789–1848, The Age of Capital, 1848–1875* and *The Age of Empire, 1875–1914.* I would add E. J. Hobsbawm, *Nations and Nationalism since 1780: Programme, Myth, Reality*, 2nd Canto ed. (Cambridge: Cambridge University Press, 1992) before them and E. J. Hobsbawm, *The Age of Extremes, 1914–1991* (New York, NY: Vintage Books, 1996) after them.
67. Raymond Allen Morrow and Carlos Alberto Torres, *Reading Freire and Habermas: Critical Pedagogy and Transformative Social Change* (New York, NY: Teachers College, Columbia University, 2002), 48–49; Notes 10–13, 21 of Chapter 24.

68. D. Keen, 'Incentives and Disincentives for Violence', in *Greed and Grievance: Economic Agendas in Civil Wars*, eds M. Berdal and D. Malone (London: Lynne Rienner, 2000), 27.
69. Mark F. Brawley, 'Political Economy of Balance of Power Theory', in *Balance of Power: Theory and Practice in the 21st Century*, eds T. V. Paul, James J. Wirtz, and Michel Fortman (Stanford, CA: Stanford University Press, 2004), 76–100.
70. Marx and Engels, *German Ideology*, 43.
71. Halliday, 'Necessary Encounter', 69–70.
72. This is a free paraphrasing of Robert W. Cox, 'Structural Issues of Global Governance: Implications for Europe', in *Gramsci, Historical Materialism and International Relations*, ed. Stephen Gill (Cambridge: Cambridge University Press, 1994), 271.
73. David McNally, 'Foreword', in *Gramsci, Political Economy and International Relations Theory: Modern Princes and Naked Emperors*, ed. Alison J. Ayers, revised ed. (New York, NY: Palgrave Macmillan, 2008), ix.

CHAPTER 17

Dependency Theory

INTRODUCTION

Disciplinary and Situational Context of Its Rise

As a strong critic of the premises and promises of capitalist modernization, the dependency literature is sometimes confused with the structuralist theory of Latin America, and its centre–periphery paradigm, upheld by scholars associated in the 1950s and 1960s with the Economic Commission for Latin America (ECLA), led by Raúl Prebisch, and the United Nations Conference on Trade and Development (UNCTAD). But structuralist thought stemming from the work of scholars in ECLA and its kindred institution Instituto Latinoamericano y del Caribe de Planificación Económica y Social (ILPES), as from the work of Neo-Marxist scholars once active within the Centro de Estudios Socio-Económicos (CESO; Centre for

Socio-economic Studies) in the University in Chile, is a strand in the dependency movement from which it soon detached itself.[1] To understand this, we would have to look at the context of the emergence of the theory.

The mid-1960s, especially 1965, was a turbulent period in North America, as well as in Latin America, for entirely different reasons. While America was restive with the landing of US marines in Santo Domingo, the explosion of the anti-Black Watts Riots in 1965, the escalation of the Vietnam War throughout the 1960s and the aftershock of the murder of President Kennedy, Latin Americans were harried with their own internal problems. A new batch of military authoritarianisms presaged the later arrival of counter-insurgency states, and the post-Second World War rising trends of capitalist accumulation and reproduction declined into a period of steep slump and crisis (affecting especially big Latin American players such as Brazil, Argentina and Mexico) in spite of the interventionist role of the state in this capital accumulation. Consequently, the structuralist model of import substituting industrialization (henceforth ISI) started losing appeal and legitimacy. It was in this context that a bunch of ideas from a multitude of authors, often disagreeing on many aspects of the diagnoses and prognoses of the crisis and prescriptions for it, shared enough commonalities to be grouped together as the dependency school/theory/approach/perspective in different perceptions. Frequently, these dependency spokesmen of different hues are termed *dependentistas*.[2]

SOURCES: MARXIST AND NON-MARXIST

The most dominant strands of the dependency position recognize the pervading influence of and debts to Marxism–Leninism (Leninism a little more than Marxism) for its categories of analysis and conceptual structures, despite some differences in their prime conceptual thrusts. Chilcote says that they 'have struggled over the past decade to integrate their ideas with a theory of Marxism'.[3] Most of the articles in his edited volume seek to apply Marxist concepts and views of modes of production and class analysis, processes of capitalism and socialism, imperialism and expropriation of surplus value on a world scale, internationalization of capital and so on in the Latin American context.[4] More importantly, some of the most iconic *dependentistas* have attested to this debt and influence. For example, Cardoso insists that the 'analyses of dependency situations in Latin America done in the second half of the [nineteen] sixties did not represent new methodological propositions', away from Marxism. And even the overhyped 'renovating influence of the North American neo-Marxist current' (principally the contribution of Baran) was 'certainly not greater than that of Marx himself, and did not "reveal" anything nor already present in the perspective of critical Latin American thought before 1960…' Lenin gets greater credit for formulating with simplicity 'what would be the core of the dependency analyses: the forms of articulation between two parts of a single mode of production, and the subordination of one mode of production to another'.[5] The subtlety of Lenin's perspective is that it views imperialism as 'a new form of the capitalist mode of production', but 'not a different mode of economic organization'. For, it depends on 'capital accumulation based on private ownership of the means of production and exploitation of the labour force'. It is just a 'new stage of capitalism'. From 'that broad picture', Lenin inferred new political tasks, tactics and strategies for socialist revolution,[6] which Cardoso sought to apply to the dependency situation of Latin America.

But the major *dependentistas* themselves (Cardoso disapproves of the epithet) mention both European and American Marxist and non-Marxist economists and thinkers as formative influences. In different phases of his work, Cardoso omits or mentions with varying degrees of emphasis Jean Paul Sartre, Louis Althusser, Georg Lukács, Antonio Gramsci, Paul Sweezy, Paul Baran, Marc Bloch, Maurice Dobb and C. Wright Mills. Osvaldo Sunkel and Pedro Paz not only quote copiously and regularly from Marx, Engels and Lenin but, apart from Lukács and Sweezy, refer to classical economists such as Adam Smith, David Ricardo, Alfred Marshall and Joseph Schumpeter, as well as many modern non-Marxist economists. Other dependency thinkers, such as Helio Jaguaribe, Guillermo O'Donnell and Defina Linck have cast their nets even wider. Some, such as historians Sergio Bagú and Caio Prado Jr., sociologists Florestan Fernandez, Pablo González Casanova and Jorge Graciarena, economists Armando Córdoba, Antonio García and Alonso Aguilar, recognize their intellectual debts to a host of preceding Latin American Marxist, neo-Marxist and other radical writers. Cardoso explicitly mentions his debts to Prado, Fernandez and historian Nelson Werneck Sodré, who championed the 'critical tradition' in Brazil. So the dependency perspective of the 1950s and 1960s is not something altogether novel in Latin America, and the ideas of Frank about a 'dual society' and of Cardoso and other dependency thinkers of an 'anti-nation inside the nation' had many sources.[7]

But dependency thinkers had also major discontinuities with past traditions, whether in Latin America or elsewhere, from 'liberal' and 'structuralist' to 'vulgar Marxist' ideas of development. The liberal tradition, starting from Smith through Walt Rostow, Wilbert Moore, Clark Kerr and so on down to the Pearson Report—*Partners in Development* (1969)—did not speak one voice. Cardoso interpreted classical, neo-classical or orthodox theories of economic development as explaining the under-industrialization of Latin American economies from the perspective of the comparative advantages accruing from 'agricultural production for export'. The Pearson Report, however, contended that the world economy is generally congenial to economic development. For, 'interdependence and economic linkages of advanced economies with less developed economies' help the latter to acquire export markets, capital and requisite technology for economic prosperity through 'trade, international aid and foreign investment'. Dependency theorists spurned both the diagnosis and the prescription because, while liberal theories stressed factors such as productivity and aggregate national product, they prioritized more 'equitable distribution among classes, regions and sectors'. Besides, against liberalism's attempts to present conventional, Western models of economic development as appropriate for Latin America, *dependentistas* wanted definitions appropriate to Latin American reality, reflecting needs of concrete people in classes, rather than abstract and impersonal wants.

Modernization theory, another branch of the liberal tradition, detected congenial socio-economic conditions for political democracy in the factors of heightened industrialization, broadening middle classes or 'sectors', and certain helpful ethos, such as 'civic' political culture and civil societies. The structural–functional version of it suggested generic timeless 'functions' of all social and political systems and sought to identify the structures that performed them in different societies. Dependency theorists, however, rubbished its tendency to treat national units as autonomous of the 'international context of national development, underdevelopment and distorted development', along with its deceitful plea for emulating European and North American models of development. They also denied any causal link between socio-economic modernization and political democracy, showing modernization theory to be perfectly compatible with military coups in Brazil (1964), Argentina (1966), and Chile and Uruguay (1973), and even bureaucratic and political authoritarianism. Dependency writers also rejected those areas of USA and even UN policy initiatives, where classical–liberal and modernization thoughts coalesced, such as the US Alliance for Progress for Latin America and, to a lesser extent, the UN Development Decade meant for all the less developed countries, as cosmetic tinkering to sidetrack more radical changes based on equality.

Rejection of the liberal principle of comparative advantage was inspired not only by Marxist thinkers but also by Raúl Prebisch, Celso Furtado, Aníbal Pinto from Latin America and by Ragnar Nurkse, Hans Singer, Gunnar Myrdal and Albert Hirschman, who opposed it in varying degrees. Prebisch argued that in the actual ground of economic relations and the positions of the principally industrial 'centre' and the predominantly 'agricultural-and-extractive' 'periphery', the principles of classical or neoclassical economics founder in the face of unequal exchange. Amid this asymmetric centre–periphery relations—underemphasized by proponents of the dynamics of comparative advantage—and unequal division of gains of trade between centre and the periphery, both development in the centre and underdevelopment in the periphery sprang from the iniquities of the international trading system and were both causally and functionally related manifestations.

The similarities and differences between the structuralist or ECLA model and the dependency approach are as multifaceted as they are nuanced. But, due to space constraints, we first state that while diagnosing what went wrong in Latin America and how it could be redressed, both stressed the importance of autonomous or self-reliant development and the role of unequal terms of trade between the advanced industrial North and Latin America as obstacles to it. Only while structuralism favoured an inward-directed developmental path based on ISI strategy to correct it, the dependency school suggested the institution of a new international economic order (NIEO), and at least some writers in it thought socialism was a way out of the impasse. I say some because eventually the dependency position got split into the *reformist* dependency perspective and the *Marxism-influenced* reading of dependency, with attendant differences in epistemology and methodology.[8]

In spite of their firm Marxist moorings, dependency thinkers also considered certain contentions of Marxists as 'vulgar, outdated, incomplete or faulty', and departed from the traditional Marxist analysis of capitalist imperialism in several important aspects. First, against Lenin's emphasis on political control as the main attribute of capitalist imperialism, they stressed economic means of subordination and substituted political colonialism with economic neocolonialism and informal control. Second, they spurned the classical Marxist view that imperialism facilitated the development of the colonized economy to an extent where it could shake off colonial bonds to argue that even if development really happens, it would be of a *dependent* kind that would not enable the country to free itself from its shackles. Third, *dependentistas* regard MNCs, especially in the manufacturing and services sector, who have displaced the international banking of 'haute finance' and colonial governments that lorded it over less developed countries in Lenin's time, as the chief mechanism of capitalistic domination and exploitation in the advanced 20th century.[9] Fourth, in the area of the analysis of unequal exchange, contrary to Marx's focus on the subjugation of one class by another in the relations of production, the dependency position 'locates surplus extraction at the level of exchanges between countries, rather than in the relationship between classes in production'. One reason of this shift may be that, notwithstanding their edge over other approaches in explaining the source of surplus value through its expropriation in the production process, Marxist studies did not pursue its ramifications in the creation of global inequality, and Marx, despite his intentions, did not carry out his analysis of the world market fully. This neglect again is traceable to Marx's belief in the technologically dynamic character of capitalism vis-à-vis pre-capitalist modes of production. So dependency theory had to remove Marxism's alleged myopia about and partial insight into the 'underdeveloping' tendencies within capitalism.[10]

MAIN TENETS AND TYPOLOGIES OF DEPENDENCY THEORY

In its most basic essentials, the dependency position visualizes the world as comprising two poles: the wealthy, industrialized countries forming the 'centre' or 'core' of the global capitalist system and poorer countries, constituting the 'satellite' or 'periphery'. Coercive regimes perpetuating low wages for labourers by subverting independent labour unions and curbing social movements preponderate in the periphery. In the context of the inability of dependent nations to constitute viable local markets for a series of products from themselves, nations in the core are their inevitable destinations. The core in turn robs them for cheap labour, raw materials and larger markets that would increase their own wealth. Besides, their own class conflicts are temporarily alleviated by their exploitation of the periphery. So dependency theorists claim that development in the centre or core is predicated on underdevelopment of the periphery.

The centre–periphery ordering and its links of exploitation travel down, in Frank's words, 'a whole chain of metropolises and satellites, which runs from the world metropolis down to the hacienda or rural merchant who are satellites of the local commercial metropolitan centre but who in turn have peasants as their satellites'.[11] It extends the capitalist link between the capitalist world and national metropolises to the regional centers (part of whose surplus they appropriate), and from these to local centers, and so on to large landowners or merchants who expropriate surplus from small peasants or tenants, and sometimes from even these latter to landless labourers exploited by them in turn.[12]

The reverse is also true. While power, natural resources and 'surplus value' extracted from cheap labour in the periphery flow bottom up along the ladder of unequal exchange, control, ideology and costly manufactured goods and services move top down. The key agents that further the situation of dependency and thrive on it are foreign capital embodied by MNCs rooted in core nations, rich classes and elites within the periphery and even national governments that assure the core of non-opposition by their masses. Proponents of the dependency perspective emphasize the global nature of capitalism, of which both the core and the periphery are parts, instead of being, as asserted by modernization theorists, 'similar entities at different stages of development'. Accordingly, they challenge the liberal belief that global capitalism is merely the outcome of economic growth to posit that it is rather the consequence of dissimilar relationships of economic development with differential dividends. The inherently unequal nature of these capitalist relationships, at both global and local levels, is underscored by the centre–periphery analogy. So, by contrast to liberal and even Marxist theories of economic development, which regarded capitalism as a homogenizing force, both dependency and world-system theorists concentrated on the inequalities that this set of economic relationships bred.

Within this generic world view, the principal propositions and emphases of the dependency position vary according to the schools they represent, whose names differ according to the typological criteria employed by commentators identifying them. For example, Roberts et al. speak of two schools. The first, spearheaded by Andre Gunder Frank, showed dependency as an inexorable tendency and permanent condition under the capitalist system, remediable only by escaping it entirely. Paul Baran, Theotonio Dos Santos, Samir Amin and other radical thinkers who shared this view contended that the global capitalist system was not inherently competitive, but was controlled by monopolies, which made it impossible for poorer economies to improve their lot through competition. The second, even after acknowledging the deleterious impacts of the situation of dependency, keeps a possibility and scope for some degree of development within this relationship, in the form of 'associated' or 'dependent development'. Having some similarities with the ISI strategy of ECLA, ILPES or CESO, this second school believed that even though dependency was a reality, it was possible to 'ameliorate its effects by pursuing development in only relative isolation from the damaging relationships with wealthy nations'. Roberts et al. consider Cardoso, who mixed a strong historical approach with mainstream dependency theories, to take them to new social and economic directions, as a good spokesman of the 'structuralist' variant of dependency thinking.[13]

Packenham typologizes dependency thinkers in terms of whether they (a) 'analyse dependency only within capitalism or within both capitalism and socialism', (b) 'see solutions to problems of dependency exclusively in either/or terms, or as questions of degree as well', (c) 'stress abstract theory and global laws or concrete, specific situations', (d) are 'mechanical and deterministic or interactive and probabilistic', (e) 'take a rigid class approach or use a more differentiated approach involving groups and class fractions as well as classes', (f) 'treat the state as purely reflective of economic interests or as having its own separate interests', (g) pursue a 'historical or ahistorical' approach, (h) 'see history as open or close ended', (h) have 'closed and unfalsifiable or open and falsifiable ways of knowing', (i) 'see solutions only within capitalism or within both capitalism and socialism', and (j) 'see scholarship as fundamentally an aspect of political struggle or as an enterprise fundamentally separate from political struggle'. While dependency thinkers widely diverge in the answers they give to these questions, Packenham thinks that still it is possible to make a broad grouping where *orthodox* dependency is detectable in tendency to choose the first options in the binarics listed above, and *unorthodox* dependency applies to those who choose 'the second set of options listed'. Packenham places Frank and sharers his views in the orthodox group, while Cardoso with upholders of his views in the unorthodox group.[14]

Kay offers a threefold typology in the backdrop of 'important differences' among dependency thinkers, despite some shared propositions: 'reformist' and 'Marxist' schools in Latin America, and a 'Caribbean dependency school'. Avowedly, Marxists are less cautious while critiquing conventional economic theory and modernization compared to the reformists; more cynical about the ECLA's '*dessarrollista* or developmentalist position' and more critical of the reformists' mistaken focus on the external causes of dependency. They blame the reactionary nature of the local bourgeoisie and the incapacity of the national–populist alliance to act as catalysts of authentic development for the failure of ISI-based industrialization. Marxists look askance at the reformists' adoption of a modified version of 'modernization-cum-developmentalist theory', and their trust in a new populist alliance seeking to reform the existing economic system, since nothing short of a socialist revolution can eradicate the problems of underdevelopment and dependency. This is spurned by reformists as utopian. Kay includes Marini, Dos Santos, Frank, Oscar Braun, Vania Bambirra, Anibal Quijano, Edelbarto Torres-Rivas, Tomás Amadeo Vasconi, Antonio Garcia, Alonso Aguilar and so on as Marxist dependency thinkers. Compared to the above two schools, the Caribbean school was more 'coherent' and 'tightly knit' because the reformist and Marxist views upheld by its individual members did not, in spite of their ideological differences, harden into 'Marxist and reformist wings, as in the Latin American school'. After admitting misgivings about 'some degree of "arbitrariness and simplification...involved"' in this classification, Kay himself questionably includes Cardoso, along with Enzo Falletto, Sunkel, Jaguaribe, Furtado, Aldo Ferrer and Pinto among *reformist* dependency thinkers.[15] After reading my discussion above of the sources of dependency thinking, you might find Cardoso's branding as non-Marxist as astonishing as branding of Furtado and Pinto, precursors of dependency thinking, as reformist *dependentistas*.

Slightly differently, Gilpin identifies three schools while 'explaining how the situation of dependency came about'. The first two of these—'exploitation' and 'imperial neglect'—are clubbable in Roberts's first school. According to the exploitation theory, of which Samir Amin is a major spokesman, the poverty of the Third World is caused by its systemic exploitation. Rather than benefiting Third-World countries, the processes of trade and investment facilitate a transfer of wealth from the Third World to the First World. The underdevelopment of the less developed countries is both causally and functionally linked to the development of the developed countries, since the modern world system functions in a way that allows the advanced core to fleece the periphery of its economic surplus. In consequence, dependence does not merely incommode the full development of the less developed countries but also leads to the progressive immiseration of their economies.

While including 'imperial neglect' as another position in dependency literature, Gilpin quotes Brown about its apparent incongruity to concede that it 'perhaps should not even be classified as dependency theory'.[16] While analysing the impact of the world economy on less developed countries, this school shows how some less developed economies, especially the least developed among them, suffered by being 'bypassed by the forces of capitalist imperialism'. The trade-and-investment-induced expansion of world capitalism, coupled with European migration, engendered an international division of labour that favoured some countries at the cost of others. But even in countries adversely affected, 19th-century capitalist imperialism created conditions of economic development through its impetus to trade and infrastructure investments, such as in ports, railways and urban settlements. But this happened only in a selected set of privileged countries. In others, where the spread of capitalism and the depth of its impact were much less, archaic modes of production survived to slow down economic progress. Yet others, fully bypassed by the process, lamented why they were not colonized by the core. So, while causing underdevelopment by nurturing unequal patterns of trade and investment, the world capitalist economy has bred a 'differential impact on the global periphery'.

The third school of 'dependent or associated development' (Roberts's second school) utilizes the evidence of the relative economic prosperity of newly industrializing countries such as Brazil, South Korea and Taiwan to contend that dependency relations can in certain circumstances make for fast economic growth, even though it is not 'true development' for many reasons. First, excessive dependence on export of raw materials in conditions of fluctuating prices breeds domestic economic instability. Second, dependent development results in maldistribution of national income, creating selfish tastes in the elites for foreign-made, luxury goods, and suppressing real needs of the masses, so that the resultant social inequalities and cultural imperialism 'reinforce the dominance of external capitalism'. Third, manufacturing investments and the consequent conditioned industrialization create 'an inefficient branch plant economy with high production costs' that decimate local entrepreneurship and technological innovation and rob the country by repatriated profits. Foreign-based undertakings gain control over key industrial sectors and flush out local firms from capital markets, ushering in inappropriate capital-intensive technology in the country. The international division between 'high-technology industries of the core and low-technology industries of the periphery' disturbs the process of 'autonomous or self-sustaining development based on domestic technology'. And the higher wages paid by MNCs to local employees distort the local labour market, leading to waste and unemployment. Apart from these evils, it necessitates authoritarian regimes, which will provide MNCs the political stability they demand, to sustain reliance on foreign capital. To sum up, the limited prosperity ensured by 'associated' or 'dependent development' is bought at too high a cost. It is not genuine and authentic development because it generates income inequalities, cultural imperialism and other deleterious consequences that mar the chances of real economic and political independence of the country.[17]

Now let us see, to what extent, these differences of approach influence the definitions of dependency, identifications of their causes and prescriptions for their removal by representative dependency thinkers.

COMMONALITIES AND DIVERGENCES OF INDIVIDUAL DEPENDENCY THINKERS IN DEFINITIONS AND IDENTIFICATION OF CAUSES OF DEPENDENCY, AND SUGGESTIONS FOR ITS CURE

Since dependency thinkers of different schools frequently overstep their limits, they do not always define dependency all too differently and, even among themselves, frequently disagree about the causes of dependency. This will be evident from two 'unorthodox' definitions of dependency from Sunkel, and two Marxist, one definition each from Dos Santos and Frank, reproduced below.

> Development and underdevelopment can therefore be understood as partial structures, but interdependent, which form a single system. A principal characteristic which differentiates

> both structures is that the developed one, to a large extent by its indigenous capacity of growth is the dominant, and the underdeveloped, due in part to the induced character of its dynamic, is dependent (Sunkel).[18]

> Both underdevelopment and development are aspects of the same phenomenon, both are historically simultaneous, both are linked functionally, and therefore, interact [with] and condition each other mutually. This results...in the division of the world between industrial, advanced or 'central' countries, and underdeveloped, backward or 'peripheral' countries (Sunkel).[19]

> By dependence we mean a situation in which the economy of certain countries is conditioned by the development and expansion of another economy to which the former is subjected. The relationship of interdependence between two or more economies, and between these and world trade, assumes the form of dependence when some countries (the dominant ones) can expand and can be self-sustaining, while other countries (the dependent ones) can do this only as a reflection of that expansion, which can have either a positive or a negative effect on their immediate development (Dos Santos).[20]

Evidently, Sunkel's two definitions largely tally with that of Dos Santos regarding the impact of interdependence and dependent countries' lack of autonomous potential for growth, since both hold that underdevelopment, or the shape of development in dependent countries, is nothing but the particular form of capitalist development there. Both of them also concur that dependency owes to the compulsive absorption of these countries by the dominant core into the world capitalist system. So their underdevelopment never replicated a comparable historical phase that the capitalist countries too once passed through. Frank reiterates the same point from his Marxist perspective, when complaining that 'ignorance of the underdeveloped countries' history' leads to the misperception that the less developed countries' pasts and present recall 'earlier stages of the now developed countries', even though 'a modest acquaintance with history' convinces us that 'underdevelopment is not original or traditional and that neither the past nor the present of the underdeveloped countries resembles in any important respect the past of the now developed countries'. These were 'never underdeveloped, though they may have been undeveloped'. Again, the lesson of historical research is that the contemporary underdevelopment of a country

> is in large part the historical product of past or continuing economic and other relations between the satellite underdeveloped and the now developed metropolitan countries. Furthermore, these relations are an essential part of the structure and development of the capitalist system on a world scale as a whole.[21]

Frank's points about the different pasts of the core and peripheral countries and explanation of their dependency in terms of the forceful incorporation of the non-capitalist world into an exploitative capitalist system are not also much different from Sunkel's, as shown below.

> The present international panorama of countries at different levels of development is not simply an aggregate of individual historical performances; the development process is not simply a race...in which some countries reached advanced stages while others stagnated or moved slower...one of the essential elements of the development of capitalism has been, from the outset, the creation of an international system which brought the world economy under the influence of a few European countries, plus the Unites States.... Development and

> underdevelopment, in this view, are simultaneous processes: the two faces of the historical evolution of the capitalist system.[22]

Comparing Sunkel's and Dos Santos' quotations,[23] we see that both portray the present situation of dependency as an inescapable and permanent stable condition caused by the entire capitalist system. Do then the main differences between the different perspectives on dependency lie in the possibility of the amount of development they allow/disallow under dependency, as well as thc possibility/impossibility that they emphasize about transforming this situation under the world capitalist system? This seems to be the case if we contrast the views of those who view dependency as a permanent form of incapacitation under capitalism (Frank, Baran, Dos Santos and Amin) and those who kept a possibility of a modicum of development under capitalism (Cardoso, Falletto, Sunkel, Jaguaribe, Furtado, Ferrer, Pinto and so on), that is, contrast the views of the *orthodox* and *unorthodox* schools as per Packenham, or the *exploitation-centred* and *dependent-development-centred* schools as per Gilpin. I shun the epithets of *reformist* and *Marxist*, finding it impossible to deprive Cardoso's thinking of any Marxist lineage, even though this is the most accepted divide. Font's branding of Frank's position as 'radical',[24] or Packenham's use of the epithet 'unorthodox' is more apt. Anyway, the reformist or rather the unorthodox strand, upholding dependent/associated development in its most noted formulation by Cardoso and Falletto, is charged with betrayal of the cause, and with selling away the concept of dependency in favour of a conservative and neoliberal version 'interdependency'. Valencia too finds Marini's critique of Cardoso justified that he regarded the dependent economy as an 'accidental occurrence' in the historical development of capitalism, instead of seeing it as an 'immanent condition' of it.[25]

To gauge the distance between these schools regarding the way out from dependency, it would be best to compare the views of Frank and Cardoso/Falletto more specifically, with the views of other *dependentistas* sharing their views thrown in when needed.

DEBATE ON THE WAY OUT OF DEPENDENCY: FRANK AND CARDOSO

In sharp contradistinction to the radicals or the unorthodox, Frank rules out the chances of peripheral countries remaining integrated with the capitalist world economy and gaining real development. His 'dual society' and 'development of underdevelopment' theses proffered the extremist solution of severing contact with Western capitalism and treading the path of revolutionary socialism. Speaking on the dependency situation of Chile and Brazil, Frank rubbished the ECLA thesis of ISI strategies, asserting that as their economies get more intensely integrated with the global capitalist system, it becomes increasingly evident that neither national capitalism nor national bourgeoisie can offer a way out of underdevelopment in Latin America. The bourgeoisie could give no leadership here since the 'progressive potential of the Chilean bourgeoisie and its state' is hamstrung 'not by any "non-capitalist" or "pre-capitalist" institutions or structure' but by 'the very capitalist structure imposed on it by its own world capitalist metropolis' and also by the vested interest the bourgeoisie develops in preserving this capitalist structure at world, national, provincial and local levels in tandem with other bourgeois vested groups.

Since the 'political tasks faced by those who would free Chile and their sister countries from underdevelopment are no less urgent and profound than the scientific ones', Frank suggested action from below, exacerbating their internal contradictions, as the only solution of this impasse. Expropriation of the economic surplus and the limitations to development emanating from exploitation by the metropolis was sure to breed contradictions between the metropolis and the Chilean bourgeoisie on the one hand, and the provincial bourgeois groups and the exploitative Chilean bourgeoisie on the other and compel the lowest rungs and weakest groups of the exploited local bourgeoisie to pursue confrontational polices against them. While these minor contradictions would only lightly impact the cohesiveness of the bourgeoisie, the contradictory development of capitalism and the resultant underdevelopment of Chile will convince the people themselves of 'both the necessity and the possibility of liberating the economy from underdevelopment and providing for the development of its people'. Frank's diagnosis was that, in our times, as 'the contradictions deepen, the process accelerates, the discontinuity destroys the system', and 'the opportunity of liberating their people and developing their civilization is at hand', the people would seize this opportunity, compelling leaders to follow. For Brazil too, he belittled any positive action from the national bourgeoisie and stressed the importance of mass action. For, the 'largest and strongest sectors' of the bourgeoisie, being 'the most dependent on the imperialist metropolis', would try to avert the limitations to development that are perpetuated by the metropolis by 'sticking their head still further into the jaws of the imperialist lion'. The bourgeoisie being 'less and less able to face these problems [of expropriation of surplus and consequent underdevelopment], the long exploited people themselves are being taught and prepared to lead the way out of capitalism and underdevelopment'.[26] In the backdrop of the political turmoil in the mid-1960s and early 1970s mentioned at the beginning, this proposal of mass action constituted 'a blank endorsement of guerrilla action and revolutionary movements' along the lines of the Cuban Revolution. With ideological support from Western fascination with Latin American revolutionaries and ideational foment from Regis Debray's *Revolution within Revolution* (1967) for the movement, dependency theory got closely 'identified with the radical approach of Frank'. That he wrote in English and published early in America also helped.[27]

But all this proved very unfortunate for Cardoso's much more nuanced approach, which was increasingly misunderstood while seeking to convince us that though capitalist production does strengthen underdevelopment, it possesses an innate dynamism that may transform the forces and relations of production in peripheral countries. Admitting thus a possibility of development, even if 'dependent', within Latin America, Cardoso's historical approach to underdevelopment abjured the economic determinism based on over-reliance on external causes that he thought crippled Frank's and his followers' approaches. He focused more on how local social practices incommode and/or promote neo-imperialism. Whether alone or in collaboration with Falletto, he scrutinized the role of alliances between foreign interests and local classes, including the role of alliances among local constellations of labour, peasants, ethnic groups, national bourgeoisie and ideologies of liberalism, nationalism and so on and argued that 'in spite of structural "determination", there is room for alternatives in history, their actualization depending not just on basic contradictions between interests, but also on the perception of new ways of turning a historical corner through "a passion for the possible"'.[28]

Not content with 'criticizing on theoretical grounds either the structural approach to socio-economic development proposed by ECLA, or the structural–functionalist models prevailing in sociological analyses, or blaming vulgar Marxism or the theory of political modernization', Cardoso and Falletto sought to focus on 'significant moments of structural change in countries characterized by different situations of dependency in Latin America'. Methodologically, rather than seeking to explain important stages of dependent societies only through the 'logic of capitalistic accumulation' from 'mechanistic conceptions of history', they wanted to explore internal causes as much as external ones and portray imperialism as 'an active and metaphysical principle' that etches out the 'paths of history on the sensitive but passive skin of dependent countries'. 'Forms of local societies', their political dynamics, 'reactions against imperialism' and efforts to discover 'alternatives', all these had to be kept in reckoning for understanding Latin American outcomes, these societies being passive but not inert. Even where imperialist penetration was brought about by 'external social forces' represented by 'multinational enterprises, foreign technology, international financial systems, embassies, foreign states, and armies, etc.', the system of domination transformed itself into an 'internal' force expressed through 'the social practices of local groups and classes' that champion foreign interests not as foreign interests but as coinciding with values and interests of their own. The distance of this approach from orthodox views becomes clearer when Cardoso and Falletto claim that 'the forms of social and economic exploitation' in Latin American countries, the degree of 'industrialization and capital accumulation' there, the relation of 'local economies to the international market' and so on can be understood not just as the consequence of a 'logic of capital accumulation' but also of particular relationships and struggles between social classes and groups at the international as well at the local level.[29]

Believing that description and analysis of contemporary forms and situations of dependent development promise to be 'the most significant contribution by *dependentistas* to the theory of capitalistic societies', Cardoso and Falletto sought to categorize situations in which a nation is overwhelmingly shackled by foreign capital or is seen even amid underdevelopment making efforts to secure a kind of political severance from the centre nations. This is because even though in circumstances of pervasive colonial dependency 'local history is reduced to a reflection of what happens in a metropolis', the resolve of local forces to resist colonialism to forge a nation involves 'an attempt to influence local history according to local values and interests'. To that extent, national underdevelopment is a dualistic condition of 'objective economic subordination to outside nations and enterprises, and at the same time, of partial attempts to cope with "national interests" through the state and social movements that try to preserve political autonomy'.[30] Accordingly, Cardoso differentiated between *autonomous developed* countries like the USA, *dependent developed* economies as Brazil, *autonomous but underdeveloped* nations such as Cuba and *dependent and underdeveloped* countries as those depicted by Frank and other radicals. Besides portraying these differential trajectories of dependent economies, getting industrialized or remaining primary producers, Cardoso identifies three forms of dependency marked by three locales of capital accumulation and three types of external imperatives from capitalism.

- An enclave economy, where production for export is strictly and openly controlled by foreign capital, generating financial dependency and externally originating capital accumulation.
- A nationally controlled economy, in which production for export is regulated by 'national' capital, engendering commercial dependency and internally originating capital accumulation.
- The 'new dependency' or the post-1950 form of dependency in which MNCs make direct investments in the industrialization of the periphery, not seeking exports but greater control over their internal markets.

These different types of dependency presuppose appropriate changes in the external phases of capitalism, being articulated with competitive capitalism, monopolistic capitalism, industrial capitalism or financial capitalism.[31] While identifying various phases in the world capitalist system and different configurations of external–internal linkages, dependency literature differentiates between (a) the 'mercantilistic' colonial era (1500–1750), (b) the era of 'outward growth' based on exports of primary products (1750–1914), (c) the era of the crisis of the liberal solution and (d) the final period of transnational capitalism. Cardoso's three types of dependency help in understanding their dynamics. In a new light, we see Cardoso and Falletto's contention that foreign investment no longer remains 'a simple zero-sum game of exploitation as was the pattern in classical imperialism', and that 'dependency, monopoly capitalism, and development are not contradictory things' anymore since 'there occurs a kind of dependent capitalist development in the sectors of the Third World integrated into the new forms of monopolistic expansion'.[32] Cardoso allows dependency theory to claim that 'there exist more dynamic forms of dependence than those characterizing enclave or quasi-colonial situations (even allowing greater degrees of manoeuver to the national states and to the bourgeoisie locally allied to the state and to the multinationals'. He is not worried by the argument that the situation is then more of interdependence than dependence. For, the possibility of development notwithstanding, close examination of the relationship of the economies marked by 'dependent-associated development' and the central economies makes it hard to miss an 'international division of labor... based on unequal degrees of wealth, on unequal forms appropriation of the international surplus, and on the monopolization of the dynamic capitalist sectors by the central countries'. The former are unmistakably distinct as 'sectors of production of capital goods and the generation of new technologies', 'most revolutionary sectors at the level of productive forces' and 'decisive in the scheme of reproduction of capital', being controlled by the 'central nuclei of multinational firms', and the external debt remaining 'oscillating but continuous'.

Quite persuasively, Cardoso analyses the '"historical agents" of social transformation' identified by both the 'stagnationist' or 'underconsumptionist' writers.[33] Cardoso finds that stagnationists are inclined to 'repeating clichés that explain little'. Among underconsumptionists, he sides with those who eschew both these 'idyllic' and 'catastrophic' visions and points out three ways in which peripheral societies could achieve development. First, when an economically dependent nation state fashions an autonomous decision-making process and rearranges its economy in non-peripheral directions, either through revolution or political reforms that impact the internal relation of forces and accelerate advancement of the stages of development; second, when nationally controlled export-oriented economies generate an amount of internal capital accumulation that allows them to pursue industrialization even amid trade dependency and, third, when a country that is dependent in its internal decision-making process, and even peripheral, being economically subordinate in the international market, experiences development through industrial expansion and multinational capital investments, especially those which facilitate technology transfer, without shaking off their dependent status, as in the case of Peru.[34]

CRITIQUE AND EVALUATION

Ever since the 1970s, dependency theory has drawn flak from modernization theory, Marxism and others, concerning its methodology, concept of dependency and policy implications. Consequently, the criticisms became so varied and vast that it sometimes lost track of the original dependency thinkers and presented partial critiques as comprehensive. Besides, since critics in the Anglo-Saxon world tended to take Frank as the sole representative of dependency theory, often criticisms targeting Frank have been mistaken as an across-the-board rebuttal of all dependency arguments, including non-Frankian analyses in the general condemnation, thereby effacing important differences between dependency thinkers.[35] Munck says that this does not 'detract from the role of Frank as iconoclastic gadfly, consummate synthesizer, and someone not afraid to move on to new problematics', but merely shows that 'his role has led to a distortion of the understanding of the dependency perspective outside Latin America'. A 'postcolonial analysis of this process would see this as another (mis)appropriation of the periphery by the center'.[36] So a good approach would be to first state the main points of critique and then see where they apply and where they do not.

Expectedly, modernization theorists, whom *dependentistas* branded as providers of a façade for Western countries' exploitation of less developed countries, counter-attacked it as 'a propaganda fragment of Marxist revolutionary ideology', 'exercises in pamphleteering' rather than 'products of scholarly work', a school that 'gave up the battle for science to lapse into rhetoric' and rather than trying to proffer 'a scientific analysis of what actually happened in Third World countries,...became an all-purpose explanation of everything that is wrong' with them. It was also dubbed 'highly abstract', logically flawed, contradictory and deterministic in its search for a general pattern, and mistakenly treating all peripheral countries as the same. Dependency thinkers were charged for their deductive approach to analyses of peripheral nations, forcing them to fit into the dependency model instead of bringing out 'the historically specific development of each particular Third-World country'. By considering dependency as a 'global phenomenon', dependency studies allegedly 'have little room left for analysis of national variants'.[37] But, from what we have shown above, the charge of homogenizing dependency in Third-World countries, ignoring analysis of national variants, may apply to the orthodox/radical position, or to Frank and his ilk, but not to the unorthodox or reformist thinkers like Cardoso.

The Marxists' first problem about the methodology of dependency studies is that these locate the expropriation of surplus in the registers of exchanges between countries and not in the relations between classes in the production process, because of which subjugation of one country by another disturbs the Marxian focus on subjugation of one class by another. Besides, while identifying the surplus transfer mechanism, the dependency perspective faces the theoretical difficulty of having no explanation for the 'source and growth of the surplus production of a society'.[38] As we can see, even this charge is only partly applicable to the unorthodox/reformist strand of dependency studies coming from Cardoso. For, he has shown how even for dependent and even peripheral countries capital accumulation is possible.[39]

Marxists moreover problematize the concept of dependency as an 'eclectic combination of orthodox economic theory and revolutionary phraseology', whose meaning is 'ever more elusive, not to say mystical' and 'totally misleading'.[40] Their objections mainly revolve around its overemphasis on external conditions, which induces neglect of the role of internal dynamics emanating from class conflict and the state. This supposedly misses the 'clarity with which classical Marxism located the question of class struggle at the centre of development and decay of capitalism'. Besides, any attempt at conceptualizing the issues of Third-World countries solely in terms of dependency allegedly leads to overlooking the most decisive processes of class formation and social relations that generate change. So, while conceding the importance of examining the transfer of surplus from the periphery, Marxists enjoin dependency researchers to introduce social classes, political struggles and the state in their framework to make understandable the mechanisms and rationale of surplus transfer. Neglect of political struggles emanates from the assumptions of the dependency school that Third-World industrialists are a comprador-bourgeoisie class thriving on foreign capital; that Third-World governments are little more than 'administrative committees' of foreign capital and the metropolitan state and that Third-World workers are a 'labour aristocracy' whose interests are served by foreign capital. In this situation, it is inconceivable that domestic classes and institutions will try to shake off the yoke of foreign domination and institute-independent development. The resultant oversight of the internal workings of interests and nascent political struggles induces dependentistas to present a mistaken picture of inert peripheries with diminutive degrees of freedom, where the exaggerated impact of external forces presents dependency as the ineluctable fate of backward countries. In this model, the dynamic of the system emanates wholly from the centre, and the 'periphery, whether originally in Europe, or today in Third-World countries, becomes a passive victim of capitalism from without'.

Other detractors of dependency theory challenge this picture of immutable nemesis in many ways. Some cite abundant historical evidence about some leeway even for dependent countries, such as 'their ability to carry out, under some circumstances, fairly drastic policies of internal and external transformation'.[41] Lall contends that 'dependency is impossible to define and cannot be shown to be causally related to the continuance of underdevelopment'.[42] But again, we see from the typology of dependency made by unorthodox and reformist scholars led by Cardoso, and Cardoso's own criticisms of Frankian dependency theory, including his point that the '"historical agents" of social transformation' identified by both the 'stagnationist' or 'underconsumptionist' writers are wrong, that the second charge too strikes them less harder.[43]

Surprisingly, the interdisciplinarity of the dependency discourse and 'its orientation towards long-term strategic policy issues' have also attracted critics who allege that its 'ambitious interdisciplinary orientation invites oversimplification', while its 'concern with strategic policy creates intense pressures to draw broad conclusions quickly, and to become committed to the conclusions once drawn', though these 'shortcomings neither excuse the weaknesses, nor invalidate the approach'.[44] For, issues of policy concern stem primarily from dependency theory's deep belief in the deleterious effects of colonialism and international division of labour, which convinces it that so long as the extant unequal exchange prevails, 'extraversion, hypertrophy, technical dependency, the development of underdevelopment, and so on' will inescapably trouble Third-World countries. This makes a radical strategy of socialist revolution the only way out of this externally imposed crippling dependency. But all critics do not consider the prospect so bleak. Judging the possibility of coexistence of dependency with development, Weeks shows that, during the 20th century, a number of countries, including Chile, China, Denmark, Ireland, Japan and North Korea, cast off the shackles of underdevelopment to strive for and achieve 'advanced capitalist development in terms of their income per capita, economic structure or economic and political power'. Alvin So shows that South Korea and Taiwan, once colonies of Japan, also managed to make rapid economic progress since the Second World War.[45] Should one important test of a theory be 'its ability to address the exceptions to its main conclusion, dependency theory would seem to fail'. But Weeks points out two policy implications of dependency theory that are counterfactual and clueless. The first suggests that 'relatively isolated countries, for example in Latin America and Sub-Saharan Africa, would be more likely to grow more "autonomously"', compared to other developing countries that are more closely tied to international trade and financial flows, though it 'contradicts historical experience'. The second is its failure to provide any explanation of the 'initial division of countries between advanced and dependent', the colonizer and the colonized. Irrespective of our unacceptance of it, the fervour with which Marxist economists have grappled with these issues is sadly missing in dependency theory. Another charge that touches the policy implications of dependency theory targets its 'functionalism', in the sense of placing structure over agency and assuming that 'the historical development and the social structure of the periphery can be explained by their functionality with Western capitalism'. Given the absence of any autonomous agency, 'dependent countries tied to the world market *cannot* develop'. This functionalist determinism is criticized by Weeks in these terms.

> However, the claim that capitalist development is impossible in the periphery is insufficient to support the claim for revolution. At best, the argument that the periphery is exploited by the centre implicitly makes a case for nationalism. If underdevelopment is due to international integration, the logical solution is not socialism, but a delinked national development strategy.... In practice, this approach leaves the state as the most important agent of national emancipation, which again is incompatible with purported socialist objectives.[46]

We see again that the points about the historical evidence of autonomous progress of the economies of Chile, China, Denmark, Ireland, Japan, South Korea, Taiwan and even North Korea in rebutting the stock branding of dependent countries as destined to underdevelopment do not apply to Cardoso's and others' reformist/unorthodox version of dependency. Further, the claim that 'relatively isolated countries...would be more likely to grow more "autonomously"' cannot explain the lamentation of bypassed undeveloped countries in the imperial neglect school.[47] And the final critique of ideological incompatibility between the two solutions prescribed by dependency theory—delinking for nationally pursued development strategies (foregrounding the national state) and the dream of a socialist revolution—can apply only to the Frankian position, not Cardoso's.

But though no shotgun critique of dependency theory could accordingly capture well the strengths and weaknesses of individual approaches or say something meaningful, such across-the-board attacks *were* made, terming it as no more 'serviceable', and therefore needing to be 'transcended',[48] or rejected outright,[49] 'vitiated by a variable combination of circular reasoning, fallacious inferences from empirical observation and a weak base in deductive theory',[50] reflecting 'the class needs of local dominant classes'[51] and meant to 'divert and dampen support for socialist revolution'.[52] The case for closure of the approach was accordingly made on widely divergent grounds of economism, utopianism, structuralism, non-Marxism, eclecticism, nationalism, populism, globalism, determinism and so on, all made plausible because dependency was 'a fluid, labile concept', lacking any 'unified political belonging', readily appropriable by dissimilar political ideologies, conveying 'quite different things to different people and in different contexts' and capable of 'being used by generals and guerrillas, nationalists and socialists'.

In its defence, dependency theory may have been 'economistic'; its orthodox version may not have added something wholly new, due to the existence of the Marxian belief of determination in the last instance; the underpinning economism may have been tied to a certain form of mechanistic analysis characteristic of functionalism and may have banished political agency. Besides, its most variants may have favoured economic nationalism, 'hardly surprising given the postcolonial situation in which it arose and the nationalist tinge of Marxism in the Third World at that time', may have been weakest in the area of specifying development alternatives and may have adopted a totalizing approach in typical modernistic fashion.[53] But these lacunae do not belittle the significance of dependency theory's concerns about the inordinately 'large net flows of resources from underdeveloped to advanced countries', dramatized by the international debt crisis of the 1980s, which emerged earlier, continued later and dispirited countries bent by debt. Even if these flows did not provide direct empirical evidence for the claims of the dependency perspective, they did point to the myopia of 'neoclassical analysis that views the international economy as harmonious' and the incompleteness of 'Marxian analyses that tend to focus overwhelmingly on class relations'.[54] Besides, in the backdrop of later, more nuanced work on dependency and strategies of its reversal,[55] it is not risky to suggest that studies of underdevelopment have moved beyond both modernization and dependency theories. Neither can answer the new questions that scholars are raising in the context of comparative studies, such as 'why countries facing similar international circumstances pursue differing development strategies?' While dependency theory focuses on external constraints to answer this question and overlooks 'domestically generated variation across countries', modernization theory emphasizes internal factors but focuses on 'broad social and cultural traits that change slowly and are only loosely connected to specific policy choices'. In contradistinction to both, the more recent literature highlights 'the roles that political coalitions, as well as bureaucracies, institutional, and political structures play in determining which development path a particular state is likely to choose'. These additional factors help to explain why some Latin American countries (such as Brazil and Mexico) have chosen inward-directed development strategies valuing autonomy, while some East Asian countries (such as

South Korea and Taiwan) have gone for outward-looking development paths centred on export promotion.[56]

CONCLUSION

This chapter examined the disciplinary and contextual origins of dependency, its Marxist and non-Marxist sources and its main tenets and typologies to find out the commonalities and divergences about definitions of dependency by individual dependentistas. It has accordingly summarized the debate on the way out of dependency as reflected in the writings of leading orthodox and unorthodox thinkers, mainly Frank and Cardoso, regarding the possibilities of development and capital accumulation, even if 'dependent', within Latin America (as per Cardoso), obviating severance from the capitalist system and social revolution as the only alternatives (as Frank reckoned). The chapter has discussed Cardoso's specification of three forms of dependency marked by three locales of capital accumulation and three types of external imperatives from capitalism (an enclave economy/a nationally controlled economy/ and the 'new dependency' or the post-1950 form of dependency). The chapter has shown how, due to these internal diversities, no shotgun critique of dependency theory can adequately capture strengths and weaknesses of individual approaches, and how later nuanced researches on dependency and strategies of its reversal have progressed beyond early crude dependency theory and its bête noir, modernization theory.

But even with all their imperfections, dependency studies were forerunners of more recent work on alternative development models and also of what has come to be known as 'post-development'.[57] Escobar, known for his diatribes against the 'invention of development', its role in 'strategies of cultural and social domination' and the anachronism of radical core–periphery models in the mid-1990s, because the politics of global trade had grown more complex, did not go to the extent of saying that the core–periphery models were no longer theoretically relevant. In the case of Latin America, trade still tended to be dominated by core–periphery patterns, even though for some of them (especially for oil exporting countries) alternative models of underdevelopment were available since, as argued by Lairson and Skidmore, they had better resources to bargain with MNCs.[58] Anyway, Escobar conceded that though dependency theories, based on concepts of dependence and unequal exchange, 'did not constitute an alternative to development, they amounted to a different view of development and an important critique of bourgeois development economics'.[59]

REVIEW QUESTIONS

1. Give examples of 'unorthodox'/reformist and Marxist definitions of dependence.
2. Explain the disciplinary and situational context of the rise of dependency theory.
3. Elaborate the Marxist and non-Marxist sources of the dependency position.

4. How would you typologize the dependency perspective? Describe the main tenets specific to the different versions of it.
5. Are there commonalities and divergences among individual dependency thinkers regarding indicators of dependency and suggestions for its eradication? If not, state why. If so, state them.
6. Evaluate dependency theory in the context of the post-development position.

NOTES AND REFERENCES

1. Cristóbal Kay and Robert N. Gywnne, 'Relevance of Structuralist and Dependency Theories in the Neoliberal Period: A Latin American Perspective', in *Critical Perspectives on Globalization and Neoliberalism in the Developing Countries*, eds. Richard Legé Harris and Melinda J. Seid (Leiden: Brill, 2000), 50; Viotti and Kauppi, *International Relations*, 406.
2. See Robert A. Packenham, *The Dependency Movement: Scholarship and Politics in Development Studies* (Cambridge, MA; London: Harvard University Press, 1992), 1–2; Robert Gilpin, *The Political Economy of International Relations* (Princeton, NJ: Princeton university Press, 1987), 291–292; Adrián Sotelo Valencia, *Sub-Imperialism Revisited: Dependency Theory in the Thought of Ruy Mauro Marini* (Leiden; Boston, MA: Brill, 2017), 25–26. I will not, however, choose any one of the epithets exclusively.
3. See Ronald H. Chilcote, 'Issues of Theory in Dependency and Marxism', in Chilcote *Dependency and Marxism: Toward a Resolution of the Debate* (Latin American Perspectives Series), ed. Ronald H. Chilcote (Boulder, CO: Westview Press, 1982), 3.
4. See particularly articles by Colin Henfrey, Carlos Johnson, Gary Nigel Howe, David Barkin and Ronaldo Munck in Chilcote, *Dependency and Marxism.*
5. See Fernando Henrique Cardoso, 'The Consumption of Dependency Theory in the United States', *Latin American Research Review* 12, no. 3 (1977): 9; 'Imperialismo y dependencia en América Latina', in *Estada y sociedad en América Latina*, ed. Fernando Henrique Cardoso (Buenos Aires: Nueva Vision, 1972), 4, both cited in Packenham, *The Dependency Movement*, 7–9.
6. See Fernando Henrique Cardoso, 'Dependency and Development in Latin America', in *An Introduction to the Sociology of 'Developing Societies'*, eds. Hamza Alavi and Teodor Shanin (New York, NY: Monthly Review Press, 1982), 112–127, especially 112.
7. All cited in Packenham, *The Dependency Movement*, 9–13.
8. Ibid., 14–17; Cristóbal Kay, *Latin American Theories of Development and Underdevelopment* (London; New York, NY: Routledge, [1989]2011), 26–28; Kay and Gywnne, 'Relevance of Structuralist and Dependency Theories in the Neoliberal Period ', 50; Valencia, *Sub-Imperialism Revisited*, 25–26.
9. Gilpin, *The Political Economy of International Relations*, 284.
10. John Weeks, 'Dependency Theory', in *The Elgar Companion to Marxist Economics*, eds. Ben Fine and Alfredo Saad-Filho (Cheltenham; Northampton, MA: Edward Elgar, 2012), 100.
11. A. G. Frank, *Latin America: Underdevelopment or Revolution* (Harmondsworth: Penguin, 1969), cited by Martin Slattery, *Key Ideas in Sociology* (Cheltenham: Nelson Thornes, 2003), 93.
12. Andre Gunder Frank, *Capitalism and Underdevelopment in Latin America: Historical Studies of Chile and Brazil* (New York, NY; London: Monthly Review Press, [1967]2009), 7–8.
13. See J. Timmons Roberts, 'Introduction', Part II, 'Dependency and Beyond', in *The Globalization and Development Reader: Perspectives on Development and Global Change,*

2nd ed., eds., J. T. Roberts, Amy Bellone Hite and Nitsan Chorev (Chichester: Wiley Blackwell, 2015), 97–100.

14. Packenham, *The Dependency Movement*, 31–32.
15. Kay, *Latin American Theories of Development and Underdevelopment*, 126–128.
16. Michael P. Brown, *After Imperialism* (New York, NY: Humanities Press, 1979).
17. Gilpin, *The Political Economy of International Relations*, 284–286. Also see Robert G. Gilpin, 'Development and Underdevelopment: Conflicting Perspectives on the Third World', in *Philosophy, History and Social Action: Essays in Honor of Lewis Feuer*, eds., S. Hook, W. O'Neill and R. O'Toole, with an autobiographical essay by Lewis Feuer (Dordrecht; Boston, MA; London: Kluwer Academic Publishers, 1988), 187–189.
18. Osvaldo Sunkel, 'Transnational Capitalism and National Disintegration in Latin America', *Social and Economic Studies* 22, no. 1 (1973): 132–176, here 136.
19. Osvaldo Sunkel and Pedro Paz, *El Subdesarrollo Latinoamericano y la Teoria del Desarrollo* (Mexico City: Latin American Institute for Economic and Social Planning, 1970), 6, cited in J. Samuel Valenzuela and Arturo Valenzuela, 'Modernization and Dependency: Alternative Perspectives in the Study of Latin American Underdevelopment', *Comparative Politics* 10, no. 4 (1978): 535–557. doi:10.2307/421571; here 544.
20. Theotonio Dos Santos, 'The Structure of Dependency', *American Economic Review* 60, no. 2 (1921): 231–236, here 231.
21. Andre Gunder Frank, 'The Development of Underdevelopment', *Monthly Review* 18, no. 4 (1969): 17–31, reproduced in Roberts, Hite and Chorev, *The Globalization and Development Reader*, 105–106.
22. Osvaldo Sunkel, 'Big Business and Dependencia: A Latin American View', *Foreign Affairs* (1972), reprinted in Viotti and Kauppi, *International Relations*, 477–889, especially 479.
23. See notes 18–20 above.
24. Mauricio A. Font, 'Introduction', in *Charting a New Course: The Politics of Globalization and Social Transformation*, ed. Fernando Henrique Cardoso (Lanham, MD: Rowman & Littlefield Publishers, 2001), 6.
25. Ruy Mauro Marini, *Dialéctica de la Dependencia* (Ciudad de México: ERA, 1973), 91, cited by Valencia, *Sub-Imperialism Revisited*, 29.
26. Frank, *Capitalism and Underdevelopment in Latin America*, xv, 118–119, 215–218.
27. Font, 'Introduction', 6.
28. Fernando Henrique Cardoso, *Dependency and Development in Latin America* (Berkeley, CA: University of California Press, 1979), xi; Suzanne Bergeron, *Fragments of Development: Nation, Gender and the Space for Modernity* (Ann Arbor, MI: University of Michigan Press, 2004), 80.
29. Cardoso, *Dependency and Development in Latin America*, xiv–xviii.
30. Ibid., 22.
31. Ramón Grosfoguel, 'Developmentalism, Modernity and Dependency Theory in Latin America', in *Coloniality at Large: Latin America and the Postcolonial Debate*, eds. Mabel Moraña and Enrique D. Dussel (Durham, NC: Duke University Press, 2008), 324.
32. Cardoso, *Dependency and Development in Latin America*, 89.
33. Stagnationists base themselves on the 'structural possibility' of revolution and foresee the 'overcoming of dependency in terms of a historical horizon, in which socialism appears as the result of growing crises peculiar to a stagnating capitalism', or they visualize a relapse into a 'new barbarism'. They believe that being based on the 'hyper-exploitation' of labour, dependent capitalism lacks the potentiality to broaden the internal market, breeds constant unemployment and marginality instead and cannot evade 'a tendency' towards stagnation and the development of underdevelopment. Frank, Marini and, 'to a certain extent', Dos Santos are upholders of this view. Contrarily, underconsumptionists either portray the rise of an inexplicable goodwill for an autonomous capitalism or 'sketch out' hopes for a

socialism whose 'historical persona' is clouded by indeterminacy. Underconsumptionists contend that, in at least certain peripheral countries, the ingress of industrial–financial capital speeds up the production of relative surplus value, expands productive forces and, even when generating unemployment in the phases of recession, absorbs unemployed labour power during cycles of expansion, thereby producing, like in central economies, a situation marked by coexistence of unemployment and recruitment, wealth and misery. See Cardoso, 'The Consumption of Dependency Theory in the United States', 19–20.

34. Fernando Henrique Cardoso, 'Associated-Dependent Development: Theoretical and Practical Implications', in *Authoritarian Brazil,* ed. Alfred Stepan (New Haven, CT: Yale University Press, 1973), 142–178.
35. Kay, *Latin American Theories of Development and Underdevelopment*, 174.
36. Ronaldo Munck, 'Dependency and Imperialism in Latin America', in *The Political Economy of Imperialism: Critical Appraisals*, ed. Ronald M. Chilcote (Lanham, MD; Boulder, CO: Rowman and Littlefield, 2000), 143.
37. Alvin Y. So, *Social Change and Development: Modernization, Dependency and World System Theories* (Newbury Park, CA: Sage Publications, 1991), 131–132.
38. Weeks, 'Dependency Theory', 100.
39. See Note 34 above.
40. Geoffrey Kay, *Development and Underdevelopment: A Marxist Analysis* (London: Macmillan, 1975), 103; Bill Warren, *Imperialism: Pioneer of Capitalism* (London: NLB, 1980), 182, 184; Sanjay Lall, 'Is "Dependence" a Useful Concept in Analysing Underdevelopment?', *World Development* 3, nos. 11–12 (1975): 808, all cited in Kay, *Latin American Theories of Development and Underdevelopment*, 174.
41. For relevant citations, see So, *Social Change and Development*, 132–133.
42. Lall, 'Is "Dependence" a Useful Concept in Analysing Underdevelopment?', 808.
43. See Note 34 above.
44. M. Bienefeld, 'Dependency and the Newly Industrializing Countries: Towards a Reappraisal', in *Dependency Theory: A Critical Reassessment*, ed. D. Seers (London: Frances Pinter, 1981), 18, cited in Kay, *Latin American Theories of Development and Underdevelopment*, 163.
45. So, *Social Change and Development*, 133–134.
46. Weeks, 'Dependency Theory', 100.
47. See Notes 16 and 17 above.
48. C. Leys, 'Underdevelopment and Dependency: Critical Notes', *Journal of Contemporary Asia* 7, no. 1 (1977): 92, in Kay, *Latin American Theories of Development and Underdevelopment*, 174.
49. R. A. Fernández and J. F. Ocampo, 'The Latin American Revolution: A Theory of Imperialism, Not Dependence', *Latin American Perspectives* 1, no. 1 (1974): 39, in Ibid.
50. D. Booth, 'Marxism and Development Sociology: Interpreting the Impasse', *World Development* 13, no. 6 (1985): 762, 764, in Ibid.
51. C. Johnson, 'Dependency Theory and Processes of Capitalism and Socialism', *Latin American Perspectives* 8, nos. 3–4 (1981): 66, in Ibid.
52. T. Angotti, 'The Political Implications of Dependency Theory', *Latin American Perspectives* 8, nos. 3–4 (1981): 127, in Ibid.
53. Munck, 'Dependency and Imperialism in Latin America', 144–145.
54. Weeks, 'Dependency Theory', 101.
55. See, for example, Charles F. Doran, George Modelski and Cal Clark, eds., *North South Relations: Studies of Dependency Reversal* (New York, NY: Praeger, 1983); Heraldo Muñoz, *From Dependency to Development: Strategies to Overcome Underdevelopment and Inequality* (Boulder, CO: Westview Press, 1981); Jason P. Abbot, *Developmentalism and Dependency*

in Southeast Asia: The Case of the Automotive Industry (London; New York, NY: Routledge, 2003).
56. Thomas D. Lairson and David Skidmore, *International Political Economy: The Struggle for Power and Wealth in a Globalizing World* (London; New York, NY: Routledge, 2017), 214.
57. Munck, 'Dependency and Imperialism in Latin America', 145.
58. See Lairson and Skidmore, *International Political Economy*, 214–216.
59. See 'New Preface', *passim*, in Arturo Escobar, *Encountering Development: The Making and Unmaking of the Third World* (Princeton, NJ: Princeton University Press, 2012), 81–82.

CHAPTER

18

World Systems Theory

CHAPTER OUTLINE

INTRODUCTION AND PHENOMENON CALLED WALLERSTEIN

Under the pressure of criticisms, dependency theory, generally, and its distinct strands, specifically, yielded place to world-systems analysis/approach/perspective/theory (WSA/WSP/WST), another important constituent of the globalist paradigm in IR and distinctly Marxist in provenance. However, its link with WST remained. Thinkers such as Christopher Chase-Dunn, Peter Evans and Gary Gereffi, earlier proponents of dependency theory, later became converts to it.[1] Many ideas integral to world-systems thinking were articulated as early as the 1960s and mumbled even in the First World War era, although its basic concepts were first developed, most systematically, by Immanuel Wallerstein.[2] Although Wallerstein first introduced this new thinking in a seminal paper of 1974, 'The Rise and Future Demise of the World Capitalist System', it was the four-volume pathbreaker, *The Modern World-system* (*MWS*; first volume published in 1974) that proclaimed the birth of this sub-discipline in the USA. Considered 'one of the best-known social scientists in the world'; 'acute observer of the most contemporary events'; author of classic and fundamental works on the history of capitalism; 'active promoter of the restructuring of the social sciences'; 'implacable critic of the most common explanations for the phenomena and processes of the "long 20th century"';[3] 'original thinker; masterful synthesizer; intellectual coordinator and collaborator; an effective institution-builder, and a tireless activist', this leading exponent of WSP had a phenomenally rich academic and organizational achievement[4] apart from the reputation as analyst and critical diagnostician of current events and processes and supporter of 'altermundialist movements'.[5] He continued to write on world affairs from his WSA perspective[6] till his death at 89 in 2019.

ROOTS OF WALLERSTEIN'S WSA

The intellectual roots of WST are interwoven with the formative influences on Wallerstein's intellectual development, comprising aversion to 'grand theory' and 'abstracted empiricism' instigated by C. Wright Mills during his Columbia University days; instruction by Georges Balandier in Sorbonne to study colonial societies holistically; impact of Frantz Fanon and Third-World radicalism, and works of Braudel and the French Annales school. Taught by Fanon and Braudel to look at capitalism differently, Wallerstein initially conducted single-country studies of African states during the pre-colonial and post-colonial times, reflecting the currently dominant modernization approach.[7] But soon, from Balandier's teaching, he developed the insight that 'the "whole" of each colonial society was but a part of a larger totality ... a world context of U.S. hegemony and Soviet challenge and of continuing asymmetrical interdependence between the first world and the third.'[8] Since the sustained poverty of many African countries could not be explained by merely looking at their individual experiences, he 'abandoned the idea of taking either the sovereign state or that vaguer concept, the national society, as the unit of analysis' since 'one could speak of social change only in social systems', and the 'only social system in this scheme was the world system'.[9]

Methodologically speaking, Wallerstein's holistic answer meshes three intermingling ideational traditions dominant in the period 1945–1970, namely 'universalist liberalism', scientistic positivism and unidirectional modernizationism'. Its core debates were 'the concept of core periphery' of ECLA and subsequently dependency theory; 'the utility of Marx's concept of the "Asiatic mode of production", a debate that took place among communist scholars'; 'the discussion among historians of Western Europe about the "transition from feudalism to capitalism"; the debate about "total history", and the triumph of the *Annales* school of historiography in France and then elsewhere.'[10] I choose the sequence of Marxism, German historical/institutional economics, *Annales* historiography and the dependency perspective.

Marxism was important in inducing him to consider socio-economic totalities as the most productive level of analysis and view them as riven by conflicts, historically mutable and endowed with systemic but contradictory attributes. It taught him to view accumulation and conflicts and class struggles resulting from it as the most important aspects of capitalist structure and its change, achievable through identification and encouragement of class forces that may be the champions of movements towards world revolution. But since Marx said very little about IP in his serious writings, Wallerstein borrowed more from Lenin, who showed that the nature of capitalism had significantly altered since the publication of *Capital* in 1867, and its international context has acquired greater importance. He accepted from Lenin's thought (a) his departure from Marx's assumption of a clear confrontation between the bourgeoisie and the proletariat throughout the world, irrespective of separate geographical realities and conflicts of interests between workers of different countries to talk about a hierarchical structure created by capitalism where a developed centre exploited an underdeveloped periphery and (b) Lenin's emphasis on labour aristocracies and inter-capitalist competition.[11] Wallerstein developed from this the insight that the "'labour aristocracy" is in a "social contract" with the true bourgeoisie, in which their collective individual remunerations are the political counterpart of their essential conservatism'.[12] He appreciated that 'when all hope was abandoned for the mythical German Revolution, Lenin turned to proclaim a new emphasis on the "East",' taking Marxism–Leninism 'from its origins as a theory of proletarian insurrection against the bourgeoisie to a new role as a theory of anti-imperialism'.[13] From Mao Zedong, Wallerstein derived the idea that class struggles survive the self-styled socialist revolutions; from Fanon, the idea that the 'fundamental difference between the position of Mao and that of Stalin was precisely in this different sense of the function of dialectic in the historical process' so that 'the national-bourgeois phase in Mao is significantly more transitory and provisional than in Stalin'. In the debate between Mao and Liu Shaoqi in the 1960s regarding the character of the Chinese People's Republic as a 'socialist state', Wallerstein chose Mao's judgement that 'the elimination of the system of ownership by the exploiting classes through socialist transformation is not equal to the disappearance of struggle in the political and ideological spheres'. Western Marxism, reflected Georg Lukács's view that 'it is not the primacy of economic motives in historical explanation that constitutes the decisive difference between Marxism and bourgeois thought, but the point of view of totality', induced him to focus on socioeconomic totalities.[14]

Regarding Germanic historical/institutional economics, Wallerstein borrowed the idea from Weber that modern interstate and (ethnonational) status group conflicts are central aspects of capitalist politics. Two other insights derived were about (a) 'the implications of the two forms of the disintegration of an empire: feudalization, as in Western Europe, and prebendalization, as in China', and (b) the importance of considering both intellectual and political challenges while making a move for a world 'substantively rational'. Among other Germanic influences, Joseph Schumpeter provided him with ideas about the 'causal importance of economic cycles' (a cycle being a process within which all elements of the economic system interact in certain characteristics ways and no one element can be singled out for the role of the prime mover) and the nature of capitalism in both in the economic and sociological sense as 'essentially one process, with the whole world as its stage', however, impermanent in the long range.[15] Polanyi gave him 'the model of three types of socio-economic totality: reciprocal, redistributive and market', which Wallerstein rechristened as 'mini-systems, world empires and world-economies'.[16]

The third methodological ballast of the French *Annales* school of history, nurtured by eponymous journal *Annales* and by Braudel, Lucien Febvre and Marc Bloch, rose 'in the 1920s as a protest' against the political bent of dominant French historiography. It insisted that historiography should be looking at a total, 'integrated picture of historical development', which, besides going below the political surface, would bring out the economic underpinnings of this development. Resurgent after 1945, ending its interwar period dormancy, this school focused more on long-range, deep and enduring historical structures. It regarded '"event-dominated" or episodic history'—in Wallersteinian parlance 'traditional idiographic, empiricist, political historiography'—as 'dust', slipped into our eyes and hiding 'real underlying structures' from them. By structure, Braudel meant 'something organized, something coherent, relatively fixed relations between social realities and groups' and 'something put together, an architecture, but even more a reality that time affects only slightly and maintains over a long period', being 'simultaneously underpinnings and obstacles'. Equally critical of the quest for 'timeless truths' and the purely nomothetic endeavours of numerous social scientists as 'mythical', Braudel avoided both extremes. Insisting on the plurality of social times, he resurrected two types of previously neglected social times: (a) 'structural time', involving 'long-lasting', though not 'eternal, basic structures' undergirding historical systems and (b) 'cyclical processes within the structures' represented by 'medium-run trends, such as the expansions and contractions of the world-economy'. Braudel, who conceptualized the 16th-century Mediterranean as a 'world-economy' and the main focus of his study, provided clues about Wallerstein's proper unit of analysis.[17] However, contrary to the reliance of the *Annales* school on primary sources in their research, Wallerstein resorts to secondary source and is accordingly more nomothetic and theoretical in his orientation and less grounded in history.[18]

The fourth methodological component, dependency theory, shared many similarities with WSA, despite some important differences. It countered both liberal/modernizationist and Marxist developmentalist traditions to offer a third path, contours of which are detailed in **Chapter 17** and are not repeated here. Wallerstein agreed with Frank on the malady of the Third World, following Lenin, ECLA and Prebisch (regarding the differentiation between the core and periphery and suggestion that the latter lags in development increased with every trading transaction because of unequal terms of trade between the primary goods and industrialized products). He accepted that capitalist development is inherently uneven and exploitative. But possibly influenced by Fanon's acerbic denunciation of the comprador neo-colonial governing elites in Third-World countries, he spurned the proposed cure. Anyway, unlike dependency theorists, he refused to focus on the exploited countries as discrete units of analysis, choosing instead to treat them as hardwired parts of a single systemic whole and accordingly spurned autarky as a viable solution for their problems. For him, escape from capitalism was an unavailable option because the markets of these countries are small and also the countries that have traded in world markets are far better off. So compared with the dependency perspective, WST is far less static and affords a chance for mobility within it in, however, a limited fashion.[19]

OVERVIEW OF WALLERSTEIN'S APPROACH

Rojas thinks the best way to grasp Wallerstein's multifaceted argumentation is to follow it through its following four major interconnected overlapping 'thematic axes', 'sometimes superimposed on one another and at other times intersecting transversally' and constituting the whole architecture of his thought:

1. A 'historical-critical axis' retells unconventionally the whole history of capitalism and modernity in terms of the crucial and path-breaking "long 16th century" (1450–1650) of Braudelian conception. It was first formulated in *MWS I*[20] and continued in later volumes to show capitalism's spread in the long 17th century,[21] its consolidation in the long 18th century[22] and maturity in the long 19th century[23] and is the most read component of Wallerstein's oeuvre. This axis is the original template of the entire WSA/WSP.
2. An axis of 'critical analysis' of major occurrences and processes of the long 20th century updates and explicates the central argument of the first axis and shows 'those realities and tendencies' in a new light, embodied in 'specific contexts of characters, events and evolutionary processes' that are parts of our lived experience. It transforms history from a 'science of the past' into an open sesame chant for 'understanding the most essential processes of our own historical century', which started roughly around 1870 and unfolding since then and will continue to evolve for many years or even decades.
3. A third axis of 'the study of immediate history' aims at 'defining possible prospective scenarios of the future evolution of the capitalist world-system', which endows since 1968 and the inauguration of WSP in 1974, international affairs and occurrences a rare degree of 'historical density' apart from relocating them in a broad comparativist frame.
4. Finally, in an axis of 'critical epistemological reflection' on our conventional modes of thinking about the social realities, we set to explore, at a higher level, reflection on the very shape of the present structure of knowledge created by capitalist modernity, which involves a critique of the intellectual division of labour of extant social sciences and the 'dominant structure of knowledge' represented by them. Compared to the preceding three axes, this axis is not temporal, but rather intersects all the three axes transversally to question and expose their unnoticed biases, predilections and 'epistemological limits' and energize the construction of 'radically new and profoundly unidisciplinary "historical social sciences"'.[24]

I would apply Rojas' map and supporting discussion while presenting thoughts, ideas and insights of Wallerstein as well as others on him whenever needed for my purpose as supplements with citations.[25]

Wallerstein's Historical-critical Thematic Axis

Historical: Past and Future of Capitalism

The historical-critical axis, featuring Wallerstein's deep and elaborate study of the global history of capitalism,[26] is the fulcrum of Wallerstein's WSA since the most important ideas, whether regarding the proper level or unit of analysis or concepts, such as systems, world-empire and world-economy emerge in the context of its unravelling. Here, Wallerstein departs from descriptive histories of the capitalist world-system to a theoretical model of the complex global itinerary of capitalism for the last 500+ years. His daring 'to think about capitalism as a global problem in its integral unity and its most general dimensions' placed him on par with Marx, Weber, Werner Sombart, Norbert Elias, Polanyi and Braudel. In *MWS I*, Wallerstein shows how a 'world-economy' first emerged in Europe during the period of 1450–1650. Before this period, there was no world-system, even in the form of a 'world-empire'.

Word Help

World-System, world-empire and world-economy as per Wallerstein:

> A world-system is a social system, one that has boundaries, structures, member groups, rules of legitimation, and coherence. Its life is made up of the conflicting forces which hold it together by tension, and tear it apart as each group seeks eternally to remold it to its advantage. It has the characteristic of an organism, in that it has a life span ... One can define the structures as being at different times strong or weak in terms of the internal logic of its functioning ... life within it is largely self-contained, and ... the dynamics of its development are largely internal.[27]

'There can be two varieties of such world-systems, one with a common political system and one without. We shall designate these respectively as world-empires and world-economies'.[28]

Before 1450–1650, in the absence of any world-empire or world-economy constitutive of any modern world-system (hereafter, MWS), a Christian civilization pervaded most of Europe, and in the second half of the Middle Ages, feudalism characterized it. Feudalism had, however, cycles of expansion and contraction. A downturn between 1300 and 1450 after a period of all-round growth between 1150 and 1300 signalled the beginning of a crisis that 'represented a conjuncture of secular trends, an immediate cyclical crisis and climatological decline'. By the first, he means saturation of the maximum level of production using existing technology; by the second, the abovementioned cyclical economic trend, and by the third, a climatic change that caused a fall in crop yields. The 'immense pressure of this conjuncture' avowedly 'made possible the enormity of the social change', manifest in a new type of surplus appropriation and ushered in the capitalist system, helped in turn by three other factors, 'an expansion of the geographical size of the world in question, the development of variegated methods of labor control for different products and different zones of the world-economy and the relatively strong state machineries in what would become core-states of the world-economy'.[29]

In this situation, leading cities in many states—Seville (Spain), Lisbon (Portugal), Antwerp (Belgium), Lyon (France), Genoa (Italy) and Hamburg (Germany)—vied more or less justifiably to be the hub of the emerging capitalist world-economy (hereafter

CW-E). But as 'Spain steadily lost not only its political imperium but also its economic centrality', and in Antwerp, 'the boom which was based on the axis with Spain ended', the new theatre shifted to Amsterdam. The 'story of the "second" 16th century is one of how Amsterdam picked up the dissolving threads of the Hapsburg Empire, creating a framework for the smooth operation of the world-economy'. Amsterdam could step in the breach, owed as much to the 'failure of England' that hamstrung England's early 'ascendancy' in the first half of the long 16th century as to the 'success of the Dutch'. 'Amsterdam became a threefold centre of the European economy: commodity market, shipping centre and capital market.' But Amsterdam's 'true forward surge' did not happen before 1590, till the Netherlands Revolution (1557–1590) was suppressed.[30]

MWS II treats a part of the long 17th century (1600–1750) as one denoting Dutch hegemony and compared to the 'long' 16th century as one of contraction rather than expansion, though not harsh enough to signify a crisis for the world-economy, being rather a period of greater entrenchment and 'strengthening of the state structures, at least in the core states and the rising semi-peripheral ones, as a way of coping with contraction'. Unlike the 1300–1450 contraction, which had led to 'acute internecine warfare among the landed nobility', wars in the 17th century, involving extensive use of mercenaries, were 'interstate rather than interbaronical'. They did not cause 'massive bleeding of the ruling strata' and thus could help the 'accretion of someone's economic strength'. Besides obvious markers, like 'Holland's Golden Age, the German upturn from the late 17th century, steady improvement in English agronomy' and unceasing economic activity here or there showed that there was no crisis. At this juncture, revealing how the role of the state becomes crucial during periods of downturn, the policies of the Swedish state helped it rise from the position of the semi-periphery to that of the core. Meanwhile, the politics of the core was marked by 'venomous trade rivalry' and 'acute commercial rivalry' between the three core powers of Britain, France and Denmark. The stagnation of the world-economy had caused the collapse of gain trade, frequent resultant wars and efforts of the British and French states to overturn Dutch hegemony. This increased pressure on peripheral regions as sources of increased surplus and resulted in increasing incorporation of the semi-periphery, such as Spain and Portugal, as 'conveyor belts for the interests of the core powers in the peripheral regions'.[31]

MWS III depicts the period 1730–1840s, following the decline of Dutch hegemony as the 'second era of the expansion of the capitalist world economy' but, unlike most contemporary commentators, does not date the true onset of 'modernity' or 'capitalism' or 'industrialism' or 'Western dominance of the world' to this period, favouring the 'long 16th century' as the moment of creation of the MWS as a CW-E.[32] The period contained three overlapping spatial-temporal zones: 'struggle' or intense inter-core rivalry of England and France for primacy between 1763 and 1815; 'incorporation of vast new zones into the world-economy' between 1750 and 1850, and 'settler decolonization of the USA' between 1763 and 1833. The Franco-British rivalry was 'crucial' because not only it was 'competition for control of a new peripheral zone of the world economy', but also the 'key policy element' that differentiated it from previous phases was 'the virtually automatic involvement' of both of them on the exact opposite side of every revolutionary development, including the French Revolution.[33] Comparing all the three important revolutions of this period, Wallerstein denied that the Industrial Revolution (1760–1840) was a revolution at all. It was rather 'a cyclical upward increase in the mechanization of industrial production' which had precedents and would occur again in future but, presently, 'accrued to the particular advantage of Great Britain' because Britain happened to defeat France in the Seven Years' War 'in its struggle to become the new hegemonic power of the world-system'.[34] The French Revolution was also not a bourgeois revolution because of the 'centrality of the lord-peasant struggle' in it (as Skocpol insisted) and 'the realities of capitalism in France as elsewhere in Western Europe long predated 1789'.[35] Together with the American Revolution, these three revolutions did not constitute a threat to the world-economy and rather 'represented its further consolidation and entrenchment'.[36]

In *MWS IV*, Wallerstein traced the triumphant march of centrist liberalism during the period 1789–1914. Liberalism 'started its life on the left of the political spectrum or at least on the centre-left'. After 1815, it 'presented itself as the opposite of the conservative thrust and was as such considered by conservatives to be 'Jacobinical'. But as liberalism 'gained momentum, support and authority as an ideology, its left credentials weakened; in some respects, it even gained the right credentials. But its destiny was to assert that it was located in the centre' as conceptualized by Constant in the 18th century. Finally, ensconced as the centrist position in the 19th century, it was still being hailed 'as the vital centre by Schlesinger (1962) in the mid-20th century'.[37] The rest of the book deals with how the period 1815–1830 could be treated as one of 'constructing the liberal state'. It absorbed class conflict between 1830 and 1875 first by building itself up as 'a strong bureaucratic state' after the death of Jacobinism in its original form in 1815 and then by rebuilding itself as the welfare state, 'after 1848', when 'capitalists fully realized' that only 'the reformist state could buffer them against the winds of worker discontent'. Expectedly, in this period, the working classes lost their opprobrious appellation of 'dangerous classes' and became citizens.[38]

The historical-critical axis does not, of course, stop at the end of the 'long 19th century' in 1914. Wallerstein has characterized the period 1945–1967 as one of American hegemony, the only last two periods of hegemony being of the United Provinces between 1620–1650, maximally up to 1672, and of the UK between 1815 and 1873.[39] By contrast, the period between 1967 and 1973 betokened beginning of the end of the world economic expansion, the start of a decline of US hegemony and, in the long-term, early indications of a possible systemic disintegration of the 500-year-old CW-E.[40] Wallerstein was sure that although the modern capitalist world system 'has lasted some 500 years, and in terms of its guiding principle of the endless accumulation of capital, it has been extremely successful, the period of its ability to continue to operate on this basis has come to an end'. And the collapse will come about in three–four decades.[41]

Thematic: Nature and Dynamics of the MWS

The trajectory of capitalism along this historical-critical axis cannot be fully understood without the help of Wallerstein's view of the system. Two defining characteristics of social systems are (a) 'life within it is largely self-contained' so that if it severs from all external influences, the internal outcomes will be identical and (b) derivatively, all changes within the system emerge from internal forces.[42] Wallerstein thinks that to be able to capture the dynamics of the world-system, 'all social sciences must be simultaneously historic and systemic'. WSA 'substitutes for the term society and the term "historical system", not as 'a mere semantic substitution' but as a deliberate attempt to purge its current centrally connotative link to state and clarify that a dynamic relationship exists between its elements. By choosing the world-system as the appropriate unit, Wallerstein wanted to analyse something larger than the modern nation state, 'something that was defined by the boundaries of an effective, ongoing division of labour'.[43] Within it, the three zones of the core, semi-periphery and the periphery 'were assigned specific economic roles, developed different class structures, used consequently different modes of labour control and profited unequally from the workings of the system'.[44] Apart from conceptual delinking from society, another reason why this world-system is a 'historical system' is that even after having 'started with spatial or geographic concerns' and a 'spatial metaphor', Wallerstein shortly discovered that space was inseparable analytically from time, and the meaningful unit for us was, therefore, one kind of TimeSpace, specifically structural TimeSpace.[45] Now, being historical, world-systems 'have lives', including a beginning, a lifespan and a demise; 'all systems, from the infinitesimally small to the universe', should be analysed as consisting of three qualitatively different moments, those of coming into existence, functioning during their 'normal' life (the longest moment) and going out of existence (the structural crisis).[46] The prefix world before any such TimeSpace does not suggest that it encompasses the whole world. The Roman Empire has been called a world-empire without extending to the whole world. Likewise, a 'world-system is not the system of the world, but a system that is a world and that can be, most often has been, located in an area less than the entire globe', and a 'world-empire (such as the Roman Empire and Han China) is a large bureaucratic structure with a single political centre and an axial division of labour but multiple cultures', while a 'world-economy is a large axial division of labour with multiple political centres and multiple cultures.'[47] For these political and cultural multiplicities, historically earlier, world-economies have tended to be quite unstable and have been frequently transformed into world-empires (China, Persia and Rome), whenever one of the competing centres of political control got the better of all others. But the modern world-economy has been more stable, thanks to the intervention of capitalism.[48]

Modern world-economies differ from world-empires in ways in which decisions on resource distribution are taken. Empires represent more 'primitive means of economic domination', based on systemic 'extraction of tribute from otherwise locally self-administered direct producers (mostly rural) that is passed upward to the centre and redistributed to a thin but crucial network of officials'. Contrastingly, in world-economies, characterized by 'vast uneven chains of integrated production structures dissected by multiple political structures', redistribution of resources occurs not via political decisions but through the framework of the transnational market mechanism where 'the accumulated surplus is distributed unequally in favour of those able to achieve various kinds of temporary monopolies in the market networks.'[49]

Within the TimeSpace of spatio-temporal systems, Wallerstein's definitions of core and periphery are very close to those of dependency theory. Core states are the most 'advantaged areas of the world-economy', characterized by the highest types of skills and the greatest doses of capital investment. The periphery, a supplier of raw materials and a source of comprehensive surplus extraction for the core, is also 'that geographical sector wherein production is primarily of lower-ranking goods (i.e., goods whose labour is less well-rewarded) but which is an integral part of the overall system of the division of labour'. Wallerstein's major modification of dependency theory's core–periphery differentiation is the addition of a *semi-peripheral* space, which is neither 'an artifice of statistical cutting points' nor 'a residual category' but is rather a 'necessary structural element in a world-economy'; 'collection points of vital skills that are often politically unpopular', and middle areas that 'partially deflect the political pressures which groups primarily located in peripheral areas might otherwise direct against core states'.[50] The division of labour between the core, semi-periphery and periphery of the CW-E is so designed that there is 'unequal exchange between the sectors but dependence of all the sectors, both economically and politically, on the continuance of this unequal exchange'.[51]

Wallerstein depended on Emmanuel's complex 20th-century Marxist theory of imperialism to argue how these three zones of the world-economy are linked to one another by this process of unequal exchange where higher levels of technology accessible to producers in the core, the relative mobility of capital vis-à-vis that of labour and the institutional capacity of workers in the core to achieve pay hikes above the subsistence level predestine an inequality of exchange between the core and the periphery for four factors. First, trade between the low-income periphery and high-income centre of the world-system is unfair and biased against the former. Second, low-income countries' undervalued wages compared to wages in high-income countries ensure that goods from the peripheral countries requiring equal amounts of labour time are available at a lower cost in the core. Third, export prices of commodities exported from low-income countries are undervalued in relation to the export prices of high-income countries. Fourth, a relationship exists between the undervaluation of labour and the undervaluation of exports in low-income countries. Emmanuel said that 'inequality of wages as such, all other things being equal, is alone the cause of the inequality of exchange', and wages are for him 'the independent variable of the system'.[52]

To dynamize this static spatial picture and impart temporal dimension to it, Wallerstein identifies four types of closely interrelated and interactive processes operative within the MWS, which shape 'the character of the historical development' of the CW-E and present distinctions between them 'as different ways of viewing historical time in a manner similar to Braudel': cyclical rhythms, secular trends, contradictions and crises.[53] Among cyclical rhythms, the most obvious and important is 'a seemingly regular process of expansion and contraction' in its entirety. Extending to 50–60 years as per current trends, these cycles, termed 'long waves' or Kondratieff cycles, indicate the regular upswings and downswings in the world-economy[54] and are, 'in fact, only medium length' among 'a whole panoply of presumed cycles of varying presumed lengths' (from 2–3 to 150–300 years). It has two phases: a Kondratieff-A period of expansion and a Kondratieff-B period of contraction. Secular trends of the system bring out the long-term development of the system, including processes such as expansion, commodification, urbanization and 'patterns of internal transformation that will eventually bring about the demise of the system'. Since the 'stagnation phases of the world-economy's rhythms are not symmetrical to its expansion phases, this results in a certain "ratchet" effect, which leads to some long-term slow upward curves'. Not denying the validity and applicability of cyclical rhythms, these are, 'rhythms of a historical system', rhythmic but not symmetrical and constitutive of the secular trends, which, 'in their contradictory development, lead to a point of bifurcation, the eventual decline of the historical system and the transition to some other historical system.' During this long process of transition, 'the cyclical rhythms of the existing system do not cease operating. Quite the contrary, it is their continued operation that is forcing the transition'.[55]

All world-systems, says Wallerstein, are beset with contradictions, which provide a key law of the motion of the world economy, being processes which compel our historical system 'to go in one direction to pursue our short-run interests and in another to pursue our middle-run interests'. Of 'two fundamental contradictions involved in the workings of the capitalist world-system', the first, which the 19th-century Marxian literature identified as the crisis of underconsumption, has been rephrased by Wallerstein in the following way: 'Whereas in the short run, the maximization of profit requires maximizing the withdrawal of surplus from immediate consumption of the majority, in the long run, the continued production of surplus requires a mass demand which can only be created by redistributing the surplus withdrawn'.

Here, the contradiction is that the short-range and long-range interests of the system make two sets of behaviour optimal. The second main contradiction, indicated by Mao's concept of socialism as a process, is

> whenever the tenants of privilege seek to coopt an oppositional movement by including them in a minor share of the privilege, they may not only eliminate opponents in the short run, but they also up the ante for the next oppositional movement created in the next crisis of the world-economy.[56]

But Wallerstein avoids the 'overused term' crisis while describing 'every downturn in any cyclical curve on any scale' and uses it only to depict 'a rare circumstance'; 'a historical system has evolved to the point where the cumulative effect of the internal contradictions make it impossible for the system to "resolve" its dilemmas by "adjustments" in its ongoing institutional patterns".' A systemic problem that can be resolved in some manner 'is not a true crisis but simply a difficulty built into the system'. True crises signify those difficulties that can be resolved 'only by going outside of and beyond the historical system of which the difficulties are a part'. So a crisis is a one-final-time occurrence in the lifespan of a historical system, foregrounding for its insiders 'a real historical choice: what kind of new historical system to build or create'.[57] Except for these periods of crisis, possibilities are much more restricted in systems, the structures of the world-economy during their 'normal' life being deeply deterministic.[58]

States and States System in the MWS

The world-system being the primary unit in Wallerstein's level of analysis, 'the creation of all the major institutions of the world', including classes, ethnic/national groups, households and the states', stems from the development of the CW-E. 'All of these structures post-date, not antedate capitalism; all are the consequence, not cause'.[59] For example, the inception of England's Industrial Revolution, which steeply increased the demand for sugar and cotton production in the Western Hemisphere, 'expanded the demand for slaves', increased the price to be paid for the accelerated demand, including the sale of firearms and created an atmosphere that was 'propitious to the creation of large state structures' and caused 'the great spurt observed in Africa in state-building from 1805–1820'.[60]

States cannot be conceived in isolation from the capitalist world-system because its 'many institutions—states and the interstate system, productive firms, households, classes and identity groups of all sorts'—constitute 'a matrix which permits the system to operate but, at the same time, stimulate both the conflicts and the contradictions which permeate the system'.[61] But still states are important. WSA is both a theory of capitalist economic development on a world scale and a theory of IP, against all Marxian demur about the possibility of separating economics and politics as autonomous sub-units, attempting a 'reconceptualization of the capitalist mode of production itself' where beyond pure market-oriented strategies for accumulation of surplus value, it is a system in which these structures pursue in tandem their politico-military and profit-seeking strategies and seek simultaneous optimization. 'Thus, the state-system, state-building and geopolitics are the political sides of the capitalist mode of production.'[62] States may be products of the world economy but are defined in their relationships with one another, which reins in even the strongest of them in their decision-making. Wallerstein is not always consistent about the nature of the trammels, which are sometimes the 'operational guidelines' of the interstate system, including 'the so-called' BOP, but at other times, is the 'rule-bound nature of the interstate system'.[63] States derive importance from their provision of an apparatus for the realization and protection of property rights, plus necessary infrastructure for the smooth functioning of the capitalist enterprises (such as in sectors of education and transportation), which these enterprises are reluctant to supply, despite their importance for resolving the contradictions which their operations engender.[64]

However, as Chase-Dunn emphasizes, 'the political system of capitalism' is not constituted by the states but by the 'larger competitive state system'. Individual states may exhibit greater or lesser inclinations towards 'politico-military aggrandizement or free-market accumulation depending on their position in the larger system', and the system, as a whole, may fluctuate between periods of more general recourse to state power and periods more marked by 'a relatively free world market of commodity exchange'.[65] Moreover, the role and functions of the state depend on its position in the spatial divisions of the CW-E and its production processes. Its first consequence is in 'state structure, the peripheral states being weakened and the core states strengthened by the ongoing process of exchange'. The second consequence is in 'different modes of labour control', dictated by the highest relative wages in the core sectors and lower relative wages in peripheral areas. Once the difference in state machinery in the context of the operation of 'unequal exchange' is established, it is 'enforced by strong states on weak ones by core states on peripheral areas'.[66]

States bear a deeper geographical reflection of core-peripheral production processes beyond this enforcement of unequal exchange. Since quasi-monopolies, major avenues of accumulation of capital 'depend on the patronage of strong states; they are largely located—juridically, physically and in terms of ownership—within such states'. Because core-like processes are normally concentrated in a few states and form the bulk of the production activity there, while peripheral processes get dispersed among a large number of states; we speak of core states and peripheral states as shorthand epithets only, remembering that 'we are really talking of a relationship between production processes'. States having a nearly even mix of core-like and peripheral products may be called semi-peripheral states, although semi-peripheral production processes are not a valid expression.

The position of states will accordingly change as quasi-monopolies 'exhaust themselves' from the status of core-like processes to become peripheral processes. The 'role of each state differs 'vis-à-vis productive processes depending on the mix of core-peripheral processes within it'. Containing an excessive share of core-like processes, strong states attempt to stress their role of protecting quasi-monopolies of them. Contrastingly, riddled with largely peripheral production processes, the very weak states find themselves incapable of doing much to correct the axial division of labour and compelled to manage with their lot. The plight of semi-peripheral states is sorrier. Under pressure from core states and passing it on to peripheral states, their major worry is how to prevent their slippage into the periphery and manage advance towards the core.[67] States' stances on free-market accumulation also differ. Hegemonic core states, enjoying a clear competitive advantage in production, advocate free trade, while peripheral states, controlling peripheral capitalist producers of low-wage goods exportable to the core, support the 'open economy' of free international exchange. Smaller core states, heavily dependent on international trade, uphold a liberal democratic order. 'Semi-peripheral states and core states contending for hegemony utilize protectionism and mercantilist monopoly to protect and expand their access to world surplus value.'[68]

Since possession of, lack of or aspiration after hegemony affects the stances of states on the nature of the international trading order, the periodic appearance of the disappearance of a hegemonic power engages Wallerstein. He, however, defines this term more narrowly and restrictively than others as 'that situation in which the ongoing rivalry between the so-called "great powers" is so unbalanced that one power can largely impose its rules and wishes in the economic, political, military, diplomatic and even cultural arenas'. It is materially rooted 'in the ability of enterprises domiciled in that power to operate more efficiently in all three economic arenas—agro-industrial production, commerce and finance', stemming from an 'edge in efficiency . . . so great that these enterprises can not only outbid enterprises domiciled in other great powers in the world market in general but quite specifically in very many instances within the home markets of rival powers themselves'. However, the edge has to be 'so significant that allied major powers are de facto client states and opposed major powers feel relatively frustrated and highly defensive vis-à-vis the hegemonic power'.[69] We have already seen how, through this restrictive definition, Wallerstein has recorded only three instances of a hegemonic power in the interstate system.[70]

Among other features of the interstate system are 'antisystemic movements' and a geoculture. Since it is 'the world-system of historical capitalism which has given rise to antisystemic movements', WSA needs to unearth 'system-wide structural processes', which have not only 'produced' the but have also simultaneously formed the constraints within which such movements have operated. For Wallerstein, these antisystemic movements have assumed two major forms: the 'social' and the 'national'. Typical of the former are unions, socialist parties and other worker organizations that have emerged from the increasing system-wide polarization between the bourgeoisie and the proletariat and exploitation of the latter by the former and have 'implicitly or explicitly challenged the triumph of capitalism. By contrast, national movements arise over internal considerations, whether protesting 'the growing polarity between the centre and the periphery', defining 'the oppression like that of one ethnonational group over another', primarily questioning 'the jurisdiction of the state' or seeking to give 'the oppressed group equal juridical status' by 'the creation of a new state, either by secession or merger'. National movements have sought to organize their activities inside particular countries for advancing their structural position within the world-system. But 'three major varieties of "new" social movements have their social bases' outside national boundaries in 'the peace/ecology/alternative lifestyle movements, the women's movements and minority rights'. But both these social and national oppositional movements have caused a 'marked increase in the structural "centralization" of the state'.[71] Wallerstein finds it 'hard to see how the antisystemic movements' could have conceivably 'incarnated any culture other than that of the capitalist world economy' and harder 'to see how they could not have been impregnated by and expressed the paired ideologies of universalism and racism–sexism'. His verdict is, 'if one considers their global activities over 150-odd years', the *telos* of these antisystemic movements 'has been essential to turn themselves into the fulfillers of the liberal dream while claiming to be its most fulsome critics'.[72]

Geoculture is not 'the superstructure of this world-economy' but 'is underside', veiled and 'more difficult to assess' but essential for the latter's nourishment. Wallerstein names it geoculture 'by analogy with geopolitics, not because it is supra-local or supranational, but because it represents the cultural framework within which the world-system operates'.[73] In *MWS IV*, Wallerstein showed how a geoculture informed by centrist liberalism was belatedly being put together. Understood as 'values that are very widely shared throughout the world-system, both explicitly and latently', geoculture was 'something that has not yet been achieved in the historical development of the MWS'.[74] The French Revolution became the harbinger of this geoculture by introducing into its foundations: 'the normality of political change and the refashioning of the concept of sovereignty', conceptually around 'citizens'. But this concept, although nominally exclusive, 'in practice excluded very many' and turned the political history of the MWS in the 19th and 20th centuries into 'the history of a debate about the line that divides the included from the excluded', following the dialectic of a coeval liberal version of universalism and racism–sexism.[75] Amid the triad of ideologies—conservatism, liberalism and socialism—which emerged in the 19th century to provide the parlance of subsequent political debates within the CW-E for this geoculture, liberalism triumphed as early as in 1848, in the first world revolution of the capitalist system, being the best legitimizer of the institutions of the capitalist system not only for 'the cadres of the system' but also for the mass of the populations.[76] But the rejection of liberalism as an ideology both in its Wilsonian and Leninist versions, after what Wallerstein calls the Revolution of 1968, especially since the 1980s, represented 'a fundamental break with the intellectual premises of the geoculture' of the CW-E. It placed the 'liberal verities' of the existing geoculture before three challenges, which are as follows:

1. A 'new intellectual focus on culture', away from economy or politics, stemming from disenchantment with the transformative claims of economic or political forms and foregrounding 'agency' against objective pressures emanating from the politico-economic domains.
2. Resurgence of the concepts of racism and sexism as 'belated recognition of a fundamental feature of the geoculture of the capitalist world-economy, despite (or even because of) its universalizing pretensions'.

3. And finally, 'the "new science," itself a direct attack on the oldest pillar of the MWS, Baconian-Newtonian science', seeking to circumvent the cultural division between science and the humanities and favouring mutual dialogue.[77]

This exploration of capitalist geoculture and the tensions in it helped Wallerstein answer the question, 'whether and how we will invent new systems that will utilize neither the ideology of universalism nor the ideology of racism–sexism'.[78]

The Three Other Axes of Wallerstein's Framework

Sadly, due to space constraints, we will not be able to do full justice to the second, third and fourth axes of Wallerstein's analysis,[79] all introduced above. Regarding the second axis of 'critical analysis' of the long 20th century (1870–2050 and beyond), Wallerstein diverts our attention from the rise and decline of socialism, the putatively defining feature of the recent past, to chart the 'long curve' that depicts the 'construction, definition, affirmation and then decadence of US hegemony'. This hegemony started around 1870, after the end of the American Civil War and France's defeat in the Franco–Prussian War; gained strength through the rivalry with Germany that reached its apex during the modern 'Thirty Years' War' (1914–1945, containing two world wars), and was solidified by US victory in it. It extended from 1945 to 1968/1972/1973, operating in a period of equilibrium till 1989, meeting an inexorable decline after the global cultural revolution of 1968 and the global economic crisis of 1972–1973, best manifest in two decadent administrations of George W. Bush.

Viewing this long stretch of time from the vantage point of US hegemony, Wallerstein belittled the existing spatio-temporal socialist phase, contending that there 'are today no socialist systems in the world-economy any more than there are feudal systems.' Socialism was seeking 'neither a redistributive world-empire nor a CW-E but a socialist world government'. The Russian Revolution was nothing but the response of a semi-peripheral country to 'the marked penetration of foreign capital' into its industrial sector and its resultant 'decline to a peripheral status', new state managers of which countered this downslide with 'the classic technique of mercantilist semi-withdrawal from the world-economy'.[80] And among alternative descriptions of the collapse of communist party regimes in East Europe in 1989 and the Soviet Union in 1991 as the 'end of the post-war epoch 1945–1989', 'end of the Communist epoch 1917–1989', 'end of the French Revolutionary epoch 1789–1989' and 'end of the ascension of the MWS, 1450–1989', Wallerstein chose the last as the best. It signified 'the final collapse of liberalism as a hegemonic ideology'. The old-fangled communist parties of the erstwhile communist bloc were the 'last serious believers in the promise of liberalism. Without them to continue to perform this function, the world's dominant strata have lost any possibility to control the world's working classes other than by force'.[81]

Preparing to study the trajectory of post-1979 US decadence equipped with insights about the 'previous hegemonic cycles of capitalist history', Wallerstein predicts that in the present competition between declining American power, a Northeast Asia with its immense capitalist development and an integrated Europe led by German power, Northeast Asia is sure to come out winner, should capitalism not be gripped by its terminal crisis. Running parallel to this central curve of declining US power, Wallerstein detects a second basic one, total decolonization of the whole planet, although this will not eliminate the composite dependence of these countries on the metropoles, and its curve will flatten just like the curve of US hegemonic decline during 1968/1972–1973, releasing pressures of global critique of Eurocentrism in all its forms.

To analyse the subsequent developments, Wallerstein divides the 'long 20th century' into two halves, the 'first' starting from 1870 and ending around epoch-making 1968–1973 and the 'second' unfolding since then to the present. The 1968 revolution, a profound worldwide upheaval between 1966 and 1969, had ramifications in the broadest domains of contemporary politics, culture, society and even quotidian life. These were the demise of Old Left movements and rise of numerous New Lefts in the dominant geocultural system; interrogation of dominant structures of knowledge following the decline of the liberal ideology; unhinging of age-old structures accepted for millennia in the cultural domain, including masculinism and patriarchy as the basis of the monogamous family, facilitation of women's liberation and a 'slow but unstoppable process of revolution in the family cell'; destabilization of 'traditional hierarchical relationships' and other mechanisms of domination in the organized dissemination of knowledge in the academic and pedagogical domains, and increase in the power of communication media in influencing the global and national public opinion and seating and unseating of domestic and foreign governments in the communicational sector.[82]

To enlighten us better about the 'second 20th century', Wallerstein embarks on his third dual axis of 'examination of the immediate history', backed by charting of 'future prospective scenarios of the capitalist world-system'. Here, Wallerstein debunks the recent rhetoric about globalization to reveal that it is 'nothing but the basic operating principle' of the CW-E.[83] The hugely hyped role of transnational organizations, planet-wide diffusion of certain cultural models, the global movement of commodities and the nearly instantaneous flow of news and information on which the claims and boasts of globalization are based have avowedly precedents in previous centuries, as the dominant role of the Dutch East India Company (from 1600 to 1750) and imposition of their languages and cultures by the Spanish and the Portuguese in the Americas or by the British in India. Even the global market network existed in previous centuries, and the invention of the telegraph and telephone were no less revolutionary in the impact than the modern Internet. So the current discourse on globalization results from 'a gigantic misreading of the current reality' and 'a deception imposed on us by powerful groups', who falsely claim that it has ushered in a new stage of the capitalist life cycle. Wallerstein calls it 'age of transition, transition not merely of a few backward countries who need to catch up with the spirit of globalization but a transition in which the entire capitalist world-system will be transformed into something else'.[84]

This 'something else', amid the world capitalist system's 'multifaceted', 'profound', terminal crisis of 'civilizational import' and projected final collapse in the next three or four decades,[85] was likely because the 'endless accumulation of capital', the sine qua non of capitalism, was possible only under 'quasi-monopolies of leading industries' backed technically by 'innovation' and 'transmogrification' of products and the 'quasi-monopolies of geopolitical power'. Since neither is sustainable in present conditions, there was no chance for the capitalist world-system to regain its equilibrium.[86] Socialism was also not a viable alternative.[87] But Wallerstein does not specify what will succeed capitalism. Against Chase-Dunn's charge that he is 'intentionally vague about the organizational nature of the new system (as was Marx)',[88] Wallerstein's defence is that as world history is in the mid of a chaotic and historical transformation predicted to unfold up to 2050, the qualitatively different non-capitalist system that will emerge from this chaos is difficult to foresee.[89]

Wallerstein's fourth axis of 'critical epistemological reflection' on the conventional modes of thinking about these chaotic social realities involves a major restructuring or 'unthinking' of the social sciences, 'structured at its inception in the middle of the 19th century', around 'a set of often unquestioned a priori assumptions'.[90] 'Unthinking' involved, first, understanding the 'turmoil' that the social sciences experienced in the 'last quarter of the 20th century' and, then, exploring the transformations that caused the reopening of many of their settled questions, thereby buttressing 'the view that 19th-century paradigms have reached their limits'.[91] Towards this, an international commission chaired by Wallerstein submitted a report where the disciplinary institutionalization and sectarianization of the social sciences were questioned with suggestions of tentative steps towards a holistic integration of them to address their myopic limitedness. They included fundamental reforms of universities, including their institutions, research programmes within university structures and university structure itself.[92] Wallerstein rejected 'an indefensibly state-centric epistemological framework' in which 'significant strands of 20th-century social science have been locked, and 'national states are viewed as self-enclosed containers of social, economic, political and cultural relations' by focusing on 'the world scale of capitalist development'. In subsequent decades, a host of globalization researchers would follow it in 'attempting to construct methodologies that are attuned to the worldwide scale of political and economic relations'.[93]

CRITIQUE AND EVALUATION

Inevitably, a grandiose scheme like Wallerstein's WSA attracted critiques along many dimensions and directions, organized below as sympathetic/internal critiques and external/radical critiques, both possessing historical and theoretical components and generating the undermentioned sub-types.

Internal Historical Critiques

Sympathetic/internal historical critics include detractors of Wallerstein's view of when the capitalist world-system first came into existence. Frank and Gills trace its history back to 'at least 5,000 years', covering a vast Afro-Eurasian mass, in which the recent dominance of Europe and the West is only a passing phase. They employ as relevant theoretical categories of WSA: (a) the concept of 'the world system itself', albeit without a hyphen, (b) the process of capital accumulation as the 'motor force' of its history, (c) the 'centre–periphery structure in and of the world (system)', (d) the 'alternation between hegemony and rivalry' and (e) long and short 'cycles of alternating ascending and descending phases'; but discover them much earlier than the 16th-century Europe. Judged by the criterion of capital accumulation, the MWS is not so very different from earlier millennia-old world systems. The centre–periphery structure, which includes but moves beyond 'the transfer of surplus between zones of the world system, is also found before 1492 as are the fourth and fifth characteristics of the world system.[94]

Following Braudel, Wallerstein differentiated between the unhyphenated and hyphenated 'world economy' and adjudged the latter as 'the largest units which will be still coherent'. But citing Wilkinson,[95] Frank and Gills contend that 'this largest unit has been much larger and older', dating far beyond the 'central civilization', constituted by the relations between Egypt and Mesopotamia in 1500 BC and identifiable through its 'political coherence'. A world system could be identified at least as far back as 3000 BC. It is immaterial if world-systems at that time were world-empires. Unlike Wallerstein, who thinks they reveal military coercion, Frank and Gills posit a far greater role for markets and choose the criteria of continuity and discontinuity for the dating of the world-system. Emphasizing discontinuity, Wallerstein, Amin and others posit that 'the mode of production or social formation of world history' made a sharp break around 1500 BC, while Frank and others affirm that capital accumulation neither began nor became ceaseless only after 1500. Their different timings of the emergence of CW-E/system stem from differences about what structures make up 'a world (-) system' in particular'. For them, 'a hierarchy of centre–periphery (and hinterland) complexes within the world system, in which surplus is being transferred between zones of the hierarchy' is enough to betoken the presence of some type of interstate division of labour.[96]

Nölke treats these critiques as internal because 'these lively debates' revolve around the use/avoidance of a hyphen between the words world economy/system and the resulting disputes about the point of emergence of the world-system 'demonstrate the topicality of the theory building inspired by Wallerstein and others' since the 1970s and are merely examples of the 'contemporary empirical and theoretical developments' in WST.[97] But there are external critiques that problematize the structure of Wallerstein's theory, including its empirical foundation and Marxian provenance.

External Historical Critiques

Wallerstein has been charged by some external critics with overemphasizing the historical evidence which highlight commonalities between the world-systems of 16th-century and present times. Problematizing the supposed link between trade with the periphery and growth of output and formation of capital at the core, O'Brien showed that international trade at the beginning of the mercantile era was limited to 'exchange across the boundaries of states located mainly on the continent of Europe'. Intercontinental trade with 'Asia, the Middle East and Africa formed only a tiny percentage of exports and imports' and must have far less if we time travelled to the 'long 16th-century' upswing and 17th-century 'crisis' decades.[98] DuPlessis pointed out that belying Wallerstein's arguments about the impact of wages on unequal exchange,[99] 'high real wages failed to push the Dutch Republic into the semiperiphery, while lower wages did not prevent Flanders from ending up there'. This indicated that Wallerstein exaggerated the role of wages and pursued a wrong method to measure them. DuPlessis shared O'Brien's view that 'only limited core–periphery trade occurred before 1750, and it was not profitable'. Besides 'overstating the magnitude of international trade', Wallerstein also 'misapprehended the way it functioned'.[100] Stinchcombe says that interstate or inter-zonal division of labour and the unequal exchange being impossible without significant volumes of trade, structuring of the world in terms of core–periphery–semi-periphery or world-system in the 16th century was a misnomer. When referring to capitalism as a system, Marx considered not only the series of problems posed by the aggregate dynamics of the falling rate of profit to capitalists, compelling them to behave in some common ways (like substituting capital for labour) but also some common distinctive solutions offered by them regarding other parts of the system (such as landowners and proletarians). Stinchcombe doubted if the world-system confronted Northern Italy, Prussia and Sweden with similar problems so as to generate 'similar tendencies in the "semi-periphery"'. In such circumstances, even if such a world-system did exist even in the 17th century, it must have been 'a ramshackle affair with a lot of random motion and ill-fitting parts going in their specific orbits', hardly able to 'be treated either in a single theory of causal change or as a chronological narrative'.[101]

The weakness of systemic properties of the previous world-system is argued through the strength of indigenous roots in the dynamics of colonialism. In its South-Asian context, the British Raj in the semi-peripheral India was 'an empire that, in critical ways, was as much Indian as British' because with the British component never exceeding 0.3 per cent of the population, including the army, British power in South Asia was compelled to rely quite extensively on extant political and economic structures.[102]

The combined weight of this evidence is threefold. First, it shows the volume of trade to have been far less crucial in restructuring societies on lines of Wallerstein's theory. Second, it brings out the strength of sub-unit autonomy vis-à-vis structural determination. Third, it shows that capitalist-type economies were not always exported to semi-peripheral countries through incorporation into the world-economy as institutions of them existed already there.[103]

External Theoretical Critiques

Theoretical critiques of Wallerstein's WSA target his detection of capitalism at the level of exchange, his anti-agency view of systems and structural determinism, the teleological nature of his approach and the resulting perception of dominance by core and absence of peripheral and semi-peripheral autonomy. Let us take these up one by one.

Wallerstein finds the basic characteristic of capitalism in the presence of appropriation of profit from the exchange: for feudalism, direct appropriation of agricultural surplus and, for capitalism, exchange of goods at the market. But for Marxists, the prime site for detecting the existence of capitalism is the production process and expropriation of a part of the surplus value produced by the labourer. Worsely rejects the 'methodological assumption that capitalism is a system in which "production is for exchange", which mistakenly locates the defining properties of capitalism in exchange and not in the relations that govern the way commodities are produced' in trade under profitability rather than in production.[104] However, production for exchange characterized other pre-capitalist societies as well,[105] and capitalism, traditionally understood as a mode of production, affords a far better view of the 'internal contradictions' that propel its dynamism in technology, structuring of class relations and 'relations between factions of capital', which generate its periodic crises'.[106]

As a structuralist theory, WSA attracts all the criticisms that structuralist schemes (as of Waltz) are susceptible to, including charges of (economic) determinism and prioritization of structure over the agency. About determinism, Skocpol says that Wallerstein's model involves a two-step reduction: first, a reduction of socio-economic structure to determination by world market opportunities and technological production possibilities, and second, a reduction of state structures and policies to determination by dominant class interests, each of which 'deprives him of crucial explanatory resources for understanding the patterns of history'. So even when we instinctively agree with Wallerstein's diagnosis of 'an enduring and exploitative division of labour' as correct, we feel that 'the theoretical reasons why it is correct must be found elsewhere' than in his market economics and economic-reductionist political sociology.[107] Zolberg and Shannon have accused him of reducing every event or development of world politics to economic factors.[108] Predictably, an indictment of Wallerstein from the perspective of agency-structure debate also questions his statement that, except during periods of crisis, the world-system's restrictions severely hamstring states, social classes and even households in their intended actions.

Apart from critics in realism and liberal theory, critics of other theoretical persuasions also find it problematic. Klink says that 'methodological collectivism renders world system theory's static and dynamic characterizations of the international system as unproblematic assertions because the collectivist ontology treats systemic-level properties as an axiomatically given phenomenon'. Additionally, if 'the properties of the world-system are ontologically prior to the states embedded within that system and if state behaviour is a function of systemic reproductive imperatives, then it must be the case that states or state decision-makers are not goal-directed entities'.[109] Kimmel finds Wallerstein's WST weakened by a 'historical teleology' in which occurrence of events is occasioned by 'a systemic need for them to happen', which substitutes 'the dynamic internal engine of social change' with 'a static reactive capacity for adaptation and system maintenance'.[110]

Wallerstein's views on the core–periphery–semi-periphery relationship, core dominance in it, and varying strengths of state structures in them have also been questioned. First, Skocpol rejects Wallerstein's finding that strong states come up only in the core area and not in the periphery. In economic terms, both the Netherlands and England were core states and strong polities for Wallerstein. Yet 'the Dutch government was simply a federation of merchant oligarchies', and the English monarchs under Tudor reign 'had no large standing armies and no bureaucratic administration that penetrated the localities'. Against these examples of weak state structures in core countries, the instances of Sweden and Prussia after 1650 show that 'a very strong state can be built on a peripheral agrarian base'. Likewise, Wallerstein was hard put to resolve the theoretical oddity of a much stronger state than of either the Netherlands or England emerging in France 'situated only partly in the core zone, partly in the semi-periphery'. He inserted 'an alternative ad hoc (and, of course, teleological) explanation of state strength' that 'France 'had to' develop a centralized bureaucratic monarchy in order to hold together her differently oriented capitalist classes'. To explain the abovementioned 'even more blatantly deviant case' of Sweden, Wallerstein supplied another ad hoc explanation that its strength did not come from its thriving commerce and industry but rather, paradoxically, from the fact that 'its agriculture was weak, and its aristocrats wished to take hold of the profits of other lands for want of being able to create them on their own.' All these rejoinders gravely weakened the force of Wallerstein's hypothesis that 'the strongest absolutisms should emerge in the core and certainly not in the periphery', highlighting Wallerstein's wrong history and problematic theory. As Skocpol says,

> If the strongest states are not always in the core and if, in fact, equally strong or stronger states can grow up in the periphery (not to mention the semiperiphery), then according to Wallerstein's own logic ... the economic division of labor cannot be presumed likely to hold together over time as a 'system' and the differential flow of surpluses to the core is likely to be disrupted.[111]

Moreover, 'neither the differential appearance of absolutist states in early modern Europe nor their effects on upon economic development are adequately explained in Wallerstein's world capitalist system theory'.[112]

Second, from an African case study, Stein shows that the presumed dominance of the Western core, stemming from technological and organizational advantages, over less advanced peripheral Africa and Asia in the late 19th century was 'not the case for the first two centuries of the European expansion in these areas. In fact, the long-term technological advantages enjoyed by Europe in the last century may well be the exception rather than the rule in the history of interregional interaction'.[113]

The concept of semi-periphery, assumed to be a stabilizing political and economic insulator between the core and the periphery, becomes problematic when

> all the major revolutions of the 20th century, which were antisystemic by intention if not necessarily in consequence, should have arisen in the semi-periphery (Russia, China, Algeria, Vietnam, Cuba), and also it should be from the semi-periphery (South Africa, Latin America and Southeast Asia) that many of the most serious ideological challenges to the world system, which cruelly expose the underlying contradictions of capitalism, continue to come.[114]

CONCLUSION AND A FINAL WORD IN VINDICATION

This chapter has discussed the roots of Wallerstein's WST in the influences of Wright Mills, Fanon, Braudel, Balandier and the four traditions of Marxism, German historical/institutional economics, Annales historiography and the dependency perspective. It has identified the four axes along with which his thought can be most fruitfully pursued to show how within the most important 'historical-critical axis', Wallerstein conceived his world-empire, world-economy and finally CW-E as the basic unit of WSA. The CW-E that according to him first emerged in Europe during the period of 1450–1650 and was detected by him at the level of exchange in the market and not at the level of production process and appropriation of a part of the surplus value and was predicted to be transformed towards the end of the 'second 20th century' into something else', although its contours could be studied only after a major restructuring of the social sciences. Wallerstein's WST was attacked both internally and externally along historical and theoretical dimensions, generating sympathetic/internal historical critiques, external historical critiques and external critiques.

The combined force of these critiques raises a question about what remains of Wallerstein as a systems thinker since his admirers far outnumber his critics. As Nölke says, in our confusing times of disciplinary sectarianization, academic fragmentation and limiting specialization, Wallerstein's success in melding 'visionary scope and provocation' with a nearly encyclopaedic grasp over historical detail is a remarkable exception'. Both as his internal and external historical critics, Nölke's should realize that exponents of a 'conceptually parsimonious theory that seeks to explain the broad outlines of world history over the last few centuries with reference to a fairly small number of variables' should learn to live with the fact that it 'cannot always do justice to the empirical minutiae'.[115]

DuPlessis echoes this sentiment after a very detailed and elaborate review of the 'censorious reception' accorded to Wallerstein's theory in *MWS I* and *II* by 'specialists in early modern European history', 'early modernists', 'economic historians' and even Marxist scholars of different hues. Besides echoing objections voiced by bourgeois historians, the latter first faulted Wallerstein's 'definition of capitalism, as essentially a system of exchange rather than production', and after berating this definition, belittled it as 'not a new position' but 'a restatement of a classic thesis extending back through Henri Pirenne and some of Marx's formulations to Adam Smith'.[116]

However, Wallerstein's fate does not depend on what Arrighi calls 'nondebates'[117] but on applications of his approach with or without modifications. These include Braudel's avowed similarity with his understanding of capitalism in his massive trilogy *Civilization and Capitalism*; unrevised adoption of his framework in a study of the dynamics of Swiss migration; extension of his insights to explore the significance of Amsterdam as a centre for distributing information for financial and investment decisions; modification of his framework for studies of the Luso–Atlantic economy, and attempts by others to synthesize Wallerstein's approach with that of proto-industrialization.[118] Apart from these, some researchers have adopted two foci of his framework to study 'incorporation' or the processes through which pre-capitalist societies are drawn into the world-system, and 'commodity chains', that is, analyses of movement of goods through the world-system.[119] Besides, some anthropologists have extended his framework to precapitalist interregional exchange to go beyond Wallerstein's emphasis on bulk commodities like foodstuff or raw materials as the cementers of economic integration to focus on 'luxury goods or preciosities'.[120] Both critics and admirers should finally remember that he has accelerated the process of diffusion and transference of concepts and terminology of dependency theory from their Latin American setting to the discursive word-historical plane and has made everyone, even laymen, aware of a world-system even if just emerging.[121] In other axes of his scheme, he has dragged history to the present and has given a view of an architectonic social science.

REVIEW QUESTIONS

1. Describe the intellectual roots of Wallerstein's WST, the four intermingling ideational traditions Wallerstein's thought meshes and the four major

interconnected, overlapping 'thematic axes' axes along which his theory can be best understood.

2. Show how Wallerstein traces the past and future of capitalism in the four volumes of his magnum opus *MWS*.
   Or
   Trace out the nature and dynamics of the MWS as given by Wallerstein.
3. Delineate the historical-thematic axis of Wallerstein's thought.
4. Comment on the importance of Wallerstein's concept of semi-periphery.
5. Comment on the evolution of states and states system in the MWS in Wallerstein's scheme.
6. Write an essay on Wallerstein's view of the decline of US hegemony and its link with the trajectory of capitalism along a historical-critical axis up to predicted final collapse.
7. Summarize the critiques of Wallerstein's WST on internal historical, external historical and external theoretical lines.

NOTES AND REFERENCES

Note: After first reference, the most frequently cited books of Wallerstein will be mentioned in acronyms, without author name.

1. J. Timmons Roberts, A. B. Hite, and N. Chorev, eds., *Globalization and Development Reader* (Hoboken, NJ: Wiley, 2007), 100.
2. Immanuel Maurice Wallerstein, *World-systems Analysis: An Introduction* (Durham: Duke University Press, 2004), 1, hereafter *WSAAI.*
3. Carlos Antonio Aguirre Rojas, 'Immanuel Wallerstein and the Critical "World-systems Analysis" Perspective,' in *Uncertain Worlds: World-Systems Analysis in Changing Times*, eds. Immanuel Wallerstein, C. A. A. Rojas, and Charles C. Lemert (Abingdon: Routledge, 2012/2016), ii.
4. W. L. Goldfrank, 'Wallerstein's World System: Roots and Contributions,' in *Routledge Handbook of World System Analysis*, eds. Salvatore J. Babones and Christopher K. Chase-Dunn (London: Routledge, 2012), 97–98.
5. See his website: https://www.iwallerstein.com/ (accessed on 06 April 2021).
6. Carlos Antonio Aguirre Rojas, 'Wallerstein and the Critical,' in *Uncertain Worlds: World-Systems Analysis in Changing Times*, eds. Immanuel Wallerstein, C. A. A. Rojas, and Charles C. Lemert (Abingdon: Routledge, 2012/2016), iii.
7. See Immanuel Wallerstein, *Africa: The Politics of Independence* (New York, NY: Vintage Books, 1961); Immanuel Wallerstein, *Africa: The Politics of Unity: An Analysis of a Contemporary Social Movement* (New York, NY: Random House, 1967); Immanuel Wallerstein, 'Left and Right in Africa,' *The Journal of Modern African Studies* 9, no. 1 (1971): 1–10; Immanuel Wallerstein, 'Africa in a Capitalist World,' *A Journal of Opinion* 3, no. 3 (1973): 1–11.
8. Goldfrank, 'Wallerstein's World System,' 98.
9. Immanuel Wallerstein, *The Modern World System I: Capitalist Agriculture and the Origins of European World-Economy in the Sixteenth Century* (With a new prologue, London: University of California Press, 1974/2011), 7, hereafter *MWS I.*
10. Wallerstein, *WSAAI*, 11.
11. Goldfrank, 'Wallerstein's World System,' 98–99; Andreas Nölke, 'World-system Theory,' in *Theories of International Relations*, eds. Siegfried Schieder and Manuela Spindler (London: Routledge, 2014), 198–199.

12. Immanuel Wallerstein, *The Essential Wallerstein* (New York, NY: The New Press, 2000), 30, hereafter *EW*.
13. Immanuel Wallerstein, *After Liberalism* (New York, NY: New Press, 1995), 154.
14. See for relevant citations about 'Fanonismo': Wallerstein, *EW*, 30–31, 79–81, 103; about Lukács: ibid., 71–72, and Wallerstein, 'The Rise and Future Demise of the World Capitalist System: Concepts for Comparative Analysis,' *Comparative Studies in Society and History* 16, no. 4 (1974): 387–415.
15. Wallerstein, *MWS I*, 57; Wallerstein, *EW*, xxii, 210, 212.
16. Goldfrank, 'Wallerstein's World System,' 99; Wallerstein, *MWS I*, 17; Wallerstein, *EW*, 75–76.
17. Wallerstein, *WSAAI*, 15; Wallerstein, *EW*, 160–169.
18. Stephen Hobden, *International Relations and Historical Sociology: Breaking down Boundaries* (London: Routledge, 2006), 144.
19. Ibid.; Goldfrank, 'Wallerstein's World System,' 99.
20. See note 9 above.
21. Immanuel Wallerstein, *The Modern World System II: Mercantilism and the Consolidation of the European World Economy, 1600–1750* (With a new prologue, Berkeley, CA: University of California Press, 1980/2011), hereafter *MWS II*.
22. Immanuel Wallerstein, *The Modern World System III: The Second Era of Great Expansion of the Capitalist World Economy* (New York, NY: Academic Press, 1989), hereafter *MWS III*.
23. Immanuel Wallerstein, *The Modern World System IV: Centrist Liberalism Triumphant, 1789–1914* (Berkeley, CA: University of California Press, 2011), hereafter *MWS IV*.
24. Rojas, 'Wallerstein and the Critical,' iv–vi.
25. Rojas' citations will come after these supplemental citations.
26. This theme is treated in Wallerstein's 4 historical treatises, *MWS I–IV*, and 11 mainly conceptual books on capitalism (6 written singly and 5 edited and/or written jointly). Solo conceptual ones are Immanuel Wallerstein, *The Capitalist World Economy* (Cambridge: Cambridge University Press, 1979); Immanuel Wallerstein, *Historical Capitalism: With Capitalist Civilization* (Brooklyn, NY: Verso, 1983); Immanuel Wallerstein, *The Politics of the World-economy: The States, the Movements and the Civilizations* (Cambridge: Cambridge University Press, 1984), henceforth *POTWE*; Immanuel Wallerstein, *Geopolitics and Geoculture: Essays on the Changing World-system* (Cambridge, New York: Cambridge University Press, 1991); Immanuel Wallerstein, *Unthinking Social Science: The Limits of Nineteenth-century Paradigms*, 2nd ed. (Philadelphia, PA: Temple University Press, 2001), henceforth *USS*; Immanuel Wallerstein, *After Liberalism* (New York, NY: The New Press, 1995); Wallerstein, *EW*; Wallerstein, *WSAAI*, and Immanuel Wallerstein, *European Universalism: The Quest for Power* (New York, NY: The New Press, 2006). Edited and/or jointly written books are, Giovanni Arrighi, Terence K. Hopkins, and Immanuel Wallerstein, *Antisystemic Movements* (Brooklyn, NY: Verso, 1989/2011); Etienne Balibar and Immanuel Wallerstein, *Race, Nation Class: Ambiguous Identities* (Brooklyn, NY: Verso, 1991); Terence K. Hopkins, Immanuel Wallerstein, and John Casparis, *The Age of Transition: Trajectory of the World System, 1945–2025* (London; Atlantic Highlands, New Jersey: Zed Books; Leichardt: Pluto Press, 1998); Immanuel Wallerstein, *The Modern World System in the Longue Durèe* (Boulder, CO: Paradigm Publishers, 2004); Immanuel Wallerstein, Randall Collins, Michael Mann, Georgi Derleugian, and Craig Calhoun, *Does Capitalism Have a Future?* (Oxford: Oxford University Press, 2013).
27. Wallerstein, *MWS I*, 347.
28. Wallerstein, *EW*, 75.
29. Wallerstein, *MWS I*, 36–38.
30. Ibid., 162, 165, 185, 199, 201, 212, 214.
31. Wallerstein, *MWS II*, 26–27, 76–77, 99, 179, 217–225, 158.
32. Wallerstein, 'New Prologue,' *MWS III*, xiv.

33. Ibid., 182, 112, 94.
34. Ibid., 22, 29–36; *MWS IV*, 275.
35. Ibid., 34, 49, 94, 111.
36. Ibid., 256.
37. Wallerstein, *MWS IV*, 1–20, especially 6.
38. Ibid., 77–141, especially 112; 143–218.
39. Wallerstein, *POTWE*, 17, 40, 181.
40. Hopkins, Wallerstein, and Casparis, *The Age of Transition*, 210–212, 226–243.
41. Wallerstein et al., *Does Capitalism Have a Future?* 11.
42. Wallerstein, *MWS I*, 347.
43. Wallerstein, *EW*, xviii, 139, 149.
44. Wallerstein, *MWS I*, 162.
45. Wallerstein, *EW*, 149–150.
46. Wallerstein et al., *Does Capitalism Have a Future?* 9–10.
47. Wallerstein, *MWS I*, 15; Wallerstein, *EW*, 54; Wallerstein, *WSAAI*, 98–99.
48. Wallerstein, *MWS I*, 15–16; Wallerstein, *EW*, 54–55, 16–17, 75–76.
49. Wallerstein, *MWS I*, 16; Wallerstein, *EW*, 139–140.
50. Wallerstein, *MWSI*, 349–350, 301–302.
51. Wallerstein, *EW*, 56.
52. Arghiri Emmanuel, *Unequal Exchange: A Study in the Imperialism of Trade*, trans. Brian Pearce (with additional comments by Charles Bettelheim, New York, NY: Monthly Review Press, 1972), 61, 64.
53. Hobden, *International Relations and Historical Sociology*, 148.
54. Wallerstein, *Geopolitics and Geoculture*, 163, 124–125.
55. Wallerstein, *EW*, 207–208; 216–217, 247–248.
56. Ibid., 123; Wallerstein, *Capitalist World Economy*, 35.
57. Wallerstein, *Geopolitics and Geoculture*, 104; *WSAAI*, 76.
58. Wallerstein, *Unthinking Social Science*, 235.
59. Wallerstein, *POTWE*, 29.
60. Wallerstein, *EW*, 61.
61. Wallerstein, *WSAAI*, x.
62. Christopher Chase-Dunn, 'Interstate System and Capitalist World-economy: One Logic or Two?' in *The Theoretical Evolution of International Political Economy: A Reader*, eds. George T. Crane and Abla Amawi (New York, NY: Oxford University Press, 1996), 147.
63. Wallerstein, *POTWE*, 38, 33.
64. Nölke, 'World-system Theory,' 202.
65. Chase-Dunn, 'Interstate System,' 147.
66. Wallerstein, *EW*, 56, 86.
67. Wallerstein, *WSAAI*, 28–30.
68. Immanuel Wallerstein, 'The Three Instances of Hegemony in the History of the Capitalist World-Economy,' *International Journal of Comparative Sociology* 24, no. 1–2 (1983): 100–108, here, 101.
69. Wallerstein, *POTWE*, 38–40.
70. See note 37 above.
71. Arrighi, Hopkins, and Wallerstein, *Antisystemic Movements*, 1, 30–32, 43, 77, 88, 111, passim.
72. Wallerstein, *EW*, xix, 285–286.
73. Wallerstein, *Geopolitics and Geoculture*, 11.
74. Wallerstein, *MWS IV*, xiii, 277. Also see Wallerstein, *EW*, 418.
75. Wallerstein, *WSAAI*, 38–41, 60–61.
76. Wallerstein, *EW*, 418.
77. Wallerstein, *Geopolitics and Geoculture*, 11–13; Wallerstein, *WSAAI*, 38–41; Wallerstein, *EW*, 277–287, 344–352.
78. Wallerstein, *EW*, 352.

79. Discussion of these three axes will draw heavily on Rojas, 'Wallerstein and the Critical,' xiii–xxxi; except for specific independent references I mention.
80. Wallerstein, *Capitalist World Economy*, 35, 30–31.
81. Immanuel Wallerstein, 'The Collapse of Liberalism,' *Socialist Register* 28 (1992): 96, 104.
82. Immanuel Wallerstein, *1968, Revolution in the World-system: Theses and Queries* (New York, NY: State University of New York at Binghamton, 1988); Immanuel Wallerstein, *The Decline of American Power: The U.S. in a Chaotic World* (London: New Press: 2003), 50, 75, 109; Wallerstein, *After Liberalism*, 68.
83. Immanuel Wallerstein, ed., 'Preface to the Second Edition,' in *Unthinking Social Science: The Limits of Nineteenth-Century Paradigms* (Philadelphia, PA: Temple University Press, 2001), viii.
84. Wallerstein, *Decline of American Power*, 45–46.
85. Wallerstein et al., *Does Capitalism Have a Future?* 2.
86. Ibid., 11–16.
87. Ibid., 6, passim.
88. Christopher Chase-Dunn, 'Continuities and Transformations in the Evolution of World Systems,' *in Comparing Globalizations: Historical and World-Systems Approaches*, ed. Thomas D. Hall (e-book, Berlin: Springer, 2018), available at: https://books.google.co.in/books?isbn=3319682199 (accessed on 06 April 2021), 20.
89. Immanuel Wallerstein, *Utopistics, Or, Historical Choices of the Twenty-first Century* (New York, NY: New Press, 1998), cited in Chase-Dunn, 'Continuities and Transformations in the Evolution of World Systems,' 20.
90. Wallerstein, *Unthinking Social Science*, 237.
91. Ibid., vi.
92. Immanuel Wallerstein, *Open the Social Sciences: Report of the Gulbenkian Commission on the Restructuring of the Social Sciences* (Stanford, CA: Stanford University Press, 1996), 103–105.
93. Neil Brenner, 'The Space of the World: Beyond State-centrism,' in *Immanuel Wallerstein and the Problem of the World: System, Scale, Culture*, eds. David Palumbo-Liu, Bruce Robbins, and Nirvana Tanoukhi (Durham, NC: Duke University Press, 2011), 101.
94. Andre Gunder Frank and Barry Gills, eds., 'The 5,000-year World System: An Interdisciplinary Introduction,' in *The World System: Five Hundred Years or Five Thousand?* (London: Routledge, 1993/1996), xix, 3–5.
95. David Wilkinson, 'Central Civilization,' *Comparative Civilizations Review* 17, no. 17 (1987): 31–59, available at: https://scholarsarchive.byu.edu/ccr/vol17/iss17/4 (accessed on 6 April 2021).
96. Andre Gunder Frank and Barry Gills, 'The Five Thousand Year World System in Theory and Praxis,' in *World System History: The Social Science of Long-Term Change*, eds. Robert. A Denemark, Jonathan Friedman, Barry K. Gills, and George Modelski (London: Routledge, 2003), 3–4.
97. Nölke, 'World-system Theory,' 208.
98. Patrick O'Brien, 'European Economic Development: The Contribution of the Periphery,' *The Economic History Review*, New Series, 35, no. 1 (1982): 1–18, especially 3–4.
99. See note 50 above.
100. Robert S. DuPlessis, 'Wallerstein, World Systems Analysis, and Early Modern European History,' *The History Teacher* 21, no. 2 (1988): 221–232, especially 225–226.
101. Arthur L. Stinchcombe, 'Review Essay: The Growth of the World System,' *American Journal of Sociology* 87, no. 6 (1982): 1389–1395, especially 1395.
102. David Washbrook, 'South Asia, the World System, and World Capitalism,' *Journal of Asian Studies* 49, no. 3 (1990): 479–508, especially 490–493.
103. Hobden, *International Relations and Historical Sociology*, 160.
104. P. Worsely, 'One World System or Three? A Critique of the World System Theory of Immanuel Wallerstein,' *Socialist Register* 17 (1980): 298–338, especially 304.

105. Robert Brenner, 'The Origins of Capitalist Development: A Critique of Neo-Smithian Marxism,' *New Left Review* no. 104 (1977): 27–32, cited in Hobden, *International Relations and Historical Sociology*, 157.
106. D. Harvey, 'The World System Theory Trap,' *Studies in Comparative International Development* 22, no. 1 (1987): 44, cited in Hobden, *International Relations and Historical Sociology*, 157.
107. Theda Skocpol, 'Wallerstein's World Capitalist System: A Theoretical and Historical Critique,' *American Journal of Sociology* 82, no. 5 (1977): 1075–1090, especially 1078–1087.
108. Aristide R. Zolberg, 'Origins of the Modern World System: A Missing Link,' *World Politics*, 33, no. 2 (1981): 253–281, especially 255; T. R. Shannon, *An Introduction to the World System Perspective*, 2nd ed. (Boulder, CO: Westview Press, 1996), 155–159.
109. Frank F. Klink, 'Rationalizing Core-Periphery Relations: The Analytical Foundations of Structural Inequality of States,' *International Studies Quarterly* 34, no. 2 (1990): 183–209, especially 184.
110. M. S. Kimmel, *Revolution: A Sociological Interpretation* (Oxford: Polity Press, 1990), 110.
111. Theda Skocpol, 'Wallerstein's World Capitalist System: A Theoretical and Historical Critique,' *American Journal of Sociology* 85, no. 5 (1977): 1084–1085, 1087; Theda Skocpol, *Social Revolutions in the Modern World* (Cambridge: Cambridge University Press, 1994), 63–65.
112. Ibid, 65.
113. Gil Stein, *Rethinking World-systems: Diasporas, Colonies, and Interaction in Uruk Mesopotamia* (Tucson, AZ: The University of Arizona Press, 1999), 17.
114. Washbrook, 'South Asia, the World System, and World Capitalism,' *The Journal of Asian Studies* 49, no. 3 (1990): 1084.
115. Nölke, 'World-system Theory,' 211.
116. DuPlessis, 'Wallerstein,' 222–227.
117. Giovanni Arrighi, 'Capitalism and the Modern World-system: Rethinking the Nondebates of the 1970's,' *Review* (Fernand Braudel Center) 21, no. 1 (1998): 113–129.
118. See for discussion and citations for these applications in DuPlessis, 'Wallerstein,' 227–229, 232.
119. William G. Martin, 'The World-systems Perspective in Perspective,' *Review* 17 (1994): 145-185, cited in Marc Stein, *Rethinking the Gay and Lesbian Movement* (London: Routledge, 2012), 15.
120. Jane Schneider, 'Was There a Pre-capitalist World System,' *Peasant Studies* 6 (1977): 20-29, cited in William G. Martin, 'The World-systems Perspective in Perspective,' 15–16.
121. DuPlessis, 'Wallerstein,' 230.

CHAPTER

19

International Political Economy*

CHAPTER OUTLINE

* This chapter is available on the companion website.

CHAPTER

20

Gender, Feminism and Women in International Relations

CHAPTER OUTLINE

INTRODUCTION: ABOUT SEMANTICS AND NON-RECOGNITION

In this approach of the globalist paradigm, the three connected words of the title are not semantically identical as regards their implications for the scope of IR as a discipline. To clarify their import, except when expressly said, by gender, I would imply the feminine one, take women's issues as bearers of feminism in IR and show how shaking off the non-recognition up to the early 1980s, questions of gender, feminism and women have first demanded increased space and then gradually exclusive attention in IR. The stable points at which they temporarily settled themselves have been thrown open time and again to link these questions with other 'critical' approaches in IR.

Whether or not women were really 'hidden from history' for '300 years',[1] there is no doubt that, with rare exceptions in the 1980s and even the 1970s,[2] their academic occultation in British and American IR textbooks and journals as late as the early 1980s was also matched by their near banishment from the arenas of international practices. In a world dominated by mainly male diplomats and international bureaucrats, there was 'little evidence to suggest that women have played much of a role in shaping foreign policy in any country in the 20th century'. In the USA in 1987, women accounted for less than 5 per cent of total foreign service ranks and occupied less than 4 per cent of administrative positions in the Department of Defense. No less importantly, entrenched attitudes belittled women, as fit for only 'human interest stuff' of military calculations or outcomes. Jean Kirkpatrick, one of the few interlopers into the charmed circle of FPDM as US ambassador to the UN in 1981, described her position as one of 'a mouse in a man's world'.[3]

There were many reasons behind this physical and ideational concealment and invisibility of women in academic IR. First, 'institutional inertia' within disciplinary IP caused shyness of the conceptual leap required to consider new categories or concepts'.[4] The resulting near-complete silence about the 'second sex' discouraged attempts at academic exploration of the three categories, even by 'refereed journals' who also barred them as gatekeepers. Second, this inertia was helped by the 'selective insulation' of IR from developments going on in other social sciences, including sociological concepts like society, or economic concepts like labour in IR, in spite of its engagement with IPE and sidelining of the burgeoning literature of women's studies in other social sciences. Third, this insulation of IR from women's studies was encouraged by the conventional disciplinary self-definition of IR in terms of the dominance of 'high politics' in it.[5] Fourth, the male-dominated nature of the 'domain of international practice', mentioned above, also strengthened academic exclusion. Finally, assumptions shared by both the discipline and the feminist literature about the irrelevance of women's studies in IR and IR in women's studies strengthened disciplinary 'gender blindness'. Mainstream IR believed that the course of relations between nations did not touch, except tangentially, women's issues (properly the subject of domestic politics). Feminism thought that its sociological and psychological preoccupation with the interpersonal, the subjective and the focused on 'the discrete society and the family or the individual' rather than nation states.[6]

SPATIAL DEBATES AND EMERGENCE OF GENDER AS A VARIABLE

In the late 1980s, feminist ideas started infiltrating IR books, journals and seminars/ conferences and finding audiences, but took a decade more to be placed in proper theoretical context. With feminist essays filling journals, panels on feminism bedecking conferences, feminist courses adorning university curricula and interrogations of the gender-neutrality of IR starting in right earnest, it seemed that IR's affair with feminism was thickening. But the tête-à-tête was not without its hiccups and hitches. Even as IR scholars (largely men) started welcoming feminist writings (largely from women) to books/journals edited by them, and even declared themselves as feminists, many feminists (mostly women) found the situation suboptimal, because feminist issues were just being stirred with IR questions in a way that left the realist malestream of the discipline untouched. Yet feminist questions could challenge 'the very terms in which IR was approached, understood and studied', as legitimately as the old questions of war and peace. The mainstream IR position against this feminist chagrin was that feminists should also accept that the value of newly admitted feminist approaches lay in their success in expanding IR's core agenda by raising important new questions, not in undermining the very foundation from which these questions sprang. The wise male scholars owlishly warned feminists against getting extortionate and unreasonable, as well as against 'asking the most uncomfortable sorts of questions'. Male scholars, like Keohane, even sought to advise their intractable feminist (female) colleagues about how to pursue a more responsible approach in IR that is also convenient for its male practitioners. One objective behind this attempt at taming of feminism by IR was constriction of the right feminist questions for adoption (in all senses), and specification of proper types, times and contexts for them, and that too by male scholars who wanted to put feminism in its proper sphere in IR, sorely perturbed and fretful at the intractability of feminism to stay put in its assigned place.[7]

Jones famously sought to circumvent the whole impasse by contending that 'feminism's primary, and seminal contribution to the study of international relations is its focus on the...incorporation of the gender variable, and the exploration of its influence on women and (to a lesser extent) society as a whole'. The contention was a double-edged sword. Apparently, it urged 'an expansion of the seminal "discovery" of feminism—the gender variable in IR—by moving beyond feminism's standard equation of *gender*, an inclusive designation, with *women/femininity*, a narrower and more restrictive one'.[8] But, as Weber argues, it would also have made feminism and feminists 'manageable' by placing them 'within one reasonable realm—gender' and placing gender itself 'within the confines of a variable', which they would now view as a 'discrete set of relationships' to be explored 'qualitatively or quantitatively'. Feminists, however, contended that conceptualization of gender as a variable is mistaken because 'one is never outside of gender', and Jones' presentation of gender as a variable makes sense only if it goes beyond claiming 'just a gender-neutral status', involving equality to all genders and claims a 'gender-free status (being outside of gender altogether)'. Weber illustrates how Jones uses the gender variable 'to construct a gendered relationship between IR and feminism', in which 'feminism is once again placed in the stereotypical feminized position as irrational, unbalanced and in need of guidance', which, if left un-chaperoned, might distract 'IR's family romance about MSW'.[9]

FEMINISM AND ITS CHARGES AGAINST THE THEORETICAL PRACTICES OF IR

This section starts with this awareness that there is not one feminism but many, with exemplars such as liberal feminism of Betty Friedan (*The Feminist Mystique*, 1963), Janet Radcliffe Richards (*The Sceptical Feminist*, 1982) and Susan Moller Okin (*Gender, Justice and the Family*, 1990); radical feminism of Germaine Greer (*The Female Eunuch*, 1970) and Kate Millet (Sexual Politics, 1970); Marxist and socialist feminism spearheaded by Juliet Mitchell (*Women's Estate*, 1971), Michèle Barret, (*Women's Oppression Today: The Marxist/Feminist Encounter*, 1988) and Lise Vogel, *Marxism and the Oppression of Women: Toward a Unitary Theory*, 1983); black feminism most famously articulated by Angela Davis (*Women, Culture and Politics*, 1990), Patricia Collins (*Black Feminist Thought*, 1990) and Bell Hooks (*Yearning: Race, Gender and Cultural Politics*, 1991) and postmodern feminism theorized by Chris Weedon (*Feminist Practice and Poststructuralist Thought*, 1987) and Alison Assiter (*Enlightened Women: Modernist Feminism in a Postmodern Age*, 1996).[10] Typologizing feminism a little differently, Tickner and Sjoberg associate Mary Caprioli and Mark Boyer ('Gender, Violence and International Crisis', 2001) with liberal feminism in IR; Sandra Whitworth (*Feminism and International Relations*, 1994; Christine Chin, *In Service and Servitude*, 1998) with critical feminism; Elisabeth Prügl (*The Global Construction of Gender*, 1999) with constructivist feminism; Charlotte Hooper (*Manly States*, 2001), with post-structuralist feminism and C. T. Mohanty ('Under Western Eyes: Feminist Scholarship and Colonial Discourse', 1988) with postcolonial feminism.[11] But before going into the nuances of critiques of IR as presently constituted by particular types of feminism, we should first state their common contentions.

The most basic critique, shared by all brands of feminism, is one which conflates the two levels at which the role of gender in the narrower and more restrictive sense of Jones can be investigated in IR: 'women as a category' and 'gender as epistemology'.[12] It says that since women were excluded from most of the classic schools of political theory, the discipline of IR suffers from 'gender bias' in its self-definition and theories of knowledge,[13] as seen in how the Hobbesian SON, the most common starting point of not only much political theory but also IRT, and its falsely 'universal models' based on 'parables of man', deftly excludes women. Quoting from Simone de Beauvoir's *The Second Sex*, Grant shows how 'the ancient image of man's battle for survival as a struggle against Mother Nature' and 'against the feminine, affective attributes and the capricious power of the state of nature' sought to hide how women 'with their mysterious powers of bringing forth life, were a symbol of power of nature over mankind'. Even Rousseau's version of a more harmonious SON was not more amenable to a feminized version of it, as could be seen from his cautionary parable of the stag hunt and the suggestions in *Emile* that the female, whose 'powers are those of the body and not of the mind', is an 'adjunct to the male'. This male domination is not much alleviated by Rousseau's description of a woman's reign in the home in *Emile* as 'a reign of gentleness'.

The second source of 'gender bias' was the concept of the state, not only in its Athenian model in ancient Hellas but also in the modern European example during the Renaissance. In Greece subordination of women and sexual division of labour consequent upon the devaluation of the processes of reproduction and management of the home, facilitated efforts to introduce and bolster new economic and political structures geared to increasing the state's economic power. Women's resultant relegation into the private sphere and banishment from public life was exemplified in Socrates's decision to send away weeping wife Xanthippe to the home while he continued his intellectual discussions before drinking the hemlock given as punishment. Although Plato allowed women to be guardians, they were not equal to their male counterparts and were assigned domestic duties. With occasional chinks, the public–private split not only disfavoured women but also enabled the state to claim a kind of morality that was different from the moral needs of individual relations and more consonant with the morality of men. A similar transition in social relations in Europe not only helped the 'consolidation of mercantile and manufacturing economies in the city states of Italy' but also brought down the high status of the feudal noblewoman, whose 'family order was [also] the public order of her class' and afforded her an independent 'sphere of her own in the church' as well. The practice of women ruling principalities in feudal society through familial rights was terminated in France by the Salic Law, which debarred women from inheriting the French crown. The resulting public–private split drowned women's experiences in Renaissance literature compared with its medieval counterpart, turning women into objects marked by affectivity before man's reasoning mind; 'symbols of virtue and human qualities', 'beautiful souls' whose protection was the duty of the valourized men. Excluded from functions of the state and the public realm, passive experiencers, receivers or even victims of the outcomes of war and other fallouts of the activities of the state, women were living examples of the false universality of the state and its gender bias.

According to Grant, security dilemma, an important concept of the realist paradigm,[14] is the third source of gender bias in IRT. It also emerged from 'a selective definition of gender roles in political society', since the task of defending the state as soldiers and citizens was monopolized by men. Besides, the concept privileged 'an abstract representation of the state' that can be employed 'as a generic model of a rational actor', from which women, emotional people and recluses in the private realm were left out. Both Rousseau's tale of the stag hunt and its neorealist use by Waltz[15] hides the fact that

> [t]he choices of the hunters are probably directly by the situation of the family; one hunter may have [had] a greater need than another to settle for a rabbit on a particular day.... In this sense, the controlled anarchy of the hunting group is a condition created for specific purposes ...'.

Besides, perhaps there would have been little difference in the perception of the security dilemma symbolized by the stag hunt if 'exceptional women' like Boadicea (the Celtic Warrior Queen), the virginal Elizabeth I (enthusing England to confront the Spanish Armada in 1588) or Margaret Thatcher (tough during the Falklands war) were in charge. But 'the real question is whether the concept of female gender role offers insight into the ways to reduce the tensions of the security dilemma'. No less important is its implication that the above view of the pitfalls of the security concerns of a state does not necessarily reflect those of the whole population of the state, and ipso facto 'the epistemological parameters of what we know as IR have been severely limited'.[16]

Feminists contend that this gender bias of IR makes its scholars impervious to the gendered effects that international processes, ranging from military and economic ones to the construction and diffusion of images of women and fashions of feminism, share with other social practices.[17] One example of this is the track record of state policy on one of the most intimate and private aspects of human life, namely the control of reproduction and birth rate as matters of international competition. Its centrality in the 19th century is manifested in Britain in Caleb Saleeby's comment in *Parenthood and Race Culture* (1910) that the 'history of nations is determined not in the battlefield but in the nursery... The politics of the future will be domestics'; and in France in Elizabeth Sloan-Chesser's remark in *Perfect Health for Women and Children* (1912) that the home was 'the cradle of the race...Empire's first line of defence'. This was endorsed in France by millions of pro-natalist postcards displaying pictures of babies sitting on the barrels of field guns.[18] In 17th-century France, the creation of large families was so much encouraged by the Church and the State that 'bearing of 10 sons was regarded as a mere trifle and several ladies boasted of having 18 children each...' (as in the city of Clermont-Ferrand).[19] And in the USSR, as late as 1944, encouragement of mothers and caregivers of large families was manifest in the new title of Mother Heroine (*Mat'-geroinia*), accompanied by new medals: the Motherhood medal (I degree for six children, II degree for five children) and the Order of Maternal Glory (I class for nine children, II class for eight and III class for seven children). The Order of Mother Heroine was bestowed by the Presidium of the Supreme Soviet on mothers who bore 10 or more children.[20] Russia has revived its policy of rewarding fertility, 18 years after it was discontinued, in an attempt to reverse a potentially disastrous demographic decline.[21] Also relevant is a 'Profamily Program' developed by the Polish state, mainly on the lines of the Vatican's Family Rights Charter, to combat persistent decline of fertility, which contained nothing much beyond political rhetoric urging higher childbearing, being 'void of any meaningful policies to help women combine work and motherhood'[22]; or Mao's satisfaction, even in overpopulated China, that 'Ren Duo, Liliang Da' (in English, 'With Many People Strength is Great'), a slogan that encouraged people to have lots of children, which led to a baby boom. In this and Mao's later utterances (one before Nehru), Schapiro finds his appreciation of China's population as a 'source of military strength and survival on the world stage'. The 600 million people inhabiting 9,600,000 sq. km of territory were conceived a good match for America's nuclear weapons. However, in 1953, Zhou Enlai was pleading for birth control and, in 1979, Hua Guofeng officially announced the implementation of the policy of one-child family.[23]

The interstate competition over birth rates later mellowed down because of the fear of global population explosion, epitomized by William Draper's 1966 plea for a 'new Manhattan project', desisting from building more atomic bombs, but 'to defuse the population bomb', and providing the title of Ehrlich and Ehrlich's famous 1968 book.[24] But, while pillorying both the former interstate competition over birth rates and the later neo-Malthusian control of state populations, feminist critiques remind one of or reiterate Foucault's concept of 'biopolitics of the population', which targets living 'populations', especially their sex.[25]

According to feminists, the language of IP also suffers from a gender bias in suggesting a 'strong conventional masculine and homophobic content' that privileges toughness and competition. Writ large in the imperial rhetoric of the late 18th and early 20th centuries, explicit in the social Darwinist creed of the right of 'virile' nations to conquer more effeminate nations, and continuing in the 'discourse and imagery' of Great Power rivalry, this language too has its roots in classic political theory. Feminists show how three different forms of the Latin maxim, 'Fortune favours the bold/brave', in Pliny ('fortēs Fortūna adiuvat': *Epistles*), Virgil ('audentīs Fortūna iuvat': *Aeneid*) and Ovid ('audentēs deus epse iuvat': *Metamorphoses*), were reworked by Machiavelli to pit 'virtu', the quality of the *vir* against the fickleness of Renaissance goddess *fortuna*, and how it is amenable to a gendered reading of the desired ability of the virile male leader (*vir virtutis*) to overpower and compel her to serve his own ends. They also show how, in urging England in 1796 to confront revolutionary France, Edmund Burke exhorted Englishmen to overcome their 'frivolity and effeminacy', how even in 'contemporary political parlance...it is insulting to be called a Pollyanna, wimp or limp-wristed' and how top female political figures such as Golda Meir, Margaret Thatcher or Jean Kirkpatrick (I add Indira Gandhi) tried not to show their difference in moral orientation (as Carol Gilligan would have preferred it)[26] but their ability in besting male morality, strength and toughness. An exception is Sirimavo Bandaranaike, who used a 'charismatic mother image'.[27] In language, the saying 'All's fair in love and war' reveals the close similarity between two Hobbesian domains, and if one decodes the language of military strategy, particularly its nuclear part, the remarkable echo of male chauvinism in analyses of weaponry and deployment becomes immediately evident.

The gender bias of IR language and the vacuity of its gender neutrality thus confirmed, I initially proceed to explore more deeply the interdigitations of women/gender and IR from the twin basic levels of 'women as a category' and 'gender as epistemology', while delineating the layers of perspectives in them.

WOMEN AS A CATEGORY

This, perhaps, easiest and most recognizable level shows how transnational processes impact women in their invisibility, how they victimize women as international actors through the joint operation of capitalism and patriarchy in the international society or system, how evocation of nationalism by nation states keeps women out of its purview, how gender-specific components of numerous areas of foreign policy discriminate against women and how the recent globalization also has impacted women. Among the transnational processes, war, with peace constitutive of IR, has had numerous implications for women. Not only were women the quintessential objects/personalized objectives of many wars since ancient times (winning back Helen in the Trojan War, avenging Draupadī's public humiliation in the Kuru–Pāṇdava war at Kurukşetra), but the country being protected during war was often conceived as a woman, and when it was a *patria*, war was waged for the defence of its women from foreign aggression. But once wars started, women were mobilized and assigned new tasks, such as reproductive, productive and even military, though to a lesser degree, and were relocated back into their homes after the war ended, as depicted in the famous film *Rosie the Riveter*. The wartime tasks that women were assigned to ranged from engineering to munitions factories.[28]

However, unlike ungendered civilians, women also suffer as rape victims during wars. An authentic gendered account of the Second World War will reveal the enormousness of the problem, even without exaggeration, as in British and American claims of rape of Belgian women by German soldiers.[29] For, apart from the authorized use of Korean and Chinese women in brothels by Japanese forces, there was brutal mass rape by Japanese soldiers in Nanking in 1937, in the very first month of occupation, of 20,000 by conservative estimates and 80,000 by liberal estimates, apart from forcible recruitment of 200,000 teenage Korean girls as 'comfort women' by some estimates. On top of this, the international silence against overwhelming historical evidence about the mass rapes of women of various ethnicities (though mostly German) by the Soviet army[30] hints that in modern wars rape is not just a by-product or side effect but a conscious instrument of strategy. The wars in former Yugoslavia buttress this point. There, rapes have been a regular feature of the wars; 'degradation and molestation of women were central to the combat'; mostly Muslim women 'of childbearing age were principal targets'; and Serb forces in Bosnia were not the only perpetrators. If they had set the trend in 1992 towards the creation of a Greater Serbia, Bosnian Croats in Western Herzegovina adopted it in the spring of 1993 to create an ethnically purified Croatian sector. Forces of the predominantly Muslim government of Bosnia also have been indicted for atrocities, 'but not as tool of government policy'. In Bosnia, the numbers of victims ranged from 20,000 (as per EC) and 50,000 (as per the Bosnian Ministry of the Interior) Croatian and Serbian Muslim women and here, as elsewhere, rape was 'systematic', a part of 'ethnic cleansing'.[31]

Among non-military international processes, economic development was one where women's existence was noticed long before other domains, even though traditional economics was blind to gender, and did not consider women as subjects of the economic sphere save as exceptions, the concept of the rational economic man being overly masculine. But apart from their role in home economy and its significance for the modus of bilateral and multilateral aid giving in developing countries, women have been deeply affected by international processes in both developed and developing countries. Cases in point are as follows: mass recruitment of women in high-tech industries in newly industrializing countries (hereafter NICs), changes in agricultural employment in the Third World and out-migration of male workers to more affluent parts of it and decomposition/decline of wage rates in the informal sector consequent on 'structural adjustment policies'. Apart from the first mentioned point, women, located mainly in the informal sector, were badly affected in all of the others, being forced to work in the least remunerative sectors while bearing the brunt of the debt repayment costs. In developed countries, industrial change facilitated the employment of women in some sectors and took them away from others, causing the formation of an urban underclass composed of women and children.

There are several pragmatic reasons why research on women in development is designed in a policy-relevant manner, urging close collaboration between feminist advocates, practitioners and feminist scholars. Revealingly, some of these researches have shown that, while the entry of women in the modern sector quickened economic development, modern technology and cash crops have improved the condition of men at their expense, showing the necessity of better educational facilities for women. These researches also showed that industrialization impacted women differently in various societies. The adoption of gender-sensitive strategies by various international aid agencies has not been able to fully eliminate gender disparities in development, partly because modernization has not undermined patriarchy. While men retain control over women's sexuality and reproductive relations, women remain weaker than men in production relations due to their limited access to global resources, as a result of which their increasing productive duties have not been compensated by a decrease in reproductive tasks. Moreover, these nagging disparities also result from the 'feminization of poverty' in the Third World due to the differential consequences of world recessions for women. Feminist pleas to remove these inequalities through positively gendered policies have thus far been given short shrift by insensitive, male-dominated

Third-World governments.[32] Elson locates the 'proximate causes' of 'male bias in development outcomes' in 'everyday attitudes and actions, in theoretical reason and in public policy', and its undergirding supports in a situation of 'integration of getting a living and raising children' to sum up the contentions of feminists on the persistence of 'male bias in the development process' beautifully in the context of even the benevolence of the ties that bind households together.

> When supposed gender neutrality masks male bias, this serves to obscure the distribution of costs and benefits of development processes between men and women...barriers that gender asymmetries constitute to the successful realization of development policy objectives. To overcome such bias it is not enough to affix 'women' as an afterthought. For that tends to obscure the differences between different groups of women, and to perpetuate the gender blindness of analytical concepts.[33]

Halliday also shows how enfranchisement of women and their entry into the political realm as electors and 'political subjects' have, in spite of their international nature, been usually presented as milestones of national progress. Scholars show that while the most shielded and sequestered aspect of social relations, the familial one, has been touched by international processes and developments in the 20th century, including changes in medicine and technologies of contraception, the invention of newer domestic technologies and the 'diffusion of new role models and ideologies of male–female and parent–child relations', the processes are filtered by changing state policies to control population. Consequently, the social position, including the religious aspect, remains unaffected, as evidenced by the impact of Islamicist movements since the 1970s and the 1980s in Islamic republics, and of the restrictions on abortion in Catholic countries on women in these countries, leading a scholarly study to state that 'the strength of feminists is vital for the promotion of abortion reform in Catholic countries'.[34] All of this induced feminists to formulate and rework their famous slogan, 'the personal is political' into 'the personal is international' by reading 'power backward and forward'; forward 'insofar as ideas about what it means to be a "respectable" woman or an "honourable man" have been shaped by colonizing trade policies, international trade strategies and military doctrines'. However, the awareness that personal relations have been internationalized can at best 'make one only guilty for not having paid enough attention to international affairs'. But 'when one reads it "the other way round," as "the international is personal," the importance of a feminist understanding of IR becomes more obvious'. For, it makes clearer that 'governments depend on certain kinds of allegedly private relationships in order to conduct their foreign affairs', such as their need for and use of the willing services of wives of diplomats for the successful negotiations of their husbands.[35]

Among political processes, even the collapse of communism in the Soviet Union and its East European satellites impacted their women, through a sudden rise in unemployment of millions of women and prostitution and pornography (encouraged by the now dominant Western freedom and modernity), the demise of welfare systems, particularly those targeted at working mothers, and the regressive 'new masculinism' which urged women to return home and nurture traditional Russian family values. On the positive side, women gained new political rights. As Molyneux so aptly said, 'The key issue is what impact the new, internationally encouraged openness in these states...will have on policies regarding women...there are indications that more traditional views of women's place in society may gain ascendancy.'[36]

From Enloe's insights about the services rendered by diplomatists' wives and the 'steady supplies of women's sexual services' along with military hardware and so on, and the way in which it depended on 'masculinized dignity and feminized sacrifice' in the service of nationhood,[37] it is easy to visualize women as important, even if unrecognized and uncredited, international actors. Despite their noticeable role in revolutionary (including the French and the Bolshevik) movements and national liberation struggles, with or without enticement through inclusion of women's concerns, women have not been given their due after victory collectively. In the Third World, women's achievement of legal equality, universal adult suffrage, rights to education (in India, women gained voting rights without 'any major debate on the question without there ever having been a movement for women's suffrage at any period of nationalist politics of India')[38] and property have but touched the tip of the iceberg of their social subjugation. All of this suggested that a national struggle in which the feminist agenda was consonant with the nationalist agenda was rare, though there should essentially be no contradiction between them but for the failure to articulate to integrate women's emancipatory goals into other nationalist goals, or for the conscious design to subordinate the former to the latter. Still, the 'sexism of new nationalism serves to discredit them and opens the way for an invigorated critique of the masculinity of ultra-nationalism, unmasked as a male fantasy of regaining power'.[39] This is because, even with enormous organizational advances of women's groups in the 20th-century world, several aspects of the authority of national liberation movement over women's politics have yet to be clarified. In South Africa, 'within the national liberation movement and its allies in the women's movement, the notion of feminism was vilified to the extent that activists joked about the "f-word"',[40] thereby supporting feminists' contention that both nationalist and socialist revolutionary movements have tended to subordinate women's causes to their goals through the specious Mazzinian logic that national independence and national interest come before the interests and privileges of any particular group within the nation, including the nation's women. But, despite its imagination as a 'deep horizontal comradeship',[41] the national community, be it old or new, contains a vertical dimension, that is, hierarchies that allow men to impose their control over women through appeals to nationalism, urging feminists to argue that its effects are different for women, and/or point to the long relationship between feminism and internationalism, whether in the formulations of Flora Tristan, Virginia Woolf or Rosa Luxemburg. Viewing gender through the prism of class, Tristan posited that 'workers' organizations had a role to play in the liberation of women, and framed her reasoning for women's rights around the benefits that free, educated women be provided to men and children of the working class.[42] Even more forthrightly, Woolf portrays a woman chiding a brother who had asked her to support the nation's war preparations, showing that the 'Our country' he refers to has 'throughout the greater part of its history...treated me as a slave; ...denied me education or any share in its possessions...still ceases to be mine if I marry a foreigner'. So, in insisting upon fighting to protect it, he is gratifying a 'sex instinct which I cannot share, to procure benefits which...probably will not share'. For she is an 'outsider' and 'in fact, as a woman, I have no country...want no country...my country is the whole world'.

This shrill rejection of nationalism has, however, some problems. Apart from instinct, exclusion from equality with men in sundry social benefits and inadequate protection by men are remediable and have been at least partly remedied under modernity, and Woolf's position runs athwart the actual history of involvement of women in nationalist and international wars. Apart from women's organizations' transnationalist campaigns across frontiers since the late 1960s, one should also recall the collective activities of *women* in the Yugoslav conflict of 1991–1993, blocking food supplies meant for other communities, which problematized 'automatic political identification or women with internationalism'.[43]

Feminists have also used Rosa Luxemburg's modification of Lenin's view of 'the right of self-determination of nations' as self-determination of the working class into a feminist Luxemburgism, where its meaning became self-determination of women in the context of national independence. However, the problems with Rosa's concept stuck to the extension too.[44]

Women's problems with nationalism are exacerbated when it is of the Islamic fundamentalist variant, which turns women literally invisible and imparts greater relevance to women's issues by compelling them to use different strategies and strike types of 'patriarchal bargains' for the different systems of male chauvinism within Islam. In the case of socialist revolutions that granted formal legal equality to women but still practised discriminatory policies in pay or positions in higher echelons of politics, science and economy (in the erstwhile Soviet Union and its satellites), women engaged in 'velvet revolutions' to end communist rule but were once again disenchanted with post-communist promises and the resultant uncertainties; they have struggled with the dislocations.[45]

In the last component of transnational processes, women in war and peace, a considerable body of theoretical literature has been woven around women's aversion to war, stemming from the contradiction between mothering and war, and the compatible image of the 'moral mother', symbolizing the 'nurturant, compassionate vision of women', distinct from male warmongers. This has facilitated an 'automatic connection between feminism and pacifism', though feminists like Enloe seek to show that the source of these stereotypical imageries is not men or women per se, but the presumed logical link between patriarchy and militarism, which has tended to forget that masculinity and femininity are complementary logical constructions both used in the cause of waging wars that disprove these gender stereotypes and inflexible sex roles, particularly because the historical record about this is inconclusive.[46] To debunk these 'superficial images of women in peace and war', the first five case studies of Macdonald's edited volume look at examples of women as members of armies or on the battlefield, and the last five chapters focus on the impacts on women and their actions of men's warfare. Macdonald says, summing these up, that because gender, peace and war are interlinked in multiple ways in social life, 'images of women—and the definition of women's lives are never irrelevant or neutral in the discourses of peace and war', and hence 'if women want to question or disrupt these definitions, they must take on, through both words and actions, the imagery itself'.[47]

The illogicality of deriving women's position on peace from their roles as mothers, insinuated in Macdonald's quote above, is clear. For, beyond participating in peace campaigns just before or during the First World War and in anti-nuclear campaigns of the 1980s, women have also entered armies, whether as combatants in contexts of resistance to occupation, supporting national–military objectives, or strengthening peacekeeping forces. The discernible trend within NATO countries of recruitment of women in peacetime armies in recent decades has generated a lively debate on how women can be integrated into military structures. The controversy over the inclusion of American women on active duty in the US attack against Panama and the Gulf War (involving some 30,000 women among half a million male soldiers) not only revealed how deep was inflexibility in attitudes but also other complex issues from feminist and other standpoints. The presence of women in armies has engendered new issues not only over their role in active fight but also about their homosexual rights, immunity against sexual harassment,[48] and other questions of identity, one highlighted by the inversion by peacekeeping women in Swedish armed forces while implementing a UNSC resolution for taking care of women in war-ravaged areas, of Gayatri C. Spivak's maxim of 'white men…saving brown women from brown men'. Here, women liberators as soldiers/officers who 'risk being subjected to violence and harassment in the international arena—by their own countrymen', making nationalism irrelevant. Rather, the 'bodies of women serve as targets for various sexual attacks in parallel to being made symbols of freedom, democracy and equality'. Also, while allowed entry into the Swedish national defence, women were 'requested to adapt' and 'balance…in the field of tension between what is considered feminine and what characterizes a (male) soldier', not participating 'on the same conditions as men', so as to risk 'crossing current notions of femininity'.[49]

Recent analyses of globalization show gender's critical impact on human groups since it 'reinforces pre-existing gender structures, barriers and relationships', just on a global scale now. This makes incomplete any study of globalization sans the status of gender in it. So feminism rubbishes the claims of mainstream perspectives and theories on globalization in sociology, economics and IR that globalization is gender-neutral or blind, pointing out that the experiences and voices of women, particularly those in the Third and Fourth Worlds, are unheard in it. To establish the 'gendered processes of global capitalism', feminists have perused development studies, critiques of neoliberalism, IR, IPE and transnational networking, and have shown how the 'gendered effects of globalization have shaped gendered ideologies, institutions, hierarchies and inequality structures', all of these hitting poor Third-World women far more than others.[50] Feminists take note of the profound effects of globalization on 'shifting production sites, labour markets, feminization of employment, daily lives and gender inequalities in the household'. As women enter and are sucked into globalized markets 'as workers, consumers and borrowers', they turn into economic agents and are increasingly treated as individuals endowed with 'choice, autonomy and responsibility'. Its avowedly corrosive effect on patriarchal relations through an emphasis on gender equality, hyped in IMF and IBRD literature, obscures the dark sides of neoliberal globalization, in which processes of 'deregulation and informalization of markets' find women being 'relegated to the lowest echelons of labour market hierarchies' and facing 'extremely exploitative conditions'. On top of this is the attendant-heavy level of commodification of women, which has had 'contradictory effects' on women, with increased choice and convenience juxtaposed with augmented burdens and increased poverty.[51] Feminist analysts of globalization have already started exploring 'the PE of globalizing beauty industries', as well as 'the fashion and apparel industries', where, first, 'Northern women's increased fashion consumption contributes to demands for Southern women's labour' and, second, through 'gendered production, reproduction and consumption in the beauty industries…the feminine gendering of the body itself is an engine of globalization'.[52]

GENDER AS EPISTEMOLOGY

Overcoming Troubles with Gender

This level[53] (which comprises accounts of feminist epistemologies and feminist critiques of entrenched IR concepts, theories and practices) is more sophisticated and difficult than the previous one, partly because gender, as noted above,[54] is a *taming* concept, contestable even in the sense of 'asymmetrical social constructs of masculinity and femininity' against evidently 'biological' male–female differences. Tickner referred to R. W. Connell's notion of a culturally defined 'hegemonic masculinity', distinguishable from 'other subordinated masculinities…sustained through its opposition to various subordinated and devalued masculinities, such as homosexuality, and more important, through its relation to various devalued femininities', to show how a host of contemporary feminists 'draw on similar, socially constructed, or engendered, relationships in their definition of gender difference'. But lately, when feminists generally employ the term *gender*, they do not mean 'biological differences between males and females', but 'a set of culturally shaped and defined characteristics associated with masculinity and femininity'.[55]

However, even this gender–sex distinction has been problematized by postmodernists, feminists and others. Butler warns, 'If the immutable character of sex is constructed, perhaps this construct called "sex" is as culturally constructed as gender…. It would make no sense, then to define gender as cultural interpretation of sex, if sex itself is a gendered category'.[56] Later, she suggested that debates concerning the theoretical priority of sexual difference, sexuality and gender 'are all crosscut by another kind of problem…namely the permanent difficulty of determining where the biological, the psychic, the discursive, the social, begin and end'.[57] Bourdieu problematizes the gender–sex distinction more when he writes that even though 'the idea that the social definition of the body, and especially of the sexual organs, is the product of social labour of construction' has become familiar to the extent of banality, due to anthropologists' research, the 'mechanism of the inversion of cause and effect…through which the naturalization of that construction takes place' is yet to be fully analysed.[58]

In non-mainstream IR, the concept of gender was being criticized on various other grounds. First, critics charged that aggressive use of the concept distracted attention from many other forms of oppression raging in global politics. Complaining against 'the production of the "Third-World woman" as a singular monolithic subject in some recent (Western) feminist texts', Mohanty said that if 'one of the tasks of formulating and understanding the locus of "Third-World feminisms" is delineating the way in which it resists and works against…"Western feminist discourse," an analysis of the discursive construction of "Third-World women" in Western feminism is an important first step'.[59] To 'discover and articulate a critique of "Western feminist" scholarship on Third-World women via the discursive colonization of Third-World women's lives and struggles', Mohanty later suggested that 'we—feminist scholars and teachers—must respond to the phenomenon of globalization as an urgent site for the recolonization of peoples, especially in the Two-Thirds World'.[60]

Second, 'confusion over the apparent conflation of sex and gender' was targeted. At the fourth World Women's Conference at Beijing, Baden and Goertz were shocked to see the extent of 'ambivalence about—or even hostility towards—the GAD [gender and development] discourse expressed by some Southern women activists', reflecting 'deeper anxieties about the imposition of what is perceived as an external agenda', and the 'virulent challenge to the concept of "gender" which came from a very different direction...conservative backlash politics', anxieties about the 'depoliticization of gender relations' and fear about the concept of gender threatening to over-politicize the relations between women and men.[61]

But, unfazed by such definitive demolitions of gender–sex distinctions, feminists stuck to the Beauvoirian and post-Beauvoirian distinctions between them, only taking gender as a *relational* concept now. Tickner's notion of 'hegemonic masculinity' survived in its relational dimension. Others sought to show how IP and institutions undergirding it themselves provide crucial anvils where masculinities and masculine identities are forged.[62] Hooper, however, besides reiterating that IR 'plays a significant role in the creation and maintenance of masculine identities', and that 'the relationship between globalization and challenges to hegemonic masculinities...may involve a reformulation of the relationship between masculinities and the international', showed how this awareness not only 'raises new questions about the relationships between different masculinities and international practices' but also about the boundaries of the discipline.[63] And Gelfer warns that 'non-Western masculinities have been the focus of majority of the work on globalization'.[64] Considering the same thing from the opposite angle, Hearn reminds us that 'a grasp of large-scale social processes and global relationships is necessary to understand men and masculinities on global scale'.[65]

In view of the above reservations about the universal categories of woman or man, as well as the operation of hegemonic Western discourses behind them, second-generation feminist thinkers are increasingly shunning attempts to explain international and global processes through generic concepts of *patriarchy* or *gender* hierarchy for examining the dynamic relationship among the global PE, the state and culturally–geographically contextualized gender relations.

Overcoming problems with gender and including it as the central factor in IP involves taking gender seriously, as constitutive of IR and as transformative of IR.

TAKING GENDER SERIOUSLY

The subtle difference of this epistemological level from engagement with women as a category comes out clearest in this statement of two scholars.

> The exclusion of women's experiences from the conceptualization of international relations has had negative consequences both for the discipline and for male and female inhabitants of the real world...has resulted in an academic field excessively focused on conflict and anarchy, and...statecraft and formulating strategy that is excessively focused on competition and fear.[66]

The resultant claim for more gender-sensitive research however raises issues that we have already touched upon in the contexts of feminist charges against theoretical practices of IR and their gender bias, as well as the discussion of women as a category. So, here, we refer briefly only to issues surrounding how, due to the occultation or misrepresentation of women in IP, and the false assumption that male experiences can serve for both men and women, women have been deemed irrelevant to global processes, despite constituting 50 per cent of the world's population. This neglect may have been caused by the fact that, even in the late 1990s, despite doing 60–67 per cent of the world's work and producing 50–75 per cent of the food, women own only 1 per cent of the world's property and resources; earn 10 per cent of the world's income; account for less than 5 per cent of the world's heads of states and a small fraction of legislative seats; make up 70 per cent of the world's poorest people; account for about 66 per cent of the world's illiterates, and 80 per cent of the world's refugees and displaced persons and constitute 75 per cent of the world's people without access to bank loans because of having no jobs or insecure jobs. Between 80 per cent and 90 per cent of the world's female workforce is unprotected by labour laws.[67] These discriminations have persisted because women are turning into an underclass of neoliberal globalization, as providers of flexible female labour in state and corporate plans for global competitiveness, facilitating the downgrading of secure and stable occupations and tasks formerly monopolized by males into their ill-paid, insecure, part-time and contractual versions. Not only 'free state' export-processing or foreign direct investment (FDI)-facilitating Special Economic Zones but also global cities that are hubs of global financial markets and economic transactions rely on discriminated female labour. Along with coloured immigrant women employed by the masculinized corporate elite and 'intimate others' of neoliberal globalization, an even murkier underside caters for the 'growth of sex tourism, *male*-order brides and, most gravely, the international trafficking of women and girls for prostitution', thereby filling the foreign exchange coffers of subordinate states in the global system. Of course, the processes of flexibilization of female labour, feminization of occupations and the global growth of a feminine underclass of 'precariats',[68] have also, through post-Fordist re-siting of TNCs, benefited mainly Southern women, for example, Bangladeshi women in transnational garment production and Mexican women in Maquiladora factories.

Apart from changing structures of global production dependent on gender relations, the portrayal of gender differences by MNCs and states in their search for global competitiveness in the consumer market solidifies gender identities and symbols, even when women's empowerment by the global media enables them to question and challenge gender divisions of labour and power in the labour market and families. The gendered character of international organizations and the domination of elite males in them (despite women now holding top policymaking positions in some of them) as well as the gendered context of global environment policies and regimes pointed out by feminist scholars, along with the recent recognition of gender justice as a norm in international society, betoken the new serious attention to gender and women as the world's biggest non-state actors for a long time.[69]

VIEWING GENDER AS CONSTITUTIVE OF IR THEORY FIELD AND ITS CONCEPTS

Some issues relevant for this section too have already been touched upon in this essay, in the contexts of feminism and its charges against the theoretical practices of IR, and of Tickner's critique of Morgenthau's realism and its six principles and their feminist reformulation, her feminist redefinitions of the concept of security, and her efforts to construct a feminist epistemology of IR in Chapter 7.[70] Beyond these merits mention, feminists' charge that all IR concepts (including power, sovereignty, autonomy, anarchy and security) are tailored from a theoretical cloth embossed with 'patriarchy'. The three levels of man, the state and the international are also premised in the patriarchal division between the public and the private and are informed by men's rather than women's experiences and forms of knowledge. The bottom line of the claim that the gender factor is not 'world-constitutive' in IR is that it 'resurrects a debilitating choice between what is private and moral, and what is public can be legitimized in the national interest'. A gender-neutral theory of IR is difficult to construct first because the insights of history and anthropology, where gender-sensitive research has made tremendous progress, are inapplicable in this field, which is not only 'ensnared by the trap of dividing the domestic and the international' and, second, because as a newcomer among social sciences, IR 'first developed as a subject when the prejudice against women was the norm'.[71] So beyond addressing Robowtham's charge by restoring 'women to history' and 'history to women', a far more challenging and uncompleted historical task in the understanding of the 'social relations of the sexes' is appreciating how 'we are all, women and men, initially humanized, turned into social creatures by the work of that domestic order to which women are primarily attached' and how 'its character and the structure of its relations order our consciousness'.[72]

For feminists, applying this historical insight for IRT would require showing how the formation of states and the expansion of an international society of states are rooted in the construction of gender differences via the entrenchment of the binaries of public/private, state/society and domestic/international, as well as rejecting the independence of domestic politics as a false basis of the boundary of the discipline of IR. For, the constant harping on anarchy outside often serves as a justificatory device for (gender) hierarchy at home and the exalted international has often been a ruse for resisting change in domestic political orders.

But, since despite these nuanced mentions of the false dichotomy between the domestic (gendered) inside and the genderless outside/international, malestream IR persists with its three distinct levels of analysis, the individual (man), the (manly) state and the (androcentric) international, feminists take up all three, rejecting the ontology of the sovereign, rational, self-interested and autonomous man exalted in realist, neorealist and liberal theory, as really a dangerously circumscribed model of agency for both IP and economy and the discipline. As Sylvester argues,

> Arguably, statecraft became mancraft…an environment in which 'man' was the interpreter and keeper of various interrelated contracts of importance to other 'men' and their creation of nation-states and theories. Sovereignty was theirs…the preserve of judging and reasoning 'men', and not contra Kenneth Waltz's conclusion…the preserve of a war-inducing but abstract system…of nonstatesmen.[73]

Likewise, Tickner considers the 'rational economic man' to be a construct which, 'while it extrapolates from roles and behaviours associated with certain Western men and assumes characteristics that correspond to the definition of hegemonic masculinity', has been unjustifiably 'used by liberal economists to represent the behaviour of humanity as a whole'. Coeval with modern capitalism, this social construct is 'based on the reduction of a variety of human passions to a desire for economic gain'.[74] Suspicious of masculine, autonomy-oriented models which disallow the importance of human relatedness and affective subjectivities, some feminists, such as Gilligan, propose 'an alternative, female model of the individual' that emphasizes connection, interdependence and interrelation, allowing for the transcendence of false terminological boundaries of autonomy and relatedness in a way where self and others do not remain 'mutually exclusive'.[75] Still, other feminists urge rejection of inflexible, gendered notions of human agency to embrace more inclusive models that emphasize both production and reproduction, reformulate rationality in less mechanistic and instrumentalist directions and, apart from honouring human relationship at all levels, view them in their relationships with nature, compelling them to redefine Morgenthau's concept of national interest and to baulk at Waltz's insistence that whether among men or states any 'automatic adjustment of interests' is inconceivable.

Truly, as late as the 1980s, feminist writers ignored the state not because of 'oversight, or failure in not developing a distinct theory of "the state"', but rather because the state did not figure prominently in the feminists' theoretical agenda. It was 'a category of abstraction' that was too aggregative, unitary and unspecific to be helpful in exploring 'the disaggregated, diverse and specific (or local) sites' that they were concerned with; and 'too blunt an instrument to be of much assistance (beyond generalizations) in explanations, analyses or the design of workable strategies'. The state was also unprivileged because, historically, feminism was distinguishable from sundry other political positions in its central focus on 'the oppression or women, as a sex is in the interests of men as a sex', with its consequent central objective being its elimination. Yet feminist theory and research inspired by it threw up political–cultural concepts such as 'policing', 'law', 'legal culture', 'medical culture', 'bureaucratic culture', 'organized crime', 'masculinity', 'violence' and 'power'.[76] But Linklater, among other critical theorists, convinced feminists that the principle of territoriality, which transversally cuts the two axes of inside/outside and public/private to legitimize the state, not only makes an unethical differentiation between men and citizens but, ever since its Greek and European Renaissance origins, the genealogy of the state has ignored the gendered spaces that constitute its public/private dimension and has thereby revealed its true nature of the principal instrument of gendered power and masculine agency and domination. After this, feminism turned averse to being implicated in liberal and Marxist views of the state and, in a decade or less, ceased making any distinction between the realist 'security state' and the post-2008–2009 'neoliberal state', both being 'legitimated through gender relations' and valuing 'masculine qualities of rationality, competitiveness and risk-taking', and support one another in these.[77]

Besides, feminist theory started showing the embroilment of even early Western state-manufacturing in

> the codification of sex/gender binaries (male–female bodies, masculine/feminine gender identities, gendered dichotomies) as foundational symbolic order; the production of oppositional gender identities in service to state-centric heterosexist reproduction and hierarchical relations (patriarchal families/households; state regulation of reproductive sexual activities); the conceptual *and* material constitution of gendered spheres of social activity (not least the public–private) that structure hierarchical divisions of authority, power, labor, and resources;

and state centralization of authority, power, accumulation and reproduction ideologically (through heterosexist language, philosophy, religion, political theory) and concretely (through the juridical and coercive powers of the state).[78]

We have already shown above how feminists critique the other constitutive concepts of IR, such as power, security, rationality and sovereignty, and the neorealist theories they support as gender-biased,[79] derived from 'androcentric accounts of men (human nature), the state and the system of states as ahistorical fixities made self-evident by reference to a gendered SON (the natural state of egoistic, rational men)',[80] epitomized in Tickner's incisive critique of the Morgenthauian and realist view of power and security.[81] Sovereignty is considered 'distorted and mystified', needing to be 'detached from the state...reconstructed and "reclaimed"'. For, the state being 'intertwined with male domination,...a sovereignty which respects and empowers women, is a sovereignty beyond the state'. So 'to study the question of gender and sovereignty is to be concerned with the problem of emancipation...of one particular group'.[82]

But, as we will see below, while critiquing mainstream IR, all schools of feminism do not stress emancipation of this 'one particular group' in the same extent and, ipso facto, are not equally transformative of IR.

GENDER AS TRANSFORMATIVE OF IR: MAINSTREAMING AND/OR EMANCIPATION OF GENDER AND DIFFERENT SCHOOLS OF FEMINISM

According to True, the extent to which gender can be transformative of IR depends on the way 'the epistemological significance of feminist IR is discussed in relation to the ontological claims of the category of "woman" by conjoining "women as an identity group" with "gender as a unit of analysis"'. For, 'gender is a *transformative* macro-political category,...because once we understand it, we can transform how it works at all levels of social and political life'.[83] Tickner and Sjoberg say that for postpositivist feminists, 'one cannot think about IR without thinking about gender, and without recognizing the transformative potential of feminist IR for the discipline'.[84] We judge below the following feminist schools just by these yardsticks.

Liberal Feminism

Liberal feminism foregrounds the subordinate position of women in global politics, investigates the causes of this subordination within a positivist framework, based on an empirical project that makes this underrepresentation visible, and shows what disadvantages women have in the agenda of IR. For example, some have used quantitative data and statistical measures to test whether there is a high positive correlation between domestic gender equality and states' recourse to violence internationally, and found one, with implications for the democratic peace thesis. But liberal feminists have been charged for focusing on women to the neglect of gender and pursuing an 'add women and stir' approach in studying IR (even though some others do bring in gender to 'explain certain policies and policy results'). Besides, postpositive feminists charge that measures resulting from their use of national parliamentary data and electoral indicators 'are inadequate for understanding gender inequality which is associated with gender role expectations that keep women out of power', even in countries conferring formal legal equality on their women. The positivistic craze of liberal feminists for 'facts' is also criticized for not paying attention to the bias in their collection of data and later distortions. Some, however, come to their defence by saying that more feminist research with an empirical orientation can also expose the reign of false beliefs and prejudices that pollute the findings of research by facilitating an enlarged perspective.[85]

Standpoint Feminism

Intent on relating the experiences and perspectives of women themselves to tell story in their voices, standpoint feminism does not, unlike liberal feminists, take for granted the marginal existence of women in the world, rather seeking to bring them '"from the margin to the centre" of IR as the subjects of knowledge'. It is postpositive in borrowing a host of insights from psychoanalytical feminism to assert that due to different modes of socialization and gender-specific experiences, such as childbearing and childrearing, women were different from men, though not necessarily inferior. Some exponents show how the formation of a gender identity for a boy or a girl involves different processes; that women's material life activity causes important epistemological consequences; and that different life-worlds of women problematize all universal theories as male-as-norm standpoint-based and gender-biased. From this perspective, Tickner critiques mainstream IR approaches because of their tainted dualism: realism through reliance on the 'rational political man' and liberalism because of its belief in the rational economic man, an offshoot of 'Enlightenment knowledge', employed 'to explain the behaviour of states in the international system'. The notion of standpoint has, however, been challenged by postmodernist feminists since 'a unified representation of women across class, racial, cultural lines' does not make practical sense.[86] The fact that many types of movements, including race, ethnicity-based, anti-imperial and queer social justice, continue to generate standpoint themes suggests that 'standpoint theory is a kind of organic epistemology, methodology, POS and social theory that can arise anywhere, whenever oppressed people gain public voice' and is, to that extent, liberating for women.[87]

Critical Feminism

Critical feminism goes beyond liberal feminists' gender-as-variable approach and, along with Marxist feminism, views gender as a 'social relationship of inequality', but distances itself from it in putting more emphasis on the power of ideas and ideologies in reproducing gender relations. It has also affinities with CT, inasmuch as some critical feminists start from Cox's portrayal of the world as historical structures constituted by the reciprocal interactions of the forces of material conditions, ideas and institutions at the three different levels of production relations, the state–society complex and historically defined world orders.[88] But beyond critical theorists, they seek to understand the world and the possibility of changes in it that mainstream

gender in various ways. While showing how the role of international associations (specifically the International Planned Parenthood Federation and the International Labour Organization [ILO]) is impacting policies ranging from labour laws to population policies and reproductive rights, Whitworth claims that understandings of gender are only partly determined by real material conditions of men and women in particular circumstances because institutions, social practices and ideas blend to sustain gender relations of inequality, which privilege patriarchal forms of power relations that enable even the weakest men to dominate women that makes gender rather than women the right focus. Chin shows, in the context of the Malaysian state-supported importation of Filipino and Indonesian female domestic workers during its modernizing years, how their service in near-slavery conditions was countenanced by the Malaysian state, thereby revealing that far from being neutral, this state was complicit in class, race and gender-based exploitation. For exposing this, and upholding change, critical feminism is emancipatory.[89]

Feminist Constructivism

Feminist constructivism's critique of the foundationalism of both liberal–positivistic and standpoint epistemologies results in social constructionist feminism. Constructivism, as discussed in Chapter 25, contends that the social world around the members of a society is constructed and shaped by them, making any prior 'true knowledge' of it a false claim. So, unlike postmodern feminism, constructivist feminism retains the concept of woman but denies that some feminist knowledge(s) can have priority over other feminist knowledge(s), and, with constructivism, regards agents and structures as co-constructed. It shows how ideas about gender influence, and are influenced by, global politics. For example, from a linguistically based feminist constructivist position, Elisabeth Prügl (*The Global Construction of Gender*) analyses the status accorded to home-based work in international negotiations and law and finds that, because it was located in the private reproductive domain of the household rather than in the public sphere of wage-based productive tasks, low wages and poor working conditions in such work were often justified for not being 'real work'. While ideas about womanhood and femininity contributed to the interpretation of such work, it took the lobbying of a host of women's NGOs to redress this state of affairs through the passage of the ILO's Housework Convention in 1996. This way, gender codifies power at every level of global politics and institutionalizes a set of linguistically based principles about how states should behave with each other and their own citizens, even as some political spaces continue to be created by negotiations which facilitate alternative, emancipatory interpretations.[90]

Feminist Poststructuralism

Poststructuralism, as we will see in greater detail in Chapter 26, revolves around meaning as codified in language, the umbilical relationship between knowledge and power, and discourses through which binaries such as strong/weak, rational/emotional and public/private, and their IR counterparts such as order/anarchy and developed/undeveloped come to possess racial and gendered implications and serve to privilege masculinity over femininity. Since, from a poststructuralist perspective, truth and meaning and forms of identity are always subject to doubt and questioning, no tall claims to construct human destinies, chart out linear histories and enforce social and political boundaries are above dispute. Accordingly, even after accepting that that IR has neglected gender the most among all institutionalized social sciences, poststructuralism looks askance at any reconstructive project (such as Tickner's attempt to feminize security) as another effort to develop another single or coherent feminist perspective that will seek centrality and drive other feminist perspectives to marginality. Since poststructuralist feminists take categories such as man and masculinity,[91] woman, gender (and even sex) to be constructed, and deny that there is any real essence to 'woman', they deny any connection between being a woman and having specific interests arising from her gender, whether at the local, national or global levels. Predictably, any idea of feminist thought serving as an emancipatory tool for gender is taken to be problematic, potentially risky, because the whole endeavour of theorizing is conceived as 'a form of domination whereby the theorist comprehends and appropriates the subject of knowledge'.[92]

Postcolonial Feminism

Postcolonialism is largely an effort to extend the insights of postmodernism and poststructuralism to the postcolonial context, which was not addressed directly except in two essays: Foucault's 'George Canguilhelm: Philosopher of Error' and Derrida's 'White Mythology: Metaphor in the Task of Philosophy'. Gayatri Spivak found the intellectual anchorage of postcolonialist thought in their 'unhesitating challenge to the universal validity of Western culture and epistemology'.[93] While on the authorial side, postcolonial feminism attempted to redress 'the marginalization and exclusion of a separate trajectory of feminist thought about race, power, culture and empire', content-wise 'current postcolonial theory still exerts a pressure on mainstream postcolonial theory in its constant iteration of the necessity to consider gender issues'. Initially, feminist postcolonial theorists criticized their male counterparts for presuming that the behaviour or attributes of British males could serve as the yardstick of that of their imperial subjects or be symbolic of the empire as a whole, as pretended by Ronald Hyam's single-minded focus on British men (*Empire and Sexuality: The British Experience*, 1994). Since early postcolonial theorists like Said largely ignored female agency and engaged with very few female writers, one feminist response has been to mainstream women's experiences in metropolises not only as colonizers but also as colonized or 'at home', while another response has been to focus on studies in masculinity to deconstruct the putative privileges of the normative–imperial male subject.[94] Postcolonial feminist writers such as Mohanty, Spivak and Kumari Jayawardena do not reject the existence of gender inequalities in specific societies; rather, their major concern is the end of such inequalities and exploitation. But, as we have shown above, their complaint was against the production of the 'Third-World woman' as a singular monolithic subject in some recent (Western) feminist texts to discover and articulate a critique of 'Western feminist' scholarship on Third-World women via the discursive colonization of Third-World women's lives and struggles.[95]

CONCLUSION

This chapter has shown how studies of feminism in IR progressed from non-recognition to circumscribed space, causing spatial debates to lead mainstream IR to introduce gender as a variable as a ruse. After recounting how feminism, through its charges against the theoretical practice of IR, has forced a serious consideration of women in IR at two levels: women as a category and gender as epistemology, and showing how, according to feminist writers, gender is not only constitutive but also transformative of IR, this essay has judged the merits of different schools of feminism against this latter yardstick. The way in which this chapter has brought out the quarrel between different schools of feminism over the meaning of women, gender and feminism at the local, domestic, international and global levels, a separate critique has become redundant.

REVIEW QUESTIONS

1. Comment on the quarrels generated in IR by the non-recognition/occultation of women/gender to allowance of limited space.
2. How did feminists react to Adam Jones' contention that 'feminism's primary and seminal contribution to the study of IR is its focus on the gender variable'?
3. What are the spatial debates that resulted from the emergence of gender as a variable in IR?
4. Summarize feminism's charges against the theoretical practices of conventional IR.
5. Comment on the perspective of women as a category as a vantage point of organizing/reconstructing IR.
6. What are the different levels of gender as epistemology as applied to IR?
7. Show what taking gender seriously and seeing it as constitutive of the IR theory field and its concepts theoretically implies.
8. In what ways can gender be transformative of IR? Show in this context the differences between liberal, standpoint, critical, constructivist and post-structuralist feminism.

NOTES AND REFERENCES

1. Sheila Robowtham, *Hidden from History: 300 Years of Women's Oppression and the Fight against It* (London: Pluto Press, 1977).
2. See Cynthia Weber, *International Relations Theory*, 3rd ed. (London; New York, NY: Routledge, 2010), 84; Fred Halliday, *Rethinking International Relations* (Hampshire; London: Macmillan, 1994), 147, 264 for the exceptions.
3. J. Ann Tickner, *Gender in International Relations: Feminist Perspectives on Achieving Global Security* (New York, NY: Columbia University Press, 1992), 1–4.
4. Margot Light and Fred Halliday, 'Gender and International Relations', in Groom and Light, *Contemporary International Relations*, 45.

5. See for the different contexts in which 'high politics' was mentioned in the book, Chapter 1 *passim*, notes 53, 75–77; note 21, Chapter 13B; note 11, Chapter 14; note 11, Chapter 21.
6. Halliday, *Rethinking International Relations*, 148–149.
7. Weber, *International Relations Theory*, 84.
8. Adam Jones, 'Does "Gender" Make the World Go Round? Feminist Critiques of International Relations', *Review of International Studies* 22, no. 4 (1996): 405–429, especially 406–407, 409.
9. Weber, *International Relations Theory*, 85–86.
10. Valery Bryson, 'Feminism', in *Contemporary Political Ideologies*, 2nd ed., eds. Roger Eatwell and Anthony Wright (London; New York, NY: Pinter, 1999), 214–230.
11. J. Ann Tickner and Laura Sjoberg, 'Feminism', in Dunne, Kurki and Smith, *International Relations Theories*, 188–192.
12. Light and Halliday, 'Gender and International Relations', 46.
13. Rebecca Grant and Katherine Newland, 'Introduction', in Grant and Newland, *Gender and International Relations*, 2.
14. See notes 41 of Chapter 1; 84 of Chapter 2; 9 of Chapter 5 and 21, 25, 26, 34, 39 of Chapter 7 for its various overtones.
15. See Note 9 of Chapter 5.
16. Rebecca Grant, 'Sources of Gender Bias in International Relations Theory', in Grant and Newland, *Gender and International Relations*, 9–16.
17. This part of feminists' charges in the following five paragraphs, minus the citations below from 18 to 27, is reconstructed from Halliday, *Rethinking International Relations* and his citations not mentioned, 149–151.
18. Neil MacMaster, *Racism in Europe: 1870–2000* (Basingstoke: Palgrave, 2001), 46–47.
19. Wendy Gibson, *Women in 17th Century France* (Basingstoke: Palgrave Macmillan, 1989), 71.
20. Tatiana Karabchuk, Kazuhiro Kumo and Ekaterina Selezneva, *Demography of Russia: From the Past to the Present* (Basingstoke: Palgrave Macmillan, 2017), 71–72.
21. Miriam Elder, 'Russia Awards "Order of Parental Glory" to Prolific Parents, *The Telegraph* (17 January 2009). Available at https://www.telegraph.co.uk/news/worldnews/europe/russia/4279145/Russia-awards-order-of-parental-glory-to-prolific-parents.html (accessed on 16 June 2019).
22. Joanna Mishtal, 'Irrational Non-reproduction? The Dying Nation and the Postcolonial Logics of Declining Motherhood in Poland', in *Reproduction and Biopolitics: Ethnographies of Governance, Rationality and Resistance*, eds. Silvia De Zordo and Milena Marchesi (London; New York, NY: Routledge, 2015), 18–19.
23. Judith Shapiro, *Mao's War against Nature: Politics and the Environment in Revolutionary China* (Cambridge: Cambridge University Press, 2001), 31–32; Jeanne Boden, *The Wall Behind China's Open Door: Towards Efficient Intercultural Management in China* (Brussels: Academic and Scientific Publishers, 2008), 104.
24. Paul R. Ehrlich and Anne H. Ehrlich, 'The Population Bomb Revisited', *The Electronic Journal of Sustainable Development* 1, no. 3 (2009): 5–13, especially 8.
25. Michel Foucault, *The History of Sexuality: An Introduction*, Vol. 1 (New York, NY: Vintage Books, [1978]1990), 139, cited in Zordo and Marchesi, *Reproduction and Biopolitics*, 3.
26. Gilligan showed that women possess a different but not inferior moral orientation compared with men. See Carol Gilligan, *In a Different Voice*, first published in 1982 (Cambridge, MA: Harvard University Press, 1993), 1, 19, 25, 73 and *passim*; Mike Cardwell, *Dictionary of Psychology* (London; Chicago, IL: Fitzroy Dearborn Publishers, 1996), 109.
27. See Blema S. Steinberg, *Women in Power: The Personalities and Leadership Styles of Indira Gandhi, Golda Meir, and Margaret Thatcher* (Quebec: Arts Insight and McGill-Queen's University Press, 2008), 8 and *passim*; J. Jensen, *Women Political Leaders: Breaking the Highest Glass Ceiling* (New York, NY: Palgrave Macmillan, 2008), 28, 164–165.

28. The whole section of women as a category draws substantially on the structure and citations of Halliday, *Rethinking International Relations*, 153–166; Light and Halliday, 'Gender and International Relations', 47–49, except the new citations, data and references.
29. In spite of a report signed by the eminent James Bryce, 'the more comprehensive postwar Belgian report counted thirty-six rapes'. See Larry Zuckerman, *The Rape of Belgium: The Untold Story of World War I* (New York, NY: New York University Press, 2003), 132–136, especially 133.
30. Maria Eriksson, *Defining Rape: Emerging Obligations for States under International Law?* (Leiden; Boston, MA: Martinus Nijhoff Publishers, 2011), 30–31; and Hua-Ling Hu, Zhang Lian-hong, 'Introduction', in *Undaunted Women of Nanking: The Wartime Diaries of Minnie Vautrin and Tsen Shui-Fang*, eds. and trans. Hua-Ling Hu and Zhang Lian-hong (Carbondale, IL: Southern Illinois University Press, 2010), 1–2. For records of un-totalled rape victims, see Timothy Brook, *Documents on the Rape of Nanking* (Ann Arbor, MI: Ann Arbor University of Michigan Press, 1999).
31. Roy Gutman, 'Foreword', in *Mass Rape: The War against Women in Bosnia-Herzegovina*, ed. Alexandra Stiglmayer (London: University of Nebraska Press, 1994), ix–xii, xix; Catharine A. McKinnon, 'Turning Rape into Pornography: Postmodern Genocide', Ibid., 73; Alexandra Stiglmayer, 'Rapes in Bosnia-Herzegovina', in Ibid., 84–86, 122.
32. For relevant citations, see Halliday, *Rethinking International Relations*, 153–154.
33. Diane Elson, 'Male Bias in the Development Process: An Overview', in *Male Bias in the Development Process*, ed. Diane Elson (Manchester: Manchester University Press, 1994), 7, 11, 13.
34. Merike Blofield, 'Women's Choices in Comparative Perspective: Abortion Policies in Late-developing Catholic Countries', *Comparative Politics* 40, no. 4 (2008): 399–419, especially 409.
35. Cynthia Enloe, *Bananas, Beaches and Bases: Making Feminist Sense of International Politics*, 2nd ed. (Berkeley, CA; Los Angeles, CA; London: University of California Press, 2014), 343, 350–352.
36. Maxine Molyneux, 'Marxism, Feminism, and the Demise of the Soviet Model', in Grant and Newland, *Gender and International Relations*, 51–63, especially 59.
37. Enloe, *Bananas*, 351.
38. Partha Chatterjee, *Nation and Its Fragments: Colonial and Postcolonial Histories* (Delhi: Oxford University Press, 1995), 131.
39. Mónica Threlfall, *Mapping the Women's Movement: Feminist Politics and Social Transformation in the North* (London: Verso, 1996), 301.
40. Shireen Hassim, *Women's Organizations and Democracy in South Africa: Contesting Authority* (Madison, WI: University of Wisconsin Press, 2006), 28.
41. See Benedict Anderson, *Imagined Communities: Reflections on the Origin and Spread of Nationalism*, first published in 1983 (London; New York, NY: Verso, 2006), 7.
42. C. G. Moses, *French Feminism in the Nineteenth Century* (Albany, NY: SUNY Press, 1984), cited and commented on in Suzanne Franzway and Mary Margaret Fonow, *Making Feminist Politics: Transnational Alliances between Women and Labor* (Urbana, IL; Chicago, IL; Springfield, MO: University of Illinois Press, 2011), 90.
43. For citation and comment on Virginia Woolf's *A Room of One's Own. Three Guineas* (Oxford: Oxford University Press, 1992), 313, see Halliday, *Rethinking International Relations*, 161–162.
44. Horace P. Davis, 'Introduction' in *Rosa Luxemburg, The National Question: Selected Writings by Rosa Luxemburg*, ed. H. P. Davis (New York, NY: Monthly Review Press, 1976), 1–45.
45. See substantial citations in Light and Halliday, 'Gender and International Relations', 48–49.
46. For relevant citations, see Ibid.

47. Sharon Macdonald, 'Drawing the Lines—Gender, Peace and War: An Introduction', in *Images of Women in Peace and War: Cross-cultural and Historical Perspectives*, eds. Sharon Macdonald, Pat Holden and Shirley Ardener (Madison, WI: The University of Wisconsin Press, 1988), 2, 3, 4–5, 23.
48. For supporting citations, see Halliday, *Rethinking International Relations*, 156–157.
49. Maud Eduards, 'What Does a Bath Towel Have to Do with Security Policy? Gender Trouble in the Swedish Armed Forces', in *Making Gender, Making War: Violence, Military and Peacekeeping Practices*, eds. Annica Kronsell and Erika Svedberg (New York, NY; London: Routledge, 2012), 61.
50. George Ritzer, *Globalization: A Basic Text* (Malden, MA: Wiley-Blackwell, 2010), 455.
51. Lourdes Beneria, Günseli Berik and Maria Floro, *Gender, Development and Globalization: Economics as If All People Mattered*, 2nd ed. (London; New York, NY: Routledge, 2003), 129–130.
52. Angela B. McCracken, *The Beauty Trade: Youth, Gender, and Fashion Globalization* (Oxford; New York, NY: Oxford University Press, 2014), 6, 78.
53. This section largely follows Jacqui True, 'Feminism', in *Theories of International Relations*, 2nd ed., eds. Scott Burchill, Andrew Linklater, Richard Devetak, Jack Donnelly, Matthew Paterson, Christian Reus-Smit and Jacqui True (Basingstoke: Palgrave, 2001), 236–262; consults her references independently and adds new ones.
54. See notes 8 and 9 above.
55. Tickner, *Gender in International Relations*, 6–7.
56. Judith Butler, *Gender Trouble: Feminism and the Subversion of Identity* (New York, NY: Routledge, 1990), 7.
57. Judith Butler, *Undoing Gender* (New York, NY: Routledge, [2004]2015), 185.
58. Pierre Bourdieu, *Masculine Domination* (Stanford, CA: Stanford University Press, 2001), 22–23.
59. Chandra Talpade Mohanty, 'Under Western Eyes: Feminist Scholarship and Colonial Discourse', in *Media and Cultural Studies: Keyworks*, Revised edition, eds. Meenakshi Gigi Durham and Douglas M. Kellner (Malden, MA; Oxford: Blackwell Publishing, [1988]2006), 396–421.
60. Chandra Talpade Mohanty, '"Under Western Eyes" Revisited: Feminist Solidarity through Anticapitalist Struggles', *Signs* 28, no. 2 (Winter 2003): 499–535, especially 501, 515.
61. Sally Baden and Anne-Marie Goertz, 'Who Needs (Sex) When You Can Have (Gender): Conflicting Discourses on Gender at Beijing', in *Feminist Visions of Development: Gender, Analysis and Policy*, eds. Cecile Jackson and Ruth Pearson (London; New York, NY: Routledge, 1998), 18–37, especially 24–25.
62. Marysia Zalewski and Jane Parpart, eds., *The 'Man' Question in International Relations* (Boulder, CO: Westview Press, 1998), cited in True, 'Feminism', 238.
63. Charlotte Hooper, *Manly States: Masculinities, International Relations, and Gender Politics* (New York, NY: Columbia University Press, 1992), 14, 16, 115 and *passim.*
64. Joseph Gelfer, 'Introduction', in *Masculinities in a Global Era*, ed. J. Gelfer (New York, NY: Springer, 2014), 4.
65. Jeff Hearn, 'Part I: Introduction', in *Rethinking Transnational Men: Beyond, between and within Nations*, eds. Jeff Hearn, Marina Blagojević and Katherine Harrison (New York, NY; Abingdon: Routledge, 2013), 27.
66. Grant and Newland, 'Introduction', 5.
67. I have reconciled here UNDP data cited by Jean Kachiga, *Global Issues in the Context of Space* (Lanham, MD: Lexington Books, 2016), 56; and other data presented by Steven C. Hackett, *Environmental and Natural Resources Economics: Theory, Policy, and the Sustainable Society* (Armonk, NY; London: M. E. Sharpe, 1998), 220; Craig A. Lockard, *Societies, Networks, and Transitions*, Vol. 3 (Boston, MA: Wadsworth Cengage Learning, 2011), 751.

68. I am borrowing the term from Guy Standing, *The Precariat: The Dangerous Class* (London; Oxford; New Delhi: Bloomsbury, [2011]2016).
69. See, for discussion and numerous citations, True, 'Feminism', 239–247.
70. See notes 44–52.
71. Grant, 'Sources of Gender Bias in International Relations Theory', 21–23.
72. Joan Kelly, *Women, History, and Theory: The Essays of Joan Kelly* (Chicago, IL; London: The University of Chicago Press, 1984), 1, 15.
73. Christine Sylvester, *Feminist Theory and International Relations in a Postmodern Era* (Cambridge: Cambridge University Press, 1994), 82.
74. Tickner, *Gender in International Relations*, 72, 82.
75. Gilligan, *In a Different Voice*, 53.
76. Judith Allen, 'Does Feminism Need a Theory of "The State"?', in *Playing the State: Australian Feminist Interventions*, ed. Sophie Watson (London; New York, NY: Verso, 1990), 22.
77. Swati Parashar, J. Ann Tickner and Jacqui True, 'Introduction', in *Revisiting Gendered States: Feminist Imaginings of the State in International Relations*, eds. S. Parashar, J. A. Tickner and J. True (New York, NY: Oxford University Press, 2018), 4.
78. V. Spike Peterson, 'Sexing Political Identities', in *Women, States and Nationalism: At Home in the Nation?* eds. Sita Ranchod-Nilsson and Mary Ann Tetreault (London; New York, NY: Routledge, 2000), 61.
79. See especially notes 14–17, 71–72 above.
80. True, 'Feminism', 254.
81. See notes 44–59 of Chapter 7.
82. J. Hoffman, *Gender and Sovereignty: Feminism, the State and International Relations* (Basingstoke: Palgrave, 2001), 4, 6, *passim*.
83. True, 'Feminism', 258.
84. J. Ann Tickner and Laura Sjoberg, 'Conclusion: Looking Forward for Feminist International Relations', in *Feminism and International Relations: Conversations about the Past, Present and Future*, eds. J. A. Tickner and L. Sjoberg (London; New York, NY: Routledge, 2011), 225.
85. Jill Steans, *Gender and International Relations: Issues, Debates and Future Directions* (Cambridge; Malden, MA: Polity Press, 2006), 12–13.
86. Steans, *Gender and International Relations*, 13–15, 81; Tickner, *Gender in International Relations*, 16, 65, 82.
87. Sandra G. Harding, 'Introduction', in *The Feminist Standpoint Theory Reader: Intellectual and Political Controversies*, ed. S. G. Harding (London; New York, NY: Routledge, 2004), 3.
88. Note 7 of Chapter 19.
89. Sandra Whitworth, *Feminism and International Relations: Towards a Political Economy of Gender in Interstate and Non-Governmental Institutions* (London: Palgrave Macmillan, 1997), 80; Steans, *Gender and International Relations*, 15–16; Tickner and Sjoberg, 'Feminism', 189–190.
90. Ibid., 190–191; and Pamela Abbott and Claire Wallace, *An Introduction to Sociology: Feminist Perspectives*, 2nd ed. (London; New York, NY: Routledge, 1997), 236–237.
91. See notes 62–65 above.
92. Tickner and Sjoberg, 'Feminism', 191; Steans, *Gender and International Relations*, 16–18.
93. Leela Gandhi, *Postcolonial Theory: A Critical Introduction* (Delhi: Oxford University Press, 1999), 26–27.
94. Reina Lewis and Sara Mills, 'Introduction', in *Feminist Postcolonial Theory: A Reader*, eds. R. Lewis and S. Mills (New York, NY: Routledge, 2003), 1–2, 6.
95. See notes 59 and 60 above.

CHAPTER

21

Green Politics

CHAPTER OUTLINE

FROM ENVIRONMENTALISM TO ECOLOGISM AND GREEN THEORY: A TERMINOLOGICAL PRELUDE

Green politics and theory is one of the newest globalist theoretical perspectives in IR and is presently distinguished from environmentalism and even ecologism. However, to assess the worth of this distinction, we need to know the meaning of these words. Environmentalism 'argues for a managerial approach to environmental problems, secure in the belief that they can be solved without fundamental changes in present values or patterns of production and consumption'. But 'ecologism holds that a sustainable and fulfilling experience presupposes radical changes in our relationship with the non-human natural world and our mode of social and political life'.[1] Paterson says, 'environmentalists, broadly speaking, accept the framework of the existing political, social, economic and normative structures of world politics and seek to ameliorate environmental problems within those structures, while Greens regard those structures as the main origin of the environmental crisis and therefore contend that they need to be challenged and transcended'. He, however, cautions that this, 'obviously crude simplification of the variety of positions adopted by those within the Green and broader environmental movement', is useful here only 'as a representation of ideal types'.[2]

But, even as ideal types, the distinction between the terms environmentalism and ecologism has not always been sustained. While considering different alternative labels for 'environmental political theory' (henceforth EPT), Gabrielson, Schlosberg, Hall and Meyer argue that in current parlance, 'green' is a broader label than 'environmental' betokening better 'field's expansive interest in the intersection of environmental concerns with those of social justice, non-violence and the valuation of the non-human world for more than instrumental purposes', against EPT's implication of the 'mere application of already formed political theories to the "issue" of the environment'. But they still retain the term to maintain the identity of the field from the positions and views of Green political parties (henceforth GPPs).[3] However, in a wider context of 'interspecies', Youatt refuses to analyse these two terms from the perspectives of shallowness and depth. 'Shallow ecology is perfectly possible as is deep environmentalism'.[4] This point would be buttressed by the fact that Eckersley's book on environmentalism and political theory stakes out an 'ecocentric approach' and starts with the impact of Green parties on it at the start,[5] while Carter's book on the 'politics of the environment', speaks of key ingredients of 'Green political thought' (GPT), the 'anthropocentric and ecocentric divide', 'holistic perspectives' and 'moral extensionism', right from the 'Introduction' to second and third chapters of the book.[6] Some explanation of why this is happening can be found in Mulvaney's words that the understandings of ecologism 'can be grouped into two schools, known as "minimalist" and "maximalist"'. In the former approach, 'the terms environmentalism and ecologism are often used interchangeably' and either 'can be used as an umbrella term, encompassing a spectrum that runs from "light green" or "ecological modernization", at one extreme, and "dark green" or "deep ecology", at the other', taking its roots, as suggested by Andrew Vincent, to the 19th century. In the latter maximalist approach, best represented by Dobson, a strict distinction between the two terms places the origins of ecologism in more recent times.[7]

It is from this maximalist position that Shellenberger and Nordhaus wrote their famous essay about the 'death of environmentalism' (although without uttering the word 'green' even once), where they identified the crisis in the fact that,

> Environmentalism will never be able to muster the strength it needs to deal with the global warming problem as long as it is seen as a 'special interest'. And it will continue to be seen as a special interest as long as it narrowly identifies the problem as 'environmental' and the solutions as technical.[8]

And in a later book (uttering the word green in passing only three times in the text and twice in references), they point out that,

'Paradoxically, it is the global ecological crises that have triggered the death of environmentalism ... the category of "the environment" ... is no longer useful. The challenge of climate change is so massive, so global, and so complex that it can be overcome only if we look beyond the issue categories of the past, and embrace a grand new vision of the future'. For, 'global warming is as different from smog in Los Angeles as nuclear war is from gang violence. The ecological crises we face are more ... tied to the basic functioning of the [global] economy than were the problems environmentalism was created to address forty years ago'.

So the dominant consensus is that environmentalism came first, and ecologism in its new avatar of Green theory came later, but both concepts were late entrants in IR. Although the environment was on the political agenda since the late 1960s,[10] it was sidelined in IR, preoccupied with 'high politics', till the escalation in transborder environmental problems from the 1970s ushered in a dedicated sub-field in IR, concerned with international environmental cooperation in the areas of management of common pool resources, such as major river systems, the oceans and the atmosphere. Scholarly pursuits in this area got a fillip from the increasing global economic and ecological interdependence, on the one hand, and from the rise of unprecedentedly global ecological problems, such as air-water-noise pollution, acid rain, thinning of the Earth's ozone layer, deforestation, salinization of inland water sources, erosion of the Earth's biodiversity and species loss, pesticide poisoning and climate change, on the other. The burgeoning field of environmental research, accordingly, concentrated on the study of environmental regimes, primarily from the newly unfolding theoretical field of neoliberalism, which added environment as an 'issue area' or new political problem, rather than a theoretical challenge to the dominant theoretical discourses of IR,[11] much as liberal feminism pursued an 'add women and stir' approach in studying IR.[12]

This resulted in the growth of the field of 'global environmental politics' (henceforth GEP). This approach (which had adherents up to the second decade of the present century) normally started with (sometimes) lurid descriptions of the state of the planet; a list of the major problems, causes and reasons of their persistence; their projected 'solutions' (where available) and so on. The litany of problems included overpopulation and poverty, water scarcity, deforestation, climate change and so on. The proximate causes were both general and specific, including the 'tragedy of the commons'; the deleterious effects of capitalism, including alienation from nature caused by it, capitalism's metabolic and ecological 'rifts' and the vices of 'ecological imperialism', over-consumption and other indicators of its unsustainability; 'car trouble'; 'the speed of fast food' (including McDonaldization and the lawsuit over criticisms of the corporations famous as 'McLibel'); 'consumer culture' and its attendant 'unsustainable consumption' (where by way of 'individualizing responsibility' the ecological impact of mobile phones and fashion was discussed); the ecological impact of hazardous substances including toxic elements, and so on.[13]

The range of issues raised by GEP is broad and does not avoid the significance of Green politics. So what really distinguishes it from Green politics? While justifying the subtitle of his book, *Problems, Policy and Practice*, Stevenson deplores that in GEP, 'these three elements are rarely aligned' and suggests that the 'health of the planet would undoubtedly be in better shape' if they were.[14] Even this criticism is not available in Paterson's version of GEP, where he stresses the dominative and accumulative practices of capitalism and the workings of global power structures in the context of the 'normal and mundane practices of modernity', as generative of environmental crises, and shows the problems and possibilities of resistance. While commenting that 'it is the network of various power structures which are mutually supportive of each other and which necessarily produce environmental crises through their interaction' and including patriarchy as one of them, Paterson admits that similar arguments have been made by Green writers, Marxists and feminists.[15] So GEP may be the 'hyphen that joins, buckle that fastens' environmentalism with Green theory and politics.

FROM ENVIRONMENTAL CONCERNS TO GREEN POLITICAL THOUGHT/THEORY

Much like feminist concerns, environmental anxieties also left their mark on most branches of social sciences, including IR. But it was not until the late 1970s and 1980s that a completely new thought structure sought to weave together and rearticulate the interrelated preoccupations of the new social movements, representing the environment, peace, anti-nuclear protests and women and fomented, since the 1980s, the formation of Green parties mostly in Europe at local, regional and national levels with ecologism, social justice, non-violence, decentralization, gender and racial equality, participatory grassroots democracy and individual human rights as central concerns.[16] With the consolidation of the diverse 'Green' ideas spearheaded by these parties, the participatory and survivalist phases of ecological thought of the preceding three decades entered what Eckersley calls its 'third emancipatory moment', marked by a 'new, ecologically inspired political orientation which raised new political questions and problematized old political responses'.[17] After entering IR in the closing decades of the 20th century, it interrogated some of the basic assumptions, units of study, frameworks of analysis and implicit values of the discipline for being ecologically blind. But in order to grasp how it happened, we need to know the ideological and conceptual ballasts of GPT.

The debates between environmentalism and the first wave of green thinking revolved around a series of well-known splits and binaries between '"value in" versus "value of" nature, ecocentrism versus anthropocentrism, organicism versus mechanicism, holism versus resourcism' and so on.[18] Ecocentrism and 'a Green theory of value' (hereafter GTV) are treated first.

Ecocentrism and Its Critiques

Eckersley thinks that most New Left thinkers treated the concept of ecocentrism in a very limited manner. While discussing 'humanity's power vis-à-vis nature', they merely asked 'who exercised such power and on whose behalf'. She traced the origins of the anthropocentric/ecocentric cleavage to an ecophilosophical cleavage 'reflected, for example, in Arne Næss's influential distinction between shallow ecology and deep ecology; Timothy O'Riordan's characterization of "technocentrism" and "ecocentrism"; the "imperialist" and "Arcadian" traditions of ecological thought identified by environmental historian Donald Worster; Murray Bookchin's distinction between "environmentalism" and "social ecology"; William Catton and Riley Dunlap's distinction between "human exemptionalism paradigm" of mainstream sociology and "new ecological paradigm" of the "post-exuberant age", and in Alan Drengson's distinction between the "technocratic" and "pernectarian" (i.e., person-planetary) paradigms'. Since they accord more fundamental logical priority to the question of the human beings' 'proper place in the rest of nature' over the 'question of what are the most appropriate social and political arrangements for human communities', ecocentric theorists question the arrogant belief that human beings 'are the sole locus of value and meaning in the world'. They take the 'ethical position' that 'all the parts of the multilayered biotic community' have intrinsic value and present the 'ecological interconnectedness' as the empirical ground for 'both empathy and caution'. This model of 'ecological interconnectedness' covers not only human–non-human relations but also human–human relations in all their entire constitutive biological, psychological and social senses. Eckersley detects three complementary manifestations of ecocentrism in the Western tradition: 'autopoietic intrinsic value theory', 'transpersonal ecology' and 'ecofeminism'. The first says that all entities displaying the property of *autopoiesis* or 'self-renewal' or 'self-generation' have intrinsic value and are 'ends in themselves', meriting 'moral consideration in their own right'. The value of not only individual organisms but also species, ecosystems and the ecosphere (as in Gaia) are granted recognition. Transpersonal ecology takes a cosmological or psychological route to change the way in which we feel and understand the world, which involves 'cultivation of a wider identification of self' through 'identification with others'. Ecofeminism, in the sense of a reassertion of the relationship between women and nature, is both 'a source of empowerment of women and the basis of a critique of the male domination of women and non-human nature.' It does not have a proper cosmology. Unlike transpersonal ecology, which bases itself on 'the tree of life', ecofeminism starts from the particularized gender experience of women.[19]

However, ecocentrism has its critics. Social constructivists find it impossible for humans to 'avoid interpreting the world from a human vantage point'. Second, ecocentrism's opposition to 'any essential hierarchy of values among human and non-human beings' supposedly renders it 'vague and difficult to apply to practical environmental conflicts'. Animal rights theorists charge that Aldo Leopold's 'land ethic' has fascist implications, while social ecologists (including Murray Bookchin) contend that ecocentrism is potentially 'misanthropic'.[20] There is some uneasiness about ecocentrism in full flow and its feasibility as a productive concept even within GPT itself. Some say that the 'anthropocentric–ecocentric dichotomy' could be reworked through Norton's useful 'convergence hypothesis' to conceptualize a reformed 'naturalistic humanism' that can support a 'stewardship ethic'. It suggests that 'a self-reflexive long-term anthropocentrism, as opposed to an "arrogant" or "strong" anthropocentrism, can secure many of the policy objectives of ecocentrism'.[21] Hayward argues that anthropocentrism is a misnomer as 'a term in criticism of environmental ethics and politics'. Many of the vices of anthropocentrism are 'better understood as instances of speciesism and human chauvinism'.[22]

Critique around GTV

Among many discrete values constituting ecocentrism, a 'GTV' deserves separate discussion because it problematizes the connection between green and specific political positions. Goodin puts ethics at the heart of the green position and distinguishes between GTV and the 'green theory of agency' (hereafter GTA). While GTV supplies the 'unified moral vision running through all the central substantive planks in the green political programme', GTA 'advises on how to go about pursuing those values'.[23] GTV is so basic to the green movement's goals and intentions that it is not worth sacrificing in the name of any preferred form of agency. Since 'core green concerns are consequentialist at the root', rather than being parts of a deontological theory concerned with particular outcomes (meaning, in Goodin's sense, protection of 'natural values'), and GTA must be seen as a separate and subsidiary component of it, in situations of conflict, GTV 'and the ends that it would have us promote, simply must—within the logic of the Greens' own theory—take priority over' GTA.[24] Essentially, it means that acceptance of green arguments about the intrinsic value of the natural world would not entail abiding by green suggestions about political arrangements. Rather, 'we can and probably should accept green political prescriptions without necessarily adopting green ideas about how to reform political structures and processes'.[25] If GTV really takes priority over GTA, 'then insisting on rotation in office greens might be pursuing a lower priority goal in preference to a higher priority one.'[26] So instead of getting wedded to any particular social choice mechanism, a GTA should (incrementally, we may say) explore all available means and choose those presumed to be most favourable to the desired outcomes. Since many of the agencies considered legitimate by the greens—including decentralization and locally rooted decisions—have proven deleterious to green outcomes, they must form parties of specific types, fight elections in the normal way and form and enter coalitions, unless they are content to remain 'an amusing parliamentary slideshow'.[27]

GTV has had its unfair and fair shares of criticisms. Interpreting its main message that 'value of the natural world can be traced only to its value to human beings and the role it plays in their lives', Barry and Frankland have placed it on the same footing as the World Commission on Environment and Development's (Brundtland Commission) report, *Our Common Future* (1987), and have inexplicably called it 'anthropocentric'.[28] Eckersley concedes that it is 'non-anthropocentric and tightly argued' but still fit for rejection, being too narrow to form a basis for GPT 'because it applies only to the non-human world'. An additional vice emerges from the 'consequentialist theory of "natural" values in GTV, due to which it 'necessarily converts questions of agency and political strategy into utilitarian calculations'. Although Goodin considers liberal democracy as the 'best available means of securing green goals', for Eckersley, 'this is a purely contingent assessment that others may not share. Monkeywrenchers, for example, would beg to differ: Tree spiking is judged to be superior to lobbying and voting when it comes to the protection of an old-growth forest'.[29]

Limits to Growth, Post-development and Degrowth

Apart from ecocentrism, the 'limits to growth' (hereafter LTG) argument is the most definitional tenet of GPT. It entered environmental discourse in the early 1970s through a famous eponymous report based on computer simulation of exponential economic and population growth in a situation of the finite supply of resources. After offering various chilling trajectories of the exponential economic and population growth of societies and their impacts, Meadows, Meadows, Randers and Behrens warned that if instead of bringing in 'self-imposed limitation', the first of the 'nature-imposed limits' were allowed to be 'imposed by the exhaustion of non-renewable resources', then 'whatever fraction of the human population remained at the end of the process would have very little left with which to build a new society in any form we can now envision'. Attempts to use of 'even the most optimistic estimates of the benefits of technology in the model did not prevent the ultimate decline of population and industry and, in fact, did not, in any case, postpone the collapse beyond the year 2100'.[30]

LTG was later attacked on many counts: inadequate empirical database, faulty mathematical structures, unnecessarily pessimistic assumptions, excessive 'emphasis on the power of computer modelling', imposed homogeneity on a diverse world and other methodological inadequacies. Besides, post-*LTG* empirical realities such as stabilization of population growth and continuous discoveries of new resource reserves were shown to refute *LTG*'s Cassandra-like warnings. The models were also attacked because of minimizing the possibilities of new technological breakthroughs and mankind's capacities of changing themselves.[31] The impact of the *LTG* argument weakened further after first hints in the 1972 Stockholm UN Conference, the notion of 'sustainable development' (hereafter SD) was popularized by the Brundtland Commission report in 1987 to collar the environment-development discourse. But under the new belief that in the 1990s, economic growth was not the primary purpose of governments and societies, Meadows, Meadows, Randers and Behrens tried to substantiate the validity of their *LTG* arguments in two books. The first (*Beyond the Limits*) attempted a '20-year update' of their *LTG* arguments by studying the developments between 1970 and 1990 and concluded that by 1992 'humanity had already overshot the limits of Earth's support capacity'. The second, *Limits to Growth: The 30 Year Update*, asserted that the 'highly aggregated scenarios of World3' model presented in *LTG* 'still appear 'after 30 years'.[32] Alongside them, between 2000 and 2010, a host of environmental economists led by Matthew Simmons asserted that *LTG* had been dismissed on wrong grounds and needed a reappraisal. But negative criticisms of *LTG*, led by S. W. Popper, continued in scientific literature as late as 2005 and 2010. Together, these warring camps brought *LTG* into relevance again[33] and was embraced by Greens. Three main aspects of *LTG* argument that were highlighted by them are (a) disbelief in technological solutions, which can only postpone the collapse but not prevent it, (b) conviction that the impact of the exponential nature of growth being so unpredictable, 'dangers stored up over a relatively long period of time can very suddenly have a catastrophic effect' and (c) 'interaction of problems caused by growth means that such problems cannot be dealt with in isolation, that is, solving one problem does not solve the rest and may even exacerbate them'.[34]

Ideas allied to the limits argument that the greens adopted are ecological footprints, Holocene and Anthropocene, green consumerism, green growth (hereafter GG), postmaterialism and a new definition of sustainability. Ecological footprints are 'a measure of the amount of nature it takes to sustain a given population over the course of a year'. The global ecological footprint (hereafter GEFP) determines the ecological assets that humanity requires to regenerate the natural resources it consumes, and when pitted against the biological capacity of the Earth, the footmetric index shows whether humanity's use of croplands, forest lands, pasture lands, built space, fisheries and energy is sustainable. According to the Global Footprint Network's 2017 annual report, the Earth's biocapacity was exceeded even in the 1970s, and since then, this ecological deficit or overshoot has accelerated to reach 50 per cent so that it needs a one-and-a-half year to reproduce what we consume in one year. GEFP is a yardstick of sustainability and limits. Holocene is the geologists' term for '12,000 years of relative climate stability' preceding Anthropocene (a term coined by Paul J. Crutzen and Eugene Stoermer in 2000), which 'encapsulates the unprecedented changes to the earth's biosphere following the industrial revolution and the last 60 years of economic activity, consumption and resource use'. Anthropocene symbolizes the profound, accelerating and demonstrated changes in the Earth's atmospheric composition, stratospheric ozone, climate system, water and nitrogen cycles, marine ecosystems, land systems, tropical forests, terrestrial biosphere and so on to measure the rate at which modern civilization is degrading the earth system. GG, signifying 'economic growth that uses natural resources in an environmentally sustainable manner', is one of the suggested minimal palliatives. It would require, on the part of humans, green consumerism or employment of 'environmental and ethical criteria in choosing whether or not to purchase a product or service'. Postmaterialism or 'the theory that, as material affluence spreads, "quality of life" indicators tend to replace material ones; fundamentally changing the political culture and values of industrializer countries' is one of the requisite assumptions that greening of the environment can happen.[35] All this brings a newer and deeper green view of sustainability, different from the environmentalist view of SD. While the Brundtland Commission defined SD as 'development that meets the needs of the present without compromising the needs of future generations to meet their needs' and still represented utilitarian ecology, the definition of the World Wildlife Fund was a lot greener and saw it as 'improving the quality of life while living within the carrying capacity of supporting systems.[36] Dobson linked sustainability to limits, by quoting Jonathon Porritt that, 'if we don't learn to live sustainably within the natural systems and limits that provide the foundation for all life forms, then we will go the same way as every other life form that failed to adapt to those changing systems and limits.'[37] Thus understood, sustainability unequivocally implies 'stabilizing and, in the industrialized countries, almost certainly reducing throughputs of materials and energy' and consequent 'wholesale reorganization of economic systems'.[38]

Greens also adopted new critiques of development, from the South, from the late 1980s onwards, including 'post-development' perspectives fueled by postmodernism and feminism to assess the ecological and social consequences of development. Convinced of the irretrievability of the concept of development, Sachs wants to write an obituary of the last four-decade-long age of it;[39] calls SD 'an oxymoron', and thinks that from the unholy 'liaison' or 'newly formed bond' between sustainability and development, 'the ailing concept' is only 'gaining another lease of life'.[40] Welford says that the cooptation and hijacking of sustainable environmentalism by corporate or governmental elites bred to a 'corporate environmentalism', 'dominant ideology' of which is 'eco-modernism and within that the tool of eco-efficiency' and which concentrates only on narrow environmental aspects of that concept',[41] depending on 'how the corporate bureaucracy engages initially with the issue' and 'provides another example of a functional rationality based on the logic of the market, being applied to green issues.'[42] How this is done has been shown graphically by Sachs in the case of the Tokyo subway. The wood-pulp shortage in Japan made wall posters of advertisements replaced by video screens, which supposedly solved the 'paper problem'. It ignored the fact that efforts 'to deal with environmental problems discretely' amid the practice of 'ongoing development undermines any ameliorative effect which a particular response may have' and is due to the 'interaction of problems caused by growth' that we have shown above.[43]

The anti-development theorists disagreed with *LTG*. 'It did not call for abandoning the race but for changing the running technique, as through replacement of the slogan "no development without sustainability" by "no sustainability without development".'[44] Besides dubbing *LTG* models as technocratic and devoid of social content, these theorists even rubbished distinctions by some environmentalists, like Daly of World Bank, between growth (quantitative increase in physical scale) and development (qualitative improvement or unfolding of potentialities) and the deduction from it that the human economy being 'a subsystem of a finite global ecosystem does not grow, even though it does develop'. Contending that 'growth of the economy cannot be sustainable over long periods of time', they regard sustainable growth as 'a bad oxymoron' and SD as 'much more apt',[45] although practitioners of SD normally take it interchangeably with sustainable growth.[46]

These critiques led to the concept of 'post-development', coined in 1991 and spearheaded by Escobar and others and an ensuing 'post-development era'. Before that, after pillorying by the dependency position in the 1960s and 1970s and by critical perspectives on development as a cultural discourse in the mid-1980s and 1990s, development was also being problematized by the post-structuralists. They contended that the post-Second World War historical discourse of development facilitated the 'creation of a vast institutional apparatus' through which it was 'deployed' and 'operated through' its 'professionalization' and 'institutionalization'. It allowed various 'forms of exclusion' of 'knowledges, voices and concerns of those whom, paradoxically, development was supposed to serve: the poor of Asia, Africa and Latin America'. For Escobar, post-development referred to (a) the 'possibility of creating different discourses of development', (b) the resultant 'need to change the practices of knowing and doing and the "political economy of truth" that defines the development regime', (c) the also consequent 'need to multiply the centres and agents of knowledge production' to bring to fore 'the forms of knowledge produced by those who are supposed to be the "objects" of development' and (e) efforts to do this 'by focusing on the adaptations, subversions and resistances that local people effect in relation to development interventions'.[47] The post-development era is not empty of change content. Rahnema says it signifies that 'the binary, the mechanistic, the reductionist, the inhuman and the ultimately self-destructive approach to change is over'. For Escobar, post-development theorists 'are interested not in development alternatives but alternatives to development' and share 'interest in local culture and knowledge; a critical stance towards established scientific discourses, and the defence and promotion of localized pluralistic grassroots movements'.[48]

That the green critique of development shares many views of post-development is evident in its argument that development necessarily involved 'enclosure' of common spaces (or *commons*) originally largely organized outside markets into private property for commodity production. This not only shifted decision-making on them from the people who depended on local resources, denied them access to *commons*, concentrated resources into fewer hands and bred inequality but also consolidated the power of the already affluent, thus instilling an 'anti-ecological dynamic' into development. Culled from the example of the modernization of English agriculture, this lesson was taken to the global level to show how in the global economy the North could exploit the South to shield itself from many deleterious socio-economic consequences of development by driving out dirty industries to the South. At the micro-level also, the process could be seen in the Green Revolution of the 1970s (e.g., in India), which discriminated against poor farmers, who could not afford its requirements, to favour the rich ones. Ingrained in this concentration of power is the politics of knowledge (POK). The commandeering of *commons* empowered and was aided by 'experts', who rubbished all local knowledge in service of new techniques and handed over their management to scientists and development experts. This process also had its global reflection in the privileging of Western technologies and knowledges over non-Western wisdom. Also relevant is how, in the context of climate change, North-to-South technology transfer through developmental aid has replicated all the deleterious consequences of development listed above. A corollary of all this, as Carolyn Merchant said, is the paradigmatic shift in the world view that allowed the transformation of nature into 'natural resources' exploitable by humans and the attendant 'rationalization' of the natural world via instrumental rationality in a way that it turns nature 'into a set of countable species', usable and worth preserving or unusable and fit for destruction.[49] In one word, this is triage versus Gaia.[50]

This Green critique of development led to the 'degrowth' social movement, which rejuvenated interest in the 'radical alternative economic thinking' inspired by LTG discourses. Beyond a critique of growth, degrowth also urges for 'a desired direction, in which societies will use fewer natural resources and will organize and live differently from today' with 'sharing', 'simplicity', 'conviviality', 'care' and 'the commons'. Degrowthers, accordingly, demand 'a controlled contraction of the economy through a radical downsizing of production and consumption and decentralization of the economy and political institutions to enable society to live within its ecological means.'[51]

Decentralization and Its Critiques

Gundersen says discussion of decentralization, the third major plank of GPT, starts with Bookchin, 'founder and principal defender of social ecology'. Without him '(n)o discussion of the politics of scale, perhaps the central institutional problematic in environmental political philosophy, would be complete'. His work 'anchors one pole in the environmental argument over appropriate political scale'.[52] Long back in 1952, he wrote that decentralization provides 'a real possibility for developing the best traditions of social life and for solving the agricultural and nutritional difficulties that have thus far been delivered to chemistry' since the 'majority of food problems of the world would be solved today by well-balanced and rounded communities, intelligently urbanized, well-equipped with industry and with easy access to the land'. Already implicit in this early work are suggestions about 'the social causes of ecological problems and the insistence on their solution by a revolutionary decentralization'. These ideas remained constant in his later books and articles, such as *Our Synthetic Environment* (1962; hereinafter, *OSE*), *Towards a Liberatory Technology* (1964; hereinafter, TLC) and *Ecology and Revolutionary Thought* (hereinafter, ERT).[53] Even the words 'delivered to chemistry' adumbrates the Green objection to the transference of environmental management to experts. In ERT, Bookchin not only mixed the critical dimension of his social ecology with a reconstructive vision of a truly libertarian socialist society, an ecological society utilizing solar and wind power for which 'the megalopolis must be decentralized', but also in an earlier version of ERT, he even issued warnings about the almost unheard problem of the greenhouse effect. He said the 'growing blanket of carbon dioxide' might bring about 'eventually a melting of the polar ice caps (possibly in two or three centuries), rising sea levels and the inundation of vast land areas', erring only in prolonging the time frame.[54] Moreover, Bookchin not only expected 'decentralization to encourage ecological sensibility and intelligence' but also 'ecological respect', first, 'through intensified interactions with nature' and, second, through 'heightened participation in the common life of the municipality'.[55] Like Schumacher, Bookchin found, 'in the small and human scale', not only 'evidence of the beautiful but also of the emancipatory', unless stolen away stealthily by planners not only by rooting out ecological technologies on which the notion materially rests but also emasculated by technocrats through delinking it from the radical social theory in which it is rooted.[56]

The influence of Bookchin's ideas is visible even in Dryzek's arguments for decentralization in his *Rational Ecology*, particularly where he claims that (a) small-scale communities are more dependent on environmental support facilities in their vicinity and accordingly more susceptible to disruptions in their environment; (b) since self-reliance and smallness abbreviate feedback channels, responses to disruptions before they escalate are enabled, and (c) these communities have a tendency to develop a social ontology that advises against instrumental modes of behaviour with nature.[57] In Bookchin's terms, they are ecocommunities.

Before going into the other less basic and sometimes more contested ideological and conceptual ballasts of GPT, we should refer to another subsidiary literature that appeared in the early 1990s seeking to employ the basic green principles discussed above to measure the consistency of the present situation with them. Called 'global ecology' (GE), this subsidiary literature differed from the normative orientation of GPT in its exploratory approach.

Global Ecology

GE has both scientific and political aspects. The scientific side revolves around 'understanding the dynamics of the linkages that exist between the vast resources of the globe'. It posits that understanding 'the resilience and response of the biota to environmental perturbations requires knowledge of the interaction between the biotic and non-biotic aspects of the Earth's surface', and GE is the science that 'considers the Earth as a single system with global dimensions, facing enormous difficulties'.[58] The founding insight of GE as the advanced awareness of 20th-century science is that the profound unity emerging from the findings of ecology and other earth sciences today has shattered the 'conventional view of isolated ecosystems' to unearth not only 'the "intradependencies" within discrete ecosystems but also the "interdependencies" between far and distant places and their relation to our everyday lives'. These teach us that 'our lives and well-being are mutually dependent on and fused with those of the bacteria in the soil, the shrubs in a remote tropical forest and the salamanders crawling on muddy pond bottoms'.[59] Its present focus is 'the biosphere or the ecosphere conceived as one unified cooperative system with numerous synergistic effects that explain the unique properties of this sphere'.[60]

Two central planks of the political side of GE, associated in the popular mind with the writings of Sachs, Pratap Chatterjee, Matthias Finger, contributors in the magazines *The Ecologist* and *Third World Resurgence*, Vandana Shiva and so on, are (a) development as the basic cause of planetary disturbances and (b) protection and reclamation of 'commons' as a means of re-greening of our environment. Convinced that the goals and objectives of the environmental movements throughout the 1980s have suffered dilution and co-optation, causing the call for 'new public virtues' in place of 'better managerial strategies', Sachs and others chose the United Nations Conference on Environment and Development (UNCED) or the Earth Summit in Rio in June 1992 as their main target of attack because it tried to make environmentalism consistent with developmentalism.[61] Sachs showed that even after 'recognizing the declining state of the environment', governments assembled at Rio 'insisted on the relaunching of development'. That is why the UNCED's Agenda 21 was replete with phrases such as 'rational use', 'sound management', 'internalizing costs', 'better information', 'increased coordination' and 'long-term prediction'. Still, by and large, 'except for some timid phrases in the hotly debated chapter "Changing Consumption Patterns",' it failed to contemplate any scaling down of material standards of living and any attempt to check the accumulation dynamics, thereby blackballing 'alternatives to development', while 'alternatives within the development are welcome'. Rather than resolving the four-fault lines of 'international environmental diplomacy, involving rights to further exploitation of nature, rights to pollution, rights to compensation and overall conflicts over diplomacy', the UNCED discussions foregrounded them.[62] As per Chatterjee, UNCED had 'raised the promotion of economic growth to a planetary imperative'. Forsaking any new vision consonant with global ecology, 'UNCED has rehabilitated technology and other cults of efficiency'[63] and legitimized the 'gospel of global efficiency'.[64] Global ecologists castigated UNCED for the sordid ways in which governments sought to bolster their power by getting mainstream environmental groups and NGOs to legitimize their actions; allowing MNCs assembled in shady groups to enter the deliberations as genuine actors; giving free public relations job for it to business groups tainted for environmental disasters caused by them, and providing privileged access to their proceedings to MNCs.[65] Against these, they sought to restore hallowed GPT values.

The second plank of GE buttressed green arguments for decentralization by giving it a politico-economical twist through moving beyond the economics of scale to a plea for the structural reorganization of political institutions so that they can be integrated into new political forms. On the positive side, the central argument of the Green economy, as most persuasively argued in *The Ecologist*'s issue 'Whose Common Future? Reclaiming the Commons' (1993), concerns the commons, as loci of the most sustainable practices currently available, and hence justifies not only resistance to their enclosure but also constructive proposals for their creations where none existed. *The Ecologist* emphatically distinguished these *commons* from the tragic, overgrazed, English medieval 'commons', fated to be overgrazed, since each herder will try to maximize the number of sheep grazed by them, making it less of commons than of an 'open access resource'. Contrastingly, *commons* are not lawless but are rather spaces use of which through community-determined rules is rooted in approximate equality between the members since power imbalances among them would make these rules less binding on some. These are governed by appropriate social and cultural norms (such as privileging common safety over accumulation and members over non-members since commons are collective goods but not public goods, spaces in both the senses of access by the state and all people). Their difference from private property systems commons is reflected, inter alia, in their stress on use values rather than exchange values. The reasons why *commons* are congenial sites for sustainable practices include (a) approximate equality in earning and power that precludes usurpation or domination of the system, (b) local scale, facilitating patterns of mutual dependence, that provide greater chances of cooperation, (c) by implication, the prevalence of ethos of recognizing everyone's dependence on everyone else and the mutual or reciprocal obligations it entails and (d) while practices relating to the accumulation of *commons* are made difficult, the chosen path is usufruct. *The Ecologist* provides ample examples of such community rules and practices in commons all over the world.[66]

WAVES OF GREEN THEORY AND ITS CRITIQUES OF THE STATE, LIBERALISM AND POLITICAL CENTRALIZATION

The attacks of GPT against mainstream IR, IPE and global politics have come in three different waves, and the effects have been cumulative. The first wave, resulting from seminal books as of Carson and Commoner, and reports such as *LTG*,[67] primarily revolved around efforts to establish ecologism as a distinct 'ideology' and GPT as a distinctive approach to politics. The second wave was marked by its debates with liberalism, feminism, CT and socialism and a new focus on key concepts of political thought such as democracy, justice, the state and citizenship. The third distinguished itself by its 'explicitly interdisciplinary and applied focus', sometimes making a reflection on many issues of concern to GPT difficult, without roping in disciplines outside political science and political theory.[68] Proponents in the first wave spiritedly decried both Western capitalism and Soviet communism, contending that both were basically two different versions of anthropocentric manifestations of the same vice of industrialism, differing only in the role reserved for the market and the state. The green critique of this industrialism extended to a broader reappraisal of the ideas of progress and modernization, propagated by post-Enlightenment social science and castigated both liberalism and doctrinaire Marxism for sheltering such anthropocentric, cornucopian and meliorist assumptions, based on the misconception that Earth's natural resources could sustain the present rate of economic growth, as also both for their optimism about scientific and technological solutions of the problems generated by human manipulation of the nature and the resultant reliance on instrumental reason.[69]

The second wave of GPT was not uniform in all its strands. For example, Eckersley took a mildly statist position, not subscribing to the views of ecosurvivalists of the 1970s regarding diminution of state-scale on Athenian or Jeffersonian lines, even as some others accepted the Leviathan only as a necessary but undesirable part of the short or medium-term transitional scenario; deplored humanity's 'limited choice between "Leviathan or oblivion"', or called for a 'legislative temperance' through 'mutual coercion, mutually agreed upon'. They and ecoanarchists were very far from Eckersley's faith in a 'Green state', which 'will be able to facilitate a shift away from growth in material energy and throughput towards qualitative or 'postmaterial' growth in accordance with a new Green index of economic welfare'. For Eckersley, a 'multi-tiered democratic political' structure, in which there was 'dispersal of political power between the centre and the periphery', rather than their concentration in either, provided 'checks and balances in both directions', down to the local communities and up to the regional and global levels. It is more 'compatible with an ecocentric world view than the simple web-like horizontal structure of ecoanarchism'. It 'recognizes the layered interrelationships between parts (social and ecological) of larger wholes', best suited for the 'superregional perspective and multilateral action by nation states' needed to 'bring about the kind of dramatic changes necessary to save the global commons'.[70] In her later book, *The Green State* (*TGS*), Eckersley explained why 'green political theorists need to think not only critically but also constructively about the state and the state system' and from a 'green demand upon the state' look at it 'not only as a good ecological trustee over its own people and territory but also as a good citizen in the international society of states'. Eckersley finally defended 'a green democratic state' not merely 'as a necessary evil but rather as a crucial mechanism for facilitating democratic negotiations in the public sphere and steering society along more ecologically sustainable lines'. While dealing with the two dimensions of the green critique of the liberal democratic state revolving around the '*state form* through which the liberal democratic ideals have been institutionalized' and its '*liberal* character', Eckersley pointed out that 'the organized coercive power of democratic states is not a totally untamed power'. Since, contrary to liberals, Green activists and theorists are readier to approve of a slew of restrictions on accepted freedoms in the areas of investment, production, consumption, mobility and property use, she suggests that despite the 'proactive role' that Green consumers may like to play 'in encouraging the greening of investment and production patterns, the important task of laying down sustainability parameters is one that should primarily belong to people acting publicly and democratically as citizens rather than as consumers'. As sustainability is 'an uncertain quest', pursuable 'in an open-minded, practical and experimental fashion', critical political ecologists should also shun their 'search for one true green path' and usurp 'the role of political communities in determining the meaning of and path towards sustainability'.

For Eckersley, with these qualifiers and conditions, accommodation of Green demands within liberalism is possible through a radicalization of political pluralism, which involves 'questioning' of the 'liberal distinctions between public and private, justice and the good' and transformation of the 'privatization of good', enabled by liberal democratic theory, by GPT's 'politicization of the private good, and the repoliticization of the public good'. One problem of liberalism is that while the fundamental liberal freedoms find expression in the form and realm of rights, environmental concerns are treated less importantly as 'matters of "the good life" and accordingly as 'non-fundamental and therefore negotiable'. But Eckersley shows how Marcel Wissenburg's innovation of the 'restraint principle', partly flowing from Rawls's 'savings principle', might tide over this shortcoming of liberalism by imposing 'a side constraint on the distribution of conditional rights', and an 'inverse restraint principle' can apply the same formula to the production of pollutants. So equipped with this green liberalism, an ecological state might be born 'within the shell of the liberal democratic state' to put ecological concerns at the heart of its activities. But despite all its innovations, the restraint principle still treats nature instrumentally and cannot provide 'ecological guarantees'; the new full-fledged rather than the emergent post-liberal ecological state should be based on ecological democracy, acting through 'a postpositive, socially and ecologically inclusive model of democratic decision-making and risk assessment'.[71]

While Eckersley's ecocentric environmentalist arguments could also be developed in a conventional liberal or liberal institutionalist perspective or the context of the global environmental governance, those raised in TGS implied moving beyond liberalism towards a post-liberal ecological state, which is still a state. She and some other Greens have even no problem with state sovereignty. To the extent its 'constitutive discourses' begins 'to absorb ecological arguments, it becomes possible to talk about the concomitant "greening of sovereignty"'.[72] Others also think that being a 'multifaceted and historically variable concept and practice, sovereignty should be unbundled, and ecological issues can be special solvents in the 'unbundling of sovereignty as a political practice' because with their 'grassroots constituency', 'scientific underpinnings', 'essential borderlessness' and 'intergenerational temporal content', ecological issues 'may be especially likely to alter the broader matrix of modernity's cultural practices'.[73]

There are, however, three other claimed environmental positions following from the LTG logic, apart from Eckersley's mildly statist one. The second of them is 'centralized authoritarianism', logically emanating from Garrett Hardin's famous metaphor of the 'tragedy of the commons'. It advocates the creation of centralized global political structures that can enforce behavioural changes in the direction of sustainability; adopts in some of its versions 'lifeboat ethics' as the appropriate choice for rich countries, and involves the principle of 'triage' or 'pulling up the ladder behind them' (as in Garrett Hardin's *Lifeboat Ethics: The Case against Helping the Poor*, 1974). Save a few exceptions, this alternative is rejected by the Greens. The third is also authoritarian but not practised on a global scale, its locale being small tightly knit communities, running on hierarchical conservative lines and aiming self-sufficiency in the use of resources since freedom and egoism is the main source of the environmental crisis. The fourth is the 'anarchist solution', accepted by most of the Greens groups as the basis of the principle of decentralization. Emanating from the programme of German Democratic Party of 1983, it envisioned global networks of small-scale self-reliant communities, which despite their close affinity with Schumacher and Sale, differed on two counts: (a) Relations within them are meant to be libertarian, egalitarian and participatory, rather than reflect anxieties generated by the 'tragedy of the commons', and (b) their orientation is meant to be internationalist.[74] This position is shared by the (Greens, right from Bookchin [who said that the state is the source of all hierarchies], to others who regard its Weberian features problematic from a Green viewpoint; or think that the state is part of the dynamic of modernity that has caused the environmental crisis).[75]

The third wave or generation of GPT brought into being and enriched by the writings of Andrew Dobson, Graham Smith, Tim Hailwood, Mathew Hayward, Humphrey, Molly Scott Cato, Tim Jackson, John Barry, David Boyle and Andrew Simms and so on questioned the conventional view of economic growth in their light. Additional academic and policy research publications from bodies such as the New Economic Foundation and the Green New Deal Group (resulting in the *Green New Deal Report*, 2008) also joined in.

The upshot of all this was launching of GPT as an applied political theory, aiming to reanalyse the empirical 'reality of the situation' in the light of old and basic ethical principles such as justice, democracy and citizenship and assess the 'appropriate ordering and respective roles and relationships between the three basic governance/ political or order-producing institutions of human societies: the state, the market and the community'. Against conservatism and liberalism which tend to uphold 'the free and self-regulating market, that is, capitalism as the best institutional form for governing the human economy' and 'Marxist forms of socialism' inclined towards 'state-based forms of economic organization and regulation', GPT 'favours and prioritizes the community and community forms of economic, cultural and political organization and regulation'. The state and the market retain value only to the extent they bolster 'community-based forms of political and economic organization and ways of life'.[76]

To some commentators on environmentalism for whom John Barry's third wave of GPT coincides with and is analogous to the 'fourth wave' of the environmental movement,[77] it is 'no less diverse than its predecessors' and has possibly a 'broader reach, largely a product of the third wave's co-optation of and by the public, the political establishment and the business community', which has made it 'even less homogeneous' but yet allows a degree of 'convergence'. Amidst a certain level of infighting between different ecological organizations working at cross purposes, this convergence cannot be said to 'connote unity of propose' or 'signify identical paths or goals'. But it does reflect 'a bending or turning together, a rapprochement, a drawing together', a convergence 'towards a coevolutionary perspective'.[78] But here a very important question arises. Does this convergence cover 'ecoterrorism'—a convenient label to tag to all radical environmental activists groups, from 'monkey wrenching' (including such acts as pulling up survey stakes, putting sand in the crankcases of bulldozers, rendering dirt roads in wild places impassable to vehicles, cutting down billboards, and removing or destroying trap lines), ecological sabotage, ecotage, eco-defense, or 'night work'[79]—and other such activities? The sweep of the term makes one commentator uneasy since groups such as Greenpeace, which publicly professed only 'bearing witness' to environmental damage could be accused of it, and activities of groups such as Earth First!, Earth Liberation Front, Animal Liberation Front and Sea Shepherd proved easily accusable of it. Indeed, around 'the mid-1990s, the term was used to label any act of sabotage committed by these groups. It became the preferred term utilized by not only their opponents but also the mainstream news media, law enforcement and politicians',[80] and after the US Congress organized hearings on the activities of Earth Liberation Front and Animal Liberation Front[81] and NATO Advanced Research Workshop published its proceedings on it,[82] ecoterrorists remained disaffected with the state.

GREEN THEORY'S TRANSNATIONAL TURN

GPT became more transnational and cosmopolitan, for Eckersley, even in its 'second wave', although for others from the third,[83] first, through its preoccupation with environmental justice (EJ) and environmental democracy and through critical rethinking about and the transnationalizing of core political scientific concepts of justice, rights, democracy, activism, citizenship and even state that rendered them deterritorialized and global. At the heart of EJ is an 'ecologically unequal exchange' (EUE),[84] in which unanswerable social agents pass off the environmental costs of their decisions to 'third parties' who are not only innocent of them but had no knowledge of or part in these ecologically risky decisions. EUE also arises when privileged social groups or states usurp more than their 'fair share' of the environment and leave for the underprivileged burdensome and gigantic 'ecological footprints'.[85] EUE is also 'seen as a process that takes away the ability of individuals and their communities to fully function through poor health, destruction of economic livelihoods and general and widespread environmental threats'.[86] Accordingly, GPT wants to bring down ecological risks and prevent their unfair externalization and displacement simultaneously. EJ finally demands (a) recognizing and admitting the 'expanded moral community' adversely affected by ecological problems into decision-making about them, (b) allowing the larger community-at-risk access to the extent of participation and critical deliberations about them, (c) adoption of a pre-emptive approach regarding policies that may place the larger community at risk, (d) 'a fair distribution of those risks that are reflectively acceptable' through democratic procedures and arrangements accommodating the viewpoints of all affected groups and advocacy organizations and (e) redress and recompense to everyone ecologically affected.[87]

Citizenship is another deterritorialized concept that facilitated the transnational turn of GPT. Dobson complains that although 'environmental problems do not confine themselves neatly to the boundaries of nation states, citizenship is most often thought of precisely in terms of these boundaries.' This necessitates a concept of 'post-cosmopolitan' citizenship, which is not only inexpressible 'in either the dominant liberal or civic-republican form of citizenship' but transcends its environmental conception where it 'has a quite specific articulation in the guise of environmental politics' to an ecological interpretation of it. While environmental citizenship 'refers to attempts to extend the discourse and practice of rights-claiming into the environmental context', ecological citizenship talks in terms of 'non-contractual' obligations or responsibility, 'inhabits the private as well as the public sphere, works with the language of virtue and is explicitly non-territorial'.[88]

Political economy is yet another source of the transnational turn of GPT. As shown in Chapter 19, political economy is inherently international or even global, not needing GPT to be so. But after LTG arguments since 1972 and the Brundtland report of 1987 succeeding it, both of which issued transnational and international calls to action, the concept of 'GG', resulting from green economics or 'greenomics', made this transnationalism clearer. GG was accepted and propagated by the United Nations Environment Programme in 2008, the OECD in 2009 and as inclusive GG by the World Bank in 2012. The World Bank document admitted that there is no 'single GG model', and GG strategies will 'vary across countries, reflecting local contexts and preferences' but advised it for all countries, rich and poor.[89]

CONCLUSION: WHAT DOES GREENING IMPLY AND INVOLVE FOR IR THEORY?

Apart from distinguishing, semantically and terminologically, environmentalism, ecologism and Green theory/politics and showing the closeness of GEP to GP, this chapter has charted the transition from particularistic environmental anxieties in social sciences to holistic Green ideas, beyond their participatory and survivalist phases, to what Eckersley called its 'third emancipatory moment'. This has been done through explications of trademark Green ideas and their critiques (such as ecocentrism; GTV versus GTA; LTG, post-development and degrowth; decentralization and ecocommunities; GE, and the variously estimated waves of environmentalism/Green theory) from the perspective of their attacks against mainstream IR, IPE and global politics, in order to assess how these helped to launch of GPT as an applied political theory. Beyond this, this chapter has looked at the factors that have facilitated GPT's transnational turn (unbundling of sovereignty; EJ, ED, EUE; deterritorialized citizenship; PE, etc.). The summary is unsatisfying but cannot be helped because of the complexities of the issues. Now, what do these excogitations contribute to our understanding of the possibilities of the greening of international relations theory (GIRT)?

GIRT owes much to the 'Third Great Debate' or 'wave' (for us, 'fourth debate'), being self-avowedly critical, problem-centred, multidisciplinary and unabashed about its normative project. While propagating EJ, ecological citizenship and democracy and a post-liberal ecological state, Greens bring to the forefront many of the voices existing at the margins of IR, such as environmental NGOs, green consumers, ecological scientists, ecological economists, GPPs, community-based groups, indigenous people and all others who have a stake in the transformation of global patterns of 'trade, aid and debt' for the sake of more sustainable life both in the North and the South. Eckersley subdivides GIRT into two wings, a green international political economy (GRIPE) and a 'green cosmopolitan theory' (GREECOSM), both of which have their intellectual moorings in CT, especially the neo-Gramscian variant of Robert Cox and the cosmopolitan 'discourse ethics' of Jürgen Habermas. So GIRT's ideal location will be in the critical/constructivist wing of the rationalism versus constructivism debate in IRT.[90]

In the ecological critique of realism offered before, it was shown that for ecologists, realist theory, as presently constituted, cannot take a 'leap of faith' towards ecologism because of vices in its thought structure.[91] This critique applies also to neorealism and neoliberalism, both of which treat GPT as a 'new issue area', absorbable within their own theoretical frameworks. While neo or structural realists give less importance to ecological concerns as matters of low politics, best left to domestic politics, neoliberals think that regimes focusing on transborder or global environmental problems will be enough for it. Both neorealism and neoliberalism being wedded to rationalist and problem-solving ways of thinking, avoid any critical-normative orientation.

Both GRIPE and GREECOSM critique the rationalist assumptions of neorealism and neoliberalism on four counts. First, they see through the normative presuppositions and purposes of rationalist approaches, including these two and the problematic environmental assumptions and ethical values they represent. Neorealism is guilty of 'normalizing' rather than interrogating the environmentally deleterious projects of nation states and arguing from their 'anarchy problématique' (AP) that, in a Hobbesian universe, it would be rash for them to pursue environmental cooperation unless assured of absolute gains from it. Besides, in the backdrop of their restrictive conception of security, Greens urge them to take human well-being and ecosystem integrity as their primary referents in place of state security. Neoliberals are guilty of reposing their trust from their Lockean presuppositions about property in international regimes that would introduce limitations of sufficiency and spoliation that would facilitate 'rational exploitation' of nature. This is assumed to balance state-sponsored development and the integrity of nature. But for Greens, their rationalist orientation not only foregrounds an anthropocentric and instrumentalist attitude towards nature but also hides their implicit acceptance of capitalist markets and sovereign states as domain assumptions in international regime negotiations and distracts attention from social structures that impede the emergence of more thorough-going environmental initiatives. Greens also direct a tirade against the neoliberal economic globalization that was the logical culminating point of neoliberalism and search for social agents who can transform its social structure in the direction of EJ and GG.

Second, Greens have lent their weight to the critical theorists and constructivists who pillory all positivist IRT and its construction of an 'AP' (as in Waltzian neorealism) which would make the Hardinian 'tragedy of the commons' seem inevitable. For Waltz, the only changing element in the international system is the distribution of 'physical capabilities of nations or alliances' and the weight of their 'combined capabilities' to change the 'polarity' of the system,[92] NSAs and normative discourses are redundant and peripheral. Greens, however, regard this 'image' as crude and comic before the fast proliferation of environmental treaty-making in the international arena. GIRT is also equally critical of the deceptive plausibility of regimes-based environmental cooperation posited by neoliberals, who in their failure to offer a normative basis of the growth of regimes, reduce them 'to the outcome of a set of interest-based bargaining by states'. Averse to such reductionism, Greens counter that environmental regimes do symbolize moral norms irreducible to such interest or capacity calculations by states. Explaining why regimes have come up to protect endangered species, the atmosphere, the oceans, the wilderness areas and so on would be impossible without reference to national cultural values and the contribution of scientists and transnational environmental advocacy networks and 'norm entrepreneurs'. For example, quite far from Keohane, Zangl traces the formation of regimes predominantly in 'the "distribution of knowledge" within the issue area under consideration'. For Young, 'epistemic communities are coalitions of scientists and policymakers—usually transnational in scope—who share a common understanding of the nature of the problem and appropriate solutions and make a concerted effort to inject their point of view into the process of regime formation'. Even scholars who highlight their role do not normally affirm that epistemic communities are crucial to the formation of regimes. They only say that 'such communities regularly constitute an important presence in cases of success'.[93] But Haas finds these communities 'causally implicated in the form and persistence of regimes' and, to justify his point, shows that, ever since the 1970s, regimes that have proliferated, arrived only through a process of social learning, which is why 'regimes negotiated in the shadow of epistemic communities and strong international institutions' alone 'have yielded patterns of comprehensive environmental management through a process of social learning'.[94]

At a more general level, however, GRIPE scholars have remained sceptical of state-sponsored regimes because of this state-centric rationalist focus, which wrongly identifies the basic source of global ecological degradation and EUE, namely the rivalry among states themselves in place of the competitive momentum of globalizing capitalism. This optical illusion disaggregates global production and consumption in a slapdash manner and therefore misses the locales where social power, responsibility and capacity for adjustment inhere. Yet the differential impacts of global capitalism on diverse communities and ecosystems create the EUEs mentioned above, where some privileged social groups leave ampler 'ecological footprints' at the cost of others. Here, identifying the states as the biggest polluters will miss the truth that free-riding consumers and financial interests outside them may reap benefits without sharing the costs. To this extent, at least, states are not the 'most meaningful units of consumption' since their aggregate figures of gross domestic product (GDP) or net resultant pollution hide gaping 'disparities of wealth, income and risks' within them. Therefore, instead of blaming states alone, GRIPE theorists advise us to focus on monitoring and allocation of accountability to 'transnational commodity chains, from investment, resource extraction, production through to marketing, advertising, retailing, consumption and disposal'. Actually, GRIPE highlights global consumption and global investment and production with equal importance.

Third, true to their focus on social agents and structures that block the emergence of more comprehensive environmental initiatives, Greens have not only singled out counterproductive environmental regimes (like the Tropical Timber Agreement, controlled by the timber industry and states engaged in the import and export of timber) and exposed the nexus between the overlapping regimes and global governance structures but have showed that international economic regimes (as in global trade) often destabilize and stifle international environmental regimes. This has generated debates between the positions of greening WTO or setting up a parallel World Environment Regime.

Finally, GIRT practitioners have examined the parts played by non-state forms of 'deterritorialized' governance, starting from the transnational efforts of environmental NGOs (such as the Forest Stewardship Council) and extending to the private governance practices of industrial and financial corporations. The upshot of all this has been a nuanced and layered matrix of environmental governance that can 'recognize new, hybrid and/or network patterns of authority that straddle state jurisdictional boundaries or, in some cases, bypass the traditional hierarchical forms of governance typical of nation states'.[95]

Carter made an interesting point about the greening of political theory, which is also applicable to GIRT that 'the mainstream political traditions can easily produce their own ecological variants'. In the backdrop of this possible theoretical routinization of the Green perspective, he examined three alternative perspectives—eco-authoritarianism, eco-reformism and Marxism–Leninism—and found them wanting. Eco-authoritarianism essentially implied a 'benevolent despotism', but there was no guarantee 'that it will remain benevolent'. Regarding eco-reformism, the 'extent and nature of the ecological problems' faced by us 'seem to militate against a reliance on gradual tampering with the present system from within'. Concerning Marxism, apart from all other defects, shortcomings or predictive weaknesses of it, 'a theory geared to human liberation on the basis of high productivity hardly seems the most appropriate foundation for green political practice'.[96]

So like feminist IRT, GIRT will also have to create its own niche within postpositivism.

REVIEW QUESTIONS

1. Comment on the statement that GEP is the 'hyphen that joins, buckle that fastens' environmentalism/ecologism with Green theory and politics, after clarifying the differences between these terms.
2. 'The debates between environmentalism and the first wave of green thinking revolved around a series of well-known splits and binaries'. Identify and comment on them.

3. Discuss ecocentrism as a major plank of Green theory.
4. Describe the rise and decline of the 'LTG' approach as a component of Green theory.
5. Trace the development of decentralization as a major tenet of Green theory from Bookchin to Dryzek.
6. Are there differences between the normative orientations of global ecology and GPT? Argue.
7. Identify the different waves of the attacks of GPT against mainstream IR, IPE and global politics.
8. What factors facilitated the transnational turn of GPT?
9. What does the greening of IRT involve?

NOTES AND REFERENCES

1. Andrew Dobson, *Green Political Thought*, 3rd ed. (Abingdon: Routledge, 2000), 3.
2. Matthew Paterson, 'Green Politics,' in *Theories of International Relations*, eds. Scott Burchill, Andrew Linklater, Richard Devetak (London: Macmillan International Higher Education, 2013), 277.
3. Teena Gabrielson, Cheryl Hall, John M. Meyer, and David Schlosberg, eds., 'Introducing Environmental Political Theory,' in *The Oxford Handbook of Environmental Political Theory* (Oxford: Oxford University Press, 2016), 7–8.
4. Rafi Youatt, 'Interspecies,' in *The Oxford Handbook of Environmental Political Theory*, eds. Teena Gabrielson, Cheryl Hall, John M. Meyer, and David Schlosberg (Oxford: Oxford University Press, 2016), 213; also see Rafi Youatt, *Interspecies Politics: Nature, Borders, States* (Ann Arbor, MI: University of Michigan Press, 2020).
5. Robyn Eckersley, *Environmentalism and Political Theory: Toward an Ecocentric Approach* (Albany, NY: State University of New York Press, 1992), 7.
6. Neil Carter, *The Politics of the Environment: Ideas, Activism, Policy*, 3rd ed. (Cambridge: Cambridge University Press, 2018).
7. Dustin Mulvaney, *Green Politics: An A-to-Z Guide* (Thousand Oaks, CL: SAGE Publications, 2011), 132.
8. Michael Shellenberger and Ted Nordhaus, 'Death of Environmentalism: Global Warming Politics in a Post-environmental World,' 2004, available at: https://grist.org/article/doe-reprint (accessed on 09 April 2021); See also Mulvaney, *Green Politics*, 91–94.
9. Ted Nordhaus and Michael Shellenberger, *Break Through: From the Death of Environmentalism to the Politics of Possibility* (Boston, MA: Houghton Mifflin, 2007), 87–88, 98, 161, 301, 324, 7–8.
10. Carter, *The Politics of the Environment*, 1.
11. Robyn Eckersley, 'Green Theory,' in *International Relations Theories: Discipline and Diversity*, eds. Tim Dunne, Milja Kurki, and Steve Smith (Scotts Valley, CA: CreateSpace, 2017), 248.
12. See note 85 of Chapter 20.
13. For this, see M. Paterson, *Understanding Global Environmental Politics: Domination, Accumulation, Resistance* (Hampshire: Macmillan Press Ltd, 2000), and Hayley Stevenson, *Global Environmental Politics: Problems, Policy and Practice* (Cambridge: Cambridge University Press, 2017), passim.
14. Stevenson, *Global Environmental Politics*, 8.
15. Paterson, *Understanding Global Environmental Politics*, 55.

16. See Jon Burchell, *The Evolution of Green Politics: Development and Change within European Green Parties* (London: Earthscan Publications Ltd, 2002), passim, especially 9–17; Dick Richardson, 'The Green Challenge: Philosophical, Programmatic and Electoral Considerations,' in *The Green Challenge: The Development of Green Parties in Europe*, eds. Dick Richardson and Chris Rootes (London: Routledge, 1995), 8.
17. Eckersley, *Environmentalism: Ecocentric*, 7–8.
18. Eric Laferrière and Peter J. Stoett, *International Relations Theory and Ecological Thought: Towards a Synthesis* (London: Routledge, 1999), 26.
19. Eckersley, *Environmentalism and Political Theory*, 17, 26, 28, 49, 53, 60–64.
20. John Barry, *Rethinking Green Politics: Nature, Virtue and Progress* (London, Thousand Oaks, New Delhi: SAGE Publications, 1999), 7–8, and Chapters 3, 5 and 7.
21. Robyn Eckersley, 'Eco-centrism,' in *International Encyclopedia of Environmental Politics*, eds. John Barry and E. Gene Frankland (London: Routledge, 2002), 143–144.
22. Tim Hayward, 'Anthropocentrism: A Misunderstood Problem,' *Environmental Values* 6 (1997), 49–63, reproduced in *Environmentalism: Critical Concepts*, Volume 2, eds. David Pepper, Frank Webster, George Revill (London: Routledge, 2003), 43–53.
23. Robert E. Goodin, *Green Political Theory* (Cambridge: Polity Press, 1992), 15.
24. Ibid., 120.
25. Ibid., 5.
26. Ibid., 146.
27. Ibid., 171.
28. John Barry and E. Gene Frankland, 'Environmental Ethics,' in *International Encyclopedia of Environmental Politics*, Edit Page (London: Routledge, 2014), 169.
29. Robyn Eckersley, 'Greening Liberal Democracy: The Rights Discourse Revisited,' in *Democracy and Green Political Thought: Sustainability, Rights and Citizenship*, eds. Brian Doherty and Marius de Geus (London: Routledge, 1996), 217.
30. Donella H. Meadows, Dennis L. Meadows, Jørgen Randers, and William W. Behrens, *Limits to Growth, A Report for Club of Rome Project on the Predicament of Mankind*, a Potomac Associates Book (New York, NY: Universe Books, 1972), 169–170, 114 and *passim.*
31. For a good summary of these critiques, see Erhun Kula, *History of Environmental Economic Thought* (London: Routledge, 1998), 140–144.
32. Donella Hager Meadows, *Beyond the Limits: Global Collapse or a Sustainable Future* (London, Sterling, VA: Earthscan Publications, 1993); Donella H. Meadows, Dennis L. Meadows, Jørgen Randers, *Limits to Growth: The 30-year Update* (London, Sterling VA: Earthscan, 2005), xii, xviii, and *passim.*
33. Ugo Bardi, *The Limits to Growth Revisited* (New York, NY: Springer, 2011), 2.
34. Dobson, *Green Political Thought*, 13, 53–59.
35. Carter, *The Politics of the Environment*, 1–9; Frank Biermann and Eva Lövbrand, 'Encountering the "Anthropocene": Setting the Scene,' in *Anthropocene Encounters: New Directions in Green Political Thinking*, eds. Frank Biermann, Eva Lövbrand (Cambridge, NY: Cambridge University Press, 2019), 1.
36. Mark Mawhinney, *Sustainable Development: Understanding the Green Debates* (Oxford: Blackwell Science, 2002), 3.
37. Dobson, *Green Political Thought*, 60.
38. Paterson, 'Green Politics,' 283.
39. Wolfgang Sachs, ed., 'Introduction,' in *The Development Dictionary: A Guide to Knowledge as Power*, ed. Wolfgang Sachs (London; Atlantic Highlands, NJ: Zed Books, 1992), 1.
40. Wolfgang Sachs, *Planet Dialectics: Explorations in Environment and Development* (London; New York: Zed Books, 1999), 56–90, 60.
41. Richard Welford, 'From Green to Golden: The Hijacking Environmentalism,' in *Hijacking Environmentalism: Corporate Responses to Sustainable Development*, ed. Richard Welford (New York, NY: Earthscan from Routledge, 1997), 16.

42. Nick Mayhew, 'Fading to Grey: The Use and Abuse of Corporate Executives' "Representational Power",' in *Hijacking*, ed. Richard Welford (New York, NY: Earthscan, 1997), 8–86.
43. See note 34 above.
44. Wolfgang Sachs, ed., 'Global Ecology and the Shadow of Development,' reproduced in *Planet Dialectics* (Atlantic Highlands, NJ Zed Books, 1993), 27, 35.
45. Herman E. Daly, 'Toward Some Operational Principles of Sustainable Development,' *Ecological Economics* 2 (1990): 1–6, especially 1, available at: https://d1wqtxts1xzle7.cloudfront.net/32257912/herman_daly_.pdf?1383853127=&response-content-disposition=inline%3B+filename%3DCommentary_TOWARD_SOME_OPERATIONAL_PRINC.pdf&Expires=1617971637&Signature=ChriDx-RP8XnR0QeatH5ZzZ57i9ZbOikm88-c8OaQr-dzC1FMWP8wdzq8B1XIz5z95cs-xVuVuOLovks57iq8fqzqlrKJ06ad~Um-ohl2VWaCV3mxpKCXQam1BjV-vnQhmZXFttVCttjufvaM1kHnB75FSlaDp3opwuDk1pBu0Sp5XxpRz3IpcBy-I~3oxhXlTKgF~oRksZ9caPeL7qjnJFusDNFOXFPHDRumsjGf4vi7AUgoJIYVBrTVbaLGWEcQb0QuffctE-96n0yUt0ta7qeyi8luMYZT75EfzgJb9piobQKhgCnD7xtuophKE-8wa5qRCkYn5o9XDqpXHNkXTw__&Key-Pair-Id=APKAJLOHF5GGSLRBV4ZA (accessed on 9 April 2021).
46. Sachs (1993) and Daly are also cited in Paterson, 'Green Politics,' 283–284.
47. Arturo Escobar, 'Post-development as a Concept and Social Practice,' in *Exploring Post-development: Theory and Practice, Problems and Perspectives*, ed. Aram Ziai (London: Routledge, 2007), 19–21; Arturo Escobar, *Encountering Development: The Making and Unmaking of the Third World* (Princeton, NJ: Princeton University Press, 1995).
48. M. Rahnema, 'Introduction,' in *The Post-Development Reader*, eds. Majid Rahnema, Victoria Bawtree (London: Zed Books, 1997), 391; Escobar, *Encountering Development*, 215; both cited in Aram Ziai, ed., 'Development Discourse and Its Critics,' in *Exploring Post-Development: Theory and Practice, Problems and Perspectives* (London: Routledge, 2007), 4–5.
49. Paterson, 'Green Politics,' 284–285.
50. Gaia is a holistic scientific consciousness plus a new gaze for realizing that 'if we are "all creatures great and small", from bacteria to whales, part of 'Gaia', the Earth, then all of us are potentially important to her well-being.' See James Lovelock, 'What is Gaia?' website reviewed and approved by Lovelock himself, www.ecolo.org/lovelock/-17k, visited on 4 February 2007. In medical science, triage means the assignment of degrees of urgency to wounds or illnesses to decide the order of treatment of a large number of patients or casualties. For ecological triage, see Peter Kareiva and Simon A. Levin, eds., *The Importance of Species: Perspectives on Expendability and Triage* (Princeton, NJ: Princeton University Press, 2003).
51. See Carter, *Politics of the Environment*, 48, 393, 402; Giacomo D'Alisa, Federico Demaria, and Giorgos Kallis, eds., 'Introduction: Degrowth,' in *Degrowth: A Vocabulary for a New Era* (London: Routledge, 2015), 2–3, and *passim*.
52. Adolf G. Gundersen, 'Bookchin's Ecocommunity as Ecotopia: A Constructive Critique,' in *Social Ecology after Bookchin*, ed. Andrew Light (New York, NY: Guilford Press, cop. 1998), 192.
53. Murray Bookchin (under pseudonym Lewis Herber), 'The Problem of Chemicals in Food,' *Contemporary Issues* 3, no. 12 (1952): 240; Janet Biehl, ed., *The Murray Bookchin Reader* (New York, NY: Black Rose Books, 1999), 6.
54. ERT in *Post-Scarcity Anarchism* (1971), 62, 74–75, and in *Anarchy Archives*, 5, cited in ibid, 7–8.
55. See Murray Bookchin, *Post-Scarcity Anarchism* (Menlo Park, CA: Ramparts Press, 1971), 41; Murray Bookchin, *Remaking Society* (1990), 197, cited in Gundersen, 'Bookchin's Ecocommunity,' 197.
56. David Macauley, 'Evolution and Revolution: The Ecological Evolution of Kropotkin and Bookchin,' in *Social Ecology After Bookchin*, ed. Andrew Light (New York, NY: Guilford Press, 1973), 322–323.

57. John Dryzek, *Rational Ecology: Environmental and Political Economy* (Oxford: B. Blackwell, 1987), Chapter 13, cited in Paterson, 'Green Politics,' 290.
58. See Mitchell B. Rambler, ed., 'Introduction,' in *Global Ecology: Towards a Science of the Biosphere* (Boston, MA: Academic Press, 1989), ix.
59. See John Harte, *The Green Fuse: An Ecological Odyssey* (Berkeley: University of California Press, 1993), xi–xii, 146, *passim*.
60. Sven Erik Jørgensen, ed., 'Preface,' in *Global Ecology* (Amsterdam: Academic Press, 2010), 1.
61. W. Sachs, *Global Ecology: A New Arena of Political Conflict* (London: Zed Books, 1993), cited in Paterson, 'Green Politics,' 280–281.
62. Sachs, *Planet Dialectics*, 27, 36, 38.
63. Pratap Chatterjee and Matthias Finger, *The Earth Brokers: Power, Politics and World Development* (London: Routledge, 1994), 173.
64. Sachs, *Planet Dialectics*, 47–56.
65. See for details, Paterson, 'Green Politics,' 280.
66. *The Ecologist* (1993), 5, 7, 9, 13, 190–191, cited in Paterson, 'Green Politics,' 290–291.
67. Rachel Carson, *Silent Spring* (Boston, MA: Houghton Mifflin, 1962); Barry Commoner, *The Closing Circle: Nature, Man and Technology* (New York, NY: Alfred A. Knopf, 1971); Donella eta al., *Limits to Growth*; cited in Mathew Humphrey, 'Green Political Theory,' in *Encyclopedia of Political Theory*, ed. Mark Bevir (Los Angeles, London, New Delhi: SAGE Publications, 2010), 573.
68. John Barry, 'Green Political Theory,' in *Political Ideologies: An Introduction*, 4th ed., eds. Vincent Geoghegan and Rick Wilford (London: Routledge, 2014), 157.
69. Eckersley, 'Green Theory,' 250–251.
70. Eckersley, *Environmentalism and Political Theory*, 15–16, 144, 174–178.
71. Robyn Eckersley, *The Green State: Rethinking Democracy and Sovereignty* (Cambridge, MA, London: The MIT Press, 2004), 8, 13, 86, 92, 95, 96, 100, 101–103, 110; Marcel L. J. Wissenburg, *Green Liberalism: The Free and Green Society* (London: UCL Press, 1998), 166, cited in ibid., 103. Also see Wissenburg, *Green Liberalism*, 126–136, 166–173, 186–191.
72. Eckersley, *Green State*, 203.
73. Karen T Litfin, ed., 'The Greening of Sovereignty: An Introduction,' in *The Greening of Sovereignty in World Politics* (Cambridge, MA: MIT Press, 1998), 2, 5, 16, 81.
74. E. F. Schumacher, *Small is Beautiful: A Study of Economics as If People Mattered* (London: Blond & Briggs, 1973); Kirkpatrick Sale, *Human Scale* (New York, NY: Coward, McCann & Geoghegan, 1980), passim.
75. Paterson, 'Green Politics,' 288–289.
76. All of them cited in Barry, 'Green Political Theory,' 157–159.
77. See Leslie Paul Thiele, *Environmentalism for a New Millennium: The Challenge of Coevolution* (New York, NY, and Oxford: Oxford University Press, 1999), 30–31.
78. Ibid.
79. Dave Foreman, *Confessions of an Eco-Warrior* (New York, NY: Crown Publishers, 1991), passim, especially Chapters 12–15.
80. Gerry Nagtzaam, *From Environmental Action to Ecoterrorism? Towards a Process Theory of Environmental and Animal Rights Oriented Political Violence* (Cheltenham, Northampton: Edward Elgar, 2017), 9–12. For instances of FBI-sponsored definition of it and its academic adoption, see Lawrence E. Likar, *Eco-Warriors, Nihilistic Terrorists, and the Environment* (Santa Barbara, CA: Praeger, 2011), 4. For stress on its criminality, see Don Liddick, *Eco-terrorism: Radical Environmental and Animal Liberation Movements* (Westport, CN: Praeger, 2006), 1–6.
81. For example, *Eco-terrorism Specifically Examining the Earth Liberation Front and the Animal Liberation Front: Hearing before the Committee on Environment and Public Works*, United States Senate, One Hundred Ninth Congress, First Session, May 18, 2005, Volume 4 (Washington, D.C., WA: U.S. Government Printing Office, 2007).

82. Hami Alpas, Simon M. Berkowicz, and Irina Ermakova, eds., *Environmental Security and Ecoterrorism* (Dordrecht: Springer, 2011).
83. From the list of scholars, she cites, it is Barry's third GPT wave and Thiele's fourth wave of environmentalism. Eckersley, 'Green Theory,' 252.
84. See R. Scott Frey, Paul K. Gellert, and Harry F. Dahms, eds., *Ecologically Unequal Exchange: Environmental Injustice in Comparative and Historical Perspective* (Cham: Palgrave Macmillan Imprint, 2019).
85. M. Wackernagel and W. Rees, *Our Ecological Footprint: Reducing Human Impact on the Earth* (Gabriola Island: New Society Publishers, 1996), cited by Eckersley, 'Green Theory,' 252.
86. David Schlosberg, *Defining Environmental Justice: Theories, Movements, and Nature* (Oxford: Oxford University Press, 2009), 80.
87. Eckersley, 'Green Theory,' 252–253.
88. Dobson, *Citizenship*, 5, 82, 89.
89. Diego A. Vazquez-Brust and Joseph Sarkis, eds., 'Green Growth: Managing the Transition to Sustainable Economies,' in *Green Growth: Managing the Transition to a Sustainable Economy: Learning By Doing in East Asia and Europe* (Dordrecht: Springer, 2012); World Bank, *Inclusive Green Growth: The Pathway to Sustainable Development* (Washington D.C., WA: The World Bank, 2012), xii, 1.
90. This section largely follows Eckersley, 'Green Theory,' 256–258, except for independent citations.
91. See for details notes 51 and 52 of Chapter 7.
92. Hedley Bull, Herbert Butterfield, and Kenneth Waltz, *Theory of International Politics*, 15, 131.
93. Bernhard Zangl, 'Regime Theory,' in *Theories of International Relations*, eds. Siegfried Schieder, Manuela Spindler (London: Routledge, 2014), 82–84; Oran R. Young, *International Governance: Protecting the Environment in a Stateless Society*, (Ithaca, NY, and London: Cornell University Press, 1994), 96.
94. Peter M. Haas, *Epistemic Communities*, 17, 175.
95. Eckersley, 'Green Theory,' 256–258.
96. Alan B. Carter, *A Radical Green Political Theory* (London: Routledge, 1999), 24–62.

CHAPTER

22

Globalization and International Relations Theory

CHAPTER OUTLINE

INTRODUCTION

As a concept, globalization's extreme popularity competes with its imprecision and contestation, for which both 'sceptics' and 'optimists' about globalization are responsible. In the times after the demise of the USSR and the collapse of Bolshevism, globalization has shoved 'postmodernism' aside as 'the social scientific master trend of a new era'.[1] As 'a fad word fast turning into shibboleth, a magic incantation, a pass key meant to unlock the gates to all present and future mysteries', it shares the fate of all 'vogue words'. The 'more experiences they pretend to make transparent, the more they themselves become opaque'.[2] Giving a mixed judgement, Held et al. call it 'the cliché of our times: the big idea which encompasses everything from global financial markets to the Internet', even as clichés 'often capture elements of the lived experience of an epoch'.[3] To Strange, it signifies 'anything from the Internet to a hamburger' and 'a polite euphemism for the continuing Americanisation of consumer tastes and cultural practices'.[4] Some regard it as a legitimizing cover or ideology for some special interests. Schirato and Webb view it as a 'discursive regime, a kind of machine that eats up anyone and anything in its path', and also as 'a set of texts, ideas, goals, values, narratives, dispositions and prohibitions, a veritable template for ordering and "evaluating" activities, which is "filled in" or inflected with the interests of whoever can access it'.[5] So Schäfer thinks it necessary to 'disentangle the current mix-up between American culture and globalization...The USA may be the avant-garde of globalization today, but Americanization happens to a cultural "other", whereas globalization happens to all cultural others *and* to America itself'.[6]

This chapter is not about globalization per se: asking 'what is it', 'when was it' or 'how much of it is there', but about if, or to what extent, globalization has posed a serious challenge to some defining assumptions of IR theory, and about how areas, theories and even paradigms of IRT have reacted to and been affected by this challenge. But this creates a problem of priority: to start with definitions of globalization first, and then explore how different theories or areas of IRT have *faced* globalization; or to first understand what is at stake for IRT in the globalization debate and then clarify for ourselves how each or all of them have faced what they *mean* by globalization? Many scholars take the first or second option. But I take the third path: first that of defining globalization properly and then assessing the divergent takes on globalization of different schools of IRT in its light, showing how they explain the driving forces and dynamics of globalization through their takes or stakes, measuring the relevance of their claims and propositions against the present 'empirics' of globalization and finally giving a verdict on the actual challenge posed by globalization for IRT.

DEFINING GLOBALIZATION ADEQUATELY

Even among those scholars who accept globalization as a material reality, rather than a pseudonym for Americanization, some underscore singular dimensions or aspects of it and proffer partial definitions. Robins's economistic definition is of 'a more advanced stage' of the 'economic and imperial expansionism of the great powers' as part of the development of the world economy. Langhorne's technology-oriented definition sees it as 'the latest stage in a long accumulation of technological advance' which has enabled human beings to 'conduct their affairs across the world, without reference to nationality, government authority, time of day or physical environment'. Bauman's spatially temporally minded definition of it is as 'time–space compression'.[7] Coupling holistic awareness with space shrinkage, Robertson calls it 'compression of the world and intensification of its consciousness as a whole'.[8] A universally acceptable definition being unachievable, some think globalization is to be studied 'within distinct disciplinary settings'. But keeping in mind that in terms of the division of the social sciences on the basis of 'analytic' categories (comprising central organizing ideas, like power for political science) and concrete, spatial categories (such as individual, group, national society and international society), the location of IR would be towards the spatial-concrete end of the analytic-concrete continuum,[9] the definition of globalization in IRT should ideally combine both space (the concrete slot of international society) and power. One such definition would be as 'broadly…the process whereby power is located in global social formations and expressed through global networks rather than through territorially based states'.[10] Another would be as 'a process (or set of processes) that embodies a transformation in the spatial organization of social relations and transactions, generating trans-continental or inter-regional flows and networks of activity, interaction and power'.[11] In two IR books (where they are quoted), these are taken to be initially adequate decisions. But are they really?

To assess the worth of the definitions given above, particularly the last two, I will start with the 'potential indices of globalization' listed by Hay as part of its semantics to show how it signifies different things to scholars talking about it (Box 22.1).[12]

Now Hay himself doubts that quite a few of these indices are exclusive to globalization. The existence and sometimes even the magnitude of cross-border flows listed in the first index are 'by no means unprecedented historically'. So what transformations of their scale and scope entitled them to be regarded as indicators of globalization? When exactly did 'cross-border transmission of infection' turn global, if not 'when the Crusaders took their West European viruses to the Holy Lands', or Christopher Columbus's crew transported their pathogens to North America? Should we reserve the term for the 'proliferation of global pandemics'

BOX 22.1
Inadequate Indices of Globalization for Hay

- Cross-border flows of goods, investment, information, holiday makers, migrant workers, asylum seekers, environmental pollutants, infectious agents and so on
- Transnational processes of political deliberation and decision-making
- Interdependence between states
- The development of a world-system whose dynamics and developmental trajectory are not reducible to the simple product of the units (states) which comprise it
- The proliferation of problems for which global solutions are required
- The development of institutions charged with responsibility for fashioning genuinely global public policy

Source: Adapted from Colin Hay, 'International Relations Theory and Globalization', in Dunne et al, International Relations Theories, 274.

resulting from the present era of mass public transportation? In Hay's support, we can point how the bacterium causing the so-called Black Death, originated in the 1330s, somewhere in East or Central Asia, to quickly travel to all over Asia, Europe and North Africa, and then in less than two decades reach the shores of the Atlantic Ocean, killing millions of people in Eurasia, England, Italy and so on. Smallpox virus was taken by an African slave sailing from Cuba to Mexico on 5 March 1520 to decimate the population of Mexico, before entering the gates of the Aztec capital Tenochtitlan and kill millions and millions there. Flu, tuberculosis and syphilis pathogens were taken by Captain James Cook and his men to completely isolated Hawaii in January 1778. Later, explorers added typhoid and smallpox. A particularly lethal variant of the flu, nicknamed the Spanish Flu, travelled from Northern France in January 1918 via war preparations to infect men and then travel to India, the USA, Middle East, Argentina, Malaya, Congo, island of Tahiti, Samoa and so on. It killed between 50 and 100 million people in less than a year. Of course, now these viruses and pathogens can travel from Congo to Tahiti or even far in less than 24 hours. Should we relate globalization to it?[13]

After presenting a motley assemblage of themes linked to the above indices, often proffered by the same author, making it hugely difficult to single out any factor that could be presented as *the* factor instantiating globalization, Hay identifies from the globalization literature four oppositional parings consisting of globalization's own and 'others'. These are as follows:

1. *National versus global:* Concerning the level at which the centre of gravity of the world system is presumed to inhere and the basic character of the cultures, economics and politics constituting the system.
2. *International versus global:* Involving the character of the supranational decision-making processes and particularly the trans instead of international form of them.
3. *Regionalization versus globalization:* Relating to the precise geographical scope and character of any particular process of integration.
4. *Protectionism/isolationism versus globalization/internationalism:* Referring to the internal or external orientation of domestic-level policymaking.[14]

While the first pairing needs little elucidation, the second emerges from the first but is still a little different, in that stress is less on the constituent units of the international system and more on the locus of decision-making. The third brings in issues that we have described in Chapter 13B while discussing the exogenous perspectives on regionalism in relation to globalization.[15] The fourth pairing reintroduces the old debate between mercantilism and liberalism, discussed in Chapter 19,[16] in the new context of globalization. It is difficult to say whether these pairings reflect the multidimensionality of the concept as Hay does or its conceptual fuzziness. To undo this, we have to extricate globalization from what Scholte says its 'redundant concepts', four of which are according to him: internationalization, liberalization, universalization and westernization. It will be evident that the first of Hay's four indices is disguised internationalization, which according to Scholte refers to 'a growth of transactions and interdependence between countries', depicting 'a more global world is one where more messages, ideas, merchandize, money, pollutants and people cross borders between national territorial units'. Many scholars (such as Hirst and

Thompson) take globalization in this sense of an intense form of internationalization. Others who attempted to measure globalization quantitatively in terms of current account transactions as a proportion of GDP (like Rodrik) or who calculated amounts of cross-border transactions between countries on the basis of scores related to FDI, international travel, membership in international organizations, international telephone traffic and so on, that too calculated on a territorial basis, to ascertain the degree of globalization of one country relative to others (Kearney), also equate the two. The globalization-as-internationalization route is, however, objectionable not just because it imposes without explaining new vocabulary on us, but also because it perniciously implies that 'world social relations are—and can only be—organized in terms of country units, state governments and national communities' and tempts us to 'ignore, marginalize and silence other modes of organization, governance and identity that exist and are highly valued by, for example, indigenous peoples, regionalists and various kinds of cosmopolitans'.[17]

The equation with liberalization reduces globalization to 'a process of removing officially imposed constraints on movements and resources between countries in order to form an "open" and "borderless" world economy', helped by the accelerated reduction or abolition of 'regulatory measures like trade barriers, foreign-exchange restrictions, capital controls and visa requirements'. But confusing the discourse on globalization with a 'debate about contemporary neoliberalist macroeconomic policies' has first, at the practical level, subjected the concept to most of the 'anti-globalization' protests around the world. Some pillory '*neoliberalist* globalization rather than globalization per se' and take 'a rejectionist, mercantilist position' that upholds '"de-globalization" to a world of autarkic regional, national or local economies', while most others propose alternative approaches such as 'counter-globalizations', 'globalization from below'[18] and 'alter globalizations'[19] that can better accommodate values of human security, social justice, democracy and so on. Second, conceptually, the language of globalization does not need to rehash the arguments for and against laissez-faire economics, since the panegyrics for free-market economics over several centuries did not require any suggestion about globalization.

To Scholte, confusion of globalization with universalization depicts 'a process of dispersing various objects and experiences to people at all inhabited parts of the earth', taking the word 'global' as synonymous with 'worldwide' or 'everywhere' and making globalization subsume 'the Georgian calendar, tobacco, business suits, the state, curry dinners, bungalows, school curricula, Barbie dolls, shotguns and so on'. Globalization as universalization supposedly implies 'standardization and homogenization', leading to 'worldwide cultural, legal and political convergence', so that some economists measure it in the extent to which specific goods and services sell at same prices across countries. Conceding that some remarkable worldwide dispersion of commodities, services and even ideas, together with substantial construction, are seen in recent times, Scholte contends that universalization has for long been studied in world history and has for Gamble characterized even our 'global prehistory'; 'world religions' have travelled continents and transoceanic trade has dispersed goods throughout the world for a millennium, all without having to invoke the concept of globalization. Besides, this misguided equation unnecessarily strengthens cultural protectionists, who while decrying globalization are complaining against one of its outcomes, and Scholte has shown later in his book that globalization can be pursued in ways that 'promote cultural diversity, revival and innovation'.

Equation of globalization with Westernization, where social structures of Western/European modernity (including capitalism, industrialism, rationalism, urbanism, individualism and so on) cover 'all of humanity, in the process destroying pre-existent cultures and local autonomy', presents it as pervasive colonization; Americanization; 'Westoxification'; 'a hegemonic discourse, an ideology of supposed progress that masks far-reaching subordination by the West of the rest' and so on. Irrefutably, the contemporary pervasive globalization has roots in forces of modernity (manifest in rationalist knowledge, capitalist production, bureaucratic governance and so on, as per Giddens). These have frequently imprinted patterns of modern, Western social relations more widely and deeply across the globe with or without violent impositions meriting description as imperialism; have involved replication of modes of governance institutions there; enlisted the aid of Western firms, mass media, academia, civil social organizations and so on, as promoters of current globalization. But, true to Robertson, it would not be proper to ignore the rationality that underlies modernity and the spread of early global consciousness it is traceable to. Moreover, before conflating Westernization and globalization, it should be remembered that, as Pettman argues, globalization can theoretically take other turns, such as Buddhist, Confucian, Islamic or possible future postmodern globalizations and historically Westernization. Modernization and colonization possess a far longer history than contemporary intense globalization, and global modernity is in some ways distinctive from extent Western modernity, being neither coeval nor coterminous.

Tracing his way forward, away from these redundant equations, Scholte introduces a fifth notion that would capture better the 'historically relatively new conditions', one that conceives globalization as 'the spread of transplanetary—and in recent times also more particularly supraterritorial—connections between people'. Like some Internet chat room and some forms of contagion, a global as transplanetary social relation is one which can connect persons in all possible inhabited spaces on earth by eliminating nearly all impediments to such transworld social contacts, enabling people to engage with co-inhabitants of the planet physically, legally, linguistically, culturally and psychologically, wherever they are with Internet connectivity. Here, the impact of the shift in the nature of social space is important. Although even transplanetary people-to-people contacts are not wholly a matter of the last few decades, contemporary transplanetary links are far denser than those of previous eras, involving many more people, much more extensiveness, intensiveness, volume and areas. But far more than the 'quantity, frequency, scope, density and depth' of these links, contemporary global connectivity and the globalization caused by it is characterized by 'a large-scale spread of supraterritoriality'. It transcends the territorial geography that was differentially represented by the four earlier misnomers for globalization through two of its qualitative characteristics: *transworld simultaneity* (extension 'anywhere across the planet at the same time') and *transworld instantaneity* (movability 'anywhere on the planet in no time'). Scholte shows in a later chapter that 'most of the rise of this supraterritoriality is recent'.[20]

For Scholte, the new 'globality' finds manifestations in communications; transplanetary movement of people; production processes involving global factories, commodity chains and so on; consumption of commodities and brands; global money and finance, organizations facilitating all these; globalized military activities, social ecology, health management; transworld law and rules; and finally, social relations facilitated by global consciousness. But he also adds six qualifiers about the assumed free rein of globality. First, the growth of transplanetary and supraterritorial connectivity does not at all imply that territorial space has become redundant and methodological territorialism should be substituted by globalism which urges exclusive focus on transplanetary relations, completely ignoring the importance of territorial spaces. For, contrary to claims by some indiscriminate globalists of a 'borderless world', territorial arrangements, governance mechanisms, ecology and identities continue to exert powerful pressures on supraterritoriality even today. There is little if any territoriality subsisting independently of supraterritoriality. Second, although 'globality is a discrete concept, it is not a discrete concrete condition'. While differentiation of multiple spheres of social spaces is productive analytically, it does not make the global 'a domain unto itself', separable from the regional, provincial layers of social space. For, the social space is not a loose potpourri of 'discrete realms', being a site of interrelation of spheres, as is the government in a country, where 'supranational, national and subnational spaces converge'. So rather than succumbing to a reified, ontological distinction between the national and the international, the 'internal' and the 'domestic', new studies of globalization should ponder over how the 'inside' and outside of countries are intertwined and infected by it. Third, this informed awareness of the interrelation of dimensions of social space should dissuade observers from raising false binaries between the global and the local, or the old domestic and international. Fourth, cultural destruction and homogenization do happen under globalization but are not 'intrinsic' to it, transplanetary and supraterritorial relations being able to digest considerable cultural heterogeneity. Fifth, while globality as transworld simultaneity can link people anywhere on the planet, 'it does not follow that it connects people *everywhere*, or everywhere to the same degree'. Finally, globalization is not politically neutral. Even the seemingly innocuous aspect of technical harmonization breeds power struggles, as manifested in the 19th-century fight between Britain and France over the passage of the prime meridian through their state capitals and the current competition between different computer operating systems offering differing degrees of initiative and control to their users. All other aspects of globalization entail power relations and conflicts among individuals, households, associations, firms, governance organizations and social structures (including age groups, civilizations, classes, genders, races, people possessing different sexual orientations and so on), just because like all other historical processes, globalization benefits some people and harms others. So because it involves 'contests between different interests and competing values', the 'spread of globality...cannot but be normatively laden and politically charged'.[21]

IRT'S STAKE IN THE GLOBALIZATION DEBATE: FROM THE PERSPECTIVES OF THE STATE, MARKET, STRUCTURE, CLASS AND CAPITAL, CONSCIOUSNESS, DISCOURSE AND POWER/KNOWLEDGE, AND GENDER

Would one perhaps vainly search for such a nuanced take on globalization in IRT? Hay says that more than in other areas or subfields of social analysis, the globalization debate in IRT is conducted in negative rather than positive terms.[22] To test the veracity of his comment, we can assess the perspectives of the different theories on each of the five bulleted points:

- The central issue for investigation in respect of globalization
- The material and/or ideational generators of global social relations
- The key actors(s) that propelled globalization
- The principal structure(s) that have produced globalization
- The core dynamic(s) of history that have driven globalization[23]

Realism/Neorealism

Sure to lose most from the concept and its claims, different variants of realism most virulently disparage the extent, qualitative novelty and the redefining features of globalization. According to one variant, HST, globalization is explicable as the way the dominant state of the time, the USA in recent history, has asserted its sway and has simultaneously designed 'an environment of controlled competition among states'. So the huge growth of transplanetary connectivity that passes for globalization exists so long as it subserves its national interests and power. In another brand of realism, globalization is best seen as a 'strategy in the contest for power between several major states in contemporary world politics', and advanced transplanetary connectivity is the outcome of the efforts by the governments of Britain, China, France, Japan, the USA and other major powers to exploit the potentials of global political and economic relations to enhance their power positions.[24] For offensive realism, even the present significant force of economic globalization in world politics would not significantly affect the pursuit of security by great powers. Mearsheimer sees no essential difference between the nature and extent of international commerce in today's global economy and that of the pre-1914 era. So if extensive international commerce could not prevent the First World War, then 'a highly interdependent world economy does not make great-power war more or less likely'. The current wave of economic globalization offers no hope that it will act as a great constraint on the severity of conflict among great powers in the coming years.[25]

Liberalism

Opposed to the realist view of globalization as a state-led process, the liberalist explanation, as a market-led extension of modernization, depends on fulfilment of two requirements: (a) technological advances, specifically in the areas of production, transportation, communications, information processing and so on to facilitate transplanetary connectivity physically; and (b) presence of suitable financial, legal, institutional, organizational mechanisms to help modern markets and liberal democracy spread globally. Accordingly, liberalists probe issues such as the impact of various state policies on the promotion or hamstringing of globalization; the role of regional institutions as facilitators or impediments; the importance of global governance structures supporting global markets and global human rights; the contribution of market self-regulation in the furtherance of globalization; and the need for constructing global firms and civil society organizations for facilitating effective global action.

Predictably for such concerns, liberalist accounts of globalization have sprung from the disciplines of business studies, economics, IPE, law and political science. Unlike accounts of it from other approaches, such as Marxism, constructivism, postmodernism and feminism, the liberalist provenance of globalization has often disguised itself as 'common sense' and fared well as the main orthodox account of globalization, with unflinching support from circles of power and underwriting by the neoliberals' prescription for globalization.[26]

Realism Liberalism Debate

Unsurprisingly, the globalization debate in IRT has raged most raucously between realism and neo or structural realism and neoliberalism or cosmopolitanism, even though other theoretical perspectives such as feminism, constructivism, CT and post-structuralism too have some stake in it. For, the latter are not ontologically rooted in the centrality or non-centrality of states, and each of them 'can be brought to bear on the world system independently of its degree of globalization; each has relevance and critical purchase in both a state-centric and non-state-centric world alike'; and each perspective contains, among its advocates, globalists and sceptics'.

But for neoliberalism and cosmopolitanism, among which the positive stake in globalization is the highest, all the fundamental premises and articles of faith and neo or structural realism have been rendered anachronistic by the following factors:

1. The sovereignty and the policymaking capacity of the nation state have been weakened considerably by the rapid growth of cross-border flows beyond the bounds of the state.
2. The proliferation of issues related with globalization (such as global climate change and global pandemics) has exposed the frailty of nation states.
3. Emergence of genuinely transnational processes, networks and institutions of global governance, state sponsored or not, stemming from such challenges has transformed the nature of world politics so much as to presage the redundancy of nation states.
4. The resultant multi-layered and multilevel political landscape is interspersed with a rather diverse set of potentially consequential actors among which the states no longer overshadow others.
5. The transnational arena of political deliberations that has ensued from these transformations has made the 'low politics', ignored by realism, increasingly more salient.
6. The mobility of capital resulting from economic globalization has not only enabled it to evade national jurisdictions but has augmented its power vis-à-vis the state.
7. The joint impact of these globalization-induced challenges presages the demise of both and the state centrality linked with it.

Hay thinks the key point in this list of challenges, namely the supposedly rapidly decreasing sovereignty and the policymaking capacity of the nation state, is wholly untenable for forgetting that 'the politics of globalization is bound up with the complex trade-off between sovereignty and the policymaking capacity. We simply cannot conflate the two'.[27] Here, Hay would probably find support from Krasner, who points out that observers and analysts anxious about 'state sovereignty being eroded by globalization...are fundamentally concerned with questions of control, not authority. The inability to regulate the flow of goods, persons, pollutants, diseases and ideas across territorial boundaries has been described as a loss of sovereignty'. To make his point, Krasner differentiates 'interdependence sovereignty' from 'domestic sovereignty'. While the loss of interdependence sovereignty does not necessarily impinge on domestic sovereignty, 'understood as the organization of authoritative decision-making', it does undermine it, 'comprehended simply as loss of control'. For, it 'is nowhere near...self-evident...that the international economy at the end of the 20th century has reached unprecedented levels of openness which are placing new and unique strains on states'. Compared to present times, international capital markets were more open before the First World War. International trade grew during the last half of the 19th century before a downslide from the first to the fifth decades of the 20th century and then an upswing in the 1950s benefiting most but not all states. International labour movements too were more open in the 19th century. But national responses to these changing international flows widely varied.[28] Krasner's point is substantiated by Stubbs's empirical findings about globalization's 'positive effects on the political sovereignty of the institutional states of Southeast Asia's "miracle economies" during the boom times', though not during others. This makes him say that 'globalization is a complicated process that does not always have the single effect of undermining or transforming or bolstering state sovereignty but rather can be responsible for producing each of these effects at different points in time'.[29] Krasner himself states the problem even more candidly:

> Interdependence sovereignty, or the lack thereof, is not practically or logically related to international legal or Westphalian sovereignty. A state can be recognized as a juridical equal by other states and still be unable to control movements across its own borders...Unregulated transborder movements do not imply that a state is subject to external structures of authority...Rulers can lose control of transborder flows and still be recognized and be able to exclude external actors.[30]

For Hay, reduction of the globalization debate in IRT to a liberal critique of the realist/neorealist ontology and to the trading of bigoted denial of globalization by and over-zealous defence of the ubiquity of globalization by neoliberals and cosmopolitanists is unfortunate. For, neither reaction captures the fluidity of the world system today, none of these opposing perspectives being more than simplifications of a complex world political reality, some or other of whose aspects they foreground. So the world system today cannot be presumed to demolish the analytical assumptions on which any of the following eight contending theories are predicated. We take up the epistemological worth of neorealist charges against pervasiveness of globalization first.

1. Not being 'unfalsifiable' and its ascendancy or decline having had little truck with 'conceptual or empirical advances' or the 'changing character of the world system', there is little guarantee that even if sufficient empirical proofs of the pervasiveness of globalization are adduced, these will prove that neorealism was not valid before nor that its contemporary challengers are ipso facto vindicated. Oppositely, if it is proven that realist/neorealist assumptions have

not been rendered obsolescent by the processes of globalization till now, this would not logically imply that it would provide the most appropriate lens to view the proclivities of globalization, since empirical evidence cannot settle ontological divergences or theoretical preferences of this kind.

2. Neorealism can restate itself or bring to the fore some formerly less salient features to create better fit with intractable realities. In terms of the realist perspective, globalization should appear to be transforming the processes of IR by questioning its power and security dimensions since by its very disposition, globalization attracts attention to the economic and technological sides of international life and to the profound changes at the levels of culture and identity. In all such cases, the accent on the global underscores the integrative aspects of international life more than the conflictual aspects and renders interstate power politics anachronistic. But in a nuanced and accommodative exchange between Barry Buzan (softly neorealist) and David Held (cosmopolitanist), Buzan accepts these contentions of globalists avowedly destabilizing realism: (a) transnational flows diminish the ease with which nation states could be glibly be described as sovereign; (b) the importance of transnational processes of governance is increasing, even if sometimes facilitated and sponsored by nation states; (c) the salience of NSAs and the low politics they represent relative to high politics are getting heightened, particularly in more interdependent parts of the world-system; and (d) world politics is experiencing a proliferation of new issues that the nation states were never comfortable enough dealing with and the constraints emanating from economic globalization have gravely harmed the domestic policymaking autonomy of nation states. But he still vindicates a kind of realism, even if qualified and moderated, on the following four planks.
   - Basically, globalization is an economic phenomenon whose manifestations are still limited to certain low-political areas never foregrounded by realism.
   - While the importance and prestige of such domains are augmented, a large chunk of international politics has continued to be realist.
   - States have quite often been found to be effectively pooling their sovereignty, under certain conditions, for designing mechanisms of transnational governance, in isolation from or parallel to the process of economic globalization.
   - However, neither such attempts at statist transnationalism nor economic globalization are countenanced by the majority of states, due to which the biggest chunk of international politics that defies globalization remains statist.

While accommodating some charges and claims from cosmopolitanists and (neo)liberals (like Nye or Keohane), this restated summation of economic globalization by Buzan, to strengthen its ground, cannot hide that these concessions too, despite their apparent generosity, 'rest on a series of assumptions about economic globalization... which are simply not tested empirically', and 'for many so-called "sceptics" evidence of the kind of economic globalization that he seems to present here is rather less forthcoming than one may think'.[31] But before sifting such evidence, let us, secondly, test the case of neoliberalism for the pervasiveness of globalization.

Besides presenting globalization as an example of the 'intensification of the pluralist challenge' in IR, neoliberalism defends a 'myth' of 'the end of history', argued by Francis Fukuyama in a 1989 essay of the same name, and his 1992 book, *The End of History and the Last Man*. In course of her critique of Fukuyama's contentions from the perspective of the 'critical IR theory', Cynthia Weber first says that in the transformation of 'classical liberal principles' into 'neoliberal expressions of globalization', three processes supposedly beneficial for the humankind are seen to occur 'simultaneously', namely economic globalization, driven mainly by free trade; political democratization resulting in transfer of power to the people; and cultural universalization (whether 'Americanization of the globe' or not). To expose the vacuity of Fukuyama's myth of 'the end of history' that turns liberalism into the global stage on which international politics in the era of 'globalization' unfurls, Weber traces the ways in which Fukuyama presents liberalism as a complete, fully evolved ideology with no actually or even potentially successful credible external ideological challengers (such as fascism, communism, religious fundamentalism or nationalism). She shows that to achieve his purpose, Fukuyama 'deflects our attention away from liberalism's own internal contradiction—the contradiction between its creation of boundless desires within individuals for the good life and its failure to fully satisfy or control these desires'. She also shows that it is only through exchanging or swapping 'economic consumption' with personal satisfaction that 'liberalism defers and displaces individual encounters with what Fukuyama admits is "the empty core of liberalism"'. She illustrates her point through her incisive analysis of a famous 1998 film, *The Truman Show* (about a television programme called *The Truman Show*) in which the hero (Truman Burbank) did not initially *know* that he was all through spending his life inside a huge television show, its episodes watched by others. But ultimately, he found for himself through some discordant and inexplicable events, and the resultant discomfiture of his (non-material) desires, that he must break out of its 'boring daily routines' to start living 'a risky, purposeful life that calls for "daring, courage, imagination and idealism"'. Weber refutes Fukuyama's depiction of post-historical politics through this following innovative analogy of the film and the purchase from it in understanding contemporary reality.

1. For Fukuyama, the 'de-ideological' era of post-history will be one of tedious 'economic calculation, the endless solving of technological problems, environmental concerns and the satisfaction of sophisticated consumer demands', which fills even Fukuyama himself with a deep nostalgia 'for the time when history existed', shared by the 'post-historical viewers' of the television show in the film. After Truman exited history (i.e., the show), viewers were left with nothing to celebrate their constructed history, with 'nowhere to project their desires into history'. They hear the director saying that this is precisely the reason why the show was 'staged in the first place' and had 'an audience growing ever since—because it is real. And that means there is no substitute for *The Truman Show*'.
2. But what *The Truman Show* analogizes and informs us is that substitutions of history by the global show of the final triumph of capitalist globalization via liberalism is simultaneously 'necessary' but 'limited'; and what it signifies for IR in an age of globalization is that those bent on studying (neo)liberalism in the post-Cold-War era should desist from considering what alternative

ideologies might re-emerge to challenge it and focus instead on how in the era of globalization, (neo)liberalism would divert our attention to its 'empty core' and regulate our desires so deftly that it will continue to 'escape our notice'.

3. So in the demonstrations against WTO in Seattle in 1999, protestors from all over the world (developed North as well as underdeveloped South) protested not only how capitalism's promise of the good life for some (in the North) comes at the expense of others (in the South), but even for those (in the North) who are supposedly benefited, how the desire for 'total freedom' has been short changed into economic one. 'While the former point of protest is an old Marxist complaint, the latter one requires no alternative ideological challenge to bring it into focus.'[32]

Weber's last point is in spite of its shortcomings vindicated, since in every major meeting of the IMF, World Bank, WTO and so on, protests against globalization have increased in intensity and spread. Examples are as follows:

- The 26th G8 summit in Okinawa, Japan in 2000, where protesters included women's rights advocates, anti-debt campaigners demanding that G8 countries fulfil their promises of debt relief for the world's poorest countries
- Greenpeace sailing its Rainbow Warriors into the exclusion zone to protest G8 logging policies
- Ten thousand people led by the South Korean Confederation of Trade Unions agitating at the Asia Europe Summit in November 2000
- A carnival of civil society groups present at the 27th G8 summit in Genoa, where the protestors ranged from 'Greek communist students, Spanish Catholic boy scouts, German environmentalists, South American indigenous rights groups, Dutch anarchists and many more'

As a direct documenter of the protests showed, eventual abatement of G8 protests was compensated by 'new cycles of protests against war, bank bailouts and austerity. Indeed, recent times have seen mounting challenges to the multilateral institutions that provide what little governance that the globe has', failures of whom make individuals form social movements, which are important to Albrecht for analysing 'the nature of the relationship between protest and political power in this era of globalization'.[33] Therefore, neither history nor ideology is over yet. Even more jarringly for proponents of the triumph of neoliberal globalization, Stiglitz asks that the differences in the appreciation of globalization between the detractors and enthusiasts or planners being so wide, 'are the protestors and the policymakers talking about the same phenomena. Are they looking at the same data? Are the visions of those in power so clouded by special and particular interests?'[34]

Structuralism

I postpone a semantic and empirical answer to Stiglitz's question till finishing consideration of other approaches in the globalization debate in the specific context of the relevance or centrality of the state and take up structuralism thirdly. As Clark points out, conceiving globalization 'as part of a redefined structuralist paradigm' may at first sight involve 'simply a reordering of the environment in which states operate'. But in the light of contentions of major parts of the dependency, interdependence or WST literature that 'states are formed by their location within the capitalist world system, the significance of the structuralist perspective goes beyond that of environmental change alone'. This literature envisions 'a new era of state formation, as part of a quasi-deterministic account of the material system within which the state is generated'. In the same way, globalization too might be conceived as a generator of 'a refined structuralist framework of this kind'. This is comparable to Buzan's concessions keeping a space for a temperate realism.

International Political Economy

IPE is the fourth theory touched by the globalization debate. For, globalization makes key questions latent within it resurface, including the relationship between the economic and political domains and their distinguishability. Here, IPE generates a key insight into one basic, if implicit, assumption of globalization theory, namely economic globalization is bound to 'spill over' into the domain of politics, and 'social and political organization' will follow the lead given by the economic. This, of course, runs athwart a well-entrenched, central belief of the liberal tradition that economics and politics are separate, responding to different stimuli and possessing different dynamics. But the globalization discourse has rehabilitated and iconized an old counterargument of Karl Polanyi that the two are dialectically linked as parts of a 'double movement' in which politics sets limits to the excesses of the free market as a protective umbrella. Clark deduces importantly from this 'prognosis that there is no linear development of globalization, but that instead recent neoliberal trends in economic policy will eventually be recontrolled by defensive political strategies. In this way, contesting interpretations of globalization lie at the heart of the most interesting controversies within IPE'.

While examining existing IR theories through the lens of globalization's impact on parts of them, Clark reminds us that in IRT, a long-standing debate between neoliberalism and neorealism, as well as between neorealism and neoliberalism, is whether attempts at explaining outcomes structure should be viewed as capable of performing all the task; if so, what is to be accommodated within the structure and what is to be kept out; and to what extent 'institutional density alters definitions of interests'. Globalization can have a fair share of the discussions even in this circumscribed set, inducing other questions such as comparability of effects of globalization with those of interdependence, and its applicability to reconsideration of the nature of international anarchy and so on. There being some approaches to globalization that visualize it in terms of 'reconfiguration of anarchy...taken to be the principal structural constraint upon state behaviour, any reshaping of it would then portend important theoretical shifts across the field as a whole', not just within neorealism.[35]

Marxism

Woven around the basic ideas of mode and relations of production, exploitation of labour by capital through expropriation of the surplus value of labour and humanity's emancipation through the revolutionary subversion and transcendence of capitalism, the Marxist view of globalization, the fifth theory of it, has been nurtured in all fields of social enquiry, but most productively in geography, IPE, political science, sociology and even a brand of economics. Instead of foregrounding either the state or the market as propellers of globalization, it brings to the focus other structures, namely class conflict and capitalism. Globalization as spread of transplanetary relations is the ultimate result of the innate tendency of capital to expand and break all spatial barriers in its efforts to, what Marx says, 'conquer the whole earth for its market'. Globalization increases the power of the capitalist bourgeoisie by providing more opportunities for profit-making through surplus expropriation. Going against both liberalist and realist explanations of globalization, the Marxists regard technological advances not as reflection of the natural human drive for economic growth but as historically concrete instances of the impulses of capitalist expansion. Similarly, the gospel of market efficiency is nothing but a smokescreen for the need of capital's global expansion, and the *mantras* of 'freedom' and 'democracy' that are used to explain the creation of the legal and institutional infrastructure of globalization are nothing but legitimating shibboleths for exploitative global capitalist relations. For, the answer of Marxism is that state policies and interstate struggles are nothing but epiphenomenal reflections of the deeply underlying forces of capitalism and class struggles, the real drivers of globalization.

Contemporary assessment of globalization in orthodox Marxist vein stresses and underscores the proliferation of transplanetary circuits of capital via global companies and commodity flows, undergirded by the consolidated transworld networks among the capitalist class and helped by the worldwide fragmentation of the working class. Neo-Marxists of the dependency and WST varieties underline the global accumulation of capital through exploitation of the 'periphery' (helped by the 'semi-periphery' in the latter) by states of the 'core'. Marxists of the neo-Gramscian variety have given the emancipatory, grave-digging role against globalizing capitalism to a host of actors representing its underbelly, not just traditional labour unions but participants in new social movements, environmentalists, peace activists, peasants and women.[36]

Constructivism

The constructivist explanation of globalization, the sixth story, shuns the methodological materialism of all the realist, liberalist and Marxist accounts. Arrived at through the ways that various social actors 'construct' their mental world, in their mind, or through intersubjective communications with others, which 'generate common understandings of reality, shared norms of social behaviour and notion of group identity and solidarity, constructivism stresses the elements of consciousness in globalization. Rosamond says that it exposes the intersubjective structure of 'anarchy', arguing that 'the social construction of a world built around unit interaction with no overarching authority has the effect of reproducing the states system as *the* defining norm of world politics'. Contrarily, the acceptance of globalization as a structural property begets notions of contingency, crisis and unbundling of the erstwhile certainties of territoriality, national forms of governance and so on'. This conjures up the possibilities of the social construction of what John Ruggie calls 'non-territorial functional spaces', and even 'post-territorial regions' that some other constructivists venture into. In this logic, augmented transplanetary connectivity has followed people's reimaginings of society on 'transworld rather than, or in addition to, country-national-state lines', and through further intersubjective dialogue down new lines, 'global-scale understandings' of social units, rules and identities.[37]

Postmodernism

Among other ideational routes to explaining globalization (the seventh), which do not ignore the role of structural power in the creation of identities, norms and knowledge, are the kindred (though not exactly synonymous) approaches of 'postmodernism', 'post-structuralism' or derivative 'postcolonialism', which are often conflated in IR. Since their affinities and differences will be discussed in Chapter 26, we ask the reader to switch to it, avoiding repetition of these here.

In their basics, through employment of the concepts of discourse, deconstruction, genealogy, power/knowledge, intertextuality and so on (all discussed in Chapter 26), these allied approaches present globalization as a reflection of how reigning power structures constitute knowledge and how some prevailing knowledge structures—'episteme' of mode of knowledge in Foucault's view—buttress certain power hierarchies by determining what is accepted as 'truth' and 'real', and what is rejected as 'mythical' and 'imagined'. Rationalism, the intellectual ballast of the 'modern' episteme, has, in all its Cartesian and subsequent senses, possessed an expansionary urge that prods it via processes of cultural imperialism to subjugate or destroy all other non-rationalist epistemologies.

From the writings of the handful of postmodernist thinkers who address the phenomenon of globalization directly, the most general proposition that can be culled is that globalization represents a transplanetary imposition of Western rationalism on indigenous cultures and other non-modern life-worlds,[38] where the power/knowledge game privileges racism, sexism and American hegemony.[39] Featherstone and Lash show how Luke regards globalization as a thoroughly 'informationalized world system', wherein the new world order of (modern) nation states is substituted by 'a set of neo-world orders in today's postmodernity of global flows', giving rise to 'virtual communities'.[40] And Luke himself says that the machinations of power, politics and ideology in the new transplanetary flows of capital, people, commodities, information and culture are reproducing a 'cybersphere/telesphere that is coextensive with, but different from, first nature in the natural biosphere and second nature in the industrial technosphere' in creating a 'new third nature of cyberspatial/televisual/informational glocality', in which the global and the local merge in new quotidian life-worlds. In place of privileging a 'geopolitical or geoeconomic global power', the global flow's 'postmodern spectra of commodification generate many different grammars across a wide band of still less understood "writings" and "readings" of planetary political processes'. The shift from 'place to flow, terrain to streams' not only infuses 'non-perspectival, anti-hierarchical and disorganizational elements into traditional spatial/industrial/national notions of sovereignty' but possession of open and uninhibited access to flows turns into a vital attribute of power, no less important than 'juridico-legal sovereignty'.[41] In an altogether different post-structuralist focus, Cameron and Palan seek to expose the 'relationship between representation and phenomena, between narrative and globalization...The relationships between *these different* narratives, and between narrative and practice', kept implicit in the majority of studies of globalization, and analysed 'often tacitly and rarely in a systematic way'. From the assumption that economics, the underlying ideational pillar of globalization, is merely 'a form of storytelling', they emphasize that even the 'imagined economies' of 'business globalization' cannot hide the fact that the 'development of the space of offshore, crucial to the meaning of globalization, does not, in any sense,...signal the death of the state'. For, 'the very possibility of an offshore economy hinges upon the existence of an "onshore," the "sovereign" state'.[42]

Feminism

Feminism, already discussed in Chapter 20, and for us the eighth and final explanation of the hidden dynamics of globalization, does not give analytical pre-eminence to the state, technology/market, capital, identity or discourse as its driver. It views globalization exclusively from the gender lens, focusing on how it impacts the social construction of masculinity or femininity. This is because while mainstream or authoritative analyses of globalization built around the above factors differ among themselves about the central features, fault lines, costs and benefits of globalization, they share one common point, 'the near total absence of any reference to women or to feminism'.[43] Accordingly, feminism exposes the extent to which women have been marginalized and silenced in global communications (far lower Internet access), global migration (mostly violated domestics or sex workers), global finance (limited access to credit), global organizations (minuscule leadership positions) and global wars (mostly auxiliaries or sufferers as rape victims).

Accordingly, many feminist accounts of globalization have emerged more as supplementary correctives to the earlier accounts discussed by us than as comprehensive accounts standing on their own right. For example, they critique:

- market-driven explanations because globalization shapes labour markets 'by reinforcing the status quo gender division of labour and undermining the ability of states to enact progressive social policies'.[44]
- the legal and institutional structure governing globalization for their insufficient attention to the 'inputs of and consequences for women'.
- political realist explanations for nurturing 'IR's family romance about man, the state and war',[45] and presenting 'an abstract representation of the state', which can be employed 'as a generic model of a rational actor', from which women were left out, this state being dependent on 'masculinized dignity and feminized sacrifice' in the service of nationhood.[46]

In the view of Marxist/neo-Marxist feminists (like Gimenez), the discourses and language of globalization, itself a 'de-politicized, euphemistic' nomenclature for the 'transplanetary spread of the capitalist mode of production', seek to hide the contradiction between the heightened global promotion of capitalism and the 'deepening inequality and decline in living standards' afflicting particularly the female population of the world. For other Marxist feminists (like Visvanathan), even among women the worst victims are those subjected to 'exploitation committed by MNCs against non-White women at the lower end of the global supply chain'.[47] Exposing the close link between masculinism and rationalist knowledge, postmodern feminists (such as Gibson-Graham) regard globalization as a '"rape script" and a masculine project'.[48] But as Peterson so candidly points out, in place of 'a definitive map (a contradiction in terms)', postmodern feminism proffers 'valuable mapping strategies—born of researching the terrain (both empirically and critically) and addressing the complexity (both conceptually and politically) of postmodernity's shifting ground(s)'.[49]

Postcolonial feminism, in its turn, brings out the subjection of women in new imperial-postcolonial contexts of globalization.[50] More radical feminist accounts, however, seek to pinpoint the relationship between 'feminization' and globalization, where feminization 'replicates a mandate of subservience', entailing, irrespective of the tasks involved, 'a logic of menialization' and ordains that globalized economic tasks be 'performed with a measure of servility'. Globalized feminization is an offshoot of masculine behaviour patterns inscribed into globalization, but is more pervasive across gender, in that patriarchy merely ordained 'women's generic subservience to men', but feminization 'renders the feminized (men and women) subservient to market imperatives, profit maximization and commodification'.[51]

Since it is evident from the brief theoretical survey above that no single approach captures the origins and nature of globalization adequately, one indirect reflector of the individual worth of each can be the real, empirical extent of contemporary globalization compared to earlier globalizations. After considering this, we can better judge their merits and shortcomings as explainers of globalization. To this, we now turn.

SCEPTICS' EMPIRICS OF CONTEMPORARY GLOBALIZATION: EXTENT AND CONSEQUENCES

Extent

This is again a key point at issue between the sceptics (including, but not confined to realists, neorealists, a few brands of structuralism, Marxists, postmodernists and feminists) and globalists/optimists (again, including but not limited to liberalists and neoliberalists). It urges greater caution about the hyperbolic and euphoric expectations in early literature about globalization and casts healthy doubts about the self-evident, evenly spread existence of globalization and its actual/potential impact on domestic policymaking. The contending positions refer overwhelmingly to economic globalization since it is more easily measurable, and the optimistic liberalist consensus has this as its primary referent.[52]

Basically, sceptics' reservations about pervasiveness revolve around three contentions[53]:

first, the present levels of global economic integration may be much higher than any point in the Cold-War period (1945–1989) but is not higher than some points in earlier two centuries. By many indices, the world economy was possibly even more integrated at the peak of the gold standard in the late 19th century than at present. Measured by the ratio of exports to national income in the USA, Western Europe and Japan since 1870, trade volumes for the USA or Europe peaked before the First World War, went on a downslide in the interwar years and experienced a surge again after 1950, but made none of them more open this measure than under the gold standard.

Net outflow of capital from the UK in the 40 years before 1914 averaged 5 per cent of GDP, against 2–3 per cent for Japan since the 1960s up to the turn of the century. By other measures, the lowering of transportation costs facilitated by railways and steamship launched Europe towards free trade during the late 20th century, bringing about a remarkable convergence towards commodity prices. Labour flows were freer too, sucking in millions of immigrants from the old world to the new. For example, immigration inflated the labour force of the USA by 24 per cent. Regarding capital mobility, the proportion of net capital outflows in GNP was steeper in the UK during the classical gold standard than in any subsequent periods.[54] So contemporary globalization has miles more to go in the line of the integration of the world economy to justify its claim of historical uniqueness.

This widely known empirically based claim can be countered by saying that globalization does place constraints on nationals and domestic policymakers formerly unbeknown to us. In his discussion of three sources of tension between the global market and domestic social stability, Rodrik points out that reduced barriers to trade and investment first deepen the asymmetry between social groups that can cross international borders freely (capitalists, high-skilled labourers, professionals and so on) and others (such as unskilled/semi-skilled labourers and middle managers). Second, globalization begets conflicts both within and among nations over domestic norms and social institutions that characterize them. Third, globalization has grievously hamstrung states in providing social insurance for their citizens and fulfilling other social obligations for them.[55] Besides, Hay cites Hirst and Thompson's important point that qualitatively, even if not quantitatively, there is significant dissimilarity between the present type of economic integration and its predecessors,[56] a point made by Krasner through his distinction between 'thin' or 'thick' versions of it. 'Globalization is the process by which globalism becomes increasingly thick'.[57]

The second, and more important, contention of the sceptics revolves around present patterns of trade integration. Citing relevant literature, Hay summarizes their arguments against globalization as follows:

- In about all parts of the world, for quite some time, intra-regional integration has been increasing at greater speed than inter-regional integration, both for trade and FDI.
- Accordingly, regionalization rather than globalization is the strongest dynamic in the world economy.
- Apart from such regionalizing tendencies, some regions within the world economy are showing signs of becoming ever more closely integrated with one another.
- Such inter-regional processes, however, are very unevenly distributed.
- Therefore, the most appropriate name for and description of such structural changes should be 'triadization' rather than globalization, the triad being comprised by the North American, Southeast Asian and European regional economies.

This fivefold rebuttal of the globalization process will be supported by theorists of 'new regionalism', discussed in Chapter 13B of this book,[58] but countered by reflectivist approaches to 'new regionalism', which claim that regionalism was nothing but an expression of 'economic globalization and prevailing forms of hegemony'.[59]

The third, and more technical, contention of sceptics is against the faulty assumption of economic policymakers in almost all national capitals of a 'fully integrated world financial market', contending that nearly all of their predictions about the world economy merit empirical testing. Hay surveys relevant literature to identify two intractable findings that have proved vexing for such predictions:

- In a fast-integrating world financial market, interest rates should converge across nations and in a completely integrated global financial market, interest-rate differentials should disappear. But neither has happened.
- In an ever more integrated financial market, the correlation between domestic savings and investment should decline steeply and in a completely integrated capital market, it should fall to zero. But neither has happened, and savings–investment correlations persist.

Consequences

These concern sceptics' case against the supposedly debilitating impact of globalization on domestic political economy. Here also, their charges are threefold. The first is the troubling 'strong and persistently positive statistical correlation' between the openness of an economy (measured by the proportion of its trade in its GDP) and various indices of its public spending, so that the most integrated economies of the world are also seen to be the highest public spenders, that is, welfare states. First detected in 1978, this troubling fact has only been more pronounced in later decades. This only shows that, in at least aggregate terms, globalization is not generating excessive downward pressures on public spending and state autonomy.

Sceptics' second and third contentions on the debilitating impact of globalization on state autonomy hang together and base themselves on the supposed tendency of international investors to use their augmented mobility under globalization to exit from economies marked by high levels of individual and corporate taxation and virulent domestic regulation and throng more congenial investment environments. But some new research has exposed the weakness of these untested hypotheses about investors' and market participants' behaviours.

For Hay, the first set of findings, highlighting the second contention, shows that levels of inward foreign investment are actually correlated not inversely but positively with public and welfare expenditure, high levels of taxation and a host of indices in the areas of labour, environmental and other regulatory standards. So reputedly the most advanced welfare states in the world 'continue to attract a disproportionate share of the inward foreign investment, disproving the myth of the obsolescence of the welfare state in the competitive globalized economy'.

The second set of findings, pertaining to the third contention of the sceptics, also given by Hay after considerable literature survey, reveals that 'investment decisions of financial market actors' are less informed, incisive and discreet than normally believed. So the fear that economic policymakers have about the wrath of international investors is sometimes misplaced, since detailed analyses of investors' decisions and preferences have shown that in choosing market policies, market actors are more concerned about levels of inflation and budget deficits and their types. When these are under reins, social policy, welfare generosity or exacting regulatory standards are less intimidating.[60]

CONCLUSION: RETURN TO THEORY FROM EMPIRICS, WHAT LIGHT DOES THE GLOBALIZED STATE RATHER THAN THE DEBATE ABOUT GLOBALIZATION AND THE STATE THROW ON THE STATE OF GLOBALIZATION

This chapter has progressed from partial definitions and inadequate indices of globalization, and extricated it from redundant concepts of internationalization, liberalization, universalization and Westernization to define it as the spread of 'transplanetary' and, 'more particularly, supraterritorial connections between people', under qualitative conditions of transworld simultaneity and transworld instantaneity. It has shown how the takes of different approaches in IRT on the pervasiveness, benefits, negative effects, biases and predilections of globalization (such as neorealism, neoliberalism, structuralism, IPE, Marxism and its variants, constructivism, postmodernism/post-structuralism, or a derivative postcolonialism, and feminism) differ. To cut through these varying perceptions, this chapter has focused on the empirics of globalization regarding both its extent and consequences. As to extent, it finds that globalization is not as extensive as (neo)liberalists claim or as narrow based as (neo)realists affirm. As to consequences, it finds that it is not as destructive of state autonomy or deleterious for states' public spending as liberalists pretend.

The theoretical pay-off of all this for (and perhaps even more for liberalism) is that globalization has not made states anachronistic even today. For both then the focus should first shift 'to the globalized state as a single unit of analysis, rather than upon globalization and the state as two distinct fields of intellectual enquiry', since 'the state occupies a middle position between the internal and external and is itself both shaped by, and formative of, the process of globalization'. Globalization also should not be taken as merely an environment in which states exist but also as 'an element within the (shifting) identity of the state'.[61] Both approaches should realize that to understand better the nuanced relation between the globalizing state and the ever integrating market, they should explore how the state is reconstituting itself under globalization, first as the 'trading state',[62] then successively as the 'enabling state'[63], the 'market state',[64] the 'Schumpeterian workfare state',[65] and most famously in the context of globalization as the 'competition' state.[66] While the ambit of these state forms and their special foci are not exactly the same, transformations of their inside and outside point to one observation by Clark that, even if raised in the specific context of the 'competition state', applies to all:

> The construction of any dichotomy between globalization and state power is bound to deceive...the important realization...is not that state powers endure, if redefined, under the impact of globalization but rather that globalization and the redefinitions of the state are essentially transcriptions of each other. To speak of globalization is then, by this very act, to address the evidence for the reconstitution of the state.[67]

But since this chapter is not just about the role of the state and market (in concert or opposition) but is about all other elements considered by other theories in IR, an eclectic approach can be proposed that would not forget how both state and market act as leaven for them. According to Scholte, 'the trend of the growth of transplanetary and supraterritorial connectivity' (probably both as a dependent and independent variable) is 'interlinked with four other developments: a shift from capitalism to hyper-capitalism in respect of production; a shift from statism to polycentrism in respect of governance; a shift from nationalism towards pluralism and hybridity in respect of identity; and a shift from rationalism towards reflective rationality in respect of knowledge'. These other elements betoken the significance and importance in the explanation of globalization: of capitalism from Marxism, identity patterns from constructivism, power/knowledge from postmodernism and gender from feminism.[68]

But it should not be presumed that the impact of the new state and the new market will not be important within each of these elements or the workings of these other elements within the new state and the new market will not be important. Mann identified and explored four threats to the contemporary nation states that are all linked with or emanating directly or indirectly from globalization: 'capitalist transformation, environmental danger, identity politics and post-militarism'. But he urged us to 'beware the more enthusiastic of the globalists and transnationalists. With little sense of history, they exaggerate the former strength of nation states; with little sense of global variety, they exaggerate their current decline; with little sense of their plurality, they downplay IR'. Mann thinks that in all the four areas of 'threat', we direly need to assess '(a) different types of impacts on different states in different regions; (b) trends weakening *and* some trends strengthening nation states; (c) trends displacing national regulation to international as well as transnational networks; (d) trends simultaneously strengthening nation-states and transnationalism'. Mann gives examples of this but we have no space to detail here. For me, more important is his observation that even though 'global interaction networks are indeed strengthening', they cannot conceal three discordant facts. First, the force of the global scale of transnational relations, partly generated by the technology and social relations of capitalism, yet now lacks the *deus ex machina* to impose a singular universalism on global networks. Second, global networks are also modestly pierced transversally by the particularities of nation states. Third, the resulting segmentation is mediated by IR. And the weakening or strengthening of this segmentation will finally depend on the tension areas or areas of tension that globalization might create or not.[69] How much may Friedman plead, the world is not flat yet.[70] It is round, and uneven with mountains, hills and plains, as ever; and the 'sonic boom' of globalization 'at Mach speed'[71] may not reverberate in every part of the planet equally.

REVIEW QUESTIONS

1. What 'redundant concepts' should globalization be extricated from to get defined adequately?
2. 'In IRT the globalization debate has raged mostly between and neo or structural realism, on the one hand, and neoliberalism or cosmopolitanism on the other'. Discuss.
3. Delineate the different takes of different theories of IR on globalization from the perspectives of the state, market, structure, class and capital, consciousness, discourse and power/knowledge, and gender.
4. What light do the empirics of globalization throw on the theories of globalization regarding the role of the globalized state in it and its real extent?

NOTES AND REFERENCES

1. Said Amir Arjomand, 'Social Theory and the Changing World: Mass Democracy, Development, Modernization and Globalization', *International Sociology* 19 (2004): 341, cited in C. el-Ojeili and P. Hayden, eds, *Critical Theories of Globalization: An Introduction* (New York, NY: Palgrave Macmillan, 2006), 1.
2. Zygmunt Bauman, *Globalization: The Human Consequences* (Cambridge: Polity, 1998), 1.
3. David Held et al., *Global Transformations: Politics, Economics and Culture* (Stanford, CA: Stanford University Press, 1999), 1.
4. Susan Strange, *Critical Theories of Globalization: An Introduction* (Cambridge: Cambridge University, 1996), xiii.
5. T. Schirato and J. Webb, *Understanding Globalization* (London: SAGE Publications, 2003), 200, cited in el-Ojeili and Hayden, *Critical Globalization*, 12–13.
6. Wolf Schäfer, 'Global Civilization and Local Cultures', in *Rethinking Civilizational Analysis*, eds Said Arjomand and Edward A Tiryakian (London: SAGE Publications, 2004), 80.
7. Kevin Robins, 'Globalization', in *The Social Sciences Encyclopaedia*, eds A. Kuper and J. Kuper, 2nd ed. (London: Routledge, 1996), 345; R. Langhorne, *The Coming of Globalization* (Basingstoke: Palgrave Macmillan, 2001), 2; Bauman, *Globalization*, 18, all cited in el-Ojeili and Hayden, *Critical Globalization*, 13, but also perused independently.
8. Roland Robertson, *Globalization: Social Theory and Global Culture* (London: SAGE Publications, 1992), 8–9, 30.
9. Marion J. Levy Jr., 'Some Aspects of "Structural-Functional" Analysis and Political Science', in *Approaches to the Study of Politics*, ed. Roland Young (Evanston, IL: Northwestern University Press, 1958), 52–65.
10. C. Thomas, 'Globalization and the South', in *Globalization and the South*, eds C. Thomas and P. Wilkin (Basingstoke: Macmillan 1997), 6, cited in Ian Clark, *Globalization and International Relations Theory* (Oxford: Oxford University, 1999), 10.
11. Held et al., *Global Transformations*, 16; also quoted in Colin Hay, 'International Relations Theory and Globalization', in *International Relations Theories: Discipline and Diversity*, eds Tim Dunne, Milja Kurki, and Steve Smith (Oxford: Oxford University Press, 2007), 277.
12. Ibid., 274.
13. Yuval Noah Harari, *Homo Deus* (London: Vintage, 2016), 7–16.
14. Hay, 'International Relations', 275–276.
15. Notes 24, 29 and 30 of Chapter 13B.
16. Notes 24–30, 43–67 of Chapter 19.
17. Jan Aart Scholte, *Globalization: A Critical Introduction*, 2nd ed. (New York, NY: Palgrave Macmillan, 2005), 54–56, for analysis and citations of P. Hirst and G. Thompson, *Globalization in Question: The International Economy and the Possibilities of Governance*, 2nd ed. (Cambridge: Polity, 1999), 7–13; D. Rodrik, *The Global Governance of Trade as If Development Really Mattered* (New York, NY: UNDP, 2001); A. T. Kearney Consultants and Foreign Policy articles of 2001–2004.
18. For details of these, see Jeremy Brecher, Tim Costello, and Brendan Smith, *Globalization from below: The Power of Solidarity* (Cambridge, MA: South End Press, 2000), 1–4.
19. See Eduardo Zachary Albrecht, *Alter-globalization in Southern Europe: Anatomy of a Social Movement* (New York, NY: Palgrave Macmillan, 2017).
20. See for these analyses and citations, C. Gamble, *Timewalkers: The Prehistory of Global Civilization* (Cambridge, MA: Harvard University Press, 1994); A. Giddens, *Consequences of Modernity* (Cambridge: Polity, 1990); Robertson, *Globalization*, 170; R. Pettman, 'Anti-Globalisation Discourse in Asia', in *Critical Theories, International Relations and the Anti-Globalisation Movement*, eds C. Eschle and B. Maiguashca (London: Routledge, 2005), 77–86, all cited in Scholte, *Globalization*, 57–67.

21. For the manifestations of globality and their limits, and the relevant citations, ibid., 67–84.
22. For this and the analysis or realism versus liberalism debate on globalization, except other references provided further, see Hay, 'IRTAG', 268.
23. Scholte, *Globalization*, 123.
24. For citations of P. M. Kennedy, *The Rise and Fall of the Great Powers: Economic Change and Military Conflict from 1500 to 2000* (New York, NY: Random House, 1987); J. S. Nye, *Bound to Lead: The Changing Nature of American Power* (New York, NY: Basic Books, 1990), and realism, see Scholte, *Globalization*, 126–127.
25. Mearsheimer, *The Tragedy of Great Power Politics*, 371.
26. Scholte, *Globalization*, 124–125.
27. Hay, 'International Relations', 268–270.
28. Stephen D. Krasner, *Sovereignty: Organized Hypocrisy* (Princeton, NJ: Princeton University Press, 1999), 12–13.
29. Richard Stubbs, 'States, Sovereignty and the Response of Southeast Asia's Miracle Economies to Globalization', in *States and Sovereignty in the Global Economy*, eds David Alden Smith, Dorothy J. Solinger, and Steven C. Topik (London: Routledge, 1999), 229–245, esp. 229, 242.
30. Krasner, *Sovereignty*, 13.
31. Hay, 'International Relations', 270–272; Clark, *Globalization*, 2.
32. Weber, *International Relations Theory*, 107–129. I think, however, that the Marxist theory of alienation potentially addresses the latter point too.
33. See April Carter, *Direct Action and Democracy Today* (Cambridge: Polity Press, 2005), 143–144; Albrecht, *Alter-globalization*, 1–2.
34. Joseph E. Stiglitz, *Globalization and Its Discontents* (New Delhi: Penguin Books India, 2003), 9.
35. Clark, *Globalization*, 3–4.
36. For numerous citations of the new breed of Marxist scholars and this analysis, see Scholte, *Globalization*, 128–129.
37. Ibid., 31; Ben Rosamond, 'Discourses of Globalization and European Identities', in *The Social Construction of Europe*, eds Thomas Christiansen, Knud Erik Jørgensen, and Antje Wiener (London: SAGE Publications, 2001), 165, for other citations and analysis.
38. For these thinkers and citations of them, see M. Foucault, *The Order of Things* (London: Tavistock, 1970); Angus Cameron and Ronen Palan, *The Imagined Economies of Globalization* (London: SAGE Publications, 2004); Arif Dirlik, *The Postcolonial Aura: Third World Criticism in the Age of Global Capitalism* (Boulder, CO: Westview, 1998); L. Ling, 'Globalization and the Spectre of Fu Manchu: White Man's Burden as Dark Irony', in *Value Pluralism, Normative Theory and International Relations*, eds J. S. Fritz and M. Lensu (Basingstoke: Palgrave Macmillan, 2000); Ó Tuathail, *Critical Geopolitics: The Politics of Writing Global Space* (London: Routledge, 1996); T. W. Luke, 'New World Order or Neo-World Orders: Power, Politics, and Ideology in Informationalizing Glocalities', in *Globalization: Social Theory and Global Culture*, eds Mike Featherstone, Scott Lash, and Roland Robertson (London: SAGE Publications, 1995); also their main points mentioned in Scholte, *Globalization*, 132–133. I have read some of them as mentioned further.
39. Ibid., for E. W. Said, David Campbell, G. Chowdhry and S. Nair, who made these points from a postcolonialist perspective.
40. Featherstone and Lash, 'Globalization, Modernity and the Spatialization of Social Theory: An Introduction', in *Globalization: Social Theory and Global Culture*, eds Mike Featherstone, Scott Lash, and Roland Robertson (London: SAGE Publications, 1995), 7.
41. Luke, 'New World Order', 90–106.
42. Cameron and Palan, *Imagined Economies*, 25, 46, 109.
43. Mary E. Hawkesworth, *Globalization and Feminist Activism* (Lanham, MD: Rowman & Littlefield, 2006/2018), 3.

44. Drucilla Barker and Susan F. Feiner, *Liberating Economics: Feminist Perspectives on Families, Work, and Globalization* (Ann Arbor, MI: University of Michigan Press, 2004), 96.
45. Weber, *International Relations Theory*, 85–86.
46. Enloe, *Bananas, Beaches*, 351. Much of Chapter 15 concerns the realist construction of IR and demystification and debunking of the state.
47. Martha E. Gimenez, 'Connecting Marx and Feminism in the Era of Globalization: A Preliminary Investigation', *Socialism and Democracy* 18, no. 1 (2004): 86; N. Visvanahan, 'Introduction to Part 1, in *The Women, Gender and Development Reader*, eds Nalini Visvanathan, Lynn Duggan, Nan Wiegersma (London: Zed Books, 1997), 23, both cited in Manfred Steger, Paul Battersby, and Joseph Siracusa, eds, *The SAGE Handbook of Globalization* (Los Angeles, CA: SAGE Publications, 2014), 61.
48. J. K. Gibson-Graham, *The End of Capitalism (as We Knew It): A Feminist Critique of Political Economy* (Oxford: Blackwell, 1996), cited in Valentine M. Moghadam, *Globalizing Women: Transnational Feminist Networks* (Baltimore, MD: Johns Hopkins University Press, 2005), 28.
49. V. Spike Peterson, 'Shifting Ground(s): Epistemological and Territorial Remapping in the Context of Globalization', in *Globalization: Theory and Practice*, eds Eleonore Kofman and Gillian Youngs (London: Pinter, 1996), 22.
50. See for example, Eliza Wing-Yee Lee, *Gender and Change in Hong Kong: Globalization, Postcolonialism, and Chinese Patriarchy* (Vancouver: UBC Press, 2003); Nicole Constable, *Maid to Order in Hong Kong: Stories of Filipina Workers* (Ithaca, NY: Cornell University Press, 1997); Kimberley Chang Campani and L. H. M. Ling, 'Globalization and Its Intimate Other: Filipina Domestic Workers in Hong Kong', in *Gender and Global Restructuring*, eds Marianne March and Ann Runyon (London: Routledge, 2000), 27–58.
51. M. E. Hawkesworth, *Globalization and Feminist Activism* (Lanham, MD: Rowman & Littlefield, 2006), 22–23.
52. See for example the contents of or articles in books like Dani Rodrik, *Has Globalization Gone Too Far?* (Washington, DC: Institute for International Economics, 1997); Gerard Caprio, ed., *The Evidence and Impact of Financial Globalization* (London: Elsevier, 2013).
53. Hay, 'International Relations', pp. 277–81 for these.
54. Rodrik, *Has Globalization*, 7–8; Robert O. Keohane and Joseph S. Nye, 'Globalization: What's New? What's Not? (And) So What?', *Foreign Affairs* (Spring 2000): 104–119, esp. 109.
55. Rodrik, *Has Globalization*, 4–6.
56. Hirst and Thompson, *Globalization in Question*, 27 ff., cited by Hay, 'International Relations', 279.
57. Keohane and Nye, 'Globalization', 108.
58. See Hay, 'International Relations', 268–270; Krasner, *Sovereignty*; Stubbs, 'States, Sovereignty'; Krasner, *Sovereignty*, 13.
59. Weber, *International Relations Theory*, 107–129.
60. See citations by Hay, 'International Relations', 281–282.
61. Clark, *Globalization*, 7–10.
62. Richard Rosecrance, *The Rise of the Trading State: Commerce and Conquest in the Modern World* (New York, NY: Basic Books, 1986).
63. Neil Gilbert and Barbara Gilbert, *The Enabling State: Modern Welfare Capitalism in America* (New York, NY: Oxford University Press, 1989).
64. Philip Bobbitt, *The Shield of Achilles: War, Peace and the Course of History* (New York, NY: Alfred A. Knopf, 2002); later further developed in Philip Bobbitt, *Terror and Consent: The Wars for the Twenty-first Century* (New York, NY: Knopf Doubleday Publishing Group, 2008).
65. Bob Jessop, *From the Keynesian Welfare to the Schumpeterian Workfare State* (Lancaster: Lancaster Regionalism Group, University of Lancaster, 1992).

66. Primarily, P. G. Cerny, 'Paradoxes of the Competition State: The Dynamics of Political Globalization', *Government and Opposition* 32, no. 2 (Spring 1997): 251–274; P. G. Cerny, 'Political Globalisation and the Competition State', in *Political Economy and the Changing Global Order*, eds R. Stubbs and G. R. D. Underhill (Oxford: Oxford University Press, 2000).
67. Clark, *Globalization*, 101.
68. Scholte, *Globalization*, 136.
69. Michael Mann, 'Has Globalization Ended the Rise and Rise of the Nation-state?', in *International Order and the Future of World Politics*, eds T. V. Paul and John A. Hall (Cambridge: Cambridge, 1999), 237–260, esp. 259–260.
70. Thomas L. Friedman, *The World Is Flat [Further Updated and Expanded, Release 3.0]: The Globalized World in the Twenty-first Century* (New York, NY: Picador/Farrar, Straus and Giroux, 2007).
71. Gregg Easterbrook, *Sonic Boom: Globalization at Mach Speed* (New York, NY: Random House Publishing Group, 2009).

SECTION 4

POSTPOSITIVIST THEORIES OF THE MIDDLE AND LEFT

CHAPTER

23

The English School as the Middle Way: Origins, Evolution and Spillover

CHAPTER OUTLINE

INTRODUCTION: THE SCHOOL, ITS MONIKER AND LOCATION

We start this chapter by informing you why this approach called the 'English School' (ES), for which a commentator celebrates its success in 'establishing a globally recognized brand name' and 'no mean feat for a non-American theory in the second half of the 20th century'.[1] The approach originated in 1959 in a tradition of systematic research conducted inside and outside the British Committee on the Theory of International Politics (BCTIP). While the group self-referentially liked to describe itself, 'directly or by implication, as belonging (a) to a classical or traditional school and (b) to a British school of IR,'[2] there are other restrictive names. Wight named it Grotian

School. Others called it liberal realism or British institutionalists. Jackson and Sørensen termed it the international society approach (henceforth, ISA).[3] Overlooked in the USA, the school was misunderstood even in its homeland by many as a local version of realism.[4] The label ES, the most widely accepted, is, however, controversial, besides being unfortunate for at least two reasons. First, whether in the classical period of the evolution of the school (the 1950s to the 1980s) or the post-classical phase (1990 onwards), some of its leading contributors were not English by birth, even if for some time or other based in British universities. Good examples are—Charles A. W. Manning (South African), Hedley Bull and J. D. B. Miller (Australian), Robert Jackson (Canadian) and Hidemi Suganami (Japanese). Second, the BCTIP, formed under the chairmanship of the Cambridge historian Herbert Butterfield, was funded by The Rockefeller Foundation of the USA.[5] Third, the label was perhaps a negative-parochial response. Crawford says that despite having generally shared with their American peers the belief that IR is a distinct and self-contained discipline, the founders of the approach were largely neglected in American courses and textbooks. Thus, while being 'reflective of but not synonymous with the British attitude to IR', proponents of the approach might have chosen the prefix "English" and the suffix "school" as a 'form of self-imposed incarceration within the American discipline' since the latter 'alone can get by without a national prefix' because of its universalist pretensions.[6] But as Third-World students, we are less concerned with the 'Englishness' of the approach or its major spokespersons and more with the distinctiveness of its research foci and its differences from the dominant paradigms of the day as an occupier of the middle ground.

EARLY ORIGINS, DEVELOPMENT AND EVOLUTION OF THE SCHOOL

It is inadequately recognized within the literature that the ES has two main lines of descent, though some scholars figure in both. First, there is the set of early post-1945 'institutionalist' scholars from the London School of Economics (LSE), including Manning, Martin Wight, Bull, Alan James and F. S. Northedge. Second, there is BCTIP, where Wight, Bull, Maurice Keens-Soper, Adam Watson and John Vincent assembled from other prominent universities in the UK.[7] Suganami identifies four interrelated groupings among the founders, proponents and converts of the school. Wight, Bull and James were in the first, LSE subgroup of the first grouping, while Wight, Bull, Watson (Bull's doctoral student at the Australian National University) and R. J. Vincent were in the second, BCTIP subgroup. The second grouping, comprising those on which the influence of the founders fell directly or indirectly as their graduate students or pupils, included Andrew Hurrell (Bull's Oxford pupil and teacher at the Keele University), Tim Dunne (Hurrell's doctoral student at Oxford), Nicholas Wheeler (Dunne's close collaborator and Vincent's critical follower), David Long and Peter Wilson (both students of James at Keele University), David Armstrong and Paul Keal (both Bull's doctoral students at the Australian National University) and (self-avowedly) Suganami. The third grouping was formed by scholars who had initially flourished independently of the ES but had later imported into their works some of its founding figures' key ideas and approaches, such as Andrew Linklater, Ian Clark and Robert Jackson. The fourth grouping consisted of scholars further outside who were initially and specially drawn by Watson's work and resolved to 'reconvene' the school after it became allegedly moribund into what they believed was a 'new ES' with 'a worldwide network of like-minded scholars, building on the achievements of the founding figures of the ES and exchanging their ideas regularly at various international conferences'.[8]

But the essence of the ES's inquiry, namely identification of the 'institutional structure of world politics organized as a society of sovereign states',[9] was created in both the two initial locales and outside. While Manning placed international society at the centre of his curriculum of IR, Wight conceptualized international society as a middle position between realist accounts of systemic logics and revolutionist accounts pleading for or auguring the downfall of the state system as a whole. Butterfield sought to institutionalize the search for this new analysis under the BCTIP, chaired by key figures of the school in the classical phase, such as Butterfield himself (till 1968), Wight (till 1972), Watson (till 1978) and Bull (till 1984, when he died) and met regularly since 1959.[10] Some scholars such as Bull, Vincent, Wheeler and Jackson also made crucial contributions in the assessment of how well the institutions of that society are functioning in the achievement of basic social goals and also what values can or should be pursued in world politics organized as a society of sovereign states. Likewise, Wight, Bull, Watson, Buzan and Little enriched another field of inquiry of the school, namely comparative study of historical states systems with or without a study of the historical evolution of the modern states system.[11]

While admitting that fixing the story of the ES into neat stages is difficult, Buzan accepts Ole Wæver's (1998) four-phase scheme setting out the main threads of its evolution. *Phase* 1 extends from 1959 (founding of BCTIP) to 1966 (featuring Butterfield and Wight's foundational text *Diplomatic Investigations*). In this phase, BCTIP fixed international society as the preferred approach to theorizing. *Phase* 2 encompasses the period 1966–1977, witnessing the publication of Bull's *The Anarchical Society* (1977) and Wight's *Systems of States* (1977), two canonical texts which facilitated the exploration of the international society in a world-historical context, added to modern classics by younger scholars like Vincent's *Nonintervention and International Order* (1974). *Phase* 3, running from 1977 to 1992, was the era of consolidation and passing over the baton to a new generation. The BCTIP phase came to an end after Bull's death, as did its formal structure of regular meetings. Its best fruits were Bull and Watson's edited volume *The Expansion of International Society* (1984) and Watson's *The Evolution of International Society* (1992). Both took Wight's comparative historical approach to a new comparative, world-historical perspective on international society, helped by other books of Vincent (*Foreign Policy and Human Rights* and *Human Rights and International Relations*, both in 1986); Miller and Vincent (*Order and Violence: Hedley Bull* and *International Relations*, 1990); editors Bull, Benedict Kingsbury and Adam Roberts, (*Hugo Grotius and International Relations*, 1990); Michael Donelan (*The Reason of States*, 1978); James Mayall (The *Community of States*, 1982); Cornelia Navari (*The Condition of States*, 1991), and so on. The christening of the ES by Roy Jones during this period inaugurated a discourse of self-reflection on the state of the school. The final Phase 4, extending from 1992 (the year of the end of the Cold War) to the present, signalled the arrival of a new generation of ES writers with little or no baptismal link to BCTIP, non-sectarian, eclectic, ready to draw on or borrow from the perspectives of systems, neorealism, regime theory, constructivism and globalization. The 1992 special issue of *Millennium* and the European Consortium for Political Research workshop at Limerick, Ireland, in the same year, culminated in B. A. Robertson's 1998 edited volume, *International Society and the Development of International Relations Theory* (1998), and announced with others that they had arrived to exploit the insights of three generations of scholars to batter down sectarian walls and build bridges for higher syntheses.[12]

THE THREE Rs AND Ss OF ES

For reasons I cannot fathom, such as ancient Romans and Indians and later day Germans (e.g., Hegel), ES theorists also love thinking in terms of three Ss. I am not accepting here a later-day tripartite classification of ES proposed by Suganami into 'structural studies, functional studies, and historical studies'[13] because it does not, in my view, well accord with the much better known and familiar Wightian classification of three Rs an three Ss and would impact the argumentative pattern of the essay. Dunne contends that intellectual ballasts of the ES are predicated on acceptance of 'three preliminary articles: (a) adherence to a given tradition of inquiry, (b) a loosely interpretive approach to the study of IR and (c) an open and manifest concern with the normative dimension of IR theorizing'.[14] For others, the foundation of the ES is a tripartite distinction between international system, international society and world society, aligned with Wight's 'three traditions' or rather three Rs of IR theory, namely realism, rationalism and revolutionism, as summarized below by Buzan:

- The international system, associated with Hobbes/Machiavelli, runs broadly parallel to neoclassical realism and neorealism, talks about power politics of the states in the background of international anarchy and accepts the ontology of states, sought to be captured through 'positivist epistemology, materialist and rationalist methodologies and structural theories'.
- International society, the main focus of ES and linked with Grotius and Rationalism, is concerned with the institutionalization of shared interest and identity amongst states and treats the creation and maintenance of shared norms, rules and institutions as central to IR theory. Although it has some similarities with regime theory, its thrust is deeper, having constitutive overtones that go far beyond surface instrumentalist implications. Although it also accepts the ontology of states, it is sought to be captured through constructivist epistemology and historical methods.
- World society, associated with Kant and revolutionism, thinks of individuals, non-state organizations and ultimately the global population as a whole as the sources of global societal identities and arrangements and places transcendence of the state system at the centre of IR theory. Its forms of universalist cosmopolitanism are equally comfortable with liberalism and communism. Some parallels with transnationalism notwithstanding, it has deeper roots in normative political theory. While disowning the ontology of states, this conceptualization cannot, because of its transnational element, privilege individuals as the only focus of inquiry. CT does not define or exhaust all the approaches to it, 'and in the Wightian mode, it is more about

TABLE 23.1 The Core Conceptual Bases of the Three Rs

Realism	*Rationalism*	*Revolutionism*
Anarchy	Society	Humanity
Power politics	Evolutionary change	Revolutionary change
Conflict and warfare	Peaceful coexistence	Anti-state utopianism
	Hopes without illusions	

Source: Robert Jackson and Georg Sørensen, 'International Society,' in *Introduction to International Relations* (Oxford, NY: Oxford University Press, 1999), 146.

historically operating alternative images of the international system than it is about capturing non-state aspects of the system'.[15] See Table 23.1 for the core conceptual assumptions/bases of the three Rs.

Wight, however, warns that no one of the above conceptualizations alone would be adequate for a full understanding of IR. What is required is the employment of all of them together and the exploration of the dialogue between them. For him, IP 'is a realm of human experience' with its distinctive repertoire of problems and language. For its study and comprehension, one has to enter this tradition and join 'in the conversation'.[16] As per Jackson, the conversation is constituted by:

> A variety of theoretical inquiries which conceive of international relations as a world not merely of power and prudence or wealth or capability or domination but also one of recognition, association, membership, equality, equity, legitimate interests, rights, reciprocity, customs and conventions, agreements and disagreements, disputes, offenses, injuries, damages, reparations and the rest: the normative vocabulary of human conduct.[17]

Understanding the society of states goes beyond the mechanical application of social science models to attempt at knowing how the people involved in IR, mainly states people, have historically perceived it. Scholars are asked to explore why these states people are prone to behave in the way they do by developing insights into the ideas and thoughts behind their foreign policies.[18] This is different from the obtrusive realist peeping over 'the shoulder' of or anticipating 'the steps a statesman—past, present or future—has taken or will take'.[19] This is because, in place of realism's methodological eavesdropping, the ES advises, as it were, a kind of participant observation.

But what is the relationship between the three Ss of ES? Jackson and Sørensen very helpfully point out that:

> The 'system of states' is a realist concept; the 'society of states' is a liberal concept. The more international relations constitute a society and the less international relations merely compose a system is an indication of the extent to which world politics forms a distinctive human civilization with its own norms and values.[20]

These words indicate that the movement from the systemic to the societal is ingrained in the epistemology of ES. But the nature of progression even within the societal framework cannot be adequately grasped unless we understand what international society means. Bull found it emerging when,

> A group of states, conscious of certain common interests and common values, forms a society in the sense that they conceive of themselves to be bound by a common set of rules in their relations with one another, and share in the working of common institutions'.[21]

Bull and Watson later defined international society as:

> A group of states (or, more generally, a group of independent political communities) which not merely form a system, in the sense that the behaviour of each is a necessary factor in the calculations of the others, but also have established by dialogue and consent common rules for the conduct of their relations, and recognize their common interest in maintaining these arrangements.[22]

But the ES does not regard international society as unchanging or state sovereignty as a fixed datum of theory, as would be evident from the distinction within the literature between first a 'pluralist account' of it, embodying a 'thin morality' and a 'solidarist' one involving a 'thick morality', generating a pluralist international society and a solidary international society.[23] In pluralist international society, the institutional structure is oriented towards preservation of the liberty of states and maintenance of order among them through instrumentally understood pluralist norms. These 'provide a structure of coexistence' based on the 'mutual recognition of states as independent and legally equal members of society'.[24] The meaning of the pluralist order would be clear if we remember that ES regards great powers, limited wars and BOPs as 'institutions', as practices that had evolved over many centuries to maintain order. For Bull, a solidary international society would involve collective enforcement of international rules and the guardianship of human rights and modification of sovereignty in a way that duty is created for members of international society to intervene forcibly to protect these rights. But while differentiating this solidarism from cosmopolitanism, for the latter's fuzziness about the institutional arrangement for delivering these values, Bull remains wary about 'premature global solidarism' and its deleterious consequences.[25] But, as Suganami argues, the pluralist–solidarist cleavage within the ES may not be as insuperable as is normally taken to be. The difference between the two stances is merely about 'what is feasible within the contemporary society of states as a whole'. Pluralists would/should not go to the extent of insisting on some 'a priori grounds that the world, as a whole, would (or should) never become solidarist, however sceptical they may be of such a transition in the near future'. Besides, a fact about pluralism that helps solidarists is that it is inherently unstable. And despite Bull's initial reservations about 'solidarism' in the matter of promotion of human rights in IR,[26] implicit in his pluralist defence of the extant world structure as a society of sovereign states was the expectation that it would be effective in securing a '"world order", defined in terms of human individuals' enjoyment of certain basic human needs, such as freedom from violence, stability of property and fulfilment of contractual obligations'. So according to Suganami, solidarism is 'immanent in the form of pluralism as endorsed by Bull', and with approval, he cites Vincent's claim that at heart, most ES thinkers are 'solidarists', although they differ about the extent to which it is here and now present in the world.[27] Moreover, Buzan expresses best the wide consensus in the ES on the relationship between pluralism and solidarism to be 'understood not as mutually exclusive positions but as positions in a spectrum representing, respectively, thin and thick sets of shared norms, rules and institutions'.[28]

ES RESEARCH AGENDA THEN AND NOW

Before we go into the research agendas of ES during the classical period and the post-classical phase, we should spell out the basics of this approach before its post-Cold-War reincarnation. A tabular presentation (Table 23.2) would most benefit my readers.

Before the end of the Cold War, the ES talked about the meaning of anarchy and order, order and justice and statecraft and responsibility in all the senses of national, international and human responsibility. Since the end of the Cold War, the research agenda of the ES has not diametrically changed. But there has been a shift in priorities in some cases and additions and alterations in others. For example, the movement away from order to justice has initiated a movement in the meaning of justice away from international justice to human justice, making what Vincent calls 'boundaries' between domestic societies and international society 'fuzzier' and putting the concept of state sovereignty under tension. Besides, 'international legitimacy' is an emerging area since the legal and social discourses on human rights have placed the state under scrutiny from both insiders and outsiders. As a result, non-intervention is no longer an unchallenged 'institution'. Besides, 'the greening' of ISA theory is a distinct cry.[29]

In the second edition of *The Anarchical Society* up to the fourth, Bull put a question before us on the basis of 'five features of contemporary world politics', namely the (a) regional integration (like in EU), (b) disintegration (such as in the USSR and former Yugoslavia), (c) expansion of private international violence (including international terrorism), (d) the growth of transnational organizations (including MNCs) and (e) 'technological' and communications-based unification of the world. The question was whether the classical society of states based on state sovereignty may be yielding place 'to a secular reincarnation of the system of overlapping or segmented authority

TABLE 23.2 Basics of ES/International Society Approach

Methodology	Humanism Interpretive mode of inquiry Historical, jurisprudential and philosophical
Core concepts	Human relations States Anarchical society State system Society of states ——> World Society
Basic values	Order Justice State sovereignty Statecraft and responsibility

Source: Adapted from Robert Jackson and Georg Sørensen, 'International Society,' in *Introduction to International Relations* (Oxford, NY: Oxford University Press, 1999), 144.

that characterized medieval Christendom'.[30] Did such a question enter the research agenda? To answer this question, we would like to throw some light on the post-Cold-War transformation of the ES to which I now turn.

Post-Cold-War Transformation of the ES

Regeneration

Georg Sørensen rightly said that amidst the 'soul searching' in IR theories after the end of the Cold War, the ES was receiving fresh attention.[31] Dunne shows that while a whole range of recent books and edited volumes in IR echo the concerns of many of the classical ES writers such as Wight, Bull, Vincent and Watson, the new writers are also, at the same time, more receptive than the founders to influences from philosophy, social theory and world history and are also less claustrophobic.[32] In my view, they also mirror many of the contentious issues highlighted in the cosmopolitan/communitarian debate about the normative presuppositions that should inform the new global order around the triangular relationship between individuals, states and the global order.[33]

Dunne's pointer to an increasing elective affinity between the research agenda of the ES and much of recent writings in IR without formally aligning with the school[34] may baffle the one who remembers that just two decades back, a leading IR scholar was constructing 'a case for closure' against the ES, though it was then 'still at its prime' with its bonds still sufficiently strong and new recruits joining. Even so the ES had appeared to him as a 'spent force' and a 'sterile regime' that lacked intellectual coherence, rigour and passion on top of being non-conversant with the increasing sophistication of international economics.[35]

But since contrary to Jones' prognosis, ES has not closed shop but has rather spread its influence over, cross-fertilized and impregnated other schools, one may wonder how it has managed it. That Bull's classic *The Anarchical Society* (1977) wields greater influence today than at birth is substantiated by diverse indicators. First, certain terms, concepts and metaphors employed by Bull, such as 'neo-medievalism' and the 'pluralist–solidarist' distinction have been taken up by integration theorists and other normative theorists to highlight the differences between different types of communities. Likewise, the concept of world society is being refurbished by a group of scholars at the universities of Darmstadt and Frankfurt. Besides, realists and constructivists alike have accepted Bull's insight that statecraft must be understood in historical and sociological contexts. This merely means that theorizing about international society has spilled over the brim of ES/ISA to soak and wet other theoretical domains. The second, though crude and numerical, indicator of ES's diasporic spread is its dominant presence in edited texts of IR. Apart from containing five essays of Bull, Linklater's massive five-volume collection of theoretical essays[36] includes at least one ES essay in each of the volumes. Dunne deduces from it that this approach has greater acceptability and clout than when Wight wrote his classic *De Systematibus Civitatum* in 1967.

Catalytic of the regeneration of the ES and its quiet spread into the guarded precincts of other schools and approaches has been the effort of other secular scholars. Since Bull's ideas of and insights into international society had changed a lot from his magnum opus *The Anarchical Society* (1977) in his later and lesser works, these have been collected by Alderson and Hurrell in an anthology[37] for the sake of a more holistic reading of Bull. Buzan and Little[38] have taken up the questions posed by Wight and later by Watson in his seminal book *The Evolution of International Society* (1992) to rework them into a truly systematic and comparative study of international systems. Bull was a little more difficult to adapt. Although Bull's less reputed essays add to our understanding of the breadth and depth of international society because of its substantial amount of material on the normative content of the rules and institutions of international society and its exploration of the relationship between European international society and the non-European world, Bull's idea of an international society is not entirely unproblematic. The most problematic is an overstatement of the difference between a system and society and exaggeration of the importance of Westphalia for the arrival of the international society and its inextricable linking with the birth of nation states,[39] making Bull a victim to what Saurin so aptly describes as the 'fallacy of misplaced concreteness'.[40] Wight did not, however, fall victim to his disciple's mistake. Aware of patterns of order that existed in many premodern states systems, Wight had preferred comparing successive historical states systems to stressing the unique characteristics of modern international society. Further, he listed 'permanent communication' and a 'degree of cultural unity' among fellow members, apart from their sovereignty, as defining characteristics of these states systems. Besides, Wight gave more attention to the status and obligations of the 'barbarian outside pre- or post-Westphalian international society'.[41]

Buzan and Little did their repair job here to bring the ES theorizing in step with post-Cold-War theoretical frontiers. They used their international systems framework based on the perspective of world history to identify 'three significant turning points in the world history of international systems'. The first happened more than 40,000 years back when hunter-gatherer bands first embarked on a form of exchange that 'resulted in long-distance movement of goods and ideas from one group to another over hundreds and sometimes thousands of miles.' The second occurred 5,500 years back, the period marked by the emergence and interaction of 'state-like units', where the mutual interactions between sets of these units provided the backbone of the 'first fully fledged international systems', the major units of which became increasingly diversified to embrace agrarian empires, nomadic empires, chiefdoms, city-states and city leagues. At the onset of the third turning point that started only 500 years ago, a new kind of political actor, the modern sovereign state emerged and after leading to the elimination of units in 'pre-international systems' and of the diversity of actors in both eras, covered the entire globe by the end of the 20th century. The international systems that had emerged and developed in the five millennia after the second turning point, now, 'coalesced remarkably swiftly' to engender a single international system dominating all the lands and seas of the Earth. This process was completed more than 150 years ago, culminating in 'the fully global international system, which in turn gave birth to the self-conscious study of IR'. But the world-historical transformation is far from complete. Amid debates about whether the Westphalian state was yielding place to a postmodern state and military-political relations are ceding primacy to industrial-economic ones, the 'historic tradition' of IR remains open.[42]

The extent to which Buzan and Little have veered away from the methodological parochialisms of IR to batter down the wall of Westphalia is remarkable. Elsewhere, Buzan tries to 'relate the concept of "international society" to structural realism and regime theory to show how they complement and strengthen each other' by first drawing 'a clear boundary' between 'international system' and 'international society' to 'enable a clear boundary to be drawn between them' and then resolving 'the nebulous position' in the existing literature on the complementarities of the two terms. Very significantly, he uses 'the logic of structural realism to show how international society can emerge as a natural product of the logic of anarchy'. He does not go the whole way with either ES or structural realism or even with Kenneth Waltz because 'the consequences of anarchy vary according to the level and type of interaction in the system'. This secular perspective teases out the theoretically rich finding that present-day international society—hybrid, global and postcolonial—in part 'stems from the Gemeinschaft international society that developed in modern Europe and imposed itself on most of the planet during its imperial heyday, and in part, it reflects a Gesellschafts process by which different cultures embedded in a system with high levels of interaction have learned to come to terms with each other'.[43]

The impact of the post-Cold-War transformation of ES is manifested also in changes in its recent research agendas. The first change was led by a 2009 book by Buzan and Gonzalez-Pelaez, although the year before saw Stivachtis's article on Europe. Now, veering away from the global level of analysis, preferred by the first generation of scholars, ES research started focusing on the regional level of analysis, extending the socio-structural theory of norms and institutions to the sub-global level. And new books and articles on different regions of the world came out in a spree by Schouenborg, Merke, Buzan and Zhang, Pourchot and Stivachtis, Kaczmarska, Tan Shek Yan, Costa Buranelli and so on.[44]

The second change, also in 2009, involved methodological cleaning, the methodology being one of the chinks in the ES armour. Navari's edited book started with the admission that a 'consideration of English School methods may seem a contradiction in terms' but warned that even if 'the classical school disdained methodology, we should not on that account suppose, however, that its members did not have the method.' Among the contributors, Andrew Jackson characterizes IR as a 'craft discipline', the basis of which is 'normative inquiry into world politics' from a stance of 'detachment'. James Mayall focuses on 'normative reasoning'. Navari points to the members' lack of interest in 'causal reasoning'. Richard Little and William Bain write on the importance of history as a methodological tool. Christian Reus-Smit points to the element of constructivism in its reasoning. Holsti concentrates on theorizing the 'causes of order'.[45] Parrat and Costa Buranelli offered important methodological insights.[46]

The third change, which takes ES 'back to the roots', is the historical dimension. ES scholars such as Aissaoui, Schulz, Costa Buranelli and Pella have supplemented Bull and Watson's and others' work on the expansion of international society.[47]

The fourth change was in the area of depiction of the relationship between primary institutions (signifying stable and routinized practices, such as sovereignty, diplomacy and international law) and secondary institutions (referring to international organizations, such as the UN and ASEAN). Pursuing the lead of Buzan, Holsti and so on, scholars such as Knudsen and Spandler worked on the mutually reinforcing relations between primary and secondary institutions.[48] A stirring cauldron indeed, but why should it symbolize any middle way? We consider that below.

WHY THE MIDDLE WAY AND WHY UNDER PRESSURE

Those who cast their lot with the ES in both the classical and post-classical phases see it as occupying, alongside constructivism, a middle ground in IR, avoiding in the classical phase the binary of idealism/liberalism and realism, and, in the postclassical phase, searching for a niche between assertive mainstream theories of neorealism and neoliberalism and the radical and resistant alternatives to them, such as CT, postmodernism or poststructuralism. Its attraction lies in offering ever broader syntheses of theories and concepts that evaded the 'either/or framing' between realism/idealism during the First Great Debate or between explanatory/interpretive dichotomy that caused the 'fourth debate' during the 1990s. In their place, ES foregrounds a broad platform that 'combines theory and history, morality and power and agency and structure'.[49] There are other reasons why it occupies the middle way. According to Costa Buranelli, the holism that the ES believes in denies 'that either agency or structure have precedence in determining the course, the content and the characteristics of world politics'. In its view, in the matter of IP, especially international society, 'defined as an arrangement with which states regulate their relations through the use and the common understanding of norms, rules, practices and institutions', what really matters is 'the co-constitution of the agents giving birth to the structure and the structure constituting the roles, the behaviours and the identities of agents'. For Jørgensen, the middle way lies in the fact that 'the English School is currently in an interregnum between orthodoxy and innovation'.[50]

But predictably, this middle position is under pressure from all sides from right to left. Even in England and within LSE, known for research in the classical tradition, Brown critiques the concept of *international society* 'identified as occupying the middle position of a triptych', the other two being *system* and *community*, as problematic, whether seen 'as a "happy medium" to be defended in its own terms or as a "second best", defensible only because no better international order is on offer'. This is because 'whichever fork of the road is taken, the route to an international society is less straightforward than the international theory tradition suggests; the viability of the middle way is open to serious question, and it may be that "international society" is a conception of the international order that is available only under very limited circumstances' to only a handful of advanced, industrial, liberal-democratic states, not to all.[51] Again, Rengger, one of the least sectarian and discipline-bound liberal theorists of IR and representative of the British tradition at its best, also asked ES to close shop since it had failed in 'resolving the problem of how to adjudicate between international and world order' because of being a middle-of-the-roader. If it chooses 'to plump for the traditional international society model, international order would always have priority', but if it chooses 'to shift to a much more strongly cosmopolitan view, they would no longer be dealing in any meaningful sense with "international society" at all' and would rather reach a point at which 'the distinctive contribution of the ES simply evaporates'. Rengger saw the same problem of intellectual trade-off faced by another 'halfway house', namely constructivist theory. His advice to it and also to ES was that 'as always, the middle of the road is just too dangerous a place to be. Sooner or later, you have to move to one side or the other'.[52]

In Waltz's canonical text for neo-realists and positivists in IR, Bull finds no mention at all, while Wight only gets a passing reference in the discussion on alternative definitions of BOP. The words 'English School' or 'international society' are absent even in the index, and ES does not even qualify as a 'reductionist theory', the worst reproach word in the book.[53]

Neumann summarizes the basic critique of Ole Wæver, doyen of the Copenhagen School of security-oriented IRT, of the ES as its failure to specify 'exactly where international society resides—is it at the level of unquestioned, given, or doxic language, at the level of the clash of inherently contested concepts or at the level of negotiating utilitarian and co-operative institutions?'. But in Neumann's judgement, 'this boils down to a critique of lacking formalism, not a substantive one'.[54]

Postmodernist Walker objects to Wight's or Bull's search for a Groatian or Humian middle road and controverts Wight's contention in one of his writings that theories of IR are marginal to political theory. He also critiques Wight's historical method because of locating 'spatial differentiation' or the ahistorical contrast between political community within and anarchy without, as 'constitutive of modern political life in the transformations of the late medieval era', even as 'the myth of an eternal tradition almost collapses in the face of sustained historical analysis'.[55] Walker castigates Bull also because Bull's 'familiar threefold categorization' of approaches to IR' cannot limit 'the expansive capacities of the middle category. Introduced as a via media between the supposed extremes of realism and revolutionism (in other versions, idealism), Bull's analysis seems to be drawn in both directions at once'.[56]

Poststructuralist Jim George regards ES as an exemplar of an unselfconscious body of historical scholarship, wedded to the empiricist belief that the story of what really happened can be told without one imposing any part himself on the narrative and then passing judgement like Wight on the intractability of IR to theorizing in any political theoretic sense. He also regarded the famous Wightian typology of realists-rationalists-revolutionists as a mere replication of the 'simplistic realist/idealist dichotomy' by locating 'another universalistic category in the centre'. The Groatian category may have mitigated the aggressiveness of power-politics realism but never overcame its positivist bias based on 'the distinction between the scholar (subject) and an anarchical world of recurrence and repetition, existing "objectively out there"'.[57]

ES BUILDS BRIDGES

It is in the backdrop of such free-flowing criticisms from all sides that the methodological and substantive innovations of ES should be evaluated. One commentator rightly says that the most elemental characteristic of the ISA 'is an interpretative orientation that bears strong resemblances to the philosophy of Hans-Georg Gadamer'.[58] If this was done inadvertently (since unselfconsciousness was the keyword of George's criticisms of Wight and Bull), then later ES scholars, led by Buzan and Little, made ample amends for it. 'One aspect of the Buzan and Little work that rests uneasily with the earlier ES research is that they are self-conscious about the way in which they are building on the research agenda for historic systems identified by Wight and Watson'.[59] We can realize the full weight of the methodological eclecticism of Buzan and Little and other new recruits. While Buzan and Little have drawn on neorealist and systems-based spices to stir their history, Reus-Smit has taken the tradition in the opposite direction of constructivism. Shifting his attention away from international systems appearing in the hoary past of 5,500 years ago, Reus-Smit focuses on comparison across the history of different kinds of international systems that appeared around the times of ancient Greece, Renaissance Italy, absolutist Europe and the modern era, in the light of the constitutive role that institutions played in determining prevailing patterns of interaction in international society. Dunne says that Reus-Smit's refined constructivism eschews the penchant of the earlier cruder version for grand theory to allow room for historical change; criticizes its inordinate emphasis on sovereignty to the neglect of 'deep constitutive values that define the social identity of the state', and refuses to trace the beginnings of modern industrial society back from Westphalia, since the 'metavalues' of its underlying constitutional structure flowed from a rigidly hierarchical social structure.[60] Dunne also cites Wheeler's researches on humanitarian intervention[61] as a very good example of the new syncretism of the ES, especially where he mixes the injunctions of CT regarding the ideal dialogue with metaphors from constructivists and insights from Wittgenstein through his study of three Cold War and four post-Cold-War studies of humanitarian intervention to build up a solidarist theory of international society,[62] beyond Bull's warning against 'premature global solidarism'. In his own words, Wheeler wanted to 'develop a comprehensive framework for deciding what is to count as legitimate humanitarian intervention; examine how pluralist and solidarist conceptions of international society shaped the diplomatic dialogue over humanitarian interventions; provide a rebuttal of realist and pluralist critiques of humanitarian intervention, and integrate legal and pluralist approaches'. This solidarist conception of international society rubbishes the pluralist contention that 'state practice' is the litmus test of legitimate humanitarian intervention'[63] and is a fine example of the 'middle way'.

CONCLUSION

I wish to conclude this essay with a long quote from Buzan which expresses my sentiments and hopes about the approach's middle way perfectly:

> (T)he English School is an underutilized research resource. The time is ripe to develop and apply its historicist, constructivist, and methodologically pluralist approach to IR.... The English School is not just another paradigm to throw into the tedious game of competing IR theories. It is instead an opportunity to step outside that game, and cultivate a more holistic, integrated approach to the study of international relations. By this I do not mean the narrow 'neo-neo' synthesis that has settled around rational choice methodology and questions of absolute versus relative gains as a way of understanding international cooperation ... the English School offers a basis of synthesizing that is both wide and deep enough to set up the foundations for a return to grand theory.[64]

It is good that 38 years after Jones pleaded for a 'closure' of the school, its most versatile pedagogue asked for a 'reconvening' and creation of a '"great conversation" around it on the lines of what Wallerstein has done around "world systems"'.[65]

REVIEW QUESTIONS

1. Describe the names, early origins and later development of the ES, including its four phases.
2. In what ways have ES theorists looked at international society? Are there more common points than differences?
3. Discuss the Wightian classification of three Rs and three Ss as a scheme that best brings out the core arguments of the ES.
4. 'Since the end of the Cold War, the research agenda of the ES has not diametrically changed. But there has been a shift in priorities in some cases and additions and alterations in others.' Comment.
5. Identify the post-Cold-War transformations of the ES.
6. How does the ES represent the middle way and why is it under pressure? How does it build bridges to offset the pressure?

NOTES AND REFERENCES

1. See Barry Buzan, 'The English School: An Underexploited Resource in IR,' *Review of International Studies* 27 (2001): 471–488, here 471.
2. Roy E. Jones, 'The English School in International Relations: A Case for Closure,' *Review of International Studies* 7 (1981): 1–13.
3. Robert Jackson and Georg Sørensen, 'International Society,' in *Introduction to International Relations* (Oxford, NY: Oxford University Press, 1999), 139–174.
4. Tim Dunne, 'The English School,' in *International Relations: Discipline and Diversity*, eds. Tim Dunne, Milja Kurki, and Steve Smith (Oxford, NY: Oxford University Press, 2007), 128.
5. Tim Dunne, 'The English School,' in *The Oxford Handbook of International Relations*, eds. Christian Reus-Smit and Duncan Snidal (Oxford, NY: Oxford University Press, 2010), 267–268.
6. Robert M. A. Crawford, 'Where Have All the Theorists Gone—Gone to Britain, Every One? A Story of Two Parochialisms in International Relations,' in *International Relations—Still an American Social Science? Toward Diversity in International Thought*, eds. Robert Crawford, Darryl S. L. Jarvis (Albany, NY: State University of New York, 2001), 231–233.
7. Linda Quayle, *Southeast Asia and the English School of International Relations: A Region-theory Dialogue* (London: Palgrave Macmillan, 2013), 4.
8. Hidemi Suganami, 'The English School in a Nutshell,' *International Studies* 1983, available at: http://www.ritsumei.ac.jp/ir/isaru/assets/file/raris/raris-09-02Hidemi_Suganami.pdf (accessed on 09 April 2021), 15–28, here 15–17.
9. Andrew Linklater and Hidemi Suganami, *The English School of International Relations: A Contemporary Reassessment* (Cambridge, MA: Cambridge University Press, 2006), 260.
10. Dunne, 'The English School,' 269–270.
11. Linklater, Suganami, *The English School of International Relations*, 260.
12. Ole Wæver, 'International Society and the Development of International Relations Theory,' cited in Buzan, 'The English School,' 473–474.
13. Suganami, 'The English School in a Nutshell,' 17–26.
14. Tim Dunne, *Inventing International Society: A History of the English School* (Basingstoke: Macmillan, 1998), 5–11.

15. Buzan, 'The English School,' 474–475; Barry Buzan, *From International to World Society? English School Theory and the Social Structure of Globalisation* (New York, NY: Cambridge University Press, 2004), 6–8.
16. Martin Wight, *International Theory: The Three Traditions*, eds. Gabriele Wight and Brian Porter (Leicester: Leicester University Press, for the Royal Institute of International Affairs, 1991), 1.
17. Robert H. Jackson, 'Pluralism in International Political Theory,' *Review of International Studies* 18, no. 3 (1992): 271–281, here 271.
18. Robert Jackson and Georg Sørensen, *Introduction to International Relations* (Oxford, NY: Oxford University Press, 1999), 140.
19. Morgenthau, *Politics among Nations,* 5–6.
20. Jackson and Sørensen, *Introduction*, 142.
21. Hedley Bull, *The Anarchical Society: A Study of Order in World Politics*, 4th ed. with Forewords by Andrew Hurrell and Stanley Hoffman (London: Macmillan International Higher Education, 1977/2012), 13.
22. Hedley Bull and Adam Watson, *The Expansion of International Society* (Oxford: Clarendon Press, 1984), 1.
23. Dunne, *Inventing International Society,* 11.
24. Kai Alderson and Andrew Hurrell, 'Introduction,' in *Hedley Bull on International Society*, eds. Andrew Hurrell and Kai Alderson (London: Macmillan, 2000), 7.
25. Nicholas J. Wheeler and Tim Dunne, 'Hedley Bull's Pluralism of the Intellect and Solidarism of the Will,' *International Affairs* 72, no. 1 (1996): 91–107; Andrew Hurrell and Kai Alderson, *Hedley Bull on International Society* (London: Macmillan, 2000), 15; Dunne, 'The English School,' 136–138.
26. For instance, in Bull, 'Society and Anarchy in International Relations,' in *Diplomatic Investigations: Essays in the Theory of International Politics*, eds. H. Butterfield and M. Wight (London: Allen and Unwin, 1966); Bull, *The Anarchical Society;* in Suganami, 'The English School in a Nutshell,' 26.
27. R. J. Vincent, *Human Rights and International Relations* (Cambridge: Cambridge University Press, 1996), in Suganami, 'Nutshell', 25.
28. Buzan, *From International to World Society?* 139–143.
29. Jackson and Sørensen, *Introduction*, 152–165, 170–172.
30. Bull, *The Anarchical Society*, 254–266.
31. Georg Sørensen, 'IR Theory after the Cold War,' in *The Eighty Years' Crisis: International Relations 1919–1999*, eds. Tim Dunne, Michael Cox, Robert Cox (Cambridge: Cambridge University Press, 1998), 30.
32. Tim Dunne, 'New Thinking on International Society,' *British Journal of Politics and International Relations* 3, no. 2 (2001): 223–244, here 223.
33. Molly Cochran, 'Cosmopolitanism and Communitarianism in a Post-Cold War World,' in *Boundaries in Question: New Directions in International Relations Research*, eds. John Macmillan and Andrew Linklater (London: Pinter Publishers, 1995), 46–47.
34. Dunne, 'New Thinking on International Society,' 224.
35. Roy Jones, 'The English School in International Relations: A Case for Closure,' *Review of International Studies*, 7 (1981): 1–13.
36. Andrew Linklater, *International Relations: Critical Concepts in Political Science*, Vol. 1–5 (London: Routledge, 2000).
37. Hurrell and Alderson, *Hedley Bull on International Society.*
38. Barry Buzan and Richard Little, *International Systems in World History: Remaking the Study of International Relations* (Oxford: Oxford University Press, 2000).
39. I refer particularly to Hedley Bull, 'The Peace of Westphalia and the Modern International System,' Lecture Series, 1982, and the series on Hedley Bull, 'The Theory and Practice of

International Relations 1648–1789, Introduction,' in *The British Committee on the Theory of International Politics* (1954–1985), ed. Brunello Vigezzi (Milan: Unicopli, 2005); both cited in Hurrell and Alderson, *Hedley Bull on International Society*, 39.

40. Julien Saurin, 'The End of International Relations? The State and International Theory in the Age of Globalization,' in *Boundaries in Question: New Directions in International Relations*, John Macmillan and Andrew Linklater (London: Pinter Publishers, 1995), 244–245.
41. Dunne, 'New Thinking,' 224–228.
42. Buzan, Little, *International Systems in World History*, 1–7.
43. Barry Buzan, 'From International System to International Society: Structural Realism and Regime Theory Meet the English School,' *International Organization* 47, no. 3 (1993): 327–352.
44. See B. Buzan and A. Gonzalez-Pelaez, *International society and the Middle East: English School Theory at the Regional Level* (London: Palgrave Macmillan, 2009); Y. A. Stivachtis, 'Civilization and International Society: The Case of European Union Expansion,' *Contemporary Politics* 14, no. 1 (2008): 71–89; L. Schouenborg, *The Scandinavian International Society: Primary Institutions and Binding Forces*, 1815–2010 (London: Routledge, 2013); F. Merke, 'The Primary Institutions of the Latin American Regional Interstate Society,' presented at the IDEAS Latin America Programme, LSE, 2011; Barry Buzan and Yongjin Zhang, *Contesting International Society in East Asia* (Cambridge: Cambridge University Press, 2014); G. Pourchot and Y. A. Stivachtis, 'International Society and Regional Integration in Central Asia,' *Journal of Eurasian Studies* 5, no. 1 (2014): 68–76; K. Kaczmarska, 'Russia's Droit de Regard: Pluralist Norms and the Sphere of Influence,' *Global Discourse* 5, no. 3 (2015): 434–448; E. Tan Shek Yan, 'Understanding African International Society: An English School Approach,' Aberystwyth University, unpublished PhD Thesis, 2013; F. Costa Buranelli, '"Do You Know What I Mean? Not Exactly!" English School, Regional International Societies and the Polysemy of Institutions,' *Global Discourse* 5, no. 3 (2015): 499–514; all cited in, Filippo Costa Buranelli, 'The State of the Art in English School,' E-International Relations, 18 September 2015, available at: https://www.e-ir.info/2015/09/18/the-state-of-the-art-of-the-english-school (accessed on 09 April 2021).
45. Cornelia Navari, 'Methods and Methodology in the English School,' in *Theorising International Society: English School Methods*, ed. Cornelia Navari (New York, NY: Palgrave Macmillan, 2009), 1–2. See 21–28, 209–226, 39–57, 78–103, 148–166, 58–77, 125–147, for the other articles referred to, in that order.
46. C. Friedner Parrat, 'Changing before Our Eyes and Slipping between Our Fingers: International Organisations and Primary Institutions,' *International Studies Association*, Annual Conference, 2014; F. Costa Buranelli, 'Explaining the Yolks: Process-tracing and the Formation of Regional International Societies,' Workshop on Regional International Societies, Roskilde University, Denmark; cited in Costa Buranelli, 'State of the Art'.
47. A. Aissaoui, 'System or Society? Ancient Near Eastern Polities (ca. 1600–1200 BCE),' International Studies Association, San Francisco, CA, 2013; C. A. Schulz, 'Civilisation, Barbarism and the Making of Latin America's Place in 19th-century International Society,' *Millennium: Journal of International Studies* 42, no. 3 (2014): 837–859; F. Costa Buranelli, 'Knockin' on Heaven's Door: Russia, Central Asia and the Mediated Expansion of International Society,' *Millennium: Journal of International Studies* 42, no. 3 (2014): 817–836; J. A. Pella Jr. 'World Society, International Society and the Colonization of Africa,' *Cambridge Review of International Affairs* 28, no. 2 (2015): 210–228; cited in Costa Buranelli, 'State of the Art'.
48. Buzan, *From International to World Society?*; K. J. Holsti, *Taming the Sovereigns: Institutional Change in International Politics* (Cambridge: Cambridge University Press, 2004); T. B. Knudsen, 'Fundamental institutional Change at the UN and the ICC: Solidarist Practices of

Law and War,' International Studies Association, New Orleans, LA, 2015; K. Spandler, 'The Political International Society: Change in Primary and Secondary Institutions,' *Review of International Studies* 41, no. 3 (2015): 601–622, doi: 10.1017/S026021051400045X, cited in Costa Buranelli, 'State of the Art'.

49. Dunne, 'The English School,' 128, 268.
50. K. E. Jørgensen, '"Things are different in Pago Pago": A Rejoinder to Ahrens and Diez,' *Global Discourse* 5, no. 3 (2015): 356–359, cited in Costa Buranelli, 'State of the Art.'
51. Chris Brown, 'International Theory and International Society: The Viability of the Middle Way?' *Review of International Studies* 21, no. 2 (1995): 183–196, especially 184, 195.
52. Nicholas J. Rengger, *International Relations, Political Theory and the Problem of Order: Beyond International Relations Theory* (London: Routledge, 2000), 92–94.
53. Waltz, *Theory of International Politics*, 117, and *passim*.
54. Iver B. Neumann, 'John Vincent and the English School of IR,' in *The Future of International* Relations, eds. Iver B. Neumann, Ole Waever (London: Routledge, 1997), 65.
55. R. B. J. Walker, *Inside/Outside: International Relations as Political Theory* (Cambridge: Cambridge University Press, 1993), 32–34.
56. Ibid., 69.
57. Jim George, '(Re)Introducing the Theory as Practice of International Relations,' in George, *Discourses of Global Politics: A Critical (Re)Introduction to International Relations* (Boulder, CO: Lynne Rienner Publishers, 1994), 81–82.
58. Roger Epp, 'The English School on the Frontiers of International Society,' in *The Eighty Years' Crisis, eds.* Michael Cox, Tim Dunne, and Ken Booth (Cambridge: Cambridge University Press, 1999), 49.
59. See Dunne, 'New Thinking on International Society,' 230. Dunne is referring to Herbert Butterfield and Martin Wight, eds., *Diplomatic Investigations: Essays in the Theory of International Politics* [for] British Committee on the Theory of International Politics (London: Allen and Unwin, 1966); M. Wight, *Systems of States* (Leicester: Leicester University Press [for] the London School of Economics and Political Science, 1977); Adam Watson, *The Evolution of International Society: A Comparative Historical Analysis* (London: Routledge, 1992).
60. Christian Reus-Smit, *The Moral Purpose of the State: Social Identity and Institutional Rationality in International Relations* (Princeton, NJ: Princeton University Press, 1999), 40–199 for international systems, and 6, 39, 153–168 for these constitutive 'metavalues'. Also see Dunne, 'New Thinking on International Society,' 230–233, for his assessment of Reus-Smit.
61. Nicholas J. Wheeler, *Saving Strangers: Humanitarian Intervention in International Society* (New York: Oxford University Press, 2000).
62. See Dunne, 'New Thinking on International Society,' 239–240.
63. Wheeler, *Saving Strangers*, 12, 52.
64. Buzan, 'English School: Underexploited,' 472.
65. Ibid., 481.

CHAPTER

24

Critical Theory: Postpositivism in International Relations

CHAPTER OUTLINE

INTRODUCTION: SIGNIFICANCE OF THE TERM 'CRITICAL THEORY' AND PARENTAGE OF THE THEORY

The admittance of Critical theory (CT) to IR is symptomatic of its 'reflectivist' turn against the reigning realist, liberal and Marxist orthodoxies, as well as against its rationalist revision by Keohane in the early 1980s (see Chapter 1 of this book). But the approaches and perspectives included by different scholars within CT being quite diverse, CT 'does not form a unity', but is rather divisible into 'at least two branches—the first centred around the Institute of Social Research, established in Frankfurt in 1923, and the second around the more recent works of Jürgen Habermas'. The first branch comprised research of the Institute spearheaded by scholars from diverse backgrounds, such as Max Horkheimer (philosophy-sociology-social psychology), Friedrich Pollock (economics-planning), Theodor Adorno (philosophy-sociology-musicology), Erich Fromm (psychoanalysis-social psychology), Herbert Marcuse (philosophy), Franz Neumann and Otto Kirchheimer (political science-jurisprudence), Leo Lowenthal (popular culture-literature), Henryk Grossman (PE), Arkadij Gurland (economics-sociology), and, at the outskirts of the Institute, Walter Benjamin (literary criticism). Horkheimer, Adorno, Marcuse, Lowenthal and Pollock formed the quintuple core of the famous 'Frankfurt School', because of the comparability and complementarity of their research, though others affiliated with the Institute too contributed significantly. Later, works of Habermas (philosophy-sociology), assisted by the writings of Albrecht Wellmer (philosophy), Claus Offe (political science and sociology) and Klaus Eder (anthropology) recast the notion of CT into the form it is known by us now.[1]

Other commentators cast the net even wider. From the perspective of literary theory, Tyson includes within the purview of CT widely divergent forms of criticisms of existing orthodoxies in Western tradition: 'psychoanalytic', 'Marxist', 'feminist', 'new', 'reader-response', 'structuralist', 'deconstructive', 'new historical and cultural', 'lesbian/gay', 'African-American' and 'postcolonial', at least the first two not being strictly postpositivist too.[2] Even within IRT, Brown treated CT as a generic category, accommodating, apart from the Frankfurt School from Horkheimer to Habermas, postmodernism, poststructuralism and feminism, because they all shared the view that the hegemonic discourses of modernity emanating from Enlightenment thought were facing a crisis.[3] But we will mainly treat the Frankfurt School and its later Habermasian developments as CT in this chapter, though not entirely neglecting other sources as supplements to the former, for two reasons.

First, some commentators make a distinction between the attitudes of CT and postmodernism/poststructuralism towards the Enlightenment Project. Both stem from the culturally pessimistic contentions of Nietzsche and Heidegger that, far from delivering emancipation, the reigning Enlightenment-driven trend in the 19th and early 20th centuries is fraught with calamities yet have two characteristic responses to this. While postmodernism wants to totally discard the Enlightenment Project, CT argues that, even though not deserving uncritical defence as before, some parts of Enlightenment can be still salvaged. Brown himself links this attitude to CT, 'capitalized to distinguish this from looser usages'. However, he equates postmodernism with CT through the unifying critique of the Enlightenment.[4]

Second, the dominant meaning given to CT in the majority of IR books is the body of thoughts represented by the thinkers of the Frankfurt School and the Institute and their appliers in IR. Shapcott pertinently urges us to note that

> ...a common distinction is made between small 'c' and large 'C' critical theory, with only the latter referring to the Frankfurt School approaches. Small 'c' includes approaches that are sceptical about the emancipatory project outlined by the Frankfurt School such as poststructuralism, (some) feminism, and critical realism... Many small 'c' approaches reject their assimilation into Andrew Linklater's project of community and have a philosophical resistance to talk of emancipation.[5]

This chapter mainly treats the large 'C' CT within IRT, keeping small 'c' approaches in/for separate chapters (such as feminism, already done, and postmodernism/poststructuralism, to be done), except where IR theorists themselves mix small 'c' elements with large 'C' critical analyses.

WHAT CRITICAL THEORISTS SAID IN ONE VOICE AMID THEIR DIFFERENCES OUTSIDE IR

Before embarking on its journey to IRT, CT aimed at a thorough restructuring of social and political theory and found its main obstacle in 'Comtean positivism...a great source of reactionary thought in the 19th century'. It regarded Enlightenment too as incomplete and 'the standard Enlightenment view as one dimensional', having 'no place in it for what makes life significant'.[6]

Refusing to identify freedom with any institutional arrangement or fixed system of thought, CT sought to uncover the 'hidden assumptions and purposes of competing theories and existing forms of practice' and asserted that thought must address the new problems and possibilities for liberation emanating from altered historical circumstances.[7] Epistemologically, critical theorists rubbished the idea of objectively valid forms of knowledge reachable 'independently of social context, innocent of prevailing practices and norms', and questioned the dichotomization of 'is and ought, fact and value, known object and knowing subject which underpinned "positivist" forms of scientific knowledge claims and associated constructs'. Borrowing from Horkheimer and Adorno's bitter critique of 'instrumental reason' that professes neutrality regarding ends, CT would rather regard 'the construction of social knowledge' as 'no less a purposive social practice than any other'. For, 'theory is permeated with social values and norms, fraught with political implications for the future, whether they are explicit or implicit'. To that extent, CT supposedly considered theories which aspire to objective truth as 'profoundly misleading', not only because they hide all 'normative commitments' which undergird their own truth claims but also because they deny that 'alternative normative values and future possible worlds are at stake in knowledge claims which the theory offers up as fact'.[8]

But all critical theorists allowed that while 'all knowledge is historically conditioned, truth claims can be rationally adjudicated independently of immediate social (i.e., class) interests'. They 'defended the possibility of an independent moment of criticism' and also 'attempted to justify CT on a non-objectivist and materialistic foundation'. They built on the notion of critique from its germinal seeds in the thoughts of Kant (about 'the conditions and limits of reason and knowledge'), Hegel (regarding reflection on the emergence of spirit) and Marx (concerning the specific socio-historical formation of capitalism and its underlying exchange), which were then refined further by the thoughts of the Frankfurt theorists and Habermas.[9]

Although most of the important early members of the Institute worked explicitly within the contours of Marxist theory, Horkheimer and Habermas were notable exceptions. Habermas built on the legacy of the Frankfurt school, but minus its baggage of Marxism and cultural pessimism. While continuing to work 'openly within the Marxist tradition', Horkheimer desisted from terming his approach as 'Marxist' to distance his dialectical method, true to Marx's conception of the 'critique', from 'vulgar (positivist) philosophy and PE'.[10] Habermas had no such compunctions. In *Knowledge and Human Interests* (1968), he claimed that the human species possesses three types of cognitive or 'knowledge-constitutive' interest: technical, practical and emancipatory, facilitating the conditions for the emergence of three types of sciences: empirical-analytic, hermeneutic and critical. These three sciences act to systematize and formalize the procedures required for the basic human activities of controlling external conditions, communicating and reflecting so that the human species may function. Accordingly, Habermas replaces Horkheimer's dichotomous division between traditional theory and CT with a trichotomous distinction between the natural sciences (foregrounding 'empiricoanalytical knowledge' and meeting the needs of prediction and control); the cultural sciences (or the historical–hermeneutic sciences, meeting the needs of understanding of meaning) and the critical science (catering for the needs of freedom from domination, emancipation and the attainment of rational autonomy).[11]

True to Horkheimer's saying that CT is engaged with 'people and all their potential', CT commits itself to identifying, critiquing and overcoming 'any social mechanisms and structures that systematically prevent people from realizing their potential'. To that end, CT 'engages both with social practice and with other social science theories'. In the domain of social practice, different types of exclusion caused by gender, race or nationality are addressed. In the domain of theory, 'non-critical' (meaning *traditional, positivistic* or *problem-solving*) theories are castigated because, while analysing the social world, these merely tinker with extant patterns of exclusion. Treating the social world as a research object amenable to explanation or technological manipulation involves presenting it as 'quasi-natural'. CT wants to expose such 'false naturalizations' and 'explain the historical contingency and fundamental changeability of social conditions previously regarded as natural' so that one might visualize options that might facilitate emancipation from exclusionary systems and 'help create *more inclusive* orders'.[12]

JOURNEY OF CRITICAL THEORY TO IR

CT first travelled to IR land in the early 1980s, through the writings of scholars such as Richard Ashley, Robert W. Cox, Andrew Linklater, John Maclean and Mark Hoffman. They raised or addressed epistemological, ontological and axiological questions, familiar in social sciences and summarized above, but normally marginalized or sidelined in mainstream IRT. The epistemological questions mostly centred around the relationship between knowledge and values, particularly focusing on the latent interests informing the major theoretical traditions of IR. The ontological questions aimed at identifying and exploring not just the relevant agents and structures in IR but also their historical transformations and 'complicity with various forms of domination and exclusion'. The normative or axiological questions, already implicitly implicated in the epistemological and ontological concerns, were mostly induced by CT's interest in emancipation. From the viewpoint of the tradition of emancipatory thinking, running from Kant through Marx to Habermas, CT decided to look into the possibilities of cleansing IR of all obstacles or impediments to universal freedom and equality.

But from the mid-1990s, a new breed of 'critical international theorists' (henceforth CRITHEOs) grew within IR itself, including Karin Fierke, Stephen Gill, Kimberly Hutchings, Mark Neufeld, Richard Shapcott and so on who drew upon the classical tradition of emancipatory thought (Aristotelian, Hegelian), but mixed it with Foucaultian, Gadamerian and Wittgensteinian perspectives and Habermasian elements. Although, eclectic in their intellectual moorings, CRITHEOs are held together by their common belief that the study of IR should be geared to an emancipatory politics, aimed at the elimination of different forms of domination and the furtherance of global freedom, justice and equality, conceptualized in terms of 'reflexive theory based on the method of immanent critique'.[13]

Explaining Late Entry of CT in IR

It surprises one that IRT took so long to admit CT, since its birth had an unmistakable international context. Frankfurt scholars had seen how post-First World War socialist uprisings in Germany petered out; fascism rose in Spain, Italy and Germany; a Bolshevik form of totalitarianism emerged in the Soviet Union and a new form of domination centred around mass culture and consumption became manifested in the exile of Adorno, Horkheimer and Marcuse.[14] Faced with the (a) installation of bureaucratic socialisms in Eastern Europe, (b) the rise of fascism in Central Europe and (c) the birth of the 'culture industry' in Western Europe, Frankfurt theorists understood the inadequacies of Marxism. Since it was no longer possible to regard the working class as the vehicle of removal of obstacles to freedom and front-line soldiers in the fight against domination, Frankfurt theorists engaged in a reconstruction of Marxism to give a better portrayal of the new situation of the ideological hegemony of capitalism and the cultural invasion of mass society.

The critiques of the 'culture industry' offered by Adorno, Horkheimer and Marcuse veered over the years between two theoretical stances. The first critique was elaborated as a supplement to the Marxist critique of capitalism, where workers, now substituted by the 'masses', were seen as 'manipulated', narcotized and depoliticized dupes of capitalist values, benumbed by the entire post-Second World War paraphernalia of quotidian leisure and life. The culture industry symbolized in all its manifestations a unified and apparently baffling design to disrupt the class struggle, and the contemporary life generated by all bearers of popular culture was 'a parody of crude capitalist greed and stupid working class gullibility'.

In the second critique, Adorno and Horkheimer, even if probably not Marcuse, despaired over the negative, libertarian tendencies of the working class and turned their attention to the capitalist mode of production as their main target. Both the bourgeois and working-class subjects slowly disappeared from their writings, and Adorno, in particular, 'moved towards a "negative dialectic", a postulate of non-identity and a remote appeal to critique as the last resort of a world without discernible hope of redemption'.[15]

Now, if Horkheimer and other theorists of the School and the Institute were worried by the intellectual and political trends of the 1920s and 1930s, the 'critical turn' in IR was induced by the tensions generated by the Second Cold War and the iniquity of the Vietnam War. Positivism was viewed as conniving in the injustice of the American involvement in the Vietnam War, with its political and moral disaster, testifying to the inadequacy of the technical reason and the vacuity of the triumph of policy 'science'. Similarly, the heightened tensions between the superpowers, and the nuclear race between them, made some observers wonder if IR itself was not disciplinarily 'contributing to the problems faced in the international realm'. Accordingly, CRITHEOs asked their mainstream colleagues to remember Cox's famous warning about theory's beneficiaries and the purposes served by theory for them (we are coming to it below) in that light to realize their own 'cognitive interests' and purposes.[16]

From Critical Theory to Critical International Theory

But when CT finally entered the IR land, it was not just as the thought of the Frankfurt School plus Habermas applied in a special field. It came with its own established concerns in the first wave, plus new concerns developed by critical international theory (hereafter CRINTHEO). Devetak affirms that as a historical phenomenon, CRINTHEO does not reveal a single unbroken line of conceptual descent from an origin in the European Enlightenment, the Frankfurt School or the Regina Coeli,[17] to the current style. Despite recognizing 'the influence and reception of these origins and their ideas', along with the impact of Nietzschean and Foucaultian genealogy, one should not

> think that the emergence of CT in international relations is the linear story of an original idea of CT extended to international relations, and in the process evolving to become critical international theory—simply applying concepts and methods originally tailored to society to international politics.[18]

In the next section, we will first show how the familiar social theoretic concerns of CT, such as the politics of knowledge (POK), emancipatory knowledge and its politics, and reconceptualization of the political community, were taken up in its application in IR.

TRANSFORMATION OF CT's CONCERNS IN CRINTHEO: FROM POLITICS OF KNOWLEDGE TO ALTERNATIVE WORLD ORDERS

True to one of its sources in the Frankfurt School plus Habermas, CRINTHEO has grappled with the questions related to POK that became relevant in IR ever since the 'third debate', and more explicitly since the 'fourth debate'. Issues integral to POK were modes of 'justification and verification of knowledge claims', questions about the methodology employed to gain knowledge, 'the scope and purpose of theory' and ontological concerns about the 'nature of the social actors and other historical formations and structures of IR'. All of these questions involved normative implications that were unfashionable in IR ever since the triumph of neorealism or structural realism here. One of the changes introduced by CRINTHEO in IR was not only prioritizations of these epistemological and ontological questions in IR but the explication of their nature in prior political conceptions of the international society or system.[19] Horkheimer's dichotomous division between theories, and its replacement by Habermas with a trichotomous distinction between three types of sciences, based on corresponding technical, practical and emancipatory 'knowledge-constitutive' interests,[20] were leads taken up by Cox to famously claim in 1981 that 'theory is always for someone and for some purpose'. This means that all theories possess a perspective, deriving from a 'specifically political time and space', whereby the world becomes 'definable in terms of nation or social class, of dominance or subordination, of rising or declining power, of a sense of immobility or of present crisis, of past experience, and of hopes and expectations for the future'. While no theory can shake off the shackles of perspective, with greater sophistication, it can reflect upon and transcend its own perspective. Still, 'the initial perspective is always contained within a theory and is relevant to explication. There is accordingly no such thing as theory in itself, divorced from a standpoint in time and space'.[21] In line with this realization, CRITHEOs refuse to treat any type of theoretical knowledge as neutral or apolitical. Hutchings shows how Cox uses the distinction made by 'Gramsci between hegemonic and counter-hegemonic discourses to capture the way in which theory is political'. He thinks that the application of the 'Hegelian–Foucauldian approach to normative international theory' can take us beyond the repetition of old debates, showing simultaneously how 'it allows the international to be conceived (the theory of politics)' and 'how it understands the nature of theorizing itself and the relation between theorist and theoretical object (the politics of theory)'.[22]

Cox regards the first purpose of theory (traditional for Horkheimer) as one of 'simple, direct response'. Aimed at guidance 'to help solve problems posed within the terms of the particular perspective which was the point of departure', it generates positivistic or *problem-solving theory* and 'takes the world as it finds it, with the prevailing social relationships and the institutions in which they are organized, as the given framework for action'. The second purpose, which is 'more reflective upon the process of theorizing itself', is prone 'to become easily aware of the perspective that gives rise to theorizing, and its relation to other perspectives (to achieve a perspective on perspectives)'. It is more willing to explore 'the possibility of choosing a different valid perspective from which the problematic becomes one of creating an alternative world', thereby engendering 'critical theory'. It is critical for questioning the prevailing world order, enquiring into its origins rather than begging the questions about institutions and social and power relations, and possible processes of change. Accordingly, unlike problem-solving theory, which is 'non-historical or ahistorical', positing a 'continuous present' with the constancy of institutions and power relations constituting its main parameters, CT is a 'theory of history', reflecting on not just the past but also on 'a continuous process of historical change'.

How is critical thinking on POK and CT as its outgrowth related to IP? Cox says that CT is 'not unconcerned with the problems of the real world'. But 'it approaches practice from a perspective that transcends that of the existing order, which problem-solving theory takes as its starting point', instead allowing for 'a normative choice in favour of a social and political order different from the prevailing order'. CT, however, circumscribes the gamut of the alternative orders after clarifying for itself their range to choose only feasible ones. This circumscription becomes relevant because the 'perspectives of different historical periods favour one or the other kind of theory'. In this connexion, Cox relates both 'problem-solving theory' and CT to temporal perspectives on IR. Thus,

> Periods of apparent stability or fixity in power relations favour the problem-solving approach. The Cold War was one such period. In international relations, it fostered a concentration upon the problems of how to manage an apparently enduring relationship between the two superpowers. However, a condition of uncertainty in power relations beckons to critical theory as people seek to understand the opportunities and risks of change. Thus, the events of the 1970s generated a sense of greater fluidity of power relations, of a many-faceted crisis, crossing the threshold of uncertainty and opening a new development of critical theory directed to the problems of world order. To reason about the possible future world orders now, however, requires a broadening of our enquiry beyond conventional international relations, so as to encompass basic processes at work in the development of social forces and forms of state, and in the structure of global political economy.

Critique of Mainstream Theories

CRINTHEO took off precisely from here. It regarded both realism/neorealism and liberal internationalism as problem-solving theories that were, ipso facto, limited. According to Cox, despite being men of great historical knowledge, both Morgenthau and Waltz were 'prone to adopt the fixed ahistorical view of the frame of action characteristic of the problem-solving theory', instead of seeing it as 'historically conditioned and thus susceptible to change' after Carr. The debate between neorealists and liberal internationalists is also nothing but a historically updated version of the 17th-century challenge thrown by 'the civil philosophy of Hobbes to the natural law theory of Grotius'.[23] Neoliberal institutionalism is also similarly tainted. 'Its epistemology has remained both positivistic and rational deductive insofar as its objects of inquiry are actors and interactions and as it attempts to account for their behaviour through models of rational choice' and 'has its starting point in the coexistence of state system and the world capitalist economy'.[24]

Other CRITHEOs either followed the Coxian version of CT or went back to Habermas to add their own versions. Linklater contends that Habermas' threefold distinction of social sciences can accommodate the three Wightian traditions of realism, rationalism (or Groatianism) and revolutionism (another name of which is CRINTHEO). They 'form a sequence of progressively more adequate approaches to world politics'. Surely, 'a theory which analyses the language and culture of diplomatic interaction in order to promote international consensus' (or rationalism, and particularly regime thinking and interdependence) is more advanced than 'a theory of recurrent forces constituted by an interest in manipulation and control' (or realism/neorealism). But far more advanced is 'an account of world politics which seeks to understand the prospects for extending the human capacity for self-determination'.[25] Shapcott shows that liberal institutionalism, the ES or Wight's Groatian approach and even constructivism are linked to Habermas's 'practical interest' and the historical–hermeneutic or cultural sciences of which it was a vehicle. Liberal institutionalism is critiqued because, apart from propagating change within, rather than of, the existing international system, and not pleading for an avowedly more 'political' world order, it merely wants movement away from neorealist anarchy to 'a highly reflexive institutionalized or mature anarchy', which is in essence 'a shift from one form of technical rationality, strategic, to another, cooperative'. The ES takes flak because, despite concentrating on the communication and agreement between the actors that turn international systems into civilized societies marked by rule-governed interstate interactions, it implicitly avoids talk of changing the system, being more amenable to normative reflection and prescription and keeping revolutionism as only one of the options. Constructivism is criticized because, despite saying (especially in its Wendtian version) that 'anarchy is what the states make it', taking IR as 'a realm of meaning and not just material power', and being preoccupied with the construction of the reigning norms in the international domain and the constitution of that domain by these norms, constructivism preserves the fact/value differentiation of the *verstehen* sociology and thereby separates questions of 'is' from 'ought'. Additionally, in spite of disclosing how such norms come into being, constructivist analysis does not possess the intellectual faculties of rational critical assessment of them.[26]

The only theory which is able to make this critical evaluation is one which knows that cognitive mechanisms are set in motion by springs of political interest, and that (as per Habermas) knowledge is *not* constituted objectively as 'a universe of facts whose law-like connection can be grasped descriptively'. Ashley's desire that 'the illusion of objectivism' is to be 'replaced with the "recognition that knowledge is always constituted in reflection of interests"' applies to political realism.[27] Obeying this foundational belief, CT, particularly its later version, not only wanted to tease out the concealed interests that colour any theory but also looked at its own goals in self-reflectiveness. True that first-generation CT, as in the writings of Horkheimer in the 1930s, looked askance at moral norms, influenced by Schopenhauer's doubts at their rational foundation, Marx's cynicism about their political potential, and Nietzsche's doubts about the consequences of morality for individuals. But ever since Habermas' and Karl Apel's second-generation CT writings of the 1960s, a reassessment and revaluation of the normative content of theory started. And now it seems to have been 'the central motive and driving force behind the deep and far-reaching conceptual definition of language, reason, subjectivity and modernity' through which the younger generation of CT sought 'to overcome what they interpreted as the impasse of this tradition'.[28]

CRINTHEO continued CT's concern with normative theory and embodied Neufield's three defining features of emancipatory theory: (a) 'theoretical reflexivity' involving the conviction that any theorization aimed at emancipation cannot stay confined to an examination of the empirical; (b) belief in the 'creative role of human consciousness: a role which goes beyond the process of knowledge production' to extend to the designing and transforming of patterns of social and political existence and (c) focus on emancipation, in tune with the general tenor of the Aristotelian project, distinguished by involvement in social criticism geared towards 'practical political activity oriented towards social transformation'. Considerations of morality cannot but be integral to theoretical reflexivity, in the sense of 'theoretical reflection on the process of theorizing itself'. Neufield insists that in the study of world politics, it is 'not that normative concerns ought to be addressed', but that 'they have always been at the centre of the subject'.[29] Menke thinks 'self-reflection consists in a bending-back-upon-itself—a referring back to itself of moral reflection that creates distance and enables critical scrutiny. Self-reflection in morality is…required when simple moral reflection proves insufficient or wrong'.[30]

Reflection on the Existing Order and the Emancipatory Project

Despite refusing to accept the existing order in its current shape, CT and CRINTHEO do not plainly ignore it. Following Marx's caution in *The Eighteenth Brumaire of Louis Bonaparte* that 'Men make their own history…not…just as they please…not…in circumstances chosen by themselves, but under circumstances directly encountered, given, and transmitted from the past',[31] they advise undertaking a detailed investigation into the present conditions, so that the order that prevails does not seem anymore as either natural or inevitable. Applying this insight to the present global configuration of power relations, CRINTHEO concentrates on how it originated, with what attendant costs, and keeps what alternative possibilities open in history. This helps fight the reigning modes of dogmatism in present theorizing, lays bare the undiagnosed assumptions that inform traditional modes of thought and reveals their complicity with extant exploitative arrangements. It denaturalizes them in order 'to consider alternatives to the prevailing order'.[32]

Reflection on the prevailing order inevitably involves a critique of the ideology which sustains it. CT learnt from Marx that 'a central task of critical theory was to criticize ideology' so as to reveal 'how the terms in which societies legitimated their arrangements clashed profoundly with existing social and political conditions', being thereby able to pinpoint 'the particular revolutionary social forces which emerged from the tension between ideology and practice'. The critique, however, is to be conducted not in Kantian abstract or utopian terms, but through 'immanent critique', following Marx and Engels' reminder that 'it is necessary to judge societies with the same terms they use to describe and legitimize themselves'.[33]

CRINTHEO's emancipatory dimension comes straight from Frankfurt School's and Horkheimer's anti-positivistic 'desire to "lend voice to suffering" and to "abolish existing misery"'.[34] Hoffman says that CT seeks to not 'simply reproduce society by description, but to understand society and change it', evincing 'both descriptive and constructive…theoretical intent' as 'both an intellectual and a social act'.[35] Accordingly, CT attacks 'the immutability thesis' of positivistic theory, which 'sanctifies historically specific configurations of power that the weak may resent'.[36] It views IR not as a field for 'hunting down immutable laws' but as one for 'exploration of the manner in which some political ideas have become political facts, whereas others have not'.[37] Again, true to Habermas' suggestion that the emancipatory interest of critical science inheres in the identification and eradication of unwelcome social confinements and constraints, Ashley highlighted the 'interest in securing freedom from unacknowledged constraints, relations of domination, and conditions of distorted communication and understanding that deny humans the capacity to make their future through full will and consciousness'.[38]

CT's, Especially Habermas', Critical Commentary on Concrete International Developments and Practices

We have already shown how the anti-democratic, authoritarian and consumerist-cultural tendencies of Europe disillusioned the earlier members of the Frankfurt School with the Marxist project of emancipation,[39] based on 'the centrality of production and class conflict'. Later members sought to retrieve the emancipatory project without being bogged down in classical Marxism but yet not losing sight of the deleterious side of capitalist modernity. Marcuse[40] first castigated the 'one-dimensional man' created by capitalism's preoccupation with the gratification of manufactured material needs, and he reposed faith in the student movement of the 1960s and struggles for national liberation and socialism in the Third World, represented as major political initiatives towards the creation of a free society.

Habermas too showed how efforts to administer capitalist societies more efficiently and economically have brought about 'colonization of the life world' via 'the encroachment of administrative rationality on everyday life'. He supported social movements, which propagated human security, equality for women and fought against environmental degradation, as heralds of a new kind of society that substituted efforts to control nature and administer society by counter-efforts to expand human freedom. In the backdrop of state systems supported by neorealism, Habermas praised the EU as an important innovation towards the creation of 'postnational communities' bound by 'shared commitments to world citizenship and cosmopolitan law', which no more prioritized the state marked by a dominant nationality or dedication to selfish interests. Besides states in Europe, there were other entities pressurized to fashion new political arrangements that would recognize the multicultural nature of modern societies. This 'post-national' development was caused by the greater mobility of people and globalization, and it facilitated the realization that democracy should be designed on world scales to endure. In his proposal for a cosmopolitan democracy that would have to thread together people and cultures that have not had a common language, common symbols or the shared history that have undergirded nation states for the past 200 years, Habermas was plainly influenced by Kant's ideal of perpetual peace and Marx's internationalism.

Evidently, Habermas has been more prone than earlier or other members of the Frankfurt School to comment on current international affairs. While desisting from theorizing current international developments towards a CRINTHEO, Habermas has in his many interviews and journalistic essays addressed some global issues, including the 1991 Gulf War, NATO's intervention over Kosovo in 1999 and the dramatic political events of the period since 11 September 2001 that led to the war in Iraq since 2003, in the context of his 'discourse theory of morality' derived from Kant's ethical doctrine.[41] He showed how the unilateral misadventure of the USA in going to war in Iraq without backing by unambiguous UNSC resolutions compromised its international normative status, created deep fissures between allies, among allies and opponents, and opened up the cauldron of international terrorism. But he did all this in the light of the Kantian project of replacing friction between states typical of SON by a constitutionalization of international law, informed by the vision of a multidimensional model of transnational and supranational governance inspired by Kantian cosmopolitanism.[42] Habermas also wrote on the crisis of the EU amid globalization and suggested its evolution away from an executive federalism and regional internationalization into a cosmopolitan community as a way out of its impasse caused by the crisis of the Eurozone threatening its very existence. 'The civilizing role of the European unification', said Habermas, 'acquires prominence especially in the light of a more far-reaching cosmopolitanism'.[43] But Habermas looked at all these developments with an open critical eye, blinkered not even by the new CT he was constructing. Habermas' political writings remained loosely tied to his 'theoretical defence of universalism'. Remarkably, 'his theory is never simply imposed on his occasional writings', and despite being a 'prodigious theory-writer Habermas has never fallen into the trap of making the facts fit the theory'. Rather, 'Habermas' political writings carry on a noticeably tense relation' with his theoretical project.[44]

It was obvious and predictable that after quarrying POK in social science and IR, and clarifying for itself its emancipatory task, CT and CRINTHEO will re-conceptualize for itself the ideal political community. To this we now turn.

RE-CONCEPTUALIZING POLITICAL COMMUNITY

CRINTHEO's rethinking of the political community proceeds from three angles: the normative (principally revolving around the philosophical critique of the state and its exclusionary and particularistic practices), the sociological (mainly urging the exploration of the origins and evolution of the modern state or states system) and the praxeological (concerning the 'practical possibilities' for redesigning IR in more emancipatory and cosmopolitan directions).[45]

The Normative/Philosophical Critical Dimension

Normative theory, marginalized in IR's self-interpretation for a long time, became a newly burgeoning field in CRINTHEO through systematic thinking on emancipation, aided by moral universalism through dialogical principles. While the avowed objective of emancipation was 'freedom to consent or to be included in open dialogue in relation to the action of all others',[46] the dialogue was true to Habermas' concept of 'ideal speech situation', one 'that is in principle open to all human beings, that accepts the prima facie equal legitimacy of all claims, and that proceeds on the assumption that... no one can be sure about who will learn from whom...'.[47] The state being its main obstacle, its normative philosophical critique in CRINTHEO starts from a Marxist-inspired attack against the naturalizing and fetishizing of the modern state by attracting attention to its 'moral deficits' coming from its complicity in the capitalist organization of the world economy. Linklater critiques the normative basis of political life built around the state from the perspectives of its 'ethical particularism', the resultant social exclusions and the discrimination it constantly makes between citizens and non-citizens or the rest of the humanity in the matter of its ethical obligations. He contrasts the 'fragmented nature of modern political and social life' with 'the communitarian character of the Greek polis' and refers to Rousseau's and later Hegel's efforts to reconcile the latter with the modern principle of individuality, and even to the early concerns of Marx about how to 'make good citizens out of modern men, men who are no longer spontaneous citizens'. Linklater is convinced that the tensions regarding men and citizens have become integral to the experience of the modern states system, ever since the emergence of moral and religious individualism has divided the Western experience of morality between two opposing viewpoints. The first regards it as a matter internal to a particular community, which is the 'source of his concrete ethical life and the particular object of his political loyalty', while according to the other the moral law it applies to humans *qua* humans and not as insiders of any specific community. Persons may 'employ their rational faculties' to stipulate their rights, duties and moral aspirations because the state is 'an incomplete moral community' and the states system is an impediment to the 'institutional expression of the human race'.

Linklater found this 'dividedness' between these opposed moral standpoints unresolved in different stages of modern international thought. The 'man–citizen dichotomy' remained a principal concern of theories of IR, generating irreconcilable assessments of the ethics of statecraft. Kant's achievement in providing an international theory could not prevent the emergence of a historicist theory of IR and a philosophical history of it, both of which sustained the difference between man and citizen in their own ways. From a romanticized and rationalist viewpoint, the historicist view posited that 'the capacities of men were inextricably linked with the forms of life in which they were involved', thereby falsely deducing that moral capabilities were likewise conditioned and shaped. This helped undermine 'the belief in a universal moral constituency required by the universality of reason'. Philosophical historians in their turn suggested a view of 'historical periodization' which placed different societies in an ascending scale of capabilities in providing men with higher levels of self-consciousness. It facilitated the distinction between man and citizen in a different way. Since the modern state allegedly made available for its citizens freedoms unattainable for members of earlier forms of association, it demanded to have created greater opportunities of individual self-determination and control over the immediate social and political environment. Linklater denies the philosophical historical claim an international turn by pointing to Rousseau's warning that the citizen's chances of living in a free and fulfilling life within states is severely hamstrung by the 'disruptive power of international events', and to Kant's cautionary statement that the world of states is necessarily a place of conflict and competition. Here, states cannot be purveyors of the good life because 'states pursue their particularistic interests and insist on their sovereign rights,...conduct their external affairs on the basis of a separation between the principles of domestic and international political life'. Both approaches kept afloat the conflict between men and citizens in both the theory and practice of IR.

From his conviction that the realization of a more complete and better form of international life is predicated on 'a radical critique of the state', which historicism failed to provide and modern natural law theory was loth to take on,[48] Linklater sought an appropriate political philosophy rooted in universal ethical reasoning and found it in the Stoic-Christian ideal, which was sidelined in the 20th century, particularly in the Cold War era, under the sway of realism. But not only the modern accounts of IR, theoretical as well as practical, but even the modern Western trends in IR were informed by its 'idea of a more embracing human community'. Sadly, within the Enlightenment tradition, none except Kant has paid this Stoic-Christian ideal of the unity of humankind its due regard, culminating into a situation where 'the limited moral community' of sovereign states continued to promote exclusion and breed estrangement, injustice, insecurity and violent conflicting among themselves, thus solidifying the false binaries of 'us' and 'them'.[49]

A way out of this divisiveness involves a 'rethinking (and questioning) of the meaning and viability of democracy and the nature of its link with the bounded nation state', and its interrogation as 'a normatively desirable mode of political organization'.[50] Linklater suggests that 'the existence of a moral community more inclusive than the sovereign state can be defended only on the basis of man's unique capacity for self-determination'.[51] But Hutchings relevantly asks whether the selves which should be 'self-determining in the international context' would only be 'the selves of the individual human being, the nation, and the state', as claimed by some normative theorists, or beyond them.[52] And Shapcott interprets Linklater's solution to the ethical particularism of existing political communities from the perspective of the relationship of self and others in them through a cosmopolitanism that 'must strike a balance between the claims of universalism and particularism'.[53] Shapcott himself, however, looks at the problem of the self in the community going beyond both the ends of the cosmopolitan/communitarian divide, woven around the 'argument whether the state or the species represent the limit of the community', and around the resultant debate about universal justice and cultural diversity. In cosmopolitans' portrayal of 'rational discussion regarding the arrangements of social life', the Kantian/Rawlsian conception of the self 'involves a significant moment of assimilation', which 'does not require the assimilation of the identity of the other'. Communitarians, however, situate supreme moral significance 'in the local or national community, or the individual's relationship to the community', to contend that citizens 'have *no* obligations to others, or more correctly, that community borders work as strict walls preventing expressions of moral solidarity and action between peoples'. So, while liberals minimize the significance of national differences, communitarians overemphasize them, and both fall short of doing 'justice to difference'. Shapcott's chosen reconciliation comes by avoiding 'some aspects of the most dominant formulations' and facilitating "adequate communication" between them', obviating a 'too-quick foreclosure of the possibilities for...a communitarian path to cosmopolitanism'.[54]

The Sociological Dimension

For Shapcott, the sociological aspect of CT is mostly interested in 'explaining and understanding the forces that shape the international order', beyond the conventional divide between idealism and realism, and realists' complaint that idealists overlooked the limitations of the era and the resilience of the international realm in reproducing itself amid reformist challenges. Since the 'practical goal' of CRINTHEO is not studying the world just as is but understanding 'how it got that way', 'how it ought to be', what possibilities does it retain about transforming it and what prospects for emancipation inhere within 'tendencies within the existing order', CT's or CRINTHEO's normative agenda is not viable without an attendant social theory that takes cognizance of the 'conditions of the age, without reifying them'. Tapping constructivist and sociological research in the diffusion of 'humanitarian, democratic and human rights norms', and historical sociology of state building, CRINTHEO buttresses Price and Reus-Smit's claim that there has been an elective affinity between critical and constructivist approaches.

One departure of CRINTHEO from CT is that, while both advocate emancipation, CRINTHEO remains largely lukewarm to Habermas' warning about the 'colonization' of the 'life world' by technical–instrumental morality and the rationality of money. For, as Martin Weber shows, while 'posing threats to freedom and increasing the risk of over-administration', such colonization also brightens the chances of having 'more universal forms of association'. The Marxian insight that the world has not always been riven by sovereign states provides not just a task but also a hope. The task entails enquiring into how the world became so divided, and the hope is the chance of knowing how it can change in the future. The task includes pinpointing all the forces that have facilitated or incommoded universalism in any given order, since, as Linklater and Suganami point out, working for emancipation requires awareness of varying levels of commitment to universalist practices evidenced in human history, through focusing in a 'comparative sociology of states systems' on when and where 'visions of the unity of the human race' influenced their development. Such investigations can be seen in the work of Rae and Keal. Rae probes after Horkheimer and Adorno's logic in the *Dialectic of Enlightenment*, the dark and progressive potentials of modernity and problematizes the emancipatory possibilities of sovereign states organized around the violent exclusion, if not effacement, of minority nonconformist identities in their citizenry.[55] I add here that, according to Rae, because of the astonishingly scant attention paid to the 'strategies of pathological homogenization and state formation', crucial questions concerning the 'relationship between state formation, sovereignty, changing forms of political legitimacy and the building of collective identities', the most talked about areas in IR, 'have not been brought to bear on the treatment of those "political misfits"'. Rather, state strategies for expulsion or worse oppressions targeted at these minority groups have been presented as internal crisis management *inside, outside* the purview of IR.[56]

Keal showed that while the focus of IR has been on the expansion of European international society to the entire world through the rivalry of states and recurrent interstate and post-Second World War intrastate wars and resultant casualties, the immense loss of lives that 'resulted from the arrival of Europeans, from the time of Columbus, in lands inhabited by non-European people' are 'frequently overlooked by the emphasis on states and interstate conflict'. CRINTHEO emphasizes here the adoption of the perspective of others. For, the relationship between Europeans and non-Europeans progressed not simply through 'the simple tale of subjugation and denial' but also 'involved a complex interaction between cultures that did not necessarily deny the agency of non-Europeans'.[57]

Linklater finds manifest in the course and present state of this comparative sociology of historical systems a unique success in ushering in higher levels of commitment to humanity as a whole, measured in terms of institutionalization of the norms of national self-determination; enactment and enforcement of universal human rights norms; codification of laws of war protecting combatants as well as non-combatants across gender and accommodation of other cosmopolitan commitments to restriction of the gamut of permissible harm to individuals. This concept of limitation of harm as the infliction of suffering on a substantial portion of humanity owes to an operative civilizing process. Linklater counters Norbert Elias' realist pessimism about it,[58] especially his assertions that (a) territorial pacification (including calming of relations between the core industrial states) and broadening of the ambit of emotional identification encompassing all or most members of the human species have made little impact on IR and (b) here decivilizing processes ultimately outdo civilizing processes. Against all despair about 'the prospects of long-term advances in the reduction of pointless suffering', Linklater shares Wight's vista of a universal moral community, which seems to have been shared by all state systems and has nearly always 'survived final conflicts, and the transition from the lawlessness of a states system in its terminal phase to a universal empire that could enforce the peace has often been greeted with relief'. Linklater urges further research that would throw light on whether attempts to create an international order preceded attempts to maintain justice in war; whether commonly held notions of 'pointless suffering' generated a common culture that eased the emergence of a society of states and whether international and cosmopolitan harm conventions appeared together, so as to better comprehend the conditions that allowed the birth of global civilizing processes in various states systems. For him, the sociology of global civilizing processes should unearth the ways different communities explored how they could further their interests sans recurrent violent or non-violent harm against each other, and to what extent their achievements in this regard 'were connected with advances in thinking that insiders and outsiders were moral equals'.[59]

These developments are important for interrogating the realist/neorealist and even the ES conceptions of the political community. The realist logic of anarchy cannot assume or accept that societies are poised towards acquiring the 'multiple identities that are critical for developing cosmopolitan harm conventions that promote cultural justice within and between states'. Surely, the ES thinking about international society reserves some—even if tangential—space for global harm concerns and civilizing processes sustaining them, but its long-held anxieties that pluralist agreements may not be able to accommodate 'solidarist' ideals have prevented it from hoping that these global harm principles will facilitate the movement from a pluralist to solidarist and then a cosmopolitan society.[60] But what Linklater reads from these developments is that 'pockets of solidarism' have already sprouted up within a pluralist international society, and 'still more intricate forms of close political cooperation have evolved within the solidarist zone of peace'. So 'a post-Westphalian configuration of states' seems within reach,[61] as is a cosmopolitan society, because 'cosmopolitan harm conventions' may be considered to have been 'immanent in the way all societies have been organized'.[62]

So, sociologically, CRINTHEO rejects the positivism and empiricism of different brands of realism that take the state of international anarchy and the resultant self-centred behaviour of states as self-generative, natural and immutable, by adopting a small 'c' version of constructivism in order to explain the social and historical production of state structures. In it, reflection 'upon change discredits old ontologies and yields an intimation of a possible new ontology', visualizing 'strategies of action in the emerging social order'. Since structures are 'socially constructed', any 'attempt to study the process of historical change' must concern itself with how 'this objective world is made and remade through changes in intersubjectivity'. Such a study again requires a focus on 'the relationship between (a) the stock of ideas people have about the nature of the world and (b) the practical problems that challenge them', together with 'the aptitude or ineptitude of ideas' to provide a means of grappling with these nagging problems.[63] The ineptitude of the ideas of realism, such as the logic of geopolitics, state-building and war, comes in sharp relief in this context. For, these ensure the survival and preservation of particularistic forms of association such as tribe, nation or state in a way that in the resultant conflictual environment, pleas for universalism are sure to be shrouded by pleas for security and stability.[64]

Cox adopts two perspectives to explain how the modern state came into being as the dominant structure of the modern political community. The first emanates from the Marxian–Gramscian view that 'World orders...are grounded in social relations', which essentially signifies that all discernible changes in military and geopolitical configurations are ultimately traceable to significant changes in the relationship between capital and labour. The second perspective is an offshoot of Vico's argument that institutions like the state are historical products, precluding pretensions that their essences are definable as *prior* to history. Rather, the definition of the state should be broadened enough to include the 'underpinnings of the political structures in civil society'. For, the state understood as the machinery of government surrounded by civil society makes up the 'hegemonic social order', comprehended as a constellation of 'material, ideology and institutions' that structures and sustains forms of world order, with their 'specific conditions of existence and dynamics'.[65] Linklater points out that in the CW-E 'system dynamics are produced by a single logic in which capitalist commodity production interacts with the processes of geopolitics, state formation and nation building'.[66] The key task of critical sociology then becomes demonstrating how structural characteristics of world orders emerge, crystallize, stabilize and get transformed, so as to judge the possibilities and guess the trajectory of the post-Westphalian world order and cosmopolitan society.

The Praxeological Dimension

The praxeological project of CRINTHEO encompasses its self-awareness as a 'practical philosophy' equipped with 'a normative critique of the present, a sketch of an alternative and better future, and a responsibility to inform praxis in the present'. Its object is to show how the cosmopolitan emancipatory values stated in the normative project and located in conditions identified in the sociological project can be developed and institutionalized in the present. Although this part of CRINTHEO is conditional to progress of research in the first two domains, it is indispensable in a theory concerned with changing the world. The philosophical catch here is how to guide action without reducing the effort to 'instrumentalism or a "programme"'.[67]

Yet another philosophical problem is how to distinguish the praxeological effort of CRINTHEO from what is going on in late 20th-century liberalism. Let us explain why this is so. We have seen that Linklater's systematic interrogation of the state as the dominant modern political community pleads for its 'triple transformation to secure greater respect for cultural differences, stronger commitments to the reduction of material inequalities and significant advances in universality', through withstanding pressures to circumscribe the bounds of the community while buoying up social tendencies that might diminish these moral deficits. But while normatively a global narrative of universal emancipation aiming at this 'triple transformation' is 'immanent within the dialogic ideal', it is only 'national commitments to the principle of equality, welfare rights and respect for cultural differences that make it viable.[68] For these, the first step of praxis is raising states to the status of good international citizens, prepared to foreground 'the welfare of the international society' over the 'relentless pursuit of its own national self-interests'.[69] Besides, states have to extend harm conventions to include bilateral, third-party and global relationships. All these require cosmopolitan foreign policies oriented towards evolving more 'inclusive arrangements for democratic governance of the international, regional and national orders', and committed to transforming the institutions of the international order in a way that would disallow redundant suffering.[70]

But, within liberalism, in the backdrop of the dilemma of the post-1991 world order, the cosmopolitan/communitarian debate over how the society of states and its conventional principles of state sovereignty and its non-intervention can be preserved while, at the same time, upholding a global system of human rights echoes many of the concerns of CRINTHEO. The central question of the debate is: 'What are the freedoms/obligations of individuals by *virtue* of their humanity versus the freedoms by *nature* of their citizenship of a state?' [Italics mine].[71] Answers to this question involve

> (1) 'a conception of the person' and the constituents of the good life for the individual (2) the question of the moral standing of the states vis-à-vis promotion of or obstructions to the good life for the individual; (3) universalism versus particularism, whether there exists an external standpoint by which moral judgements can be made across cultures.

In this debate, cosmopolitans such as Beitz and Pogge take individuals as the only moral persons and deny any moral relevance of states, but communitarians such as Janna Thompson argue, much like Linklater, that a state has a moral personality if it 'protects, enhances or makes possible the national life that people value'.[72] This debate echoes many of the concerns of CRITHEOs.

Where CRINTHEO is distinct and different from advanced liberalism is in the direction it sets for its reconfiguration of the political community beyond the frontiers of the sovereign state, through suggesting a 'more complex multi-tiered structure of governance' and reconstructing the state and its tasks within 'alternative frameworks of political action that reduce the impact of social exclusion'. Devetak thinks that the triple transformation first requires identifying the processes that augur well for the dismantling of 'the nexus between sovereignty, territory, citizenship and nationalism, and moving towards more cosmopolitan forms of governance'.[73] This will end what Linklater calls the 'destructive fusion' brought about by the modern state by promoting wider dialogical communities and propagating what Linklater and Shapcott call a 'thin cosmopolitanism' that would accommodate universal claims as well as justice to difference. The basis of this thin cosmopolitanism would not only be a Habermasian 'discourse ethics' (as with Linklater) but also a Todorovian emphasis on removing obstacles to the self's 'way of knowing and conversing with the other', and a Gadamerian solution of 'reaching an understanding on the subject matter of a conversation' by first working out its common language (as with Shapcott).[74] Being inclusionary, democratic and informed by moral–practical reasoning, discourse ethics has three implications for the alchemical transmutation of world politics: the ability to offer general guidance for democratic decision-making processes through its 'consent-oriented, deliberative approach', the ability to steer political processes away from violent conflict and the ability to offer 'a means of criticizing and justifying the principles by which humanity organizes itself politically'.[75]

A BRIEF CRITIQUE AND EVALUATION

Writing a critique of a theory that calls itself 'critical' looks a bit audacious but is still apposite, as will be clear from what follows. When Hoffman and later Linklater introduced CT in the inter-paradigm debate and hailed it as the harbinger of the fourth paradigm of IRT, the academic prospect seemed bright. But once one moves beyond optimistic announcements to actual theoretical production, CT becomes not always easily distinguishable from other brands of progressive thought, whether in social sciences or IR, as already shown in the context of the similarity of Linklater's and Thompson's view of rights-promoting states as moral international citizens.[76] Another example is the difficulty of distinguishing Hoffman's cosmopolitan discourse ethics from similar formulations by Todorov, Gadamer and even Charles Beitz, Henry Shue or Nicholas Onuf, the last three being exponents of CT only in small 'c'.[77] Navari also speaks of 'cosmopolitan ethic' in the constructivist context of intervention as a factor in the construction of the state.[78] Again, the radical PE upheld by Cox, Hayward Alker and Thomas Biersteker, and Linklater, may apparently be seen as post-Marxist in eschewing the 'positivist epistemology of classic Marxist theories of imperialism', but are, as pointed out by Kubálková and Cruickshank, and later admitted by Cox, traditional Marxist in content.

In these circumstances, it is unsurprising that CT will indistinguishably merge with the broader progressive theories of IR, since its goal of recasting Enlightenment was shared by them also. As Brown says ironically, 'The most distinctive feature of Critical IR lies in its programmatic self-justification, and this becomes of particular importance not in contest with the Enlightenment thought but with respect to "critics" of the Enlightenment Project'. These critics first came from the Right, but are now increasingly being seen also in the Left, ranging from Marxist to post-Marxist and postmodern writings in IR.[79]

Among Marxists, Bottomore says that contrary to the original objective of the Frankfurt School and the Institute of promoting interdisciplinary research, 'the range of its interests became in fact extremely limited' and except for the brief period when Carl Grünberg was the director, 'historical studies played no part in its work and no historian was closely allied its activities'. This jettisoning of history flowed from the belief that the Frankfurt School, as it had developed under the influence of Adorno and Horkheimer, took social theory primarily, if not only, as 'a critique of the present time'. Apart from history, economic analysis was also sidelined. Except for Henryk Grossmann (famous for his study of 1929 study of capitalist accumulation and breakdown, and never a core member of the School, being impervious to the dialectical, neo-Hegelian approach of the School), Franz Neumann (whose association was brief) and economic policy analyst Friedrich Pollock, the School remained cool about theoretical economics. Judgements about class, given by the School in its mature stage, and also by 'neocritical theorists', seemed unsupported by facts, as manifested in its prognosis of the 'decline or disappearance of the working class as a political force' in the backdrop of the development of working class movements and parties in Western countries, which arguably had turned '*more* rather than less socialist' during the 20th century since 1945 to the end of the 1970s. This class blindness was also reflected in Marcuse's diagnosis of American exceptionalism in 'the long absence from American society of a politically organized working class'.[80]

Among liberal critics, Held cites Perry Anderson's and Göran Therborn's view that the limitations of CT overshadow their achievements, and that remaining within the 'problematic' of CT would entail risking 'intellectual paralysis', because Frankfurt School's CT was marked by 'a failure to produce a genuine reconciliation of theory and practice'. Anderson thought that CT symbolized 'method as impotence; art as consolation, pessimism as acquiescence', and a deviation from the 'path of true science'. To Therborn, CT's 'underlying structure' revealed a 'double reaction of science and politics to philosophy'. It also lacked 'a close connection with the practical activity of the proletariat'. Held also found in Adorno's and Horkheimer's extensive participation in the multi-author *Authoritarian Personality* (first published in 1950) a 'complete capitulation to bourgeois social psychology in theory, method and political conclusions'. He cites Marxist critic Phil Slater complaining that the front-ranking students of the Institute failed to connect concretely with the class struggles in Germany.[81]

Among Frankfurt School theorists, Habermas has drawn the most flak. One set of charges came from the feminists. Led by Nancy Fraser, feminists of all hues from Marxists to poststructuralists, problematized Habermas' theorization of the public and private spheres, communicative rationality and so on from the perspectives of its gender blindness and gender-based exclusion.[82] MacKendrick deduces from the way Habermas' writings in the 1970s started drifting away from the critical spirit of the Frankfurt School in his later writings of the 1980s and 1990s 'that he was veering "into the realm of what could be called conformist CT"', which frequently 'read more like an apology for existing forms of liberal democratic regimes than a critical account of their pathologies'.[83] This tendency was diagnosed by Fraser too from a feminist angle.[84] Among poststructuralists, Habermas' concept of 'domination-free communication' has been regarded by Rorty as a merely 'good way to restate the traditional liberal claim that the only way to avoid perpetuating cruelty within social institutions' is by maximizing liberal freedoms and opportunities.[85] Habermas' concept of the 'ideal speech situation', or 'discursive rationality', functioning as the 'centrepiece' of his theory, is criticized by Connolly for symbolizing simultaneously 'the ideal of enlightened politics and the threatened closure of public space for its realization'. Untrammelled by 'any concrete political practice, it provides a sanctuary of sorts for political reflection', a place where we find 'the idealized speech of stoics frozen out of effective participation in public life'. This is a severe indictment that goes to the core of the 'speculative'[86] nature of the Habermasian project.

CONCLUSION

This chapter has discussed the parentage and emergence of CT and its general contentions before its late entry in IR, its transformation thereafter into CRINTHEO and the resultant change of theoretical priority from Habermasian POK to alternative world orders of Cox, Linklater, Ashley, Shapcott and so on, in the course of which it reconceptualized the political community from normative, sociological and praxeological angles, in the course of which, according to critics, CRINTHEO became difficult to distinguish from advanced liberal theory. In such circumstances, it should not be surprising that the mantle of emancipatory critique is now passing on to small 'c' CT. If we look at recent books on it, large 'C' critical theorists are no more dominant there.

In one book, among 32 thinkers, only Adorno, Benjamin and Habermas find place.[87] In another, among nine thinkers, only Habermas is there.[88] Postmodernists/poststructuralists, poststructuralist feminists and other radical philosophical schools have earned the epithet 'critical'.

REVIEW QUESTIONS

1. Write a brief note on the parentage of CT, distinguishing between the large 'C' and small 'c' versions of it.
2. From what critical theorists said in one voice outside IR, both before and after CT's its late entry in IR, point out the unchanging elements of CT and CRINTHEO.
3. Describe the connections between CT's contention about POK and CRINTHEO's concerns about alternative global orders.
4. How does Cox relate both 'problem-solving theory' and CT to temporal perspectives on IR?
5. Summarize CRINTHEO's critique of mainstream IRTs, assessment of the existing order and visualization of the emancipatory project.
6. Discuss the normative, sociological and praxeological dimensions of CRINTHEO's reconceptualization of the political community.
7. Attempt an evaluation of CT.
8. Assess Habermas as a critical theorist.

NOTES AND REFERENCES

1. David Held, *Introduction to Critical Theory: Horkheimer to Habermas* (Berkeley, CA; Los Angeles, CA: University of California Press, 1980; Cambridge: Polity Press, 2004), 14; Stephen Eric Bronner, *Critical Theory: A Very Short Introduction* (New York, NY: Oxford University Press, [2011]2017), 3.
2. Lois Tyson, *Critical Theory Today: A User-Friendly Guide*, 2nd ed. (New York, NY; London: Routledge, 2006), *passim.*
3. Chris Brown, '"Turtles All the Way Down": Anti-Foundationalism, Critical Theory and International Relations', *Millennium* 23, no. 2 (1994): 213–236, especially 217.
4. Chris Brown, 'Critical Theory and Postmodernism in IR', in Groom and Light, *Contemporary International Relations*, 57–58.
5. Richard Shapcott, 'Critical Theory', in Reus-Smit and Snidal, *The Oxford Handbook of International Relations*, 329.
6. Charles Taylor, *Sources of the Self: The Making of the Modern Identity* (Cambridge: Cambridge University Press, [1989]1996), 382–383.
7. Stephen Eric Bronner, *Critical Theory: A Very Short Introduction*, 2nd ed. (Oxford: Oxford University Press, 2017), 1–2.
8. All quotes are from Rupert, 'Marxism and Critical Theory', 157.
9. Held, *Introduction to Critical Theory*, 15–16.
10. Stanley Aronowitz, 'Introduction', in *Critical Theory: Selected Essays*, ed. Max Horkheimer, trans. Matthew J. O'Connell and others (New York, NY: Continuum Pub. Corp., [1982]2002), xii–xiii.

11. See Rick Roderick, *Habermas and the Foundations of Critical Theory* (London: Macmillan Education, 1986), 50–56.
12. Christoph Humrich, 'Critical Theory', in Schieder and Spindler, *Theories of International Relations*, 269.
13. Richard Devetak, 'Critical Theory', in Burchill, Linklater, Devetak, Donnelly, Paterson, Reus-Smit and True, *Theories of International Relations*, 155–156.
14. See Perry Anderson, *Considerations on Western Marxism* (London: New Left Books, 1976), cited in C. el-Ojeili and P. Hayden, *Critical Theories of Globalization: An Introduction* (Basingstoke; New York, NY: Palgrave Macmillan, 2006), 7.
15. Mark Poster, *Critical Theory and Poststructuralism: In Search of a Context* (Ithaca, NY: Cornell University Press, 1989), 1–2.
16. Shapcott, 'Critical Theory', 331–332.
17. The prison in Rome where Antonio Gramsci was kept in solitary confinement.
18. Richard Devetak, *Critical International Theory: An Intellectual History* (Oxford: Oxford University Press, 2018), 4–5.
19. Devetak, 'Critical Theory', 158–159.
20. See Note 11 above.
21. Robert W. Cox, 'Social Forces, States and World Orders: Beyond International Relations Theory', *Millennium—Journal of International Studies* 10, no. 2 (1981): 126–155, here 128. Available at http://mil.sagepub.com/cgi/content/refs/10/2/126 (accessed on 17 October 2019).
22. Kimberly Hutchings, *International Political Theory: Rethinking Ethics in a Global Era* (London; Thousand Oaks, CA; New Delhi: Sage Publications, 1999), 69, 93.
23. Cox, 'Social Forces', 128–132.
24. Robert W. Cox, 'Multilateralism and World Order', *Review of International Studies* 18, no. 2 (1992): 161–180, here 172–173.
25. Andrew Linklater, *Beyond Realism and Marxism: Critical Theory and International Relations* (Basingstoke: Macmillan, 1990), 10.
26. Shapcott, 'Critical Theory', 332–334.
27. Richard Ashley, 'Political Realism and Human Interests', *International Studies Quarterly* 25, no. 2 (1981): 204–236, here 207 (Symposium in honour of Hans J. Morgenthau).
28. Christoph Menke, 'Critique and Self-Reflection: The Problematization of Morality', in *Critical Theory: Current State and Future Prospects*, eds. Peter Uwe Hohendahl and Jaimey Fisher (New York, NY; Oxford: Berghahn Books, 2001), 119–120.
29. Mark A. Neufeld, *The Restructuring of International Relations Theory* (Cambridge: Cambridge University Press, 1995), 20, 40, 108.
30. Menke, 'Critique and Self-Reflection', 125.
31. Excerpted in McLellan, *Marx*, 329.
32. Devetak, 'Critical Theory', 160–161; *Critical International Theory*, 129.
33. Andrew Linklater, 'Critical Theory', in *International Theory for the Twenty-First Century: An Introduction*, ed. Martin Griffiths (London; New York, NY: Routledge, 2007), 50.
34. M. Horkheimer, 'Materialism and Morality', in *Between Philosophy and Social Science*, ed. M. Horkheimer (Cambridge, MA: MIT Press), 32, cited in Ibid., 56.
35. M. Hoffman, 'Critical Theory and the Inter-Paradigm Debate', in *The Study of International Relations: The State of the Art*, eds. Hugh C. Dyer and Leon Mangasarian (New York, NY: Palgrave Macmillan in association with *Millennium: Journal of International Studies*, 1989), 63.
36. Andrew Linklater, 'Achievements of Critical Theory', in *International Theory: Positivism and Beyond*, eds. Steve Smith, Ken Booth and Marysia Zalewski (Cambridge; New York, NY: Cambridge University Press, 1996), 282–283.
37. M. Banks, *Conflict in World Society* (Brighton: Wheatsheaf, 1984), 4, cited in Linklater, 'Critical Theory', 7.

38. Ashley, 'Political Realism and Human Interests', 227.
39. See notes 14–16 above.
40. 'Herbert Marcuse, *One Dimensional Man: Studies in the Ideology of Advanced Industrial Society* (London: Routledge and Kegan Paul, 1964/ London and New York: Routledge, 2013), passim.
41. Linklater, 'Critical Theory', 47–49.
42. See Jürgen Habermas, *The Divided West* (Hoboken, NJ: John Wiley and Sons, 2014), *passim.*
43. Jürgen Habermas, *The Crisis of the European Union: A Response,* trans. Ciaran Cronin (Cambridge: Polity, 2012), 11 and *passim.*
44. Max Pensky, 'Editor's Introduction', *The Postnational Constellation: Political Essays,* ed. Jürgen Habermas, trans., Max Pensky (Cambridge: Polity, 2011), ix.
45. This section draws on Shapcott's scheme elaborated by Devetak. See Shapcott 'Critical Theory', 335–341; Devetak, 'Critical Theory', 164–175. But their cited references below have been accessed independently.
46. Shapcott, 'Critical Theory', 335–336.
47. Richard Linklater, 'The Changing Contours of Critical International Relations Theory', in *Critical Theory and World Politics,* ed. Richard Wyn Jones (Boulder, CO: Lynne Rienner Publishers, 2001), 28.
48. Andrew Linklater, 'Men and Citizens in International Relations', *Review of International Studies* 7, no. 1 (1981): 23–37.
49. Andrew Linklater, *Men and Citizens in the Theory of International Relations* (London; Basingstoke: Palgrave Macmillan, 1982), 21–23, 28, 97.
50. Hutchings, *International Political Theory,* 125, 154.
51. Linklater, 'Preface', *Men and Citizens in the Theory of International Relations,* ix.
52. Hutchings, *International Political Theory,* 122.
53. Richard Shapcott, *Justice, Community and Dialogue in International Relations* (Cambridge; New York, NY: Cambridge University Press, 2001), 83.
54. Ibid., serially, 14, 130, 30–31, 118, 39, 26, 33, 12, 31.
55. R. Price and Christian Reus-Smit, 'Dangerous Liaisons: Critical International Theory and Constructivism', *European Journal of International Relations* 4, no. 3 (1998): 259–294; Martin Weber, 'The Critical Social Theory of the Frankfurt School, and the "Social Turn" in IR', *Review of International Studies* 31, no. 1 (2005): 195–209; Linklater and Suganami, *The English School of International Relations,* 231; Heather Rae, *State Identities and the Homogenisation of Peoples* (New York, NY: Cambridge University Press, 2002); Paul Keal, *European Conquest and the Rights of Indigenous Peoples: The Moral Backwardness of International Society* (Cambridge: Cambridge University Press, 2003); all cited with the above comments by Shapcott, 'Critical Theory', 337–338.
56. Rae, *State Identities and the Homogenisation of Peoples,* 14–15.
57. Keal, *European Conquest and the Rights of Indigenous Peoples,* 24–25.
58. See Andrew Linklater, 'Norbert Elias, the "Civilizing Process" and the Sociology of International Relations', *International Politics* 41 (2004): 3–35. Available at https://doi.org/10.1057/palgrave.ip.8800067; 'Process Sociology and International Relations' (2011). Available at https://doi.org/10.1111/j.1467-954X.2011.01978.x; 'Norbert Elias, Process Sociology and International Relations'. Available at https://www.e-ir.info/2012/05/29/norbert-elias-process-sociology-and-international-relations/ (all accessed on 28 September 2020).
59. Andrew Linklater, *The Problem of Harm in World Politics: Theoretical Investigations* (New York, NY: Cambridge University Press, 2011), x, 18–20, 232, 240, 244.
60. Ibid., 9, 128, 131, 128, 138.
61. Andrew Linklater, *Transformation of Political Community: Ethical Foundations of the Post-Westphalian Era* (Cambridge: Polity, 1998), 207.

62. Linklater, *The Problem of Harm in World Politics*, 111.
63. R. W. Cox, 'Towards a Post-Hegemonic Conceptualization of World Orders: Reflections on the Relevancy of Ibn Khaldun', in *Governance without Government: Order and Change in World Politics*, eds. James N Rosenau and Ernst Otto Czempiel (Cambridge: Cambridge University Press, [1992]2000), 136, 138.
64. Linklater, *Beyond Realism and Marxism*, cited by Shapcott, 'Critical Theory', 339.
65. R. W. Cox, 'Gramsci, Hegemony and International Relations: An Essay on Method', Millennium 12, no. 2 (1983): 141, 164, 173; Cox, 'Social Forces', 133.
66. Linklater, *Beyond Realism and Marxism*, 190.
67. Shapcott, 'Critical Theory', 340.
68. Linklater, *Transformation of Political Community*, 3, 106, 165.
69. Andrew Linklater, *Critical Theory and World Politics: Citizenship, Sovereignty and Humanity* (London; New York, NY: Routledge, 2007), 69.
70. For Andrew Linklater, 'The Problem of Harm in World Politics: Implications for the Sociology of States Systems', *International Affairs* 78, no. 2 (2002): 319–338; and comments with examples in Shapcott, 'Critical Theory', 341.
71. Molly Cochran, 'Cosmopolitanism and Communitarianism in a Post-Cold War World', in *Boundaries in Question: New Directions in International Relations*, eds. John MacMillan and Andrew Linklater (London; New York, NY: Pinter Publishers, 1995), 43. Note how 'virtue' is interestingly counterposed in an unstated anti-Machiavellian manner to 'nature' in the quote.
72. See Charles Beitz, *Political Theory and International Relations* (Princeton, NJ: Princeton University Press, 1979), 7; Thomas Pogge, *Realizing Rawls* (Ithaca, NY: Cornel University); Janna Thompson, *Justice and World Order: A Philosophical Inquiry* (London: Routledge, 1992), 177, cited in Ibid., 47.
73. Devetak, *Critical International Theory*, 147.
74. See Note 53 above.
75. See Devetak, 'Critical Theory', 171–175.
76. See Note 71 above.
77. See Brown, 'Critical Theory and Postmodernism in IR', 59.
78. Cornelia Navari, 'Intervention, Non-Intervention and the Construction of the State', in *Political Theory, International Relations, and the Ethics of Intervention*, eds. Ian Forbes and Mark Hoffman (Basingstoke: Macmillan, 1993), 55.
79. Brown, 'Critical Theory and Postmodernism in IR', 59.
80. Tom Bottomore, *The Frankfurt School and Its Critics*, first published in 1984 (London; New York, NY: Routledge, 2002), 72–75.
81. Held, *Introduction to Critical Theory*, 354–355.
82. See Johanna Meehan, ed., *Feminists Read Habermas: Gendering the Subject of Discourse* (London; New York, NY: Routledge, 1995), *passim*.
83. Kenneth MacKendrick, *Discourse, Desire, and Fantasy in Jürgen Habermas' Critical Theory* (New York, NY; Abingdon: Routledge, 2008), 1–2.
84. Nancy Fraser, 'What's Critical about Critical Theory', in Meehan, *Feminists Read Habermas*, 21–55.
85. See Richard Rorty, *Contingency, Irony and Solidarity* (Cambridge: Cambridge University Press, [1989]1999), 66–67.
86. William E. Connolly, *Politics and Ambiguity* (Madison, WI: Wisconsin University Press, 1987), 52–71, especially 52–53, 71.
87. See Jenny Edkins and Nick Vaughan-Williams, eds., *Critical Theorists and International Relations* (London; New York, NY: Routledge, 2009).
88. Simon Tormey and Jules Townshend, *Key Thinkers from Critical Theory to Post-Marxism* (London; Thousand Oaks, CA; New Delhi: Sage Publications, 2006).

CHAPTER

25

Constructivism in International Relations as Another Middle Ground*

CHAPTER OUTLINE

Introduction: Nature of the Approach and Its Middling
  Why and How the Constructivist Ground Is in the Middle?
Context and Genealogy
Minimal, Core or Signature Argument of Constructivism
Dinosaurs Crossing the Minimal Core: Wendt, Onuf and Kratochwil
  Wendt
  Onuf
  Kratochwil
Types of Constructivism
Applications of Constructivism in IR
Conclusion: Towards a Critique and Evaluation

* This chapter is available on the companion website.

CHAPTER

26

Postmodernism or Post-structuralism in International Relations

CHAPTER OUTLINE

AN ALIEN APPROACH

For many IR scholars, 'postmodernism' in IR is not just in the mainstream but the 'latest bête noire of IR',[1] as the equation of the international and intertextual in the title of a famous IR book bears out.[2] The evident influences on this book, coming from Foucault, Derrida, Lacan, Kristeva, Barthes and Baudrillard 'are, in more than one sense, "foreign"' to a discipline known for its Anglo-American provenance. The places where these influences are most visible are in discourse analysis, genealogy, deconstructionism and textuality through all of which postmodernists have sought to interrogate, problematize and reconceptualize the 'reality' foregrounded by IR.[3] Because of the challenges postmodernism has posed to the foundational assumptions of IR, either directly or through other approaches influenced by it (such as postmodern feminism),[4] many scholars are worrying about how to defend the discipline against its invasion.[5]

POSTMODERNISM AND POST-STRUCTURALISM: TERMS AND THEORIES, ORIGINS AND REASONS BEHIND CONFLATION

Literary theorists Federico De Onis Sánchez (in *Antologia de la poesia espanola e hispanoamericana*, 1934) and Dudley Fitts (in *Anthology of Contemporary Latin-American Poetry*, 1942) first used the term postmodernism in reaction to the latent modernism of Latin-American poetry. D. C. Somervell meant by it a historical cycle in Western civilization, originating around 1875 (in his first-volume abridgement of Arnold Toynbee's *A Study of History*, 1947). American poets and/or literary theorists used it in literary contexts: Charles John Olson in the 1950s, Irving Howe and Harry Tuchman Levin in 1959 and 1960, and Leslie Aaron Fiedler and Ihab Habib Hassan in the 1960s. From literature, the term moved to art, music, dance, architecture, urban planning and cultural tendencies of all types[6] and the prosaic social sciences, including IR.

In IR, the word postmodernism is used in various senses, including the periodizational, as by Appiah (in a query about the prefix 'post'),[7] Coker, Connolly as well as Der Derian in a later work (using, however, vague 'late modern' in place of postmodern). However, Der Derian and Shapiro tag postmodern IR with literary theory and postpositivist continental philosophy.[8] Modernism symbolized 'the predominant cultural style of the period from the 1890s to the outbreak of the Second World War', bringing together crystallized ideas and values in painting, sculpture, music, architecture, design and literature of that period', plus the resultant 'upheavals in political, sociological, scientific, sexual and familial orders in Europe and the USA'. It was in reaction to these multiple manifestations of the fixities of modernism that postmodernism appeared after the Second World War, highlighting the 'indeterminate, pluralistic and ever more globalized culture of the Cold-War world', which necessitated a specifically eclectic stance on the cultural context. Thus understood, postmodernism represents 'the cultural forms inspired by the conditions of accelerated time and space and hyper-consumerism that we experience in the globalized era some call "postmodernity"', rather than any break or disjuncture with modernity.[9]

Although Ashley considers the term post-structuralism synonymous with postmodernism,[10] it arose primarily in the domain of philosophy, claiming that the concepts and approaches of the 20th-century European thought 'cannot be understood in isolation from a 'social and political event in thought', which became resurgent in the early 1960s, marked by the publication of Deleuze's *Nietzsche and Philosophy* (1962), ebbing out a little around the time of publication of Lyotard's *The Postmodern Condition* (1979). As a successor to structuralism, 'it is a form of relativism' which 'celebrates the death of the subject'; is 'a post-metaphysical form of inquiry that has utterly displaced the truth'; is 'stylistically obtuse'; 'refuses all claims to normativity', and 'transforms critical practice into textual play'.[11] Rather than signifying '"anti-structuralism", it was a philosophical position that developed out of structuralism (in the French sense of the word), sharing in many ways more with structuralism than with its detractors.[12] But still, there is a rationale of conflation between postmodernism and post-structuralism: 'While "postmodernity" is the cultural, economic, social and political formation within modernity that results from changes in time-space relations, post-structuralism is one of the interpretative analytics that critically engages with the production and implication of these transformations.'[13] While postmodernism refers to the 'current historical, social and cultural epoch', post-structuralism is merely 'an aspect of the postmodern era'.[14]

Key Terms of Postmodernism/Post-structuralism

In an article about the application of postmodernism/post-structuralism in IR, I will only briefly acquaint my readers with the basic, primary level concepts of both, detailed below, which make them distinctive. Secondary level concepts emerging from the application will be taken up when discussing it.

'Power/knowledge' is a Foucauldian concept, culled from Plato's *Theaetetus*, adversarial to the scientific approach to knowledge and cognition and has an affinity with Kant's caution (in *Toward Perpetual Peace*) that possession of power by some inevitably pollutes the free play and judgement of reason by others. Foucault, however, mocked any equation of the expressions 'knowledge is power' or 'power is knowledge' attributed to him, saying 'studying their relation is precisely my problem.... I do not identify them'.[15] In Foucault's genealogical analysis of forms of rationality and their subservience to 'a microphysics of power',[16] power is 'productive' because it appears when 'discourses constitute particular subject positions as the "natural" ones'.[17] Power constitutes subjectivity because being ubiquitous and capillary, it 'reaches into the very grain of individuals, touches their bodies and inserts itself into their actions and attitudes, their discourses, learning processes and everyday lives'.[18] After much groping for it between 1971 to 1974 in his lectures at the Collège de France (in *Penal Theories and Institutions*, *The Punitive Society* and *Psychiatric Power*), Foucault succeeded in unearthing the social and political matrices which hitched together the fields of power and knowledge through the concepts of 'discipline' and 'panopticism' in *Discipline and Punish* (1975). It showed the individual social agent as a by-product of the operation of mechanisms of power/knowledge. Applying the underlying mechanism of Jeremy Bentham's 1823 model of the transparent prison, *panopticon*, Foucault focuses on the techniques and mechanisms of power that employ them, and shows in the process how social institutions exercise power and discipline over the bodies and souls of their subjects through moving from a 'network of gazes that supervised one another' to a 'perfect disciplinary apparatus', which 'would make it possible for a single gaze to see everything constantly'.[19] This 'disciplinary hypothesis' which harked back to yet deviated from the argument of *The Archaeology of Knowledge* now contended that the functioning of these discourses 'created' the individual subject as the appendant of the case data that they gathered, tracked and monitored,[20] as the 'intendants', 'syndics' and guards 'did during a plague in a French town at the end of the 17th century'.[21]

The concept of 'discourse' shows how disciplinary power strives to generate conceptions of subjectivity and identity. The discourse emphasizes the role of language as a system of socially shared codes in making sense of the world.[22] Discourse alludes to the concatenation of representations and practices through which meanings are generated, identities formed, social relations crystallized and political and ethical outcomes rendered more or less plausible. But this does not signify that language is everything, with no reality outside it, and the external and the material does not count at all.[23] Foucault thinks that 'discourse, in general, and scientific discourse, in particular, is so complex in reality that we not only can but should approach it at different levels and with different methods'.[24] I would take this complex concept minimally here as 'little more than textual and intellectual irreverence in an attempt to be a spanner in the works of modernity'.[25]

Foucault's concept of 'genealogy', first spelt out in *Discipline and Punish* and *History of Sexuality*, is a different 'style of historical thought which exposes and registers the significance of power-knowledge relations,'[26] termed by Foucault as 'effective history' (wirkliche Historie) because it relativizes all conceptions of truth and solidity and, 'within a process of development, places everything considered immortal in man'. Effective history 'studies what is closest but in an abrupt dispossession so as to seize it at a distance' and is aware of its 'interested character'. It is a 'history of the present',[27] basically, a style of inquiry that seeks to interpret the present by invoking the past. Genealogy is central to Foucault's interest in Nietzsche's radical attack against the concept of origins; although Nietzsche's philosophical method was no essay in genealogy, despite the title of his book *The Genealogy of Morality* containing the word. Foucault's genealogy stems partly from his own earlier work in 'archaeology', which aimed at exposing discontinuities and differences in the development of ideas without causally relating, interpreting or evaluating them. However, genealogy is quite ready to interpret and evaluate causes. As a sociocultural project, genealogy has three allied but distinct domains or aspects, symbolizing truth, power and ethics. The first domain relates to 'a historical ontology of ourselves', wherein we 'constitute ourselves as subjects of knowledge'. The second yields 'a historical ontology of ourselves in relation to a field of power through which we constitute ourselves as subjects acting on others'. The third generates "a historical ontology in relation to ethics through which we constitute ourselves as moral agents".[28]

Genealogy being 'a history of the knowledge and the metastories which furnish other stories with validity and coherence' from its perspective, everything in the present 'including that which is thought to be timeless, unchanging, given or original' is historical.[29] Genealogy historicizes even phenomena thought to be beyond history in the process of exhuming things and thoughts thought to have been entombed and concealed from view. It evokes Benjamin's concept of excavation and memorializing, where a man seeking 'to approach his own buried past must conduct himself like a man digging', unafraid 'to return again to the same matter; to scatter it as one scatters earth.... For the "matter itself" is no more than the strata which yield their long-sought secrets only to the most meticulous investigation'.[30] Accordingly, genealogy cannot but dig up counter-histories that reveal the mechanisms of exclusion and concealment which facilitate the teleological concept of history as a fused and monochromatic story with fixed beginning, midpoint and ending. Its innate perspectivism questions our capacity to pinpoint these beginnings and endings, and its natural anti-essentialism insists on the spatiotemporal context of all knowledge. Genealogy holds that lacking any 'universal frame of reference or overarching perspective', we are fated to face a plurality of perspectives'. Let us read here Nietzsche's famous maxim,

> There is only a perspective seeing, only a perspective 'knowing'; and the more affects we allow to speak about one thing, the more eyes, different eyes, we can use to observe one thing, the more complete will our 'concept' of this thing, our 'objectivity' be.[31]

It not only warns about the possibility of different perspectives on the same world but warns us against '(t)he "true world" and the "apparent world"—that means the mendaciously invented world and reality'.[32] This remaining perspectivism is described by Derrida as 'textuality'.

Its seeds coming from Ferdinand de Saussure, Roland Barthes, Julia Kristeva and so on, 'intertextuality' essentially means that we comprehend the social world as constituted by texts, themselves forming an 'intertext' through their connections to preceding texts, making it impossible in the postmodern era to speak of originality in artistic creations. True to the term's original meaning of 'a tissue, a woven fabric', it betokens 'relationality, interconnectedness and interdependence'. From its origins in Kristeva's melding of the works of Saussure and Mikhail Bakhtin, via its post-structuralist development in the works of Barthes, its structuralist elaboration in the writings of Gérard Genette and Michael Riffaterre and its feminist and postcolonial theoretic adaptations, intertextuality became a conceptual standard-bearer of all postpositivist and postmodernist thought. While seeds of the realization that in the postmodern epoch 'reproduction takes over from authentic production' were present even in the writings of Marxist critics such as Terry Eagleton and Fredric Jameson, it was Jean Baudrillard who naturalized the term in postmodernist literature through his concept of simulacrum, a word adopted from Plato, to refer to a copy that has no original,[33] yet becoming truth in its own right: the hyperreal. Baudrillard credits Benjamin for capturing this process in cinema, photography, contemporary mass media and so on, where 'the original no longer even exists since things are conceived from the beginning as a function of their unlimited production'.[34]

Of two textual strategies of postmodernism, 'deconstruction' and 'double reading', deconstruction is 'not a method applied to the text to produce the reading' but is 'just a situation and event of reading', arising in its very moment, not existing separately from the text and aiming 'to rethink the conceptual and non-conceptual foundations of the Western tradition from the bottom up'. In *Of Grammatology*, Derrida said that the structuring of the entire Western thought and tradition since Plato and Aristotle through binary oppositions (such as man/woman, black/white, voice/silence and speech/writing) is misleading and false. These couplings are far from being true opposites in which one term is the equal but contrasting complement of the other. Rather, one (here, the first) of these pairs of terms is privileged over the others.[35] While the privileged term nearly always 'connotes a presence, propriety, fullness, purity or identity which the other lacks (e.g., sovereignty as opposed to anarchy),' deconstruction seeks to show the vacuity of these oppositions. Because 'each term always already depends on the other', the privileged term nearly always gains its legitimacy by disowning its dependence on the subordinate term. To expose the falseness of the oppositions of these binary terms, Derrida interrogates their relationship with the lens of 'structural parasitism and contamination'. Since 'each term is structurally related to and already harbours the other', the difference *between* them is always undercut by the revealed difference *within* them.[36]

Derrida's concepts of 'difference', 'supplementarity' and 'freeplay' in *Of Grammatology* also interrogate the purity of terms. He regards the concept of origin or nature as 'nothing but the myth of addition, of supplementarity annulled by being purely additive'; 'the myth of the effacement of the trace, that is to say of an originary différance that is neither absence nor presence, neither positive nor negative'.[37] Freeplay signifies 'the disruption of presence' as 'an interplay of absence or presence'. But in its radical conceptualization, it must be 'conceived of before the alternative of presence or absence; being must be conceived as presence or absence beginning with the possibility of freeplay and not the other way round'.[38] But while critical of the 'ideal purity' of these terms and of their underlying language, Derrida avowedly never subscribed to a 'kind of "all or nothing" choice between the pure realization of self-presence and complete freeplay or undecidability'. His only point about these privileged and underprivileged terms was that there is no stability but only degrees of stabilizations. Parasitic contamination 'once again broaches and breaches all these relations'.[39] For Derrida, the image of this contaminated relation is also reflected in the 'relations between the framed and the frame, *panergon* (alongside or subsidiary, ornament) and *ergon* (work)', their relation 'mirroring yet distancing relation of différance'. Beyond designating the manner in which the establishment of any system qua system suggests a beyond to it, the logic of parergonality entails the inclusion of 'the parasitic contamination of inside and outside, external and internal, interior and exterior distinctions. And this can be generalized from the merest example of an exemplar which cannot be exemplified'.[40] So deconstruction refers to 'the attempt to "account", in a certain manner, for a heterogeneous variety or manifold of nonlogical contradictions and discursive inequalities of all sorts that continues to haunt and fissure even the successful development of philosophical arguments and their systematic exposition'.[41]

'Double reading' is a natural corollary of deconstruction since the tension between stability attainments and destabilizations can be captured only by undertaking two readings of any writing. Derrida shows its need by raising the question, 'If the same premises lead to evaluations that are apparently contradictory, what does that tell about the system of reading and hierarchization at work?' This impasse points to the importance of finding some way of thinking the opposites together without resorting to the false resolution of 'simply neutralizing the differences' within them, thereby avoiding both *neutralizations* of the binary oppositions. Double reading, at the same time, 'faithful and violent', achieves this. While the first reading is nothing but 'repetitive', attempted within the limits of the system or institution, its foundational assumptions and modes of ratiocination', demonstrate how these attain desired stability effects. The second reading, however, rebounds or springs back upon itself, interrogates its own motives, focuses on what was excluded, systematically or institutionally in the first reading. As Nealon clarifies, the 'second movement of the double reading is, generally speaking, the intervention of an outside or excluded term within the very constitution of wholeness'.[42] To Devetak, it is a 'counter-memorializing reading that unsettles the first by applying pressure to the diagnosed points of instability in a text'. As a mode of deconstruction, it aims to show how even when a discourse or social institution is put together, 'it is already threatened with its own undoing'.[43]

As to 'subjectivity and identity' and the role of power (all related concepts) in their creation, postmodernism/post-structuralism stands apart from not only mainstream approaches but even emancipation-oriented CT. Foucault informs us that the goal of his two-decades-long research 'has not been to analyse the phenomena of power' but 'to create a history of the different modes by which, in our culture, human beings are made subject' through 'three modes of objectification'. The first mode has given itself the status of sciences and is exemplified in the 'objectivizing of the speaking subject in *grammaire générale*, philosophy, and linguistics' or 'objectivizing of the productive subject', as depicted in economics, or even objectivizing of the living subject as shown in history or biology. The second mode involves objectivizing of the subject in 'dividing practices' that depicts the subject as either 'divided inside himself' or divided from others' as the mad from the sane, the sick from the healthy, the criminals from the good boys and so on. The third mode lies in the way the individual turns itself into a subject as, for example, in the domain of sexuality.[44]

Foucault's thinking on the second mode constitution of the subject is in accord with the post-structuralist thinking on dualisms which structure the human cognition, particularly with Derrida's thinking on deconstruction where the outside/ exterior/*panergon* constitutes the inside/interior/*ergon*.

To Foucault, while the 'modern individual—objectified, analysed and fixed—is a historical achievement', and there is no 'universal person on whom power has performed its operations and knowledge and its inquiries',[45] his identity is also a function of this form of power. It applies itself to the immediate everyday life which categorizes him, attaches him to his own individuality and identity and makes him a subject in two senses: (a) 'subject to someone by control and independence and (b) 'tied to his own identity by a conscience or self-knowledge'.[46] This power, as we have shown before, is more productive than repressive, and apart from theorizing disciplinary power, Foucault also shows how sexuality was constructed as an instrument for the extension of biopower through the technology of confession of the individual subject. 'Foucault analyses the particular technology and the discourse of the subject involved in the confession, just as he has analysed those which rely on discipline. He places both in a broader grid of interpretation, that of bio-power.'[47]

Postmodernism/Post-structuralism: Application of Concepts in IR

It is really interesting to see how the concepts discussed above have been applied to IR theory. Ashley applies one aspect of the 'power-knowledge' nexus, when drawing upon the Foucauldian parallelism of the 'rule of immanence' between knowledge of the state and that of 'man' to say that 'modern statecraft is modern mancraft', located at the heart of the ontological intersection of three concepts that constitute traditional IR theory, namely sovereignty, anarchy and statecraft. Ashley's 'reworking' of these three concepts shows that their meanings, functions and relationships to one another cannot be comprehended without grasping their ontological debt to an apparitional figure of 'modern reasoning man'.[48] First, in his four propositions, Ashley shows about sovereignty that:

1. 'In "its general form", the modern construct of sovereignty invoked by heroic practices is not centred upon God or upon monarchy but upon man'.
2. Even though 'modernist discourse invests the sovereign figure of man with a will and capacity to transcend those historical conditions that would deny his total freedom', it does not constitute him 'as a spectator situated outside history' but as one 'who is problematically involved in history'.

3. The 'figure of sovereign man need not lose courage in the face of his historical limitations because these limitations are not exterior and imposed upon him' but reversible through reason to his advantage.
4. The image of the sovereign figure of man riddled with limitations 'supplies the constitutive principle of both (a) the modern state as sovereign *subject* of rational collective action and (b) domestic society as object domain subordinated to the state's sovereign gaze'.

So while Ashley's first three propositions see the modern construct of sovereignty is rooted in the 'heroic figure of the reasoning man,'[49] his fourth proposition reveals its impact on the state-society dichotomy, helping Ashley's 'explorations of the complicity of the scholarship in the practices of statecraft' in the inventory of the numerous contributions of post-structuralism to the field of IR.[50]

Taken together, the 'power/knowledge' factor and 'genealogy' generate this important insight that many of the problems and issues discussed in IR 'are not just matters of epistemology and ontology but power and authority; they are struggles to impose authoritative interpretations of international relations'.[51] Simultaneously with writing a 'history of the present' and attempting a 'narrativizing of reality', genealogy also focuses on the undiscovered elements of the past. Regarding the history of the present, someone might genealogically pore over the discourse of climate change through asking who were permitted to speak and make decisions at meetings like the UN Climate Change Conference held in 2011 in Durban and then ask what constructions of 'the climate' and of 'global responsibility' held sway there, and how they connected with past discourses; or regarding the Arab Spring, he/she would ask who represented 'the people' there.[52] There have also been Nietzschean genealogical studies of diplomacy, notably in two books of Der Derian[53] in *OD* as 'a genealogy of the Western estrangement' applied to the 'supposed crisis in which diplomacy finds itself'. He thinks the 'circularity' of genealogy would best unearth 'how a (Western) diplomatic culture was constructed' and then 'projected as universally and unproblematically applicable in the last quarter of the 20th century'. Der Derian's 'six interpenetrating paradigms' of diplomacy trace out the 'origins and transformations of diplomacy' till our date, neglected by realists. Arguing that diplomacy neither contains 'an essence of common sense' nor possesses 'an origin that can be chronologically and geographically filled', Der Derian presents it as an array of practices, power struggles and truth disputations that is a tale of mediation of estrangement: 'mediation of estranged individuals, groups and entities'; 'mediation of estranged peoples organized in states which interact as a system' in modern times, and generally mediation of 'an estranged and alienated international realm'. He studies diplomatic culture as 'mediation of estrangement by symbolic power and social constraints'. The six diplomatic paradigms are mytho-diplomacy, proto-diplomacy, diplomacy, anti-diplomacy, neo-diplomacy and techno-diplomacy.[54] The parametric concepts of alienation and estrangement and the variables of type of mediation employed are central to each paradigm, associated with the different histoico-cultural influences and fundamental social values of different loosely defined time periods. Among them, the first two paradigms are located in a Judeo–Christian trajectory, starting from the 'mytho-diplomacy' of the fall from the grace of God and the granting of mediating powers between the earthly cities and the heavenly city to the Church, post-St Augustine's iconic 5th century CE classic *City of God*. It emphasizes the influence of

Judeo–Christians perspectives on diplomatic discourses, amid the 'struggles of an estranged Christianity both within the Holy Roman Empire and outside it, in its confrontation with the hated other (Islam)'. By contrast, the third and fourth paradigms depict the more tangled period of the breakdown of Christendom and the rise of a modern state system. The fifth focuses on the discernible impact of both the French and Russian revolutions upon diplomatic culture and the sixth theme, which continues till the present times, captures the transformation of 'traditional' diplomatic practices in the age of 'technodiplomacy'.[55]

Among the paradigms, mytho-diplomacy relates to (one-sided sacral) mediation between estranged man and God and estranged tribes/peoples (Jews/others, Christians/Muslims) through sacred symbols and normative knowledge employed predominantly by priests and generating sub-paradigms Jewish and Christian (Augustinian, institutionalized by the papacy). Proto-diplomacy depicts the mediation of estrangement of the newly formed city-states, primarily in Italy, from one another and from the hegemonic empires at the end of the Middle Ages and the early onset of Renaissance in an acute condition of anarchy. Much as the Augustinian paradigm before—which mediated estrangement between a mythical unity and an actual divided reality, as well as between two mythical units (Islam/Christianity)—proto-diplomacy proffered a unilateral mediation of a one-sided estrangement, even though secular or desacralized and based on *raison d'état*. Contrary to these, the third paradigm, 'diplomacy', contained mediation between national states, each with its own monarch, bereft of antiquated mediations by the papacy or emperor, and compelled to resort to reciprocal secular *raison d'état*-based legitimations, causing interdigitation of the diplomatic system based on permanent residence and the state system. Contrary to 'diplomacy', which concerns mediation of estranged states, anti-diplomacy attempts mediation of estrangement between strata (classes or nation and monarchy) strata within or across states from the perspective of mankind's universal mediation from a Utopian condition of universal brotherhood and legitimizes itself through a one-sided secularized mythical Utopia, replacing diplomacy's earlier horizontality by verticality in highlighting man's fall from a universal Utopia. Neo-diplomacy, the fifth paradigm, is the international reification of anti-diplomatic theory through its evocation of a revolutionary mediation that aspires to unity between peoples and classes across borders, as exemplified in the French and Russian revolutions. Similarly, with anti-diplomacy, it also rests on a one-sided secularized mythical Utopia. The last point is techno-diplomacy, which addresses the 'immediate question of how technology, in the sense of technical invention applied to social relations, has transformed the relevant mediation of estrangement'.[56]

This genealogical study effectively lacerates the conventional and entrenched view that 'realistic' diplomatic practice should hark back 'to some essentialized past, some universalized common sense or simple historical precedent' since it shows that in every turn of its development diplomacy is given shape by the 'matrix of tensions, ideas and conflicts' that invests its dominant discourse with power/knowledge. In *Antidiplomacy*, this idea is more explicitly discussed in the context of the independence struggles of the Baltic states during and after the breakup of the Soviet Union.[57] Der Derian's achievement is showing through 'suspicion' buttressed by historical research that the present meaning of any concept hides complexities that only 'interpretative history' can exhume.[58]

Among the two concepts of 'textuality' and 'intertextuality', the first has been used to textualize IR through a rereading of its historic and analytic tradition—not by dismissing the dominant readings but by showing that these are also possible alternative *readings*, and superiority of the former is not derived from any better match with 'an essential (real) meaning' but only from 'a discursive strategy intrinsically connected to the dominant form of (socio-historical) knowledge'. Of course, alternative readings of major realist texts were present even before postmodernists/post-structuralists arrived on the scene. Waltz pointed out the 'contemporaneity' of Thucydides experienced by Hobbes and Louis J. Halle, even in the age of nuclear weapons and superpowers.[59] Keohane detected undisturbed linearity in the writings of Thucydides, Morgenthau and Waltz.[60] From Wight to Gilpin, scholars have taken Thucydides and his *History of the Peloponnesian War* (HOTPWA) as the fountainhead of realism, leading Doyle to term Thucydides' position as 'complex realism' and assert that 'Thucydides belongs to the realists. They belong to him'. But other commentators (such as Donnelly and Boucher) think that HOTPWA is not every inch a realist text, and certain parts of it (like the Melian Dialogue) have been handpicked by realists for 'privileging'.[61] Alker would not consider the Melian Dialogue even as a minor source point of realism. Even after his penchant for 'scientific history', Thucydides offers a dialectical view characteristic of the 'philosophically serious students of the sophists, not the logical positivism or amoral realism in terms of which so many of us have been trained to see the past, nor the ambassadorial sophistry to which some of us still aspire', and 'his historiography combines a commitment to factual accuracy with what we would now call a dramaturgical perspective on human affairs'.[62]

Predictably, postmodernists vigorously carried forward this initiative. Rob Walker, for example, objected to 'simple submission to the caricature' of a tradition of IR in depicting Machiavelli since he 'can be read in ways that problematize the most basic assumptions on which claims about tradition is based'. The objective is not just understanding 'what Machiavelli really said' to reveal the extent of the caricature but 'to indicate one way of identifying some of the discursive practices that have turned a historical problem into an ahistorical apology for the violence of the present'.[63] The problem with the vacuous ahistorical linearity or realism in the great texts detected by Keohane and others is that 'the differences between accounts of political life in classical Greece and early-modern Europe are more interesting than the tenuous assertions of continuity between Thucydides, Machiavelli and Hobbes as a tradition of international political theory'. Walker thinks because this is not appreciated and rather than seeing political realism 'as a complex site of philosophical puzzles and contradictions', it is perceived as a 'banal tradition stretching from Thucydides to Morgenthau'; great realist thinkers such as Thucydides, Machiavelli, Hobbes, Rousseau and others 'appear to us as quite unproblematic figures, often in disguises that make them quite unrecognizable to anyone who examines the textual evidence we have of them'.[64]

To explain this mismatch between the disguised Machiavelli—a leading realist icon', situated 'in traditional folklore on one side of the great logocentric divide, Others (idealists, domestic political theorists, ideologues, etc.) and the contrary textual evidence about him—George shows that the 'dominant reading of *The Prince*' appears suddenly problematic when one theme 'marginalized in traditional discourse', that of 'the issue of virtū, and the problem of violence in the pursuit of a life of virtū, which is the major focus of *The Prince*' and is boldly taken up. Then, it reveals that the realist-revered gospel of state-centric realism is nothing but a guide to the nation-building problems of the new Renaissance states. Further, when another great silence on Machiavelli is broken by bringing into the reading list other works of Machiavelli, such as the *Discourses on Livy*, *The History of Florence* and *The Art of War*, then the diehard realist of the IR tradition comes out as a complete Renaissance scholar preoccupied not with 'the anarchic state system per se', as the tradition would have it, but with 'the classical (Greek) conception of the (domestic) polis—part of the very realm (dichotomously) separated from the "international" by the Tradition that proclaims Machiavelli as its own'. The dominant reading is further problematized when one takes into cognizance Machiavelli's avowed distaste for all 'universalist schemes and notions of transhistorical structural laws'. This (double reading) is aimed at, '(i)llustrating that the "great texts" of International Relations can be read in ways entirely contrary to their realized disciplinary treatment is consequently, to open up space for other ways of reading *global life*, effectively and powerfully blocked off under a foundationalist textual regime'.[65]

Switching from textualizing IR anti-disciplinarily by rereading great IR texts to the application of intertextuality to global life, we see Hansen looking at declarations issued by international institutions such as NATO, EU and the UN all of which repeat previous announcements and statements made by these bodies and even by their country members. But intertextuality acts in subtler ways. For example, the words 'the Balkans' evoke 'ancient hatred', drawing on an intertext where they are inscribed as premodern or barbaric. Intertextuality also makes images or occurrences which are not explicitly written or spoken about so that a presidential meeting before TV cameras sends signs to read and understood within the larger text of diplomacy. Similarly, non-mention, or scarcity of references to the USSR in Cold-War time, NATO declarations does not hide its anti-Soviet foundational purpose. But intertextuality also implies that reliance of present texts on past texts in an intertext does not imply that despite being copies, present texts are not simultaneously unique but related. For example, the Muhammad cartoons originally published in the Danish newspaper in September 2005 have been reproduced in countless newspapers and online news portals with so many different readings that they have little correspondence with the original readings when they were first printed.[66]

But that would not hinder one in relating a long-drawn series of events to the *Jyllands-Posten* cartoons (some would even bung in Salman Rushdie's 1988 novel *The Satanic Verses*) in a wide intertext chain of Muhammad baiting and reactions to it. These include (a) the Charlie Hebdo cartoons of the prophet on 9 February 2006, titled 'Muhammad Overwhelmed by Fundamentalists' and its relation to recent news of the post-election introduction of sharia law in Libya and the victory of the Islamist party in Tunisia; (b) firebombing of the newspaper's office in November 2011; (c) the second series of Muhammad cartoons (some of them even nude caricatures of him) in a September 2012 issue of the newspaper; (d) the 7 January 2015 attack by two Islamist gunmen on the Paris headquarters of Charlie Hebdo and 12 deaths of staff cartoonists from it; (e) cartoonist Renald Luzier's explanation of a weeping Muhammad drawn by him in the front page of a January 2015 issue of the newspaper, revolving around the words 'all is forgiven', and (f) anti-Islam Dutch politician Geert Wilders' cancellation of a November 2018 Muhammad cartoon contest initially planned by him on 30 August 2017.[67]

The whole intertext chain would also warn us about another thing. It is that since 'states actually take culture seriously, even if it is "just fiction"', post-structuralists also take popular culture seriously. Der Derian used the intertext of popular spy novels (including novels such as by ex-intelligence agent John le Carré and ex-CIA operative Charles McCarry), journalism and academic writings for deconstructing diplomacy.[68] Cynthia Weber not only used 'popular films' and TV shows to drive home her insights into the mainstream and critical theories[69] but also critically interrogated the popular image of American culture to make her point that US military policies towards the Caribbean and Latin America between 1959 and 1994 represented 'a series of displacements of castration or castration anxiety'.[70]

The post-structuralist concepts of 'deconstruction' and 'double reading' have been used in IR primarily to problematize the notion of state sovereignty. But to grasp the context and full force of this critique, it will be better to assess, first, the purchase of double reading on the realist concept of 'AP', understood as 'the political and intellectual problems that emerge from the international anarchy between states', being 'the product of an absence, the lack of a world government or final authority that can legitimately govern the plural states of the global order'.[71] This deduction has been questioned before, for instance, by constructivists and Wendt, who wrote on 'divergent logics of different types of anarchy'.[72] For mainstream IR, AP is at once 'the ontological constant for those wishing to understand the relations between autonomous political units and the principal block to a better world', a position which misses 'the potential emancipatory value of the concept'.[73]

Postmodernists/post-structuralists deconstruct the deduction from *AP* of 'not just an empty concept of anarchy' but a depiction of IR as power politics, marked by self-interest, *raison d'état* and unavoidable recourse to force. Ashley first reiteratively 'reads' the realist depiction of IP as 'a realm dominated by anarchy, not community ... a pluralistic sphere of multiple independent vantage points, each with its own independent voice, each having its own sense of a whole and each ready to check or resist others' attempts to impose an encompassing rationalist model', a sphere which allows a critical attitude towards the domestic sphere but not toward the international, where trendy 'Parisian readings of Nietzsche and Heidegger' are thought to be inapplicable because 'the void of community at the heart of global political life' has been discovered long back by theorists and practitioners.[74] He, then, asks: How AP 'works', 'gains significance in our culture' and 'comes to be recognized as a powerful representation of a predicament so compelling and so self-evident that it seems to command attention'? And ii) how has the discourse on *AP* in the course of its maturation revealed its own 'rhetorical strategies' and wrecked the very foundations of the perspective it defends and through that is clearing up 'potentially productive avenues of inquiry' till now blocked off by it? The first question is important because the theoretical discourse of *AP* hides from our view and begs the greater part of the question it seeks to resolve, namely 'the problem of order in the absence of an orderer'. Regarding the first part of this question, whether world politics is rightly characterized through the attribute of 'the absence of a central agency of rule visibly engaged in the issuing of commands and the enforcing of political order', Ashley agrees. But the other part of it, concerning the discourse's foundational axiom that the configuration of world political authority involves a number of 'already given' states and national societies invested with 'identical sovereign presence', is a 'practical matter' closely connected with the problem of order in modern political life and is, according to him, far from settled.

Ashley's answer to the second question is that AP's theoretical discourse can make this basic claim only because it relies on a knowledgeable 'heroic practice' that brings to fore an easily understandable hierarchical opposition of sovereignty and anarchy, where sovereignty is 'privileged as a higher reality and regulative ideal'. Besides it, anarchy is a derivative, 'parergonal' and negative term, signifying a failure to match this heroic ideal. So the second aspect of Ashley's reply to the question of the successful working of the AP discourse is that it spotlights and replicates the very knowledgeable 'heroic practice' that participants in its discourse should have but never have questioned. Even while observing the deep void of global politics caused by the 'absence of an arching sovereign presence capable of imposing a unique and coherent rational narrative of order', they desist from foregrounding 'the play of ambiguity, contingency, chance and open-minded eventuation in their interpretations of global political possibilities'.[75]

It is in answer to his two questions concerning the way the AP discourse might enfeeble or impair its own foundations that Ashley brings his strategy of double reading. His first reading, pervading his answer to the first question, 'follows the model of the "monologue"', while his answer to the second question hinges on the 'model of the "dialogue"'. The interpretative-monological model 'mimics'/apes the dominant discourse replicated in AP, as a 'well-bounded text' with a 'hard-core unity', downplaying 'its ambiguous, dynamic and contingent connections' to an array of 'marginal' themes and focusing instead on the 'heroic practice' itself, not as a practice existing by its own right 'but as a kind of "deep structure"'. But the resultant dilemmas of the first reading, consisting of an underscoring of its presumed boundaries, consistency, clarity of purpose at the expense of historicity, vitality, reliance upon 'the arbitrary play of knowledgeable practices in its relations to the "other" texts of a pluralistic culture' and the crippling either/or choice regarding the discourse so read, is expressed in a nutshell by Ashley as 'the blackmail of the heroic practice'. It led him on to the second dialogical reading, which overturns the sovereignty/anarchy dichotomy, privileging the latter over the former and gives primacy to 'practice over structure, surface over depth and historical movement over stasis'. The second reading shows how 'differences, discontinuities and conflicts that might be found "within" all places and times' are 'converted into an absolute difference "between" a domain of domestic society, understood as an identity and a domain of anarchy, understood as at once ambiguous, indeterminate and dangerous'. To do that, domestic sovereign societies must efface all traces of anarchy resident within them, as also of all 'transversal struggles', which are in Ashley's view, 'conflicts that traverse all political boundaries because they are conflicts over the interpretation of the sovereign man in whose terms states, domestic societies and their political boundaries shall be defined'.[76]

The impact of this critique is enormous in revealing that the boundaries between sovereignty and anarchy are indefensible, and the difference inhering within them is more important than the difference between them. There are spaces of sovereignty in anarchy, just as there are spaces of anarchy in sovereignty. But to paint life outside the state as chaotic and bereft of rule, 'internal difference is repressed and converted into external difference'.[77] In short, sovereignty is contaminated by anarchy. The deleterious consequences of the AP for the discipline as also for the 'practice' of IR are manifested in its anarchical premises, which fed the Cold-War logic for decades on both sides of the East/West divide; encouraged the costliest arms race in human history; justified brutal repression of people's aspirations with the bogey of revolutionary socialism; legitimated the truncheon in the hands of the world's 'policeman' till the late 1980s, and perpetuated in IR 'a hierarchical distinction' between a rational and meaningful (i.e., scientifically knowable and behaviourally mediatable) inside 'and that which is "outside" the realm of rational meaningful discourse and is a danger to it'.[78]

Deconstruction of sovereignty is another crucial area of application because of interrogating the normality of sovereign states, exercising state power as a legitimate use of state violence backed by law in strictly delimited territorial boundaries. Unsurprisingly, 'the most perplexing problems associated with the concept of sovereignty arise when this convergence on a monopoly of power and legitimate authority in a specific country is challenged, whether on the basis of externality (by other competing sovereignties, which, by definition, are not supposed to be in the same place at once) or of hierarchical conceptions of authority (against which the exclusive claims of sovereignty were articulated in the first place)'.[79] For both of these two points, Weber's question is very apt: '"How are sovereign functions represented?" Power and knowledge organized so that sovereign foundations are discursively constructed? How intervention justifications participate in the construction of sovereign foundations, be they domestic (citizenries), or international (epistemic communities)?'[80]

So postmodernists' interests in the sovereignty issue generally revolve around 'the connections between these articulations of sovereignty' and the normalized/unchallenged status of the sovereignty theme within realism, which turns it into 'an effectively ahistorical, universalized component of an "art of the possible" bounded by power politics logic' and acts as a source of closure in IR. To force open this closure, postmodernists first relocate the sovereign state in a much bigger discursive frame, starting with the emergence of the post-Kantian sovereign man,[81] as mentioned above.[82] Derrida questions in his cryptic way, while interpreting D. H. Lawrence's poem *Snake*, in the context of a discussion on 'political sovereignty and animality' and applying the argument of the 'first comer' and the 'second comer':

> Once we have recognized that the sovereign is in the end the first comer, the one who comes before me, the other before who is before me, are we to reconstitute a logic of sovereignty, a scene of sovereignty, by simply displacing sovereignty from me to the other ... in other words, should the deconstruction of sovereignty limit itself to deconstructing sovereignty as my sovereignty, but in order to transfer to the other, or should the idea of sovereignty in general should be contested here?[83]

Obviously, Derrida is talking about the arrogation of sovereignty by what Ashley would call 'the modern state, as sovereign "subject" of rational collective action' and its transference from the sovereign man and the polluted 'heroic practice'. And Walker thinks that in IR, the concept of sovereignty lacks sufficient contestation. Even if its meaning might be taken as 'marginally contestable by constitutional lawyers and other connoisseurs of fine lines, for the most part, state sovereignty expresses a commanding silence', pretending that 'some problems of political life' are, at least, 'simple and settled'.[84] In this sense, the issue of state sovereignty is far more interesting than it looks in its present presentation because the 'conventional story can be given slightly different readings in relation to the discursive spaces that are themselves defined by the principle of state sovereignty'. And while showing us a 'world of sovereignty/lack of sovereignty of supposedly autonomous states in an unregulated contest of wills', postmodernism teaches us that 'sovereignty is both constitutive of the system and a problem to be overcome'.[85]

'Identity', the last key term, has been mostly studied in the context of foreign policy. Conventional, realist IR links foreign policies to the rational aspirations of states for security, economic well-being and some security-oriented altruism. But post-structuralists contend that foreign policies are not drawn from some stable state object but do instead rely on and produce particular understandings of state, through constituting the identity of self-as-state or state-as-self via the construction of threats, dangers and challenges to it—constituting the Other(s). This leads us to the politics of representation because the way we represent others shapes our representation of ourselves and the foreign policies we adopt. Shapiro's work on the way the USA has represented Central America, particularly Guatemala, as the threatening source of otherness for its security discourse is a case in point because it was this politics of representation that enabled the USA to avoid answering the inevitable question of how a small country like Guatemala could pose such a big danger to the mighty USA. To George, for the 'modernist constitution of the identity/difference dichotomy', where the self or shell of a state (as in the case of the USA) is constituted and is wound in terms of a security discourse (AP) and all states of the world are arranged someplace in this threat perception as in a bagatelle board, some countries can come to acquire disproportionate importance in discursive terms.

How the politics of representation operates textually is demonstrated by *The Kissinger Report* (1984), fully implicated in constructing a US identity in a world of threatening Others, conjuring up the cultural contempt of the conquistadors for the Indian peoples described in Todorov's *The Conquest of America* (1984).[86] The politics of representation also informed the debates within the EU about whether Turkey should be accepted as a new member, which basically boiled down to if Turkey was a European country and whether a country could ever be European and Muslim at the same time. The manner in which EU members addressed this question reflected how EU countries constructed not only the identity of Turkey but also their own.[87]

Campbell links identity as a 'performative' concept (meaning, having no ontological status apart from the various acts which constitute it).[88] Rather than asking how US foreign policy furthers its national interest, Campbell enquires into how 'through the inscription of foreign-ness, US foreign policy helps produce and reproduce the political identity of the doer supposedly behind the deed'.[89] This involves retheorization of the conventional understanding of foreign policy 'as the external orientation of pre-established states with secure identities' into 'one of the boundary-producing practices central to the production and reproduction of the identity in whose name it operates'. It revolves around the distinction between two understandings of foreign policy. In the first, foreign policy can be deemed to allude to the existing practices of differentiation or modes of exclusion which turn their objects into 'foreign' while dealing with them. In this meaning of it, foreign policy is dissociated from the state as a specific 'resolution of the categories of identity and difference' for application to all apparent encounters between the self and the other occurring in different sites of ethnicity, race, class, gender and geography. These are all modes of foreign policy 'within', in lowercase, which have operated through paradigms of sovereignty and identity constitution spatio-temporarily. Traversing all levels of social organization from those of personal relationships to global orders, foreign policy in this meaning generates 'conventional dispositions' wherein 'a particular set of representational practices' offers resources from which to extract 'modes of interpretation employed to handle new situations of ambiguity or contingency'. Operation of the process is best studied in the USA, a land known for 'intolerance of ambiguity at all levels of social life', ranging from local communities to the global order, instantiated in 'a hierarchical ordering of the self and other through figurations of disease and pollution'. Here, the first understanding of foreign policy furnishes the 'discursive economy or conventional matrix of interpretations' in which the second understanding of 'Foreign Policy' (in uppercase) becomes operational, where 'Foreign Policy as state-based' is not as involved in the 'constitution of identity' as the first meaning. 'Rather Foreign Policy serves to reproduce the constitution of identity made possible by 'foreign policy' and to contain challenges to the identity which results'.[90]

In this sense, the Cold War was also a 'struggle related to the production and reproduction of identity', taking the shape in the West as 'an ensemble of practices in which an interpretation of danger, crystallized around objectification of communism and the Soviet Union', acted as a 'code for the inscription of multiple boundaries between the "civilized" and the "barbaric", the "normal" and the "pathological"'[91] and facilitated an immurement of the identity of the USA in a Cold-War logic of modernist sovereignty and the AP. The resultant 'discourses of danger' covered such themes as environmental disasters throughout Eastern Europe in the last four decades; drugs and the war on it; Japanese economic policies and 'the problematization of Japan as a national security threat'; 'contemporary representations of AIDS in which iconography associated syphilis, homosexuals, Africans, drug addicts and inner-city residents are melded into an all-encompassing discursive formation', and sometimes a 'logic of socio-medical discourse' bypassing the nature of the disease to emphasize 'a sense that disease is always from somewhere else'. These discursive practices are combined in a kind of 'discursive economy' by blurring the boundaries of inside/outside, even though their constitutive 'practices of otherness and the strategies of differentiation' are different.[92] In other cases, the discourse of danger facilitates a 'transference of the differences within the state to differences between the states', manifest in how 'the discursive practices of the "war on drugs" serve to inscribe the frontiers of the USA'.[93] What is common to these danger discourses is 'an evangelism of fear', 'cardinal for the constitution of states' identity but providing its most 'conspicuous' 'apocalyptic mode'[94] in US foreign policy. However, the role of fear in the writing of the state is in no way peculiar to the USA. Because, for the vast majority of contemporary states, existing only by virtue of their ability to constitute themselves as imagined communities, the process of imagination has been centrally rooted in 'the operation of discourses of danger which, by telling us what to fear, have been able to fix who "we" are'.[95]

These post-structuralist/postmodernist concepts have destabilized realist readings of the great texts of IR and irretrievably mutilated realist IR centred on sovereignty, anarchy, statecraft, diplomacy, security and foreign policy. They have exposed how state-actor approaches have 'obscured the historical constitution and reconstitution' of the sovereign state as the 'primary mode of subjectivity in world politics', creating thereby what Devetak says, a 'quasi-phenomenology' of the state thing, underlying genealogy of which accounts for its destabilization and the deferral of the complete realization of its subjectivity. This genealogical quasi-phenomenology of the state phenomenon is presented along the four axes of its origination: violence, boundary inscription, deconstruction of identity expressed in security and foreign policy discourses and revealed statecraft. Although the last two elements have been discussed above, their quasi-phenomenological implications bear repetition.[96]

Post-structuralist Quasi-phenomenological Problematization of the Sovereign State

Violence

Although modernist versions of sovereignty belittle the role of violence in state-making by invoking the example of rational law-governed democratic governments, post-structuralists (such as Campbell and Dillon) point out the ambivalent and ambiguous relations between modern politics and violence by claiming that since 'the political subject of violence is a reasoning subject, the complicity of reason' in his violence cannot be omitted. The state stages a 'theatre of political conflict in which the representation of the violence is integral to the conflict itself'. So 'violence is both the practice which constructs the refuge of the sovereign community and the condition from which the citizens of that community must be protected', simultaneously malady evil and cure.[97] While exploring how sovereign states 'use violence to defend and advance their interests amid a hostile anarchic world', Bradley and Klein want strategic studies to consider 'the extent to which states rely upon violence to constitute themselves as states and to impose differentiation between the internal and the external' and 'the constitutive role of violence in the making of states which act strategically upon the world'.[98]

This genealogical reference to the generative role of violence cannot be confused with the treatment of violence in traditional literature (such as the force theory of the origin of the state) or with the endemic presence of violence in the AP because the wars that 'begat' the states or their sovereigns were not constitutive but 'configurative wars' and 'positional wars'. It was only in constitutive wars, however, 'the very ontology of the units—that is to say, what kind of units they would be—was still at issue', as manifested in the Wars of Religion.[99] But statist violence is not only pre- but post-constitutive, although their forms 'may indeed vary in different societies, in part reflecting how their mechanisms of social control—what Gramsci called their "trench systems"—protect states from political and economic threats'.[100] The representational complexities and intricacies of violence are contentiously brought out by Edkins, who locates the Nazis, concentration camps, NATO and refugees together on the same continuum of violence.[101]

Boundaries

The problematization must include their boundaries, naturalized in political, scientific and IR literature, and a renewed focus on the 'boundary question'. Knowing that a political subject is constructed by the delineation of physical, symbolic and ideational boundaries and convinced that 'the prevailing mode of political subjectivity' in IR represented by the sovereign state is as unnatural as it is unnecessary, postmodernists regard marking off of boundaries as 'not an innocent and pre-political act' and against assumptions of innocence, regard world geography as not a natural product but an outcome of 'histories of class struggle between competing authorities over the power to organize occupy and administer space'.[102] As Harley points out, a map (and cartography) also reflects the power/knowledge nexus, whether when 'produced under the banner of cartographic science' or when 'it is an overt propaganda exercise', true to Foucault's caution that some 'practical implications of maps fall into the category of what Foucault has defined as "surveillance", notably those connected with warfare, political propaganda, boundary-making or the preservation of law and order'.[103]

Accordingly, postmodernists/post-structuralists disbelieve any political space prior to boundary-inscription since it is boundaries which segregate an interior, stable and sovereign space from an exterior, pluralistic and anarchical space. Although the defining moment in statecraft that turns space into a place through what Ó Tuathail terms 'social inscription of global place' around a nationalist imaginary, boundaries are deeply ambiguous. Even while offering a refuge from 'violation and violence', the barriers and fences they create are also sustained by 'cruelty and violence', a fact that generates quite a few ethical and moral questions.[104]

Identity

The boundary between the 'inside' and 'outside' of the state, although already discussed in the context of problematization of the sovereign state, may merit a few additional words in the context of problematization of the sovereign state, being also a matter of identity inscription. Campbell has shown that '(t)he state has never been a stable ground upon which a fixed identity has been secured against danger' since 'the variety of state forms throughout modernity have always been a historically contingent panoply of practices which have served to constitute identity through the negation of difference and the temptation of otherness'.[105] Among these identity-bestowing practices, tourism is one that gets implicated in the state's spatial conception of security through identification of external threats and dangers (thereby engendering a view of the state as a secure place) by branding some places as safe or unsafe. As a result, even such 'opposed social practices such as war and tourism' get tied together in a 'global security discourse'.[106]

The three themes of violence, boundaries and sovereign statehood can be captured by Derrida's concept of 'ontopology', defined as 'an axiomatics linking indissociably the ontological value of present-being (*on*) to its *situation*, to the stable and presentable determination of a locality, the *topos* of territory, native soil, city and body in general'.[107] It was employed by Campbell in the context of the Bosnian war to show how its intense violence was aimed at a perfect fit between ontology and topos, its underlying desire being inscription of a 'coherent, bounded monocultural community', not aberrant but a logical extension of the ontopological norm, the violent 'ethnic cleansing' being targeted at achieving an unambiguous territorial identity.[108] Similarly, Dalby views the Cold War in terms of a 'geopolitical "scripting" or "geo-graphing", which hinged on' discourses of the Other, how 'their' place is different from 'ours' and as such they operate to situate places in political space, creating other places in specific relation to 'our' place. 'Crucially, the Other is the external threat against which internal identity is formulated'.[109]

Statecraft

We have already shown above that underlying modern statecraft there is modern mancraft.[110] While repeating the concept in the context of post-structuralist problematization of the state, we are interested in two of their questions: (a) 'How is the sovereign state naturalized'? and (b) 'How is it made to appear as if it had an essence'? Ashley answers the first question through *his* non-Gramscian concept of hegemony, as 'an ensemble of normalized knowledgeable practices, identified with a particular state or domestic society that is regarded as a practical paradigm of sovereign political subjectivity and conduct', and operates as an 'exemplary model' and a regulative ideal, although it is by no means natural. As a holder of subjectivity, the state's sovereignty is linked to certain 'historically normalized interpretations of its competencies' and the prerequisites and limits of its actualization and authorization.[111] As for the second question, Ashley looks at the state's performative adoption and passage of various domestic and foreign policies subsumed under the word 'statecraft' that emphasizes the craft part. Against the conventional understanding that the state precedes and is prior to the craft as a fully formed entity, Ashley says that the 'task of international critical inquiry is misconstrued' if it stops at 'an attempt to come to grips with the natural structures, the covering laws or the genetic code existing prior to and independent of the international political practices they generate or represent'. Rather from a genealogical perspective, there cannot be subjects, fully formed identical egos, having an existence prior to practice. To that extent, the subject itself represents 'a site of power political contest'.[112] In Weber's words, 'sovereign nation states are not pre-given subjects but subjects in process, and all subjects in process (be they individual or collective) are the ontological effects of practices, which are performatively enacted'.[113] It is in this sense that Campbell speaks of 'metaBosnia', that is, the panoply of practices or incessant production or Bosnia as state/subject through which Bosnia took shape.[114] This shows that the 'representational, narrative and discursive practices associated with trauma' possess the potentiality not only of forming forms of identity and community but also 'for transforming identities and renegotiating political affiliations, potentially, so as to form communities of responsibility beyond the nation state'.[115] Anyway, Campbell asserts, 'Whether we are talking of "the body" or "the state" or particular bodies or states, the identity of each is performatively constituted'.[116] As Devetak summarizes beautifully,

> This post-structuralist understanding leads to an interpretation of the state as an effect produced by the ceaseless work carried out in service of a 'yet-to-be-completed' state identity … 'an historically emergent and always contested product of multiple practices' … 'not a fixed, pre-given, once-and-for-all creation, but an ongoing political accomplishment' never 'finished as entities', but 'always in a process of becoming'.[117]

CRITIQUE AND EVALUATION

Since postmodernism/post-structuralism has taken on for bashing the entire corpus of mainstream IR theories, it is not surprising that they would also get some flak back from all core or peripheral approaches of IR, generating thereby a huge body of critique. I cannot afford to dwell on them elaborately and would merely state the main lines of criticism.

Among the realists, Keohane's charge that reflective approaches (which include postmodernists) 'are less well-specified as theories'—clearly than rationalists, although they have also been urged 'to become well-developed research programmes'—since 'their advocates have been more adept at pointing out what is omitted in rationalistic theory than developing theories of their own with prior intent,'[118] boils down to asking postmodernists to cease being postmodernists. Methodologically, equally valid is Rosenau's contention that the applicability of postmodernism to literature and social sciences varies considerably. In the humanities, subjectivity and speculation can be allowed to be 'playful and interesting', but in the social sciences, they have to be 'more rigorous and analytical, grounding conclusions on reason and evidence of one sort or another'. So here, the verdict is qualified. Postmodernism may have made substantial contributions on *substantive* themes, having provided 'fascinating insights' across a wide-ranging array of themes, because of its focus on 'the non-obvious, left out and generally forgotten in a text' and scrutiny of the 'unsaid, overlooked, understated and never overtly recognized'. As examples of this, Rosenau points to the themes covered by the postmodernist special issue of a journal: 'surveillance, simulation and computer-assisted wargaming, the acceleration of weapons-systems delivery, alliance politics, arms transfers, the local politics of ecological and anti-nuclear movements, the politics of international debt and the production and transformation of political institutions', among many others. But when it comes to *methodological* reconstruction, postmodernism is, from a 'modernist perspective' (read positivistic) 'seriously flawed and epistemologically dubious' because the 'most extreme, uncompromised formulations' of post-modernism yields mostly frivolous results'.[119]

Two scholars from the perspective of critical realism have hinted that the intellectual popularity of postmodernism was due to its ambiguity and incoherence. It 'was never clear entirely, exactly, what postmodernism was (is)', leading some of its leading spokespersons to avoid the label. Contrarily, because of postmodernism's exultant celebration of 'diversity, difference, ambiguity and contradiction', it was but to be expected that 'wildly conflicting theory, practices and alleged knowledge might fly under the same designation and be labelled of doing so.[120]

Marxists' grouse with postmodernism is not confined to its downgrading of economic variables. Marxists, like Eagleton, criticize postmodernism's monomaniac focus on language that reduces everything to discourse in an apolitical frivolity, leading one 'to set up language itself as an alternative to the social problems which plagued one to renounce, gloomily or triumphantly, the traditional notion that one wrote *about* something, *for* somebody and to make language itself its cherished object'.[121] Jameson used the Marxist theory of capitalism to brand postmodernism as 'the cultural logic of late capital'.[122]

Even though there are post-structuralists/postmodernists among feminists, some feminists criticize the 'masculinity of postmodernist/post-structuralist theory and the texts considered central in its debates'. Brodribb comments that 'feminist postmodernism offers little support to a critical analysis of masculine ideology'. Feminist postmodernists consider their work done after reading and representing Foucault, Derrida, Lacan, even Nietzsche and Freud. 'It is impossible to understand feminist postmodernism without reference to the writing it has nominated as central: masculine texts.'[123]

Speaking from the perspective of the state of animal rights in philosophical and literary studies, Steiner not only critiques the anthropocentrism of postmodernism but exposes 'a fatal limitation of postmodernism/post-structuralism' lying at its philosophical core, namely its reliance on 'two notions that are fundamentally incompatible with one another: a commitment to the indeterminacy of meaning and a sense of justice that presupposes the very access to a sense of determinacy that postmodern epistemology dismisses as illusory'. According to him, postmodern appeals to justice are inherently incoherent because they eschew 'humanistic notions' of agency and responsibility.[124]

CONCLUSION

After tracing the origins of the terms postmodernism and post-structuralism, discussing their key concepts and their applications in IR, and assessing the quasi-phenomenological problematization of the sovereign state that they have facilitated, this chapter has summarized the kinds of charges levelled against postmodernists, even though it warns in conclusion that it is impossible for postmodernism/post-structuralism to answer most of the charges of the realist, Marxist or other modernist paradigms of IR without re(-)forming itself into its 'other'. For, while the latter view theory as tools of explanation, control and prediction to be placed aloft the facts and occurrences of international politics, to unravel their meanings and reveal their patterns of repetition and causal connections, postmodernists view 'theory as inculpated in these facts and events'.[125] The very view of the functions of theory and the role of the theorist is reversed here. A focus on 'investigating the role of theorists and theory in representing some actors as more significant than others' turns theory into 'an object of analysis' from 'a tool of analysis'.[126] Theorists are no longer neutrally above the fracas of international politics, archiving the facts, investigating the histories or devising remedies for problems ailing global politics. Rather, they '*are* international politics, the actors who make up those practices and reproduce them' in their quotidian activities.[127]

REVIEW QUESTIONS

1. Comment on the origins of the terms postmodernism and post-structuralism and the senses in which it is taken in IR theory.
2. Explain the key of postmodernism/post-structuralism, showing their utility in IR theory.
3. Show how post-structuralists have attempted a rereading of the great texts of IR.
4. How have post-structuralists attempted to apply their major concepts to irretrievably pillory realist concepts of sovereignty, anarchy, statecraft, diplomacy, security and foreign policy?

5. Comment on the post-structuralist quasi-phenomenological problematization of the sovereign state.
6. State the main lines of criticism of postmodernism/post-structuralism.

NOTES AND REFERENCES

1. Richard Devetak, 'Postmodernism,' in *Theories of International Relations*, eds. Scott Burchill, Andrew Linklater, and Richard Devetak (London: Macmillan International Higher Education, 2013), 81. The scheme and organization of this chapter draws heavily on it.
2. James Der Derian and M. Schapiro, *International/Intertextual Relations: Postmodern Readings in World Politics* (Lexington: Lexington Books, 1989).
3. Jim George, 'Thinking Beyond International Relations: Postmodernism—Reconceptualizing Theory in Practice,' in *Discourses of Global Politics: A Critical (Re)Introduction to International Relations*, ed. Jim George (Boulder, CO: Lynne Rienner Publishers, 1994).
4. For example, Christine Sylvester, *Feminist Theory and International Relations in a Postmodern Era* (Cambridge: Cambridge University Press, 1994).
5. See Darryl S. L. Jarvis, *International Relations and the Challenge of Postmodernism: Defending the Discipline* (Columbia, SC: University of South Carolina Press, 2000).
6. Ihab Hassan, 'The Question of Postmodernism,' *Performing Arts Journal* 6, no. 1 (1981): 30–37, here 30–31, doi: https://www.jstor.org/stable/i363012 (accessed on 09 April 2021); for Olson see: https://www.britannica.com/biography/Charles-Olson (accessed on 09 April 2021).
7. See Kwame Anthony Appiah, 'Is the Post-in Postmodernism the Post-in Postcolonial?' *Critical Inquiry* 17, no. 2 (1991): 336–357.
8. Christopher Coker, 'Postmodernity and the End of the Cold War: Has War Been Disinvented?' *Review of International Studies* 18, no. 3 (July 1992): 189–198; William E. Connolly, *Identity/Difference: Democratic Negotiations of Political Paradox* (Ithaca, NY: Cornel University Press, 1991); Der Derian and Schapiro, *International/Intertextual* Relations; all cited in Brown, 'Critical Theory and Postmodernism in IR,' 56.
9. David Campbell, 'Poststructuralism,' in *International Relations: Discipline and Diversity*, eds. Tim Dunne, Milja Kurki, and Steve Smith (Scotts Valley, CA: CreateSpace, 2017), 211–212.
10. Richard K. Ashley, 'Living on Border Lines: Man, Poststructuralism, and War', in *International/Intertextual Relations*, eds. James Der Derian and M. Schapiro (Lexington: Lexington Books, 1989), 259–321.
11. Simon Lumsden, 'Poststructuralism and Modern European Philosophy,' in *Edinburgh Companion to Poststructuralism*, eds. Benoît Dillet, Iain Mackenzie, and Robert Porter (Edinburgh: Edinburgh University Press, 2013), 23, and Benoît Dillet, Iain Mackenzie, and Robert Porter, 'Introduction,' in *Edinburgh Companion to Poststructuralism* (Edinburgh: Edinburgh University Press, 2013), 2.
12. O. Wæver, 'Identity, Communities and Foreign Policy: Discourse Analysis as Foreign Policy Theory,' in *European Integration and National Identity: The Challenge of the Nordic States*, eds. Lene Hansen and Ole Waever (London: Routledge, 2002), 23.
13. Campbell, 'Poststructuralism,' 212.
14. Graham Allen, *Intertextuality*, 2nd ed. (London: Routledge, 2000/2011), 176.
15. Michel Foucault, *Politics, Philosophy, Culture: Interviews and Other Writings, 1977–1984*, ed. Lawrence D. Kritzman (London: Routledge, 1990/1988), 43.
16. Lawrence D. Kritzman, ed., 'Introduction,' in *Politics, Philosophy, Culture: Interviews and Other Writings, 1977–1984* (London: Routledge, 1990/1988), xviii.

17. Lene Hansen, 'Poststructuralism,' in *The Globalization of World Politics: An Introduction to International Relations*, eds. John Baylis, Steve Smith, and Patricia Owens (Oxford: Oxford University Press, 2014).
18. Michel Foucault, *Power/Knowledge: Selected Interviews and Other Writings, 1972–1977*, ed. Colin Gordon (New York, NY: Pantheon Books, 1980), 30.
19. Michel Foucault, *Discipline and Punish: The Birth of the Prison*, 2nd ed. (New York, NY: Vintage Books, 1995), 170–227, especially 154, 171–173.
20. Eric Paras, *Foucault 2.0: Beyond Power and Knowledge* (New York, NY: Other Press, 2006/2019), available at: https://books.google.co.in/books/about/Foucault_2_0.html?id=gfe_DwAAQBAJ&source=kp_book_description&redir_esc=y (accessed on 09 April 2021), 11.
21. Foucault, *Discipline and Punish*, 195.
22. Michel Foucault, *The Order of Things: An Archaeology of the Human Sciences* (London: Routledge Classics, 2002), 104.
23. Campbell, 'Poststructuralism,' 216–217.
24. Foucault, *The Order of Things*, 'Foreword to the English Edition,' xv.
25. D. S. L. Jarvis, *International Relations and Challenge of Postmodernism: Defending the Discipline* (Columbia, SC: University of South Carolina Press, 2000), 55.
26. Devetak, 'Postmodernism,' 183.
27. Foucault, 'Nietzsche, Genealogy, History,' in *The Foucault Reader*, ed. Paul Rabinow (Harmondsworth: Penguin, 1984), 87–90; Foucault, *Discipline and Punish*, 22, 28, 30–31.
28. Alan Rosenberg and Joseph Westfall, 'Introduction,' in *Foucault and Nietzsche: A Critical Encounter*, eds. Joseph Westfall and Alan Rosenberg (London: Bloomsbury, 2018), 9, 62.
29. Jens Bartelson, *A Genealogy of Sovereignty* (Cambridge: Cambridge University Press, 1996), 74.
30. Walter Benjamin, 'Excavation and Memory,' in *Walter Benjamin: Selected writings*, eds. Marcus Paul Bullock, Michael William Jennings, Howard Eiland, and Gary Smith (Cambridge, MA: Belknap Press of Harvard University Press, 2004), 576.
31. Friedrich Nietzsche, *On the Genealogy of Morals and Ecce Homo*, trans. Walter Kaufmann (New York, NY: Vintage Books, 1989), Third Essay, Section 12, 119.
32. Ibid., 218.
33. Allen, *Intertextuality*, 5–6, 169, 177.
34. Jean Baudrillard, *Simulacra and Simulation* (Ann Arbor, MI: University of Michigan Press, 1994), 99–100.
35. Martin McQuillan, 'Introduction: Five Strategies of Deconstruction,' in *Deconstruction: A Reader*, ed. Martin McQuillan (New York: Routledge, 2001), 6, 8.
36. Devetak, 'Postmodernism,' 187.
37. Jacques Derrida, *Of Grammatology*, 40th anniversary ed. (Baltimore, MD: Johns Hopkins University Press, 1974/2016), 181.
38. Derrida, 'Structure, Sign, and Play in the Discourse of the Human Sciences,' in *The Structuralist Controversy: The Languages of Criticism and the Sciences of Man*, ed. R. M. E. Donato (Baltimore and London: John Hopkins Press, 1982), 263–264.
39. Jacques Derrida, *Limited Inc* (Evanston, IL: Northwestern University Press, 1988), 115, 100.
40. Irene E. Harvey, 'Derrida, Kant, and the Performance of Parergonality,' in *Derrida and Deconstruction*, ed. Hugh J. Silverman (London: Routledge, 1989), 68–69, 63. Note here the affinity of panergon with Baudrillard's *simulacrum*.
41. Rodolphe Gasché, 'Infrasructures and Systematicity,' in *Deconstruction and Philosophy: The Texts of Jacques Derrida*, ed. John Sallis (Chicago, IL: University of Chicago Press, 1987), 4.
42. Jacques Derrida, 'The Age of Hegel,' trans. Susan Winnett, in *Demarcating the Disciplines*, ed. Samuel Weber (Minneapolis, MN: University of Minnesota Press, 1987), 21; Jacques

Derrida, *Positions* (University of Chicago Press, 1982), 41, both cited in Jeffrey Thomas Nealon, *Double Reading: Postmodernism after Deconstruction* (Ithaca, NY: Cornell University Press, 1993), 17–18, 33.

43. Devetak, 'Postmodernism,' 188.
44. Michel Foucault, 'Afterword,' in *Michel Foucault: Beyond Structuralism and Hermeneutics, with an Afterword by Michel Foucault*, eds. Hubert L. Dreyfus and Paul Rabinow (Chicago, IL: University of Chicago Press, 1982/2013), 208–209.
45. Hubert L. Dreyfus and Paul Rabinow, *Michel Foucault: Beyond Structuralism and Hermeneutics, with an Afterword by Michel Foucault* (Chicago, IL: University of Chicago Press, 1982/2013), 159–160.
46. Foucault, 'Afterword,' 212.
47. Ibid., 169.
48. Cynthia Weber, 'Interruption Ashley,' *Review of International Studies* 36, no. 4 (2010): 975–987, here 980.
49. Richard Ashley, 'Living on the Border Lines: Man, Post-structuralism and War,' in in *International/Intertextual Relations*, eds. James Der Derian and M. Schapiro (Lexington: Lexington Books, 1989), 303.
50. Richard Ashley, 'The Powers of Anarchy: Theory, Sovereignty and the Domestication of Global Life,' in *International Theory: Critical Investigations*, ed. James Der Derian (London: Macmillan, 1995), 106–111.
51. Ashley, 'The Achievements of Post-structuralism,' in *International Theory: Positivism and Beyond*, eds. Steve Smith, Ken Booth and Marysia Zalewski (Cambridge: Cambridge University Press, 1996), 245–246.
52. Hansen, 'Poststructuralism,' 173.
53. These are James Der Derian, *On Diplomacy: A Genealogy of Western Estrangement* (Oxford: Blackwell, 1987); Der Derian, *Antidiplomacy: Spies, Terror, Speed, and War* (Hoboken, NJ: John Wiley & Sons, Inc., 1992), hereinafter *Antidiplomacy.*
54. Der Derian, *On Diplomacy*, 1, 4–6, 42.
55. Jim George, ed., 'Thinking Beyond International Relations: Poststructuralism—Reconceptualizing Theory as Practice,' in *Discourses of Global Politics: A Critical (Re) Introduction to International Relations* (Boulder, CO: Lynne Rienner Publishers, 1994), 198.
56. Jef Huysmans, 'James Der Derian: The Unbearable Lightness of Theory,' in *Future of International Relations*, eds. Ole Wæver, Iver B. Neumann (Abingdon: Taylor & Francis, 1997), 344–347.
57. George, 'Thinking Beyond,' 199.
58. Der Derian, *On Diplomacy*, 3.
59. Kenneth Waltz, Hedley Bull, and Herbert Butterfield, *Theory of International Politics* (Long Grove, IL: Waveland Press, 1979), 65–66, 127, 187.
60. Robert Keohane, ed., 'Realism, Neorealism and the Study of World Politics,' in *Neorealism and its Critics* (New York, NY: Columbia University Press, 1986), 7, 12.
61. Michael Doyle, Jack Donnelly, and David Boucher cited in Gabriella Slomp, 'The Origins of Realism Revisited,' in *The Ashgate Research Companion to Ethics and International Relations*, ed. Patrick Hayden (Farnham: Ashgate Publishing, 2009), 13–16.
62. H. R. Alker Jr., 'The Dialectical Logic of Thucydides' Melian Dialogue,' *American Political Science Review* 82 (1988): 805–820, especially 805.
63. R. B. J. Walker, *Inside/Outside: International Relations as Political Theory* (Cambridge, NY: Cambridge University Press, 1993), 31.
64. Ibid., 66, 79, 92.
65. George, 'Thinking Beyond,' 192–195.
66. Hansen, 'Poststructuralism,' 174–175.
67. See https://www.theguardian.com/world/video/2015/jan/13/charlie-hebdo-cartoonist-prophet-muhammad-video; https://www.mcall.com/sdut-charlie-hebdo-muhammad-

cover-luz-2015jan13-story.html; https://www.aljazeera.com/news/2018/8/30/geert-wilders-cancels-prophet-muhammad-cartoon-contest and https://www.youtube.com/watch?v=yVT9SdZDjoQ (all accessed on 09 April 2021).

68. Sungju Park-Kang, *Fictional International Relations: Gender, Pain and Truth* (London: Routledge, 2014), 35.
69. See Cynthia Weber, *International Relations Theory* (London: Routledge, 2001), 9, 104, 107-29, 271–272.
70. Cynthia Weber, *Faking it: U.S. Hegemony in a 'Post-Phallic' Era* (Minneapolis, MN: University of Minnesota Press, 1999), 2, 50–51, 108, 122 and *passim*.
71. Alex Prichard, *Justice, Order and Anarchy: The International Political Theory of Pierre Joseph Proudhon* (London: Routledge, 2013), 20.
72. See notes 26 and 59 of Chapter 25.
73. Prichard, *Justice, Order and Anarchy*, 20–21.
74. Richard Ashley, 'The Geopolitics of Geopolitical Space: Toward a Critical Social Theory of International Politics,' *Alternatives: Global, Local, Political* 12, no. 4 (1987): 403–434, especially 412–413.
75. Richard Ashley, 'Untying the Sovereign State: A Double Reading of the Anarchy Problematic,' *Millennium* 17, no. 2 (1988): 227–262.
76. Ashley, 'Living on the Borderlines,' 270.
77. Thomas Diez, Ingvild Bode, and Aleksandra Fernandes da Costa, *Key Concepts in International Relations* (Thousand Oaks, CL: SAGE Publications, 2011), 170.
78. George, 'Thinking Beyond,' 203–204.
79. Walker, *Inside/Outside*, 67, 165–166.
80. Cynthia Weber, *Simulating Sovereignty: Intervention, the State and Symbolic Exchange* (Cambridge: Cambridge University Press, 1995), 30.
81. George, 'Thinking Beyond,' 200–201.
82. See Richard Ashley, 'Living on the Border Lines: Man, Post-structuralism and War,' in in *International/Intertextual Relations*, eds. James Der Derian and M. Schapiro (Lexington: Lexington Books, 1989), 303.
83. Jacques Derrida, *The Beast and the Sovereign*, vol. 1 (Eds.) Michel Lisse, Marie-Louise Mallet, and Ginette Michaud, trans. Geoffrey Bennington (Chicago and London: University of Chicago Press, 2009), Ninth Session, 236–245.
84. R. B. J. Walker, 'On the Discourses of Sovereignty: Gender and Critique in the Theory of International Relations,' in *Gendered States: Feminist (re)visions of International Relations Theory*, ed. V. Spike Peterson (Boulder, CO: Lynne Rienner, 1992), 179–202, especially 179.
85. Walker, *Inside/Outside*, 168–169, 172.
86. Michel J. Shapiro, ed., 'The Constitution of the Central American Other: The Case of Guatemala,' in *The Politics of Representation: Writing Practices in Biography, Photography and Policy Analysis* (Madison, WI: University of Wisconsin Press, 1987). The discussion is largely based on George, 'Thinking Beyond,' 204–207.
87. Hansen, 'Poststructuralism,' 179.
88. David Campbell, *Writing Security: United States Foreign Policy and the Politics of Identity* (Minneapolis, MI: University of Minnesota Press, 1992), 9.
89. Ibid., vii.
90. Ibid., 75–76.
91. Ibid., 195–196.
92. Ibid., 197, 253, 99, 206, 225, 239, 93, 98, 99, 250.
93. Ibid., 210.
94. Ibid., 153.
95. Ibid., 195.

96. Devetak, 'Postmodernism,' 190. The next section will largely draw on him, although, except when otherwise stated, I have perused the references cited by him independently. For his scheme and supporting citations, see 190–198.
97. D. Campbell and M. Dillon, 'Introduction,' and 'Postface: The Political and the Ethical,' in *The Political Subject of Violence* (Manchester; New York, NY: Manchester University Press, 1993), 2, 161, 15.
98. Bradley S. Klein, *Strategic Studies and World Order: The Global Politics of Deterrence* (Cambridge: Cambridge University Press, 1994), 37–38.
99. John Gerard Ruggie, 'Territoriality and Beyond: Problematizing Modernity in International Relations,' *International Organization* 47, no. 1 (1993): 139–174, especially 162–163, 174.
100. Fernando Coronil and Julie Skurski, *States of Violence* (Ann Arbor, MI: University of Michigan Press, 2006), 126–127.
101. See J. Edkins, 'Sovereign Power, Zones of Indistinction, and the Camp,' *Alternatives* 25, no. 1 (2000): 19, cited in Devetak, 'Postmodernism,' 191–192.
102. Gearóid Ó Tuathail, *Critical Geopolitics: The Politics of Writing Global Space* (Minneapolis, MN: University of Minnesota Press, 1996), 1, cited in Devetak, 'Postmodernism,' 193.
103. J. B. Harley, 'Maps, Knowledge, and Power,' in *The New Nature of Maps: Essays in the History of Cartography*, ed. Paul Laxton, Introduction by F. H. Andrews (Baltimore, MD: Johns Hopkins Press, 2001), 55.
104. Devetak, 'Postmodernism,' 193.
105. Campbell, *Writing Security*, 196.
106. Debbie Lisle, 'Consuming Danger: Reimagining the War/Tourism Divide,' *Alternatives* 25, no. 1(2000): 91–116, cited in Devetak, 'Postmodernism,' 194.
107. Jacques Derrida, *Specters of Marx: The State of the Debt, the Work of Mourning and the New International* (London: Routledge, 1994/2006), 102–103.
108. David Campbell, *National Deconstruction: Violence, Identity, and Justice in Bosnia* (Minneapolis, MN: University of Minnesota Press, 1998), 168–170, 13.
109. Simon Dalby, *Creating the Second World War: The Discourse of Politics* (London: Pinter, 1990; London, Oxford, New York, NY: Bloomsbury, 2016), 39.
110. See Cynthia Weber, 'Interruption Ashley,' *Review of International Studies* 36, no. 4 (2010): 975–987, here 980; Richard Ashley, 'Living on the Border Lines: Man, Post-structuralism and War,' in in *International/Intertextual Relations*, eds. James Der Derian and M. Schapiro (Lexington: Lexington Books, 1989), 303.
111. R. K. Ashley, 'Imposing International Purpose: Notes on a Problematic of Governance,' in *Global Change and Theoretical Challenges: Approaches to World Politics for the 1990s*, ed. James N. Rosenau and Ernst-Otto Czempiel (Lexington, MA: Lexington Books, 1988), 269, 267, cited in Devetak, 'Postmodernism,' 196.
112. R. K. Ashley, 'The Geopolitics of Geopolitical Space: Toward a Critical Social Theory of International Politics,' *Alternatives* 12, no. 4 (1987): 408, 410.
113. Cynthia Weber, 'Performative States,' *Millennium* 27 (1998): 77–97, here 78.
114. David Campbell, 'MetaBosnia: Narratives of the Bosnian War,' *Review of International Studies* 24, no. 2 (1998): 261–281.
115. Emma Hutchison, *Affective Communities in World Politics: Collective Emotions after Trauma* (Cambridge: Cambridge University Press, 2016), 136.
116. Campbell, *Writing Security*, 8.
117. Richard Devetak, 'Incomplete States: Theories and Practice of Statecraft,' in *Boundaries in Question*, eds. Andrew Linklater and John MacMillan (London: Pinter Publishers, 1995), 32. The words in double quotes are from Ashley, 'Geopolitics of Geopolitical Space,' 410; Wendt, 'Anarchy Is What States Make of It: The Social Construction of Power Politics,' *International Organization* 46, no. 2 (1992): 413; Campbell, *Writing Security*, 11.
118. Hans Keohane, 'International Institutions: Two Approaches,' *International Studies Quarterly* 32 (1988): 379–396, here, 393.

119. Pauline Marie Rosenau, *Post-Modernism and the Social Sciences: Insights, Inroads, and Intrusions* (Princeton, NJ: Princeton University Press, 1992), 167–169.
120. Jose Lopez and Garry Potter, eds., 'Introduction,' in *After Postmodernism: An Introduction to Critical Realism*(London: The Athlone Press, 2001), 5.
121. Terry Eagleton, *Literary Theory: An Introduction* (Minneapolis, MN: University of Minnesota Press, 2008), 121.
122. Fredric Jameson, *Postmodernism, Or, The Cultural Logic of Late Capitalism* (Durham, NC: Duke University Press, 1991/2003).
123. Somer Brodribb, *Nothing Mat(T)ers: A Feminist Critique of Postmodernism* (North Melbourne: Spinifex, 1992/1993), ix.
124. Gary Steiner, *Animals and the Limits of Postmodernism* (New York, NY: Columbia University Press, 2013), 4.
125. Jarvis, *IR and the Challenge of Postmodernism*, 26.
126. Campbell, 'Poststructuralism,' 218.
127. Jarvis, *IR and the Challenge of Postmodernism*, 26.

INDEX